Study Guide

Wendine Thompson-Dawson
Monmouth College

Edward Scahill
University of Scranton

MICROECONOMICS

Second Edition

R. Glenn Hubbard
Anthony O'Brien

PEARSON
Prentice Hall

Upper Saddle River, New Jersey 07458

VP/Editorial Director: Natalie Anderson
Acquisitions Editor: David Alexander
Senior Development Editor: Lena Buonanno
Assistant Editor: Christina Volpe
Associate Managing Editor: Suzanne DeWorken
Senior Operations Specialist: Arnold Vila

PEARSON
Prentice
Hall

10 9 8 7 6 5 4 3 2

ISBN-13: 978-0-13-8132804
ISBN-10: 0-13-8132801

Contents

Preface

Why You Should Use the Study Guide

This Study Guide has been written for use with *Microeconomics, Second Edition,* by R. Glenn Hubbard and Anthony Patrick O'Brien. The textbook and Study Guide both apply economic principles to real-world business and policy examples. The Study Guide summarizes the material covered in the main text and provides you with additional exercises to help you practice interpreting graphs, analyzing problems, and applying the economic concepts you learn to real-life situations. The Study Guide will be especially helpful to you if this is your first course in economics. You can use many of the key concepts you will learn to other economics and business courses you take.

Study Guide Contents

Each of the 18 chapters of the Study Guide contains the following components:

1. Chapter Summary

A brief summary of the material in the textbook.

2. Learning Objectives

Several learning objectives appear at the beginning of each textbook chapter. These learning objectives are listed in the Study Guide along with a brief description.

3. Chapter Review

This offers you a synopsis of each of the sections in each chapter. Reading the Chapter Reviews is a great way to reinforce your understanding of the material in the textbook and prepare for examinations.

4. Helpful Study Hints

These are found in the Chapter Review. There is at least one *Hint* for each major chapter section. The *Hints* will help you understand economic principles and their application through the use of examples that are different from those in the textbook. *Hints* also refer you to features in the textbook – for example, *Solved Problems, Making the Connection*, and end-of-chapter *Problems and Applications* – that relate to the topics covered in the Chapter Review.

5. Solved Problems

The textbook includes worked-out problems, usually two or three per chapter, each of which is tied to one of the learning objectives. Each of the Study Guide chapters includes one or more additional Solved Problems.

6. Key Terms

Each of the corresponding textbook chapter's bold key terms is defined.

7. Self-Test

This section of the Guide will help you prepare for quizzes and exams. There are 40 multiple-choice questions, five short answer questions and 15 true/false questions for each chapter. The answers to all questions appear at the end of the Self-Test.

More Study Resources for You

Here are two other resources you can use in addition to this Study Guide to help you understand economic concepts and build your skills solving problems and exercises

myeconlab

Get Ahead of the Curve

MyEconLab, located at **www.myeconlab.com**, puts you in control of your learning through a collection of testing, practice, and study tools tied to the online, interactive version of the textbook and other media resources.

Within MyEconLab's structured environment, you practice what you learn, test your understanding, and pursue a personalized Study Plan generated from your performance on Sample Tests and tests created by your instructor. MyEconLab has the following key features:

- Sample Tests, two per chapter
- Personal Study Plan
- Tutorial Instruction
- Graphing Tool

Sample Tests

Two Sample Tests for each chapter are pre-loaded in MyEconLab, enabling you to practice what you have learned, test your understanding, and identify areas in which you need to do further work. You can study on your own, or you can complete assignments created by your instructor.

Personal Study Plan

Based on your performance on tests, MyEconLab generates a personal Study Plan that shows where you need further study. The *Study Plan* consists of a series of additional practice exercises with detailed feedback and guided solutions and keyed to other tutorial resources.

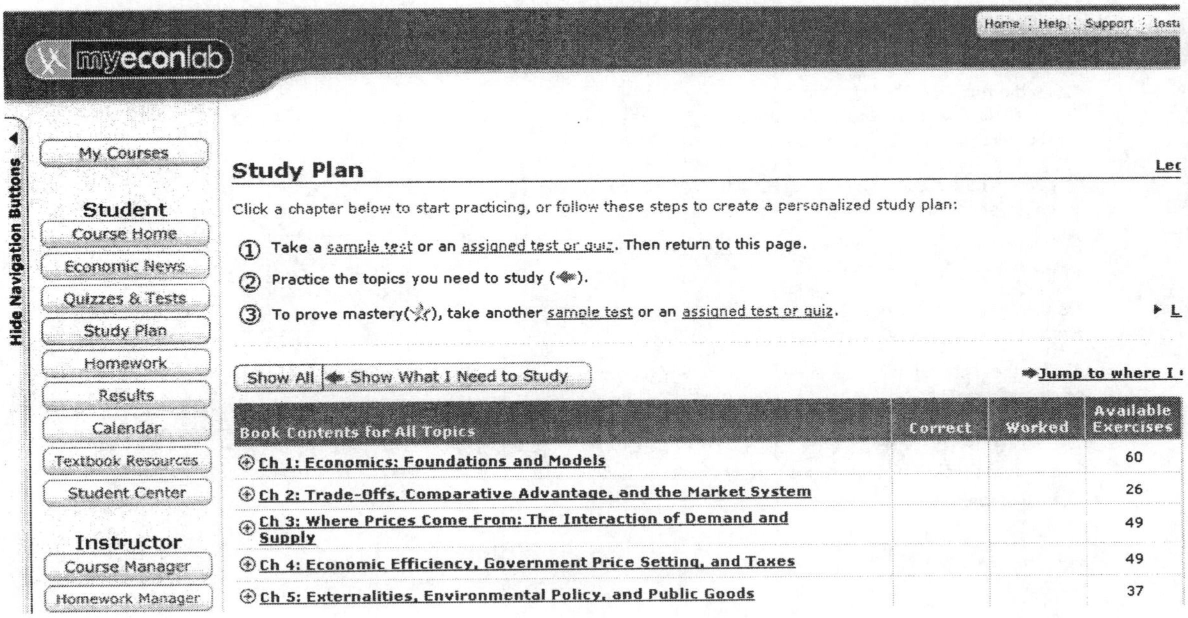

Tutorial Instruction

Launched from many of the exercises in the *Study Plan*, MyEconLab provides tutorial instruction in the form of step-by-step solutions and other media-based explanations.

Graphing Tool

A graphing tool is integrated into the Tests and Study Plan exercises to enable you to create and manipulate graphs. This feature helps you understand how concepts, numbers, and graphs connect.

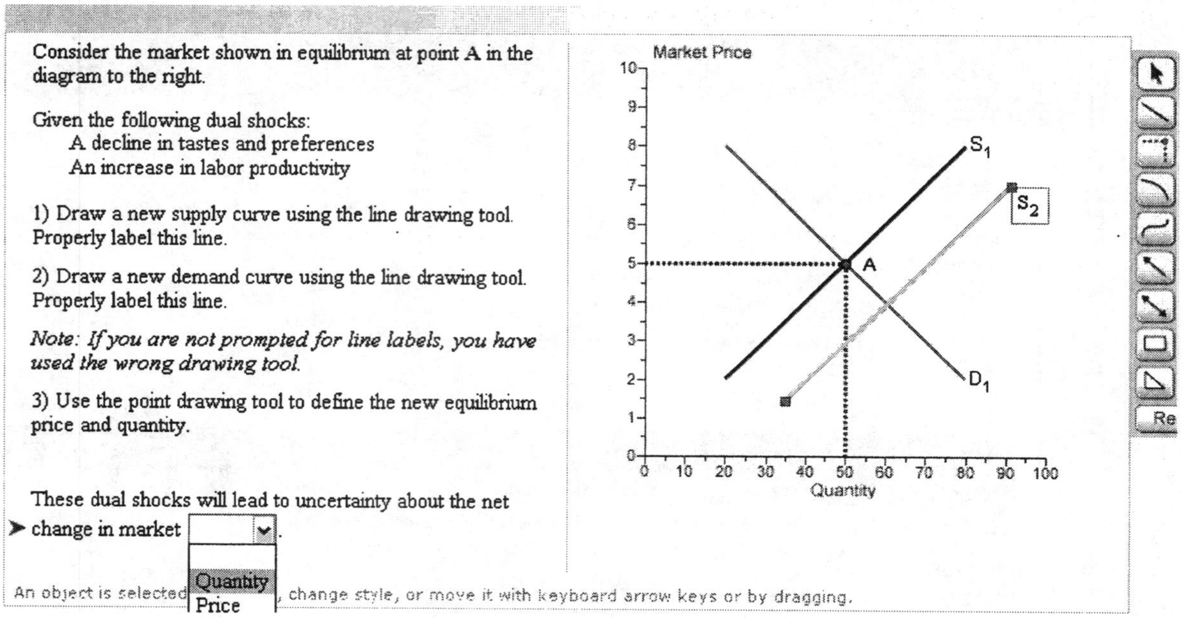

Additional MyEconLab Tools

MyEconLab also includes the following additional features:

1. **Economics in the News**—weekly news article updates during the school year of news items with links to sources for further reading and discussion questions.
2. **eText**—while working in the Study Plan or completing homework assignments, part of the tutorial resources available is a link directly to the relevant page of the text so the student can review the appropriate material to help them complete the exercise.
3. **Glossary**—a searchable version of the textbook glossary with additional examples and links to related terms.
4. **Glossary Flashcards**—every key term is available as a flashcard, allowing students to quiz themselves on vocabulary from one or more chapters at a time.
5. **Ask the Author**—email economic related questions to the author.
6. **Research Navigator (CourseCompass version only)**—extensive help on the research process and four exclusive databases of credible and reliable source material, including *The New York Times*, the *Financial Times*, and peer-reviewed journals.

Vango Notes

Study on the go with VangoNotes (**www.VangoNotes.com**), detailed chapter reviews in downloadable MP3 format. Now wherever you are and whatever you're doing, you can study on the go by listening to the following for each chapter of your textbook:

- Big Ideas: Your "need to know" for each chapter
- Practice Questions: A gut check for the Big Ideas—tells you if you need to keep studying
- Key Terms: Audio "flashcards"—help you review key concepts and terms
- Rapid Review: Quick-drill session—use it right before your test
- *VangoNotes* are **flexible**: Download all the material (or only the chapters you need) directly to your player. And *VangoNotes* are **efficient**: Use them in your car, at the gym, walking to class, wherever you go. So get yours today, and get studying.

Study Tips

1. ***Read the textbook chapter – but don't just read the chapter***. To do well in your economics course, you must learn to apply what you learn and not just memorize definitions and read graphs. Both the textbook and the Study Guide have a number of features that allow you to apply and understand what you learn. Take advantage of these learning aids. Economics is a participant sport, not a spectator sport. Use your pencil. Draw graphs, don't just look at them. Try the calculations. Use your calculator.

2. ***Attend class and ask questions***. Take this course as seriously as your instructor does. Taking days off will not help you do well in any course and is poor preparation for your life after graduation. Many students are hesitant to ask questions during or outside of classroom meetings because they feel they are the only ones who do not understand a topic (this is almost never true) or that their instructors feel they have better things to do (this is almost never true as well). Your instructor will appreciate the effort you make to learn what can be a challenging subject.

3. ***Don't leave the subject in the classroom.*** The key to doing well in your course is to understand how to apply economic concepts in real-world situations. Learning economics is similar to learning a new language. You will become fluent in the economic way of thinking only after you learn to recognize and apply concepts found in newspaper articles, magazines, and everyday conversation.

4. ***Organize a study group***. If possible, study with other students in your class. Participating in a study group can help you learn economics – students will bring different insights to the group – and make learning more enjoyable. Explaining a topic to a friend will help you discover areas where you need to spend more study time.

Chapter 1

Economics: Foundations and Models

Chapter Summary

People must make choices as they try to attain their goals. These choices usually mean that people must accept trade-offs among various competing objectives due to society's limited resources. **Economics** is the study of the choices people make to attain their goods, given their scarce resources. Economists assume that people are rational, respond to economic incentives, and make decisions at the margin. Economists construct **models**, simplified versions of some aspect of economic life, to analyze economic issues such as how buyers and sellers make decisions.

Every society faces the economic problem of limited resources. Therefore, society can produce only limited quantities of goods and services. Societies face trade-offs and must consider the opportunity costs of decisions, particularly when answering the three fundamental questions any economy must answer:

1. *What* goods and services will be produced?
2. *How* will the goods and services be produced?
3. *Who* will receive the goods and services?

Societies organize their economies in two main ways to answer these questions. A society can have a **centrally planned economy** characterized by extensive government decision making. Or, a society can have a market economy where resource allocation is determined by the decisions of households and firms interacting in markets. All high-income democracies have market economies or mixed economies. A **mixed economy** is a market-based economy with some government intervention. Market economies tend to allocate resources more efficiently than do centrally planned economies, but efficient outcomes may not be perceived as fair. Determining what is a fair or equitable outcome calls for the application of **normative analysis** – *what ought to be*. **Positive analysis** is concerned with *what is*. While most or all economists can agree on the results of positive economic analysis, their opinions often differ on *what ought to be*.

Microeconomics is the study of how individual choices are made by households, firms, and the government. **Macroeconomics** is the study of the economy as a whole.

The Appendix to Chapter 1 provides a review of basic mathematical tools and techniques that will be applied through the textbook.

Learning Objectives

When you finish with this chapter, you should be able to:

1. **Discuss these three important ideas: People are rational. People respond to incentives. Optimal decisions are made at the margin.** Economists use these ideas to analyze the way people make decisions. These ideas are especially important in analyzing what happens in markets, which is the primary focus of economic analysis.

2. **Discuss how an economy answers these questions: *What* goods and services will be produced? *How* will the goods and services be produced? *Who* will receive the goods and services?** Every society must answer these questions because the resources available to produce goods and services are scarce. Even nations with abundant supplies of natural resources cannot produce enough goods and services to satisfy the desires of all their citizens. Therefore, societies face trade-offs. Producing more of one good or service means producing less of another good or service.

3. **Understand the role of models in economic analysis.** Economic models are created by applying the scientific method to economic data. These models are simplified versions of reality used to analyze real-world issues. Economic models are used to explain issues such as whether or not outsourcing has been good or bad for the U.S. economy. This is a complex question that requires more than one model to explain different aspects of the issue.

4. **Distinguish between microeconomics and macroeconomics.** Economic decision-making is grouped into two areas. Microeconomics is the study of how households and firms make choices, interact in markets, and how the government attempts to influence their choices. Macroeconomics studies the economy as a whole, including topics such as inflation, unemployment, and economic growth.

5. **Become familiar with important economic terms.** This chapter includes descriptions and definitions of important terms that will be used in other chapters of the textbook.

Appendix: Review the use of graphs and formulas. Graphs simplify economic ideas and make the ideas concrete so they can be applied to real-world problems. Whether or not your instructor assigns the appendix, it is a good idea to read it because it will help you understand how to read and interpret the many graphs that appear throughout the book.

Chapter Review

Chapter Opener: What Happens When U.S. Firms Move to China? (pages 2-3)

In 2004, executives of 3Com Corporation decided to build a new network switch for corporate security systems in China. Part of the rationale for these executives was to save money: Chinese engineers receive lower salaries than engineers in the United States. 3Com is one of many U.S. firms that have established manufacturing, service, and design operations in other countries. This practice is often called *outsourcing*. An understanding of economics will help you to understand outsourcing and many other important issues that you hear in the news and in classes.

The textbook describes how economics is used to answer many important questions, including whether or not a firm should outsource. All of these questions represent a basic economic fact of life: people must make choices as they try to attain their goals. These choices occur because of scarcity, which is the most fundamental economic concept. The resources available to any society – for example, land, and labor – to produce the goods and services its citizens want are limited. Society has to choose which goods and services will be produced and who will receive them.

Helpful Study Hint

At the beginning of each chapter in this textbook is a chapter opener that describes an economic issue facing one or more real-world companies. You will find other special features throughout the book. For instance ***An Inside Look*** appears at the end of each chapter. This feature analyzes a topic related to the chapter opener using a magazine or newspaper article. Questions are included at the end of each article to test your knowledge of the topic. In this chapter, ***An Inside Look*** discusses whether the United States should be concerned about competition from high-tech firms in China and India. The article argues that fear of competition from China and India is exaggerated because the United States has many advantages that should allow it retain many high-skilled, high wage jobs.

The ***Economics in YOUR Life!*** feature asks whether it is likely that you will experience a job loss due to outsourcing. Think about this question as you read the chapter. The authors will answer this question at the end of the chapter.

1.1 LEARNING OBJECTIVE

1.1 Three Key Economic Ideas (pages 4-7)

Learning Objective 1 Discuss these three important ideas: People are rational. People respond to incentives. Optimal decisions are made at the margin.

Economics examines how people interact in markets. A **market** refers to a group of buyers and sellers of a good or service and the institution or arrangement by which they come together to trade. Economists make three important assumptions about the way people interact in markets. First, people are rational. This means that buyers and sellers use all available information to achieve their goals. Second, people act in response to economic incentives. Third, optimal decisions are made at the margin. The terms "marginal benefit" and "marginal cost" refer to the additional benefits and costs of a decision. Economists reason that the best, or optimal, decision is to continue any activity up to the point where the marginal benefit (or *MB*) equals the marginal cost (*MC*). In symbols, we can write $MB = MC$.

Helpful Study Hint

The image many people have of a market is a supermarket, neighborhood store, or shopping mall. But some markets do not have an easily identifiable image. Many people make online purchases with their computers. In these markets, buyers and sellers do not see each other and may be located hundreds of miles from one another. For some goods (for example, books and CDs), is it not necessary for buyers to see or test merchandise before they buy it. For other goods (clothing, food, automobiles), some personal contact is important. In many of these cases, sellers have a physical location to which buyers must travel to try out the product. There are also markets in which sellers travel to their buyers. Pharmaceutical salespersons who visit doctors' offices are one well-known example.

In the movie *Wall Street,* Gordon Gekko, a ruthless businessman played by Michael Douglas, proclaims "Greed is good." You should not assume that the phrase "people respond to economic incentives" means that people are greedy. The phrase "people respond to economic incentives" is an objective statement or a statement shown to be true rather than a belief or opinion. In contrast, Gordon Gekko's statement was subjective; he stated his opinion that "greed is good." Economists do not believe people are motivated solely by monetary incentives. Many people voluntarily devote their time and financial resources to friends, family members and charities.

See the ***Making the Connection*** "Will Women Have More Babies if the Government Pays Them To?" for a discussion of how economic incentives may alter people's behavior. Some countries have been experiencing a decline in birth rates, which will mean a decrease in population growth and future tax revenues. In some countries, the birth rate has fallen below the replacement level, which means that the population will actually begin shrinking. Some countries have begun to provide incentives to encourage women to have babies. There is evidence that this is working in Estonia, but it may be too early into the program to know if it will be successful.

The first ***Solved Problem*** is at the end of this section of the textbook. Each ***Solved Problem*** helps you understand one of the chapter's learning objectives. The authors use a step-by-step process to show how you can solve the problem. Additional Solved Problems, different from those that appear in the textbook, are included in each chapter of this Study Guide. ***Solved Problem 1-1*** in the textbook is an example of how Apple can use marginal analysis to decide whether to increase output. To make this decision, Apple must compare the additional benefit – the margin benefit – generated by producing the extra output to the additional cost – marginal cost – from the production of that output. If the additional (or marginal) benefit is greater than the marginal cost, then Apple should produce more iPods.

1.2 LEARNING OBJECTIVE

1.2 The Economic Problem That Every Society Must Solve (pages 8-11)

Learning Objective 2 Discuss how an economy answers these questions: *What* goods and services will be produced? *How* will the goods and services be produced? *Who* will receive the goods and services?

The basic economic problem any society faces is that it has only a limited amount of economic resources and so can produce only a limited amount of goods and services. Societies face **trade-offs** when answering the three fundamental economic questions:

1. *What* goods and services will be produced?
2. *How* will the goods and services be produced?
3. *Who* will receive the goods and services?

Societies organize their economies in two main ways. A **centrally planned economy** is an economy in which the government decides how economic resources will be allocated. From 1917 to 1991, the Soviet Union was the most important centrally planned economy. Today Cuba and North Korea are among the few remaining centrally planned economies. A **market economy** is an economy in which the decisions of households and firms interacting in markets allocate economic resources. The United States, Canada, Western Europe, and Japan all have market economies. Privately owned firms must produce and sell goods and services consumers want to stay in business. An individual's income is determined by the payments he receives for what he has to sell.

Helpful Study Hint

In a planned economy, government officials or "planners" are responsible for determining how much of each good to produce, who should produce it, and where it should be produced. In contrast, in a market economy no government official determines how much corn, wheat, or potatoes should be produced. Individual producers and consumers interact in markets for these goods to determine the answers to *What*? *How*? and *Who*? The role of government in a market economy is similar to that of an umpire in a baseball game. Government officials can pass and enforce laws that allow people to act in certain ways but do not participate directly in markets as consumers or producers.

The high rates of unemployment and business bankruptcies of the Great Depression caused a dramatic increase in government intervention in the economy in the United States and other market economies. Some government intervention is designed to raise the incomes of the elderly, the sick, and people with limited skills. In recent years, government intervention has expanded to meet social goals such as protection of the environment and the promotion of civil rights. The expanded role of government in market economies has led most economists to argue that the United States and other nations have **mixed economies** rather than market economies.

Market economies tend to be more efficient than planned economies because market economies promote competition and voluntary exchange. There are two types of efficiency. **Productive efficiency** occurs when a good or service is produced at the lowest possible cost. **Allocative efficiency** is a state of the economy in which production represents consumer preferences. Specifically, every good or service is produced up to the point where the marginal benefit that the last unit produced provides to consumers is equal to the marginal cost of producing it. Inefficiencies do occur in markets for three main reasons. First, it may take time for firms to achieve productive efficiency. Second, governments may reduce efficiency by interfering with voluntary exchanges in markets. Third, production of some goods may harm the environment when firms ignore the costs of environmental damage.

Society may not find efficient economic outcomes to be the most desirable outcomes. Many people prefer economic outcomes they consider fair or equitable even if these outcomes are less efficient. Equity is the fair distribution of economic benefits.

Helpful Study Hint

There are many examples of government regulation on private markets in the United States. The sale and use of cocaine and other drugs is illegal, and the sale of cigarettes is allowed only to people 18 years and older. Between 1920 and 1933, the production and sale of alcoholic beverages was also illegal in the United States.

Extra Solved Problem 1-2

Chapter 1 includes a Solved Problem. Here is an extra Solved Problem to help you build your skills solving economic problems.

Supports Learning Objective 2: Discuss how an economy answers these questions: *What* goods and services will be produced? *How* will the goods and services be produced? *Who* will receive the goods and services?

Giving Advice to New Government Leaders

Suppose that a developing nation is experiencing a change in government leadership. Prior to this change the nation had a centrally planned economy. The new leaders are willing to try a different system if they can be convinced that it will yield better results. They hire an economist from a nation with a market economy to advise them and will order their citizens to follow this advisor's recommendations for change. The economist suggests that a market economy replace central planning to answer the nation's economic questions (*what*, *how* and *who*?).

a. What will the economist suggest the leaders order their citizens to do?

b. Do you believe the leaders and citizens will accept the economist's suggestions?

SOLVING THE PROBLEM

Step 1: **Review the chapter material.**
The problem concerns the choice of economic system a nation must make, so you may want to review the section "Centrally Planned Economies versus Market Economies," which begins on page 9 in the textbook.

Step 2: **What will the economist suggest the leaders order their citizens to do?**
Market economies allow members of households to follow their self-interest in selecting which occupation to enter and which goods and services to purchase. Market economies also allow privately owned firms to follow their self-interest in selecting which goods and services to produce. Therefore, the economist would ask the leaders of the poor country to not issue any orders. Government officials should ordinarily not attempt to influence individual decisions made in markets.

Step 3: **Do you believe the leaders and citizens will accept the economist's suggestions?**
Even democratically elected rulers, especially those with previous experience with significant government involvement in the nation's resource allocation, will find it difficult to accept the

new system. They may wonder how self-interested individuals will produce and distribute goods and services so as to promote the welfare of the entire nation. This new system requires a significant reduction in the government's power to influence people's lives. History has shown that government officials are often reluctant to give up this power. Acceptance is most likely to occur when the rulers have some knowledge of the successful operation of a market economy in other countries. Most ordinary citizens are more likely to accept the economist's suggestions because they will have more freedom to pursue their own economic goals. However, those who benefited from the previous system will resist change.

1.3 LEARNING OBJECTIVE

1.3 Economic Models (pages 11-15)

Learning Objective 3 Understand the role of models in economic analysis.

Models are simplified versions of reality used to analyze real-world situations. To develop a model, economists generally follow five steps.

1. Decide on the assumptions to be used in developing the model.
2. Formulate a testable hypothesis.
3. Use economic data to test the hypothesis.
4. Revise the model if it fails to explain well the economic data.
5. Retain the revised model to help answer similar economic questions in the future.

Models rely on assumptions because models must be simplified to be useful. For example, models make behavioral assumptions about the motives of consumers and firms. Economists assume that consumers will buy the goods and services that will maximize their satisfaction and that firms will produce the goods and services that will maximize their profits.

An **economic variable** is something measurable that can have different values, such as the wages of software programmers. A *hypothesis* is a statement that may be correct or incorrect about an economic variable. An economic hypothesis usually states a causal relationship where a change in one variable causes a change in another variable. For example, "outsourcing leads to lower wages for software programmers" means that an increase in the amount of outsourcing will reduce the wages of software programmers. **Positive analysis** is analysis concerned with what is and involves questions that can be estimated. **Normative analysis** is analysis concerned with what ought to be and involves questions of values and basic assumptions.

Helpful Study Hint

For a good explanation of what a model is and how models are used in economics, read the first section of the Appendix to Chapter 1.

A feature introduced in Chapter 1 of the text – ***Making the Connection*** – describes a debate between two prominent economists over outsourcing. ***Making the Connection*** features in other chapters relate concepts described in the text to recent business stories.

Positive economic analysis deals with statements that can be proved correct or incorrect by examining facts. If your instructor stated that "It is snowing outside," it would be easy to determine whether this statement is true or false by looking out a window. Normative analysis concerns statements of belief or opinion. If your instructor wants to go skiiing that evening and states that "It *should* be snowing outside today," you could not prove the statement wrong because it is a statement of *opinion*. It is important to recognize the difference between these two types of statements. The feature ***Don't Let This Happen to You!*** appears in each chapter to alert you to mistakes often made by economics students. To reinforce the difference between positive and normative statements, review ***Don't Let This Happen To YOU!*** "Don't Confuse Positive Analysis with Normative Analysis," where the minimum wage law is discussed. Positive analysis can show us the effects of the minimum wage law on the economy, but it cannot tell us whether the policy is good or bad. Nor can positive analysis tell us whether we should increase or decrease the minimum wage. The discussion of whether a policy is good or bad will depend on an individual's values and experiences and falls under the realm of normative analysis.

1.4 LEARNING OBJECTIVE

1.4 Microeconomics and Macroeconomics (page 15)

Learning Objective 4 Distinguish between microeconomics and macroeconomics.

Microeconomics is the study of how households and firms make choices, how they interact in markets, and how the government attempts to influence their choices. **Macroeconomics** is the study of the economy as a whole, including topics such as inflation, unemployment, and economic growth.

1.5 LEARNING OBJECTIVE

1.5 A Preview of Important Economic Terms (pages 15-16)

Learning Objective 5 Become familiar with important economic terms.

This chapter introduces twelve economic terms that will each be covered in depth in future chapters. Those terms are: entrepreneur, innovation, technology, firm, goods, services, revenue, profit, household, factors of production, capital, and human capital.

Helpful Study Hint

At the beginning of the chapter, you read the ***Economics in YOUR Life!*** question: "Are You Likely to Lose Your Job to Outsourcing?" The authors answer the question at the end of the chapter. Jobs are continuously created and eliminated in the U.S. economy. Only a small percentage of jobs are outsourced, so, even though you are likely to lose your job once or twice during your career, it will probably *not* be due to outsourcing.

Appendix

Using Graphs and Formulas (pages 24-35)

LEARNING OBJECTIVE: Review the use of graphs and formulas.

Graphs of One Variable

Bar charts, pie charts and time-series graphs are alternative ways to display data visually. Figures 1A-1 and 1A-2 illustrate how relationships are often easier to understand with graphs than with words or tables alone.

Graphs of Two Variables

Both microeconomics and macroeconomics use two-variable graphs extensively. You need to understand how to measure the slope of a straight line drawn in a graph. The slope of a straight line can be measured between any two points on a line because the slope of a straight line has a constant value, so we don't need to worry about the value of the slope changing as we move up and down the line. Slope can be measured as the change in the value measured on the vertical axis divided by the change in the value measured on the horizontal axis. In symbols, the slope formula is written as $\Delta y/\Delta x$. The formula is also described as "rise over run." The usual custom is to place the variable y on the graph's vertical axis and the variable x the horizontal axis. If the slope is negative, then the two variables are inversely related. If the slope is positive, then the two variables are positively related. We can show the effect of more than two variables in a graph by shifting the line representing the relationship between the first two variables. For example, we can draw a graph showing the effect of a change in the price of pizza on the quantity of pizza demand during a given week. We can then shift this line to show the effect of an change in the price of hamburgers on the quantity of pizza demanded.

Formulas

The formula for a percentage change of a variable over time (or growth rate) is:

$$\frac{Value_2 - Value_1}{Value_1} \times 100\%$$

The formula for the area of a rectangle is Base x Height. The formula for the area of a triangle is ½ x Base x Height.

Key Terms

Allocative efficiency. A state of the economy in which production is in accordance with consumer preferences; in particular, every good or service is produced up to the point where the last unit provides a marginal benefit to society equal to the marginal cost of producing it.

Centrally planned economy. An economy in which the government decides how economic resources will be allocated.

Economic model. A simplified version of reality used to analyze real-world economic situations.

Economic variable. Something measurable that can have different values, such as the wages of software programmers.

Economics. The study of the choices people make to attain their goals, given their scarce resources.

Equity. The fair distribution of economic benefits.

Macroeconomics. The study of the economy as a whole, including topics such as inflation, unemployment, and economic growth.

Marginal analysis. Analysis that involves comparing marginal benefits and marginal costs.

Market. A group of buyers and sellers of a good or service and the institution or arrangement by which they come together to trade.

Market economy. An economy in which the decisions of households and firms interacting in markets allocate economic resources.

Microeconomics. The study of how households and firms make choices, how they interact in markets, and how the government attempts to influence their choices.

Mixed economy. An economy in which most economic decisions result from the interaction of buyers and sellers in markets but in which the government plays a significant role in the allocation of resources.

Opportunity cost. The highest-valued alternative that must be given up to engage in an activity.

Normative analysis. Analysis concerned with what ought to be.

Positive analysis. Analysis concerned with what is.

Productive efficiency. The situation in which a good or service is produced at the lowest possible cost.

Scarcity. The situation in which unlimited wants exceed the limited resources available to fulfill those wants.

Trade-off. The idea that because of scarcity, producing more of one good or service means producing less of another good or service.

Voluntary exchange. The situation that occurs when both the buyer and the seller of a product are made better off by the transaction.

Self-Test

(Answers are provided at the end of the Self-Test.)

Multiple-Choice Questions

1. Which of the following questions could be answered using economics?
   a. "How are the prices of goods and services determined?"
   b. "How does pollution affect the economy, and how should government policy deal with these effects?"
   c. "Why do firms engage in international trade, and how do government policies affect international trade?"
   d. All of the above are economic questions.

2. Which of the following statements best describes scarcity?
   a. Scarcity studies the choices people make to attain their goals.
   b. Scarcity is a situation where unlimited wants exceed limited resources.
   c. Scarcity is an imbalance between buyers and sellers in a specific market.
   d. Scarcity refers to a lack of tradeoffs.

3. When you think of an arrangement or institution that brings buyers and sellers of a good or service together, what are you thinking of?
   a. Marginal analysis
   b. A market
   c. Scarcity
   d. Rational behavior

4. Fill in the blanks. In economics, as well as in life, optimal decisions are made ___________.
   a. once all costs have been considered
   b. only when all benefits have been considered
   c. in their totality
   d. at the margin

5. In Solved Problem 1-1: "Should Apple produce an additional 300,000 iPods?" which of the concepts below is most applicable in solving the problem?
   a. The concept of what a market is
   b. Rational behavior and how people respond to economic incentives
   c. Marginal analysis
   d. The concept of scarcity and tradeoffs

6. Which of the following is not among the fundamental economic questions that every society must solve?
   a. What goods and services will be produced?
   b. How will the goods and services be produced?
   c. What goods and services will be exchanged?
   d. Who will receive the goods and services produced?

7. What types of economies require that we answer the questions of what, how, and for whom to produce goods and services?
   a. Market economies
   b. Centrally planned economies
   c. Mixed economies
   d. All of the above

8. In what type of economy does the government decide how economic resources will be allocated?
   a. In a market economy
   b. In a mixed economy
   c. In a centrally planned economy
   d. In none of the above

9. Which of the following is the best classification for the economies of the United States, Canada, Japan, and Western Europe?
   a. Market economies
   b. Mixed economies
   c. Centrally planned economies
   d. None of the above

10. Which of the following terms best relates to a fair distribution of economic benefits?
    a. Productive efficiency
    b. Allocative efficiency
    c. Voluntary exchange
    d. Equity

11. Which of the following is achieved when a good or service is produced up to the point where the marginal benefit to consumers is equal to the marginal cost of producing it?
    a. Productive efficiency
    b. Allocative efficiency
    c. Equality
    d. Equity

12. Which of the following terms summarizes the situation in which a buyer and a seller exchange a product in a market and, as a result, both are made better off by the transaction?
    a. Productive efficiency
    b. Allocative efficiency
    c. Voluntary exchange
    d. Equity

13. What does an economy achieve by producing a good or service at the least possible cost?
    a. Productive efficiency
    b. Allocative efficiency
    c. Voluntary exchange
    d. Equity

14. Which of the following best describes the characteristics of models used in economics?
    a. Models are approximations to reality that capture as many details as possible.
    b. Models are usually complex abstractions of reality that simulate practical problems.
    c. Models are demonstrations of how economic concepts and theories accurately predict real situations.
    d. Models are simplifications of reality that include only essential elements and exclude less relevant details.

15. Which of the following is not an essential component of an economic model?
    a. Assumptions
    b. Hypotheses
    c. Variables
    d. Normative statements

16. What is the purpose of an economic hypothesis?
    a. To establish a behavioral assumption
    b. To establish a causal relationship
    c. To make a statement based on fact
    d. To determine the validity of statistical analyses used in testing a model

17. What type of economic analysis is concerned with the way things ought to be?
    a. Positive analysis
    b. Marginal analysis
    c. Normative analysis
    d. Rational behavior

18. What type of statement would "A minimum wage actually reduces employment" be considered?
    a. A positive statement
    b. A marginal statement
    c. A normative statement
    d. An irrational conclusion

19. Which of the following is an example of a positive question?
    a. Should the university offer free parking to students?
    b. Should the university provide more financial aid assistance to students?
    c. If the college increased tuition, will class sizes decline?
    d. Should the college cut tuition to stimulate enrollments?

20. Which of the following questions can be answered using normative economic reasoning?
    a. If the college offers free parking, will more students drive to campus?
    b. If the college provided more financial aid, would more students go to college?
    c. If the college hires better qualified instructors, will more students attend?
    d. Should the college cut tuition in order to stimulate enrollments?

21. Which of the following involves an estimation of the benefits and costs of a particular action?
    a. Positive economics
    b. Normative economics
    c. The market mechanism
    d. An irrational conclusion

22. What type of assessment is one where a person's values and political views form part of that assessment?
    a. A positive assessment
    b. A normative assessment
    c. A microeconomic assessment
    d. A macroeconomic assessment

23. Fill in the blank: ____________ is the study of how households and businesses make choices.
    a. Microeconomics
    b. Macroeconomics
    c. A market mechanism
    d. Marginal analysis

24. Which of the following covers the study of topics such as inflation or unemployment?
    a. Microeconomics
    b. Macroeconomics
    c. Both microeconomics and macroeconomics give equal emphasis to these problems.
    d. None of the above

25. What is the name given to the development of a new good or a new process for making a good?
    a. An invention
    b. An innovation
    c. Entrepreneurship
    d. Capital

26. What is the name given to the practical application of an invention?
    a. A model
    b. An innovation
    c. Voluntary exchange
    d. Capital

27. What is the stock of computers, factory buildings, and machine tools used to produce goods better known as?
    a. Physical capital
    b. Technology
    c. Innovation
    d. Goods and services

28. Human capital is similar to physical capital because
    a. both represent the value of money as a productive resource.
    b. both are financed by the profits of firms.
    c. both are productive resources.
    d. both represent changes in technology.

29. Which of the following graphs shown below is the graph of a single variable?

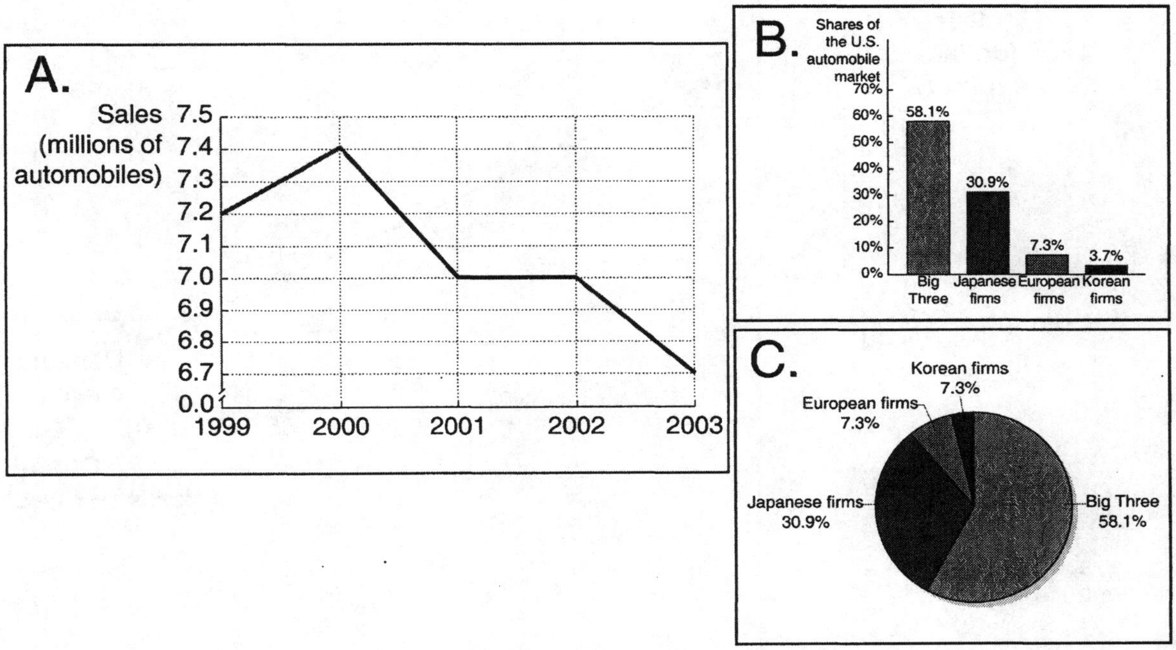

a. A
b. B
c. C
d. All of the above.

30. Which of the following is a graph of the relationship between two variables?

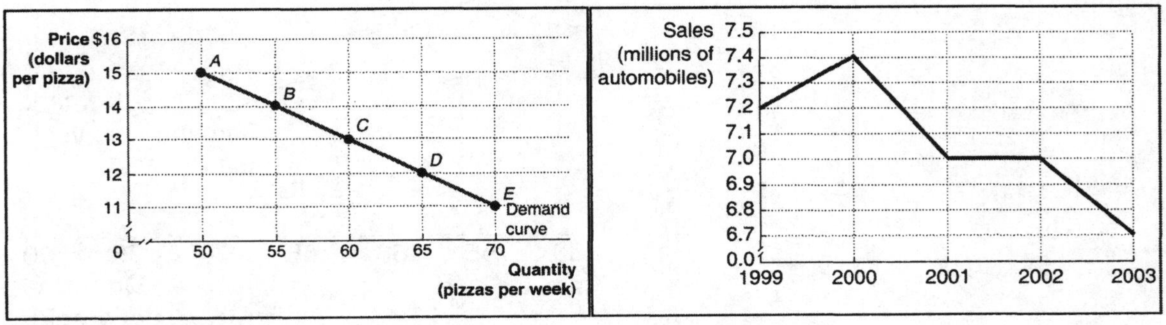

a. The graph on the left
b. The graph on the right
c. Both graphs
d. Neither graph

31. Fill in the blanks. The slope of a straight line equals the change in value on the ____________ axis ____________ by the change in the value of the other axis between any two points on the line.

a. horizontal; multiplied
b. horizontal; divided
c. vertical; multiplied
d. vertical; divided

32. Refer to the graph below. What is the value of the slope of this line?

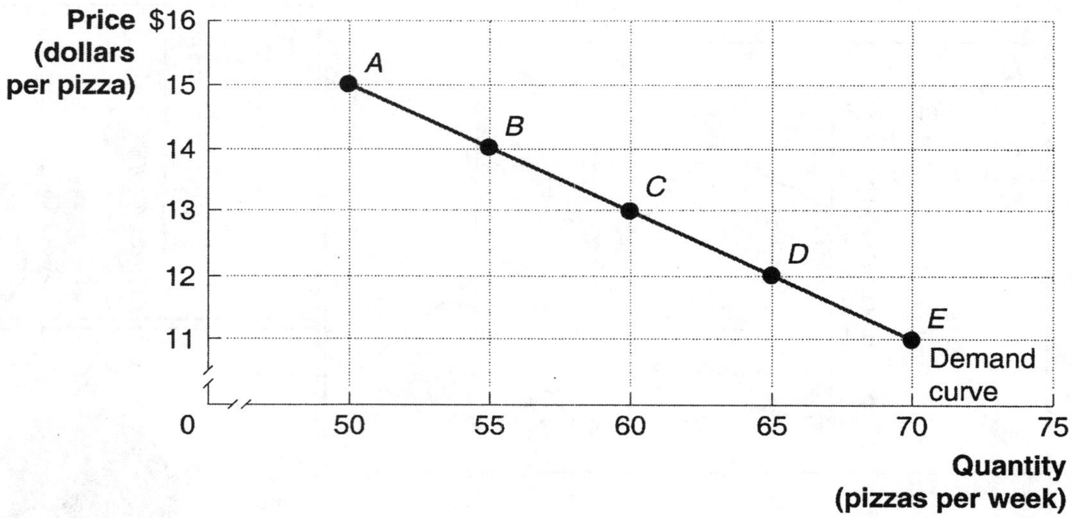

a. −5
b. −1/5
c. −1
d. There is insufficient information to compute the slope of this line.

33. Refer to the graph below. Which variable explains why the line shifts to the right?

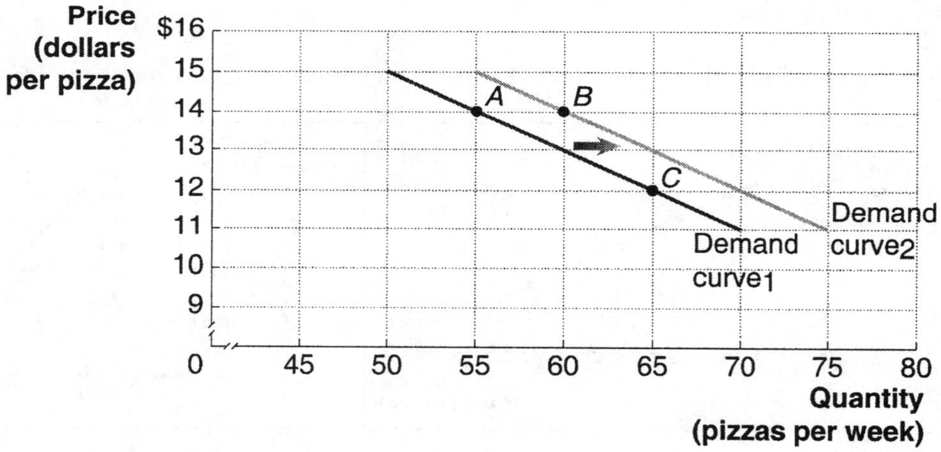

a. The price of pizza
b. The quantity of pizza
c. A third variable other than the price or quantity of pizza
d. All of the above.

34. Refer to the graph below. How many variables are involved in explaining the move from point *A* to point *C* on this graph?

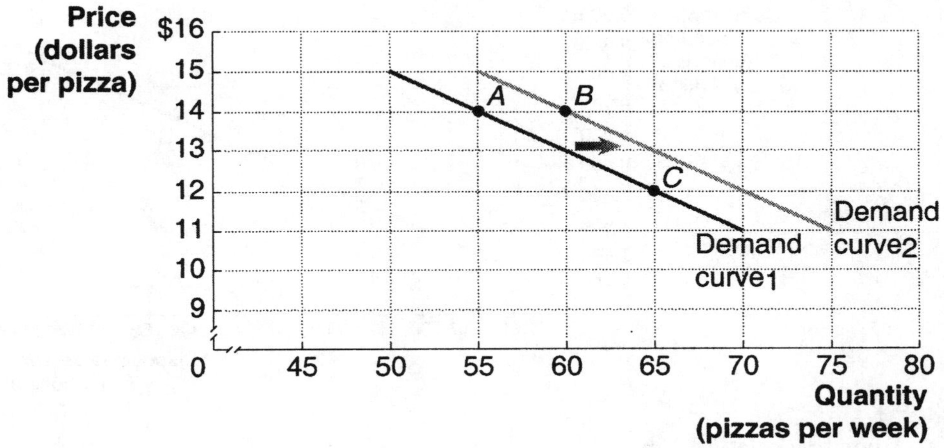

a. One
b. Two
c. Three
d. More than three, at least four.

35. Suppose that there are three variables involved in the graph below: (1) quantity, (2) price, and (3) a third variable. Which of those variables causes the move from point *A* to point *D* in the graph?

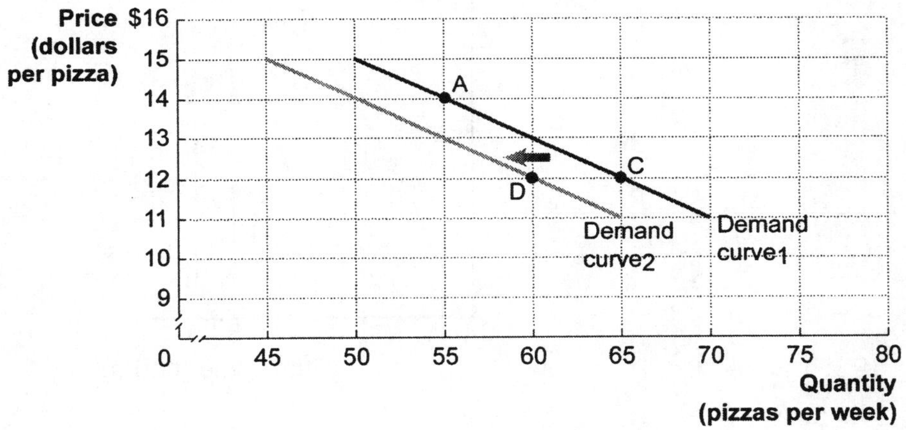

a. The first variable, quantity.
b. The second variable, price.
c. The third variable.
d. Either a. or b.

36. Refer to the graph below. What is the best descriptor of the relationship between disposable personal income and consumption spending?

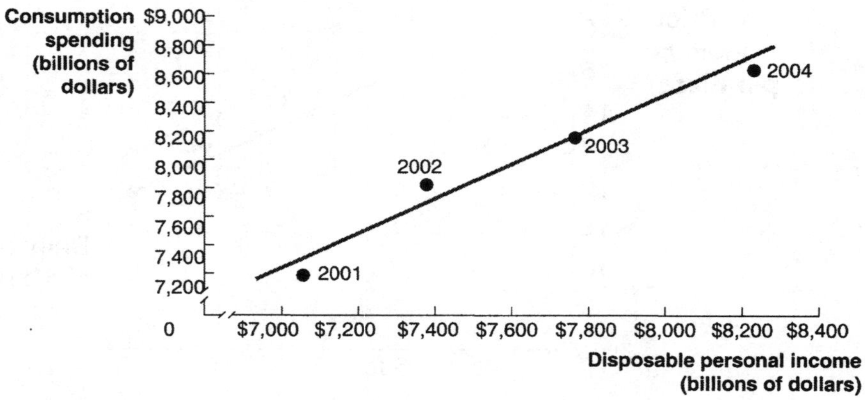

a. A positive relationship
b. A negative relationship
c. A relationship that is sometimes positive and sometimes negative
d. A relationship that may be positive and negative, but sometimes neither positive nor negative

37. Refer to the graph below. What can be said about the value of the slope of this curve?

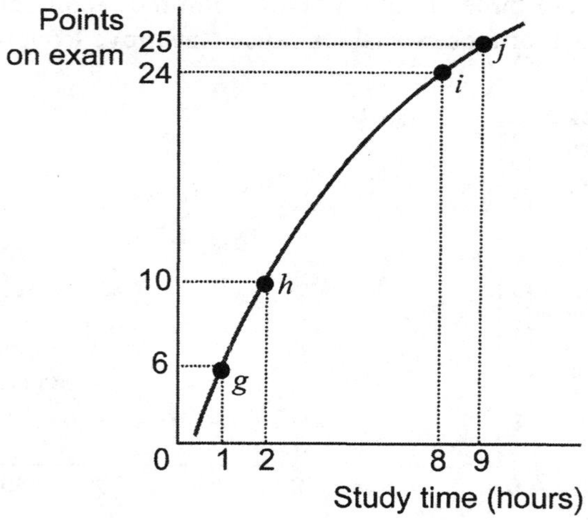

a. The value of the slope is greater between points *i* and *j* than between points *g* and *h*.
b. The value of the slope is greater between points *g* and *h* than between points *i* and *j*.
c. The value of the slope is the same between any two points along the curve.
d. It is difficult to establish the value of the slope because the relationship is not linear.

38. Let V_1 equal the value of a variable in period 1, and V_2 equal the value of the same variable in period 2. What is the rate of growth between periods 1 and 2?
a. $[(V_1 + V_2)/2]\text{x}100$
b. $[(V_2 - V_1)/V_1]\text{x}100$
c. $(V_2 - V_1)/(V_1 + V_2)$
d. $V_2 - V_1$

39. Refer to the graph below. Which of the formulas below must you apply in order to compute the grey area shown on the graph?

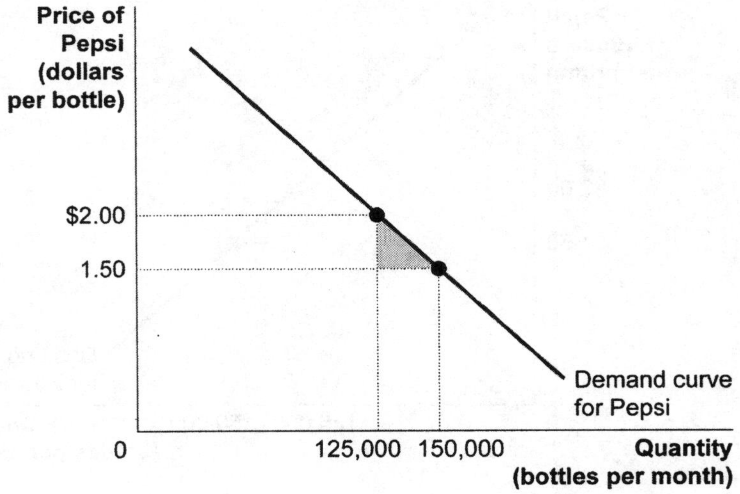

a. Base x Height
b. ½ x Base x Height
c. Both of the above
d. None of the above

40. Refer to the graph below. What is the name of the area contained in rectangle A?

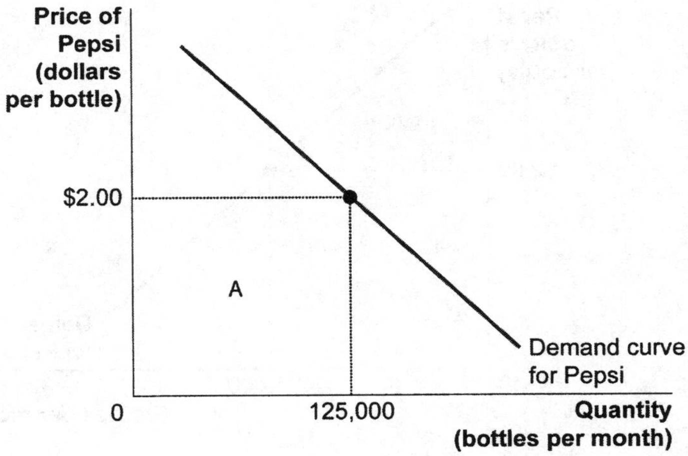

a. Total cost
b. Total revenue
c. Price
d. Average cost

41. Refer to the graph below. What is the value of the grey area shown on the graph?

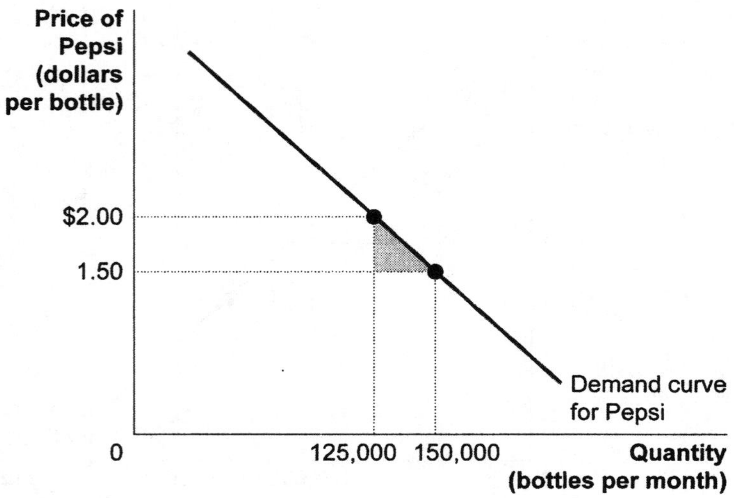

a. $300,000
b. $225,000
c. $62,500
d. $6,250

42. Refer to the graph below. What is the value of the area contained in rectangle A?

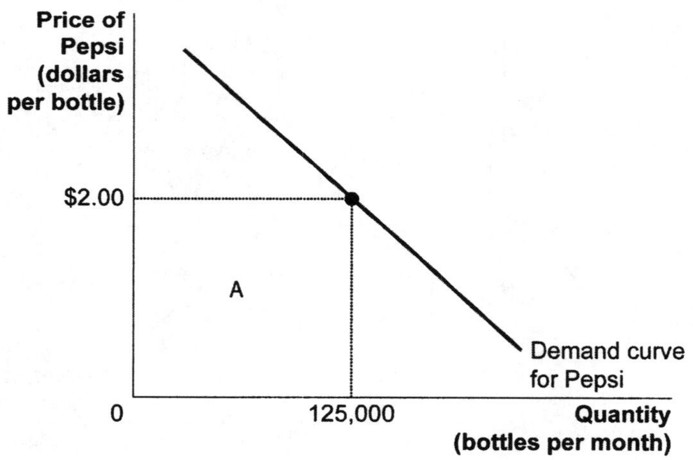

a. $2.00.
b. $125,000
c. $250,000
d. There is not enough information to determine the area.

Short Answer Questions

1. Why do economists distinguish between financial capital and physical capital?

2. Explain the difference between productive efficiency and allocative efficiency.

3. Economists rely on economic models and tests of hypotheses to analyze real-world issues. The use of models and hypothesis testing is common in the natural sciences such as physics and chemistry. Yet, economics is considered a social science, not a natural science. Why?

4. Write an example of a positive statement and an example of a normative statement.

5. Duncan Grant, a freshman economics student at John Borts University, claimed that fresh water is a necessity for all human beings. When asked by his economics instructor if he would be willing to buy a 16 ounce bottle of water for $5.00, Duncan declined. What economic principle would explain Duncan's refusal to buy something that he insists is a necessity?

True/False Questions

T F 1. Stating a hypothesis in an economic model is an example of normative analysis.
T F 2. An entrepreneur is someone who works for a government agency.
T F 3. Economists assume that human beings respond only to economic incentives.
T F 4. In a centrally planned economy the goods and services produced are always distributed equally to all citizens.
T F 5. Equity is achieved when economic benefits are equally distributed.
T F 6. A mixed economy is an economy in which the three fundamental questions (*What? How? Who?*) are answered by a mixture of consumers and producers.
T F 7. Both market economies and centrally planned economies face trade-offs when producing goods and services.
T F 8. When economists assume people are rational, this means that consumers and firms use available information in order to achieve their goals.
T F 9. Government intervention in the United States economy increased dramatically as a result of the Great Depression.
T F 10. Economists use normative analysis to argue that the minimum wage law causes unemployment.
T F 11. Microeconomics is the study of how households and firms make choices, how they interact in markets and how the government attempts to influence their choices.
T F 12. The slope of a straight line is the same at any point.
T F 13. To measure the slope of a nonlinear curve at a particular point one must draw a straight line from the origin to the point. The slope of this line is equal to the slope of the curve at that point.
T F 14. All societies face the economic problem of having a limited amount of economic resources.
T F 15. Economic models can help analyze simple real-world economic situations but are of little value in analyzing complicated economic situations.

Answers to the Self-Test

Multiple-Choice Questions

Question	Answer	Comment
1	d	In this textbook, we use economics to answer questions such as those found in all of the choices given.
2	b	This is the textbook definition of scarcity.
3	b	The question is precisely the definition of a market.
4	d	The textbook presents three important ideas: People are rational; people respond to economic incentives; optimal decisions are made at the margin.
5	c	In solving the problem, consider that optimal decisions are made at the margin. An activity should be continued to the point where the marginal benefit is equal to the marginal cost.
6	c	The three questions are: What goods and services will be produced? How will the goods and services be produced? Who will receive the goods and services?
7	d	These questions refer to the economic problem *every* society must solve.
8	c	A centrally planned economy is an economy in which the government decides how economic resources will be allocated.
9	b	A mixed economy is an economy in which most economic decisions result from the interaction of buyers and sellers in markets, but where the government plays a significant role in the allocation of resources.

10	d	Equity, or fairness, refers to the fair distribution of economic benefits.
11	b	This is a state of the economy in which production reflects consumer preferences; in particular, every good or service is produced up to the point where the last unit produced provides a marginal benefit to consumers equal to the marginal cost of producing it.
12	c	This is a situation that occurs in markets when both the buyer and the seller of a product are made better off by the transaction.
13	a	This occurs when a good or service is produced at the lowest possible cost.
14	d	Economic models are simplified versions of some aspects of economic life used to analyze an economic issue.
15	d	Normative statements are not components of an economic model.
16	b	An economic hypothesis is usually about a causal relationship, or how one thing causes another.
17	c	Normative analysis is analysis concerned with "what ought to be."
18	a	Positive statements describe "what is."
19	c	This question objectively examines a relationship between tuition and class sizes, or "what is."
20	d	This is a question of "what ought to be."
21	a	Positive analysis uses economic models to estimate gains and losses. Positive questions are questions that can be tested.
22	b	A normative statement is a matter of "what ought to be," not "what is," and this is determined by one's values and beliefs.
23	a	Microeconomics is the study of how households and businesses make choices, how they interact in markets, and how the government attempts to influence their choices.
24	b	Macroeconomics is the study of the economy as a whole, including topics such as inflation, unemployment and economic growth.
25	a	An invention is different from an innovation.
26	b	An innovation is the application of an invention.
27	a	In economics, capital refers to physical capital.
28	c	Human and physical capital are used to produce goods and services.
29	d	The bar chart, pie chart, and time series graph are all graphs of a single variable.
30	a	This graph shows the relationship between two variables: price and quantity demanded.
31	d	The slope of a line equals the value on the vertical axis divided by the value on the horizontal axis.
32	b	Along this line, the value of the slope is the same between any two points. As an example, as we move from B (55, 14) to C (60, 13), the value of rise is (13-14) = -1 and the value of the run is (55-60) = -5. Then, the value of the slope is -1/5.
33	c	Shifting a line involves taking into account more than two variables on a graph. In this case, something other than the price of pizza has changed, causing the demand curve to shift to the right, and showing the quantity of pizza demanded is greater for each of the prices shown.
34	a	The movement from A to C is explained by one and only one thing: a change in price. The (price, quantity demanded) combination at A is different from that at C, but the movement from A to C is explained by a change in only one variable: price.
35	c	A shift of the demand curve is caused by a change in something other than price, such as a change in income. For each price, quantity demanded is less than it was before.
36	a	An upward sloping line shows that the relationship between two variables is positive, i.e. the variables change in the same direction.

37	b	As you move upward along the curve, the value of the slope decreases. The slope between g and h is (10-6)/(2-1) = 4 and the slope between i and j is (25-24)/(9-8) = 1.
38	b	This is the formula for computing a percentage change.
39	b	You are computing the area of a triangle, which is ½ x Base x Height.
40	b	Total revenue equals price x quantity, which is the area of the rectangle (Base x Height).
41	d	The area of the triangle is ½ x ($2.00 - $1.50) x (150,000 – 125,000) = $6,250.
42	c	The area of the rectangle is equal to $2.00/bottle x 125,000 bottles = $250,000, which is $250,000 in total revenue.

Short Answers

1. Economists distinguish financial capital and physical capital because only physical capital (for example, machinery, tools and buildings) is a productive resource. Financial capital includes stocks, bonds, and holdings of money. Financial capital is not part of a country's capital stock, because financial capital does not produce output.

2. Productive efficiency is the situation in which a good or service is produced at the lowest possible cost. Allocative efficiency is a state of the economy in which production reflects consumer preferences. Every good or service is produced to the point at which the last unit provides a marginal benefit to consumers equal to the marginal cost of producing it.

3. Economics, unlike physics and chemistry, is a social science because it applies the use of models and hypothesis testing to the study of the interactions of people.

4. Positive statements are statements or facts, or statements that can be proven to be correct or incorrect. Example: "Abraham Lincoln was the 15th president of the United States." (This is a false statement – Lincoln was the 16th president). A normative statement is an opinion or a statement of what should or ought to be. Example: "The United States should elect a female as president of the United States."

5. The principle that best describes Duncan's refusal to pay for the bottle of water is marginal analysis. The total benefit to people from fresh water is very high but the marginal benefit of water – the benefit to Duncan from an additional 16 ounces of water – is very low. Duncan probably is not very thirsty. If Duncan had not had anything to drink for two days the benefit to him of the next 16 ounces of water he drinks will be much higher.

True/False Answers

1. F A hypothesis is a testable statement about how the world is.
2. F An entrepreneur is someone who operates a business.
3. F Economists believe people respond to incentives.
4. F The distribution of goods and services is determined by the government and that need not be equal.
5. F People differ on what they believe is equitable or fair.
6. F A mixed economy is one in which government influence on the choices of buyers and sellers is greater than in a market economy.
7. T All economies face trade-offs due to scarce resources.
8. T
9. T See the section titled "The Modern 'Mixed' Economy" on page 10.
10. F Economists would use positive economics analysis to address this issue.
11. T This is the definition of microeconomics.
12. T
13. F The slope of a point on a nonlinear curve is measured by the slope of a tangent to the curve at that point.
14. T
15. F Economic models provide a basic foundation for use in the analysis of both simplistic and complicated economic situations.

Chapter 2

Trade-offs, Comparative Advantage, and the Market System

Chapter Summary

A nation can produce only limited quantities of goods and services because it has scarce resources. Economists use the **production possibilities frontier** (*PPF*) to analyze the opportunity costs and trade-offs that nations, firms, and individuals face as a result of **scarcity**. The *PPF* is a curve that illustrates the combinations of two goods a nation can produce using all of its economic resources and a current state of technology in a given time period. The more resources that are devoted to an activity, the smaller the payoff to devoting additional resources to that activity. Production possibilities frontiers can be used to demonstrate the benefits of specialization in production and trade for two individuals or two nations.

Markets enable buyers and sellers of goods and services to come together to trade. The **circular-flow diagram** shows how buyers (households) and sellers (firms) interact in both product and factor markets. Free markets exist when governments place few restrictions on how a good or service can be produced and sold or on how a factor of production can be employed.

Entrepreneurs, those who own and operate businesses, are critical to the working of a market system. The businesses they operate produce goods and services consumers want. The entrepreneur decides how these goods and services should be produced to yield the most profit. Entrepreneurs organize factors of production and risk their own funds to start businesses. Successful entrepreneurs are rewarded for their efforts with profits, but most entrepreneurs, including many who later meet with success, suffer financial losses and business failures if they do not satisfy consumers' wants. Although government does not restrict how firms produce and sell goods and services in a free market, it is essential that government protect an individual's right to private property in order for a market system work well.

Learning Objectives

When you finish this chapter, you should be able to:

1. **Use a production possibilities frontier to analyze opportunity costs and trade-offs.** Each point on a production possibilities frontier represents a combination of two goods that can be produced by using all of a nation's available resources given the state of technology and during a specific time period. Along the frontier, an increase in production of one good requires a decrease in production of the other good. Production possibilities frontiers usually appear bowed outward because marginal opportunity costs typically increase as the production of any good or service rises.

2. **Understand comparative advantage and explain how it is the basis for trade.** Comparative advantage explains why a person is better off specializing in the production of the good or service that he or she can produce at a lower opportunity cost than another person. Each person can then trade for the good or service the other person produces.

3. **Explain the basic idea of how a market system works.** In a market system, buyers and sellers in product markets and resource markets are free to trade with few restrictions on how a good or service can be sold or how a factor of production can be employed. Individual buyers and sellers are assumed to act in rational, self-interested ways.

Chapter Review

Chapter Opener: Managers Making Choices at BMW (pages 36-37)

The managers at firms such as BMW (Bavarian Motor Works) must make decisions regarding the production and marketing of their products. These decisions include the location of manufacturing plants and the production methods used at these plants. Because BMW is a German firm, there are good reasons to locate factories in Germany. However, locating factories in other countries can reduce manufacturing costs (for example, by paying lower wages). Locating in countries where the automobiles are sold also reduces the risk that foreign governments will impose import restrictions.

Helpful Study Hint

The authors use a production possibilities frontier to illustrate BMW's decision to produce Z4 roadsters and X5 sports utility vehicles. See Figure 2-1. An ***Inside Look*** at the end of the chapter uses the concepts explained in the chapter to analyze BMW's production decisions during 2007. BMW generated a new production possibilities frontier (*PPF*) due to technological change and is moving in the direction of producing on the new *PPF*. As production increases, BMW is substituting the production of SUVs for coupes.

Economics in YOUR Life! "The Trade-offs When You Buy a Car" asks whether there is a relationship between gas mileage and safety and whether we can increase both safety and the mileage. Keep this question in mind as you read the chapter. The authors will answer this question at the end of the chapter.

2.1 LEARNING OBJECTIVE

2.1 Production Possibilities Frontiers and Opportunity Costs (pages 38-44)

Learning Objective 1 Use a production possibilities frontier to analyze opportunity costs and trade-offs.

A **production possibilities frontier** (*PPF*) is a curve showing the maximum alternative combinations of two products that may be produced with available resources. The slope of a *PPF* is used to measure the opportunity cost of increasing the production of one good along the frontier relative to the other good.

The slope of a linear frontier and the opportunity cost of moving along the frontier are constant. But convex or "bowed out" production possibilities frontiers represent a more likely outcome. A convex *PPF* means marginal opportunity costs rise as more and more of one good is produced. For example, starting from point *A* in Figure 2-2 and moving downward to points *B* and *C*, the slope of the frontier becomes steeper and steeper. This means that the cost of producing one more automobile (the number of tanks that must be given up as resources are transferred to automobile production) is greater at each point.

Along a production possibilities frontier, resources and technology are fixed. If there is an increase in the available resources or an improvement in the technology used to produce goods and services, the *PPF* will shift outward. The economy will be able to produce more goods and services, which means the economy has experienced economic growth. **Economic growth** is the ability of the economy to produce increasing quantities of goods and services. Growth may lead to greater increases in production of one good than another.

Helpful Study Hint

Solved Problem 2-1 will help you draw a *PPF* and understand how a linear *PPF* illustrates opportunity costs incurred in production. Be sure you understand how slope is measured along the frontier and that this slope represents the opportunity cost of substituting the production of one good for the production of another.

Making the Connection "Trade-offs: Hurricane Katrina, Tsunami Relief, and Charitable Giving" describes a sobering example of the opportunity cost of making donations to charitable organizations when aid is solicited as a result of a natural disaster. Households and firms typically have a fixed budget for charities, and contributions to one charitable cause will diminish the supply of funds available to another charitable cause. When natural disasters strike, the focus for charitable giving becomes the relief fund for that disaster and other charitable causes typically see a reduction in giving.

2.2 LEARNING OBJECTIVE

2.2 Comparative Advantage and Trade (pages 44-49)

Learning Objective 2 Understand comparative advantage and explain how it is the basis for trade.

By specializing in production and engaging in trade, individuals can enjoy a higher standard of living than would be possible if these individuals produced everything they consumed. Specialization in production is so common that most people take for granted that they must trade income earned from their own labor to buy the services of plumbers, carpenters, medical doctors, and stock brokers. Specialization makes trade necessary. **Trade** is the act of buying or selling.

Absolute advantage is the ability of an individual, firm, or country to produce more of a good or service than competitors using the same amount of resources. **Comparative advantage** is the ability of an individual, firm, or country to produce a good or service at a lower opportunity cost than other producers. An individual country should specialize in the production of the good or services in which it has a comparative advantage, and then trade this good to other countries for goods in which it does not have a comparative advantage.

Helpful Study Hint

Don't Let This Happen to You! clarifies the differences between absolute and comparative advantage using the example of individuals picking apples and picking cherries. A country has the absolute advantage in the production of a good if the country can produce more of the good, while the comparative advantage in the production of a good goes to the country that can produce the good relatively inexpensively (that is, with the lower opportunity cost). In the simple case with two goods, a country can have an absolute advantage in the production of both goods, but the country will only have a comparative advantage in the production of only one of the two goods.

Solved Problem 2-2 describes the benefits realized when a nation specializes in the production of a good for which it has a comparative advantage. In the problem, the United States has a comparative advantage in producing honey, while Canada has a comparative advantage in producing maple syrup. Each country should specialize in producing the good for which it has a comparative advantage and trade some of that good for the other good. With trade, the United States and Canada can consume outside of their *PPFs*.

Most examples of absolute and comparative advantage are similar to the hypothetical examples in section 2.2 of the textbook. This is due, in part, to the difficulty of identifying people who have an absolute advantage in two different areas. But the career of Babe Ruth offers a good example of someone with an absolute advantage in two activities who was still ultimately better off specializing in the activity in which he had a comparative advantage. Before he achieved his greatest fame as a home run hitter and outfielder with the New York Yankees, Ruth was a star pitcher with the Boston Red Sox. Ruth may have been the best left-handed pitcher in the American League during his years with Boston (1914-1919), but he was used more and more as a fielder in his last two years with the team. In fact, he established a record for home runs in a season (29) in 1919 when he was still pitching. The Yankees acquired Ruth in 1920 and made him a full-time outfielder. The opportunity cost of this decision for the Yankees was the wins Ruth could have earned as a pitcher. But because New York already had skilled pitchers, the opportunity cost of replacing Ruth as a pitcher was lower than the cost of replacing him as a hitter. No one else on the Yankees could have hit 54 home runs, Ruth's total in 1920; the next highest Yankee total was 11. It can be argued that Ruth had an absolute advantage as both a hitter and pitcher in 1920 but a comparative advantage only as a hitter.

2.3 LEARNING OBJECTIVE

2.3 The Market System (pages 50-56)

Learning Objective 3 Explain the basic idea of how a market system works.

A **market** is a group of buyers and sellers of a good or service and the institution or arrangement by which they come together to trade. **Product markets** are markets for goods, such as computers, and services, such as medical treatment. **Factor markets** are markets for the factors of production, such as labor, capital, natural resources, and entrepreneurial ability. A **circular-flow diagram** is a model that illustrates how participants in markets are linked. The diagram demonstrates the interaction between firms and households in both product and factor markets. Households buy goods and services in the product market and provide resources for sale in the factor market, while firms provide goods and services in the product market and buy resources in the factor market. A **free market** is a market with few government restrictions on how a good or service can be produced or sold, or on how a factor of production can be employed.

Entrepreneurs are an essential part of a market economy. An **entrepreneur** is someone who operates a business, bringing together the factors of production – labor, capital, and natural resources – to produce goods and services. Entrepreneurs often risk their own funds to start businesses and organize factors of production to produce those goods and services consumers want.

The role of government in a market system is limited but essential. Although government in a market economy imposes few restrictions on the choices made by consumers, resource owners, and firms, government protection of private property rights is necessary for markets to operate efficiently.

Property rights are the rights individuals or firms have to the exclusive use of their physical and intellectual property, including the right to buy or sell it. New technology has created challenges to protection of property rights. Unauthorized copying of music and other intellectual property in cyberspace reduces the rewards to creativity and may reduce the amount of such activity in the future.

Helpful Study Hint

Consumers seldom know the identity of the people who produce the products they buy. The impersonal and decentralized character of markets is illustrated very well by the discussion of the production of Apple's iPod found in ***Making the Connection*** "A Story of the Market System in Action: How Do You Make an iPod?" The iPod contains 451 parts. Many of the manufacturers of the components of the iPod do not know what the final product will be. No one person at Apple knows how to produce all of these components, so Apple relies heavily on its suppliers.

The role of government in a free market economy can be compared to that of an umpire or referee in a sporting event. The most vocal critics of these officials would not argue they are not needed. It would not take long for a professional football or baseball game to turn into a shouting match (or worse!) if players were allowed to enforce the rules of their own games. On the other hand, the quality of sporting events suffers when officials bar players, coaches, or managers from participating in contests for frivolous reasons. ***Making the Connection***

"Property Rights in Cyberspace: YouTube and MySpace" reinforces the need for government protection of property rights and the difficulties associated with enforcing intellectual property rights. Material can easily be uploaded to and posted on the Internet. Once on the Internet, the material can be easily downloaded, reproduced, reposted, and the like. It is highly unlikely that you will get caught for piracy when reproducing the material for your personal use, so these intellectual property rights are nearly impossible to protect.

The stories of successful businesses such as Microsoft and Google can give a misleading impression about the risks of business ownership. Many businesses fail. The National Restaurant Association estimates an 80 percent failure rate for independently owned restaurants within their first two years of operation. The average work week for many small business owners is much longer than that of the average employee – 80 hours is not uncommon – and owners often borrow heavily to start and maintain their businesses.

At the start of the chapter, ***Economics in YOUR Life!*** "The Trade-offs When You Buy a Car" asks whether there is a relationship between gas mileage and safety and whether we can increase both safety and the mileage rate. You can analyze these questions using a *PPF*. The trade-off between safety and gas mileage can be depicted by looking at a given *PPF*. We know that bigger, heavier cars are safer, but they also have worse gas mileage. We could get a combination of safety and fuel mileage that is outside the given *PPF* by improvements in the technology used in manufacturing automobiles. This would give us a new *PPF* and an increase in both safety and gas mileage.

Extra Solved Problem **2-3**

The chapter includes 2 Solved Problems. Here is an extra Solved Problem to help you build your skills solving economic problems.

Supports Learning Objective 2-3: Explain the basic idea of how a market system works.

Adam Smith's "Invisible Hand"

Alan Krueger, an economist at Princeton University, has argued that Adam Smith "...worried that if merchants and manufacturers pursued their self-interest by seeking government regulation and privilege, the invisible hand would not work its magic..."

Source: Alan B. Krueger, "Rediscovering the Wealth of Nations," *New York Times*, August 16, 2001.

a. What types of regulation and privilege might merchants and manufacturers seek from the government?

b. How might these regulations and privileges keep the invisible hand from working?

SOLVING THE PROBLEM

Step 1: Review the chapter material.
This problem is about how goods and services are produced and sold and how factors of production are employed in a free market economic system as described by Adam Smith in *An Inquiry into the Nature and Causes of the Wealth of Nations.* You may want to review the section "The Gains from Free Markets," which begins on page 52 in the textbook.

Step 2: Answer question (a) by noting the economic system in place in Europe in 1776.
At that time, governments gave guilds – associations of producers – the authority to control production. The production controls limited the amount of output of goods such as shoes and clothing as well as the number of producers of these items. Limiting production and competition led to higher prices and fewer choices for consumers. Instead of catering to the wants of consumers, producers sought the favor of government officials.

Step 3: Answer question (b) by contrasting the behavior of merchants and manufacturers under a guild system and a market system.
Because governments gave producers the power to control production, producers did not have to respond to consumers' demands for better quality, more variety, and lower prices. Under a market system, producers who sell goods of poor quality at high prices suffer economic losses; producers who provide better quality goods at low prices are rewarded with profits. Therefore, in a market system it is in the self-interest of producers to address consumer wants. This is how the invisible hand works in a free market economy, but not in eighteenth century Europe.

Key Terms

Absolute advantage. The ability of an individual, firm, or country to produce more of a good or service than competitors, using the same amount of resources.

Circular-flow diagram. A model that illustrates how participants in markets are linked.

Comparative advantage. The ability of an individual, firm, or country to produce a good or service at a lower opportunity cost than competitors.

Economic growth. The ability of the economy to produce increasing quantities of goods and services.

Entrepreneur. Someone who operates a business, bringing together the factors of production – labor, capital, and natural resources – to produce goods and services.

Factor markets. Markets for the factors of production, such as labor, capital, natural resources, and entrepreneurial ability.

Factors of production. The inputs used to make goods and services.

Free market. A market with few government restrictions on how a good or service can be produced or sold or how a factor of production can be employed.

Market. A group of buyers and sellers of a good or service and the institution or arrangement by which they come together to trade.

Opportunity cost. The highest-valued alternative that must be given up to engage in an activity.

Product markets. Markets for goods – such as computers – and services – such as medical treatment.

Production possibilities frontier (*PPF*). A curve showing the maximum attainable combinations of two products that may be produced with available resources and current technology.

Property rights. The rights individuals or firms have to the exclusive use of their property, including the right to buy or sell it.

Scarcity. The situation in which unlimited wants exceed the limited resources available to fulfill those wants.

Trade. The act of buying or selling.

Self-Test

(Answers are provided at the end of the Self-Test.)

Multiple-Choice Questions

1. What is the name given to the highest-valued alternative that must be given up to engage in any activity?
   a. Scarcity
   b. The production possibilities frontier
   c. Opportunity cost
   d. A tradeoff

2. What happens if a country produces a combination of goods that uses all of the resources available in the economy?
   a. The country is operating on its production possibilities frontier.
   b. The country is maximizing its opportunity cost.
   c. The country has eliminated scarcity.
   d. All of the above

3. Refer to the graph below. Which of the following combinations is unattainable with the current resources available in this economy?

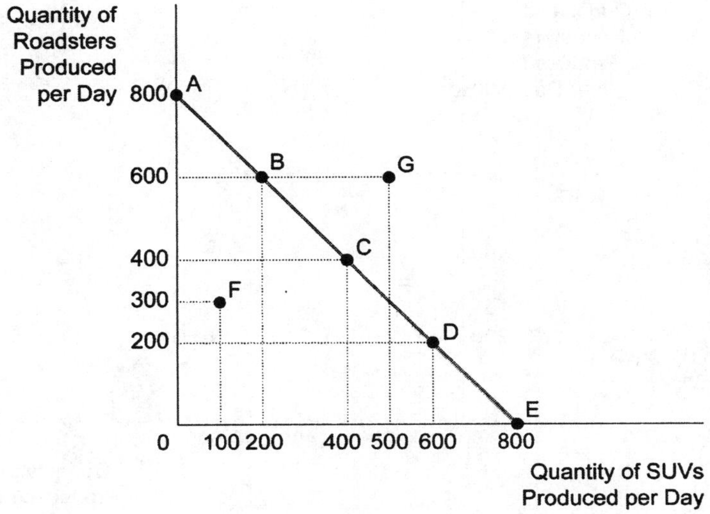

a. Combination G
b. Combination F
c. Combinations A or E
d. All of the above. None of the combinations above can be attained with current resources.

4. Refer to the graph below. Which of the following combinations is inefficient?

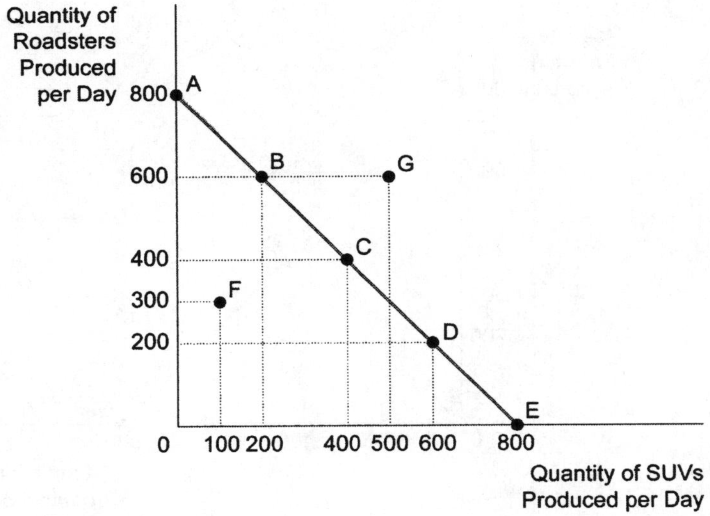

a. Combination G
b. Combination F
c. Combinations A or E
d. Both F and G

5. Refer to the graph below. Which of the following best represents the situation in which BMW *must* face a tradeoff between producing SUVs and producing roadsters?

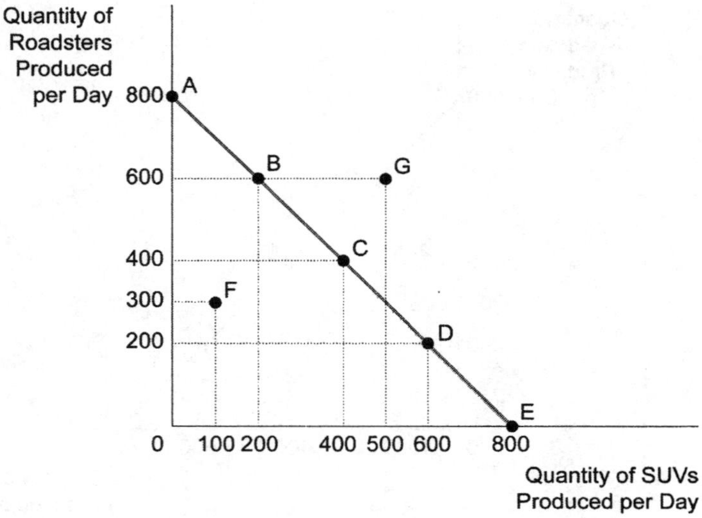

a. Any point on the graph represents that tradeoff.
b. Moving from B to C
c. Moving from F to B
d. Moving from C and G

6. Refer to the graph below. How many roadsters are produced at the point where BMW produces 800 SUVs?

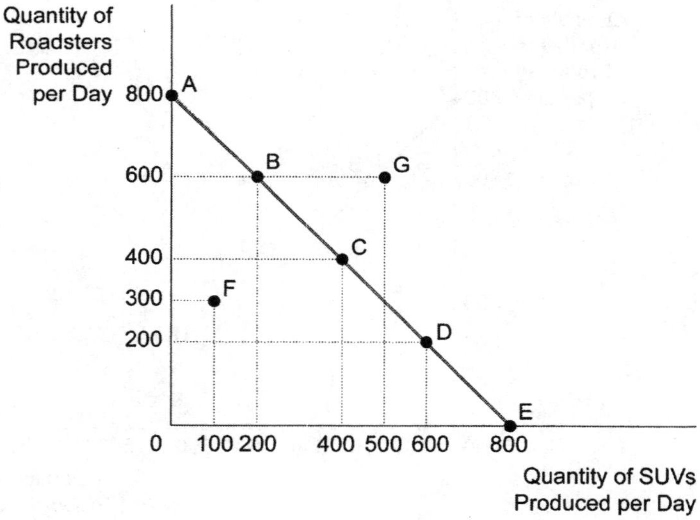

a. Zero
b. Any amount up to 800
c. Exactly 800
d. 400

7. Refer to the graph below. What is the opportunity cost of moving from point B to point C?

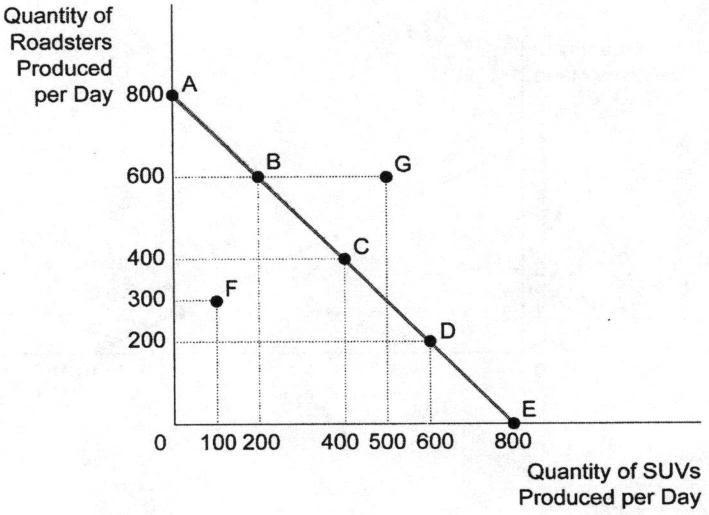

a. 200 SUVs
b. 400 SUVs
c. 200 roadsters
d. 400 roadsters

8. Refer to the graph below. The graph shows the data from Solved Problem 2-1. What is the opportunity cost of switching from Choice D to Choice E?

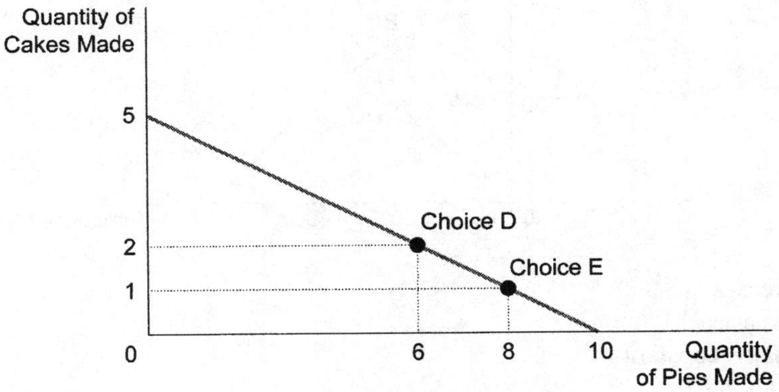

a. Two pies
b. Eight pies
c. Two cakes
d. One cake

9. Refer to the graph below. The graph is a representation of the data in Solved Problem 2-1. In this problem, what is the opportunity cost of producing five cakes?

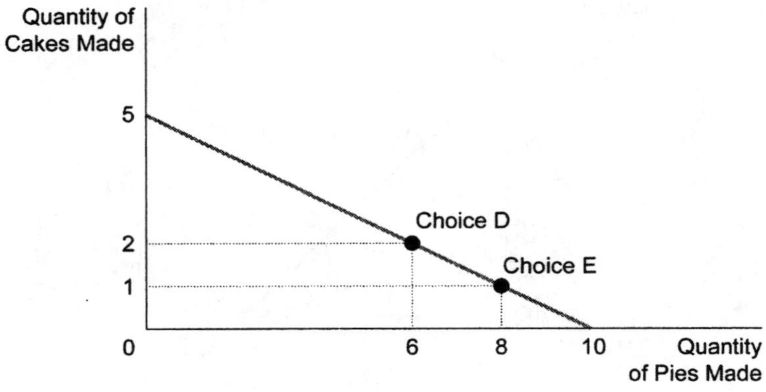

a. Zero cakes
b. Zero pies
c. Ten pies
d. There is insufficient information to answer the question.

10. Refer to the graph below. As you move from point A to point B and then to C on this graph, what happens to the marginal opportunity cost?

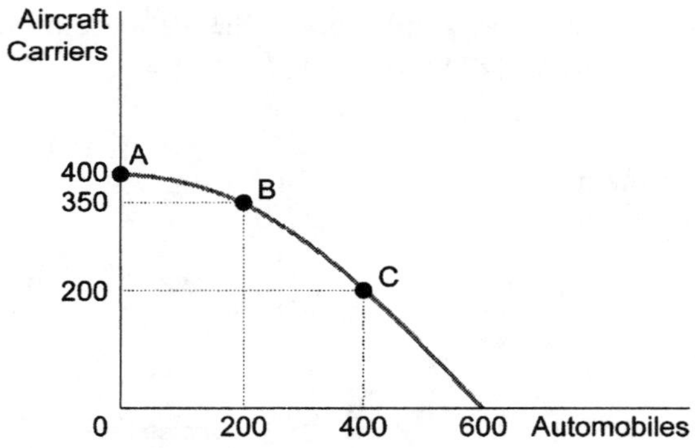

a. It increases
b. It decreases
c. It remains constant
d. It equals zero

11. Refer to the graph below. What is the opportunity cost of producing 400 aircraft carriers?

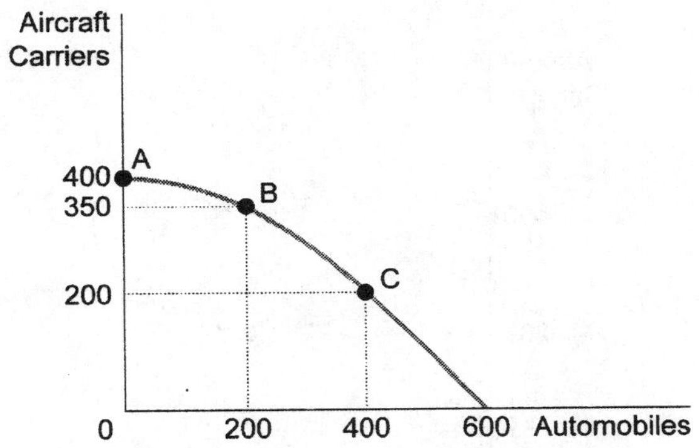

a. 200 automobiles
b. 50 aircraft carriers
c. 200 automobiles
d. 600 automobiles

12. Refer to the graph below. What is the opportunity cost of moving from point B to point C?

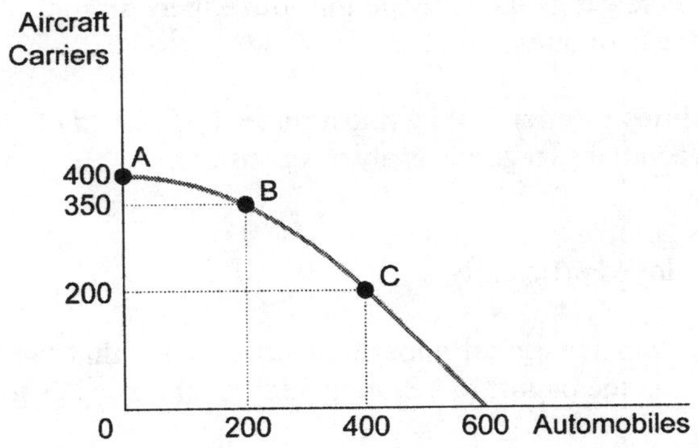

a. 200 automobiles
b. 400 automobiles
c. 50 aircraft carriers
d. 150 aircraft carriers

13. Refer to the graph below. Precisely what does the term "increasing marginal opportunity cost" mean in this graph?

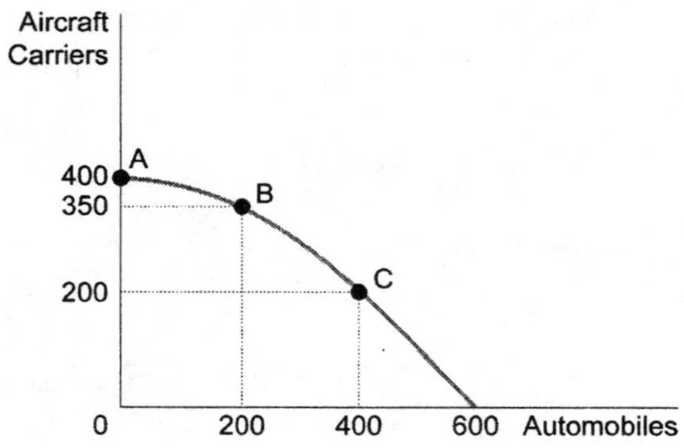

a. It means that there is a higher opportunity cost of producing either aircrafts or automobiles, so long as the quantity produced of that good is decreasing.
b. It means that there is a higher opportunity cost of producing either aircrafts or automobiles, so long as the quantity produced of that good is increasing.
c. It means that increasing the production of aircrafts results in higher automobile production costs, such as the costs of labor and capital to build automobiles.
d. It means that increasing the production of either aircrafts or automobiles creates more opportunities in the economy.

14. A production possibilities frontier will be linear instead of bowed out if
a. the tradeoff between the two goods is always constant.
b. no tradeoffs exist.
c. unemployment is zero.
d. resources are employed efficiently.

15. The principle of increasing marginal opportunity cost states that the more resources devoted to any activity, the __________ the payoff to devoting additional resources to that activity.
a. smaller
b. greater
c. proportional
d. more instant

16. Refer to the graphs below. Which graph best represents an improvement in the technology used to make automobiles?

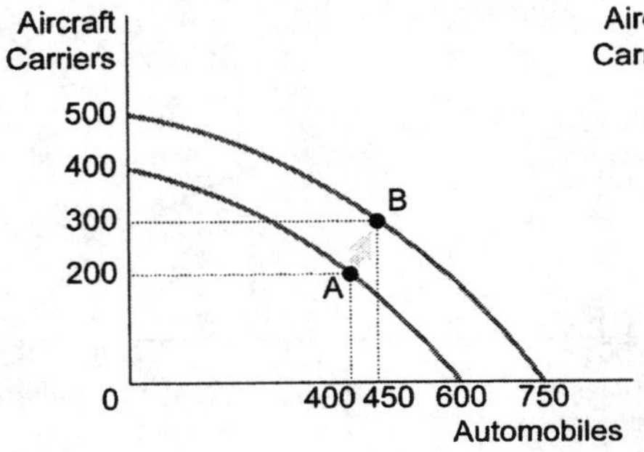

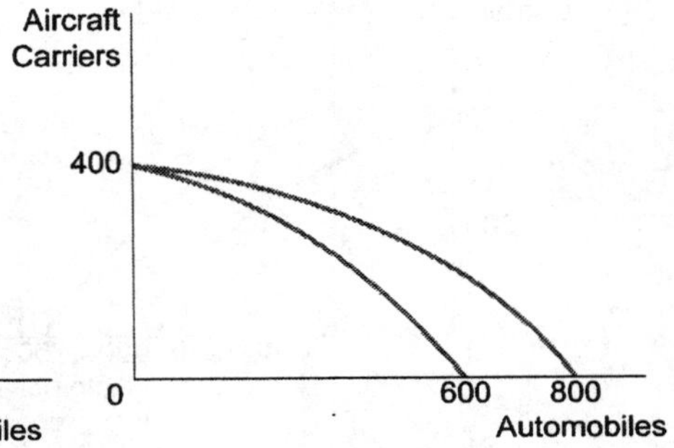

a. The graph on the left
b. The graph on the right
c. Both graphs
d. Neither graph

17. Refer to the graphs below. Which graph best represents an increase in the economy's resources?

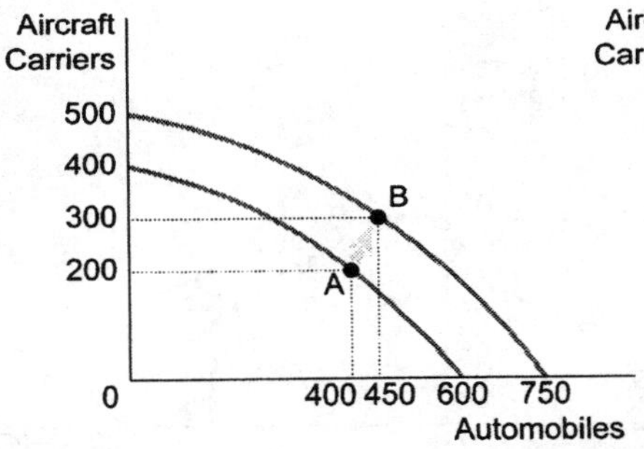

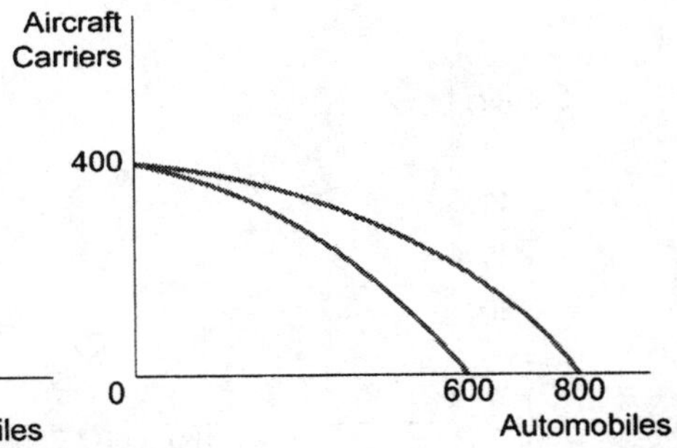

a. The graph on the left
b. The graph on the right
c. Both graphs
d. Neither graph

18. Refer to the graphs below. Which graph best represents the concept of *economic growth*?

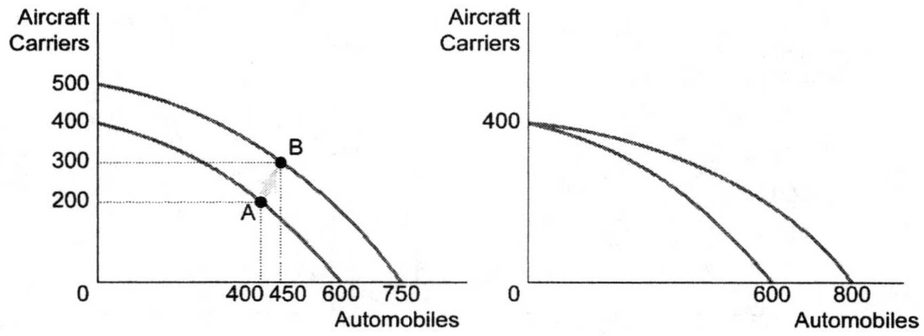

a. The graph on the left
b. The graph on the right
c. Both graphs
d. Neither graph

19. Refer to the graphs below. Which of the following could have caused the outward shift of the curve in the graph on the left side?

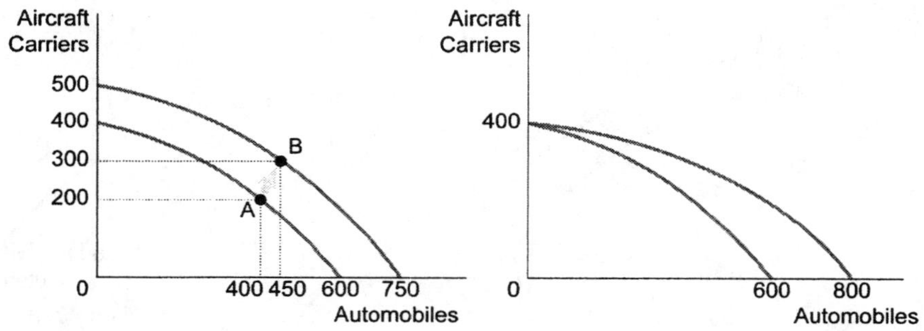

a. An increase in technology that affects the production of both aircraft carriers and automobiles.
b. Technological change that affects only the aircraft carrier industry.
c. Unemployment in the economy
d. A change in the cost of producing automobiles.

20. Which of the following would create economic growth, that is, shift the production possibilities frontier outward?
a. An increase in the available labor.
b. An increase in technology that affects the production of both goods.
c. An increase in the available natural resources.
d. All of the above

21. According to textbook section 2.2 on trade, which of the following statements is most consistent with positive economic analysis?
    a. The United States would be better off being self-sufficient, so we don't have to rely on other nations for certain goods.
    b. The United States would be better off if we specialize in the production of some goods, and then trade some of them to other countries.
    c. We should produce at home the goods that we now import—that way we can generate additional jobs here at home.
    d. We should establish trade with friendly countries and avoid trade with our enemies.

22. *Absolute advantage* is the ability of an individual, firm, or country to
    a. produce more of a good or service than competitors using the same amount of resources.
    b. produce a good or service at a lower opportunity cost than other producers.
    c. consume more goods or services than others at lower costs.
    d. reach a higher production possibilities frontier by lowering opportunity costs.

23. If a country has a *comparative advantage* in the production of a good, then that country
    a. also has an absolute advantage in producing that good.
    b. should allow another country to specialize in the production of that good.
    c. has a lower opportunity cost in the production of that good.
    d. All of the above

24. Refer to the graphs below. Each graph represents one country. Which country has a comparative advantage in the production of shirts?

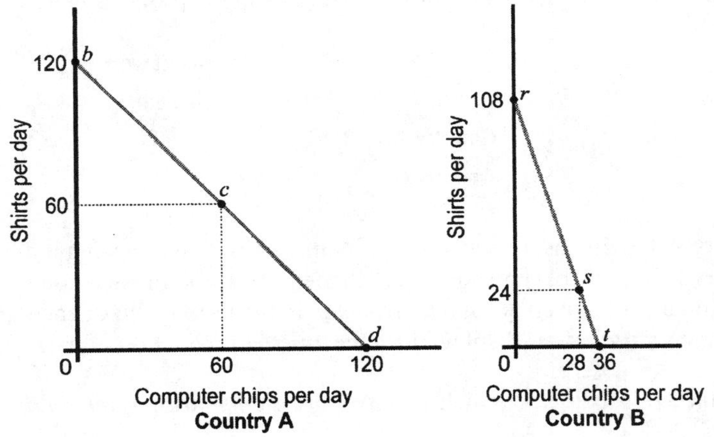

    a. Country A
    b. Country B
    c. Neither country
    d. Both countries

25. Refer to the graphs below. Each graph represents one country. Which country should specialize in the production of chips?

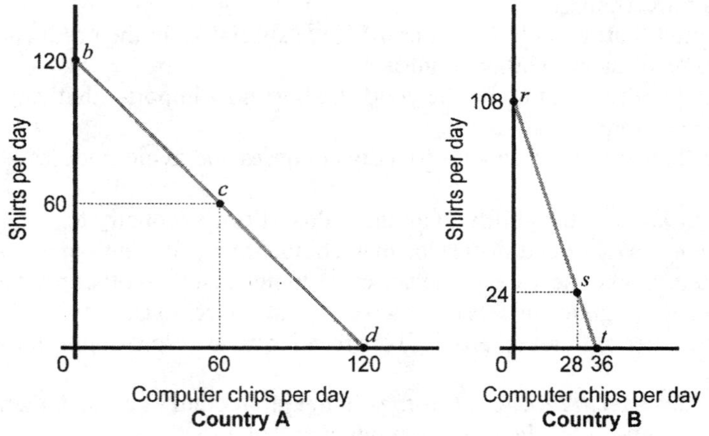

a. Country A
b. Country B
c. Neither country; they both should produce some chips and some shirts.
d. Both countries should specialize in the production of chips.

26. The table below shows the quantity of two goods that a worker can produce per day in a given country. Which country has an *absolute advantage* in the production of each good?

	Output per day of work	
	Food	Clothing
Country A	6	3
Country B	1	2

a. Country A has an absolute advantage in the production of each good.
b. Country B has an absolute advantage in the production of each good.
c. Both countries have an absolute advantage in the production of each good.
d. Neither country has an absolute advantage in the production of each good.

27. Consider the table below. Which country has a *comparative advantage* in the production of each good?

	Output per day of work	
	Food	Clothing
Country A	6	3
Country B	1	2

a. Country A has a comparative advantage in the production of both goods.
b. Country B has a comparative advantage in the production of both goods.
c. Country A has a comparative advantage in the production of food.
d. Country B has a comparative advantage in the production of food.

28. Refer to the graphs below. If you have a comparative advantage in the production of apples, what point would best represent your production with trade?

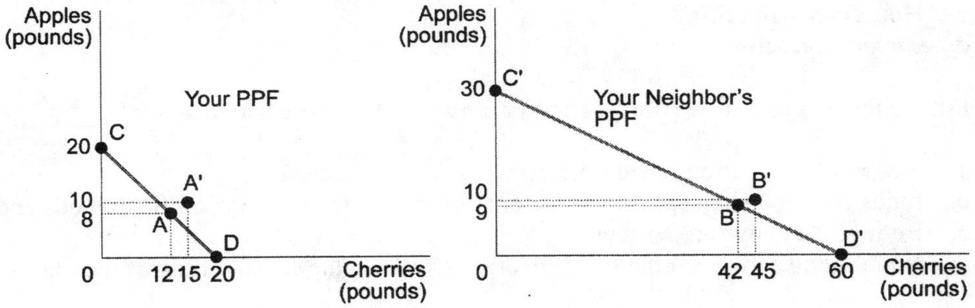

a. A
b. A'
c. C
d. D

29. Refer to the graphs below. What is point B' on your neighbor's *PPF* curve?

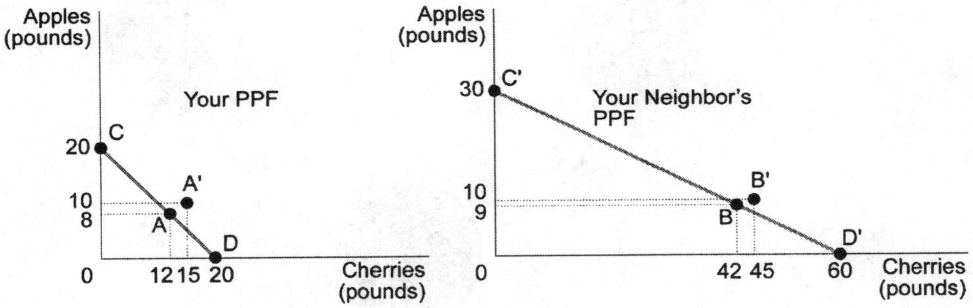

a. Point B' is your neighbor's production before trade.
b. Point B' is your neighbor's consumption before trade.
c. Point B' is your neighbor's production after trade.
d. Point B' is your neighbor's consumption after trade.

30. Which of the following refers to markets where goods such as computers or services such as medical treatment are offered?
a. Product markets
b. Essential markets
c. Factor markets
d. Competitive markets

31. In which markets are factors of production, such as labor, capital, natural resources, and entrepreneurial ability traded?
a. In product markets
b. In essential markets
c. In factor markets
d. In competitive markets

32. Which of the following comprises the two key groups of participants in the circular flow of income?
   a. Product markets and factor markets
   b. Government and the financial sector
   c. Households and firms
   d. Buyers and sellers

33. Fill in the blanks. In a simple circular flow model, there are flows of _________ and flows of _________.
   a. factors of production; goods and services
   b. funds received from the sale of factors of production; spending on final goods and services
   c. Both of the above are correct.
   d. None of the above. Actually, there are no flows in the circular flow of income.

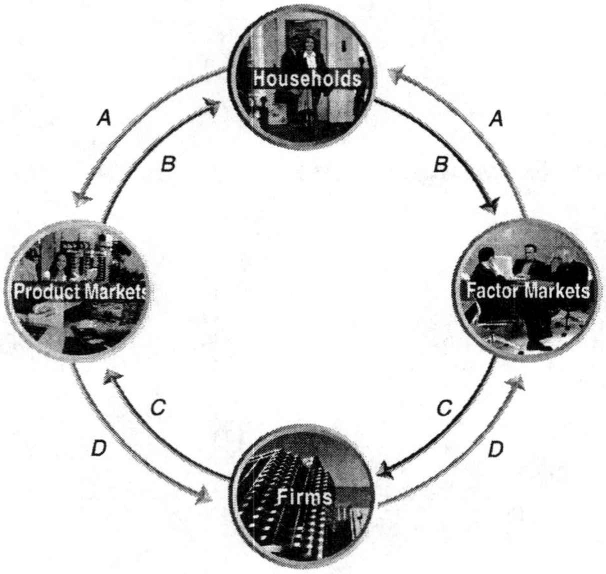

34. In the circular-flow diagram above, which arrow shows the flow of goods and services?
   a. A
   b. B
   c. C
   d. D

35. In the circular-flow diagram above, which arrow shows the flow of spending by households?
   a. A
   b. B
   c. C
   d. D

36. In the circular-flow diagram on the previous page, which arrow shows the flow of factors of production?
    a. A
    b. B
    c. C
    d. D

37. In the circular-flow diagram on the previous page, which arrow shows the flow of income paid to the factors of production?
    a. A
    b. B
    c. C
    d. D

38. According to Adam Smith, which of the following is true?
    a. Markets work because producers, aided by government, ensure that neither too many nor too few goods are produced.
    b. Market prices can come to reflect the prices desired by all consumers.
    c. Individuals usually act in a rational, self-interested way.
    d. All of the above.

39. According to Adam Smith, which of the following is the instrument the invisible hand uses to direct economic activity?
    a. Price
    b. Government regulation
    c. Financial markets
    d. Cost

40. According to Adam Smith, which of the following is necessary for the proper functioning of the market system?
    a. For markets to work, people should take into account how their decisions affect society as a whole.
    b. For markets to work, government should help citizens make the right decisions.
    c. For markets to work, people must be free to pursue their self-interest.
    d. For markets to work, people and government need to coordinate their decisions.

41. What is the role of an entrepreneur?
    a. To operate a business that produces a good or service.
    b. To bring together the factors of production—labor, capital, and natural resources.
    c. To take risks.
    d. All of the above

42. In a free market system, which of the following groups brings together the factors of production—labor, capital, and natural resources—in order to produce goods and services?
    a. The government
    b. Entrepreneurs
    c. Lobbyists
    d. Politicians

43. Which of the following is critical for the success of a market system?
    a. To allow individuals or firms to have exclusive use of their property.
    b. To prevent individuals from buying or selling their property depending on the circumstances.
    c. Either choice above.
    d. To allow the government to determine the optimal use of private property.

44. Generally speaking, for a market system to work, individuals must
    a. be very cautious in their approach to saving and investment.
    b. take risks and act in rational, self-interested ways.
    c. be able to evaluate and understand all available options.
    d. consult people who have experience.

45. What are patents and copyrights designed to do?
    a. Prevent entrepreneurs from earning excessive profits.
    b. Eliminate unnecessary duplication whenever it arises.
    c. Protect intellectual property rights.
    d. All of the above

46. What is the outcome of enforcing contracts and property rights in a market system?
    a. Increased economic activity
    b. Decreased economic activity
    c. No change or no effect on economic activity
    d. An unpredictable but definite effect on economic activity

47. If a market system functions well, which of the following is necessary for the enforcement of contracts and property rights?
    a. Powerful political connections
    b. An independent court system
    c. Action by government to prevent the exercise of certain property rights
    d. All of the above

Short Answer Questions

1. Does the story about Apple's production of the iPod imply that people must cooperate with one another in order for specialization in production and trade to occur? Explain.

____

____

____

____

____

2. Comment briefly on the following statement: "The circular-flow diagram implies that the income household members receive is directly related to the market value of the resources they own."

3. How has the emergence of companies such as Napster and Kazaa changed the manner in which music companies and artists market their CDs?

4. Some companies have had success selling goods and services through the Internet, but others have failed. What types of goods or services would consumers prefer to buy in stores rather than online?

5. In the explanation of Adam Smith's argument in favor of replacing the guild system with a market system, the textbook states that "*the key to understanding Smith's argument is the assumption that individuals usually act in a rational, self-interested way.*" Did Smith believe that the success of a market system requires that people act selfishly?

True/False Questions

T F 1. In his book *An Inquiry into the Nature and Causes of the Wealth of Nations*, Adam Smith argued that a guild system was the most efficient way for a nation to coordinate the decisions of buyers and sellers.

T F 2. The story about Apple's production of the iPod shows how production requires the coordinated activities of many people, spread around the world.

T F 3. A nation with an absolute advantage in the production of two goods will usually have a comparative advantage in only one of the goods.

T F 4. A production possibilities frontier that is bowed outward illustrates increasing marginal opportunity costs.

T F 5. Technological advances always benefit the production of all goods and services equally.

T F 6. It is possible to have an absolute advantage in producing a good without having a comparative advantage.

T F 7. Households are suppliers of the factors of production that are used by firms to produce goods and services.

T F 8. The circular-flow diagram is used to explain why the opportunity cost of increasing the production of one good is the decrease in production of another good.

T F 9. The 5th and 14th amendments to the U.S. Constitution guarantee property rights.

T F 10. Opportunity cost refers to the all of the alternatives that must be given up to engage in an activity.

T F 11. The popularity of Napster and Kazaa was due to the difficulty music companies and artists had in protecting intellectual property rights.

T F 12. Private contributions to the relief effort following the December 2004 tsunami led to an increase in donations for the homeless and poor as donors realized the need to fund other charities.

T F 13. Because the governments of Hong Kong, Estonia, and Singapore impose few restrictions on economic activity, the economies of these countries approximate free market economies.

T F 14. The Bavarian Motor Works Company has always produced its automobiles in Germany in order to supervise production and employ German workers, who have high levels of technical skills.

T F 15. The marginal opportunity cost along a linear (straight-line) production possibilities frontier is constant.

Answers to the Self-Test

Multiple-Choice Questions

Question	Answer	Comment
1	c	Opportunity cost is the highest-valued alternative that must be given up to engage in an activity. Refer to page 39 of the textbook.
2	a	The production possibilities frontier is a curve showing all the attainable combinations of two products that may be produced with available resources.
3	a	In order to produce the combination G, the economy needs more machines, more workers, or more of both.
4	b	This combination is attainable but inefficient because not all resources are being used. Refer to page 39 of the textbook.
5	b	A move along the curve shows the sacrifice associated with increasing the quantity of SUVs, or the amount by which roadsters will have to be reduced.
6	a	Point E describes this choice. Point E shows that 800 SUVs are produced when zero roadsters are produced.
7	c	Opportunity cost is what you sacrifice. As you move from point B to point C, the production of SUVs increases, and the quantity of roadsters sacrificed to do so is 200.
8	d	As you move from D to E, you increase the production of pies by 2 and sacrifice one cake. Refer to pages 40-41 of the textbook.
9	c	Opportunity cost is what you sacrifice. If Rosie produced zero cakes, Rosie could make 10 pies.

10	a	The sacrifice associated with producing more automobiles is ever greater. Refer to Figure 2-2 on page 39.
11	d	Either the economy produces 400 aircraft carriers or it produces 600 automobiles with the same amount of resources.
12	d	The economy can now produce 400 automobiles instead of 200. In order to produce these additional 200 automobiles, the economy produces 200 aircraft carriers instead of 350 (an opportunity cost of 350 – 200 = 150 aircraft carriers).
13	b	As the economy moves down the production possibilities frontier, it experiences increasing marginal opportunity costs because increasing automobile production by a given quantity requires larger and larger decreases in aircraft carrier production.
14	a	A linear production possibilities frontier has a constant slope and, therefore, a fixed opportunity cost.
15	a	This is the principle of increasing marginal opportunity cost.
16	b	An improvement in the technology used to make automobiles causes a shift of the production possibilities frontier along the horizontal axis.
17	a	This graph shows that something affects both the production of automobiles and the production of aircraft carriers, such as an increase in resources or better technologies.
18	c	These graphs show an increase in the production of one or both goods. This increase in the productive capacity of the economy is referred to as *economic growth*.
19	a	Economic growth is the ability of the economy to produce increasing quantities of goods and services.
20	d	All of the above factors create economic growth.
21	b	If a nation produced everything it consumed, it would not depend on any other nation for its livelihood. Although self-sufficiency sounds appealing, countries are better off if they specialize in the production of some products and trade some of them to other countries. Refer to the section of the book entitled "Comparative Advantage and the Gains From Trade" on page 47.
22	a	Absolute advantage is the ability of an individual, firm, or country to produce more of a good or service than competitors using the same amount of resources.
23	c	The country with a lower opportunity cost of production has a comparative advantage in the production of that good.
24	b	The opportunity costs are as follows: The opportunity cost of shirts is: 1 chip for country A, and 1/3 chip for country B. The opportunity cost of chips is: 1 shirt for country A and 3 shirts for country B. Country B has a comparative advantage in the production of shirts because it sacrifices fewer chips to produce one shirt. Country B should therefore produce shirts.
25	a	The opportunity costs are as follows: The opportunity cost of shirts is: 1 chip for country A, and 1/3 chip for country B. The opportunity cost of chips is: 1 shirt for country A and 3 shirts for country B. Therefore, country A has a comparative advantage (or lower opportunity cost) in the production of chips because it sacrifices fewer shirts to produce one chip. Country A should therefore produce chips.
26	a	Country A can produce more food and more clothing in one day than Country B.
27	c	A worker in Country A can produce 6 times as many units of food as a worker in Country B, but only 1.5 as many units of clothing. Country A is more efficient in producing food than clothing relative to Country B.
28	c	If you have a comparative advantage in the production of apples, you would specialize entirely in the production of apples.
29	d	After trade, you and your neighbor can consume more than you can produce.
30	a	Goods and services are exchanged in product markets.

31	c	The focus here is on the types of markets where households and firms interact. Read page 50.
32	c	A household is all the individuals in a home. Firms are suppliers of goods and services.
33	c	In the circular flow of income there are flows of funds and spending, and also flows of factors of production and goods and services.
34	b	Goods and services flow from firms to the households through the product market.
35	a	Spending on goods and services flows from households to firms through the product market.
36	c	Factors of production flow from households to the firms through the factor market.
37	d	Income flows from firms to the households through the factor market.
38	c	Individuals usually act in a rational, self-interested way. Adam Smith understood that people's motives can be complex.
39	a	Price represents both the value of the good to consumers and the cost (to producers) of making those goods.
40	c	Individuals usually act in a rational, self-interested way. When people act in their own self-interest, the right quantity of goods will be produced.
41	d	The role of an entrepreneur is to operate a business and take risks in bringing together the factors of production—labor, capital, and natural resources—in order to produce goods and services.
42	b	In a market system, entrepreneurs bring together the factors of production—labor, capital, and natural resources—in order to produce goods and services.
43	a	The legal basis for a successful market is property rights. Property rights are the rights individuals or firms have to the exclusive use of their property, including the right to buy or sell it.
44	b	Risk taking is an essential ingredient of entrepreneurship and this risk taking is essential for the market system to function well.
45	c	Property rights are very important in any modern economy.
46	a	Much business activity involves someone agreeing to carry out some action in the future. For a market to work, business and individuals have to rely on contracts.
47	b	Independence and impartiality on the part of judges are very important.

Short Answer Responses

1. Cooperation is essential for specialization and trade but it is an impersonal cooperation. It is not necessary for business owners, workers, suppliers and consumers to know or see one another. In fact, many of these individuals can be located thousands of miles away from each other, live in different countries and speak different languages. Their cooperation is due to their self-interest, not their regard for one another's welfare.

2. This is true. In order for household members to earn income to buy the goods and services they want, they must first sell their resource services to firms who purchase these services in factor markets. The market value of factor services determines the income resource owners receive.

3. Traditional music companies face competition from firms such as Napster and Kazaa that can offer downloaded music at low prices. And consumers can purchase online one or two songs rather the entire CD that contains the songs they want. Music companies must offer more attractive options for consumers and consider lowering prices on the CDs they sell. Artists can market directly to consumers through their own web sites rather than through music companies as they have done in the past.

4. Many consumers are reluctant to buy items they cannot see, touch or taste before buying. Clothing, food and automobiles are usually purchased after close inspection.

5. Smith did not believe that self-interest was the sole motive nor did he believe that self-interest was synonymous with selfishness. People are motivated by a broad range of factors, but when they buy and sell in markets, monetary rewards usually provide the most important motivation. Note that people may give to charity due to their own self-interest such as tax breaks and a good feeling about oneself.

True/False Answers

1. F Adam Smith explained the inefficiencies of the guild system and explained how markets were more efficient.
2. T See Making the Connection "A Story of the Market System in Action: How Do You Make an iPod?" on page 53.
3. T A nation can only have the comparative advantage in the production of one of the two goods being compared.
4. T As the slope of the frontier becomes steeper, the opportunity cost of obtaining one more unit of one good increases.
5. F Technological advances often affect the production of some goods (those that use the advances most) more than others.
6. T Absolute advantage is about who produces more, while comparative advantage is about who produces the good relatively inexpensively.
7. T See the section titled "The Circular Flow of Income" on page 50.
8. F A production possibilities frontier, not the circular flow diagram, illustrates opportunity cost in production.
9. T Refer to page 54 for a discussion of the U.S. Constitution.
10. F See the definition of opportunity cost on page 39 of the textbook.
11. T See a discussion of similar companies, such as YouTube and MySpace, on page 55 in the textbook.
12. F Donations to other charities were reduced as people donated to the tsunami relief effort. See Making the Connection "Trade-offs: Hurricane Katrina, Tsunami Relief, and Charitable Giving" on page 41.
13. T The countries that are mentioned in this problem are in the list of examples of free markets in the textbook.
14. F The Chapter Opener discusses the BMW plant in Spartanburg, South Carolina.
15. T The change in the opportunity cost per each additional unit of the good being produced; i.e. the marginal opportunity cost; is constant along a linear *PPF*.

Chapter 3

Where Prices Come From: The Interaction of Demand and Supply

Chapter Summary

The model of demand and supply explains how prices are determined in a market system. The main factor affecting the demand for a product is its price. A **demand schedule** is a table that lists various prices of a product and the quantities that would be demanded at those prices. A **demand curve** shows this same relationship in a graph. The **law of demand** is the negative relationship between price and **quantity demanded**, holding everything else constant. A change in the price of the product causes a movement along the demand curve and is called a change in the quantity demanded. Other factors that affect demand include prices of related goods (**substitutes** and **complements**), income, tastes, population and **demographics**, and expected future prices. A change in any of these will shift a product's demand curve and is called a change in demand.

The most important factor affecting the supply of a product is its price. A **supply schedule** is a table that lists various prices of a product and the quantities that would be supplied at those prices. A **supply curve** shows this same relationship in a graph. The **law of supply** is the positive relationship between price and **quantity supplied**, holding everything else constant. A change in the price of the product causes a movement along the supply curve and is called a change in the quantity supplied. Other factors that affect supply include prices of inputs, technological change, prices of substitutes in production, expected future prices, and the number of firms in the market. In response to a change in any one of these factors, there will be a change in supply or a shift in the supply curve.

The equilibrium price is the price that will make the quantity demanded be equal to the quantity supplied. This occurs where the supply curve and demand curve intersect. A **surplus** exists when the price charged is above the equilibrium price. A **shortage** exists when the price charged is below the equilibrium price. When the market price is not the equilibrium price, the price will adjust toward the equilibrium price. When the price charged equals the equilibrium price, both consumers and producers are willing to exchange the same quantity of the product and there is no further movement in the market price.

An increase in demand increases equilibrium price and increases the equilibrium quantity. A decrease in demand decreases equilibrium price and decreases the equilibrium quantity. An increase in supply decreases equilibrium price and increases the equilibrium quantity. A decrease in supply increases equilibrium price and decreases the equilibrium quantity.

Learning Objectives

When you finish this chapter, you should be able to:

1. **Discuss the variables that influence demand**. Many factors influence the willingness of consumers to buy a particular product. Among these factors are the income they have to spend and the effectiveness of advertising campaigns of the companies that sell products consumers want. The most important factor in consumer decisions, though, is the price of the product. It is important to note that demand refers not to what a consumer wants to buy but what the consumer is both willing and able to buy. In other words, it's not only what consumers want but also what they can afford.

2. **Discuss the variables that influence supply**. Just as many variables influence consumer demand, many variables influence the willingness and ability of firms to sell a good or service. Among these variables are the prices of inputs used in production and the number of firms in the market. The most important variable that affects firms is the price of whatever they sell.

3. **Use a graph to illustrate market equilibrium.** Economists use graphs to show how demand and supply interact in a competitive market to establish equilibrium. The graph of a competitive market shows that quantity demanded equals quantity supplied at the equilibrium price. When the price is greater than the equilibrium price, a surplus exists. In response to the surplus, the market price will fall to the equilibrium level. When the price is less than the equilibrium price, a shortage exists. In response to the shortage, the market price will rise to the equilibrium level.

4. **Use demand and supply graphs to predict changes in prices and quantities**. Demand and supply in most markets change constantly. As a result, equilibrium prices and quantities change constantly. Graphs show the impact on competitive market equilibrium of increases and decreases in demand and supply.

Chapter Review

Chapter Opener: Apple and the Demand for iPods (pages 66-67)

Apple is a leading seller of digital music players in the United States. Apple's ability to sell iPods is affected by the sales of music from Apple's iTunes website and by the competition's sales of digital music players. Apple currently sells its music on iTunes at a price significantly lower than competitors and at a very low profit margin in order to increase its sales of iPods. Many consumers are choosing to purchase music phones as these provide both a digital music player and a telephone. Apple's success depends on the ability of its executives to analyze and react to changes in the demand and supply of its products.

Helpful Study Hint

Apple and the market for digital music players are used throughout the chapter to demonstrate changes in demand and supply and how they affect prices. ***Making the Connection*** "Apple Forecasts the Demand for iPhones and Other Consumer Electronics" describes Apple's efforts to forecast the demand for the new iPhone in order to determine the price to charge and the expected profit the firm will receive. Apple's projections may or may not be correct, and this could affect the success of the company. At the end of this chapter, ***An Inside Look*** describes how Apple and AT&T may benefit from teaming up to supply the iPhone.

Economics in YOUR Life! asks what would happen to your consumption of iPods and Zunes if the prices of these digital music players changed or if the prices of the music downloaded from iTunes and Zune Marketplace changed. Keep this question in mind as you read the chapter. The authors will answer this question at the end of the chapter.

3.1 LEARNING OBJECTIVE

3.1 The Demand Side of the Market (pages 68-75)

Learning Objective 1 Discuss the variables that influence demand.

Although many factors influence the willingness and ability of consumers to buy a particular product, the main influence on consumer decisions is the product's price. The **quantity demanded** of a good or service is the amount that a consumer is willing and able to purchase at a given price. A **demand schedule** is a table showing the relationship between the price of a product and the quantity of the product demanded. A **demand curve** shows this same relationship in a graph. Since quantity demanded always increases in response to a decrease in price, this relationship is called the **law of demand**. The law of demand is explained by the substitution and income effects. The **substitution effect** is the change in the quantity demanded of a good that results from a change in price, making the good more or less expensive relative to other goods that are substitutes. The **income effect** is the change in the quantity demanded of a good that results from the effect of a change in the good's price on consumer purchasing power.

Ceteris paribus ("all else equal") is the requirement that when analyzing the relationship between two variables – such as price and quantity demanded – other variables must be held constant. When one of the non-price factors that influence demand changes, the result is a shift in the demand curve – an increase or decrease in demand. The most important non-price factors that influence demand are prices of related goods (substitutes and complements), income, tastes, population and demographics, and expected future prices.

Substitutes are goods and services that can be used for the same purpose, while **complements** are goods that are used together. A decrease in the price of a substitute for a good, such as iPods, causes the quantity demanded of the substitute, such as Microsoft's Zune music player, to increase (a move along the demand curve for Zunes), which causes the demand for iPods to fall. A fall in demand means that the demand curve for iPods will shift to the left. An increase in the price of Zunes causes the quantity of Zunes demanded to decrease, shifting the demand curve for iPods to the right. Changes in prices of complements have the opposite effect. A decrease in the price of a complement for iPods causes the quantity demanded of the complement, say music downloads from iTunes, to increase, shifting the demand curve for iPods to the right. An increase in the price of downloads on iTunes causes the quantity of downloads demanded to decrease, shifting the demand curve for iPods to the left.

The income that consumers have available to spend affects their willingness to buy a good. A **normal good** is a good for which demand increases as income rises and decreases as income falls. An **inferior good** is a good for which demand increases as income falls and decreases as income rises. When consumers' tastes for a product increase, the demand curve for the product will shift to the right, and when consumers' tastes for a product decrease, the demand curve for the product will shift to the left.

As population increases, the demand for most products increases. **Demographics** are the characteristics of a population with respect to age, race, and gender. As demographics change, the demand for particular goods will increase or decrease because as different demographic groups become more prevalent in the population their unique preferences will become more prevalent in the market. If enough consumers become convinced that a good will be selling for a lower price in the near future, the demand for the good will decrease in the present. If enough consumers become convinced that the price of a good will be higher in the near future, the demand for the good will increase in the present.

Helpful Study Hint

Students often confuse a change in quantity demanded with a change in demand. Only one variable, the price of a good or service, can cause changes in the quantity demanded of that good or service. This change is described as a movement along a demand curve. Notice that the price of the good or service is on the vertical axis. Changes in demand are caused by changes in nonprice factors. A change in any of these factors causes a shift in the demand curve. Constant repetition is essential to understand this important difference. Use ***Making the Connection*** "Why Supermarkets Need to Understand Substitutes and Complement" and ***Making the Connection*** "Companies Respond to a Growing Hispanic Population" to find examples of factors that change demand. Be sure you understand why it is demand and not quantity demanded that changes. Supermarket managers must have a clear understanding of which goods are substitutes and which are complements when deciding what to stock on the shelf. If a product is eliminated because there are other substitutes on the shelf, the demand for a complement to the eliminated product is likely to fall. Companies must also consider the changing demographics of the population and adjust their resources to meeting the needs of the growing demographic groups.

Take time to study Figure 3.3, which shows the difference between a change in demand and a change in quantity demanded. Also take time to study Table 3.1, which lists all the variables that shift market demand curves.

Extra Solved Problem **3-1**

Chapter 3 of the textbook includes two Solved Problems. Here is an extra Solved Problem to help you build your skills solving economic problems.

Supports Learning Objective 3-1: Discuss the variables that influence demand.

Suppose that Bob needs to buy an automobile. Bob has decided to purchase a new Miata convertible. Bob's neighbor tells him that Mazda will be offering a $3,500 rebate on all its automobiles starting next month.

a. Assuming that Bob can wait until next month to buy an automobile, what effect will the rebate have on Bob's demand for the Miata?

b. Which of the variables that influence demand would explain Bob's change in demand?

SOLVING THE PROBLEM

Step 1: Review the chapter material.
This problem is about variables that shift market demand, so you may want to review the section "Variables That Shift Market Demand," which begins on page 70 in the textbook.

Step 2: Answer question (a).
Bob's demand for the Miata will decrease now and increase next month as he will wait to make his purchase in order to take advantage of the rebate.

Step 3: Answer question (b).
Other things being equal, as the expected future price of the Miata falls, the demand for Miatas will fall in the present time period.

3.2 LEARNING OBJECTIVE

3.2 The Supply Side of the Market (pages 75-79)

Learning Objective 2 Discuss the variables that influence supply.

Many variables influence the willingness and ability of firms to sell a good or service. The most important of these variables is the price of the good or service. **Quantity supplied** is the amount of a good or service that a firm is willing to sell at a given price. A **supply schedule** is a table that shows the relationship between the price of a product and the quantity of the product supplied. A **supply curve** shows this same relationship in a graph. The **law of supply** states that, holding everything else constant, increases in the price of the good or service cause increases in the quantity supplied and decreases in the price of the good or service cause decreases in the quantity supplied.

Variables other than the price of the product affect supply. When any of these variables change, a shift in supply – an increase or a decrease in supply – results. The following are the most important variables that shift supply: prices of inputs used in production, technological change, prices of substitutes in production, expected future prices, and the number of firms in the market.

If the price of an input (for example, labor or energy) used to produce a good rises, the supply of the good will decrease and the supply curve will shift to the left. If the price of an input decreases, the supply of the good will increase and the supply curve will shift to the right. **Technological change** is a positive or negative change in the ability of a firm to produce a given level of output with a given amount of inputs. A positive technological change will shift a firm's supply curve to the right, while a negative technological change will shift a firm's supply curve to the left.

An increase in the price of an alternative good (B) that a firm could produce instead of producing good A will shift the firm's supply curve for good A to the left. If a firm expects the price of its product will rise in the future, the firm has an incentive to decrease supply in the present and increase supply in the future. When firms enter a market, the market supply curve shifts to the right. When firms exit a market, the market supply curve shifts to the left.

Helpful Study Hint

The law of supply may seem logical because producers earn more profit when the price they sell their product for rises. But consider Figure 3-4 and the following question: "If Apple can earn a profit from selling 40 million players per month at a price of $200, why not increase quantity supplied to 45 million and make even more profit?" The upward slope of the supply curve is due not only to the profit motive but the increasing marginal cost of printers. (Increasing marginal costs were discussed in Chapter 2.) Apple will increase its quantity supplied from 40 to 45 million in Figure 3-4 only if the price it will receive is $250, because the cost of producing 5 million more players is greater than the cost of the last 5 million players.

As with demand and quantity demanded, be careful not to confuse a change in quantity supplied (due only to a change in the price of a product) and a change in supply (a shift of the supply curve in response to one of the non-price factors). Constant reinforcement of this is necessary. Be careful not to refer to an increase in supply as "a downward shift" or a decrease in supply as "an upward shift." Because demand curves are downward-sloping, an increase in demand appears in a graph as an "upward shift." But because supply curves are upward-sloping, a *decrease* in supply appears in a graph as an "upward shift." You should always refer to both changes in demand and supply as being "shifts to the right" for an increase and "shifts to the left" for a decrease to avoid confusion.

Take time to study Figure 3.6, which shows the difference between a change in supply and a change in quantity supplied. Also take time to study Table 3.2, which lists all the variables that shift market supply curves.

Extra Solved Problem **3-2**

Supports Learning Objective 3-2: Discuss the variables that influence supply.

To (Soy)bean or not to (Soy)bean ?

Television programming in Illinois features many commercials aimed at farmers. Ads for fertilizer, seed, and farm equipment are as common as commercials for laundry soap and soft drinks. Much of the nation's corn is grown in Illinois, but the climate and soil conditions in the state are well-suited for growing soybeans as well. Each year, a farmer must decide how many acres of land to plant with corn and how many acres to plant with soybeans.

a. If both crops can be grown on the same land, why would a farmer choose to produce corn rather than soybeans?

b. Which of the variables that influence supply would explain a farmer's choice to produce soybeans or corn?

SOLVING THE PROBLEM

Step 1: Review the chapter material.
This problem is about variables that shift supply, so you may want to refers to the section "Variables That Shift Supply," which begins on page 77 of the textbook.

Step 2: Answer question (a).
Among the factors that would influence a farmer's choice is the expected profitability of the two crops. A farmer will grow corn rather than soybeans if he expects the profits from growing corn will be greater than those earned from growing soybeans.

Step 3: Answer question (b).
Other things being equal, as the price of soybeans falls relative to the price of corn, the supply of corn would rise. Because corn and soybeans are substitutes in production, the variable "prices of substitutes in production" is the one that would explain the farmer's choice.

3.3 LEARNING OBJECTIVE

3.3 Market Equilibrium: Putting Demand and Supply Together (pages 79-82)

Learning Objective 3 Use a graph to illustrate market equilibrium.

The purpose of markets is to bring buyers and sellers together. The interaction of buyers and sellers in markets results in firms producing goods and services consumers both want and can afford. At **market equilibrium,** the price of the product makes quantity demanded equal quantity supplied. A **competitive market equilibrium** is a market equilibrium with many buyers and many sellers. The market price (the actual price you would pay for the product) will not always be the equilibrium price. A **surplus** is a situation in which the quantity supplied is greater than the quantity demanded, which occurs when the market price is above the equilibrium price. Firms have an incentive to increase sales by lowering price. As the market price is lowered, quantity demanded will rise and quantity supplied will fall until the market reaches equilibrium.

A **shortage** is a situation in which quantity demanded is greater than the quantity supplied, which occurs when the market price is below the equilibrium price. Some consumers will want to buy the product at a higher price to make sure they get what they want. As the market price rises, the quantity demanded will fall – not everyone will want to buy at a higher price – and quantity supplied will rise until the market reaches equilibrium. At the competitive market equilibrium, there is no reason for the price to change unless either the demand curve or the supply curve shifts.

Helpful Study Hint

It's very important to understand how demand and supply interact to reach equilibrium. Remember that adjustments to a shortage or a surplus represent changes in quantity demanded (not demand) and quantity supplied (not supply). ***Solved Problem 3-3*** and problem 3.4 in the Problems and Applications at the end of the chapter address this topic. In ***Solved Problem 3-3***, we see how the demand and supply for the letters written by Lincoln and Booth determine the price for the letters written by each author. Because the supply is low relative to the demand for Booth's letters, his letters sell for a high equilibrium price. Similarly, because the supply of Lincoln's letters is large relative to the demand, his letters sell for a lower equilibrium price. Market or actual prices are easy to understand because these are the prices consumers are charged. You know the price you paid for a CD because it is printed on the receipt. But no receipt has "equilibrium price" written on it.

To help you understand what an equilibrium price and quantity are, it may help to use an analogy. Suppose you were to push an inflated ball under the surface of a sink filled with water. If you were to release the ball it would move quickly to the surface. If you were to hold the ball above the sink and drop it, the ball would fall to the surface. The surface of the water is the equilibrium position for the ball. A market equilibrium is the position a market will move towards if there is a shortage or surplus.

3.4 LEARNING OBJECTIVE

3.4 The Effect of Demand and Supply Shifts on Equilibrium (pages 83-88)

Learning Objective 4 Use demand and supply graphs to predict changes in prices and quantities.

When the supply curve shifts, the equilibrium price and quantity change in the opposite direction. Increases in supply result from the following non-price factor changes: a decrease in an input price, positive technological change, a decrease in the price of a substitute in production, a lower expected future product price, and an increase in the number of firms in the market. A decrease in supply results in a higher equilibrium price and a lower equilibrium quantity. Decreases in supply result from the following non-price factor changes: an increase in an input price, negative technological change, an increase in the price of a substitute in production, a higher expected future product price, and a decrease in the number of firms in the market.

When the demand curve shifts, the equilibrium price and quantity shift in the same direction. Increases in demand can be caused by any change in a variable that affects demand *except price*. For example, demand will increase if the price of a substitute rises, the price of a complement falls, income rises (for a normal good), income falls (for an inferior good), population increases or the expected future price of the product rises. A decrease in demand results in a lower equilibrium price and lower equilibrium quantity. Decreases in demand can be caused by any change in a variable that affects demand *except the price of the product itself.* For example, demand will decrease if the price of a substitute falls, the price of a complement rises, income falls (for a normal good), incomes rises (for an inferior good), population decreases, or the expected future price of the product falls.

Helpful Study Hint

Use the following features to conduct your own research on how changes in demand and supply affect prices:

- ***Making the Connection*** "The Falling Prices of LCD TVs"
- ***Solved Problem 3-4*** on lobsters
- Problem 4.5 on watermelons in the Problems and Applications section

Visit stores that sell these items and find out their market prices. For flat screen televisions, compare the market price you find with the expected prices as described in ***Making the Connection*** "The Falling Prices of LCD TVs." ***Solved Problem 3-4*** shows how the demand and supply for lobsters changes during different times of the year and the effect of those changes on the equilibrium price. In the spring, the demand and supply are both low and the equilibrium price is relatively high. In the summer, the demand for lobsters increases, but the supply of lobsters increases relatively more. This causes the summer price for lobsters to be lower than the equilibrium price in the spring. For lobsters and watermelon, ask sellers how current prices compare with prices at different times of the year. Draw demand and supply graphs that represent the market conditions you observe. You can ask your instructor if your analysis is correct.

In ***Don't Let This Happen to YOU!*** "Remember: A Change in a Good's Price Does *Not* Cause the Demand or Supply Curve to Shift," the textbook reiterates the idea that a change in the price of a good causes a movement along the curve under analysis. For example, an increase in supply will cause the equilibrium price of the good to rise. This increase in the price of the good will cause a movement up along the demand curve, or a decrease in the quantity demanded. This is not a change in demand and not a shift in the curve.

The section ***Economics in YOUR Life!*** in this chapter asks what would happen to your consumption of iPods and Zunes if the prices of these digital music players changed or if the prices of the music downloaded from iTunes and Zune Marketplace changed. Because the Zune and the iPod are substitutes, if the price of one of the players increased, the demand for the other music player would increase. For example, if the price of the Zune increases, the demand curve for the iPod would shift to the right. Similarly, the price of complements, such as music downloaded from iTunes or Zune Marketplace, affects the demand for the digital music players. For example, if the price of music downloads on iTunes falls, the demand for iPods would increase and the demand for Zunes would decrease.

Key Terms

Ceteris paribus ("all else equal"). The requirement that when analyzing the relationship between two variables – such as price and quantity demanded – other variables must be held constant.

Competitive market equilibrium. A market equilibrium with many buyers and sellers.

Complements. Goods and services that are used together.

Demand curve. A curve that shows the relationship between the price of a product and the quantity of the product demanded.

Demand schedule. A table showing the relationship between the price of a product and the quantity of the product demanded.

Demographics. The characteristics of a population with respect to age, race, and gender.

Income effect. The change in the quantity demanded of a good that results from the effect of a change in the good's price on consumers' purchasing power.

Inferior good. A good for which the demand increases as income falls and decreases as income rises.

Law of demand. The rule that, holding everything else constant, when the price of a product falls, the quantity demanded of the product will increase, and when the price of a product rises, the quantity demanded of the product will decrease.

Law of supply. The rule that, holding everything else constant, increases in price cause increases in the quantity supplied, and decreases in price cause decreases in the quantity supplied.

Market demand. The demand by all the consumers of a given good or service.

Market equilibrium. A situation in which quantity demanded equals quantity supplied.

Normal good. A good for which the demand increases as income rises and demand decreases as income falls.

Perfectly competitive market. A market that meets the conditions of (1) many buyers and sellers, (2) all firms selling identical products, and (3) no barriers to new firms entering the market.

Quantity demanded. The amount of a good or service that a consumer is willing and able to purchase at a given price.

Quantity supplied. The amount of a good or service that a firm is willing and able to supply at a given price.

Shortage. A situation in which the quantity demanded is greater than the quantity supplied.

Substitutes. Goods and services that can be used for the same purpose.

Substitution effect. The change in the quantity demanded of a good that results from a change in price, making the good more or less expensive relative to goods that are substitutes.

Supply curve. A curve that shows the relationship between the price of a product and the quantity of the product supplied.

Supply schedule. A table that shows the relationship between the price of a product and the quantity of the product supplied.

Surplus. A situation in which the quantity supplied is greater than the quantity demanded.

Technological change. A positive or negative change in the ability of a firm to produce a given level of output with a given amount of inputs.

Self-Test

(Answers are provided at the end of the Self-Test.)

Multiple-Choice Questions

1. Refer to the graph below. The point of $250 and 35 million players represents a point on the market demand curve for digital music players. Which of the following interpretations of this point on the graph is correct?

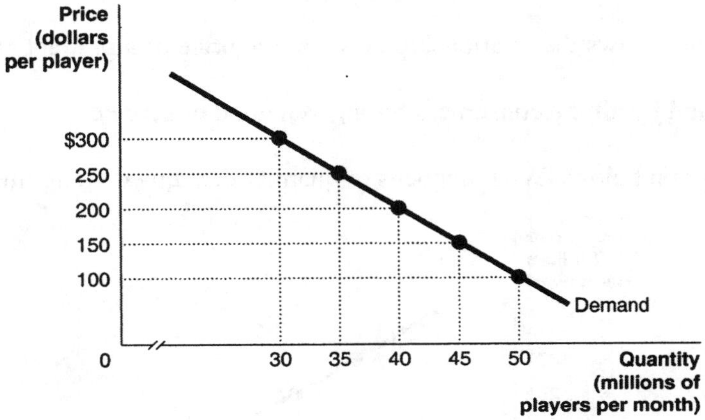

   a. The dot shows that consumers spend a total of $250 on 35 million players each month.
   b. When one player costs $250, consumers buy 35 million of them per month.
   c. When one player costs $250, suppliers sell 35 million of them per month.
   d. At $250, quantity demanded equals quantity supplied.

2. What does the term *quantity demanded* refer to?
   a. The total amount of a good that a consumer is willing to buy per month.
   b. The quantity of a good or service demanded that corresponds to the quantity supplied.
   c. The quantity of a good or service that a consumer is willing and able to purchase at a given price.
   d. None of the above.

3. Which of the following is the correct definition of *demand schedule*?
   a. The quantity of a good or service that a consumer is willing to purchase at a given price.
   b. A table showing the relationship between the price of a product and the quantity of the product demanded.
   c. A curve that shows the relationship between the price of a product and the quantity of the product demanded.
   d. The demand for a product by all the consumers in a given geographical area.

4. Which of the following is the correct definition of *demand curve*?
   a. The quantity of a good or service that a consumer is willing to purchase at a given price.
   b. A table showing the relationship between the price of a product and the quantity of the product demanded.
   c. A curve that shows the relationship between the price of a product and the quantity of the product demanded.
   d. The demand for a product by all the consumers in a given geographical area.

5. Which of the following is the correct definition of *market demand*?
   a. The quantity of a good or service that a consumer is willing to purchase at a given price.
   b. A table showing the relationship between the price of a product and the quantity of the product demanded.
   c. A curve that shows the relationship between the price of a product and the quantity of the product demanded.
   d. The demand by all the consumers for a given good or service.

6. Refer to the graph below. What happens to quantity demanded along this demand curve?

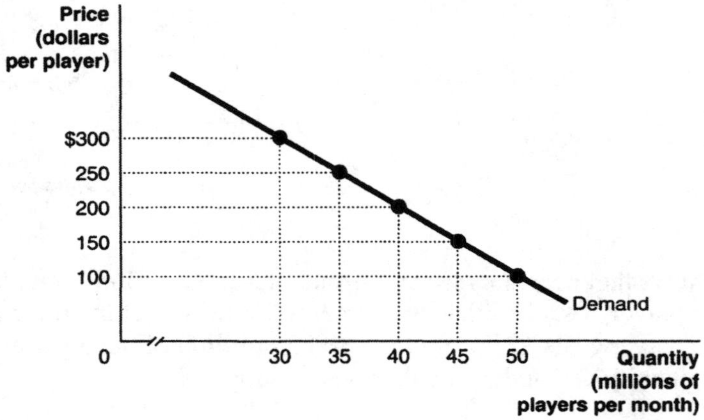

   a. It increases as the price increases.
   b. It increases as the price decreases.
   c. It may increase or decrease as the price increases.
   d. It is not related to price.

7. Refer to the graph below. Along the demand curve, what happens to the quantity demanded as the price falls from $250 to $200 per player?

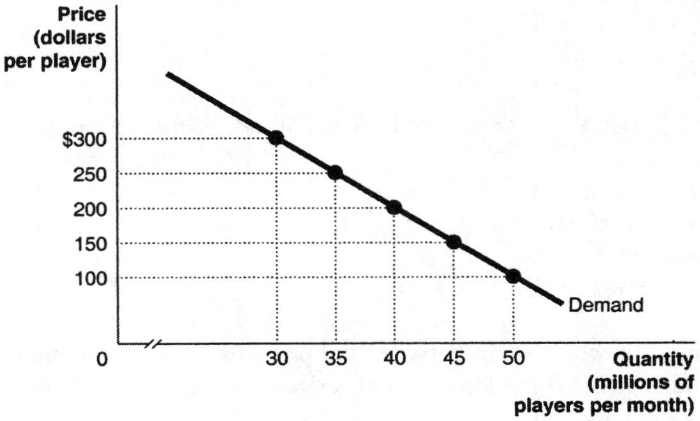

a. The quantity demanded rises from 35 million to 40 million players per month.
b. The quantity demanded falls from 40 million to 35 million players per month.
c. We cannot predict the change in the quantity demanded without the supply curve.
d. The change in the quantity demanded is not related to a change in price.

8. When the price of a digital music players rises, the quantity of digital music players demanded by consumers falls. According to this statement, what do we call the demand curve for digital music players?
a. Unpredictable
b. Upward sloping
c. Downward sloping
d. An exception to the law of demand

9. Which of the following explains why there is an inverse relationship between the price of a product and the quantity of the product demanded?
a. The substitution effect
b. The income effect
c. The law of demand
d. The price effect

10. What is the *law of demand*?
a. The law of demand states that a change in the quantity demanded, caused by changes in price, makes the good more or less expensive relative to other goods.
b. The law of demand states that a change in the quantity demanded, caused by changes in price, affects a consumer's purchasing power.
c. The law of demand states that, holding everything else constant, when the price of good falls, the quantity demanded will increase, and vice versa.
d. The law of demand is the requirement that when analyzing the relationship between price and quantity demanded, other variables must be held constant.

11. Which of the following best describes how changes in price affect a consumer's purchasing power?
    a. The law of demand
    b. The substitution effect
    c. The income effect
    d. The term *ceteris paribus*

12. Which of the following best describes how consumers consider buying other goods when the price of a good rises?
    a. The law of demand
    b. The substitution effect
    c. The income effect
    d. The term *ceteris paribus*

13. When analyzing the relationship between the price of a good and quantity demanded, other variables must be held constant. Which term best describes such an assumption?
    a. The law of demand
    b. The substitution effect
    c. The income effect
    d. *Ceteris paribus*

14. Refer to the graphs below. Each graph refers to the demand for digital music players. Which of the graphs best describes the impact of an increase in the price of a substitute good?

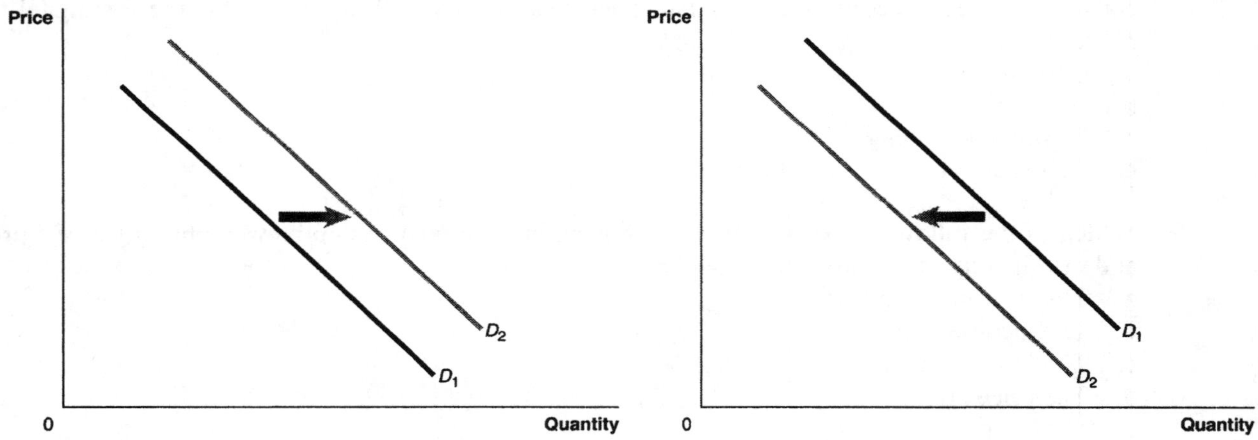

    a. The graph on the left
    b. The graph on the right
    c. Both graphs
    d. Neither graph

15. Refer to the graphs below. Each graph refers to the demand for digital music players. Which of the graphs best describes the impact of an increase in the price of a complementary good?

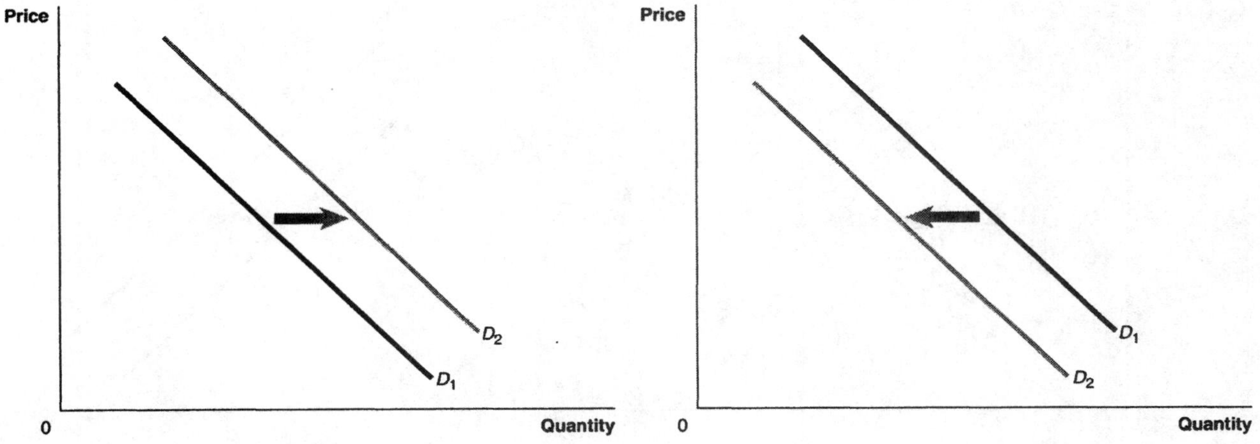

a. The graph on the left
b. The graph on the right
c. Both graphs
d. Neither graph

16. Refer to the graphs below. Each graph refers to the demand for digital music players. Which of the graphs best describes the impact of an increase in income, assuming that printers are a normal good?

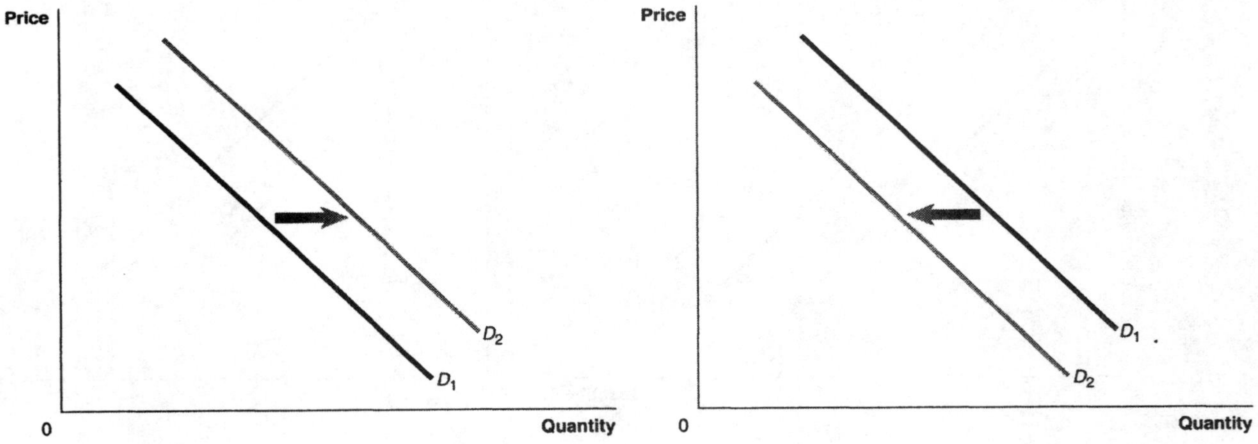

a. The graph on the left
b. The graph on the right
c. Both graphs
d. Neither graph

17. Refer to the graphs below. Each graph refers to the demand for digital music players. Which of the graphs best describes the impact of an increase in the *taste* for digital music players?

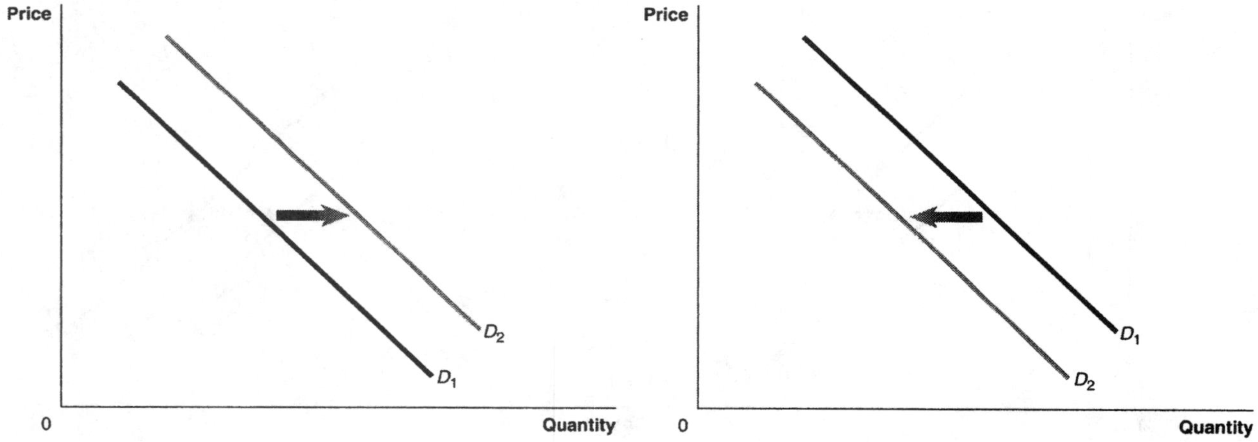

a. The graph on the left
b. The graph on the right
c. Both graphs
d. Neither graph

18. Refer to the graphs below. Each graph refers to the demand for digital music players. Which of the graphs best describes the impact of an increase in population?

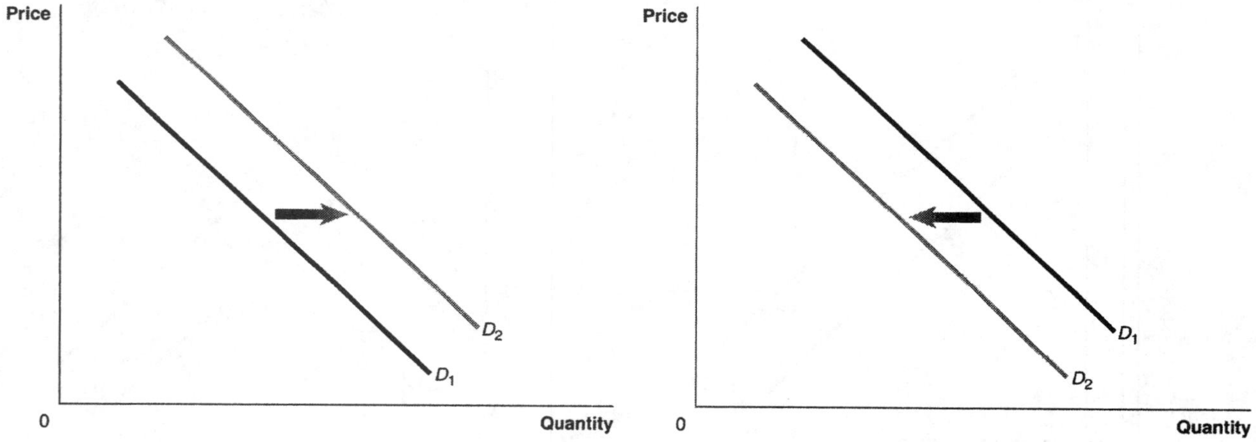

a. The graph on the left
b. The graph on the right
c. Both graphs
d. Neither graph

19. Refer to the graphs below. Each graph refers to the demand for digital music players. Which of the graphs best describes the impact of an increase in the expected price of digital music players in the future?

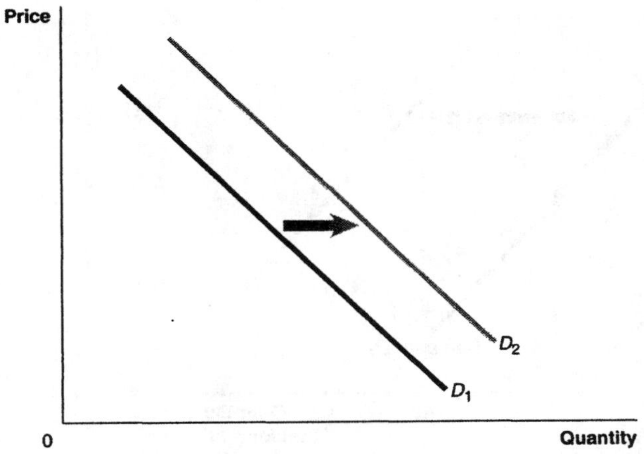

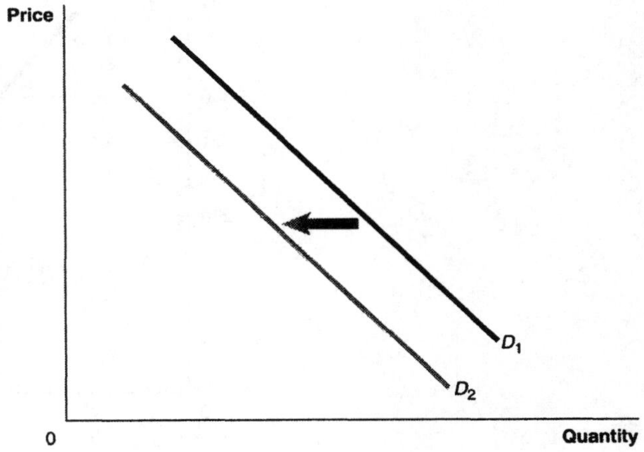

a. The graph on the left
b. The graph on the right
c. Both graphs
d. Neither graph

20. When two goods are *complements*, which of the following occurs?
a. The two goods can be used for the same purpose.
b. The two goods are used together.
c. The demand for each of these goods increases when income rises.
d. The demand for each of these goods increases as income falls.

21. When two goods are *substitutes*, which of the following occurs?
a. The two goods can be used for the same purpose.
b. The two goods are used together.
c. The demand for each of these goods increases when income rises.
d. The demand for each of these goods increases as income falls.

22. What is an *inferior good*?
a. A good for which demand increases as income rises.
b. A good for which demand decreases as income rises.
c. A good that cannot be used together with another good.
d. A good that does not serve any real purpose.

23. What is a *normal good*?
a. A good for which demand increases as income rises.
b. A good for which demand decreases as income rises.
c. A good that can be used together with another good.
d. A good that does serves more than one purpose.

24. Refer to the graph below. Which of the following moves best describes a *change in demand*?

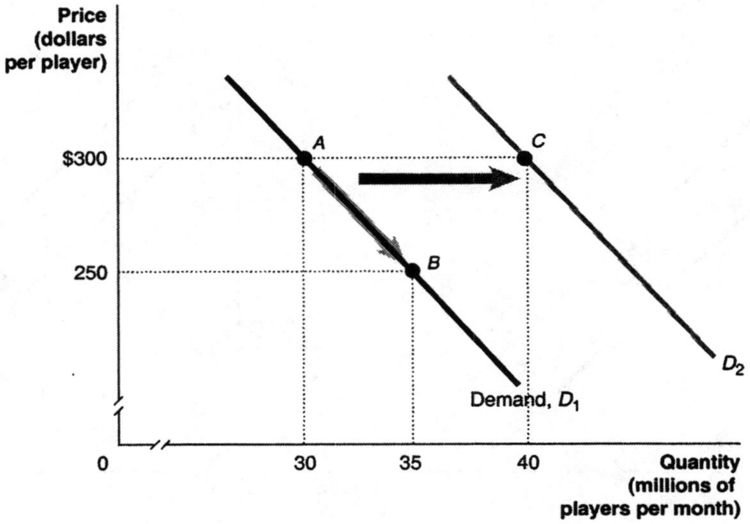

a. The move from *A* to *B*
b. The move from *A* to *C*
c. Either the move from *A* to *B* or from *A* to *C*
d. The move from *B* to *A*

25. Refer to the graph below. Which of the following moves best describes a *change in quantity demanded*?

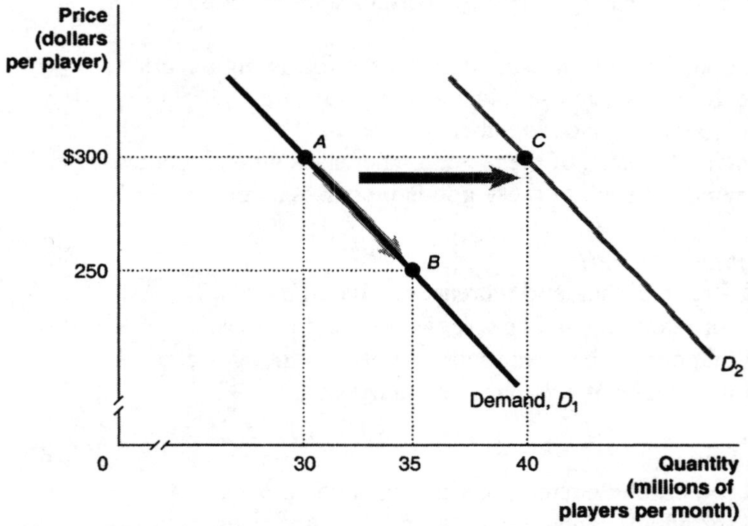

a. The move from *A* to *B*
b. The move from *A* to *C*
c. Either the move from *A* to *B* or from *A* to *C*
d. The move from *B* to *C*

26. Refer to the graph below. Which of the following moves best describes what happens when there is a change in a determinant of the demand for digital music players other than the price of players?

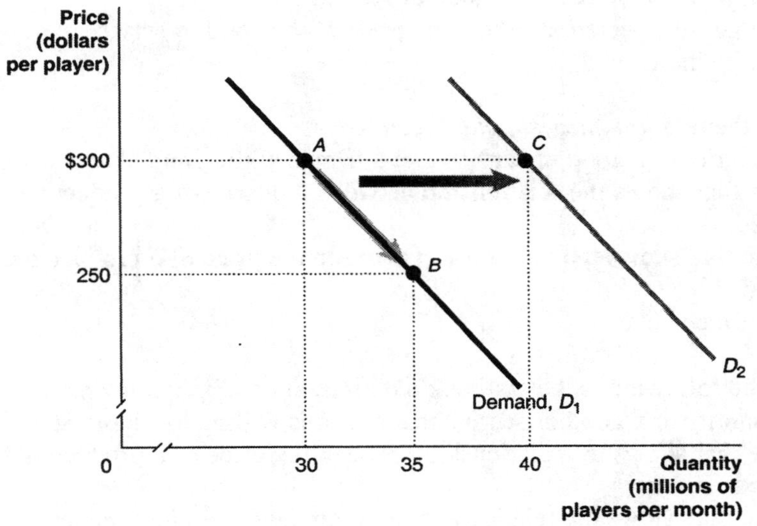

a. A move from *A* to *B*
b. A move from *A* to *C*
c. Either the move from *A* to *B* or from *A* to *C*
d. None of the above

27. Refer to the graph below. Which of the following moves best describes what happens when a change in the price of digital music players affects the market demand for players?

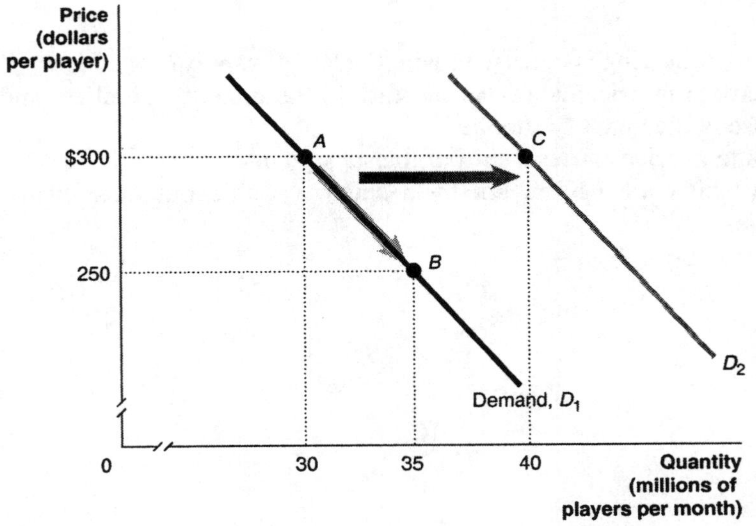

a. A move from *A* to *B*
b. A move from *A* to *C*
c. Either the move from *A* to *B* or from *A* to *C*
d. None of the above

28. Which of the following would NOT shift the demand curve for a good or service?
    a. A change in the price of a related good
    b. A change in the price of the good or service
    c. A change in expectations about the price of the good or service
    d. A change in income

29. What does the term *quantity supplied* refer to?
    a. The quantity of a good or service that a firm is willing and able to supply at a given price.
    b. A table that shows the relationship between the price of a product and the quantity of the product supplied.
    c. A curve that shows the relationship between the price of a product and the quantity of the product demanded.
    d. None of the above

30. Which of the following is the textbook's definition of *supply schedule*?
    a. The quantity of a good or service that a firm is willing to supply at a given price.
    b. A table that shows the relationship between the price of a product and the quantity of the product supplied.
    c. A curve that shows the relationship between the price of a product and the quantity of the product demanded.
    d. None of the above

31. Which of the following is the textbook's definition of *supply curve*?
    a. The quantity of a good or service that a firm is willing to supply at a given price.
    b. A table that shows the relationship between the price of a product and the quantity of the product supplied.
    c. A curve that shows the relationship between the price of a product and the quantity of the product supplied.
    d. None of the above

32. Which of the following is consistent with the law of supply?
    a. An increase in price causes an increase in the quantity supplied, and a decrease in price causes decrease in the quantity supplied.
    b. A change in price causes a shift of the supply curve.
    c. Supply shifts are caused not by a single variable but most likely by a number of different variables.
    d. All of the above

33. Refer to the graphs below. Each graph refers to the supply for digital music players. Which of the graphs best describes the impact of an increase in the price of an input?

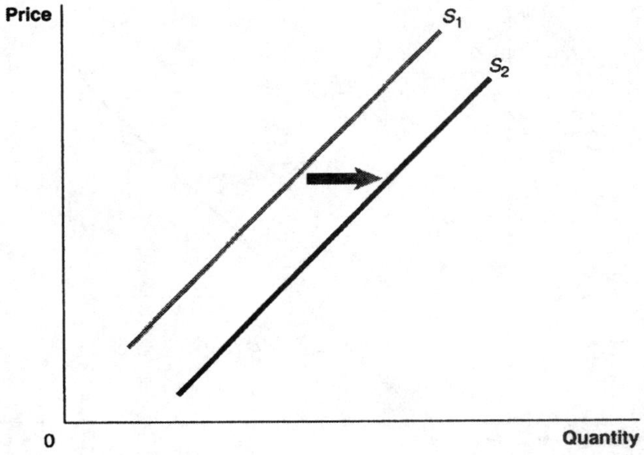

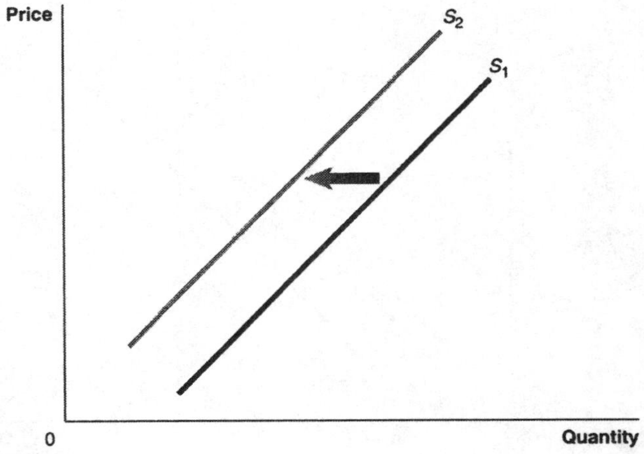

a. The graph on the left
b. The graph on the right
c. Both graphs
d. Neither graph

34. Refer to the graphs below. Each graph refers to the supply for digital music players. Which of the graphs best describes the impact of an increase in productivity?

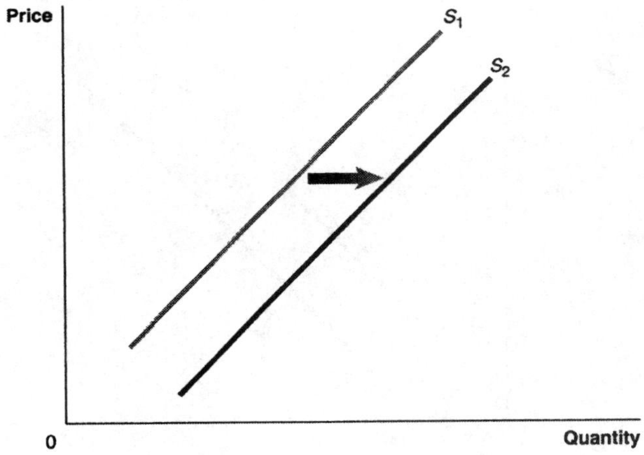

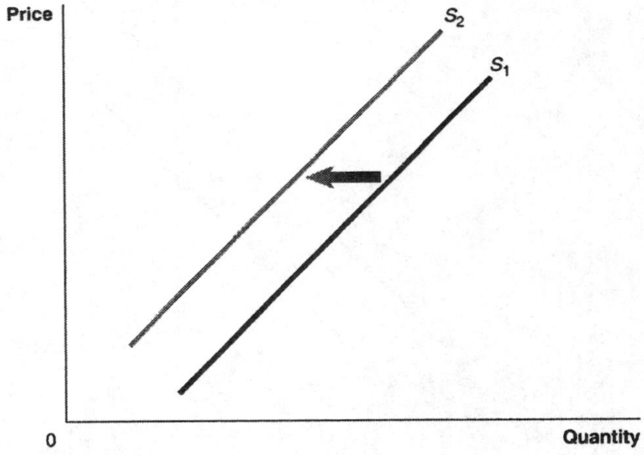

a. The graph on the left
b. The graph on the right
c. Both graphs
d. Neither graph

35. Refer to the graphs below. Each graph refers to the supply for digital music players. Which of the graphs best describes the impact of an increase in the price of a substitute in production?

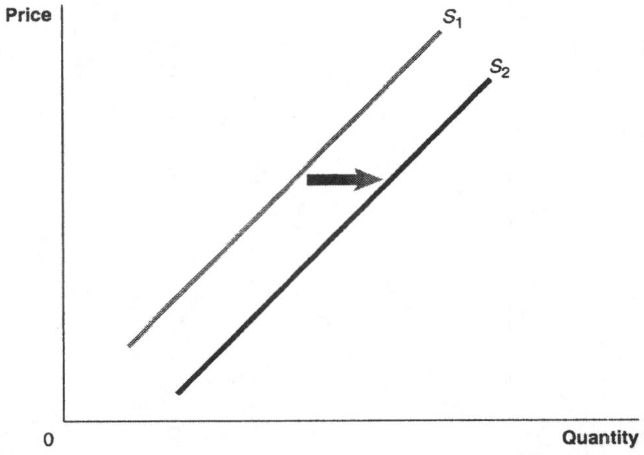

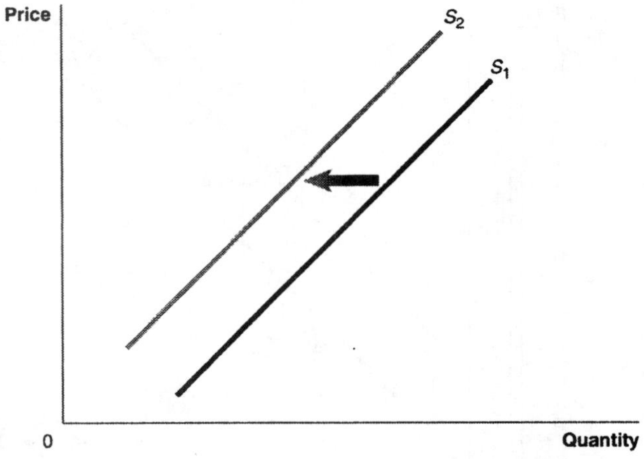

a. The graph on the left
b. The graph on the right
c. Both graphs
d. Neither graph

36. Refer to the graphs below. Each graph refers to the supply for digital music players. Which of the graphs best describes the impact of an increase in the expected future price of the product?

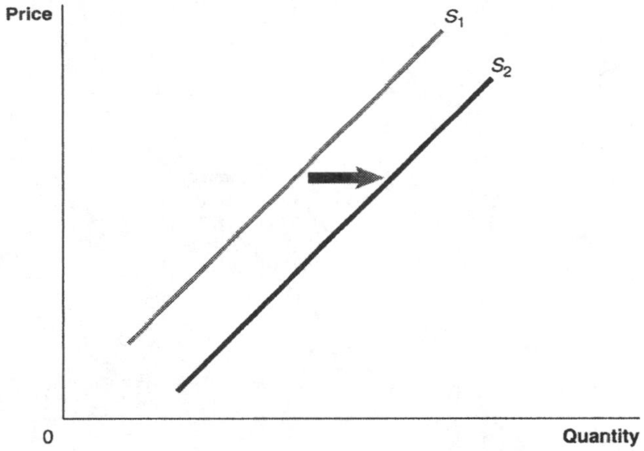

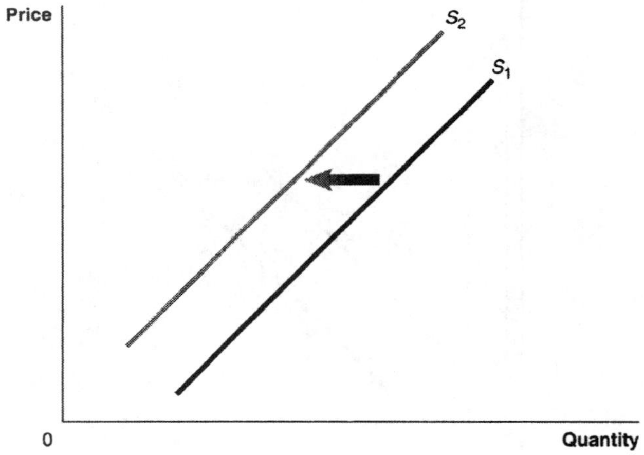

a. The graph on the left
b. The graph on the right
c. Both graphs
d. Neither graph

37. Refer to the graphs below. Each graph refers to the supply for digital music players. Which of the graphs best describes the impact of an increase in the number of firms in the market?

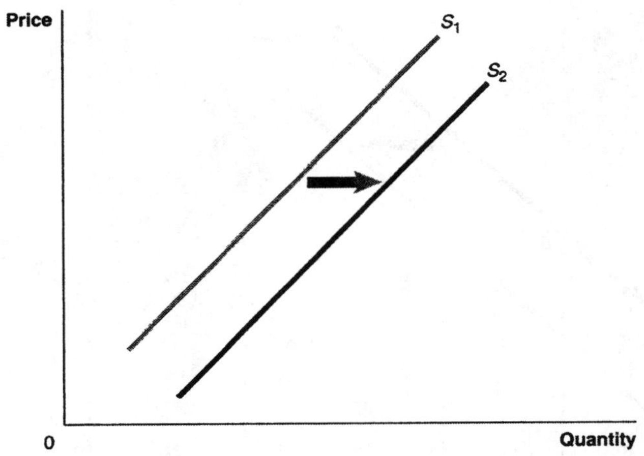

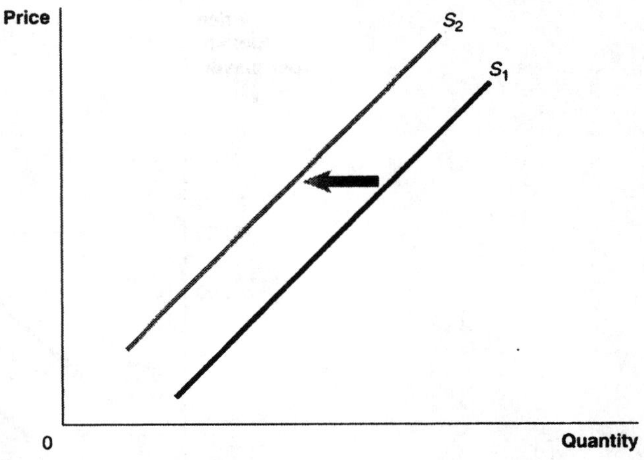

a. The graph on the left
b. The graph on the right
c. Both graphs
d. Neither graph

38. Refer to the graph below. Which of the following moves best describes what happens when there is a change in a determinant of the supply for digital music players other than the price of players?

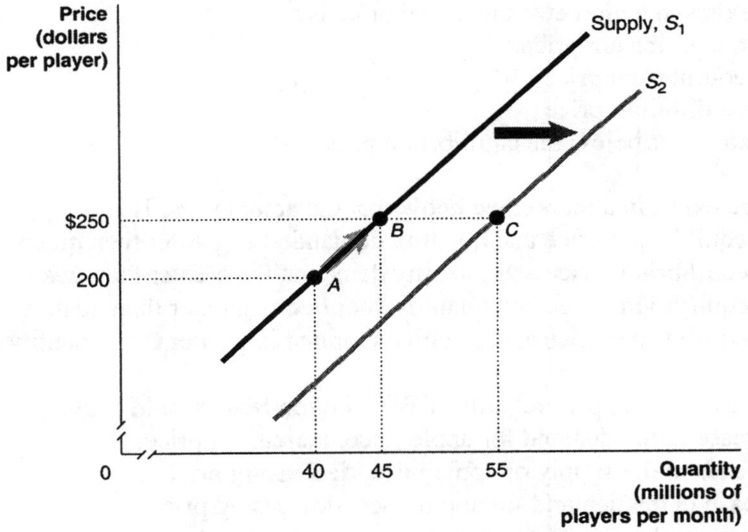

a. A move from A to B
b. A move from A to C
c. Either the move from A to B or from A to C
d. None of the above

39. Refer to the graph below. Which of the following moves best describes what happens when a change in the price of digital music players affects the market supply for players?

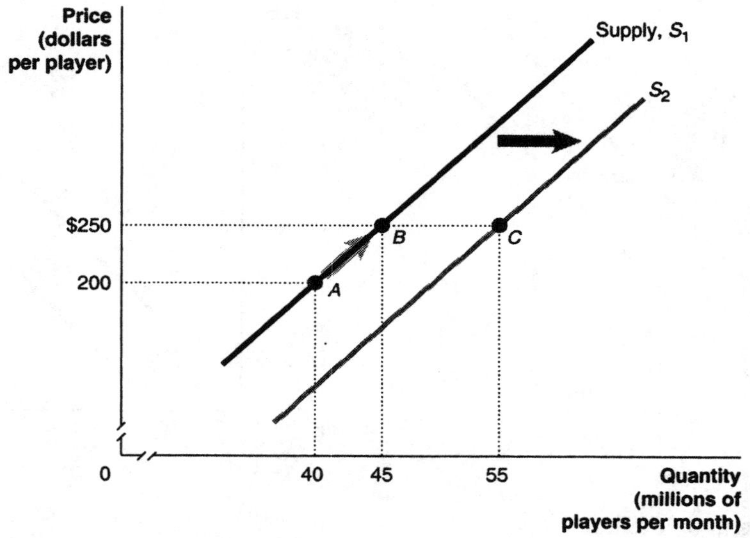

a. A move from *A* to *B*
b. A move from *A* to *C*
c. Either the move from *A* to *B* or from *A* to *C*
d. None of the above

40. A surplus exists in a market if the actual price is
a. equal to equilibrium price.
b. below equilibrium price.
c. above equilibrium price.
d. either above or below the equilibrium price.

41. If a shortage exists in a market we know that the actual price is
a. below equilibrium price and quantity demanded is greater than quantity supplied.
b. above equilibrium price and quantity demanded is greater than quantity supplied.
c. above equilibrium price and quantity supplied is greater than quantity demanded.
d. below equilibrium price and quantity supplied is greater than quantity demanded.

42. An early frost in the apple orchards of Washington State would cause
a. an increase in the demand for apple juice, increasing price.
b. an increase in the supply of apple juice, decreasing price.
c. a decrease in the demand for apple juice, decreasing price.
d. a decrease in the supply of apple juice, increasing price.

43. Which of the following would definitely result in a higher price in the market for tennis shoes?
a. demand increases and supply decreases
b. demand and supply both decrease
c. demand decreases and supply increases
d. demand and supply both increase

44. Suppose that the income of buyers in a market increases and a technological advancement also occurs. What would we expect to happen in the market for a normal good?
    a. The equilibrium price would increase, but the impact on the amount sold in the market would be ambiguous.
    b. The equilibrium price would decrease, but the impact on the amount sold in the market would be ambiguous.
    c. Equilibrium quantity would increase, but the impact on equilibrium price would be ambiguous.
    d. Both equilibrium price and equilibrium quantity would increase.

Short Answer Questions

1. What evidence can be used to support the following statement? "Tickets to the World Series and the Super Bowl do not sell at their equilibrium prices."

____

____

____

____

____

2. In response to a surplus, a firm will lower a product's price until the quantity supplied equals quantity demanded. But prices of some goods will fall more quickly than others. What type of good would a firm lower the price of quickly in response to a surplus?

____

____

____

____

3. Explain the difference between a shortage and scarcity.

____

____

____

____

4. During 2007 there were over 80,000 people on waiting lists for kidney, lung, and other organ transplant operations. By law, organ donors and their families in the United States may not be paid for the donated organs. If payments for organ donations were made legal in the United States, would this affect the demand or the quantity demanded for organ transplants demanded?

5. The demand for health care in the United States is expected to rise throughout the first part of the twenty-first century. Which of the variables that influence market demand is most responsible for this expected increase?

True/False Questions

T F 1. A market demand curve demonstrates the quantity that each consumer is willing to buy at each possible price.

T F 2. The law of demand states that, holding everything else constant, increases in price cause decreases in demand.

T F 3. The price of lobsters is higher in the spring than in the summer, even though demand is greater in summer. The lower summer price results from increases in the supply of lobsters in the summer.

T F 4. As a result of a surplus, the price in a market will fall; quantity supplied falls and quantity demanded rises until the new equilibrium is reached.

T F 5. An increase in income causes demand for a normal good to increase.

T F 6. It is better for a supermarket to remove a slow-selling good from its shelves if it is a substitute for another good than if it is a complement with another good.

T F 7. Inferior goods are goods that are of lesser quality than other similar goods.

T F 8. Substitution and income effects are used to explain the law of supply.

T F 9. A negative technological change will shift the supply curve for a product to the left.

T F 10. Increases in the supply of flat-screen televisions led to lower prices and increased quantity demanded for these televisions.

T F 11. An increase in the price of a complement for good A will decrease the demand for good A.

T F 12. When Microsoft decided to start producing the Zune music player, the market supply curve for players shifted to the left.

T F 13. An increase in the demand for digital music players will cause an increase in the price of digital music players and an increase in the supply of digital music players.

T F 14. A change in price will not cause a change in demand or supply.

T F 15. Competitive markets have many buyers and many sellers.

Answers to the Self-Test

Multiple-Choice Questions

Question	Answer	Comment
1	b	In this example, the quantity of players demanded per month is 35 million when the price per player is $250.
2	c	Quantity demanded is the quantity purchased per period of time for a given price.
3	b	The demand schedule is a table, not a curve or a single amount of quantity demanded at a given price.
4	c	This is the definition of *demand curve*.
5	d	This is the definition of *market demand.*
6	b	The demand curve is downward sloping. There is an inverse relationship between price and quantity demanded. Price and quantity demanded move in opposite directions.
7	a	The demand curve is downward sloping, so as the price falls the quantity demanded rises.
8	c	The consumers' demand curve is downward sloping. There is an inverse relationship between price and quantity demanded. Price and quantity demanded move in opposite directions.
9	c	The law of demand states that there is an inverse relationship between the price of a product and the quantity of the product demanded.
10	c	According to the law of demand, there is an inverse relationship between the price of a product and the quantity of the product demanded.
11	c	Along with the substitution effect, the income effect helps to explain why a demand curve is downward sloping. (Note that the income effect only works in this direction for normal goods.)
12	b	The substitution effect, along with the income effect, helps to explain why a demand curve is downward sloping. (Note that the income effect only works in this direction for normal goods.)
13	d	The term *ceteris paribus* means controlling variables during an analysis.
14	a	This graph shows an increase in demand. When the price of a substitute good rises, the demand for the good in question also rises.
15	b	Demand decreases when the price of a complementary good increases.
16	a	This graph shows an increase in demand. When income rises, the demand for any normal good also rises.
17	a	This graph shows an increase in demand. When tastes for a product rise, the demand for the good in question also rises.
18	a	This graph shows an increase in demand. When population rises, the demand for the good in question also rises.
19	a	This graph shows an increase in demand. When the expected future price of a product rises, the demand for the good in question today also rises.
20	b	Complementary goods work together.
21	a	The two goods can be used in place of each other.
22	b	The term inferior good means consumers will buy less of a good as income rises.

23	a	The term normal good means consumers will buy more of a good as income rises.
24	b	By definition, anything that causes a demand curve to shift also causes a change in demand.
25	a	By definition, anything that causes movement along a single demand curve also causes a change in quantity demanded. And the only factor that can change quantity demanded is a change in the price of the product.
26	b	When any variable that affects demand changes, demand shifts. (The sole exception to this rule is changes in the price of the product.)
27	a	By definition anything that causes movement along a single demand curve also causes a change in quantity demanded. And the only factor that can change quantity demanded is a change in the price of the product.
28	b	A change in the price of a good or service does not cause a shift in the demand curve. It would cause a movement along the demand curve.
29	a	*Quantity supplied* is the quantity of a good or service that a firm is willing to supply at a given price. When any variable that affects demand changes, demand shifts. (The sole exception to this rule is changes in the price of the product.)
30	b	A table that shows the relationship between the price of a product and the quantity of the product supplied is called the *supply schedule*. By definition anything that causes movement along a single demand curve also causes a change in quantity demanded. And the only factor that can change quantity demanded is a change in the price of the product.
31	c	A curve that shows the relationship between the price of a product and the quantity of the product supplied is called a supply curve. *Quantity supplied* is the quantity of a good or service that a firm is willing to supply at a given price.
32	a	This is the law of supply. A table that shows the relationship between the price of a product and the quantity of the product supplied is called the *supply schedule*.
33	a	This graph shows a decrease in supply. When the price of an input increases, supply decreases.
34	b	This graph shows an increase in supply. When productivity increases, supply increases.
35	a	This graph shows a decrease in supply. When the price of a substitute in production increases, supply for the good in question decreases because more of the substitute is produced and less of the good in question is produced.
36	a	This graph shows a decrease in supply. When the expected future price of a product increases, supply for the good in question decreases today because less of the good will be produced today and more will be produced in the future in order to take advantage of the higher price in the future.
37	b	This graph shows an increase in supply. When the number of firms in the market increases, market supply increases.
38	b	A determinant of supply other than price will cause a shift in the supply curve. In this case, the supply increases or the supply curve shifts to the right.
39	a	If the price of a good changes that will cause a movement along the supply curve. This movement from *A* to *B* is an increase the quantity supplied.
40	c	If the actual price is above the equilibrium price, the quantity supplied is greater than the quantity demanded, so there is a surplus.
41	a	If the actual price is below the equilibrium price, the quantity demanded is greater than the quantity supplied, so there is a shortage.
42	d	If there is a frost, it will destroy the apples, which will cause the price of apples to rise. Since apples are an input in the production of apple juice, the supply of apple juice will decrease.
43	a	The price will rise when the demand increases and the supply decreases, though the effect on the equilibrium quantity will be ambiguous.

44 c Both the demand and supply shift right, which will cause an increase in the equilibrium quantity and an ambiguous effect on the price.

Short Answer Responses

1. Tickets for these events typically sell out soon after they are offered to the public. Many of these tickets are later resold at prices higher than the original prices buyers paid for them. This implies that the quantity demanded for the tickets is greater than the quantity supplied at the original prices. The prices the tickets are first sold at are below their equilibrium levels. (Event promoters often price tickets this way to create additional publicity about the event.)

2. Prices of perishable goods such as fresh fish, baked goods, milk, and fruit are likely to be lowered quickly. A key factor is the product's durability. Services are the most perishable products, but a head of lettuce is not much more durable. On the other hand, cars and home appliances can be stored as inventories for quite some time without spoiling.

3. A shortage exists when the price for a product is less than the equilibrium price. If the price is allowed to rise to its equilibrium level, the shortage will be eliminated. But the product will be scarce whether the market price is above, below, or equal to its equilibrium value. Every economic product is scarce because unlimited human wants exceed society's limited productive resources.

4. Because the price of organs and transplant operations would rise, this would affect quantity demanded rather than demand. An increase in the price of organs and transplant operations would typically decrease the quantity demanded. But it is unlikely that the quantity demanded would change very much, if at all, because there are no good substitutes for the operations. And it's unusual for the transplant recipient to pay for the operation since surgery is usually covered by health insurance. This makes demand even less responsive to changes in price.

5. Demographics are most responsible for this change. As more members of the so-called "baby boomer" generation reach retirement age, their demand for health care will increase. (Most health care spending is for care of those over age 60.)

True/False Answers

1. F The demand curve shows the quantity that all consumers would collectively demand at each possible price.
2. F Increases in price cause decreases in quantity demanded, not demand.
3. T Even though demand increases in the summer, the supply increases even more.
4. T A surplus would cause firms to want to decrease their supply to reduce their inventories. As the price falls the quantity demanded increases and the quantity supplied decreases.
5. T A normal good is one for which as income rises the demand increases.
6. T If the good is a substitute, consumers will buy the related good instead. If it is a complement and you remove it from the shelf they will no longer buy the complement.
7. F Inferior goods are ones that you buy less of as your inferior rises.
8. F Substitution and income effects explain the law of demand.
9. T If something causes technology to decrease, the supply will decrease.
10. T As the supply increases, the market price will fall, which will cause a movement down the demand curve, i.e. there will be an increase in the quantity demanded.

11. T Complements are consumed together, such as coffee and creamer. If the price of one increases, consumers will buy less of the related good.
12. F An increase in the number of suppliers for digital music players will cause an increase in supply.
13. F An increase in demand for digital music players will cause an increase in the supply of digital music players, but it will not increase the supply. It will increase the quantity supplied.
14. T A change in price causes a change in the quantity demanded or quantity supplied, not demand or supply.
15. T A competitive market must have many buyers and many sellers.

Chapter 4

Economic Efficiency, Government Price Setting, and Taxes

Chapter Summary

Governments of over 200 cities in the United States have placed ceilings on the maximum rent some landlords can charge for their apartments. Governments also impose taxes in some markets. To understand the economic impact of government in markets, it is necessary to understand consumer surplus and producer surplus.

Consumer surplus is the dollar benefit consumers receive from buying goods and services at market prices that are less than the maximum prices they would be willing to pay. **Producer surplus** is the dollar benefit producers receive from selling goods and services at prices greater than the minimum prices they would be willing to accept. **Economic surplus** is the sum of consumer surplus and producer surplus. In a competitive market with no externalities, the equilibrium price for a good or service occurs where the marginal cost of the last unit produced and sold is equal to the marginal benefit consumers receive from the last unit bought. Therefore the equilibrium quantity produced in a competitive market is economically efficient. At this equilibrium level of output, economic surplus is maximized.

In some markets, producers lobby for government action to set a legal price greater than the equilibrium price – a **price floor**. Some consumers lobby the government to force firms to charge a price lower than the equilibrium price – a **price ceiling**. Price floors were established in agricultural markets in the United States during the Great Depression. The minimum wage is another example of a price floor. For most occupations, it is illegal for an employer to pay less than the minimum wage established by Congress. Price ceilings are most often found in the markets for apartments in various cities. You're probably more familiar with these ceilings under their usual name: *rent control.* Compared to the competitive equilibrium, price ceilings and price floors reduce economic efficiency.

A tax on the sale of a good or service also reduces economic efficiency. **Tax incidence** is the actual division of the burden of a tax between buyers and sellers. The incidence of a tax depends on how responsive producers and consumers are to the price change caused by the tax.

Learning Objectives

When you finish this chapter, you should be able to:

1. **Distinguish between the concepts of consumer surplus and producer surplus.** Consumer surplus is the benefit consumers receive from paying a price lower than the maximum price they would be willing to pay. Producer surplus is the benefit a firm receives from selling a good or a service at a price higher than the minimum the firm would be willing to accept. Economic surplus is the consumer surplus plus producer surplus.

2. **Understand the concept of economic efficiency.** Maximum economic efficiency results when the marginal benefit received by consumers from the last unit bought equals the marginal cost to producers from selling the unit. An economically efficient outcome occurs when a competitive market equilibrium is reached.

3. **Explain the economic effect of government-imposed price ceilings and price floors.** Though total economic surplus is maximized when a competitive market equilibrium is reached, individual consumers would rather pay a price lower than the equilibrium price and individual producers would rather charge a higher price. Producers or consumers who are dissatisfied with the equilibrium price can lobby government to legally require a different price. When the government intervenes it can aid sellers by requiring a price above equilibrium, a price floor, or it can aid consumers by requiring a price below equilibrium, a price ceiling. Price floors and ceilings reduce economic efficiency, causing a deadweight loss.

4. **Analyze the economic impact of taxes.** Whenever a government places a tax on a good or service, economic efficiency is reduced. Some of the reduction in economic surplus due to the tax becomes revenue for the government while the rest of the reduction is a deadweight loss, that is, a net reduction in economic surplus that is not transferred to government or anyone.

Chapter Review

Chapter Opener: Should the Government Control Apartment Rents? (pages 98-99)

Rent control is an example of a price ceiling. Rent controls exist in about 200 cities in the United States. Although the rules that govern rent control are complex and vary by city, rent control drives up the demand and price for apartments not subject to the controls. Like any price control, rent control also has many unintended consequences including lower quality of rent-controlled units, black markets, and unwanted, inefficient side conditions.

Helpful Study Hint

Read ***Solved Problem 4-3*** and ***An Inside Look*** from this chapter to reinforce your understanding of the impact of rent control on the demand and supply of apartments.

Economics in YOUR Life! asks if rent control makes it easier for you to find an affordable apartment. Keep this question in mind as you read the chapter. The authors will answer this question at the end of the chapter.

4.1 LEARNING OBJECTIVE

4.1 Consumer Surplus and Producer Surplus (pages 100-105)

Learning Objective 1 Distinguish between the concepts of consumer surplus and producer surplus.

Consumer surplus is the difference between the highest price a consumer is willing to pay and the price the consumer actually pays. **Producer surplus** is the difference between the lowest price a firm would be willing to accept and the price it actually receives. Consumer and producer surplus represent the net benefits consumers and producers receive from buying and selling a good or service in a market.

Marginal benefit is the additional benefit to a consumer from consuming one more unit of a good or service. The height of a market demand curve at a given quantity measures the marginal benefit to someone from consuming that quantity. Consumer surplus refers to the difference between this marginal benefit and the market price the consumer pays. Total consumer surplus is the difference between marginal benefit and price for all quantities bought by consumers. Total consumer surplus is equal to the area below the demand curve and above the market price for the number of units consumed.

Marginal cost is the additional cost to a firm of producing one more unit of a good or service. The height of a market supply curve at a given quantity measures the marginal cost of this quantity. Producer surplus refers to the difference between this marginal cost and the market price the producer receives. Total producer surplus equals the area above the supply curve and below price for all quantities sold.

Helpful Study Hint

You probably have bought something you thought was a bargain. If you did, the difference between what you would have been willing to pay and what you did pay was your consumer surplus. Consumers differ in the value they place on the same item but typically pay the same price for the item. Those who value an item the most receive the most consumer surplus. Because the marginal cost of producing a good rises as more is produced, and price will equal marginal cost only for the last unit of output sold, price must be greater than the marginal cost of producing all but the last unit of output. Therefore, firms will earn producer surplus on all but the last unit sold. Be sure you understand Figure 4-5 and Figure 4-6 and the explanation of these figures in the textbook.

Extra Solved Problem **4-1**

Chapter 4 of the textbook includes two Solved Problems. Here is an extra Solved Problem to help you build your skills solving economic problems.

Consumer and Producer Surplus for the NFL Sunday Ticket

Supports Learning Objective 4-1: Distinguish between the concepts of consumer surplus and producer surplus.

Making the Connection "The Consumer Surplus from Satellite Television" explained consumer surplus using the example of customers of DirecTV and the DISH Network, both providers of satellite television. But only DirecTV offers its customers the option of subscribing to the NFL Sunday Ticket. In 2007, subscribers to this service paid $229 for the right to watch every regular season NFL Sunday game broadcast except for those games played on Sunday evenings. For fans that have moved to cities that don't broadcast their favorite team's games, this option is very attractive. Local television stations offer games played by teams with the most local interest. A long-time fan of the New York Giants or Denver Broncos who moved to Illinois would likely have to settle for watching the Chicago Bears most Sunday afternoons – unless he had signed up for the DirecTV NFL Sunday Ticket.

Team Marketing Report estimated that the 2005 average ticket price for NFL games for all teams was $58.95 and the per-game average Fan Cost was about $330 (this amount includes four average price tickets, four small soft drinks, two small beers, four hot dogs, two game programs, parking and two adult size caps). Each NFL team plays eight regular-season games in their home stadium.

a. Estimate the value of consumer surplus for the NFL Sunday Ticket for a representative fan.

b. Estimate the value of producer surplus for the NFL Sunday Ticket.

Source: www.teammarketing.com

SOLVING THE PROBLEM

Step 1: Review the chapter material.
This problem is about consumer and producer surplus, so you may want to review the section "Consumer Surplus and Producer Surplus," which begins on page 100 in the textbook.

Step 2: Identify the maximum price a consumer would pay for the NFL Sunday Ticket.
The consumers who benefit most from the NFL Sunday Ticket are those who have the strongest demand to watch their favorite team play on Sundays. Assume that an average season ticket holder found out prior to fall 2005 that he was being transferred by his employer to a location that required him to forego season tickets for himself and three other family members. Using the Team Marketing estimate, he would save $330 for each home game that he and his family would no longer attend. Therefore, his total saving would be $330 x 8 = $2,640. This is an estimate of the maximum price he would pay for the NFL Sunday Ticket. (Note that he would also be able to watch his team's away games but would probably be able to view these games from his home at no additional cost if he had not moved).

Step 3: Estimate the value of consumer surplus.
For the average season ticket holder and his family, an estimate of the consumer surplus is: $2,640 − $229 = $2,411. Note that each family member who no longer attended home games can watch these games at home.

Step 4: Identify the minimum price DirecTV would accept for the NFL Sunday Ticket.
The NFL Package is offered to existing DirecTV customers as an additional viewing option. Therefore, only trivial additional costs are incurred by DirecTV. The customer's billing must be adjusted to include this option, and the service must be "switched on" for this customer. Assume that these costs and an economic profit sufficient to compensate DirecTV for offering this service is $30. Assume that the marginal cost is zero so that the minimum price DirecTV would accept for the NFL Sunday Ticket is $0.

Step 5: Estimate the value of producer surplus.
Because DirecTV receives $229 for the NFL Sunday Ticket its producer surplus for this customer is $229 – $0 = $229.

4.2 LEARNING OBJECTIVE

4.2 The Efficiency of Competitive Markets (pages 105-107)

Learning Objective 2 Understand the concept of economic efficiency.

Economic surplus is the sum of consumer and producer surplus. When equilibrium is reached in a competitive market, the marginal benefit equals the marginal cost of the last unit sold. This is an economically efficient outcome. If less than the equilibrium output were produced, the marginal benefit of the last unit bought would exceed its marginal cost. If more than the equilibrium quantity were produced, the marginal benefit of this last unit would be less than its marginal cost. We can also think of the concept of economic efficiency in terms of economic surplus. When in equilibrium, the willingness of the consumer to pay for the last unit is equal to the lowest price a firm will be willing to accept. If less than the equilibrium output were produced, the willingness to pay for the last unit bought would exceed the minimum price that firms would be willing to accept. If more than equilibrium quantity were produced, the willingness to pay of this last unit would be less than the minimum price that producers would accept.

Economic efficiency is a market outcome in which the marginal benefit to consumers of the last unit produced is equal to its marginal cost of production and where the sum of consumer and producer surplus is at a maximum. A **deadweight loss** is the reduction in economic surplus that results when a market is not in competitive equilibrium.

Helpful Study Hint

Figure 4-7 illustrates the deadweight loss from production at a nonequilibrium point in a competitive market. You should understand that when the quantity of chai tea cups sold is 14,000 instead of 15,000, there is a loss of both producer surplus and consumer surplus.

Extra Solved Problem 4-2

Chapter 4 of the textbook includes two Solved Problems. Here is an extra Solved Problem to help you build your skills solving economic problems.

Supports Learning Objective 4-2: Understand the concept of economic efficiency.

Suppose that the tickets for a Kelly Clarkson concert just went on sale in your local area. The tickets are selling for $25 each, the equilibrium price. Suppose that the willingness to pay of the last consumer to buy a ticket was $50 and the minimum that the producer was willing to accept was $10.

a. Is this market outcome economically efficient?

b. If not, what would need to occur for this market to become economically efficient?

SOLVING THE PROBLEM

Step 1: Review the chapter material.
This problem is about economic efficiency, so you may want to review the section "The Efficiency of Competitive Markets," which begins on page 105 in the textbook.

Step 2: Compare the minimum price that the concert producer is willing to accept to the price the consumer is willing to pay.
Because the value to the consumer of the last ticker sold is higher than the minimum price that the producer is willing to accept, the market is not efficient. The willingness to pay by the consumer must be equal to the minimum price that the producer is willing to accept in order for efficiency to be maximized.

Step 3: Determine what needs to occur in the market for the market to become efficient.
Because the willingness to pay is greater than the minimum the firm is willing to accept, there is additional consumer and producer surplus that could be gained by increasing the number of tickets sold. The number of tickets sold should increase until the willingness to pay of last consumer is equal to the minimum that the producer is willing to accept.

4.3 LEARNING OBJECTIVE

4.3 Government Intervention in the Market: Price Floors and Price Ceilings (pages 107-115)

Learning Objective 3 Explain the economic effect of government-imposed price ceilings and price floors.

Though the net benefit to society is maximized at a competitive market equilibrium, individual consumers would be better off if they could pay a lower than equilibrium price and individual producers would be better off if they could sell at a higher than equilibrium price. Consumers and producers sometimes lobby government to legally require a market price different from the equilibrium price. These lobbying efforts are sometimes successful. During the Great Depression of the 1930s, farm prices fell to very low levels. Farmers were able to convince the federal government to raise prices by setting price floors for many agricultural prices.

A **price floor** is a legally determined minimum price that sellers may receive. A price floor encourages producers to produce more output than consumers want to buy at the floor price. The government often buys the surplus, which is equal to the quantity supplied minus the quantity demanded, at the floor price. The government may also pay farmers to take some land out of cultivation, which would decrease supply. The marginal cost of production exceeds the marginal benefit, and there is a deadweight loss, which represents a decline in efficiency due to the price floor.

A **price ceiling** is a legally determined maximum price that sellers may charge. Price ceilings are meant to help consumers who lobby for lower prices. Consumers typically lobby for price ceilings after a sharp increase in the price of an item on which they spend a significant amount of their budgets (for example, rent or gasoline). At the ceiling price, the quantity demanded is greater than the quantity supplied so that the marginal benefit of the last item sold (the quantity supplied) exceeds the marginal cost of producing it. Price ceilings result in a deadweight loss and a reduction of economic efficiency. Price ceilings create incentives for black markets. A **black market** refers to buying and selling at prices that violate government price regulations.

With any price floor or price ceiling, there are winners and losers from the policy. The deadweight loss associated with a given policy tells us that the gains to the winners are outweighed by the losses to the losers.

Helpful Study Hint

An interesting question to consider is why politicians maintain agricultural price supports despite the significant costs their constituents pay for these programs. Part of the explanation is that because each individual incurs a small fraction of the total cost, it is hardly worth the trouble to register a complaint to lawmakers. But the benefits of price floors are concentrated among a few producers who have a strong incentive to lobby for the continuation of the price supports. Politicians act quite rationally by ignoring the interests of those who pay for these programs.

You may be swayed by the argument that a price ceiling is justified because its intent is to help low-income consumers afford a price-controlled product. Though some low-income consumers may be among those who buy the product, there is no guarantee of this. Suppose you were a landlord who owned an apartment subject to rent control. As a result, there are 5 potential tenants for one apartment you have to rent. The potential tenants include a male college student, a single female school teacher with a pet dog, a low-income retail worker with a spouse and two children, a medical doctor, and a lawyer. Assume that you can select any one of these as your tenant. Would you select the retail worker? What about the college student?

4.4 LEARNING OBJECTIVE

4.4 The Economic Impact of Taxes (pages 115-120)

Learning Objective 4 Analyze the economic impact of taxes.

Government taxes on goods and services reduce the quantity produced. A tax imposed on producers of a product will shift the supply curve up by the amount of the tax. Consumers pay a higher price for the product, and there will be a loss of consumer surplus. Because the price producers receive after paying the tax falls, there is also a loss of producer surplus. The imposition of a tax will also cause a deadweight loss. **Tax incidence** is the actual division of the burden of the tax between buyers and sellers. The incidence of a tax is not dependent on who is legally required to collect and pay the tax. Tax incidence is determined by the degree to which the market price rises as a result of a tax. This rise, in turn, is determined by the willingness of suppliers to change the quantity of the good or service they offer and the willingness of consumers to change their quantity demanded as a result of the tax.

Helpful Study Hint

Estimating the impact of cigarette taxes is more complicated than it appears from Figure 4-10. This is because state excise taxes on cigarettes vary widely. In 2007, the tax per pack ranged from 17 cents in Missouri to $2.58 in New Jersey. In addition, some counties and cities impose their own taxes. The variation in taxes creates a black market that reduces legal sales of cigarettes and tax revenue in states with the highest tax rates. Bootleggers can earn illegal profits by buying cigarettes in states with low tax rates and selling them to retail stores in states with the highest taxes. A disturbing example of cigarette bootlegging was reported in 2002 when a suspected terrorist was found guilty by a federal court of buying cigarettes in North Carolina and selling them in Michigan where the per-pack tax differential was about 70 cents. Revenue from the illegal cigarette sales was allegedly used to fund Hezbollah, a terrorist organization with headquarters in the Middle East.

Helpful Study Hint

Economics in YOUR Life! asked if you are more likely to find an affordable apartment in the city with rent control? Although rent control can keep rents lower than they might otherwise be, it can also lead to a permanent shortage of apartments. You may have to search for a long time to find a suitable apartment, and landlords may even ask you to give them payments "under the table," which would make your actual rent higher than the controlled rent. Finding an apartment in a city without rent control should be much easier, although the rent may be higher.

Key Terms

Black market. A market in which buying and selling take place at prices that violate government price regulations.

Consumer surplus. The difference between the highest price a consumer is willing to pay and the price the consumer actually pays.

Deadweight loss. The reduction in economic surplus resulting from a market not being in competitive equilibrium.

Economic efficiency. A market outcome in which the marginal benefit to consumers of the last unit produced is equal to its marginal cost of production and in which the sum of consumer surplus and producer surplus is at a maximum.

Economic surplus. The sum of consumer surplus and producer surplus.

Marginal benefit. The additional benefit to a consumer from consuming one more unit of a good or service.

Marginal cost. The additional cost to a firm of producing one more unit of a good or service.

Price ceiling. A legally determined maximum price that sellers may charge.

Price floor. A legally determined minimum price that sellers may receive.

Producer surplus. The difference between the lowest price a firm would be willing to accept and the price it actually receives.

Tax incidence. The actual division of the burden of a tax between buyers and sellers in a market.

Appendix

Quantitative Demand and Supply Analysis (pages 131-135)

LEARNING OBJECTIVE: Use quantitative demand and supply analysis.

Quantitative analysis supplements the use of demand and supply curves with equations. An example of the demand and supply for apartments in New York City is

$$Q^S = -450{,}000 + 1{,}300P$$

$$Q^D = 3{,}000{,}000 - 1{,}000P$$

Q^D and Q^S are the quantity demanded and quantity supplied of apartments per month, respectively. The coefficient of P in the first equation equals the change in quantity supplied for a one dollar per month change in price.

$$\frac{\Delta Q^S}{\Delta P} = 1{,}300$$

The coefficient of the price term in the second equation equals the change in quantity demanded for a one dollar per month change in price.

$$\frac{\Delta Q^S}{\Delta P} = -1{,}000$$

At the competitive market equilibrium quantity demanded equals quantity supplied

$$Q^D = Q^S \text{ or}$$

$$3{,}000{,}000 - 1{,}000P = -450{,}000 + 1{,}300P$$

Rearranging terms and solving for P yields the price at which quantity demanded equals the quantity supplied. This is the equilibrium price.

$$3{,}000{,}000 + 450{,}000 = 1{,}300P + 1{,}000P$$

$$3{,}450{,}000 = 2{,}300P$$

$$P = \$1{,}500$$

Substituting the equilibrium price into the equation for either demand or supply yields the equilibrium quantity.

$$Q^D = 3{,}000{,}000 - 1{,}000(1{,}500)$$

$$Q^D = 3{,}000{,}000 - 1{,}500{,}000$$

$$Q^D = 1{,}500{,}000$$

$$Q^S = -450{,}000 + 1{,}300\text{P}$$

$$Q^S = -450{,}000 + 1{,}300\ (1{,}500)$$

$$Q^S = 1{,}500{,}000$$

The demand equation can be used to determine the price at which the quantity demanded is zero.

$$Q^D = 3{,}000{,}000 - 1{,}000P$$

$$0 = 3{,}000{,}000 - 1{,}000P$$

$$-3{,}000{,}000 = -1{,}000P$$

$$P = (-3{,}000{,}000)/(-1{,}000)$$

$$P = \$3{,}000$$

The supply equation can be used to determine the price at which the quantity supplied equals zero.

$$Q^S = -450{,}000 + 1{,}300P$$

$$0 = -450{,}000 + 1{,}300P$$

$$450{,}000 = 1{,}300P$$

$$P = \$346.15$$

Helpful Study Hint

The equations highlight an oddity of demand and supply analysis. The dependent variable in most graphs is the Y variable, or the variable measured along the vertical axis, while the independent or X variable is measured along the horizontal axis. Economists assume that price changes cause changes in quantity, so the dependent variable appears on the left hand side of the demand and supply equations. In turn, the coefficient of the price terms in these equations equals the change in quantity divided by a one unit change in price ($\Delta Q/\Delta P$). Unfortunately, for historical reasons, our demand and supply graphs have it backwards, with price on the vertical axis and quantity on the horizontal axis.

Calculating Consumer Surplus and Producer Surplus

Demand and supply equations can be used to measure consumer and producer surplus. Figure 4A-1 uses a graph to illustrate demand and supply. Because the demand curve is linear, consumer surplus is equal to the area of the blue triangle in Figure 4A-1. The area of a triangle is ½ multiplied by the base of the triangle multiplied by the height of the triangle, or

$$\tfrac{1}{2} \times (1{,}500{,}000) \times (3000 - 1{,}500) = \$1{,}125{,}000{,}000.$$

Producer surplus is calculated in a similar way. Producer surplus is equal to the area above the supply curve and below the line representing market price. The supply curve is a straight line, so producer surplus equals the area of the right triangle:

$$\tfrac{1}{2} \times (1{,}500{,}000) \times (1{,}500 - 346) = \$865{,}500{,}000$$

Producer surplus in the market for rental apartments in New York City is about $865 million.

Economic surplus is the sum of the consumer surplus and the producer surplus, so economic surplus is as follows:

$$\$1{,}125{,}000{,}000 + \$865{,}500{,}000 = \$1{,}990{,}500{,}000$$

Self-Test

(Answers are provided at the end of the Self-Test.)

Multiple-Choice Questions

1. What is the name of a legally determined minimum price that sellers may receive?
   a. A price ceiling
   b. A price floor
   c. Marginal benefit
   d. Consumer surplus

2. What is the name of a legally determined maximum price that sellers may charge?
   a. A price ceiling
   b. A price floor
   c. Marginal benefit
   d. Consumer surplus

3. Which of the following is the definition of *consumer surplus*?
   a. The additional benefit to a consumer from consuming one more unit of a good or service.
   b. The additional cost to a firm of producing one more unit of a good or service.
   c. The difference between the highest price a consumer is willing to pay and the price the consumer actually pays.
   d. The difference between the lowest price a firm would have been willing to accept and the price it actually receives.

4. Which of the following is the definition of *producer surplus*?
   a. The additional benefit to a consumer from consuming one more unit of a good or service.
   b. The additional cost to a firm of producing one more unit of a good or service.
   c. The difference between the highest price a consumer is willing to pay and the price the consumer actually pays.
   d. The difference between the lowest price a firm would have been willing to accept and the price it actually receives.

5. Which of the following is the definition of *marginal benefit*?
   a. The additional benefit to a consumer from consuming one more unit of a good or service.
   b. The additional cost to a firm of producing one more unit of a good or service.
   c. The difference between the highest price a consumer is willing to pay and the price the consumer actually pays.
   d. The difference between the lowest price a firm would have been willing to accept and the price it actually receives.

6. Which of the following is the definition of *marginal cost*?
   a. The additional benefit to a consumer from consuming one more unit of a good or service.
   b. The difference between the highest price a consumer is willing to pay and the price the consumer actually pays.
   c. The additional cost to a firm of producing one more unit of a good or service.
   d. The difference between the lowest price a firm would have been willing to accept and the price it actually receives.

7. Refer to the graph below. What name other than *demand curve* can you give this curve?

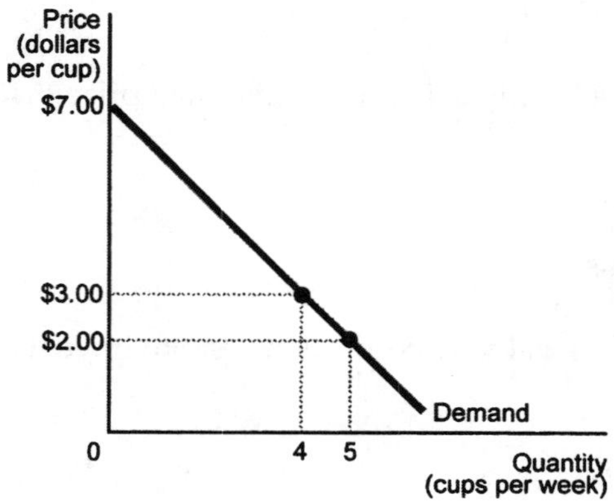

   a. The marginal cost curve
   b. The marginal benefit curve
   c. Consumer surplus
   d. The price-equilibrium curve

8. Refer to the graph below. The graph shows an individual's demand curve for tea. At a price of two dollars, the consumer is willing to buy five cups of tea per week. More precisely, what does this mean?

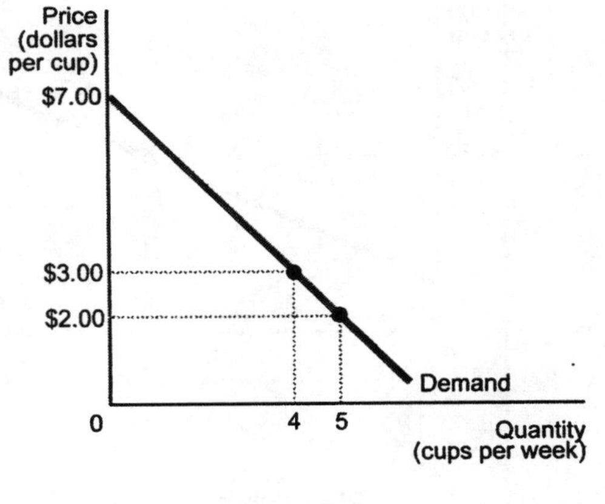

a. It means that marginal benefit equals marginal cost when five cups are consumed.
b. It means that the total cost of consuming five cups is $2.00.
c. It means that the marginal cost of producing five cups is $2.00.
d. It means that the marginal benefit of consuming the fifth cup is $2.00.

9. If the average price that cable subscribers are willing to pay for cable television is $208, but the actual price they pay is $81, how much is *consumer surplus* per subscriber?
a. $208 + $81
b. $208 – $81
c. $81 + $127
d. $81

10. Refer to the graph below. The graph shows the market demand for satellite TV service. If the market price is $81, which consumers receive consumer surplus in this market?

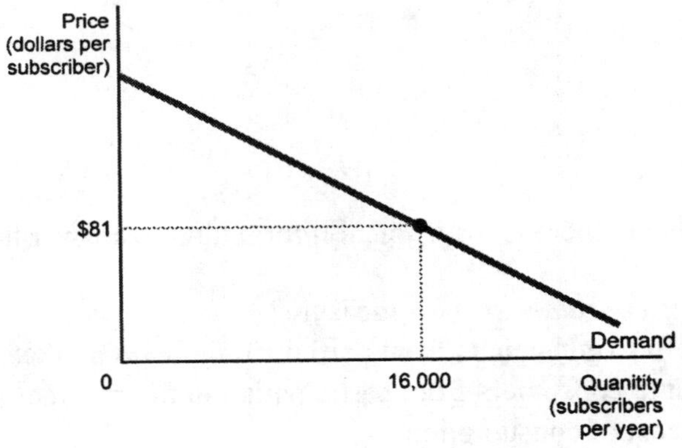

a. Those willing to pay something less than $81
b. Those willing to pay exactly $81
c. Those willing to pay more than $81
d. All of the above

11. Refer to the graph below. When market price is $2.00, how much is the *producer surplus* obtained from selling the 40th cup?

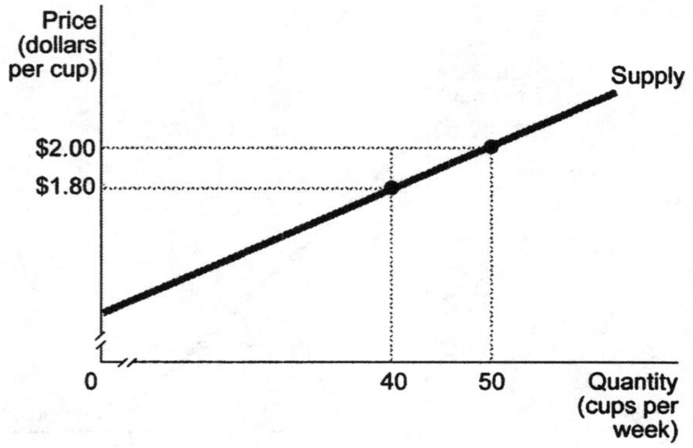

a. $72.00
b. $1.80
c. $0.20
d. $36.00

12. Refer to the graph below. How much is the marginal cost of producing the 50th cup?

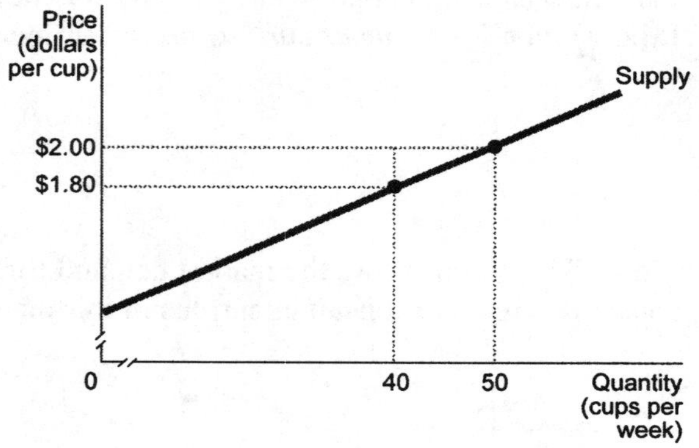

a. $100.00
b. $0.20
c. $2.00
d. None of the above; there is insufficient information to answer the question.

13. Precisely what does *consumer surplus* measure?
   a. The *total* benefit to consumers from participating in the market
   b. The *net* benefit to consumers from participating in the market
   c. The marginal cost of consumption
   d. The efficiency of competitive markets

14. Precisely what does *producer surplus* measure?
   a. The *total* benefit to producers from participating in the market
   b. The *net* benefit to producers from participating in the market
   c. The marginal cost of production
   d. The efficiency of competitive markets

15. Refer to the graph below. To achieve economic efficiency, which output level should be produced?

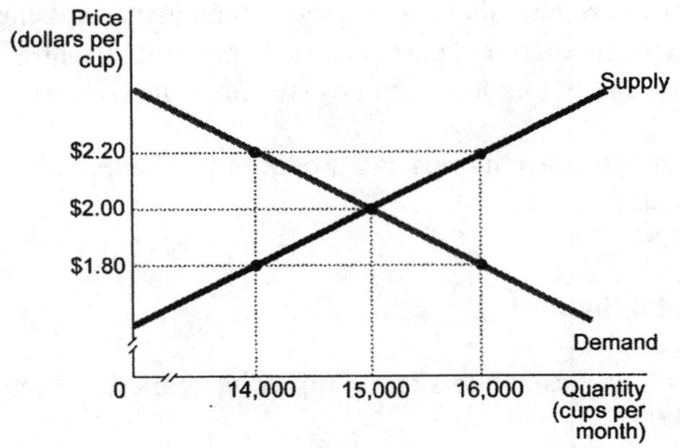

a. 14,000 cups per month, because at this level of output, marginal benefit is greater than marginal cost.
b. 15,000 cups per month, because at this level of output, marginal benefit is equal to marginal cost.
c. 16,000 cups per month, because at this level of output, marginal benefit is less than marginal cost.
d. Any of the output levels above is efficient.

16. Refer to the graph below. When should the level of output be reduced in order to increase economic efficiency?

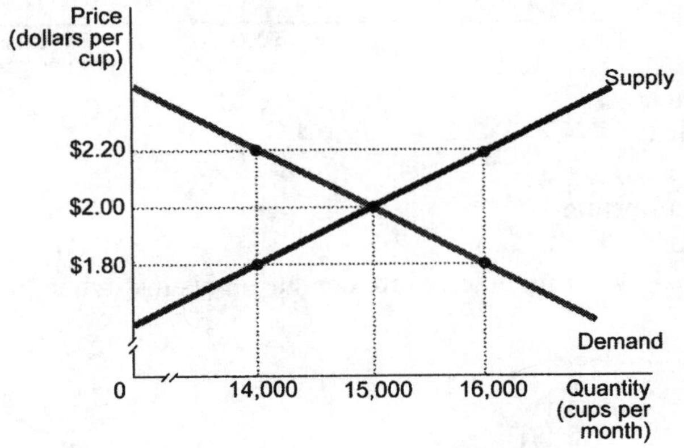

a. If 14,000 cups were produced
b. If 15,000 cups were produced
c. If 16,000 cups were produced
d. Never; output should always increase in order to increase economic efficiency.

17. When is output inefficiently low?
a. When marginal benefit is greater than marginal cost.
b. When marginal cost is greater than marginal benefit.
c. When marginal cost is equal to marginal benefit.
d. Any of the above; output can be inefficiently low at any time.

18. When a competitive market is in equilibrium, what is the economically efficient level of output?
    a. Any output level where marginal benefit is greater than marginal cost.
    b. Any output level where marginal cost is greater than marginal benefit.
    c. The output level where marginal cost is equal to marginal benefit.
    d. Any of the above; any output level can be efficient or inefficient.

19. What does the sum of consumer surplus and producer surplus equal?
    a. Economic efficiency
    b. Economic surplus
    c. A deadweight loss
    d. Competitive equilibrium

20. Refer to the graph below. Assume this is a competitive market. Which of the following *does not* exist when the price is $2.00?

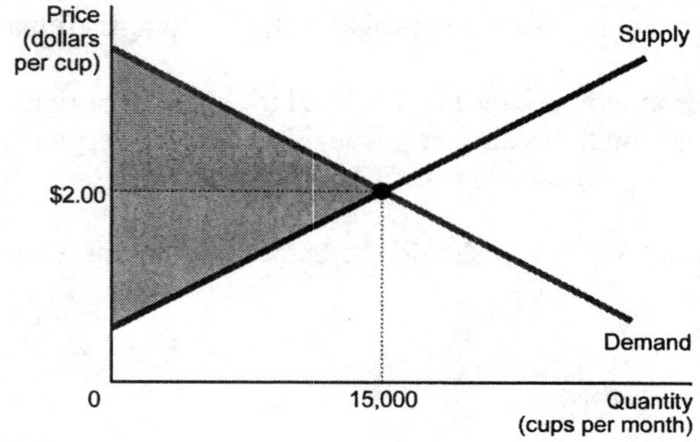

    a. Economic efficiency
    b. Economic surplus
    c. A deadweight loss
    d. Competitive equilibrium

21. Refer to the graph below. How much producer surplus is lost when the price is $2.20?

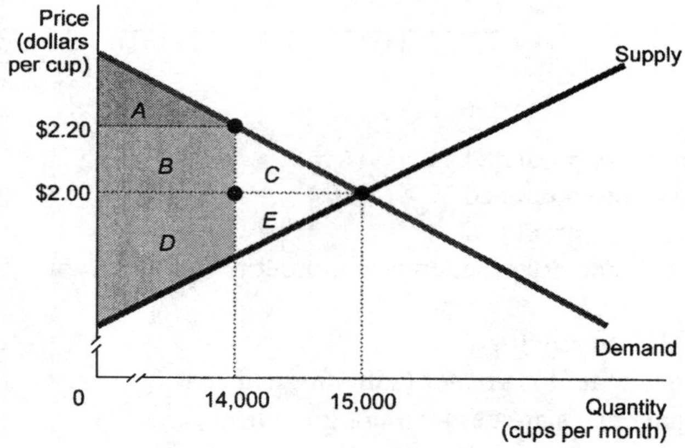

    a. Area E
    b. Area $C + E$
    c. Area D
    d. Area $B + D$

22. Refer to the graph below. Which area equals producer surplus when price is $2.20?

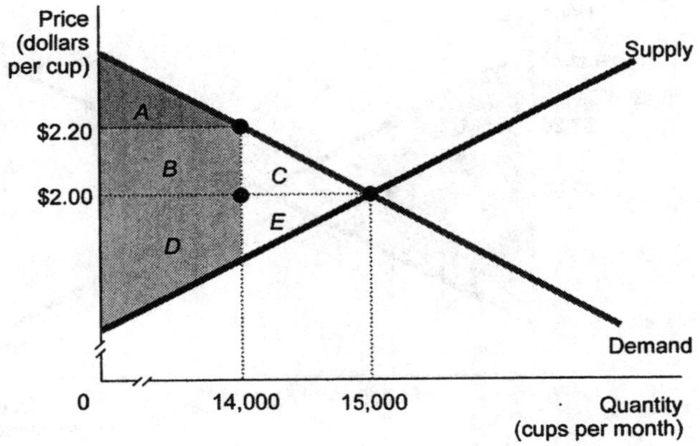

a. Area E
b. Area $C + E$
c. Area $D + E$
d. Area $B + D$

23. Refer to the graph below. Which area equals consumer surplus when price is $2.00?

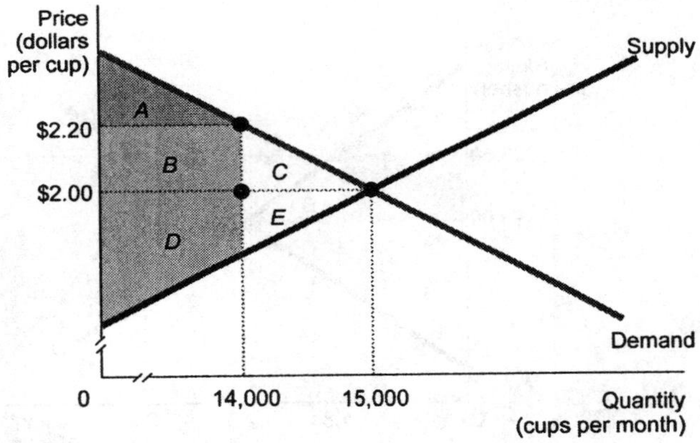

a. Area A
b. Area $B + C$
c. Area $A + B + C$
d. Area $B + C + D$

24. Refer to the graph below. Which area equals consumer surplus when price is $2.20?

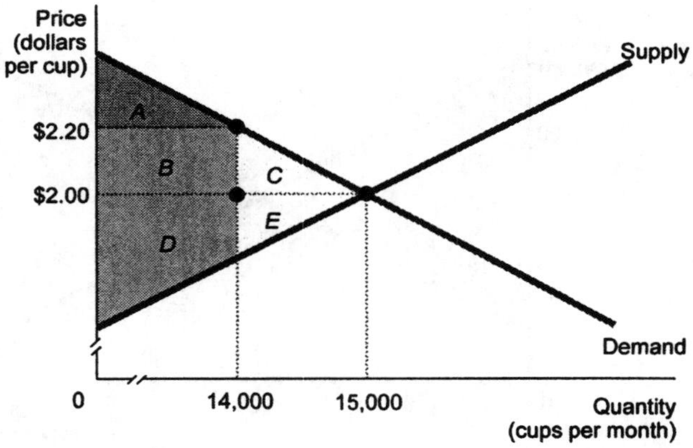

a. Area *A*
b. Area *B*
c. Area *C*
d. Area *D*

25. Refer to the graph below. After a price of $3.50 is imposed by the government in this market, what meaning do we give to area *A*?

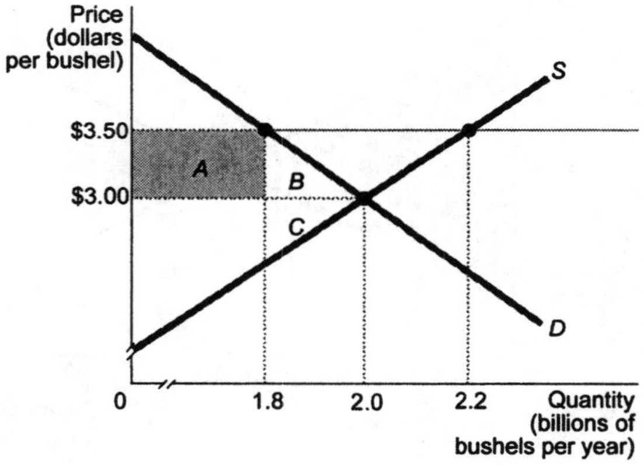

a. Area *A* is consumer surplus transferred to producers.
b. Area *A* is additional consumer surplus that goes to existing consumers in the market.
c. Area *A* is a deadweight loss.
d. Area *A* is a surplus of wheat.

26. Refer to the graph below. After a price of \$3.50 is imposed by the government in this market, what meaning do we give to area *B* + *C*?

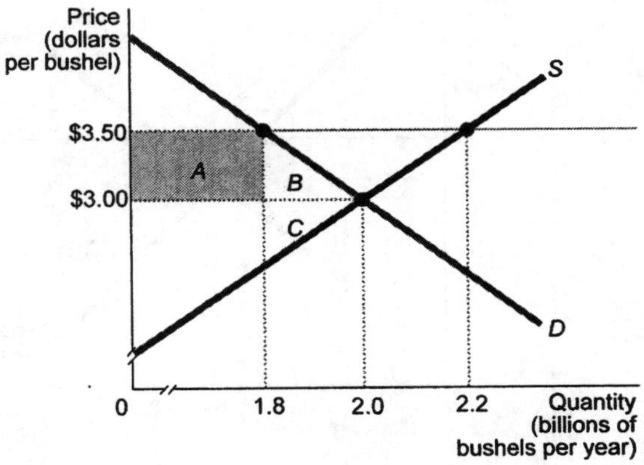

a. Producer surplus transferred to consumers
b. Additional consumer surplus to existing consumers in the market
c. Deadweight loss
d. A surplus of wheat

27. Refer to the graph below. According to this graph, the existence of a minimum wage in the market for low-skilled workers results in:

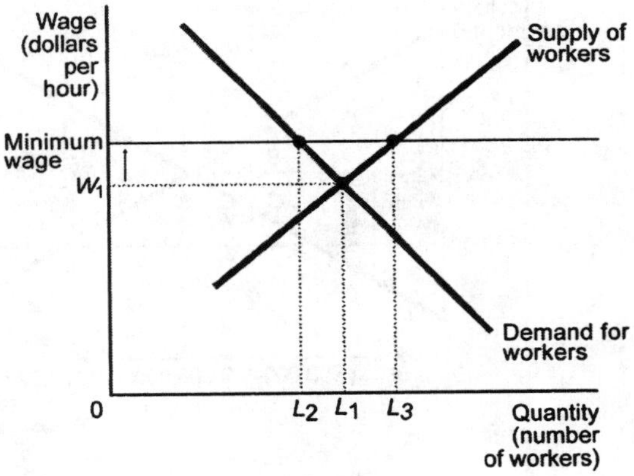

a. An increase in wages and employment
b. An increase in wages but lower employment
c. A decrease in wages but higher employment
d. A decrease in wages and employment

28. Refer to the graph below. According to this graph, the existence of a minimum wage in the market for low-skilled workers results in:

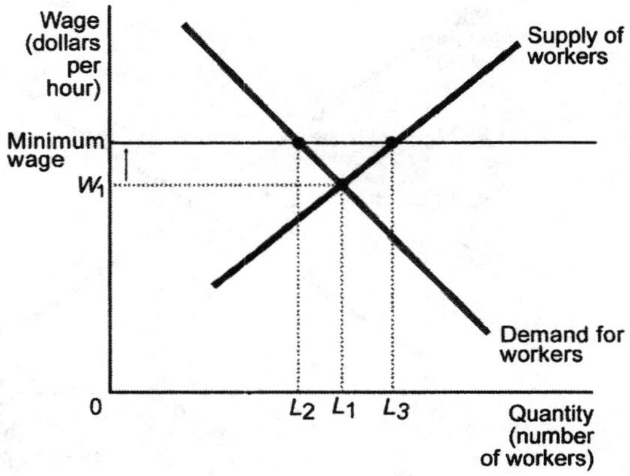

a. A shortage of workers
b. A surplus of workers
c. Neither a shortage nor a surplus of workers
d. A scarcity of workers

29. Refer to the graph below. After the rent control is imposed, area *A* represents:

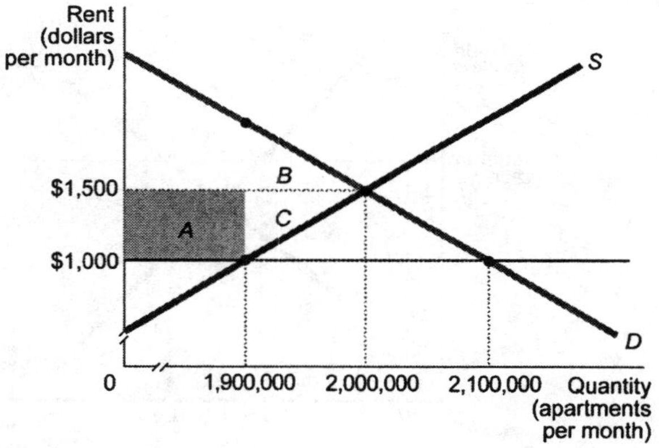

a. Consumer surplus transferred from renters to landlords
b. Producer surplus transferred from landlords to renters
c. A deadweight loss
d. A shortage of apartments

30. Refer to the graph below. After the rent control is imposed, which area represents a deadweight loss?

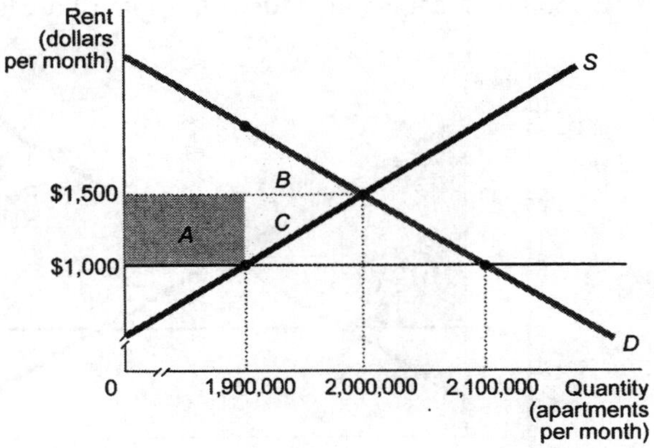

a. *A*
b. *A* + *B* + *C*
c. *B* + *C*
d. An area other than *A*, *B*, or *C*

31. Which of the following statements is correct?
a. There is a shortage of every good that is scarce.
b. There is no shortage of most scarce goods.
c. Scarcity and shortage mean pretty much the same thing to economists.
d. None of the above statements are correct.

32. Which of the following terms corresponds to a market in which buying and selling takes place at prices that violate government price regulations?
a. Price conspiracy
b. Scalping
c. Competitive market
d. Black market

33. Refer to the graph below. Suppose that this market is operating under the established rent control of $1,000 per month. Then, a black market for rent-controlled apartments develops, and the apartments then rent for $2,000 per month. What meaning does the sum of areas *A* + *E* have in this situation?

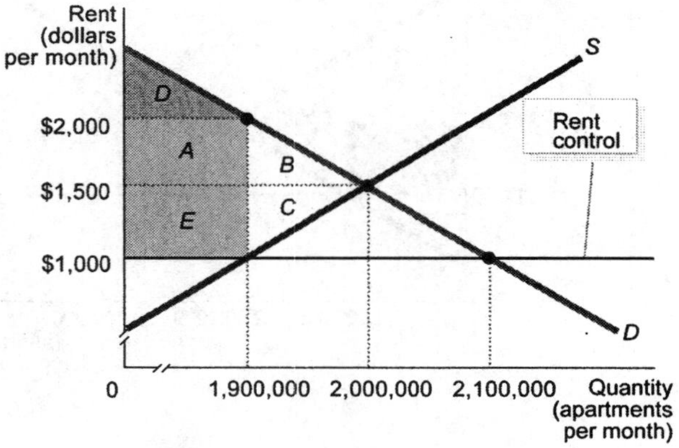

a. Consumer surplus transferred from renters to landlords
b. Producer surplus transferred from renters to landlords
c. Deadweight loss
d. A surplus of apartments

34. Refer to the graph below. When a black market for rent-controlled apartments develops, what is the area of deadweight loss?

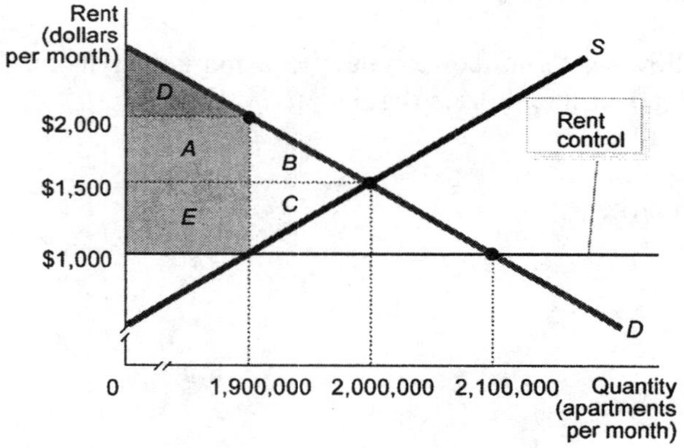

a. None; the deadweight loss disappears.
b. *B* + *C*
c. *A* + *E*
d. *D*

35. When the government imposes price floors or price ceilings, which of the following occurs?
a. Some people win
b. Some people lose
c. There is a loss of economic efficiency
d. All of the above

36. The term *tax incidence* refers to
   a. the type of product the tax is levied on.
   b. the amount of revenue collected by the government from a tax.
   c. the actual division of the burden of a tax.
   d. the actual versus the desired impact of a tax burden.

37. Refer to the graph below. What price do producers receive after this tax is imposed?

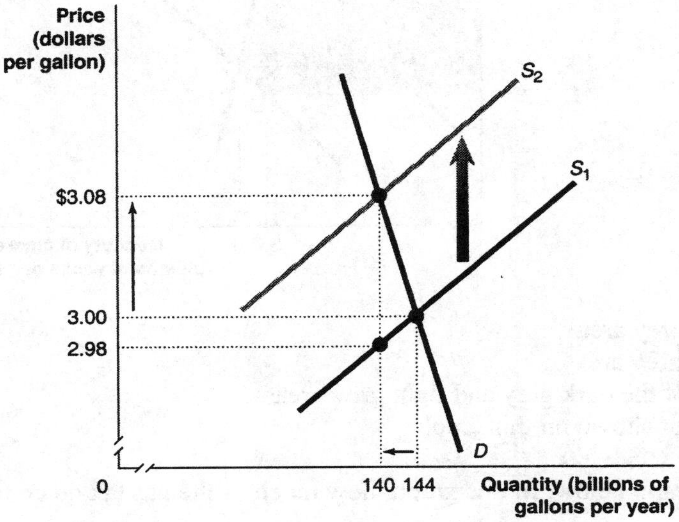

   a. $1.98
   b. $2.98
   c. $3.08
   d. None of the above

38. Refer to the graph below. What area corresponds to the *excess burden* from the tax?

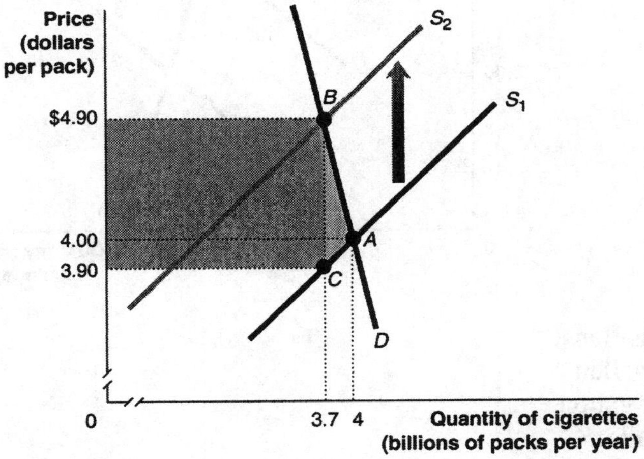

   a. The dark grey area
   b. The light grey area
   c. The sum of the dark grey and light grey areas
   d. An area not shown on this graph

39. Refer to the graph below. What area corresponds to the revenue collected by the government from the tax?

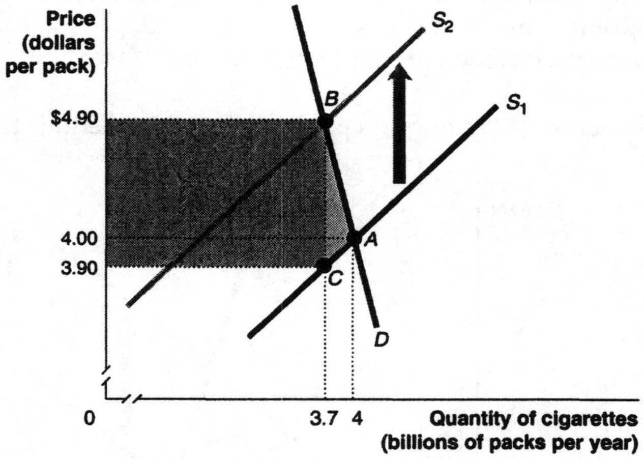

a. The dark grey area
b. The light grey area
c. The sum of the dark grey and light grey areas
d. An area not shown on this graph

40. Refer to the graph below. In this graph, how much of the gas tax do consumers pay?

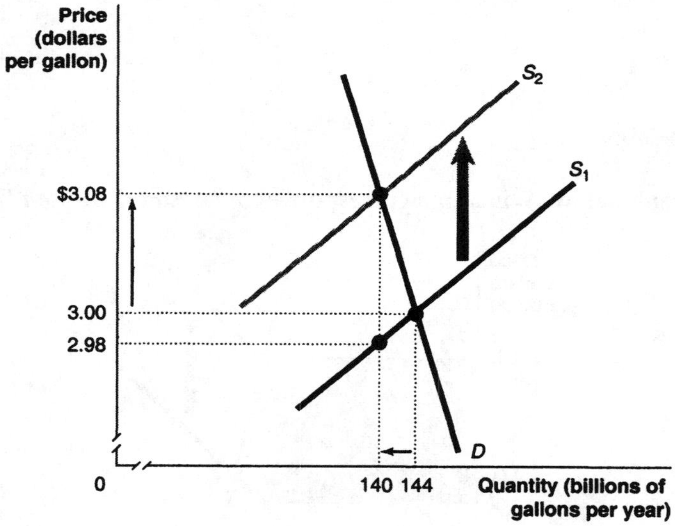

a. 2 cents per gallon
b. 8 cents per gallon
c. 10 cents per gallon
d. $1.50 per gallon

41. Refer to the graphs below. In each of the graphs below, a curve has shifted as a result of a new social security tax. In which graph does the employer pay the social security tax?

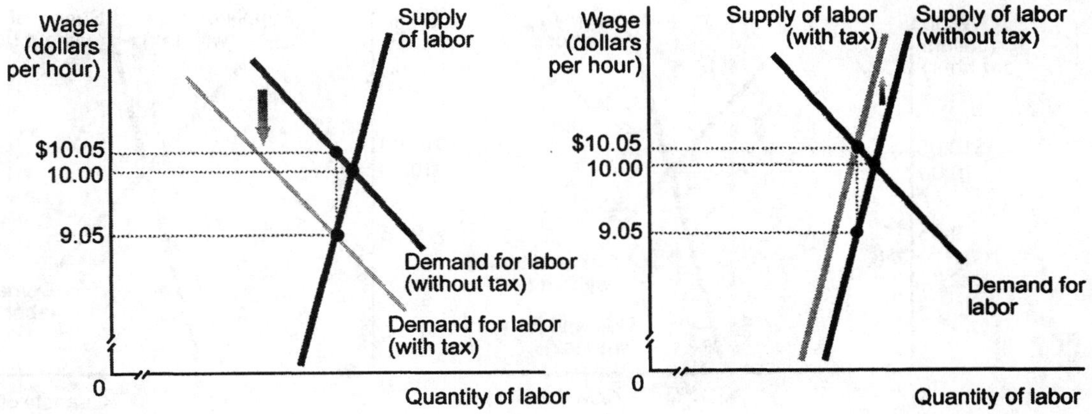

a. In the graph on the left
b. In the graph on the right
c. In both cases
d. In neither case

42. Refer to the graphs below. In each of the graphs below, a curve has shifted as a result of a new social security tax. In which graph do the workers pay the social security tax?

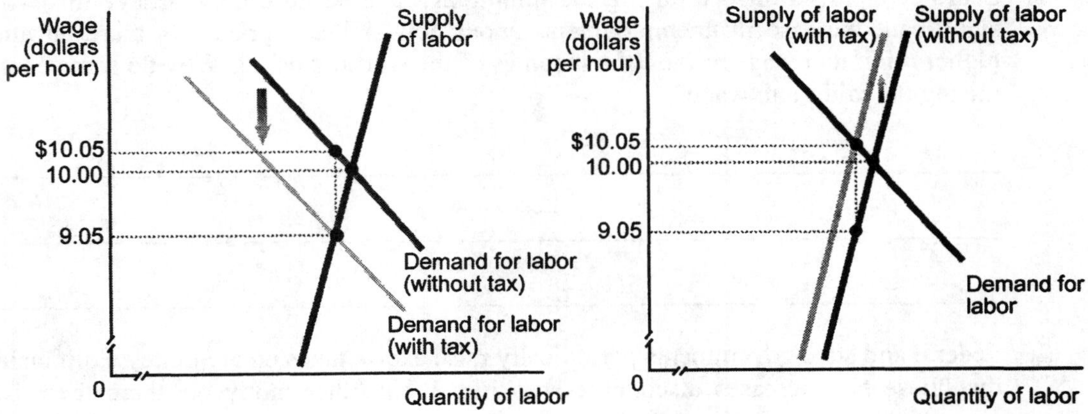

a. In the graph on the left
b. In the graph on the right
c. In both cases
d. In neither case

43. Refer to the graphs below. In each of the graphs below, a curve has shifted as a result of a new social security tax. In which graph is the tax incidence larger on workers?

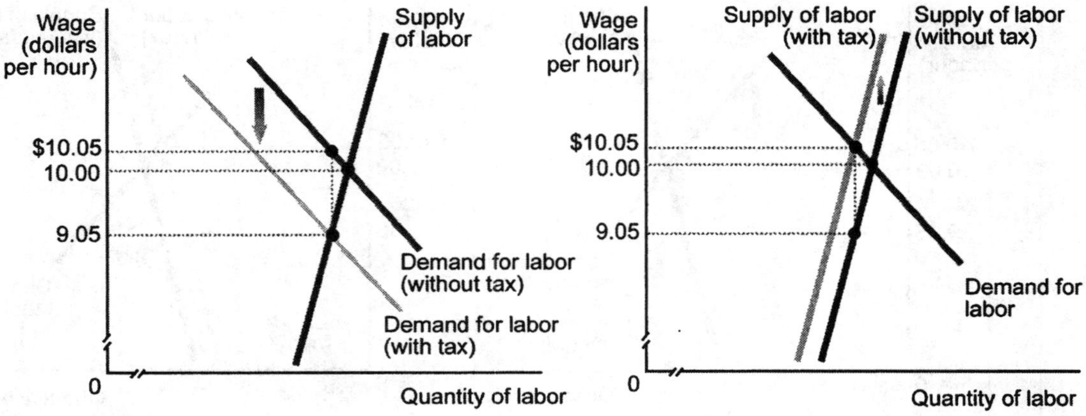

a. In the graph on the left
b. In the graph on the right
c. In neither case because the workers are not affected by the tax
d. In both cases the tax incidence is the same

Short Answer Questions

1. Some economists oppose raising the minimum wage because they believe this would lead to a significant increase in unemployment among low-skilled workers. Is there an alternative to a higher minimum wage to raise the incomes of the working poor? Why do some economists favor raising the minimum wage?

____

____

____

2. Federal and state governments periodically raise excise taxes on cigarettes. Politicians often argue that these tax increases discourage smoking. What other motive is there for raising taxes on cigarettes?

____

____

____

3. One effect of rent control in New York City is a reduction in the number of apartment buildings. If rent control were eliminated, would this result in an increase in the number of apartment buildings and, therefore, lower rents for apartment dwellers?

____

____

4. Price floors have been imposed in markets for dairy products such as milk and cheese. Surplus dairy products are bought by the government to maintain the floor price. These surplus products must be stored in some location. As an alternative to storage, suppose a program was established to distribute surplus dairy products freely to the elderly and poor. Would this eliminate the government's storage problem?

____

____

____

5. The federal government has made several attempts to reduce agricultural surpluses that result from price floors. One such attempt was a program that paid farmers to reduce the amount of land they devoted to planting crops subject to price floors. What was the reason for the failure of this program? (Hint: Use one of the "three important ideas" from Chapter 1 to answer this question.)

____

____

____

True False Questions

T F 1. The total amount of consumer surplus in a market is equal to the area under the demand curve.

T F 2. Government intervention in agriculture in the United States increased significantly as a result of the Great Depression.

T F 3. A study of fast food restaurants in New Jersey and Pennsylvania found that increases in the minimum wage caused larges increases in unemployment.

T F 4. Those people who lose because of rent control include landlords who abide by the law.

T F 5. It was Oliver Wendell Holmes who once said "Taxes are what we pay for a civilized society."

T F 6. The deadweight loss from a tax is equal to the revenue collected by government from the tax.

T F 7. Consumers will pay all of an increase in a sales tax only if the demand curve is a horizontal line at the market price.

T F 8. Economists who have studied the incidence of the social security tax have found that the tax burden is shared equally by employers and their employees.

T F 9. A tax is efficient if it imposes a small excess burden relative to the tax revenue it raises.

T F 10. One effect of rent control in New York City and London has been a large reduction in the number of apartment buildings.

T F 11. The Freedom to Farm Act was passed in Congress in 1996 to phase out price floors and government purchases of agricultural surpluses.

T F 12. Producer surplus refers to the surplus goods that result from price floors.

T F 13. Positive economic analysis is used to determine the economic results of price ceilings and price floors. Whether these price controls are desirable or not is a normative question.

T F 14. The earned income tax credit reduces the amount of tax lower income wage earners pay to the federal government.

T F 15. Economic efficiency results when the total benefit to consumers is equal to the total cost of production.

Answers to the Self-Test

Multiple-Choice Questions

Question	Answer	Comment
1	b	A price floor is a legally determined minimum price that sellers may receive.
2	a	A price ceiling is a legally determined maximum price that sellers may charge.
3	c	Consumer surplus is the area under the demand curve and above the established price level.
4	d	Producer surplus is the area above the supply curve and below the established price level.
5	a	See the definition of marginal benefit on page 100 of the textbook.
6	c	See the definition of marginal cost on page 103 of the textbook.
7	b	Marginal benefit is the additional benefit to a consumer from consuming one more unit of a good or service, and price is a measure of that additional benefit, so the demand curve is also the marginal benefit curve.
8	d	The willingness of a consumer to pay $2 for five cups of tea per week means that the fifth cup consumed is worth exactly $2.00 to the consumer.
9	b	Consumer surplus is the difference between the price a consumer is willing to pay and the price actually paid.
10	c	These consumers participate in the market and receive consumer surplus equal to the difference between the highest price the consumers are willing to pay and the price they actually paid.
11	c	Producer surplus is the difference between the lowest price a firm would have been willing to accept ($1.80) and the price it actually receives ($2.00).
12	c	Price equals marginal cost, or the additional cost to a firm of producing one more unit of a good or service.
13	b	Consumer surplus measures the *net* benefit to consumers from participating in the market, not the total benefit.
14	b	Producer surplus measures the *net* benefit to producers from participating in the market, not the total benefit.
15	b	To achieve maximum efficiency, output should be produced up until the marginal benefit to consumers is equal to the marginal cost to producers.
16	c	In this case, decreasing the level of output would increase efficiency. As output decreases, the gap between marginal cost and marginal benefit decreases, until the two are equal at 15,000 units of output.
17	a	This occurs when output is less than equilibrium output.

18	c	In this case, the current output level yields maximum economic efficiency; the market is in equilibrium, and the sum of consumer surplus and producer surplus yields the largest possible value.
19	b	The sum of consumer surplus and producer surplus is equal to the sum of the areas above the supply curve and below the demand curve up to a certain quantity of output produced.
20	c	In this case, the equilibrium output level yields maximum economic efficiency; the market is in equilibrium, and the sum of consumer surplus and producer surplus yields the largest possible value. There is no deadweight loss.
21	a	Area E is the producer portion of the deadweight loss.
22	d	Producers capture some of the consumer surplus after market price increases to $2.20.
23	c	Consumer surplus is the area below the demand curve and above the price out to the number of units sold.
24	a	Consumer surplus is the area below the demand curve and above the price out to the number of units sold.
25	a	Producers capture some of the consumer surplus after market price increases to $3.50.
26	c	After the price of $3.50 is imposed by government, some producers and consumers no longer participate in the market, so a deadweight loss is created.
27	b	The minimum wage causes an excess of quantity supplied over quantity demanded, which corresponds to additional unemployment.
28	b	The minimum wage causes an excess of quantity supplied over quantity demanded, or a surplus of workers.
29	b	The lower price at which the first 1,900,000 apartments are rented benefits consumers who would have paid more in the absence of the rent control. So producer surplus is transferred from landlords to renters.
30	c	In the absence of the rent control, more landlords and renters would have participated in the market. This area shows that loss.
31	b	Scarcity and shortage are not the same thing. A shortage is the difference between quantity demanded and quantity supplied of a good. Scarcity exists as long as the resources used to produce one thing could be used to produce another. There is no shortage of most scarce goods.
32	d	A market where buying and selling takes place at prices that violate government price regulations is the textbook definition of *black market*. Price scalping (b) is not always illegal.
33	a	Renters would have paid $1,000 but now pay more. When price rises, consumer surplus decreases and producer surplus increases.
34	b	The black market does not change the deadweight loss.
35	d	Price controls have the consequences mentioned in all of these answers.
36	c	Tax incidence in the division of the responsibility of a tax between buyers and sellers.
37	b	Producers charge a price of $3.08 and give the government $0.10, leaving them effectively with $2.98 per gallon sold.
38	b	The *excess burden* from the tax is equivalent to the deadweight loss created by the tax.
39	a	That amount of revenue equals ($4.90 – $3.90) x 3.7 = $3.7 billion.
40	b	Consumers pay a price of $3.08, which is an 8-cent increase in price from the $3.00 equilibrium price. Producers receive $3.08 from consumers, pay 10 cents to the government, and keep $2.98 per pack.
41	a	The demand curve represents employers.

42	b	Supply represents workers. When workers are assessed a tax, the supply curve shifts to the left.
43	d	It does not matter who pays the tax to the government, the tax incidence will remain the same.

Short Answer Responses

1. Opponents of the minimum wage argue that raising the minimum wage will reduce employment, especially among workers with the least skills. An alternative policy is the earned income tax credit. Workers who do not owe any federal taxes receive payments from the federal government. This program increases the incomes of low-skilled workers without the risk of increasing unemployment. Despite these arguments against the minimum wage and the clear evidence from positive economic analysis that a higher minimum wage reduces employment, a few economists still favor raising the minimum wage. They base their argument on normative economics. First, they believe the benefits of higher wages to those still employed outweigh the costs to those thrown into unemployment. This is a value judgment; you are free to agree or disagree. Second, they argue that many low-income workers miss the earned income tax credit because they don't file tax returns.

2. Because cigarettes are addictive many smokers will pay higher prices for cigarettes rather than reduce the quantity they purchase. This results in greater government revenue from the cigarette taxes. Taxes on cigarettes and alcohol (often called "sin taxes") do not affect as many people as a sales tax or income tax. Therefore, politicians do not face as much public opposition to tax increases on these products.

3. Although this result is likely to occur eventually, it will take time for the elimination of rent controls to affect the quantity of apartments in New York City. The immediate effect would likely be an increase in rents on existing apartments. This is one reason why many New Yorkers oppose the elimination of rent control.

4. In fact, such as program was initiated in the 1980s. Although the storage problem is partially alleviated, some of the dairy products that are given away freely replace purchases made by the elderly and poor.

5. The "important idea" that can be used to answer this question is: people respond to economic incentives. Given the opportunity to reduce the amount of land they used to grow crops, many farmers removed their least productive land from production and planted more on the land they did use. This program resulted in greater money payments to farmers – for the land they did not cultivate – and a smaller than expected reduction in crops harvested and sold.

True/False Answers

1. F The total amount of consumer surplus in a market is equal to the area under the demand curve above the market price.
2. T The government supported prices for the farmers because of the extremely low recession prices on agricultural goods.
3. F This study found only small increases in unemployment as a result of minimum wage increases.
4. T Producer surplus is typically reduced by rent control.
5. T

6. F Government revenue is not a deadweight loss. This revenue will be used to provide goods and services to the economy.
7. F Consumers will pay all of an increase in a sales tax if the demand curve is a vertical line.
8. F Economists have found that the burden falls almost entirely on workers.
9. T The tax revenue will be used for the provision of goods and services.
10. T Landlords often sell or convert their buildings to other uses in order to avoid rent control regulations.
11. T
12. F Producer surplus is the net benefit producers receive from participating in the market.
13. T Positive analysis tells us the cost and benefits associated with particular policy measures.
14. T The earned income credit is seen by some as a good alternative to the minimum wage.
15. F Economic efficiency results when the marginal benefit to consumers of the last unit produced equals the marginal cost of production.

Chapter 5

Externalities, Environmental Policy, and Public Goods

Chapter Summary

An **externality** is a benefit or cost that affects someone not directly involved in the production or consumption of a good or service. Negative externalities are costs imposed on individuals not directly involved in producing or consuming a good or service. Positive externalities are benefits received by individuals not directly involved in producing or consuming a good or service. When there is a negative externality as the result of production, the market supply curve understates the full economic cost, the **social cost**, of production. Economic efficiency would be increased if less of the good or service were produced. When there is a positive externality, the market demand curve understates the full economic benefit, the **social benefit**, from consumption and too little of the good is produced.

Negative and positive externalities lead to **market failure**. The absence of private **property rights** or the lack of sufficient enforcement of existing property rights is the underlying cause of externalities and other forms of market failure. Private solutions are possible and efficient if there are low transactions costs. When private solutions to externalities are not feasible, government intervention may be required. For example, if a negative externality is present, government can impose a tax equal to the additional external costs (the difference between the social cost and the private cost). When there are positive externalities, government can provide a subsidy to consumers equal to the external benefits.

To reduce pollution, governments have often used a **command and control approach**. With this approach, the government sets specific quantitative limits on each pollutant emitted, or the government may dictate the installation of specific pollution control devices. One notable exception to the command and control approach was the U.S. government's attempt to reduce acid rain pollution using a market-based approach. In the Clean Air Act of 1990, Congress required electric utilities to reduce their emissions of sulfur dioxide, a major cause of acid rain. The success of the sulfur dioxide program, which used a system of tradable permits, has led some to suggest that a similar program be used to reduce emissions of so-called "greenhouse gases" that contribute to global warming.

Other reasons for government intervention may include cases in which products are *rival* or *excludable*. **Rivalry** occurs when consumption of one unit of a good precludes its consumption by someone else. **Excludability** means that anyone who does not pay for a good cannot consume it. Because common resources are not privately owned, they are often non-rival, non-excludable, or both. There is a tendency for these common resources to be overused. This result is called the **tragedy of the commons**. One person's use of a common resource can impose costs on others, as when one person adding a cow to a common field reduces the grass available to eaten by other people's cows. Because the private cost of using a common resource is less than the social cost, the market equilibrium for the resource occurs where the marginal cost exceeds the marginal benefit. Left to its own devices, the market equilibrium will result in too much of the common resource being consumed. Government intervention in this market may involve restricting access to the common resource.

Learning Objectives

When you finish this chapter you should be able to:

1. **Identify examples of positive and negative externalities and use graphs to show how externalities affect economic efficiency.** A negative externality causes the social cost of production of a good or service to exceed the private cost borne by the producer. The social cost includes the private cost and the external cost from production. A negative externality causes output to exceed the economically efficient amount. A positive externality causes the social benefit from consuming a good or service to exceed the private benefit. The social benefit includes the private benefit received by the consumer and the external benefit. A positive externality causes output to be less than the economically efficient amount.

2. **Discuss the Coase Theorem and explain how private bargaining can lead to economic efficiency in a market with an externality.** Private bargaining can result in an efficient solution to problems arising from externalities if the transactions costs from the bargaining are low. Private parties to the bargaining agreement must have full information regarding the benefits and costs associated with the externality, and all parties must be willing to accept a reasonable agreement.

3. **Analyze government policies to achieve economic efficiency in a market with an externality.** When private efforts to solve externality problems fail, government intervention may be warranted. When there is a negative externality in production, government can impose a tax equal to the cost of the externality. When there is a positive externality in consumption, government can give consumers a subsidy equal to the value of the externality. Government may use direct controls to deal with externalities such as imposing a quantitative limit on the amount of pollution firms are allowed to emit. Government can also use a market-based approach by setting up a system of tradeable emissions allowances to reduce pollution.

4. **Explain how goods can be categorized on the basis of whether they are rival or excludable and use graphs to illustrate the efficient quantities of public goods and common resources.** Rivalry occurs when one person's consumption of a good prevents anyone else from consuming it. Excludability means that anyone who has not paid for a good cannot consume it. A good that is rival and excludable is a private good, and markets can supply the efficient quantity of the good without government intervention. If a good is not rival or excludable markets, are not likely to produce the efficient quantity of the good. A public good is both nonrivalrous and nonexcludable. A public good is usually supplied by the government. A common resource is rival but not excludable. Since no one owns a common resource, it will often be overused.

Chapter Review

Chapter Opener: Economic Policy and the Environment (pages 136-137)

Economic analysis is a useful tool in formulating efficient pollution policies. The Duke Energy Corporation is a participant in the federal government's program to reduce acid rain emissions through a market-based approach. Duke and other utility companies are allowed to trade emissions allowances.

Each allowance permits the holder to emit one ton of sulfur dioxide. Utilities are free to buy and sell allowances so long as they end up with one allowance for every ton of sulfur dioxide they emit.

Helpful Study Hint

Making the Connection "Can Tradable Permits Reduce Global Warming?" and ***An Inside Look*** discuss how the government can apply the lessons from the sulfur dioxide reduction program to the more complex problem of reducing carbon dioxide emissions to reduce global warming. ***An Inside Look*** discusses the carbon emissions permit scheme introduced in the European Union, where permits were issued to firms that emit carbon dioxide. Those firms can choose to use the permits or sell the permits in the market to firms who are interested in buying them. Too many permits were issued, so the scheme did not work. A second phase of the program is being implemented, where fewer pollution permits will be issued. The hope is that the price of the permit will be high enough that people will switch from coal to natural gas, which will reduce carbon dioxide emissions.

Is there such a thing as a "good" or "best" level of carbon emissions and other types of pollution? Or, should there be *no* pollution at all? ***Economics in YOUR Life!*** at the start of this chapter poses these questions. Keep the questions in mind as you read the chapter. The authors will answer the questions at the end of the chapter.

5.1 LEARNING OBJECTIVE

5.1 Externalities and Economic Efficiency (138-141)

Learning Objective 1 Identify examples of positive and negative externalities and use graphs to show how externalities affect economic efficiency.

An **externality** is a benefit or cost that affects someone who is not directly involved in the production or consumption of a good or service. Positive externalities refer to benefits received from a good or service by consumers who do not pay for them. Negative externalities refer to costs incurred by individuals not involved in the production or consumption of a good or service. Externalities interfere with the economic efficiency of market equilibrium by causing a difference between the private cost of production and the social cost, or between the private benefit from consumption and the social benefit.

A **private cost** is a cost borne by the producer of a good or service. A **social cost** is the total cost of production, including both the private cost and any external cost. A **private benefit** is the benefit received by the consumer of a good or service. A **social benefit** is the total benefit from consuming a good, including both the private benefit and any external benefit.

A negative externality causes the social cost of production for a good to be greater than the private cost. As a result, more than the economically efficient level of output is produced. A positive externality causes the social benefit from the production of a good to be to be greater than the private benefit. As a result, less than the economically efficient level of output is produced. Externalities result from the absence of property rights for resources (for example, air) or inadequate legal enforcement of property rights. **Property rights** are the rights individuals or businesses have to the exclusive use of their property, including the right to buy or sell it.

Market failure refers to situations where the market fails to produce the efficient level of output. Figure 5-1 illustrates the effect of acid rain on the market for electricity and the deadweight loss that occurs due to a negative externality. Figure 5-2 illustrates the impact of a positive externality in the market for a college education and the deadweight loss caused by this externality.

Helpful Study Hint

In chapter 4, you learned that the equilibrium price in a competitive market results in the economically efficient level of output, where marginal benefit equals marginal cost. In this chapter we learn that sometimes a competitive market does not produce the economically efficient level of output.

In America in the 1950s, summertime was a time of fear and anxiety for many parents; this was the season when children by the thousands became infected with the infectious and crippling disease poliomyelitis, or polio. Jonas Salk, Albert Sabin, and their colleagues developed a vaccine for polio in 1955. Their research provides a good example of a positive externality. Parents whose children receive polio vaccines would gladly pay for research that provided this protection. If parents paid even a small amount ($5 per child), the total would run into the hundreds of millions of dollars for the scientists' efforts. Of course, no market mechanism exists to transfer revenue from these parents to the researchers. As a result, markets produce less medical research than people are willing to pay for.

Source: http://www.achievement.org/autodoc/page/sal0bio-1

Extra Solved Problem **5-1**

Chapter 5 of the textbook includes two Solved Problems. Here is an extra Solved Problem to help you build your skills solving economic problems.

Supports Learning Objective 5-1: Identify examples of positive and negative externalities and use graphs to show how externalities affect economic efficiency.

The Influenza Pandemic of 1918

From 1914 to 1918, World War I caused over 8 million military deaths, a total that dwarfed the number of deaths suffered in any previous war in history. But this total is much lower than the number of people who died during the influenza pandemic of 1918-19. There were at least 20 million, perhaps as many as 40 million, victims of the so-called "Spanish Flu" or "La Grippe." Ironically, many American soldiers who survived the war would carry the influenza virus home with them from Europe. An estimated 675,000 Americans died during the pandemic, ten times the number who died in the war. With no known cure for the deadly disease, public health officials distributed gauze masks for people to wear in public. Stores were forbidden to hold sales and railroads refused to carry passengers who did not have signed certificates stating that they were free of the virus. There were serious shortages of health care workers, morticians, and gravediggers, conditions not unlike those experienced during the Black Death of the Middle Ages.

a. Draw a graph illustrating the demand and supply for research directed at finding a cure for a highly contagious disease such as the 1918 flu. Assume that all research efforts are funded through private markets.

b. Describe how an externality causes an equilibrium level of output that is not economically efficient.

Source: "The Influenza Pandemic of 1918." http://www.stanford.edu/group/virus/uda/

SOLVING THE PROBLEM

Step 1: Review the chapter material.
This problem is about externalities and efficiency, so you may want to review the section "Externalities and Economic Efficiency," which appears on page 138 in the textbook.

Step 2: Draw a graph to illustrate the externality associated with privately funded research to cure malaria.

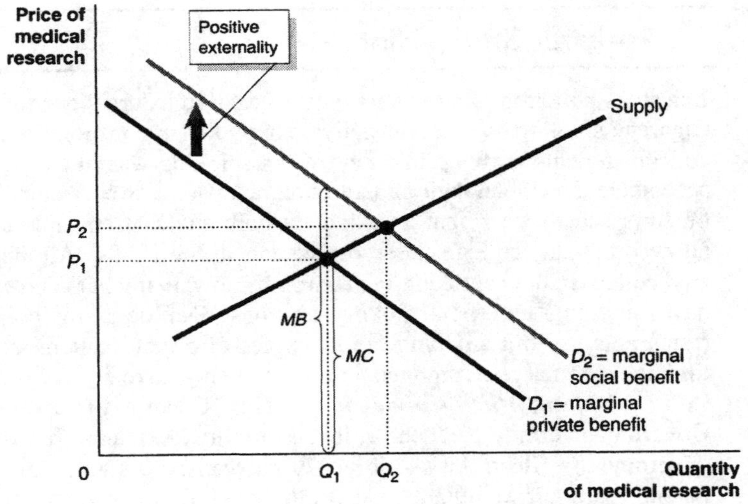

Step 3: Describe how the externality causes a deviation from economic efficiency.
There is a positive externality associated with medical research because of the external benefits the research generates. Assume that researchers had found a cure for the so-called "Spanish Flu" in 1918 at the beginning of the pandemic. The benefits to those people who would be protected from contracting the deadly disease would be substantial. If we estimate the benefit at $100 for each person, the external benefits range in the billions of dollars. Of course, medical research is by nature uncertain and scientists and doctors can work many years without finding a cure for any disease. Private hospitals and research laboratories are likely to receive a relatively small amount of the social benefit from their efforts. As the graph in Step 2 shows, the demand curve for medical research that includes only private benefits will be below the demand curve that includes all social benefits. The private market equilibrium price and quantity would be P_1 and Q_1. At this point the marginal (social) benefit (*MB*) would exceed the marginal cost (*MC*). The economically efficient level price and quantity would be P_2 and Q_2 where marginal (social) benefit is equal to marginal cost.

5.2 LEARNING OBJECTIVE

5.2 Private Solutions to Externalities: The Coase Theorem (pages 141-147)

Learning Objective 2 Discuss the Coase Theorem and explain how private bargaining can lead to economic efficiency in a market with an externality.

Ronald Coase argued that private bargaining may improve inefficient market results caused by externalities. The **Coase Theorem** states that if transactions costs are low, private bargaining will result in an efficient solution to the problem of externalities. **Transactions costs** are the costs in time and other resources that parties incur in the process of agreeing to and carrying out an exchange of goods and services. Successful application of the Coase Theorem requires that the bargaining parties have full information regarding the costs and benefits associated with the externalities and are willing to accept a reasonable agreement. In practice, private solutions are often not feasible because transactions costs are too high.

Helpful Study Hint

Industrial pollution is an example of a negative externality in production. Cigarette smoking causes a negative externality in consumption. Today's college students grew up in an era when smoking was much less socially acceptable than when their parents and grandparents were young. You may be surprised to learn that smoking by both students and instructors was allowed in many college classrooms as late as the 1970s. Although few, if any, colleges allow smoking in classrooms now, many bars and restaurants have smoking and non-smoking sections. Decisions by colleges and restaurants to limit smoking are examples of private actions designed to limit the external costs smokers impose on non-smokers.

Making the Connection "The Clean Air Act: How a Government Policy Reduced Infant Mortality" explains that the federal government's Clean Air Act of 1970 has caused a significant reduction in six main air pollutants. As pollution fell due to the Act, infant mortality also fell.

In the ***Don't Let This Happen to YOU!*** "Remember That It's the Net Benefit That Counts" the authors remind us that even though the total benefit to society would be largest if we reduced all pollution to zero, this would not be economically efficient. To find the economically efficient amount of pollution reduction we should compare the marginal benefit to the marginal cost of each unit of pollution reduction. If the marginal benefit is greater than the marginal cost, then an additional unit of pollution reduction should be pursued. Pollution reduction should continue until the maximum net benefit to society is reached, which occurs when the marginal benefit of the last unit of reduction equals the marginal cost of that unit of pollution reduction.

Making the Connection "The Fable of the Bees" discusses a traditional example of externalities. Beekeepers and apple growers realized that honeybees could use the nectar from apple trees to produce honey and that bees are useful in pollinating apple trees. Private solutions to this externality have been reached so that there are about $14 billion worth of crops pollinated by bees annually now through bee rental programs.

Extra Solved Problem 5-2

Chapter 5 of the textbook includes two Solved Problems. Here is an extra Solved Problem to help you build your skills solving economic problems.

Supports Learning Objective 5-2: Discuss the Coase Theorem and explain how private bargaining can lead to economic efficiency in a market with an externality.

The Dog Next Door

Assume that your next-door neighbor owns a large dog named "Rufus" that spends a significant amount of the night in the backyard. While in the yard, Rufus barks continuously and prevents you from getting a good night's sleep. Consider an attempt by you and your neighbor to come to an agreement that would deal with this negative externality.

a. What would you be willing to pay the neighbor to have him get rid of Rufus? What would the neighbor require in payment to get rid of Rufus?

b. Who will pay? Will you pay the neighbor to get rid of his dog or will he pay you to listen to the dog bark?

SOLVING THE PROBLEM

Step 1: Review the chapter material.
This problem is about private solutions to externalities, so you may want to review the section "Private Solutions to Externalities: The Coase Theorem," which begins on page 141 in the textbook.

Step 2: Consider the value to you of being able to sleep, and consider the value of Rufus to the neighbor.
You would be willing to pay the neighbor a dollar amount up to the value of the bark-free nights. Your neighbor would only agree to get rid of Rufus if you paid him an amount greater than the value he places on owning Rufus.

Step 3: Compare the value you place on quiet nights to the value the neighbor places on the ownership of the dog.
If the neighbor values the ownership of his dog more than you value a good night's rest, the neighbor will pay you to listen to Rufus' barking. If you value a good night's rest more than the neighbor values owning Rufus, you will pay the neighbor to get rid of his dog. But who pays also depends on the local government's regulations on barking dogs. If your town has a strict rule against dogs being allowed to bark at night, then your neighbor may have to pay you to allow him to keep his barking dog. In this case you would only accept the payment if it is greater than the value you place on a good night's sleep.

5.3 LEARNING OBJECTIVE

5.3 Government Policies to Deal With Externalities (pages 147-152)

Learning Objective 3 Analyze government policies to achieve economic efficiency in a market with an externality.

In the absence of private solutions to externalities, government intervention may be warranted. To achieve economic efficiency, governments may intervene in different ways. The government may impose a **Pigovian tax** or provide a **subsidy** to cause consumers and firms to internalize the externalities associated with production and consumption. The tax or subsidy would be equal to the dollar amount of the externality. To reduce pollution, governments have often used a command and control approach. A **command and control approach** refers to government-imposed quantitative limits on the amount of pollution firms are allowed to generate. Under this approach, the government may require installation of specific pollution control devices. Since 1990, a market-based approach of tradable permits has reduced emissions of sulfur dioxide from electric utilities at lower than expected cost. The success of this approach has led economists to advocate more extensive use of market-based approaches, and less use of command and control policies.

Helpful Study Hint

Economists working for the private research group Resources for the Future (RFF) are among the strongest supporters of a system of tradable emissions allowances to reduce the problem of acid rain. One of the difficulties of formulating environmental policy is placing a dollar value on environmental damage; for example, the breathing difficulty people with asthma experience due to sulfur dioxide pollution. Economists at RFF have pioneered techniques for measuring the value of things for which no market price exists. RFF has an excellent web site (www.rff.org) that you can use to access discussion papers, publications, and Congressional testimony regarding a wide range of environmental issues.

Solved Problem 5-3 provides an example of a government-imposed tax to deal with a negative externality. If the government imposed a tax equal to the value of the externality, the tax would increase the cost to the producer up to the point where it equals the social cost. This would cause the production of toilet paper to fall from the equilibrium level to the efficient level of production.

Making the Connection "Can Tradable Permits Reduce Global Warming?" discusses the beliefs of some scientists regarding global warming. Some scientists believe that the recent increase in global temperatures is due to the production of greenhouse gases. Tradable pollution permits for CO_2 could be an efficient way to reduce greenhouse gases and combat global warming. Tradable permits allow those who can reduce their pollution for less than the market price of the permits to sell their permits and cut their pollution, while firms that cannot cheaply reduce emissions will buy permits and continue to pollute.

5.4 LEARNING OBJECTIVE

5.4 Four Categories of Goods (pages 152-162)

Learning Objective 4 Explain how goods can be categorized on the basis of whether they are rival or excludable and use graphs to illustrate the efficient quantities of public goods and common resources.

Goods may be classified into four categories based on whether or not their consumption is rival and/or excludable. If I consume one more unit of a product and that means you cannot consume the same unit, the product is called **rival.** If anyone who wants to consume one unit of a product must pay for that unit, the product is **excludable**. Products can be either rival or nonrival and excludable or nonexcludable. This gives us four possible combinations of characteristics.

A **private good** is a good that is both rival and excludable. The economically efficient quantity of a private good can be supplied in a market without government intervention. Quasi-public goods are goods that are excludable but not rival. A **common resource** is a good that is rival but not excludable. There are typically externalities associated with common resources. A **public good** is a good that is both nonrivalrous and nonexcludable. **Free riding** refers to benefiting from a good without paying for it. Because of free riders, public goods are usually supplied by government rather than private firms.

In contrast with private goods, each consumer will consume the same quantity of a public good as every other consumer. The demand for a public good is determined by adding the price each consumer is willing to pay for each quantity of the good. Because no consumer can be excluded from receiving the good, it is difficult to determine consumers' true preferences and willingness to pay because of the free rider problem. Governments typically provide public goods, such as national defense, and determine the quantity supplied through cost-benefit analysis or a political process.

Helpful Study Hint

According to the U.S. Department of Agriculture, the average American consumes 223 pounds of beef, pork, and chicken annually. Despite the large and continuing demand for meat, we don't read news reports about shortages of cows, pigs, and chickens. In contrast, there are occasional media reports of over-fishing and the possible extinction of some animal species. When resources are privately owned, owners have incentives to use the resources efficiently. For example, producers have strong incentives to maintain the stocks of cows, pigs, and chickens to ensure future supplies. Property rights to some parts of oceans, rivers, lakes, and habitat areas of endangered species don't exist or are poorly enforced. On the other hand, some formerly endangered species have been saved from extinction by simply granting the property rights of the herd to a particular group.

Making the Connection "Should the Government Run the Health Care System?" presents the debate as to whether the United States should have a centralized health care system instead of the government-subsidized private system that exists. There are a number of positive and negative externalities that may justify further intervention. However, some economists support the current private system because of the incentives it provides for innovation.

Solved Problem 5-4 "Determining the Optimal Level of Public Goods" shows how we aggregate individual demand curves to determine the optimal level of public goods. The demand curves are summed vertically to create a marginal social benefit curve, and the optimal quantity is determined by the intersection of the marginal social benefit curve with the marginal social cost curve.

At the start of the chapter, ***Economics in YOUR Life!*** asked you to consider if there's a "best" level of pollution. Scientists disagree about how much carbon emissions are contributing to the damage from climate change. In addition, the cost of reducing carbon emissions depends on the method of reduction used. As a result, neither the marginal cost curve nor the marginal benefit curve for reducing carbon emissions is known with certainty. This uncertainty makes it difficult for policymakers to determine the correct level of carbon emissions and is the source of much of the current debate. In any case, economists agree that the total cost of *completely* eliminating carbon emissions is much greater than the total benefits.

Key Terms

Coase Theorem. The argument of economist Ronald Coase that if transactions costs are low, private bargaining will result in an efficient solution to the problem of externalities.

Command and control approach. An approach that involves government imposing quantitative limits on the amount of pollution firms are allowed to emit or requiring firms to install specific pollution control devices.

Common resource. A good that is rival but not excludable.

Excludability. The situation in which anyone who does not pay for a good cannot consume it.

Externality. A benefit or cost that affects someone who is not directly involved in the production or consumption of a good or service.

Free riding. Benefiting from a good without paying for it.

Market failure. A situation in which the market fails to produce the efficient level of output.

Pigovian taxes and subsidies. Government taxes and subsidies intended to bring about an efficient level of output in the presence of externalities.

Private benefit. The benefit received by the consumer of a good or service.

Private cost. The cost borne by the producer of a good or service.

Private good. A good that is both rival and excludable.

Property rights. The rights individuals or businesses have to the exclusive use of their property, including the right to buy or sell it.

Public good. A good that is both nonrivalrous and nonexcludable.

Quasi-public good. A good that is excludable but not rival.

Rivalry. The situation that occurs when one person's consuming a unit of a good means no one else can consume it.

Social benefit. The total benefit from consuming a good or service, including both the private benefit and any external benefit.

Social cost. The total cost of producing a good, including both the private cost and any external cost.

Tragedy of the commons. The tendency for a common resource to be overused.

Transactions costs. The costs in time and other resources that parties incur in the process of agreeing to and carrying out an exchange of goods or services.

Self-Test

(Answers are provided at the end of the Self-Test.)

Multiple-Choice Questions

1. What is the cost that affects someone who is not directly involved in the production or consumption of a good called?
   a. Private cost
   b. Indirect cost
   c. An externality
   d. All of the above fit that definition

2. What is the term used to describe the *total* cost of producing a good?
   a. Private cost
   b. Social cost
   c. Externality
   d. All of the above fit that definition.

3. What is the difference between private benefit and social benefit?
   a. An external benefit
   b. Private cost
   c. Social cost
   d. A negative externality

4. What is the benefit received by the consumer of a good or service called?
   a. Private benefit
   b. Social benefit
   c. Private cost
   d. A positive externality

5. Refer to the graphs below. In which of these markets is an externality present?

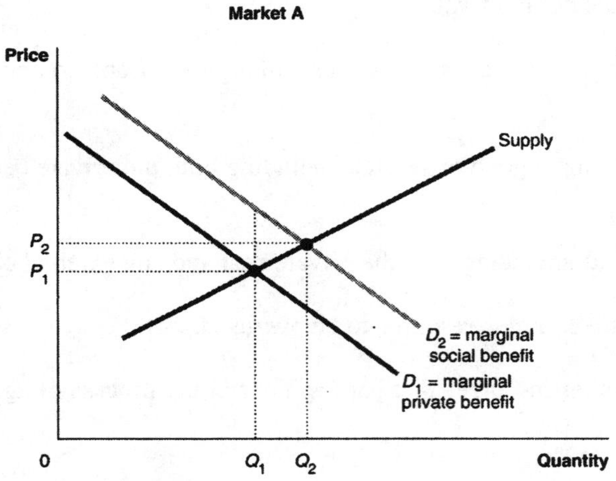

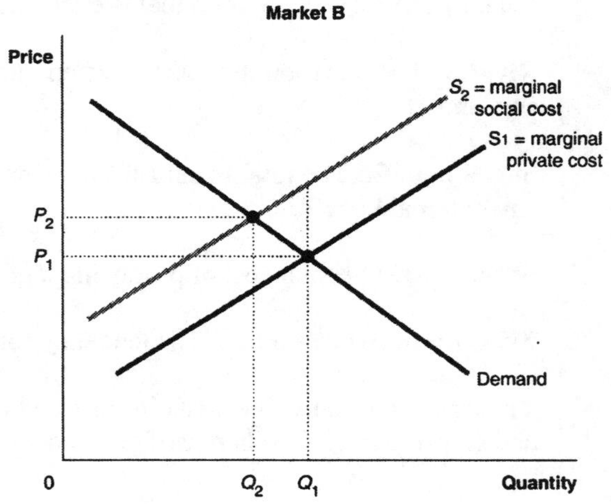

a. In the market on the left
b. In the market on the right
c. In both markets
d. Neither market exhibits an externality.

6. Refer to the graphs below. Only one statement below is entirely correct. Which one?

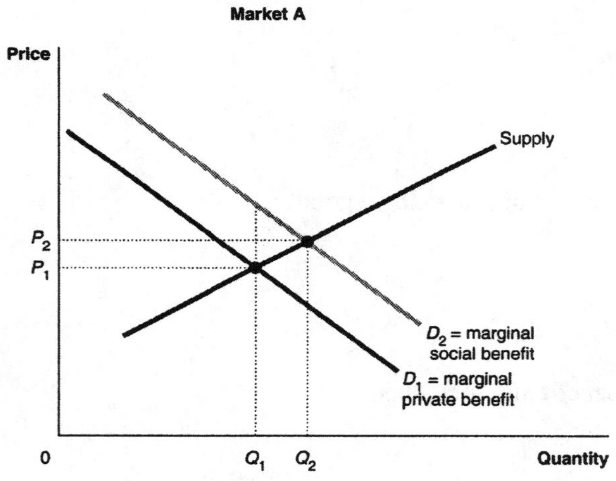

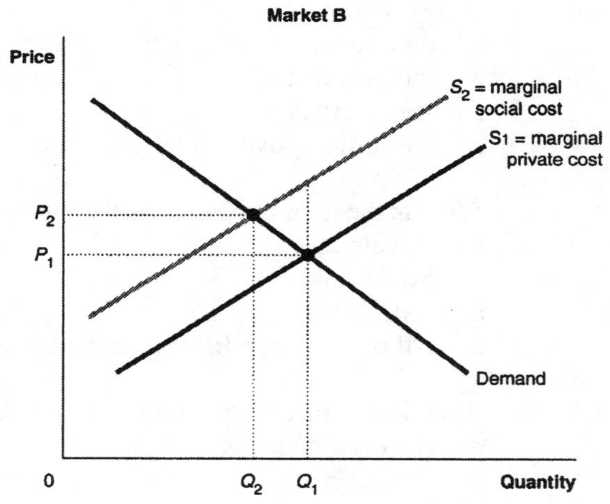

a. Market A exhibits a negative externality because the private benefit exceeds the social benefit.
b. Market B exhibits a negative externality because the social cost exceeds the private cost.
c. Market A exhibits a negative externality because the social benefit exceeds the private benefit.
d. Market B exhibits a positive externality because the private cost exceeds the social cost.

7. Refer to the graphs below. In which of the markets is the quantity Q_1 less than the economically efficient quantity?

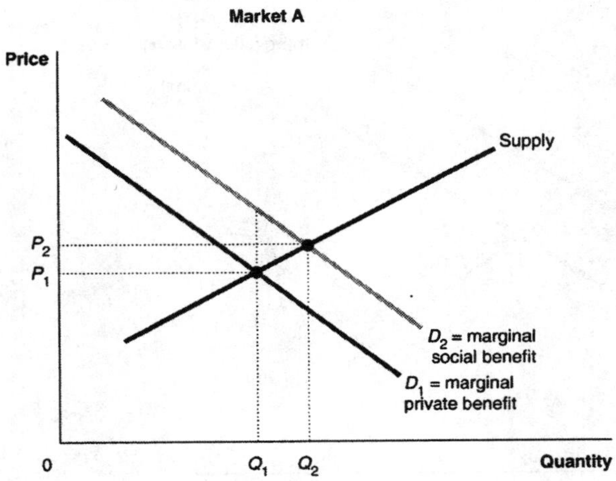

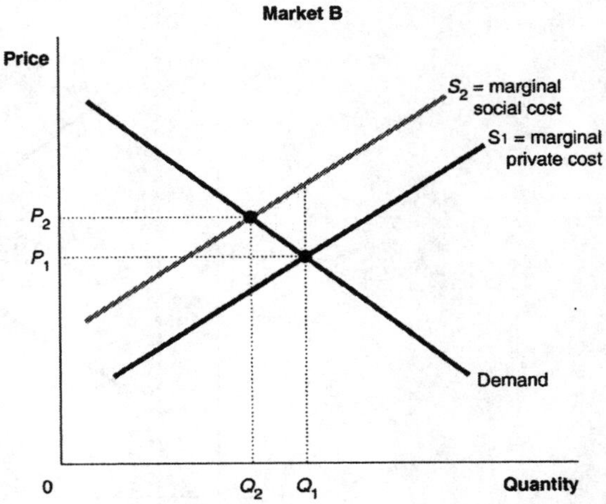

a. In market A
b. In market B
c. In both markets
d. In neither of the two markets

8. Refer to the graph below. What term would you ascribe to the magnitude of the arrow in the graph?

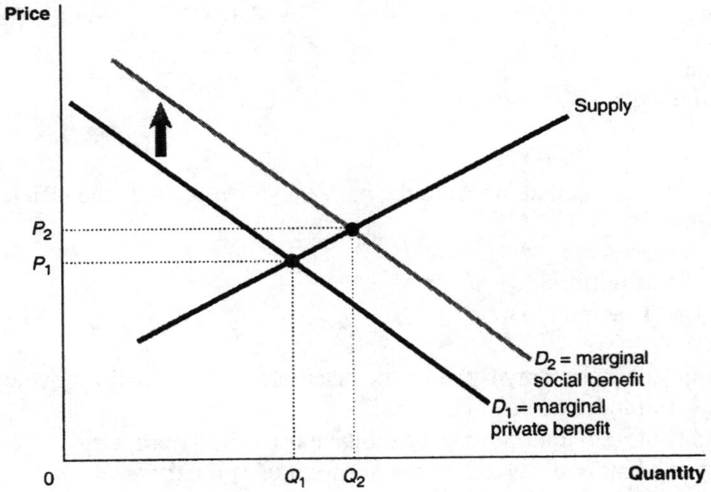

a. A positive externality
b. A negative externality
c. Private cost
d. Social cost

9. Refer to the graph below. When an externality is present, which combination of price and quantity does the market yield without intervention?

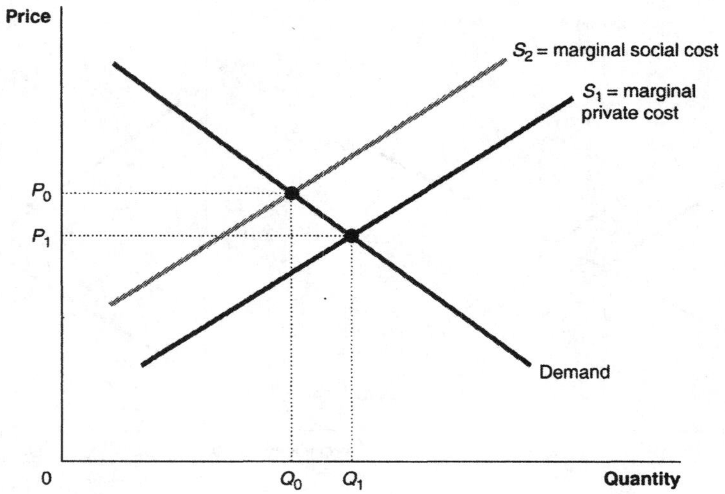

a. P_0, Q_0
b. P_1, Q_1
c. P_0, Q_1
d. P_1, Q_0

10. Fill in the blanks. When a negative externality is present in producing a good or service, ___________ of the good or service will be produced at market equilibrium.
a. too much
b. too little
c. the optimal quantity
d. none

11. What is the situation called in which the market fails to produce the efficient level of output?
a. An externality
b. Market failure
c. External disequilibrium
d. The Coase Theorem

12. When we talk about property rights in the discussion of externalities, which rights do we refer to?
a. The rights of individuals to pollute
b. The rights of individuals to have exclusive use of their property
c. The rights of individuals to buy but not sell their property
d. All of the above

13. What are the sources of externalities and market failure?
a. Incomplete property rights
b. The difficulty of enforcing property rights in certain situations.
c. Both a. and b.
d. Lack of understanding of the market system

14. What type of solution to externalities is the Coase Theorem?
    a. A private solution to externalities
    b. A public solution to externalities
    c. The only solution to externalities
    d. The least preferred solution

15. Which of the following statements is correct according to Ronald Coase's argument for dealing with externalities and market failure?
    a. In some situations, a private solution to the problem of externalities can be found.
    b. Only public solutions exist for solving externalities.
    c. Completely eliminating an externality is almost always the most efficient solution.
    d. The only cure to externalities is taxation.

16. Which of the following is correct?
    a. Completely eliminating an externality is usually not economically efficient.
    b. As reductions in pollution increase, the additional benefits will decline.
    c. When levels of pollution are high, the marginal benefit of reducing pollution is also high.
    d. All of the above

17. The *net benefit* to society from reducing pollution is equal to
    a. the sum of the benefits of reducing pollution and the costs.
    b. the difference between the benefits and the costs.
    c. the additional benefit plus the additional costs.
    d. the quantity of pollution, such as the tons of reduction in sulfur dioxide.

18. If we are considering further reductions in pollution, what rule should we follow in order to maximize the net benefit to society?
    a. The marginal benefit from another ton of reduction should be greater than the marginal cost.
    b. The marginal benefit from another ton of reduction should be less than the marginal cost.
    c. The marginal benefit from another ton of reduction should be equal to the marginal cost.
    d. The marginal benefit from another ton of reduction should equal zero.

19. Refer to the graph below. Which of the following is true when the reduction in sulfur dioxide equals seven tons?

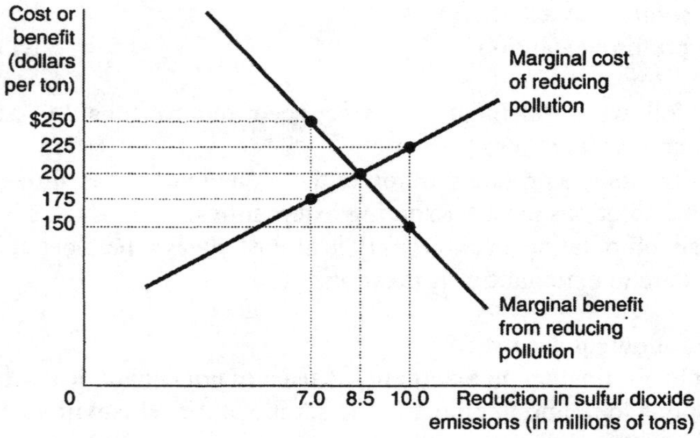

a. The marginal benefit of reducing sulfur dioxide emissions is greater than the marginal cost.
b. Further reductions will make society worse off.
c. The optimal amount of pollution reduction has been found.
d. All of the above

20. Refer to the graph below. Which of the following is true when the reduction in sulfur dioxide equals ten tons?

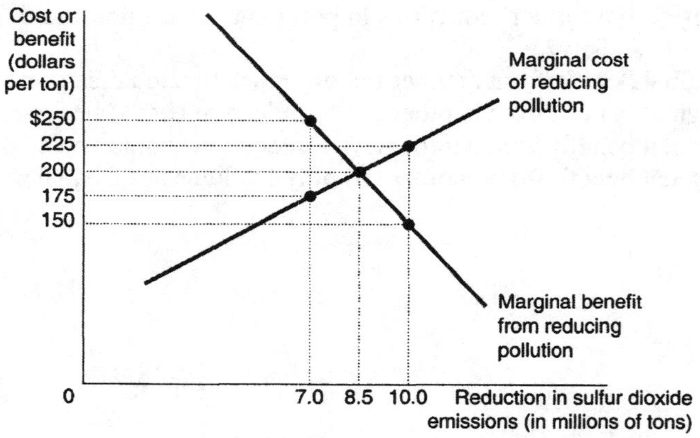

a. The marginal benefit of reducing sulfur dioxide emissions is greater than the marginal cost.
b. Further reductions will make society worse off.
c. The optimal amount of pollution reduction has been found.
d. All of the above

21. Refer to the graph below. How much reduction in sulfur dioxide can be considered economically efficient?

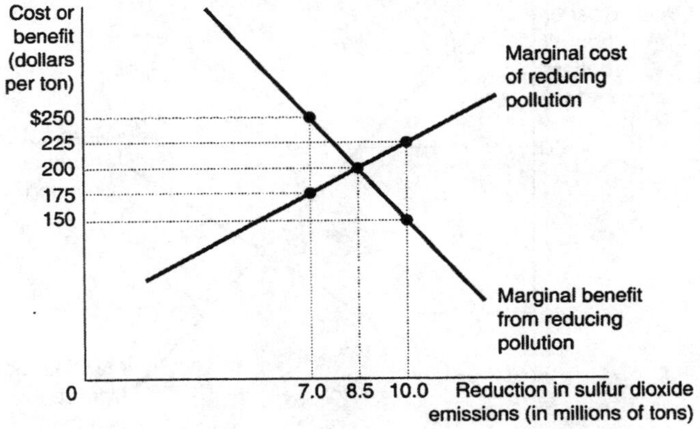

a. 7.0 tons
b. 8.5 tons
c. 10.0 tons
d. All of the above

22. Refer to the graph below. What area represents the *total benefit* of increasing the reduction of sulfur dioxide from 7.0 million to 8.5 million tons of sulfur dioxide?

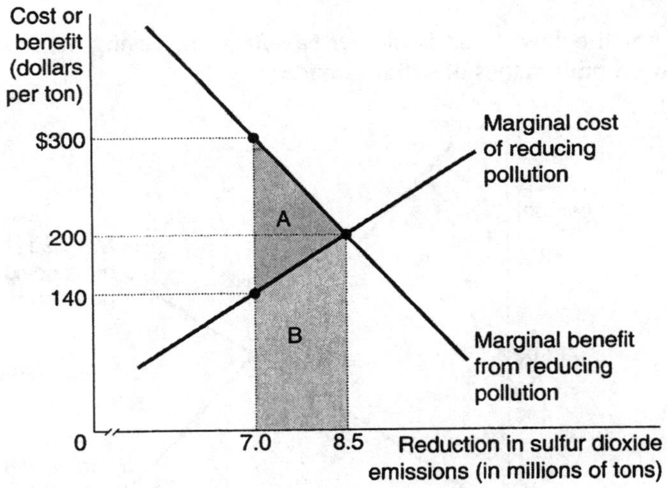

a. Area *A*
b. Area *B*
c. Area *A* + *B*
d. None of the above; the graph shows only marginal benefit.

23. Refer to the graph below. What area represents the *total cost* of increasing the reduction of sulfur dioxide from 7.0 million to 8.5 million tons of sulfur dioxide?

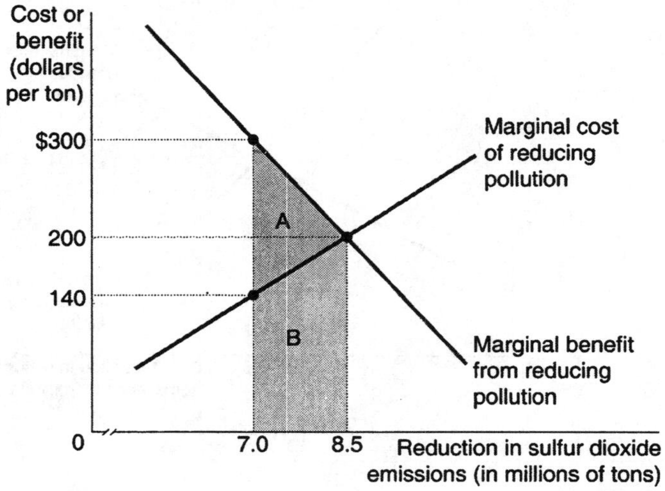

a. Area *A*
b. Area *B*
c. Area *A* + *B*
d. None of the above; the graph shows only marginal benefit.

24. Refer to the graph below. What is the *net benefit* of increasing the reduction of sulfur dioxide from 7.0 million to 8.5 million tons of sulfur dioxide?

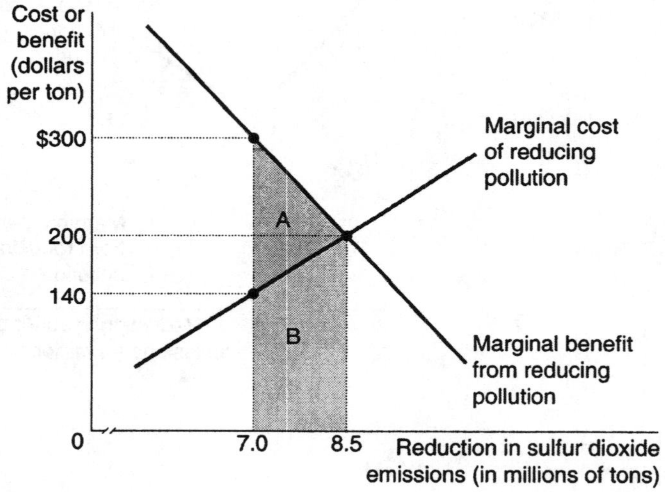

a. Area *A*
b. Area *B*
c. Area *A* + *B*
d. None of the above; the graph shows only marginal benefit.

25. Refer to the graph below. How much is the *net benefit* (in millions) of increasing the reduction of sulfur dioxide from 7.0 million tons to 8.5 million tons?

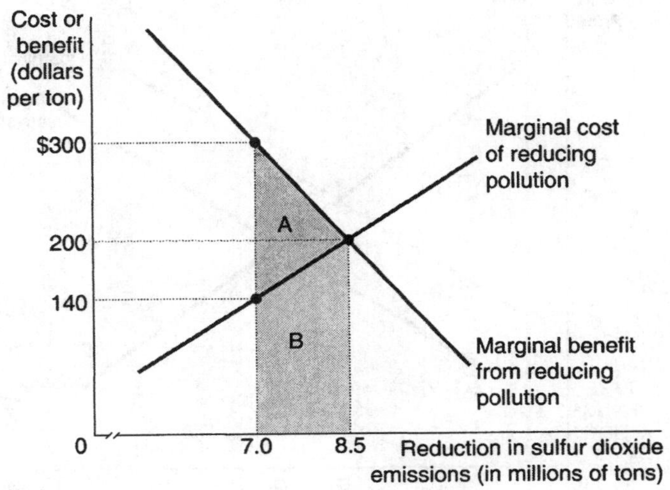

a. $255
b. $120
c. $200
d. None of the above

26. Which of the following assertions is made by Ronald Coase in finding an efficient solution to the problem of negative externalities?
a. The solution usually depends on which party has a legal property right in the dispute.
b. The solution does not depend on who has the property rights in the dispute.
c. If we are to find a solution, property rights could not be enforced because they distort efficiency.
d. In finding a solution, property rights are usually ignored.

27. Fill in the blanks. When there are many people involved, the transactions costs are often _______ than the net benefits from reducing the externality. In such cases, a private solution to an externality problem _______ feasible.
a. higher; is
b. higher; is not
c. lower; is
d. lower; is not

28. Fill in the blanks. According to the Coase Theorem, if transactions costs are ________, private bargaining will result in an __________ solution to the problem of externalities.
a. low; efficient
b. low; inefficient
c. high; efficient
d. high; optimal

29. Refer to the graph below. Which of the following best represents a tax equal to the value of the negative externality?

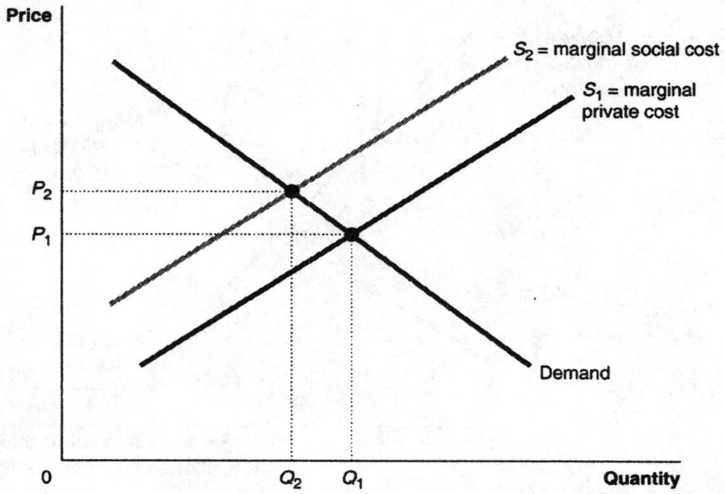

a. S_1
b. S_2
c. The vertical distance (or arrow) between S_1 and S_2
d. $P_2 - P_1$

30. Refer to the graph below. After the negative externality has been internalized, which point would best represent market equilibrium?

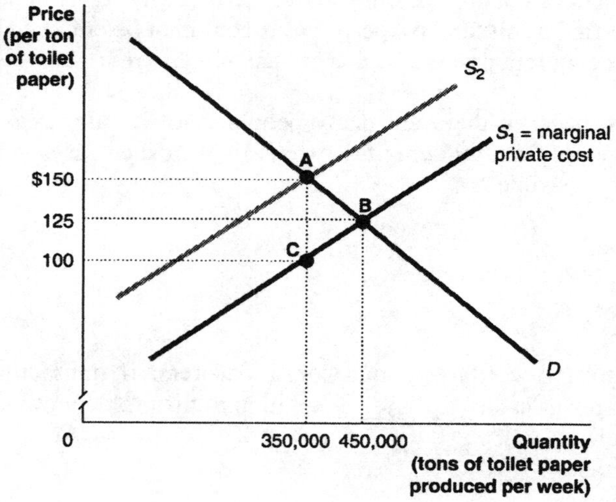

a. Point *A*
b. Point *B*
c. Point *C*
d. None of the above

31. Refer to the graph below. To bring about social efficiency, what should the magnitude of the arrow in the graph be equal to?

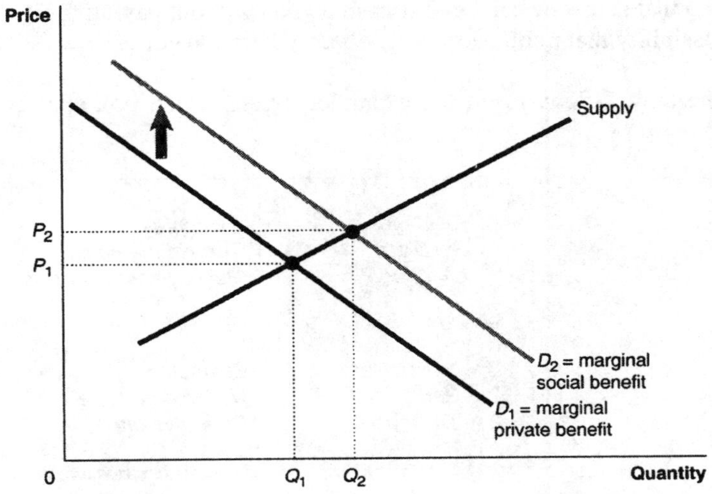

a. The amount of a subsidy
b. The amount of a tax
c. The amount of a price increase
d. The social benefit of education

32. What is the focus of a *command and control approach* to reducing pollution?
a. Imposing taxes intended to bring about an efficient level of output in the presence of externalities.
b. Offering subsidies intended to bring about an efficient level of output in the presence of externalities.
c. Imposing quantitative limits on the amount of pollution firms are allowed to generate.
d. Trading licenses to pollute for cash payments.

33. When firms sell their pollution permits in the tradable emissions allowances market, which of the following does not occur?
a. Over time, pollution will be completely eliminated.
b. The social cost of pollution reduction is reduced.
c. All firms that participate in the market benefit.
d. The total amount of pollution is the same as if the permits were not tradable.

34. What does the term *excludability* refer to?
a. A situation in which one person's consumption of a good means that no one else can consume it.
b. The fact that anyone who does not pay for a good cannot consume it.
c. The idea that someone can benefit from a good without paying for it.
d. The possibility that public goods may become private goods.

35. What does the term *rivalry* refer to?
a. A situation in which one person's consumption of a good means that no one else can consume it.
b. The fact that anyone who does not pay for a good cannot consume it.
c. The idea that someone can benefit from a good without paying for it.
d. The possibility that public goods may become private goods.

36. What does the term *free riding* refer to?
    a. A situation in which one person's consumption of a good means that no one else can consume it.
    b. The fact that anyone who does not pay for a good cannot consume it.
    c. The idea that someone can benefit from a good without paying for it.
    d. The possibility that public goods may become private goods.

37. Refer to the table below. From the examples given, which box applies to the concept of *common resources*?

A: *Examples:* *Big Macs* *Levi's Jeans*	B: *Examples:* *Tuna in the ocean* *Public pasture land*
C: *Examples:* *Cable TV* *Toll road*	D: *Examples:* *National defense* *Court system*

a. A
b. B
c. C
d. D

38. Refer to the table below. Which of the boxes applies to goods that are excludable and nonrival?

A: *Examples:* *Big Macs* *Levi's Jeans*	B: *Examples:* *Tuna in the ocean* *Public pasture land*
C: *Examples:* *Cable TV* *Toll road*	D: *Examples:* *National defense* *Court system*

a. A
b. B
c. C
d. D

39. Refer to the graphs below. What procedure does this series of graphs show?

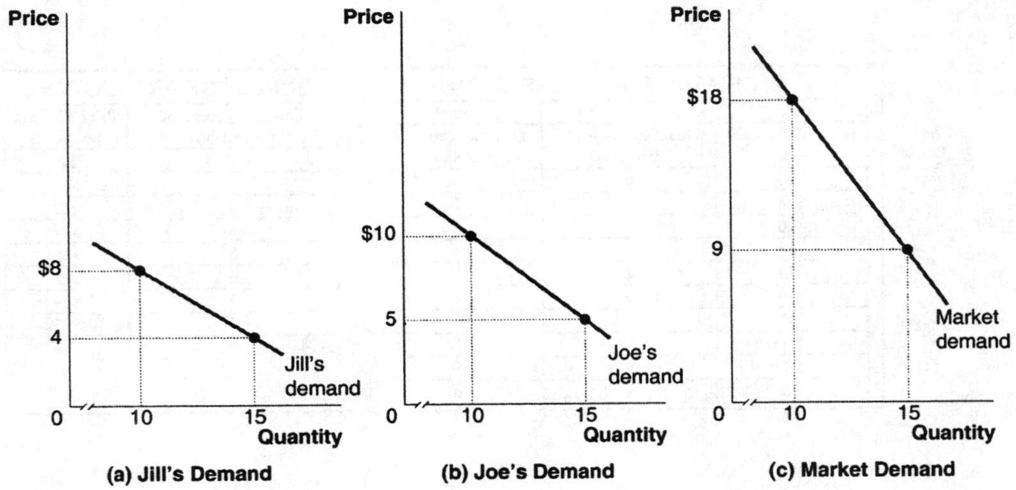

a. The construction of market demand for a private good
b. The construction of market demand for a public good
c. The construction of market demand for a rival good
d. The construction of market demand for an excludable good

40. Refer to the graph below. Which quantity is the optimal quantity of this public good?

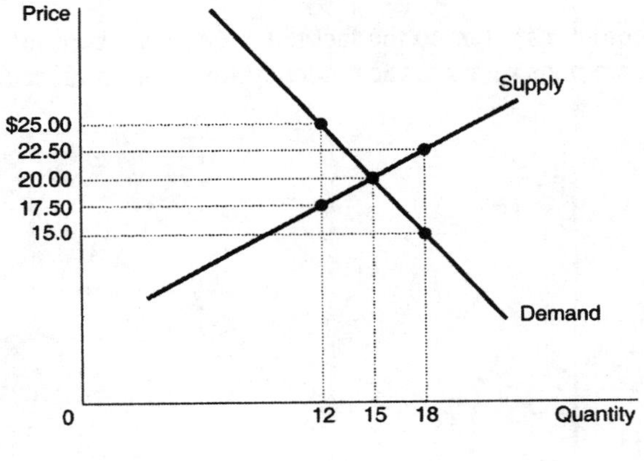

a. 12 units
b. 15 units
c. 18 units
d. None of the above

41. Refer to the table below. The table refers to the Solved Problem on page 158 in the textbook. How many hours of protection maximize economic surplus?

DEMAND FOR PROTECTION

	Joe	Jill
Price (dollars per hour)	Quantity (hours of protection)	Quantity (hours of protection)
$20	0	1
$18	1	2
$16	2	3
$14	3	4
$12	4	5
$10	5	6
$8	6	7
$6	7	8
$4	8	9
$2	9	10

SUPPLY OF PROTECTION

Quantity (hours of protection)	Price (dollars per hour)
1	$8
2	$10
3	$12
4	$14
5	$16
6	$18
7	$20
8	$22
9	$24

a. 1 hour
b. 9 hours
c. 5 hours
d. 6 hours

42. What is the *tragedy of commons*?
a. The tragedy of commons refers to the fact that some people benefit from a good without paying for it.
b. The tragedy of commons is the tendency for some goods to be excluded from public consumption.
c. The tragedy of commons refers to the fact that a good can be rival but nonexcludable.
d. The tragedy of commons refers to the tendency for a common resource to be overused.

43. Refer to the graphs below. Which graph best describes the move from an inefficient use of a common resource to an efficient use of it?

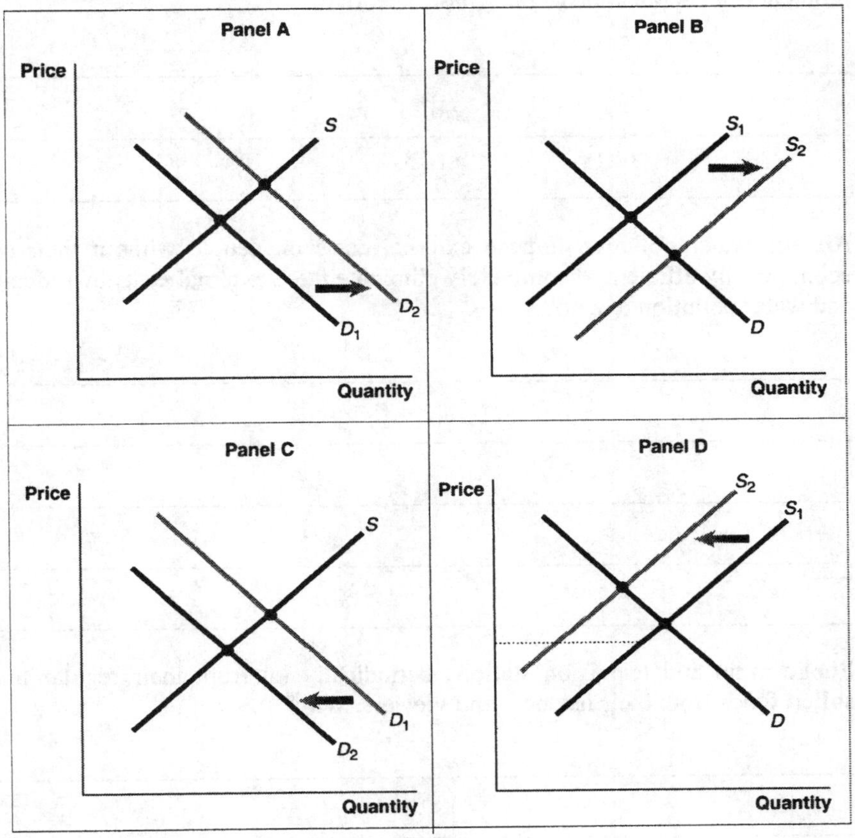

a. A
b. B
c. C
d. D

Short Answer Questions

1. Explain why the marginal benefit from reducing air pollution in the United States in 1970 were greater than the marginal benefit of reducing air pollution an equivalent amount would be today.

____

____

____

2. Steven Cheung of the University of Washington has written about the positive externalities associated with beekeeping and apple growing. Explain why the solution to this externalities problem is an application of the Coase Theorem.

____

____

____

3. Air and water pollution impose external costs on people without their consent. Why isn't it economically efficient to completely eliminate these external costs by reducing the amounts of air and water pollution to zero?

____

____

____

____

____

4. Public radio and television stations periodically interrupt their regular broadcast schedules to solicit funds from their listeners and viewers. Why?

____

____

____

____

____

5. Ronald Coase argued that private solutions can solve externality problems without government intervention. Why is government intervention used more often than private bargaining to solve externality problems?

____

____

____

____

True/False Questions

T F 1. The benefits of reducing air pollution are much higher today than in 1970 because the level of air pollution has increased since 1970.

T F 2. The Coase Theorem proves that government intervention is necessary to solve externalities problems.

T F 3. A common resource is a good that is excludable but not rival.

T F 4. A quasi-public good describes a good that it is excludable but not rival.

T F 5. The federal government rather than private firms provide national defense because consumers of national defense have an incentive to be free riders.

T F 6. Congress authorized a command and control approach to reducing sulfur dioxide emissions by electric utilities in 1990.

T F 7. A social benefit is the private benefit plus any external benefit from consuming a good or service.

T F 8. In the two years following the passage of the Clean Air Act of 1970 there was a decline in infant mortality in the United States.

T F 9. If the marginal cost of reducing emissions of some pollutant is greater than the marginal benefit, society will be better off if these emissions are increased.

T F 10. A.C. Pigou received the 1991 Nobel Prize in Economics for his work on finding private solutions to problems arising from externalities.

T F 11. Government payments to students to attend college are one way to internalize a positive externality.

T F 12. The 1983 requirement by the federal government to install catalytic converters on all new automobiles is an example of a command and control approach to reducing pollution.

T F 13. The actual cost to electric utilities companies of complying with Congress' program to reduce sulfur dioxide emissions in 2010 is greater than was originally estimated by the General Accounting Office in 1994.

T F 14. Most European governments favor a system of tradable emissions permits to reduce carbon dioxide emissions. The U.S. government favors a program that would require individual countries to reduce emissions by a specified amount.

T F 15. The demand for a public good is determined by adding the price each consumer is willing to pay for each quantity of the public good.

Answers to the Self-Test

Multiple Choice Questions

Question	Answer	Comment
1	c	An externality is a benefit or cost that affects someone who is not directly involved in the production or consumption of a good or service.
2	b	The total cost of producing a good is the social cost. The social cost is the private cost plus any external cost resulting from production, such as the cost of pollution.
3	a	A positive externality causes there to be a difference between the *private benefit* from consumption and the *social benefit.*
4	a	The private benefit is the benefit received by the consumer of a good or service.
5	c	There is a difference between private and social benefits and/or costs in both markets.
6	b	When the social cost is greater than the private cost of production, the market suffers from a negative externality.

7	a	The economically efficient quantity of output in market A is Q_2, where the private cost equals the social benefit.
8	a	An external benefit exists when the social benefit is greater than private benefit. The private market produces less than the efficient quantity.
9	b	The free market fails to account for external costs. The market produces too much output and charges too low a price when external costs are present.
10	a	When there is a negative externality in producing a good or service, too much of the good or service will be produced at market equilibrium.
11	b	Market failure refers to situations where the market fails to produce the efficient level of output. (Answer a. is incorrect because an externality is only one type of market failure.)
12	b	Property rights refer to the rights individuals or businesses have to the exclusive use of their property, including the right to sell it.
13	c	A main conclusion in the textbook is that externalities and market failures result from incomplete property rights or the difficulty of enforcing property rights in certain situations.
14	a	According to Coase, under some circumstances private solutions to the problem of externalities will occur.
15	a	According to Coase, under some circumstances private solutions to the problem of externalities will occur.
16	d	It is important to recognize that completely eliminating an externality is usually not economically efficient. For example, if emissions of sulfur dioxide fall to low levels, even people with asthma will no longer be affected. Further reductions in sulfur dioxide will have little additional benefit.
17	b	The *net benefit* to society from reducing pollution is equal to the difference between the benefit of reducing pollution and the cost.
18	c	It is optimal to reduce pollution up to the point where the marginal benefit of the last unit of pollution eliminated is equal to the marginal cost of eliminating that unit.
19	a	If the marginal benefit of reducing sulfur dioxide emissions is greater than the marginal cost, further reductions will make society better off.
20	b	Further reductions have an additional cost which is greater than the additional benefit. If the marginal benefit of reducing sulfur dioxide emissions is less than the marginal cost, further reductions will make society worse off. Refer to Figure 5-3.
21	b	The economically efficient quantity is found where marginal benefit is equal to marginal cost.
22	c	The total benefit equals the area under the marginal benefit curve.
23	b	The total cost equals the area under the marginal cost curve.
24	a	The net benefit equals the total benefit minus the total cost.
25	b	The value of the benefits is \$375 million or (1.5 million tons x \$200 per ton) + (½ x 1.5 million tons x \$100 per ton). The value of the costs is \$255 million (or (1.5 million tons x \$140 per ton) + (1/2 x 1.5 million tons x \$60 per ton)). If the people who would benefit from a reduction in pollution could get together, they could offer to pay the electric utilities \$255 million to reduce the pollution to the optimal level. After making the payment, they would still be left with a net benefit of \$120 million. Since the net benefit (see previous question) equals area A, the value of net benefits is equal to (\$300 – \$140) x 0.5 x 1.5 million = \$120 million.
26	a	Rights determine who pays for the externality.
27	b	When there are many people involved, the transactions costs are often higher than the net benefits from reducing the externality, so the cost of transacting ends up exceeding the gain from the transaction. In such cases, a private solution to an externality problem is not feasible.

28	a	The Coase Theorem states that if transactions costs are low, private bargaining will result in an efficient solution to the problem of externalities.
29	c	The amount of tax imposed by government is the length of the upward arrow on the graph. The tax is equal to the difference between private cost and social cost.
30	a	At point *A* marginal social cost equals marginal benefit.
31	a	When there is a positive externality, a subsidy can bring about the efficient level of output.
32	c	In a *command and control approach* to reducing pollution, quantitative limits are set on the amount of pollution that firms are allowed to generate.
33	a	The tradable allowances will not reduce pollution emissions to zero.
34	b	For example, private goods are excludable.
35	a	Definition of rival.
36	c	Definition of free riding.
37	b	Common resources are rival and nonexcludable.
38	c	These goods are quasi-public goods.
39	b	To arrive at a demand curve for a public good we don't add quantities at each price, as with a private good. Instead, we add the price each consumer is willing to pay for each quantity of the public good. This gives us a value for the total dollar amount consumers as a group would be willing to pay for that quantity of the public good.
40	b	The optimal quantity of a public good will occur where the demand curve intersects the supply curve. When this quantity is produced, the sum of consumer surplus plus producer surplus is maximized.
41	d	For example, for every hour beyond 6, the supply curve is above the demand curve. Therefore, the additional benefits received will be less than the additional cost of supplying these hours. This results in a deadweight loss and a reduction in economic surplus. Joe is willing to pay $8, and Jill is willing to pay $10, for 6 hours of protection. Their total willingness to pay is equal to the price needed ($18) to provide six hours or protection. Joe and Jill are willing to pay more than the price needed to provide fewer than 6 hours of protection, but they are not willing to pay more than the price needed to provide more than 6 hours of protection.
42	d	The tragedy of the commons is the tendency for a common resource to be overused. A modern example is the forests in many poor countries.
43	d	As Figure 5-12 in the textbook describes, an upward shift in the supply curve reflects the adjustment from private cost to social cost, which eliminates the deadweight loss associated with overuse.

Short Answer Responses

1. Since the passage of the Clean Air Act in 1970, emissions of the six main forms of air pollution have fallen by almost half. With the lower level of air pollution the marginal benefit (due to the reduction in illness, etc.) of reducing air pollution by an equivalent amount today would be much less.

2. Cheung noted that intervention by government was not necessary to address the problem because beekeepers and apple growers came to their own solution. Contracts are written between these two groups that specify payments between the parties.

3. The marginal cost of reducing the last amounts of air and water pollution – the amounts that would remain when nearly all forms of pollution were eliminated – would be very high. It might be necessary, for example, to ban all automobiles. The marginal benefit from reducing the last amounts of pollution would be low.

4. Public radio and television do not rely heavily on funding from commercial sponsors to cover their costs of production. Fund-raising programs are designed to solicit membership contributions to cover programming costs, but such contributions are voluntary. Free riding is common since people can enjoy programming without making contributions.

5. For most externalities problems, the number of individuals affected would require complex and costly private solutions. Often these parties do not have complete information regarding the costs and benefits associated with the externalities. Under these circumstances private solutions are not feasible.

True/False Answers

1. F The level of air pollution is lower today than in 1970.
2. F Coase Theorem states that private individuals may arrive at their own solutions to externalities.
3. F A common resource is rival but not excludable.
4. T This is the definition of quasi-public goods.
5. T As with many goods, the government provides the good due to free riders.
6. F In 1990, Congress enacted the tradable emissions allowances program.
7. T This is the definition of social benefit.
8. T See *Making the Connection* "The Clean Air Act: How a Government Policy Reduced Infant Mortality" on page 142.
9. T Reduce emissions up to the point where the marginal benefit from reduction is equal to the marginal cost of pollution reduction.
10. F Ronald Coase received the Nobel Prize in Economics in 1991.
11. T These government payments are Pigovian subsidies to help students internalize the positive externality associated with consuming education.
12. T See page 150 of the textbook.
13. F The actual cost of the program is much lower than original estimates.
14. F The United States refused to sign the Kyoto Treaty, which required countries to reduce emissions by some fixed percentage. This would indicate that the U.S. government is not in favor of these blanket reductions.
15. T See page 157 of the textbook.

Chapter 6

Elasticity: The Responsiveness of Demand and Supply

Chapter Summary

Elasticity measures how much one variable responds to changes in another variable. The **price elasticity of demand** measures the responsiveness of the quantity demanded of a good or service to changes in its price. Price elasticity of demand is calculated by dividing the percentage change in quantity demanded by the percentage change in the product's price. Demand can be either elastic, inelastic, or unit elastic.

Demand curves slope downward. That means any increase in price (a positive change) will cause a decrease in quantity demanded (a negative change). Dividing a negative number by a positive number always equals a negative number. Price elasticity of demand is always negative. Because all economists know this, they often don't bother writing the minus sign. If you ever encounter a price elasticity of demand that is positive, the first thing you should do is write a minus sign in front of the number. When we say that one price elasticity is "larger" than another, we mean larger in absolute value (that, is, when the negative value is turned into a positive value).

There are five main determinants of the price elasticity of demand for a good:

1. *Availability of close substitutes*: The more substitutes for a good, the larger the price elasticity of demand.
2. The *passage of time*: Demand becomes more elastic as more time passes.
3. *Luxuries versus necessities*: The demand curve for a luxury is more elastic than the demand curve for a necessity.
4. The *definition of the market*: A narrowly defined good will have a more elastic demand than a broadly defined good. For example, the demand for one brand of toothpaste is more elastic than the demand for toothpaste as a product.
5. *Share of the good in the consumer's budget*: The larger the share of the good in the consumer's budget, the more elastic the demand for that good will be.

Business owners should be aware of the price elasticity of demand for their product because of the effect of elasticity on the company's total revenue. **Total revenue** equals price per unit multiplied by the number of units sold. If demand is elastic, then when price increases, total revenue decreases, and when price decreases, total revenue increases. (Price and total revenue move in opposite directions.) If demand is inelastic, an increase in price will increase total revenue and a decrease in price will decrease total revenue. (Price and total revenue move in the same direction.)

There are two other measures of demand elasticity economists often use. The **cross-price elasticity of demand** equals the percentage change in the quantity demanded of one good divided by the percentage change in price of a related good. The sign of the cross-price elasticity is positive for two substitute goods and negative for two complements. The **income elasticity of demand** equals the percentage change in the quantity demanded for a good or service divided by the percentage change in income. The sign of the income elasticity will be positive for a normal good and negative for an inferior good.

The **price elasticity of supply** equals the percentage change in quantity supplied divided by the percentage change in price. The price elasticity of supply will always be a positive number (or will equal zero if supply is perfectly inelastic).

Learning Objectives

When you finish this chapter, you should be able to:

1. **Define the price elasticity of demand and understand how to measure it.** The price elasticity of demand for a good is equal to the percentage change in quantity demanded divided by the percentage change in price. Economists use percentage changes when measuring the response of quantity demanded to a change in the price of a good because percentage changes are not dependent on units of measurement. Demand is elastic when the percentage change in quantity demanded is greater than the percentage change in price, so the price elasticity of demand is greater than 1 in absolute value. Demand is inelastic when the percentage change in quantity demanded is less than the percentage change in price, so the price elasticity is less than 1 in absolute value. Demand is unit-elastic when the percentage change in quantity demanded is equal to the percentage change in price, so the price elasticity is equal to 1 in absolute value.

2. **Understand the determinants of the price elasticity of demand.** The key determinants of the price elasticity of demand for a good are the availability of close substitutes for the good, the passage of time, whether the good is a necessity or a luxury, the definition of the market for the good, and the share of good in the consumer's budget.

3. **Understand the relationship between the price elasticity of demand and total revenue.** Knowledge of the price elasticity of demand is important because it allows a firm to predict how a change in the price of a good it sells will affect its total revenue. An increase in price will decrease total revenue if demand is elastic but will increase total revenue if demand is inelastic. A decrease in price will increase total revenue if demand is elastic but will decrease total revenue if demand is inelastic.

4. **Define the cross-price elasticity of demand and the income elasticity of demand, and understand their determinants and how they are measured.** The cross-price elasticity of demand measures the percentage change in the quantity demanded of one good divided by the percentage change in the price of another good. The cross price elasticity will be positive for two products that are substitutes and will be negative for two products that are complements. The income elasticity of demand measures the percentage change in the quantity demanded of a product divided by a percentage change in income. A normal good will have a positive income elasticity, while an inferior good will have a negative income elasticity.

5. **Use price elasticity and income elasticity to analyze economic issues.** Knowledge of income elasticity values can be used to predict changes in the demand for products during expansions and recessions. The price elasticity and income elasticity for agricultural products explains why the number of farms and farmers have declined over time. Price and income elasticities are used to analyze the responses of consumers to changes in prices of alcoholic beverages, cigarettes, and illegal drugs.

6. **Define the price elasticity of supply and understand its main determinants and how it is measured.** The price elasticity of supply measures the responsiveness of firms to changes in the prices of the products they sell. This elasticity is measured by dividing the percentage change in the quantity supplied by the percentage change in the price of a product. The elasticity of supply is affected by the ease or difficulty firms have in altering the use of resources used in production. In general, supply curves will be more elastic the longer the period firms have to respond to price changes.

Chapter Review

Chapter Opener: Do People Care about the Prices of Books? (pages 172-173)

The book publishing industry, formerly dominated by relatively small firms owned and run by the families that founded them, has changed to an industry with firms that have become part of multinational corporations. Publishers have to be careful about how many copies of a book they publish because they give bookstores the right to return unsold books, which is not the case in most other businesses. Barnes & Noble, for example, can return unsold copies of Harry Potter to its publisher, Scholastic. The book publishing industry demonstrates the importance to firms of taking into account the price elasticity of demand when setting price. Choosing the best price for a book can make the difference between making a profit or suffering a loss.

Helpful Study Hint

At the end of this chapter, ***An Inside Look***, "Borders Slashes Buyers Rewards, Cuts Discounts," analyzes changes in the Borders Rewards Program for its repeat buyers. The previous discount system applied to the Christmas buying season and did not seem to increase sales. The new system is designed to provide frequent purchasers with discounts throughout the year in hopes that this will increase Borders' sales. The total revenue for Borders will increase if the price elasticity of demand for their books is high enough in absolute value.

Economics in YOUR Life! asks how sensitive you are to price when purchasing a book and if Barnes & Noble's discounting of *Harry Potter and the Deathly Hallows* will help them sell a lot of books. Keep these questions in mind as you read the chapter. The authors will answer these questions at the end of the chapter.

6.1 LEARNING OBJECTIVE

6.1 The Price Elasticity of Demand and Its Measurement (pages 174-180)

Learning Objective 1 Define the price elasticity of demand and understand how to calculate measure it.

The **price elasticity of demand** is the responsiveness of the quantity demanded to a change in price, measured by dividing the percentage change in the quantity demanded of a product by the percentage change in the product's price. All elasticity formulas are stated as ratios of two percentage change values. Because of the law of demand, the sign of the price elasticity of demand is always negative. When economists refer to one elasticity being "larger" than another, they mean larger in absolute value (with the negative value turned into a positive value). So, for example, an elasticity of −3 is larger than an elasticity of −2.

Elastic demand means the percentage change in quantity demanded is greater than the percentage change in price, so price elasticity is greater than 1 in absolute value. **Inelastic demand** means the percentage change in quantity demanded is less than the percentage change in price, so price elasticity is less than 1 in absolute value. **Unit-elastic demand** means the percentage change in quantity demanded is equal to the percentage change in price, so price elasticity is equal to 1 in absolute value.

Because the value of the price elasticity of demand is different for each price and quantity combination, the *mid-point formula* is used to calculate elasticity values. In this formula, the change in quantity that results from a price change, $(Q_2 - Q_1)$ or ΔQ, is divided by the average of the quantities $(Q_2 + Q_1)/2$ to calculate the percentage change in quantity demanded. The percentage change in price is calculated by dividing the change in price, $(P_2 - P_1)$ or ΔP, by the average of these prices $(P_2 + P_1)/2$. The elasticity values obtained with the mid-point formula are the same for either a price increase or price decrease between P_2 and P_1.

There are two extreme cases of elasticity. A **perfectly inelastic demand curve** is vertical. If price elasticity of demand is zero, a change in price will not cause quantity demanded to change. A **perfectly elastic demand curve** is horizontal. If price elasticity of demand is very large (approaching infinity), even the smallest change in price will cause a very large change in quantity demanded (also approaching infinity).

Helpful Study Hint

Your understanding of elasticity may be increased by rewriting the formula given in the textbook as:

$$E(lasticity) = \frac{\dfrac{\Delta Q}{Q_1 + Q_2}}{\dfrac{\Delta P}{P_1 + P_2}} = \frac{\Delta Q}{\Delta P} \times \frac{P_1 + P_2}{Q_1 + Q_2}$$

Because the slope of a linear, or straight line, demand curve is constant and can be written $\Delta P / \Delta Q$, the elasticity formula can be written as:

$$E = (1/slope) \times \frac{P_1 + P_2}{Q_1 + Q_2}$$

This formula illustrates several important points: (1) Elasticity is not equal to the slope of a linear demand curve. (2) Although a linear demand curve has a constant slope, the elasticity will be different for every segment of the demand curve. (3) Because relatively high values for price are associated with relatively low values for quantity demanded (and vice versa) the absolute values for elasticity will be high at high prices (demand is elastic) and relatively low at low prices (demand is inelastic). This can be shown by substituting price and quantity values for a given demand curve into the rewritten formula and observing the change in the ratio of $(P_2 + P_1)$ to $(Q_2 + Q_1)$.

Solved Problem 6-1 in the textbook gives you an opportunity to practice calculating the price elasticity of demand using an example of a Harry Potter book. If the price elasticity of demand is greater than 1 in absolute value, then demand is price elastic. If the price elasticity of demand is less than 1 in absolute value, then demand is price inelastic.

Don't Let This Happen to YOU! "Don't Confuse Inelastic with Perfectly Inelastic" reminds you that a demand curve that is perfectly inelastic is different from a demand curve that is inelastic. If the price of the good decreases, the quantity demanded would increase a relatively small amount (compared to the change in price) if demand is inelastic, but the quantity demanded would not change at all if the demand is perfectly inelastic.

6.2 LEARNING OBJECTIVE

6.2 The Determinants of the Price Elasticity of Demand (pages 180-182)

Learning Objective 2 Understand the determinants of the price elasticity of demand.

There are five key determinants of the price elasticity of demand: (1) The availability of close substitutes, (2) the passage of time, (3) whether the product is a necessity or luxury, (4) the definition of the market, and (5) the share of the consumer's budget accounted for by purchases of the product.

The availability of close substitutes is the most important determinant of price elasticity of demand. In general, the price elasticity of demand for a product will be more elastic the more substitutes there are for the product or the closer the substitutes are to the product. Time is an important factor because consumers do not adjust their buying habits immediately following a price change. The more time that passes, the more elastic the demand for a product becomes. The demand for a luxury is more elastic than the demand for a necessity. The more narrowly the market for a product is defined, the more elastic the demand will be. The larger portion of a consumer's budget that a good accounts for, the more elastic the demand for a good is.

Helpful Study Hint

It is useful emphasize two important points. First, each of the five determinants should be considered separately from the others. A product that consumes a small part of a consumer's budget (this suggests demand would be relatively inelastic) may have several good substitutes (this suggests demand would be relatively elastic). Second, changes in the market price of any product will result in different values for price elasticity because each point on a demand curve will have a different price elasticity. Estimates of the price elasticity of demand, such as those cited in the text for breakfast cereals, utilize market prices for products at a particular time. Different market prices will usually result in different elasticity estimates.

Making the Connection "The Price Elasticity of Demand for Breakfast Cereal" shows how the definition of the market affects the price elasticity of demand for the good. Post Raisin Bran is a very narrowly defined good and has an estimated price elasticity of demand of –2.5; which means it is very elastic. All family breakfast cereals are part of a more broadly defined market and have a less elastic demand. The market for all breakfast cereals is price inelastic and is the broadest of the markets for breakfast cereals discussed in the article.

Extra Solved Problem **6-2**

Chapter 6 of the textbook includes three Solved Problems. Here is an extra Solved Problem to help you build your skills solving economic problems.

Supports Learning Objective 2: Understand the determinants of the price elasticity of demand.

Hailing a Cab in the Big Apple

In New York City, the government sets the fares that taxi drivers can charge. In early 2002, some taxi drivers were upset when Mayor Michael Bloomberg proposed a fare increase. One driver was quoted as saying, "I get scared that we will start to lose passengers if rates go up and not gain a cent."

a. What was the driver assuming about the price elasticity of demand for taxi rides?
b. Which of the five determinants of elasticity would be the most important determinant of the price elasticity of demand for taxi rides in New York City?

SOLVING THE PROBLEM

Step 1: Review the chapter material.
This problem is about the price elasticity of demand, so you may want to review the section "The Determinants of the Price Elasticity of Demand," which begins on page 180 in the textbook.

Step 2: Interpret the taxi cab driver's assumption regarding the price elasticity of demand for taxi rides.
The driver asserted that if the price of a cab ride rose, the quantity demanded of rides would fall ("…we will start to lose passengers…"), but that the revenue he would receive from fares would be constant ("…we will…not gain a cent"). Therefore, the driver is assuming demand for cab rides is unit-elastic. Or, if by "not gain a cent" the driver was actually predicting his revenues would fall, then he is assuming the demand for cab rides is elastic.

Step 3: Determine which of the determinants of the elasticity of taxi cab rides in New York City is the most important.
The most important determinant of the price elasticity of demand is typically the availability of substitutes. On most occasions consumers can choose to travel by subway, bus, or taxi. Some consumers may drive their own automobiles. For many residents and tourists driving their own cars is impractical or more expensive than the others because of the difficulty and expense associated with finding parking spaces.

Source: Jayson Blair, "Some Taxi Drivers Say a Fare Increase Would Be Bad for Business," New York Times, February 24, 2002.

6.3 LEARNING OBJECTIVE

6.3 The Relationship between Price Elasticity of Demand and Total Revenue (pages 182-186)

Learning Objective 3 Understand the relationship between the price elasticity of demand and total revenue.

Changes in price and quantity demanded cause changes in the total revenue received by firms. **Total revenue** is the total amount of funds received by the seller of a good or service, calculated by multiplying price per unit by the number of units sold. This is also total spending on the product by consumers. Changes in total revenue are related to the price elasticity of demand. If demand is elastic, a change in price (increase or decrease) will result in a change in total revenue in the opposite direction. If demand is inelastic, a change in price will result in a change in total revenue in the same direction as the change in price. When demand is unit-elastic, a change in price (increase or decrease) results in no change in total revenue.

Helpful Study Hint

The relationship between elasticity and changes in revenue is very important. Setting and changing the price of a product are among the most important decisions firms make. But firms may not know the elasticity of demand for a product before a pricing decision is made. One way to estimate the elasticity is through a market experiment. ***Making the Connection*** "Determining the Price Elasticity of Demand for DVDs by Market Experiment" describes how variations in the prices of DVDs can be used to help determine the price elasticity. This experimentation is especially important for new products where a firm cannot rely on the past relationship between price and quantity demanded.

Solved Problem 6-3 explains how price and total revenue do not always move in the same direction. If demand is price inelastic, then price and total revenue do move together. However, if the demand is price elastic, then price and total revenue will move in the opposite direction from one another, with revenue falling when price increases and rising when price decreases. Work end-of-chapter problem 3.8, which describes how elasticity can be determined by the change in revenue that follows a price change.

6.4 LEARNING OBJECTIVE

6.4 Other Demand Elasticities (pages 186-188)

Learning Objective 4 Define the cross-price elasticity of demand and the income elasticity of demand, and understand their determinants and how they are measured.

The **cross-price elasticity of demand** is the percentage change in quantity demanded of one good divided by the percentage change in price of the other good. Because substitutes are products that can be used for the same purpose, an increase in the price of one of the products will lead to an increase in the quantity demanded of the substitute product. Therefore, the cross-price elasticity of demand will be positive.

Complements are products that are used together. An increase in the price of a product will lead to a decrease in the quantity demanded of its complement. Therefore, the cross-price elasticity of demand for these goods will be negative.

The **income elasticity of demand** is a measure of the responsiveness of quantity demanded to changes in income, measured by the percentage change in quantity demanded divided by the percentage change in income. An increase in income leads to an increase in the quantity demanded of a normal good. Therefore, the income elasticity of demand for a normal good is positive. A good is a luxury if the income elasticity is greater than 1. A good is a necessity if the income elasticity is positive but less than 1. A good is inferior if the quantity demanded falls when income increases. Therefore, the income elasticity of demand for an inferior good is negative.

Helpful Study Hint

It is important not to confuse one type of elasticity with another. Review the list of the different elasticities in ***Making the Connection*** "Price Elasticity, Cross-Price Elasticity, and Income Elasticity in the Market for Alcoholic Beverages" and be sure you understand what these elasticities imply. This article provides a comparison of the elasticities for wine, beer, and spirits. Beer has a negative income elasticity of demand, which puts it in the inferior good category. Wine and spirits have income elasticities greater than one, so they are in the luxury goods category. Beer is price inelastic and the cross-price elasticities between beer and wine and spirits are positive, which means that wine and spirits are substitutes for beer. You can test your understanding by completing problem 4.8 on page 205 in the textbook.

Assume that the price elasticity of demand for iPods is −2.5. Are iPods a normal good? (Answer: You cannot determine whether iPods are normal or inferior by knowing only the price elasticity. The income elasticity of demand for iPods gives you this information.)

Extra Solved Problem 6-4

Chapter 6 of the textbook includes three Solved Problems. Here is an extra Solved Problem to help you build your skills solving economic problems.

Supports Learning Objective 4: Define the cross-price elasticity of demand and the income elasticity of demand, and understand their determinants and how they are measured.

The Demand for Margarine

Suppose that the table below gives the demand this month for margarine in the city of Breadville. Each of the quantity columns, (b) and (c), is a different demand schedule. Column (a) shows the price of margarine. Column (b) shows the quantity demand of margarine for a fixed price of butter and a fixed income. Comparing columns (b) and (c), we can see the price of butter rises.

(a) price of margarine (dollars per pound)	(b) Quantity demanded (price of butter is $1.00 per pound and family income is $30,000) [hundreds of pounds]	(c) Quantity demanded (price of butter is $1.60 per pound and family income is $30,000) [hundreds of pounds]
$1.60	24.02	32.91
1.40	25.00	34.25
1.20	26.18	35.87
1.00	27.65	37.89
0.80	29.57	40.51

a. Calculate the cross-price elasticity of demand for margarine using the midpoint formula given a change in the price of butter from $1.00 per pound to $1.60 per pound. (Hint: use columns (b) and (c).)

b. What can you say about the relationship between margarine and butter?

SOLVING THE PROBLEM

Step 1: Review the chapter material.
This problem is about the other elasticities of demand, so you may want to review the section "Other Demand Elasticities," which begins on page 186 of the textbook.

Step 2: Calculate the cross-price elasticity of demand using the midpoint method.
You can choose to analyze any row in the table, and you will get the following results. The price of butter rises from $1.00 to $1.60 per pound, while the quantity demanded of margarine rises from 24.02 hundred pounds to 32.91 hundred pounds. The cross-price elasticity of demand is 0.68.

Step 3: Interpret the cross-price elasticity of demand.
Because the cross-price elasticity of demand is positive, we know that margarine and butter are substitutes. We can also see that the response of the quantity demanded of margarine to the price change in butter is relatively small, which means that an increase in the price of butter did not cause consumers to strongly switch from buying butter to buying margarine.

6.5 LEARNING OBJECTIVE

6.5 Using Elasticity to Analyze the Disappearing Family Farm (pages 189-191)

Learning Objective 5 Use price elasticity and income elasticity to analyze economic issues.

The demand for many agricultural commodities (for example, wheat) is price inelastic, while the income elasticity for these commodities is low (positive but less than one). Technological change has caused large increases in the supply of agricultural commodities over time. Because of the low income elasticity of demand for these commodities, demand has increased much less than supply. This has resulted in decreases in the relative prices of many agricultural commodities and falling revenues for farmers. At the same time, the technological improvements have meant fewer farmers are needed to produce agricultural commodities.

Helpful Study Hint

The decline in the relative price of agricultural products is an example of how knowledge of elasticity explains an important economic and social issue. ***Solved Problem 6-5***, "Using Price Elasticity to Analyze Policy toward Illegal Drugs," is another excellent application of elasticity to an economic issue. How much consumption of cocaine will be affected by a change in price depends on the price elasticity of demand for cocaine. If the price elasticity is high in absolute value, the decrease in price that would result from legalization could nearly triple consumption. If the price elasticity is low, there will be only a slight increase in cocaine consumption. You can test your understanding by completing related problems 5.2 and 5.3 on page 206 in the textbook.

6.6 LEARNING OBJECTIVE

6.6 The Price Elasticity of Supply and Its Measurement (pages 191-197)

Learning Objective 6 Define the price elasticity of supply and understand its main determinants and how it is measured.

The **price elasticity of supply** is the responsiveness of the quantity supplied to a price change, measured by dividing the percentage change in the quantity supplied of a product by the percentage change in the product's price. Because of the law of supply, this elasticity will have a positive numerical value. The longer the time period firms have to respond to a price change, the greater the elasticity of supply.

Helpful Study Hint

Making the Connection "Why Are Oil Prices So Unstable?" explains how the elasticity of demand and supply affects the price of oil. In the short run, demand and supply are both relatively inelastic, so a reduction in the supply of oil will cause a large increase in the price of oil, but only a small change in the equilibrium quantity of oil produced and consumed. In the long run, consumers and firms have time to adjust their consumption preferences and productive capacity, so the demand and supply curves are relatively elastic. A change in the supply of oil has a smaller effect on the equilibrium price of oil in the long run.

At the start of the chapter, ***Economics in YOUR Life!*** asked how sensitive you are to price when purchasing a book and if Barnes & Noble's discounting of *Harry Potter and the Deathly Hallows* will help them sell a lot of books. If you read all the earlier books in the series as soon as they came out, you are very likely to consider purchasing the book even at a high price. However, if you usually wait to purchase inexpensive paperback editions of books you like to read, you are more likely to purchase the hardcover book when Barnes & Noble discounts it. The answer to the second question depends on the prevalence of this last type of consumer. The more price-conscious consumers there are in the market, the more responsive to price the quantity demanded for the hardcover version will be, and the more likely it is for Barnes & Noble's revenue to increase in response to the drop in price.

Extra Solved Problem **6-6**

Chapter 6 of the textbook includes three Solved Problems. Here is an extra Solved Problem to help you build your skills solving economic problems.

Supports Learning Objective 6: Define the price elasticity of supply and understand its main determinants and how it is measured.

Ethanol and Biodiesel

Suppose that this summer your state government passes an immediate tax rebate to all citizens who use ethanol and biodiesel fuels in their automobiles. This causes the demand for ethanol and biodiesel to increase significantly. The main inputs for these alternative fuels are soy and corn. Because the supply of corn and soy are fixed for a given summer, the supply of these alternative fuels is fixed.

a. What is the price elasticity of supply when the supply of a good is fixed?

b. Explain what happens to the equilibrium price and quantity of alternative fuels in the summer that this rebate is introduced using a demand and supply graph.

SOLVING THE PROBLEM

Step 1: **Review the chapter material.**
This problem is about the price elasticity of supply, so you may want to review the section "The Price Elasticity of Supply and Its Measurement," which begins on page 191 in the textbook.

Step 2: **Interpret the fixed supply of alternative fuels and what that means in terms of the price elasticity of supply.**
If the supply is fixed, the quantity supplied is constant regardless of the market price, that is, supply is perfectly inelastic and is a vertical line. A vertical line has a price elasticity of supply of zero.

Step 3: **Apply the increase in demand and the vertical supply curve to the market for alternative fuels.**
The equilibrium quantity will be unaffected, and the increase in demand will cause an increase in the market price. Note that over time the elasticity of supply will increase, and the supply curve will become flatter, causing the quantity to increase in the long-run with a smaller increase in price.

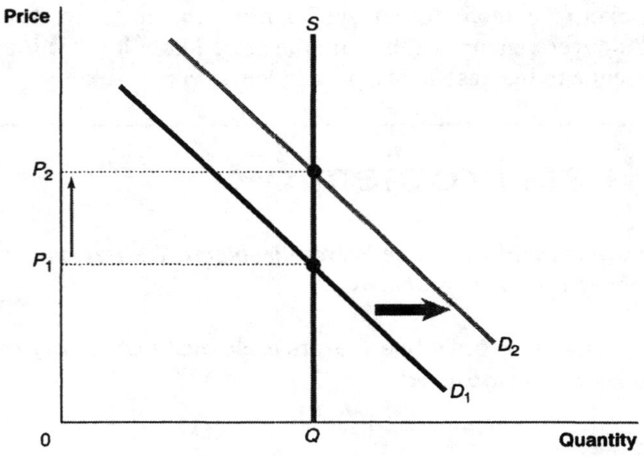

Key Terms

Cross-price elasticity of demand. The percentage change in quantity demanded of one good divided by the percentage change in the price of another good.

Elastic demand. Demand is elastic when the percentage change in quantity demanded is *greater* than the percentage change in price, so the price elasticity is *greater* than 1 in absolute value.

Elasticity. A measure of how much one economic variable responds to changes in another economic variable.

Income elasticity of demand. A measure of the responsiveness of quantity demanded to changes in income, measured by the percentage change in quantity demanded divided by the percentage change in income.

Inelastic demand. Demand is inelastic when the percentage change in quantity demanded is *less* than the percentage change in price, so the price elasticity is *less* than 1 in absolute value.

Perfectly elastic demand. The case where the quantity demanded is infinitely responsive to price, and the price elasticity of demand equals infinity.

Perfectly inelastic demand. The case where the quantity demanded is completely unresponsive to price, and the price elasticity of demand equals zero.

Price elasticity of demand. The responsiveness of the quantity demanded to a change in price, measured by dividing the percentage change in the quantity demanded of a product by the percentage change in the product's price.

Price elasticity of supply. The responsiveness of the quantity supplied to a change in price, measured by dividing the percentage change in the quantity supplied of a product by the percentage change in the product's price.

Total revenue. The total amount of funds received by a seller of a good or service, calculated by multiplying price per unit by the number of units sold.

Unit-elastic demand. Demand is unit-elastic when the percentage change in quantity demanded is *equal to* the percentage change in price, so the price elasticity is equal to 1 in absolute value.

Self-Test

(Answers are provided at the end of the Self-Test.)

Multiple Choice Questions

1. What do economists use the concept of elasticity for?
   a. To explain how producers respond to consumers' needs
   b. To measure how one economic variable responds to changes in another economic variable
   c. To define the slope of supply and demand curves
   d. All of the above

2. If you know the value for price elasticity of demand, then which of the following can you can compute?
   a. The effect of a price change on the quantity demanded
   b. The responsiveness of the quantity supplied of a good to changes in its price
   c. The price elasticity of supply
   d. All of the above

3. What is the name given to the responsiveness of the quantity supplied of a good to changes in its price?
   a. Price elasticity of supply
   b. Price elasticity of demand
   c. Income elasticity
   d. Cross-price elasticity

4. Who benefits from the concept of elasticity?
   a. Business managers
   b. Policy makers
   c. Both business managers and policy makers
   d. Neither business managers nor policy makers; only economists benefit from it

5. How is the responsiveness of the quantity demanded to a change in price measured?
   a. By dividing the percentage change in the product's price by the percentage change in the quantity demanded of a product
   b. By multiplying the percentage change in the product's price by the percentage change in the quantity demanded of a product
   c. By dividing the percentage change in the quantity demanded of a product by the percentage change in the product's price
   d. By multiplying the percentage change in the quantity demanded of a product by the percentage change in the product's price

6. Which of the following measures is more sensitive to the units chosen for quantity and price?
   a. Price elasticity of demand
   b. Price elasticity of supply
   c. The slope of a demand or supply curve
   d. The eventual equilibrium in the market

7. How do economists avoid confusion over units in the computation of elasticity?
   a. By using index numbers rather than whole numbers
   b. By using percentage changes rather than simple differences
   c. By using aggregate values rather than single values
   d. By using the same number as the value of the slope of the curve

8. Which of the following statements about the slope and the price elasticity of demand is/are correct?
   a. The slope is calculated using percentage changes in quantity and price, whereas elasticity is calculated using simple numerical changes.
   b. The slope is calculated using changes in quantity and price, whereas elasticity is calculated using percentage changes.
   c. Both the slope and elasticity must be calculated using percentage changes.
   d. Neither the slope nor the value of elasticity can be calculated using simple numerical changes.

9. Which of the following is true about the value of price elasticity of demand?
   a. The value is always negative
   b. The value is always positive
   c. The value may be positive or negative depending on the value of the slope of the demand curve
   d. The value is positive when the slope is negative and vice versa

10. In comparing price elasticities of demand, we are usually interested in their relative size. What is the best way to make these comparisons?
    a. To drop the minus sign and compare absolute values
    b. To compare the signs (positive or negative) of various elasticity values, regardless of absolute value
    c. To avoid comparing absolute values, regardless of the sign (positive or negative)
    d. To compare demand elasticities to supply elasticities

11. What happens when the quantity demanded is very responsive to changes in price?
    a. The percentage change in quantity demanded will be greater than the percentage change in price.
    b. The percentage change in quantity demanded will be less than the percentage change in price.
    c. The percentage change in quantity demanded will be equal to the percentage change in price.
    d. The percentage change in quantity demanded will be unrelated to the percentage change in price.

12. What happens when the quantity demanded is very responsive to changes in price?
    a. The price elasticity of demand will be greater than 1 in absolute value.
    b. Demand is inelastic.
    c. There are few substitutes for the good in question.
    d. All of the above

13. Which of the following is true if quantity demanded is not very responsive to price?
    a. The percentage change in quantity demanded will be less than the percentage change in price.
    b. The price elasticity of demand will be less than 1 in absolute value.
    c. Demand is inelastic.
    d. All of the above

14. Refer to the graph below. If the demand is elastic and you start at point *A*, what is the result of a cut in the price from $30 to $20?

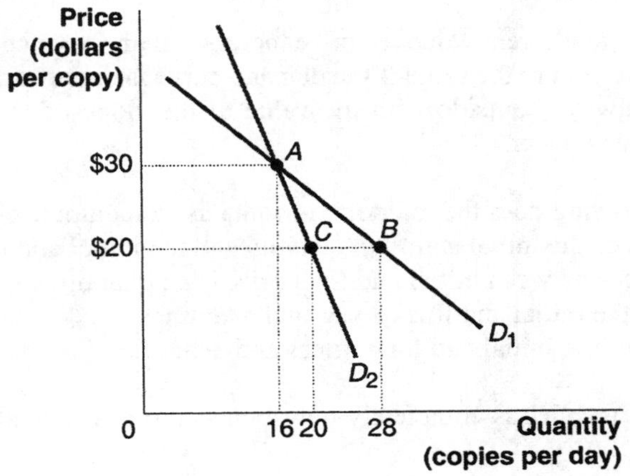

a. A move to point *B*
b. A move to point *C*
c. A move to either point *B* or point *C*
d. No move at all

15. Refer to the graph below. If the demand is inelastic and you start at point *A*, what is the result of a cut in the price from $30 to $20?

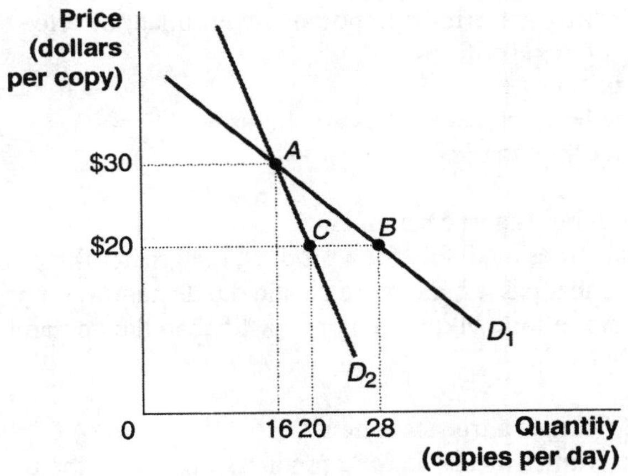

a. A move to point *B*
b. A move to point *C*
c. A move to either point *B* or point *C*
d. No move at all

16. Which of the following would occur when calculating price elasticity between two points on a demand curve if we are not using the midpoint formula?
    a. The value of elasticity we get is the same whether we apply it to price increases or to price decreases.
    b. We would get a different value for price increases than for price decreases.
    c. The values we get are the same if the demand curve is downward sloping.
    d. The values always coincide with the value of the slope of the demand curve, especially if the demand curve is linear.

17. Which of the following does the midpoint formula use to compute elasticity?
    a. The averages of the initial and final quantity and the initial and final price.
    b. The differences between initial and final prices and quantities.
    c. The sums of the initial and final prices and quantities.
    d. The product of the initial and final prices and quantities.

18. When quantity demanded is completely unresponsive to price, what is the value of price elasticity of demand?
    a. Zero
    b. 1
    c. A number between zero and 1
    d. A negative number

19. If demand is perfectly elastic, then what is the impact of an increase in price?
    a. A decrease in quantity demanded to zero.
    b. No change in quantity demanded.
    c. A change in quantity demanded exactly equal to the change in price.
    d. A very small change in quantity demanded.

20. Which of the following is the most important determinant of price elasticity of demand?
    a. The availability of substitutes
    b. The passage of time
    c. The difference between necessities and luxuries
    d. The definition of the market

21. Which of the following is a true statement?
    a. The more substitutes available for a product, the greater the price elasticity of demand.
    b. The more time that passes, the more elastic the demand for a product becomes.
    c. The demand curve for a luxury is more elastic than the demand curve for a necessity.
    d. All of the above

22. Which of the following is a true statement?
    a. The fewer substitutes available for a product, the greater the price elasticity of demand.
    b. The more time that passes, the more inelastic the demand for a product becomes.
    c. The demand curve for a luxury is less elastic than the demand curve for a necessity.
    d. The more narrowly defined a product is, the larger the price elasticity of demand.

23. The price elasticity for a particular brand of raisin bran is, in absolute value,
    a. larger than the elasticity for all family cereals.
    b. the same as the elasticity for all family cereals.
    c. smaller than the elasticity for all types of breakfast cereals.
    d. neither larger nor smaller than the elasticity for any other type of cereal.

24. What is true about elasticity for a good that comprises a smaller fraction of the average consumer's budget?
    a. The price elasticity of demand for that good is smaller.
    b. The price elasticity of demand for that good is larger.
    c. Changes in the price of that good are insignificant.
    d. The quantity of that good consumed is larger relative to the quantity of other goods.

25. What is total revenue?
    a. The total amount of funds a firm receives from selling a good or service.
    b. An amount calculated by multiplying price per unit by the number of units sold.
    c. An amount that increases when price increases if demand is inelastic.
    d. All of the above

26. When demand is price-inelastic, what is the relationship between price and total revenue?
    a. They move together.
    b. They move in inversely.
    c. They always remain unchanged.
    d. They are entirely unrelated.

27. When demand is price-elastic, what is the relationship between price and total revenue?
    a. They move together.
    b. They move inversely.
    c. They move in unpredictable directions.
    d. They don't move at all.

28. Refer to the graphs below. In which of the graphs does a price decrease lead to an increase in total revenue?

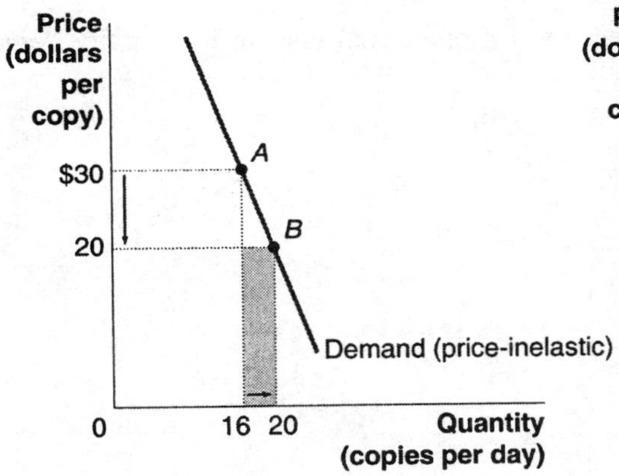

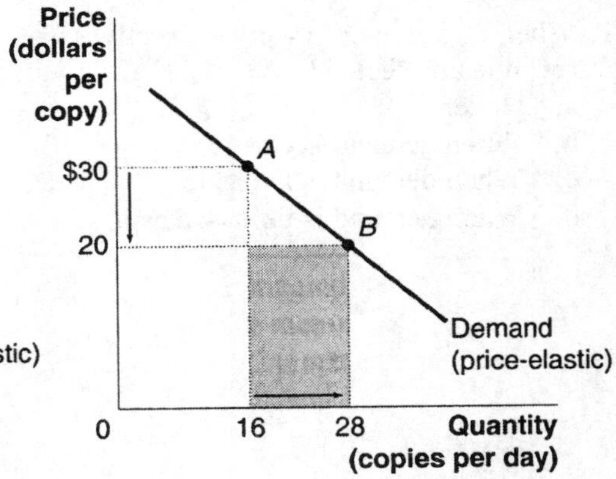

    a. In the graph on the left
    b. In the graph on the right
    c. In both graphs
    d. In neither graph

29. When an increase in the quantity demanded is not large enough to make up for a decrease in price, total revenue falls. Which graph is more applicable to this statement?

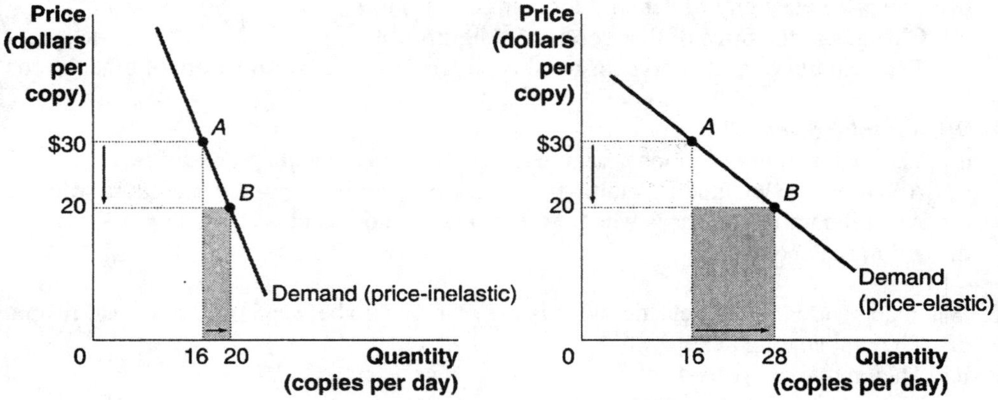

a. The graph on the left
b. The graph on the right
c. Both graphs
d. Neither graph

30. What is the effect of a cut in price when demand is inelastic?
a. An increase in total revenue
b. A decrease in total revenue
c. No effect on total revenue
d. A change in total revenue by an amount equal to the cut in price.

31. When is a change in price exactly offset by a proportional change in quantity demanded, leaving revenue unaffected?
a. Never
b. When demand is elastic
c. When demand is inelastic
d. When demand is unitary elastic

32. Refer to the graph below. What happens to price elasticity as we move down the demand curve?

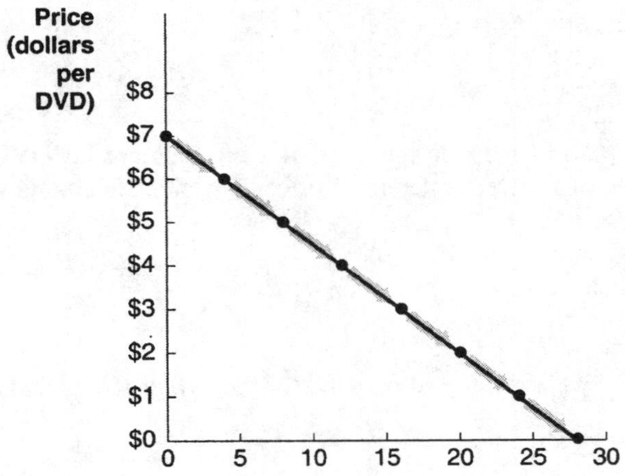

a. It rises.
b. It falls.
c. It remains the same.
d. It rises up to the midpoint, and then it falls.

33. Refer to the graph below. What happens to total revenue as we move down the demand curve?

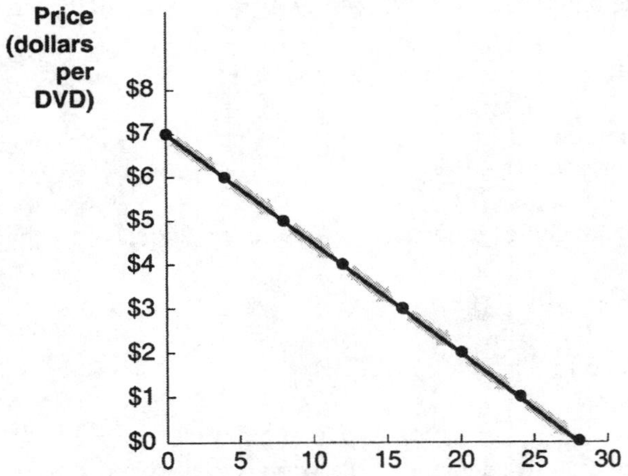

a. It rises.
b. It falls.
c. It remains the same.
d. It rises up to the midpoint, and then it falls.

34. Fill in the blanks: An increase in the price of a substitute for iPods will lead to __________ in quantity demanded of iPods, so the cross-price elasticity of demand will be __________.
    a. an increase; positive
    b. an increase; negative
    c. a decrease; positive
    d. a decrease; negative

35. Fill in the blanks: An increase in the price of a complement for DVDs will lead to __________ in the quantity demanded of DVDs, so the cross-price elasticity of demand will be __________.
    a. an increase; positive
    b. an increase; negative
    c. a decrease; positive
    d. a decrease; negative

36. What is the cross-price elasticity of demand for the two products that are unrelated?
    a. Zero
    b. 1
    c. Infinite
    d. Negative

37. If Amazon.com raises its prices by 10 percent and, as a result, the quantity of books demanded on BarnesandNoble.com increases by 35 percent, what do consumers consider the two Web sites to be?
    a. Close substitutes
    b. Close complements
    c. Unrelated
    d. Identical

38. If the quantity demanded of a good increases as income increases, what can we say with certainty about the good?
    a. It is a necessity.
    b. It is a luxury.
    c. It is a normal good.
    d. It is an inferior good.

39. If the quantity demanded of a normal good is very responsive to changes in income, what is the good considered?
    a. A necessity.
    b. A luxury.
    c. A substitute good.
    d. An inferior good.

40. What is true about quantity demanded if a good is considered a *necessity*?
    a. It is very responsive to changes in income.
    b. It is not very responsive to changes in income.
    c. It is unrelated to changes in income.
    d. It is always the same regardless of price changes.

41. Which of the following is true about what happens to the quantity demanded of an *inferior* good?
    a. It rises when income rises.
    b. It falls when income increases.
    c. It does not change with changes in price.
    d. It does not change with changes in income.

42. Suppose that an innovation in harvesting technology increases the supply of corn. Corn farmers will experience an increase in total revenue when
    a. the supply of corn is inelastic.
    b. the supply of corn is elastic.
    c. the demand for corn is inelastic.
    d. the demand for corn is elastic.

Short Answer Questions

1. From the chapter opener: "…there is no difference between \$22 and \$23…If you want a book in translation from a Czech writer, you are going to buy the book – price is not a factor if you really want it." If the price of a book is unimportant, what does this imply about the price elasticity of demand for the book?

____

____

____

2. Phil Sanders, an economics major who recently graduated from a local college, was hired as a consultant by the Middletown City Council. A member of the Council proposed lowering fares for public transportation (buses and trolleys). He reasoned that the lower price would increase both the number of people using public transportation and revenue from fares. The increased revenue would be used to buy new buses. When he estimated price elasticities of demand, Sanders found that the price elasticity of demand for both bus and trolley service was −0.6. What advice should Sanders give the City Council?

____

____

____

3. Assume that economic growth causes incomes to rise in the United States by 5 percent. Use the income elasticities of demand from ***Making the Connection*** "Price Elasticity, Cross-Price Elasticity, and Income Elasticity in the Market for Alcoholic Beverages" on page 188 in the textbook to estimate the change in the quantities demanded for beer, wine, and spirits.

____

____

____

4. The Los Angeles Lakers basketball team and the Los Angeles Kings hockey team play their home games in the Staples Arena. The seating capacity of the Arena is just under 19,000. Although Lakers games are often sold out, the number of tickets sold to Kings games, some concerts, and other non-sports events is often less than 14,000. What is the price elasticity of supply for the Staples Arena?

____

____

5. A low income elasticity of demand for wheat is one of the reasons given in the textbook for the reduction in the number of family farms in the United States. Why is the income elasticity for wheat low? Is wheat an inferior good?

____

____

____

True/False Questions

T F 1. The price elasticity of demand measures the responsiveness of demand for a product to a change in the product's price.
T F 2. The demand for all breakfast cereals is more elastic than the demand for a specific brand of cereal.
T F 3. If the demand for a product is elastic, a decrease in price results in an increase in revenue.
T F 4. The cross-price elasticity of demand for two complements is positive.
T F 5. The mid-point formula is used to ensure that there is only one value of the price elasticity of demand between two points on the same demand curve.
T F 6. One reason for the decline in wheat prices from 1950 to 2006 (measured in terms of prices in 2006) is a price elasticity of demand that is less than 1 in absolute value.
T F 7. During recessions, the demand for inferior goods will rise.
T F 8. If the supply for a product is inelastic, an increase in price will increase total revenue.
T F 9. A supply curve that is a horizontal line is perfectly elastic.
T F 10. If a product has a unit elastic demand curve, an increase in income does not affect revenue.
T F 11. The demand for a good will be more elastic, the larger the share of a good in the average consumer's budget.
T F 12. A perfectly elastic demand curve will be a horizontal line.
T F 13. A perfectly inelastic demand curve will have a price elasticity equal to 1 in absolute value.
T F 14. A good with an income elasticity of demand equal to 1.2 is a normal good.
T F 15. A good with an income elasticity of demand equal to 1.2 is a luxury good.

Answers to the Self-Test

Multiple-Choice Questions

Question	Answer	Comment
1	b	Economists use the concept of elasticity to measure how one economic variable responds to changes in another economic variable.
2	a	For this reason, elasticity is an important concept for managers and policy makers.
3	a	The responsiveness of the quantity supplied of a good to changes in its price is called price elasticity of supply.
4	c	Elasticity is an important concept not just for business managers but for policy makers as well.
5	c	The responsiveness of the quantity demanded to a change in price, measured by dividing the percentage change in the quantity demanded of a product by the percentage change in the product's price.
6	c	The measurement of slope is sensitive to the units chosen for quantity and price. For this reason we use percentage changes to compute responsiveness.
7	b	Percentage changes are not dependent on units of measurement.
8	b	The value we compute for the slope can change dramatically depending on the units we use for quantity and price. To avoid this confusion over units, economists use percentage changes when measuring the price elasticity of demand.
9	a	If we calculate the price elasticity of demand for a price cut, the percentage change in price will be negative and the percentage change in quantity demanded will be positive. Similarly, if we calculate the price elasticity of demand for a price increase, the percentage change in price will be positive and the percentage change in quantity will be negative. Therefore, the price elasticity of demand is always negative.
10	a	In comparing elasticities, we are usually interested in their relative size. So, we often drop the minus sign and compare their absolute values.
11	a	In other words, the value of elasticity will be greater than one, so the numerator will be greater than the denominator in the elasticity formula.
12	a	If the quantity demanded is responsive to changes in price, the percentage change in quantity demanded will be greater than the percentage change in price, and the price elasticity of demand will be greater than 1 in absolute value. In this case, demand is elastic.
13	d	When the quantity demanded is not very responsive to price, however, the percentage change in quantity demanded will be less than the percentage change in price, and the price elasticity of demand will be less than 1 in absolute value. In this case, demand is inelastic.
14	a	An elastic demand curve is relatively flat. Therefore, the drop in price will cause a move along the flatter (or elastic) demand curve.
15	b	An inelastic demand curve is relatively steep. Therefore, the drop in price will cause a move along the steeper (or inelastic) demand curve.
16	b	We could run into a problem because we get a different value for the price elasticity of demand for price increases than for price decreases. To avoid this problem, we use the midpoint formula to compute elasticity.
17	a	The midpoint formula uses the average of the initial and final quantity and the initial and final price to compute elasticity.
18	a	If a demand curve is perfectly inelastic, an increase in price causes the quantity demanded to remain the same, so there is no (or zero) response in quantity demanded.

19	a	Refer to table 6-1 on page 179 in the textbook.
20	a	The textbook asserts that the availability of substitutes is the most important determinant of the price elasticity of demand.
21	d	All of these statements are correct. Read pages 180-181 in the textbook.
22	d	The price elasticity of demand for a narrowly defined market (e.g., *Tide* has many substitutes) will be greater than the price elasticity of demand for a broadly defined market (laundry detergent).
23	a	The more substitutes available for a product, the greater the price elasticity of demand. Also, the more narrowly defined a product is, the larger the price elasticity of demand.
24	a	Goods that take only a small fraction of a consumer's budget tend to have inelastic demand. For example, the share of the average consumer's budget that is spent on salt is very low. As a result, even a doubling of the price of salt is likely to result in only a small decline in the quantity of salt demanded.
25	d	Total revenue is the total amount of funds a firm receives from selling a good or service. Total revenue is calculated by multiplying price per unit by the number of units sold.
26	a	An increase in price raises total revenue, and a decrease in price reduces total revenue.
27	b	An increase in price reduces total revenue, and a decrease in price raises total revenue.
28	b	In the graph on the right the increase in revenue from decreasing price equals 12 copies (28 − 12) multiplied by \$20, or \$240. This is greater than the decrease in revenue from decreasing price ((\$30 − \$20) x 16 = \$160).
29	a	This demand curve is inelastic. Refer to Figure 6-2 on page 183 in the textbook.
30	b	When demand is inelastic, a cut in price will decrease total revenue.
31	d	When demand is unit-elastic, a change in price is exactly offset by a proportional change in quantity demanded, leaving revenue unaffected. Therefore, when demand is unit elastic, neither a decrease in price nor an increase in price affects revenue.
32	b	At higher prices, demand is more elastic, and at lower prices, demand is less elastic and eventually becomes inelastic.
33	d	Total revenue is highest at the midpoint of the demand curve and decreases as the price moves away from the midpoint price.
34	a	An increase in the price of a substitute will lead to an increase in demand for the substitute product, so the cross-price elasticity of demand will be positive.
35	d	An increase in the price of a complement will lead to a decrease in demand for the complementary product, so the cross-price elasticity of demand will be negative.
36	a	If the two products are unrelated, the cross-price elasticity of demand will be zero.
37	a	If the percentage change in demand for books from BarnesandNoble.com is greater than the percentage change in the price of books from Amazon.com, then the two websites are considered by consumers to be close substitutes.
38	c	If the demand for a good increases as income increases, then the good is a normal good. Normal goods are often further subdivided into luxury goods and necessity goods.
39	b	A good is a luxury if demand is very responsive to changes in income, so that a 10 percent increase in income results in more than a 10 percent increase in demand. Expensive jewelry or vacation homes are examples of luxuries.
40	b	A good is a necessity if demand is not very responsive to changes in income, so that a 10 percent increase in income results in less than a 10 percent increase in demand. Food and clothing are examples of necessities.

41	b	A good is inferior if demand falls when income increases. Ground beef with a high fat content is an example of an inferior good.
42	d	An increase in supply with cause a decrease in the equilibrium price and an increase in the equilibrium quantity. In order of total revenue to increase the equilibrium quantity must go up by more than the equilibrium price as we move along the demand; i.e. demand must be elastic.

Short Answer Responses

1. If the price of a book really makes no difference to consumers, then the demand curve for the book would be perfectly inelastic and would be drawn as a vertical line at the quantity demanded. However, this type of demand curve is rare. Not only would there be no decrease in quantity demanded if the price rose above $22; but there would be no increase in quantity demanded if the price decreased below $22. Although price may not matter to some book buyers it is likely that other buyers would respond to price changes.

2. Sanders should advise the City Council members to not lower price, as this would result in lower revenue from fares. In fact, if the Council wishes to increase revenue the proper course would be to raise fares since demand is inelastic. However, Council members may wish to forego the fare increase for other reasons. It is likely that many lower income residents of Middletown use public transportation and Council members may not wish to place the financial burden of paying for new buses on them.

3. To determine the changes in quantity demanded it is necessary to multiply the income elasticity for these three goods by the percentage change in income. The income elasticities are: beer (−0.09), wine (5.03) and spirits (1.21). Multiplying these values by 5% (0.05) yields the following changes in quantity demanded: beer (−0.5%), wine (+25.2%) and spirits (+6.1%).

4. Assuming that temporary seating is not added to or removed from the Staples Arena for different events, the price elasticity of supply is zero. This means that the supply curve is a vertical line at the quantity supplied of 19,000. The number of tickets sold for different events reflects quantity demanded, not quantity supplied.

5. Wheat has a low income elasticity because there is a small increase in the demand for goods made from wheat as incomes rise. Wheat would be an inferior good only if demand decreased as incomes rose. This was not the case from 1950 through 2006. The income elasticity of demand for wheat was positive but less than 1.

True/False Answers

1. F The price elasticity of demand measures the responsiveness of quantity demanded to price changes.
2. F The more narrow the market, the more elastic the demand for the product.
3. T With an elastic demand, the price and total revenue move in the opposite direction of one another.
4. F Cross-price elasticity of demand is negative for complements.
5. T See page 176.
6. T See Figure 6-4 on page 189.
7. T As income falls, the demand for inferior goods increases.

8. F If demand, not supply, is inelastic, then an increase in price will increase total revenue.
9. T See Table 6-5 on page 195.
10. F A product has a unit elastic demand curve if changes in price, not income, do not affect revenue.
11. T If the good is a large share of the budget and the price increases, we consume a lot less of the good; i.e. the income demand is elastic.
12. T See Table 6-1 on page 179.
13. F A perfectly inelastic demand curve will have a price elasticity equal to zero.
14. T If income elasticity is positive, then the good is a normal good.
15. T A luxury good has an income elasticity of more than 1.

Chapter 7

Firms, the Stock Market, and Corporate Governance

Chapter Summary

This chapter examines the organization of business firms, how these firms raise funds to finance their operations, and how they provide information to their owners (both actual and prospective). In the United States, there are three legal types of firms: (1) **sole proprietorships,** (2) **partnerships,** and (3) **corporations.**

Owners of sole proprietorships and partnerships have **unlimited liability**, which means that if the firm goes bankrupt, the owners' personal assets can be seized by anyone the firm owes money to. In the early nineteenth century, state legislatures recognized that unlimited liability interfered with the ability of firms to raise money and passed laws allowing firms to be organized as corporations. Corporations limit the financial liability of firm owners to the amount of their investment in the firm. Limited liability and the ability to raise funds through the sale of corporate stock are key advantages of the corporate form of organization. Corporations are, on average, larger than the other types of businesses. Their size contributes to the difficulty of organizing and managing them.

Corporations are owned by shareholders who elect a board of directors to represent their interests. The directors appoint managers to run the day-to-day operations of the firm. The separation of ownership from control creates an incentive for managers to pursue their own interests, rather than the interests of shareholders. This conflict of interest is referred to as the principal-agent problem.

Stock refers to a financial security that represents partial ownership of a firm. Investors who buy shares of stocks buy part ownership of the firm. Corporations usually choose to keep some part of their profits as retained earnings and pay the remainder as dividends to shareholders. When a corporation's future profits are expected to rise, its stock's share price will rise, providing shareholders with a capital gain. A bond is a financial security that represents a promise to make one or more future payments that are fixed in money terms. Corporations that sell bonds must make promised payments to their bondholders before paying any dividends. Stockholders make an open-ended commitment of funds to the corporations they own so the firm is not obligated to return their funds at any particular date.

Daily buying and selling of stocks and bonds mostly involves existing rather then new issues. Trading takes place in "exchanges" and does not generate new funds for companies whose stocks are being bought and sold. To raise funds through the sale of stocks and bonds, a firm's managers must persuade potential buyers that the firm is profitable. The Securities and Exchange Commission requires U.S. firms that sell stocks and bonds to report their performance in financial statements using generally accepted accounting principles. The firm's income statement and balance sheet provide the public with information regarding the firm's profits or losses, and its assets and liabilities.

The importance of accurate financial statements was highlighted by a series of financial scandals that came to light in 2001 and 2002. Executives of Enron, WorldCom, and other firms falsified financial statements to make their firms appear more profitable than they were. In response to these scandals, the Sarbanes-Oxley Act was passed in 2002 to increase the accountability of corporate officers for the accuracy of their firm's financial statements.

Learning Objectives

When you finish this chapter you should be able to:

1. **Categorize the major types of firms in the United States.** There are three legal categories of firms in the United States. A sole proprietorship is owned by a single individual. Partnerships are firms owned jointly by two or more persons. A corporation can have any number of owners. The main point of creating a corporation is to construct a legal form of business that provides owners with limited liability.

2. **Describe the typical management structure of corporations and understand the concepts of separation of ownership from control and the principal-agent problem.** Corporations are owned by their shareholders, the owners of the corporation's stock. Shareholders elect a board of directors who represent their interests and appoint managers who run the day-to-day operations of the firms. Since top management usually does not own a large share of their firm's stock, they may have an incentive to decrease profits in order to pursue their own interests.

3. **Explain how firms obtain the funds they need to operate and expand**. Firms can raise funds from profits earned from their operations by taking on partners or new owners who invest in the firms and by borrowing. Firms raise external funds directly through financial markets or indirectly through banks and other financial intermediaries.

4. **Understand the information provided in corporations' financial statements.** A firm's income statement summarizes its revenues, costs, and profit over a period of time. A firm's balance sheet summarizes its financial position on a particular day. A balance sheet lists a firm's assets and its liabilities. The value of a firm's assets minus its liabilities equals its net worth.

5. **Understand the role of government in corporate governance**. Several firms including Enron and WorldCom were caught falsifying their financial statements and engaging in deceptive accounting practices. In response to these accounting scandals, new legislation – the Sarbanes-Oxley Act – was enacted. The Act mandates that chief executive officers of corporations personally certify the accuracy of their financial statements and requires financial analysts and auditors to disclose any conflicts of interest that would limit their independence in evaluating a firm's financial condition.

Appendix: Understand the concept of present value and the information contained on a firm's income statement and balance sheet. Your instructor may assign this appendix.

Chapter Review

Chapter Opener: Google: From Dorm Room to Wall Street (pages 208-209)

In 2004, the founders of Internet search engine Google sold part of their firm to outside investors by offering stock to the public. This decision gave the firm a much needed infusion of cash to allow for future growth, and growth for Google has increased the challenges in managing a large firm. Other firms made news in

2001 and 2002 due not to their success but through their involvement in accounting scandals that resulted in the passage of federal legislation intended to improve the accuracy of corporations' financial statements.

Helpful Study Hint

The popularity of Google's stock offering resulted in rich rewards for Google's founders and a huge inflow of funds that the firm can use for future growth. ***An Inside Look*** at the end of this chapter describes the compensation that the owners and the CEO receive and shows the movement in Google's stock price in from 2004 to 2007. Growth has meant that Google's ownership no longer rests solely in the hands of its founders, Larry Page and Sergey Brin. CEO Eric Schmidt is responsible for the operation of the business. To decrease the principal-agent problem, Schmidt receives only a small salary; most of his compensation comes from increases in Google's stock price because Schmidt owns many shares of Google.

Economics in YOUR Life! asks if it is too risky to own the stock of a firm like Google. Keep this question in mind as you read the chapter. The authors will answer this question at the end of the chapter.

7.1 LEARNING OBJECTIVE

7.1 Types of Firms (pages 210-212)

Learning Objective 1 Categorize the major types of firms in the United States.

In the United States, there are three basic legal structures a firm can assume. A **sole proprietorship** is a firm owned by a single individual and not organized as a corporation. A **partnership** is a firm owned by two or more persons and not organized as a corporation. Owners of sole proprietorships and partnerships have control of their day-to-day operations but they are subject to unlimited liability. There is no legal distinction between the owners' personal assets and those of the firms they own. As a result, employees or suppliers have a legal right to sue if they are owed money by these firms, even if this requires the owners to sell their personal assets.

A **corporation** is a legal form of business that provides owners with limited liability. **Limited liability** is the legal provision that shields owners of a corporation from losing more than they have invested in the firm. The profits of corporations are taxed twice in the United States, and corporations are more difficult to organize and run than sole proprietorships and partnerships. Despite these disadvantages, limited liability and the possibility of raising funds by issuing stock make corporations an attractive form of business.

Helpful Study Hint

Corporations are often described as "publicly owned." This phrase means that corporations are owned by members of the general public, not that they are owned by the government.

Making the Connection "What's in a 'Name'? Lloyd's of London Learns about Unlimited Liability the Hard Way" explains that the shareholders of Lloyd's of London did not have the limited liability that is enjoyed by corporate shareholders. The "Names," or owners of Lloyd's, learned they were not protected by corporate status when the company experienced significant losses and the Names were required to pay this money out of their own pockets. Many Names went bankrupt, while others committed suicide.

Extra Solved Problem 7-1

Chapter 7 in the textbook includes two Solved Problems. Here is another Solved Problem to help you build your skills solving economic problems.

Supports Learning Objective 1: Categorize the major types of firms in the United States.

The Risks of Private Enterprise: Lloyd's of London's "Names" and Enron's Shareholders

The first *Making the Connection* of chapter 7 describes the sad fate that befell investors ("Names") in the Lloyd's of London insurance company in the late 1980s and 1990s. Another section of the chapter described the scandal that drove Enron into bankruptcy in 2002 and caused billions of dollars in shareholder losses.

a. What characteristics of each firm's form of business organization were responsible for the financial losses suffered by the owners of these two firms?

b. How did the nature of these losses differ for each firm?

SOLVING THE PROBLEM

Step 1: Review the chapter material.
This problem is about firms and corporate governance, so you may want to review "Types of Firms," which begins on page 210 in the textbook, and the section "Corporate Governance Policy," which begins on page 221.

Step 2: Evaluate the losses suffered by investors in Lloyd's of London and the characteristic of the firm's form of business organization that was responsible for the size of these losses.
Making the Connection "What's in a "Name"? Lloyd's of London Learns about Unlimited Liability the Hard Way" describes Lloyd's of London as a partnership. A disadvantage of a partnership, as well as sole proprietorships, is the unlimited personal liability of the owners of the firm. The liability Lloyd's partners, or Names, incurred went beyond the amount of funds they invested in the company. Therefore, when the insurance company was hit with a series of financial losses, some of the Names suffered severe personal financial losses.

Step 3: Evaluate the losses suffered by Enron shareholders and the characteristic of the firm's form of business organization that was responsible for these losses.
Although Enron eventually became bankrupt, its shareholders' losses were limited to the amount of funds they had invested in the firm. But the management of Enron was able to engage in highly questionable business practices, the consequences of which were hidden through misleading financial statements. This is a manifestation of the principal-agent problem. The separation of management and ownership inherent in a corporate form of

organization allowed Enron's managers to pursue strategies contrary to the interests of the firm's shareholders.

7.2 LEARNING OBJECTIVE

7.2 The Structure of Corporations and the Principal-Agent Problem (pages 212-214)

Learning Objective 2 Describe the typical management structure of corporations and understand the concepts of separation of ownership from control and the principal-agent problem.

Corporate governance is the way corporations are structured and the effect that structure has on the firm's behavior. Shareholders in a corporation elect a board of directors to represent their interests. The board of directors appoints a chief executive officer (CEO) to run day-to-day operations and may appoint other top managers. Managers may serve on the board of directors (they are referred to as inside directors). Outside directors are directors who do not have a management role in the firm. In corporations, there is a **separation of ownership from control.** In most large corporations the top management, rather than the shareholders, control day-to-day operations. The separation of ownership from control is an example of a **principal-agent problem**, a problem caused by an agent pursuing his own interests rather than the interests of the principal who hired him.

Helpful Study Hint

Although the principal-agent problem is a serious one, managers who pursue their own goals at the expense of the firm's best interests risk the scrutiny of institutional investors (for example, mutual funds and pension funds). Unlike many shareholders who have modest stock holdings, institutional investors may hold a significant percentage of a firm's outstanding shares. These large investors can (and sometimes do) demand that a board of directors make strategic or personnel changes if the firm's performance is unsatisfactory, and they may cause a drop in share prices by selling some or all of their stock holdings.

Read ***Solved Problem 7-2*** in the main text to strengthen your understanding of the principal-agent problem. This Solved Problem explains how the principal-agent problem is easily extended to the relationship between management and workers. Managers would like workers to work as hard as possible, while workers would sometimes prefer to shirk. It may be difficult for management to determine whether a worker is working sufficiently hard or not.

7.3 How Firms Raise Funds (pages 214-218)

Learning Objective 3 Explain how firms obtain the funds they need to operate and expand.

To finance expansion, firms can use some of their profits, called retained earnings, rather than pay the profits to owners as dividends. Firms may obtain external funds in two ways. **Indirect finance** is the flow of funds from savers to borrowers through financial intermediaries such as banks. Intermediaries raise funds from savers to lend to firms and other borrowers. **Direct finance** is the flow of funds from savers to firms through financial markets. Direct finance usually takes the form of the borrower selling a financial security to a lender.

A financial security is a document that states the terms under which the funds have passed from the buyer of the security to the borrower. There are two main types of financial securities. A **bond** is a financial security that represents a promise to repay a fixed amount of funds. When a firm sells a bond to raise funds, it promises to pay the purchaser of the bond an interest payment each year for the term of the loan as well as the final payment (or principal) of the loan. The interest payments on a bond are referred to as **coupon payments**. The **interest rate** is the cost of borrowing funds, usually expressed as a percentage of the amount borrowed. If the coupon is expressed as a percentage of the face value of the bond, we have the coupon rate of the bond.

If the face value of a bond is $1,000 and the annual interest payment on the bond is $60, then the coupon rate is

$$\frac{\$60}{\$1{,}000} = 0.06 \text{ or } 10 \text{ percent}$$

A **stock** is a financial security that represents partial ownership of a firm. As an owner of the firm, a shareholder is entitled to a share of the corporation's profits. Management decides how much profit to reinvest in the firm (retained earnings). The remaining profits are paid to stockholders as **dividends**. Owners receive **capital gains** when there are increases in the price of a firm's shares.

There is a broad market for previously owned stocks and bonds. Changes in the prices of these financial instruments represent future expectations of the profits likely to be earned by the firms that issued them. Changes in the prices of bonds issued by a corporation reflect investors' perceptions of the firm's ability to make interest payments as well as the prices of newly issued bonds. A previously issued bond with a coupon payment of $80 and a principal of $1,000 is less attractive than a newly issued bond with a coupon payment of $100 and a principal of $1,000. The price of the previously issued bond must fall, and its interest rate must rise, to induce investors to buy it.

Helpful Study Hint

The double taxation of corporate profits—once via the corporate profits tax and again via the income tax on shareholders' dividends—gives corporations an incentive to raise funds more through debt (bonds) than equity (stocks). Some economists have criticized the corporation profits tax because it gives corporations an incentive to incur debt solely to reduce taxes.

Don't Let This Happen to YOU! "When Google Shares Change Hands, Google Doesn't Get the Money" explains the difference between primary and secondary markets for stocks and bonds. In the primary market, stocks and bonds are sold by the issuing companies and the issuing company receives the funds. In the secondary market, stocks and bonds are resold by investors and the investors receive the funds from the sales.

Making the Connection "Following Abercrombie and Fitch's Stock Price in the Financial Pages" provides a thorough explanation of how to read the stock pages in the newspaper using Abercrombie and Fitch as an example.

Extra Solved Problem **7-3**

Chapter 7 in the textbook includes two Solved Problems. Here is an extra Solved Problem to help you build your skills solving economic problems.

Supports Learning Objective 3: Explain how firms obtain the funds they need to operate and expand.

Google's Stocks

On October 25, 2007, Google's stock closed at a price of $668.51 per share and the trading volume for the day was 5,789,704. The trading volume is the number of shares that traded on the secondary market for that day.

a. How much financial capital did the trading of these stocks raise for Google to use for expansion?

b. How could Google raise additional funds for growth?

SOLVING THE PROBLEM

Step 1: **Review the chapter material.**
This problem is about how firms raise funds, so you may want to review the section "How Firms Raise Funds," which begins on page 214 in the textbook.

Step 2: **Discuss the secondary market for stocks and the impact on funds available for Google to expand.**
In the feature *Don't Let This Happen to YOU!* entitled "When Google Shares Change Hands, Google Doesn't Get the Money" you will find a description of secondary markets. The majority of stocks that are bought and sold on a daily basis are being traded in the secondary market. Trading in the secondary market does not raise additional funds for Google.

Step 3: **Consider the options that Google has to raise funds for growth.**
There are three main options for a firm to obtain funds for growth. A firm can save some of its profits, called retained earnings. They can borrow money from a bank. Or they can issue more stocks or bonds and sell them directly to the public. All of these options are available to Google.

Source: http://quotes.nasdaq.com/asp/summaryquote.asp?symbol=GOOG%60&selected=GOOG%60

7.4 **LEARNING** OBJECTIVE

7.4 Using Financial Statements to Evaluate a Corporation (pages 219-221)

Learning Objective 4 Understand the information provided in corporations' financial statements.

A firm must accurately disclose its financial condition to enable potential investors to make informed decisions about the firm's stock and bond offerings. The Securities and Exchange Commission (SEC) requires publicly owned firms to report their performance according to generally accepted accounting principles.

There are two main types of financial statements. An **income statement** is a financial statement that sums up a firm's revenues, costs, and profit over a period of time. The income statement is used to compute the firm's **accounting profit**, which is the firm's net income measured by revenue minus operating expenses and taxes paid. A **balance sheet** is a financial statement that sums up a firm's financial position on a particular day, usually the end of a quarter or year. The balance sheet summarizes a firm's assets and liabilities. An **asset** is anything of value owned by a person or a firm. A **liability** is anything owed by a person or a firm. The difference between the value of assets and liabilities is the firm's net worth.

Helpful Study Hint

Making the Connection "A Bull in China's Financial Shop" explains that although China is experiencing economic growth, its financial markets are still struggling to perform efficiently. Loans for investment and future growth are typically being made to those with political connections, rather than those firms that would receive the funds in a well-functioning financial market. There are a significant number of loans going unpaid being funds are being allocated on the basis of political connections rather than economic efficiency. Many economists doubt whether the Chinese economy can continue its rapid growth without efficient financial markets.

Extra Solved Problem **7-4**

Chapter 7 in the textbook includes two Solved Problems. Here is an extra Solved Problem to help you build your skills solving economic problems.

Supports Learning Objective 4: Understand the information provided in corporations' financial statements.

Accounting Profit versus Economic Profit

Suppose that Sally decides to open a business. Opening Sally's Sassy Salon will cost $200,000 for the necessary capital equipment. Sally is considering two options for financing her new beauty salon. The first option she is considering is to borrow $100,000 and take $100,000 from her savings. The second option is to take $200,000 from her savings to start the business. Suppose that her savings account is earning 5 percent interest and the loan that her bank offered her also has a 5 percent interest rate.

a. What is the explicit cost of opening Sally's Sassy Salon is she chooses the first option? If she chooses the second option? What is the implicit cost of opening Sally's Sassy Salon using the first option? The second option?

b. Which option will give Sally the higher economic profit? The higher accounting profit?

SOLVING THE PROBLEM

Step 1: **Review the chapter material.**
This problem is about financial statements, so you may want to review the section "Using Financial Statements to Evaluate a Corporation," which begins on page beginning on page 219 in the textbook.

Step 2: **Determine the implicit and explicit costs of each option.**
The explicit costs would be costs that require an outlay of money, for example, the interest on the loan, and the implicit costs would be the foregone interest on her savings. The first option has an explicit cost of 0.05 x $100,000 = $5,000 and an implicit cost of 0.05 x $100,000 = $5,000. The second option has no explicit cost and has 0.05 x $200,000 = $10,000 in implicit costs.

Step 3: **Evaluate the economic and accounting profit for Sally's Sassy Salon.**
Assuming that her revenue will be unaffected by her choice of how she finances her new firm, we can see that the explicit cost of the second option is lower than the first option. This means that the second option would have a higher accounting profit. If we consider all of the costs, both explicit and implicit, then we are calculating the economic profit. In this case, the explicit cost plus implicit cost is the same for both options, so the economic profit would be the same for either option.

7.5 LEARNING OBJECTIVE

7.5 Corporate Governance Policy (pages 221-224)

Learning Objective 5 Understand the role of government in corporate governance.

During 2001 and 2002, the importance of providing accurate financial information through financial statements was illustrated by several major financial scandals. The Sarbanes-Oxley Act of 2002 was passed in response to these scandals. The act requires corporate directors and chief executive officers to have greater accountability for the accuracy of their firms' financial statements. The Sarbanes-Oxley Act created a Public Company Accounting Oversight Board to oversee the auditing of public companies' financial reports.

Helpful Study Hint

One result, likely an unintended one, of the Sarbanes-Oxley Act was to increase the demand for newly hired accountants. For example, the accounting firm Ernst and Young hired 4,500 undergraduate accounting students in 2005, an increase of 30 percent from the previous year.

Source: "Jobs: Accountants are kings among grads," *CNNMoney*, June 5, 2005. http://money.cnn.com/2005/06/pf/accountant.jobs.reut/index.htm?ccc=yes

Solved Problem 7-5 describes the characteristics of a good board of directors. The majority of the board should be independent outsiders who have no business connections with the firm. The auditing and compensation committees should be made up entirely of outsiders in order to protect the best interest of the shareholders. The directors who are affiliated with the firm should own stock because, as stockholders, they will share the same goal as other stockholders to maximize profits.

Helpful Study Hint

Economics in YOUR Life! asked if owning stock in a company such as Google is risky. The principal-agent problem adds to your risk. But the rewards to owning stock can also be substantial because you are likely to earn a higher return on your investment over the long run than if you had put your money in a bank account. Buying stock of well-known companies, such as Google, that are closely followed by Wall Street investment analysts helps to reduce the principal-agent problem.

Key Terms

Accounting profit. A firm's net income measured by revenue less operating expenses and taxes paid.

Asset. Anything of value owned by a person or a firm.

Balance sheet. A financial statement that sums up a firm's financial position on a particular day, usually the end of a quarter or a year.

Bond. A financial security that represents a promise to repay a fixed amount of funds.

Corporate governance. The way in which a corporation is structured and the effect a corporation's structure has on the firm's behavior.

Corporation. A legal form of business that provides the owners with limited liability.

Coupon payment. An interest payment on a bond.

Direct finance. A flow of funds from savers to firms through financial markets, such as the New York Stock Exchange.

Dividends. Payments by a corporation to its shareholders.

Economic profit. A firm's revenues minus all of its costs, implicit and explicit.

Explicit cost. A cost that involves spending money.

Implicit cost. A nonmonetary opportunity cost.

Income statement. A financial statement that sums up a firm's revenues, costs, and profit over a period of time.

Indirect finance. A flow of funds from savers to borrowers through financial intermediaries such as banks. Intermediaries raise funds from savers to lend to firms (and other borrowers).

Interest rate. The cost of borrowing funds, usually expressed as a percentage of the amount borrowed.

Liability. Anything owed by a person or a firm.

Limited liability. The legal provision that shields owners of a corporation from losing more than they have invested in the firm.

Opportunity cost. The highest-valued alternative that must be given up to engage in an activity.

Partnership. A firm owned jointly by two or more persons and not organized as a corporation.

Present value. The value in today's dollars of funds to be paid or received in the future.

Principal-agent problem. A problem caused by an agent pursuing his own interests rather than the interests of the principal who hired him.

Separation of ownership from control. A situation in a corporation in which the top management, rather than the shareholders, control day-to-day operations.

Sole proprietorship. A firm owned by a single individual and not organized as a corporation.

Stock. A financial security that represents partial ownership of a firm.

Stockholders' equity. The difference between the value of a corporation's assets and the value of its liabilities; also known as net worth.

Appendix

Tools to Analyze Firms' Financial Information (pages 233-241)

LEARNING OBJECTIVE: Understand the concept of present value and the information contained on a firm's income statement and balance sheet.

Using Present Value to Make Investment Decisions

Most people value funds they have today more highly than funds they will receive in the future. **Present value** is the value in today's dollars of funds to be paid or received in the future. Someone who lends money expects to be paid back the amount of the loan and some additional interest. If someone lends $1,000 for one year at 10 percent interest, the value of money received in the future is:

$$\$1{,}000 \times (1 + 0.10) = \$1{,}100$$

Dividing this expression by (1 + 0.10) and adjusting terms:

$$\$1{,}000 = \frac{\$1{,}000}{(1.10)}$$

Writing this more generally:

$$\text{Present Value} = \frac{\text{Future Value}}{(1+i)}$$

The present value formula for funds received any number of years in the future (*n* represents the number of years) is:

$$\text{Present Value} = \frac{\text{Future Value}}{(1+i)^n}$$

The present value formula can be used to calculate the price of a financial asset. The price of a financial asset should be equal to the present value of the payments to be received from owning that asset. The general formula for the price of a bond is:

$$\text{Bond Price} = \frac{\text{Coupon}_1}{(1+i)^1} + \frac{\text{Coupon}_2}{(1+i)^2} + \ldots + \frac{\text{Coupon}_n}{(1+i)^n} + \frac{\text{Face Value}_n}{(1+i)^n}$$

In this formula,

Coupon_1 is the coupon payment, or interest payment, to be received after one year.
Coupon_2 is the coupon payment after two years.

$Coupon_n$ is the coupon payment in the year the bond matures.
Face Value is the face value of the bond to be received when the bond matures.
The interest rate on comparable newly issued bonds is *i*.

The price of a share of stock should be equal to the present value of the dividends, or the profits paid to shareholders, investors expect to receive as a result of owning the stock. The general formula for the price of a stock is:

$$\text{Stock Price} = \frac{\text{Dividend}_1}{(1+i)} + \frac{\text{Dividend}_2}{(1+i)^2} + \ldots$$

Unlike a bond, a stock has no maturity date, so the stock price is the present value of an infinite number of dividend payments. Unlike coupon payments which are written on the bond and can't be changed, dividend payments are uncertain. If dividends grow at a constant rate, the formula for determining the price of a stock is:

$$\text{Stock Price} = \frac{\text{Dividend}}{(i\text{-Growth Rate})}$$

Dividend refers to the dividend currently received and Growth Rate is the rate at which dividends are expected to grow.

Going Deeper Into Financial Statements

Corporations disclose substantial information about their business operations and financial position to investors. This information is provided for two reasons. First, participants in financial markets demand the information. Second, some of this information meets the requirements of the U.S. Securities and Exchange Commission. The key sources of information about a corporation's profitability and financial position are its income statement and balance sheet. Income statements summarize a firm's revenues, costs and profit over a time period (for example, one year). These statements list the firm's revenues and its cost of revenue (also called its costs of sales or cost of goods sold). The difference between a firm's revenues and costs is its profit. Operating income is the difference between revenue and operating expenses. Investment income is income earned on holdings of investments such as government and corporate bonds. The net income firms report on income statements is referred to as their after-tax accounting profit.

A balance sheet summarizes a firm's financial position on a particular day. An asset is anything of value owned by the firm. A liability is a debt or obligation owed by the firm. **Stockholders' equity** is the difference between the value of a corporation's assets and the value of its liabilities, also known as net worth. Balance sheets list assets on the left side and liabilities and new worth or stockholders' equity on the right side. The value on the left side of the balance sheet must equal the value on the right side. Current assets are assets the firm could convert into cash quickly. Goodwill represents the difference between the purchase price of a company and the market value of its assets. Current liabilities are short-term debts. Long-term liabilities include long-term bank loans and outstanding corporate bonds.

Key Terms – Appendix

Present value. The value in today's dollars of funds to be paid or received in the future.

Stockholders' equity. The difference between the value of a corporation's assets and the value of its liabilities; also known as net worth.

Self-Test

(Answers are provided at the end of the Self-Test.)

Multiple-Choice Questions

1. Which of the following statements is true?
   a. In the United States most firms are organized as corporations.
   b. In the United States there are more partnerships than sole proprietorships.
   c. In the United States corporations account for the majority of total revenue and profits earned by all firms.
   d. All of the above

2. Which of the following types of firms have limited liability?
   a. A corporation
   b. A sole proprietorship
   c. A partnership
   d. All of the above

3. Which of the following sets of firms are likely to be partnerships?
   a. Technology and telecommunications firms
   b. Law and accounting firms
   c. Public utilities, such as the power company and the gas company
   d. All of the above

4. Which of the following is true about liability for a corporation?
   a. The owners of a corporation have limited liability.
   b. The owners of a corporation have unlimited liability.
   c. The owners of a corporation may or may not be subject to unlimited liability.
   d. The owners of a corporation do not face any constraints with regard to liability issues.

5. In which of the following cases is there a legal distinction between the personal assets of the owners of the firm and the assets of the firm?
   a. Sole proprietorships
   b. Partnerships
   c. Corporations
   d. In both the case of sole proprietorships and the case of partnerships

6. When a corporation fails, which of the following is true?
   a. The owners can always lose more than the amount they invested in the firm.
   b. The owners can never lose more than the amount they had invested in the firm.
   c. The owners will always lose less than the amount they had invested in the firm.
   d. What the owners lose is unrelated to liability laws.

7. In the United States, how many times are corporate profits taxed?
   a. Once
   b. Twice
   c. Three times
   d. Often more than three times

8. Refer to the Figure 7-1 in the textbook. Which type of firms account for the majority of revenue earned in the United States in 2007?
   a. Sole proprietorships
   b. Corporations
   c. Partnerships
   d. None of the above

9. Refer to the Figure 7-1 in the textbook. Which type of firm accounts for the majority of the profits earned by different business organizations in the United States in 2007?
   a. Sole proprietorships
   b. Partnerships
   c. Corporations
   d. None of the above

10. Fill in the blanks. According to the textbook, there are more than _________ corporations in the United States, but only _________ have annual revenues of more than $50 million.
    a. 20 million; 1.2 million
    b. 18 million; 2 million
    c. 8 million; 10,000
    d. 5 million; 26,000

11. How much of the total corporate profits in the United States is earned by large firms?
    a. About 10 percent of all U.S. corporate profits
    b. One-half of all U.S. corporate profits
    c. Almost 85 percent of all U.S. corporate profits
    d. 99 percent of all U.S. corporate profits

12. What is *corporate governance*?
    a. Corporate governance is a structure imposed on all corporations by the Securities and Exchange Commission.
    b. Corporate governance is the way in which corporations are structured and the impact a corporation's structure has on the firm's behavior.
    c. Corporate governance is the division of business firms between proprietorships, partnerships, and corporations.
    d. Corporate governance is the relationship between corporations and the government officials in the states in which firms operate.

13. What term do economists use to refer to the conflict between the interests of shareholders and the interests of top management?
    a. Corporate governance
    b. A principal-agent problem
    c. Gold plating
    d. Capture theory

14. How can a firm obtain the funds for an expansion?
    a. By reinvesting profits
    b. By taking on one or more partners who would invest in the firm
    c. By borrowing funds from relatives, friends, or a bank
    d. All of the above

15. Which of the following refers to a flow of funds from savers to firms through financial markets?
    a. Indirect finance
    b. Direct finance
    c. Business finance
    d. Financial borrowing

16. What is the name given to the interest payments on a bond?
    a. Coupon payments
    b. The cost of borrowing funds
    c. The face value of the bond
    d. Capital gains

17. What are the payments by a corporation to its shareholders?
    a. Stocks
    b. Dividends
    c. Retained earnings
    d. Interest

18. Which instruments account for most of the funds raised by borrowers in the United States?
    a. Equity instruments
    b. Debt instruments
    c. Capital instruments
    d. Secondary-market instruments

19. According to the textbook, which of the following are valuable sources of information for corporations that are considering raising funds?
    a. Primary markets
    b. Secondary markets
    c. Tertiary markets
    d. All markets equally

20. What are markets in which newly issued claims are sold to initial buyers by the borrower called?
    a. Primary markets
    b. Secondary markets
    c. Tertiary markets
    d. Initial public offerings

21. In the United States, what market trades the stocks and bonds of the largest corporations?
    a. The Nasdaq
    b. The New York Stock Exchange
    c. The American Stock Exchange
    d. The Chicago Board of Trade

22. Which of the following is the most important of the over-the-counter markets?
    a. The New York Stock Exchange
    b. The American Stock Exchange
    c. The Nasdaq
    d. The S & P 500

23. In the United States the Securities and Exchange Commission requires publicly owned firms to report their performance in financial statements using standard methods. What are these methods called?
    a. Standard and Poor's Accounting Standards
    b. Generally accepted accounting principles
    c. Moody's Investors Service Standards
    d. U.S. Standard Financial Practices

24. If investors are more optimistic about the firm's profit prospects, and the firm's managers want to expand the firm's operations as a result, what will happen to the price of the company's stock?
    a. It will rise.
    b. It will fall.
    c. It will remain constant.
    d. It may rise for a while, then fall.

25. If a bond has a face value of $1,000 and pays a coupon of $70 per year, what is the coupon rate?
    a. 70
    b. $7
    c. 7%
    d. 70%

26. To answer the three basic questions: what to produce, how to produce it, and what price to charge, what does a firm's management need to know?
    a. The firm's revenues and costs
    b. The value of the property and other assets the firm owns
    c. The firm's debts, or other liabilities, that it owes to another person or business
    d. All of the above

27. Which of the following sums up a firm's revenues, costs, and profit over a period of time?
    a. The balance sheet
    b. The income statement
    c. The firm's accounting profit
    d. The firm's economic profit

28. An *income statement* starts with the firm's revenue and subtracts its expenses and taxes paid. What is the remainder called?
    a. Net income, which is the accounting profit of the firm
    b. Gross income, which is the economic profit of the firm
    c. Implicit cost
    d. Explicit cost

29. Which of the following is considered an *explicit cost*?
   a. The cost of labor
   b. The cost of materials
   c. The cost of electricity
   d. All of the above

30. What term do economists use to refer to the minimum amount that investors must earn on the funds they invest in a firm, expressed as a percentage of the amount invested?
   a. Opportunity cost
   b. The normal rate of return
   c. Explicit cost
   d. Economic profit

31. Accounting profit is equal to which of the following?
   (i) Total revenue – explicit costs
   (ii) Total revenue – opportunity costs
   (iii) Economic profit + implicit costs
   a. (i) only
   b. (ii) only
   c. (iiii) only
   d. (i) and (iii) only

32. In which of the following industries do investors require a higher rate of return?
   a. In more risky industries
   b. In less risky industries
   c. In more established industries, such as electric utilities
   d. In any industry; investors always need to receive high rates of return regardless of the type of investment or the risk involved.

33. Which of the following statements is correct?
   a. Economic profit equals the firm's revenues minus its explicit costs.
   b. Accounting profit equals the firm's revenues minus all of its costs, implicit and explicit.
   c. Accounting profit is larger than economic profit.
   d. All of the above

34. What is a balance sheet?
   a. A summary of a firm's financial position on a particular day
   b. A summary of revenues, costs, and profit over a particular period of time
   c. A firm's net income measured by revenue less operating expenses and taxes paid
   d. A list of anything owed by a person or business

35. What do you obtain by subtracting the value of a firm's liabilities from the value of its assets?
   a. Income
   b. Net worth
   c. Economic profit
   d. Accounting profit

36. Which set of incentives does the top management of a corporation have?
    a. An incentive to attract investors and to keep the firm's stock price high
    b. An incentive to attract investors and to keep the firm's stock price low
    c. An incentive to discourage investors and to keep the firm's stock price high
    d. An incentive to discourage investors and to keep the firm's stock price low

37. Which of the following is true? Top managers who are determined to cheat and hide the true financial condition of their firms can
    a. easily deceive investors, but never outside auditors.
    b. deceive outside auditors, but never investors.
    c. deceive investors, and sometimes also deceive outside auditors.
    d. deceive other managers, but never the company's investors or its outside auditors.

38. The landmark Sarbanes-Oxley Act of 2002 strengthened the expertise with financial information required of corporate directors and mandated that
    a. chief executive officers personally certify the accuracy of financial statements.
    b. financial analysts and auditors shall disclose whether any conflicts of interest might exist that could limit their independence in evaluating a firm's financial condition.
    c. managers shall be held accountable and face stiff penalties (including long jail sentences) for not meeting their responsibilities.
    d. All of the above

39. The creation of the Public Company Accounting Oversight Board is the most noticeable corporate governance reform under the Sarbanes-Oxley Act. What is the mission of this special national board?
    a. To oversee the auditing of public companies' financial reports
    b. To oversee the writing of financial reports
    c. To oversee the behavior of corporate officers
    d. All of the above

40. What does the term "insiders" refer to in the realm of corporate management?
    a. Insiders are auditors who have access to the corporation's financial statements.
    b. Insiders are members of top management who also serve on the board of directors.
    c. Insiders are managers who have connections with people on independent auditing boards.
    d. An insider is anyone who is not part of a public corporation but who knows something that the public at large does not know.

Short Answer Questions

1. Owners of successful sole proprietorships may choose to become corporations in order to raise money to finance expansion and limit the owner's liability. But this will also subject the firm to the principal-agent problem. Why don't sole proprietorships face the principal-agent problem?

____

____

____

2. Why did the passage of the Sarbanes-Oxley Act lead to an increase in the demand for accountants?

3. In addition to salary and benefits, the compensation of the top managers of many corporations often includes of shares of company stock or options to buy the stock at a favorable price. Why?

4. Explain why a firm that reports a profit on its income statement may suffer an economic loss.

5. Publicly owned firms in the United States are required to report their performance in financial statements using generally accepted accounting principles. These statements are examined closely by private firms and investors. Why did the public disclosure of the statements of Enron and WorldCom fail to provide investors with advance warning of serious financial problems that resulted in billions of dollars of shareholders' losses?

True/False Questions

T F 1. In the United States, Standard and Poor's requires publicly owned firms to report their performance in financial statements.

T F 2. If investors expect a firm to earn economic profits, the firm's share price will rise, providing a dividend for shareholders.

T F 3. Indirect finance refers to raising funds through financial intermediaries such as banks.

T F 4. A disadvantage of organizing a firm as a sole proprietorship or a partnership is that owners have limited liability.

T F 5. A disadvantage of organizing a firm as a corporation is that the firm is subject to the principal-agent problem.

T F 6. Profits that are reinvested in a firm rather than paid to the firm's owners are called retained earnings.

T F 7. The most important of the so-called "over-the-counter" stock markets is the New York Stock Exchange.

T F 8. The value someone gives today to money she will receive in the future is called the future payment's present value.

T F 9. The price of a bond is equal to the present value of dividends, or the profits paid out by the firm that issues the bond.

T F 10. The unexpected rise in the price of Google stock in 2004 led to the passage of the Sarbanes-Oxley Act.

T F 11. Over 70 percent of firms in the United States are sole proprietorships.

T F 12. The day-to-day operations of a corporation are run by the firm's board of directors.

T F 13. An advantage of organizing a firm as a partnership is that the partners share the risks of owning the firm.

T F 14. The legal and financial problems incurred by Enron, WorldCom, and other well-known firms were due to the unlimited liability of the firms' owners.

T F 15. Economic profit is equal to a firm's revenue minus its operating expenses and taxes paid for a given time period.

Answers to the Self-Test

Multiple-Choice Questions

Question	Answer	Explanation
1	c	Based on data for 2007, corporations accounted for 84 percent of revenue and 59 percent of the profits earned by all firms in the United States. See Figure 7-1.
2	a	The owners of corporations have limited liability, while sole proprietorships and partnerships have unlimited liability. Read page 210 in the textbook.
3	b	Partnerships are firms owned jointly by two or more—sometimes many—persons. Most law and accounting firms are partnerships.
4	a	Most large firms are organized as corporations. A corporation is a legal form of business that provides the owners with limited liability.
5	c	Unlimited liability means there is no legal distinction between the personal assets of the owners of the firm and the assets of the firm. In sole proprietorships and partnerships, the owners are not legally distinct from the firms they own.
6	b	Limited liability is the legal provision that shields owners of a corporation from losing more than they have invested in the firm.

7	b	Corporate profits are taxed twice—once at the corporate level and again when investors receive a share of corporate profits, or (revenues less expenses).
8	b	Although only 20 percent of all firms are corporations, corporations account for the majority of revenue and profits earned by all firms.
9	c	Corporations account for a majority of the total revenue and profits earned by businesses.
10	d	There are more than 5 million corporations in the United States, but only 26,000 have annual revenues of more than $50 million. We can think of these 26,000 firms—including Microsoft, General Electric, and Exxon-Mobil—as representing "big business."
11	c	There are more than 5 million corporations in the United States, but only 26,000 have annual revenues of more than $50 million. We can think of these 26,000 firms—including Microsoft, General Electric, and Exxon-Mobil—as representing "big business." These large firms account for almost 85 percent of all U.S. corporate profits.
12	b	The way in which corporations are structured and the impact a corporation's structure has on the firm's behavior is referred to as corporate governance.
13	b	The fact that top managers do not own the entire firm means they may have an incentive to decrease the firm's profits by spending money to purchase private jets or schedule management meetings at luxurious resorts. This problem occurs when agents—in this case, a firm's top management—pursue their own interests rather than the interests of the principal who hired them—in this case, the shareholders of the corporation.
14	d	All of the above are ways in which firms raise the funds they need to expand operations.
15	b	A flow of funds from savers to firms through financial markets is known as direct finance. Direct finance usually takes the form of the borrower selling the lender a financial security.
16	a	A coupon payment is the interest payment on a bond, usually expressed as a percentage of the amount borrowed.
17	b	Dividends are payments by a corporation to its shareholders.
18	b	Although you hear about the stock market fluctuations each night on the evening news, debt instruments actually account for more of the funds raised by borrowers. In mid-2004, the value of debt instruments in the United States was about $20 trillion compared to $12 trillion for equities.
19	b	According to the textbook, secondary markets are valuable sources of information for corporations that are considering raising funds.
20	a	Primary markets are those in which newly issued claims are sold to initial buyers by the borrower.
21	b	In the United States, the stocks and bonds of the largest corporations are traded on the New York Stock Exchange.
22	c	The stocks of many computer and other high-technology firms—including Microsoft and Intel—are traded on the Nasdaq.
23	b	In most high-income countries, government agencies establish standard requirements for information that is disclosed in order for publicly owned firms to sell stocks and bonds. In the United States this government agency is the Securities and Exchange Commission. To maintain consistency, all firms are required to use generally accepted accounting principles.

24	a	Changes in the value of a firm's stocks and bonds offer important information for a firm's managers, as well as for investors. An increase in the stock price means that investors are more optimistic about the firm's profit prospects, and the firm's managers may wish to expand the firm's operations as a result.
25	c	The coupon rate is always expressed as a percentage of the face value. If the face value is $1,000 and this corporate bond pays a coupon of $70.00 per year, then the coupon rate is 7.00 percent.
26	d	To answer these questions, a firm's management needs the following information: The firm's revenues and costs, the value of the property and other assets the firm owns, and the firm's debts, or other liabilities that it owes to another person or business.
27	b	A firm's income statement sums up the firm's revenues, costs, and profits over a period of time.
28	a	A firm's net income is revenue less expenses and taxes paid in a given time period.
29	d	Firms pay explicit labor costs to employees. They have many other explicit costs as well, such as the cost of the electricity used to light their office buildings.
30	b	Economists refer to the minimum amount that investors must earn on the funds they invest in a firm, expressed as a percentage of the amount invested, as a normal rate of return.
31	d	You can calculate accounting profit by taking the revenue and subtracting out the explicit costs. This is equivalent to taking economic profit and adding back in the implicit costs.
32	a	The necessary rate of return that investors must receive to continue investing in a firm varies from firm to firm. If the investment is risky, investors will require a high rate of return to compensate them for the risk.
33	c	Because accounting profit excludes some implicit costs, it will be larger than economic profit.
34	a	A firm's balance sheet sums up its financial position on a particular day, usually the end of a quarter or a year.
35	b	We can think of the net worth as what the firm's owners would be left with if the firm were closed, its assets were sold, and its liabilities were paid off. Investors can determine a firm's net worth by inspecting its balance sheet.
36	a	The top management of a firm has at least two reasons to attract investors and keep the firm's stock price high. First, a higher stock price increases the funds the firm can raise when it sells a given amount of stock. Second, to reduce the principal-agent problem, boards of directors will often tie the salaries of top managers to the firm's stock price or to the profitability of the firm.
37	c	This is what the textbook argues in "Corporate Governance Poly," beginning on page 221 in the textbook.
38	d	Each of the responses is a provision of the Sarbanes-Oxley Act.
39	a	The board's mission is to promote the independence of auditors to ensure they disclose accurate information.
40	b	"Insiders" are members of top management who also serve on the board of directors.

Short Answer Responses

1. The principal-agent problem is used to describe the consequence of separating ownership and management. There is no such division with a sole proprietorship and no principal-agent problem because the principal is also the agent!

2. The Act requires senior executives of publicly owned firms to have greater accountability for the accuracy of their firms' reporting and created a board to oversee the auditing of companies' financial reports. Because of the financial scandals of 2001 and 2002, there is a demand on the part of government officials and analysts for transparent and accurate financial information.

3. Tying the compensation of managers to the stock price of the firms they manage provides a greater incentive to pursue strategies that enhance profitability. Members of corporate boards of directors choose this form of compensation, in part, in response to the principal-agent problem.

4. An income statement reports a firm's accounting profit, which is net income measured by revenue minus explicit costs—operating expenses and taxes paid—over a period of time. Since the income statement does not account for the implicit costs incurred by the firm, accounting profit will be greater than economic profit. Remember, economic profit is computed by subtracting both explicit and implicit costs from total revenue.

5. Ultimately the accuracy of a firm's statements is dependent on the integrity of corporate officials and the accountants who audit these statements. There is strong evidence that some corporate officials deliberately chose to provide incomplete and misleading information in their financial statements in order to persuade analysts that their firms were more profitable than the actually were.

True/False Answers

1. F This is the responsibility of the Securities and Exchange Commission.
2. F An increase in the share price results in a capital gain.
3. T This is the definition of indirect finance.
4. F These firms have unlimited liability.
5. T The managers of a corporation are typically not the owners, so the principal-agent problem is likely to arise.
6. T This is the definition of retained earnings.
7. F The most important "over-the-counter" market is the National Association of Securities Dealers' Automated Quotation System (NASDAQ).
8. T See the definition of present values in the Appendix to Chapter 7.
9. F This statement confuses stocks with bonds.
10. F The Sarbanes-Oxley Act came about to prevent future accounting scandals like those of Enron and WorldCom in 2001.
11. T See Figure 7-1 on page 212.
12. F The Chief Executive Officer of a corporation is appointed by the Board of Directors to conduct the day-to-day operations.
13. T See pages 210 and 211.
14. F The legal problems resulted due to the stock incentive system associated with top management's pay. The capital gains and dividends that these managers received on their own units of stock were higher due to their manipulation of the accounting information.
15. F This is the definition of accounting profit.

Chapter 8

Comparative Advantage and the Gains from International Trade

Chapter Summary

Over the past 50 years, international trade has grown significantly as many governments reached agreements to reduce tariffs and other trade barriers. In Chapter 2, you learned about comparative advantage. **Comparative advantage** shows that individuals, firms, and countries will be made better off by producing goods and services for which they have a lower opportunity cost than competitors and trading for those goods and services for which they have a higher opportunity cost. Absolute advantage is the ability of an individual, firm, or country to produce more of a good or service than competitors when using the same amount of resources. Nations develop comparative advantages for different reasons including a favorable climate, the availability of natural resources, an abundance of labor or capital, and access to superior production technologies.

On average, countries benefit from trade, but while some firms and workers benefit from international trade, others do not. When a country becomes more open to trade, the profits of firms that produce the same goods that are imported will fall and some of the firms' workers may lose their jobs. Those harmed by trade often lobby their governments to impose import restrictions. Despite the gains that exist from **free trade**, nations still sometimes impose trade restrictions that result in higher prices for traded goods. Trade restrictions usually are in the form of **tariffs, quotas, voluntary export restraints,** and other non-tariff barriers. Although tariffs and quotas save jobs in the countries that impose them, the employment gains often are achieved at a high cost.

After World War II, the United States and Europe negotiated treaties to reduce the high tariff rates imposed during the Great Depression. Recent discussions have focused on expanding trade in services and products that incorporate intellectual property, rather than trade in goods. The **World Trade Organization** (WTO) was established in 1995 to facilitate these negotiations. Opposition to liberalization of international trade and investment, also known as **globalization**, grew in the 1990s. Supporters of the anti-globalization movement want to protect domestic industries from competition and believe globalization unfairly favors the interests of high-income countries.

The United States government has extended protection to some domestic industries due to allegations of dumping by foreign companies. **Dumping** refers to selling a product for a price below its cost of production.

Multinational enterprises conduct operations in more than one nation. They may open offices in a foreign country to avoid tariffs on exports; to gain access to raw materials available in other nations; to gain access to low-cost labor; to minimize foreign exchange risk; and/or to respond to competition from other firms in their industry.

Learning Objectives

When you finish this chapter, you should be able to:

1. **Discuss the role of international trade in the U.S. economy.** From 1950 to 2007, both exports and imports have steadily increased as a fraction of U.S. gross domestic product. Each year, the United States exports about 50 percent of its wheat crop, 40 percent of its rice crop and 20 percent of its corn crop. About 20 percent of U.S. manufacturing jobs depend directly or indirectly on exports.

2. **Understand the difference between comparative advantage and absolute advantage in international trade.** Absolute advantage is the ability of a country to produce more of a good than other countries using the same amount of resources. However, comparative advantage is the key to determining specialization and trade. Countries have a comparative advantage in production when they can produce a good or service at a lower opportunity cost than other producers. Countries are better off if they specialize in producing the goods for which they have a comparative advantage. They can then trade for the goods for which other countries have a comparative advantage.

3. **Explain how countries gain from international trade.** By trading, nations are able to consume more than they could without trade. This is possible because total world production of traded goods increases after trade. Shifting production to the more efficient country – the one with the comparative advantage – increases total production. (Remember, every country has a comparative advantage in producing at least one good or service.) The sources of comparative advantage include a favorable climate or supplies of natural resources; relatively abundant supplies of labor and capital; access to technology; and external economies.

4. **Analyze the economic effects of government policies that restrict international trade.** Government restrictions on international trade, such as tariffs and quotas, reduce the foreign competition faced by domestic firms. By limiting competition, trade restrictions raise the domestic price of a good above the world price. Trade restrictions help domestic producers but harm domestic consumers and reduce economic efficiency. Costs imposed by the high prices paid by consumers almost always exceed the value of the jobs saved by trade barriers.

5. **Evaluate the arguments over trade policy and globalization.** Advocates for policies that restrict trade (protectionism) argue that free trade reduces employment by driving domestic firms out of business and forces firms to pay lower wages to compete with firms in other industries. However, no economic study has found a connection in the long run between the total number of available jobs and the level of protection for domestic industries. Rather than lowering wages, free trade raises living standards by increasing economic efficiency.

Appendix: Understand why firms operate in more than one country. Your instructor may assign this appendix.

Chapter Review

Chapter Opener: Is Using Trade Policy to Help U.S. Industries a Good Idea? (pages 242-243)

Although trading between states in the United States is not controversial, trading between countries meets with a significant amount of opposition. The United States Congress enacted a tariff on Brazilian ethanol, so that this cheaper alternative fuel becomes unaffordable in the United States. There is also a quota on the importation of sugar into the United States in order to preserve jobs in the domestic sugar industry. The quota resulted in higher sugar prices for consumers, including firms, such as candy manufacturers, that use sugar as an input to produce other products. As a result, Life Savers and other candy products are no longer produced in the United States but in other countries where the costs of production are lower.

Helpful Study Hint

Advocates for quotas stress how quotas will increase employment in the protected industry, but minimize their impact on prices and on employment in other industries. Tables 8-5 and 8-6 compare the number of jobs saved and the cost to consumers per year for each of these jobs in different markets as a result of tariffs and quotas. At the end of this chapter, ***An Inside Look*** examines the impact of reducing trade restrictions between the United States and South Korea. If the bilateral agreement is ratified by the governments of both countries, U.S. car consumers and Korean car producers will gain. Likewise, U.S. producers of food and Korean consumers of food will gain. The domestic producers of the goods that will be imported will lose.

Economics in YOUR Life! asks how sugar companies have convinced Congress to enact the sugar quota and why very few people who buy and use sugar have ever heard of the quota. Keep this question in mind as you read the chapter. The authors will answer this question at the end of the chapter.

8.1 LEARNING OBJECTIVE

8.1 The United States in the International Economy (pages 244-247)

Learning Objective 1 Discuss the role of international trade in the U. S. economy.

Imports are goods and services bought domestically but produced in other countries. A **tariff** is a tax imposed by a government on imports. **Exports** are goods and services produced domestically but sold to other countries. Tariff rates in the United States have fallen, and international trade has increased significantly since 1930. The United States is the world's largest exporter, although exports and imports are a smaller fraction of GDP in the United States than in most other countries.

Helpful Study Hint

International trade is a controversial topic among politicians and the general public. You may have formed opinions about trade based on comments made through newspaper and magazine articles and conversations with family and friends. In every country there are winners and losers from international trade. Read ***Making the Connection*** "How Expanding International Trade Has Helped Boeing" for a discussion of how one U.S. firm has benefited from trade. The increase in trade around the world has helped Boeing because the Boeing 747 can be used for long-range freight transportation.

Extra Solved Problem **8-1**

Chapter 8 in the textbook includes two Solved Problems. Here is an extra Solved Problem to help you build your skills solving economic problems.

Supports Learning Objective 1: Discuss the role of international trade in the U. S. economy.

Paper Tariffs Canceled

U.S. manufacturers of glossy paper requested tariffs on glossy paper imported from Chinese firms. This request was made because U.S. firms feel that the subsidies paid by the Chinese government to Chinese paper manufacturers has given them an unfair advantage over U.S. firms. The Bush Administration responded to the concerns of the U.S. producers by imposing tariffs on the imported glossy paper. The U.S. International Trade Commission canceled the tariffs, saying that there was not significant evidence that the U.S. manufacturers had been harmed by the Chinese subsidies.

Source: Steven R. Weisman, "U.S. Trade Panel Rejects Tariff on Chinese Paper," *The International Herald Tribune*, November 22, 2007.

Explain the impact that the tariff on glossy paper would have had on U.S. imports and exports.

Step 1: Review the chapter material.
This problem asks you to interpret the effect of trade on the United States., so you may want to review section "The United States in the International Economy," which begins on 244 of the textbook.

Step 2: Explain the impact on imports and exports if the tariff were to remain in place.
A tariff will cause Chinese glossy paper to become more expensive in the United States. This makes it more difficult for Chinese firms to compete with U.S. firms. The tariff would cause imports to fall and U.S. firms would be able to sell more paper at a higher price. However, U.S. firms that use glossy paper in producing catalogs, calendars, and other products would find their costs rising, which might lead them to raise prices and reduce production and employment.

8.2 LEARNING OBJECTIVE

8.2 Comparative Advantage in International Trade (pages 247-248)

Learning Objective 2 Understand the difference between comparative advantage and absolute advantage in international trade.

Comparative advantage is the ability of an individual, firm or country to produce a good or service at a lower opportunity cost than another individual, firm, or country. Mutually beneficial trade between two parties is possible when they specialize in the production of the goods and services for which they have a comparative advantage and trade for the goods and services for which they have comparative disadvantage in production. Comparative advantage is the basic argument in favor of free domestic as well as free international trade.

Helpful Study Hint

Absolute advantage and comparative advantage were explained in chapter 2 on pages 46-47. Review ***Solved Problem 2-2*** on page 48 from that chapter as well as the example of comparative advantage illustrated in Tables 8-1 and 8-2 on page 248 to ensure you understand these two concepts.

Extra Solved Problem 8-2

Chapter 8 in the textbook includes two Solved Problems. Here is an extra Solved Problem to help you build your skills solving economic problems.

Supports Learning Objective 2: Understand the difference between comparative advantage and absolute advantage in international trade.

Suppose that the United States and China each produce only two goods, wheat and shirts. Further assume that these two countries use only labor to produce the two goods. Use the productivity information in this table to answer the questions below.

	Output per hour of work	
	Wheat	**Shirts**
United States	2 bushels	10 shirts
China	1 bushel	8 shirts

a. Who has the absolute advantage in the production of wheat? Shirts?

b. Who has the comparative advantage in the production of wheat? Shirts? What good should the United States specialize in? What good should China specialize in?

Step 1: Review the chapter material.
This problem is about comparative advantage, so you may want to review the section "Comparative Advantage in International Trade," which begins on page 247 in the textbook.

Step 2: Determine who has the absolute advantage in the production of each good.
To determine absolute advantage, you should begin by looking at each good individually and ask yourself the question "Who can produce more of the good?" The United States can produce more wheat than China, so the United States has the absolute advantage in the production of wheat. The United States can also produce more shirts, so the United States also has the absolute advantage in the production of shirts.

Step 3: Determine who has the comparative advantage in the production of each good by calculating opportunity costs.
In order for the United States to produce 1 bushel of wheat, it must give up 5 shirts, while China has to give up 8 shirts for the same bushel of wheat. The United States gives up less to produce wheat, so it has the comparative advantage in the production of wheat. To produce 1 shirt, the United States must give up 1/5 of a bushel of wheat, while China only gives up 1/8 bushel of wheat. Therefore, China has the comparative advantage in the production of shirts.

Step 4: Determine specialization by looking at the comparative advantage.
To receive gains from trade, countries should specialize in the good in which they have a comparative advantage and then trade that good for goods from other countries. In this case, the United States should specialize in the production of wheat and China should specialize in the production of shirts.

8.3 LEARNING OBJECTIVE

8.3 How Countries Gain From International Trade (pages 249-255)

Learning Objective 3 Explain how countries gain from international trade.

The gains from trade can be illustrated with an example of two countries that produce the same two goods under conditions of autarky. **Autarky** is a situation where a country does not trade with other countries. When each country specializes in the production of the good for which it has a comparative advantage and trades some of this good for some of the good produced by the other country, (a) total production of both goods can be greater than it would be under conditions of autarky and (b) total consumption of both goods in both countries can be greater with trade than under conditions of autarky.

The **terms of trade** is the ratio at which a country can trade its exports for imports from other countries. Although countries as a whole are made better off from trade, trade can harm firms and workers in industries that produce goods at a higher cost than foreign competitors.

Helpful Study Hint

Read ***Solved Problem 8-3*** "The Gains From Trade," which describes the gains from trade in David Ricardo's famous cloth and wine example. In this example, Portugal and England each gain from trade. Portugal can specialize in wine, while England specializes in the production of cloth. The two countries can make themselves better off through trade Be sure you understand the example in the textbook where Japan and the United States are both able to consume more cell phones and MP3 players after trade than under autarky.

In reality, countries do not specialize completely in the goods in which they have the comparative advantage. This lack of complete specialization is because some goods are not traded internationally, opportunity costs increase as production increases, and consumers in different countries have different preferences for products. There are several reasons why a country may have a comparative advantage in producing a particular good. A firm in one country may have a relatively low opportunity cost in the production of a good because of favorable climate, abundant supplies of certain natural resources, or relatively abundant supplies of labor or capital. Another source of comparative advantage is superior technology in one country. Comparative advantage may also result from external economies. **External economies** are reductions in a firm's costs that result from an expansion in the size of an industry.

Helpful Study Hint

Raymond Vernon provided a classic example of the importance of external economies. Anyone who lives in or has visited New York City, Manhattan in particular, knows that prices for most goods and services are higher there than in most other cities. Real estate and transportation are expensive, streets are crowded, and firms must pay employees a premium to compensate for the high cost of living. Yet, the garment and financial industries located in Manhattan continue to thrive despite these disadvantages. For both of these industries, ready access to suppliers, customers, and competitors are important assets. Personal contacts and face-to-face meetings are critical to the success of doing business. The large market size and concentration of related businesses offered by New York City are more important assets than the lower cost of real estate and transportation offered by locations outside of Manhattan. See ***Making the Connection*** "Why is Dalton, Georgia, the Carpet-Making Capital of the World?" for another example of external economies.

The carpet industry has clustered in Dalton, Georgia, to take advantage of skilled workers and suppliers who specialize in servicing the carpet industry.

Don't Let This Happen to YOU! "Remember That Trade Creates Both Winners and Losers" explains that international trade may be a win-win situation for countries, but that not all individual consumers and producers are winners. Because there is a net gain to society from international trade, some of the gains to the winners could be used to compensate the losers.

8.4 LEARNING OBJECTIVE

8.4 Government Policies that Restrict International Trade (pages 255-262)

Learning Objective 4 Analyze the economic effects of government policies that restrict international trade.

Free trade refers to trade between countries that is free from government restrictions. Free trade policies offer benefits to consumers of imported goods and allow for a more efficient allocation of resources than is possible when international trade is restricted by tariffs or other trade barriers. But free trade also harms domestic firms that are less efficient than their foreign competitors.

A **tariff** is a tax on imports imposed by the government. A **quota** is a numerical limit imposed by the government on the quantity of a good that can be imported into a country. A **voluntary export restraint** is an agreement negotiated between two countries that places a numerical limit on the quantity of a good that can be imported by one country from the other country. A *non-tariff barrier* is a government restriction on international trade other than a quota, voluntary export restraint, or tariff. The imposition of these barriers to free trade create a deadweight loss for the domestic economy.

Helpful Study Hint

Figures 8-6 and 8-7 illustrate the deadweight losses that result from the imposition of a tariff or quota. Tables 8-5 and 8-6 describe the costs of trade restrictions in a different but compelling manner. The tables list estimates of the per-job cost to consumers of saving jobs in industries protected by trade restrictions. Those who favor restrictions on international trade must be willing to argue that these high costs of preserving jobs in domestic industries are justified. See ***Solved Problem 8-4***, "Measuring the Economic Effect of a Quota," for additional practice with analyzing the deadweight losses associated with a quota. If the United States imposes a quota on the number of apples that can be imported into the country, the price of apples will increase and the quantity of apples that can be purchased will decrease. This causes a decrease in consumer surplus and a deadweight loss to the economy.

8.5 LEARNING OBJECTIVE

8.5 The Argument over Trade Policies and Globalization (pages 262-267)

Learning Objective 5 Evaluate the arguments over trade policy and globalization.

Debates over the merits of free trade and policies to restrict trade date back to the beginning of the United States. After World War II, government officials from the United States and Europe negotiated an international agreement to reduce trade barriers and promote free trade. Some interest groups began to oppose free trade policies in the 1990s. You have probably heard the term globalization. **Globalization** refers to the process of countries becoming more open to foreign trade and investment. Opposition to globalization is based on the fear that low-income countries are at risk of losing their cultural identity as multinational countries sell Western goods in their markets and relocate factories in their countries to take advantage of low-cost labor.

Protectionism is demanded by those who wish to preserve domestic jobs in certain industries or who believe that certain domestic industries should be protected from foreign competition for reasons of national security. **Dumping** refers to selling a product for a price below the cost of production. If a country is able to establish that foreign firms have dumped products on the domestic market, then they are allowed under international agreements to impose tariffs on these products. The **World Trade Organization (WTO)** is an international organization that oversees international trade agreements.

Helpful Study Hint

Arguments for and against free trade and globalization offer you an opportunity to analyze important policy issues in an objective manner.

You may have formed opinions about these issues after reading or seeing reports of low wages and poor working conditions offered by multinational corporations in developing countries. ***Making the Connection*** "The Unintended Consequences of Banning Goods Made with Child Labor" explains how in some developing countries the alternative to working in a multinational firm is begging or illegal activity. As incomes rise in countries, families rely less on child labor…

Making the Connection "Has NAFTA Helped or Hurt the U.S. Economy?" discusses the effects of NAFTA on the U.S. economy. Even though in the United States there were both winners and losers from NAFTA, there was an overall gain to the economy. U.S. firms have become more efficient and consumers have been able to buy greater quantities of goods at lower prices.

Extra Solved Problem **8-5**

Chapter 8 in the textbook includes two Solved Problems. Here is an extra Solved Problem to help you build your skills solving economic problems.

Supports Learning Objective 5: Evaluate the arguments over trade policy and globalization.

Sunlight! Bah, Humbug!

Arguments over international trade are nothing new. Alexander Hamilton called for the protection of so-called "infant industries" in the United States, and farming interests have long lobbied for trade restrictions to prevent consumers from buying cheaper food products from abroad. Although the countries and industries change over time, the arguments over trade restrictions have not. The 19th century French economist, Frédèric Bastiat, satirized French opponents of free trade in writing a petition to the French government supposedly from the manufacturers of "candles, waxlights, lamps, candlesticks, street lamps…generally of everything connected with lighting": Bastiat's "petition of the candlemakers" has been reprinted many times and often appears in textbooks because of its clever theme as well as its applicability to the arguments of 21st century "petitioners."

> We are suffering from the intolerable competition of a foreign rival, placed, it would seem, in a condition so superior to ours for the production of light that he absolutely inundates our national market with it at a price fabulously reduced. The moment he shows himself, our trade leaves us – all consumers apply to him; and a branch of native industry, having countless ramifications, is all at once rendered completely stagnant. This rival…is no other than the sun…
>
> What we pray for is, that it may please you to pass a law ordering the shutting up of all windows, skylights, dormer-windows, outside and inside shutters, curtains, blinds…all openings, holes, chinks, clefts, and fissures by or through which the light of the sun has been in use to enter houses, to the prejudice of the meritorious manufacturers with which we flatter ourselves we have accommodated our country – a country which, in gratitude, ought not to abandon us now to strife so unequal.

Source: Frédèric Bastiat, *Social Fallacies*, translated by Patrick James Stirling, Santa Anna, CA: Register Publishing, 1944, pp. 60-61.

Cite arguments from chapter 8 that are similar to those raised in Bastiat's petition.

Step 1: Review the chapter material.
This problem is about arguments over trade policies, so you may want to review the section "The Argument over Trade Policies and Globalization," which begins on page 262 of the textbook.

Step 2: Cite arguments from chapter 8 that are similar to those raised in Bastiat's petition.
In describing protectionism the textbook notes that:

> For as long as international trade has existed, governments have attempted to restrict it to protect domestic firms...protectionism causes losses to consumers and eliminates jobs in domestic industries that use the protected product...Supporters of protectionism argue that free trade reduces employment by driving domestic firms out of business...jobs are lost, but jobs are also lost when more-efficient domestic firms drive less-efficient domestic firms out of business...No economic study has ever found a connection in the long run between the total number of jobs available and the level of tariff protection for domestic industries.

Source: page 264.

As Bastiat might have said: "plus ça change, plus c'est la même chose." ("The more things change, the more they stay the same.")

Helpful Study Hint

Economics in YOUR Life! "Why Haven't You Heard of the Sugar Quota?" explains why individual citizens and politicians don't care much about the sugar quota. The sugar quota costs U.S. consumers about $2 billion per year, which works out to be about $7.50 per person. The individual citizen is not likely to be informed about the quota and its effects; and, even if he was informed, it is unlikely that he would take much action for $7.50 per year. Politicians have no incentive to alter the policy as voters are unlikely to protest and the sugar industry continues to press for the quota to stay in place.

Key Terms

Absolute advantage. The ability to produce more of a good or service than competitors when using the same amount of resources.

Autarky. A situation in which a country does not trade with other countries.

Comparative advantage. The ability of an individual, a firm, or a country to produce a good or service at a lower opportunity cost than competitors.

Dumping. Selling a product for a price below its cost of production.

Exports. Goods and services produced domestically but sold to other countries.

External economies. Reductions in a firm's costs that result from an increase in the size of an industry.

Foreign direct investment. The purchase or building by a domestic firm of a facility in a foreign country.

Foregin portfolio investment. The purchase by an individual or firm of stocks or bonds issued in another country.

Free trade. Trade between countries that is without government restrictions.

Globalization. The process of countries becoming more open to foreign trade and investment.

Imports. Goods and services bought domestically but produced in other countries.

Multinational enterprise. A firm that conducts operations in more than one country.

Opportunity cost. The highest-valued alternative that must be given up to engage in an activity.

Protectionism. The use of trade barriers to shield domestic firms from foreign competition.

Quota. A numerical limit imposed by a government on the quantity of a good that can be imported into the country.

Tariff. A tax imposed by a government on imports.

Terms of trade. The ratio at which a country can trade its exports for its imports from other countries.

Voluntary export restraint (VER). An agreement negotiated between two countries that places a numerical limit on the quantity of a good that can be imported by one country from the other country.

World Trade Organization (WTO). An international organization that enforces international trade agreements.

Appendix

Multinational Firms (pages 277-282)

LEARNING OBJECTIVE: Understand why firms operate in more than one country.

Multinational Firms

Multinational enterprises are firms that conduct operations in more than one country. Two innovations made it possible for firms to coordinate operations on several continents. The first was the completion of the transatlantic cable in 1866, which made possible instant communication by telegraph between the United States and Europe. The second was the development of more efficient steam engines, which reduced the cost and increased the speed of long ocean voyages.

Foreign direct investment is the purchase or building by a domestic firm of a facility in a foreign country. **Foreign portfolio investment** is the purchase by an individual or firm of stocks or bonds issued in another country. In the early 20th century, most U.S. firms expanded abroad through foreign direct investment because the stock and bond markets in other countries were often too poorly developed to make foreign portfolio investment practical.

Today, most large U.S. corporations have established facilities overseas because they expect to increase their profitability by doing so. Firms might expect to increase their profits though overseas operations for five reasons:

1. To avoid tariffs or the threat of tariffs.
2. To gain access to raw materials.
3. To gain access to low-cost labor.
4. To minimize exchange-rate risk.
5. To respond to industry competition.

Most newly established U.S. firms begin by selling only in the United States. If successful, they will begin to export, using foreign firms to market and distribute their products. If firms' exporting efforts are successful, they may establish their own overseas marketing and distribution networks. Finally, the firms will establish their own production facilities in foreign countries.

Firms face costs from expanding into foreign markets that differ from the costs of operating in domestic markets. One problem is that tastes differ between consumers in foreign and domestic markets. Products that are popular in one country may not be as popular in another country because of cultural differences or foreign government restrictions.

U.S. firms possess certain competitive advantages when operating in foreign countries. Some firms, such as Coca-Cola and McDonald's, have strong name recognition. Some firms possess a significant technological edge over foreign rivals and other firms have developed efficient, low-cost production methods. Some firms have proven to be better at designing and rapidly bringing to market new products than their foreign competitors.

Helpful Study Hint

Many people believe that when U.S. firms locate production facilities in other countries the level of employment and wages in the U.S. decline. ***Making the Connection*** "Have Multinational Corporations Reduced Employment and Lowered Wages in the United States?" explains that wages of U.S. workers are determined by their productivity. Competition from low-wage workers in other countries has little impact on the wages of U.S. workers. Because in the U.S. economy about 31 million jobs are created and 29 million jobs disappear every year, workers who lose jobs at one firm, whether due to foreign competition or some other factor, can eventually find jobs at other firms with, on average, little effect on the workers' wages.

Key Terms – Appendix

Foreign direct investment. The purchase or building by a domestic firm of a facility in a foreign country.

Foreign portfolio investment. The purchase by an individual or firm of stocks or bonds issued in another country.

Multinational enterprises. Firms that conduct operations in more than one country.

Self-Test

(Answers are provided at the end of the Self-Test.)

Multiple-Choice Questions

1. The sugar quota in the United States creates winners and losers. Which of these groups end up being a winner?
   a. U.S. producers of sugar
   b. U.S. companies that use sugar
   c. U.S. consumers
   d. All of the above

2. Which of the following has contributed to forming a global marketplace?
   a. The falling costs of shipping
   b. Cheaper and more reliable communications and the Internet
   c. Fast, cheap, and reliable air transportation
   d. All of the above

3. Over the past 50 years, what has happened to tariff rates?
   a. Tariff rates have risen
   b. Tariff rates have fallen
   c. Tariff rates have remained the same
   d. Tariffs rates have fluctuated up and down

4. Goods and services produced domestically, but sold to other countries are called
   a. imports.
   b. exports.
   c. tariffs.
   d. net exports.

5. Which of the following is true about the importance of trade in the U.S. economy?
   a. Exports and imports have steadily declined as a fraction of U.S. GDP.
   b. While exports and imports have been steadily rising as a fraction of GDP, not all sectors of the U.S. economy have been affected equally by international trade.
   c. Only a few U.S. manufacturing industries depend on trade.
   d. All of the above

6. Refer to the graph below. The figure is a representation of the pattern of U.S. international trade. Which trend line shows exports?

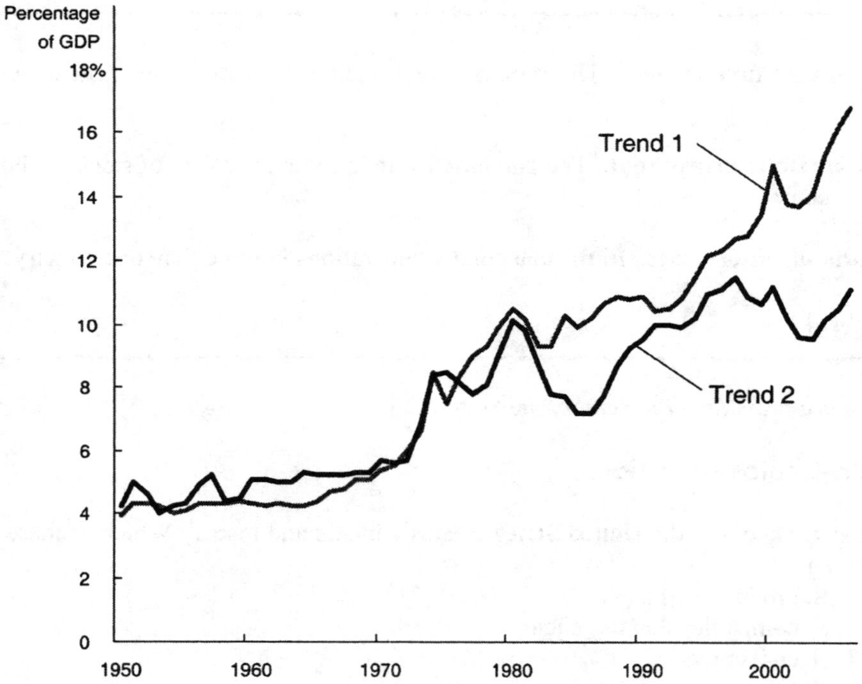

   a. Trend 1
   b. Trend 2
   c. Both lines show exports.
   d. Both lines show imports.

7. Refer to the bar graph below. The graph shows the eight leading exporting countries. The values are the shares of total world exports of merchandise and commercial services. In which of the four positions does the United States come in?

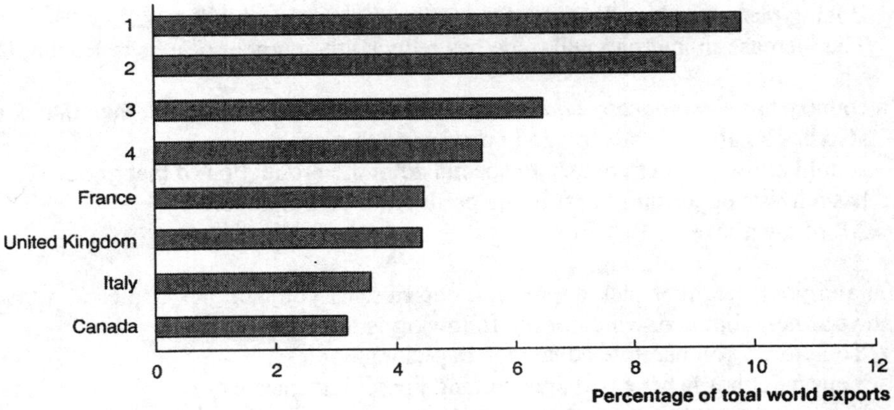

a. 1
b. 2
c. 3
d. 4

8. Refer to the bar graph below. The graph shows the importance of international trade to several countries. In which position does the United States come in?

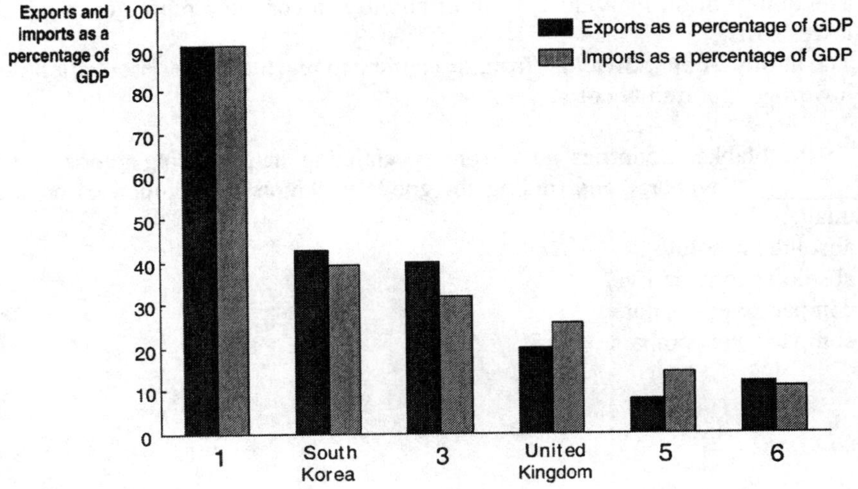

a. Position 1
b. Position 3
c. Position 5
d. Position 6

9. Select the answer that best fits the story in "Making the Connection: How Expanding International Trade Has Helped Boeing."
   a. Outsourcing has played a significant role in the slow employment growth in the United States.
   b. The production and use of the Boeing 747 has increased due to international trade.
   c. Boeing has moved production of the 747 to Korea to reduce costs.
   d. The increase in international trade has reduced the number of jobs in Boeing factories.

10. If a country has a *comparative advantage* in the production of a good, then that country
    a. also has an absolute advantage in producing that good.
    b. should allow another country to specialize in the production of that good.
    c. has a lower opportunity cost in the production of that good.
    d. All of the above

11. You and your neighbor pick apples and cherries. If you can pick apples at a lower opportunity cost than your neighbor can, which of the following is true?
    a. You have a comparative advantage in picking apples.
    b. Your neighbor is better off specializing in picking cherries.
    c. You can then trade some of your apples for some of your neighbor's cherries and both of you will end up with more of both fruit.
    d. All of the above

12. What is *absolute advantage*?
    a. The ability of an individual, firm, or country to produce more of a good or service than competitors using the same amount of resources.
    b. The ability of an individual, firm, or country to produce a good or service at a lower opportunity cost than other producers.
    c. The ability of an individual, firm, or country to consume more goods or services than others at lower costs.
    d. The ability of an individual, firm, or country to reach a higher production possibilities frontier by lowering opportunity costs.

13. Fill in the blanks. Countries gain from specializing in producing goods in which they have a(n) ___________ advantage and trading for goods in which other countries have a(n) _____________ advantage.
    a. absolute; absolute
    b. absolute; comparative
    c. comparative; absolute
    d. comparative; comparative

14. This case is similar to the one in Solved Problem 8-3. Consider the table below. The table shows the quantity of two goods that a worker can produce per day in a given country. Which country has an *absolute advantage*?

	Output per day of work	
	Food	Clothing
Country A	6	3
Country B	1	2

a. Country A has an absolute advantage in the production of both goods.
b. Country B has an absolute advantage in the production of both goods.
c. Both countries have an absolute advantage in the production of both goods.
d. Neither country has an absolute advantage in the production of either good.

15. This case is similar to the one in Solved Problem 8-3. Consider the table below. Which country has a *comparative advantage*?

	Output per day of work	
	Food	Clothing
Country A	6	3
Country B	1	2

a. Country A has a comparative advantage in the production of both goods.
b. Country B has a comparative advantage in the production of both goods.
c. Country A has a comparative advantage in the production of food.
d. Country B has a comparative advantage in the production of food.

16. In the real world, specialization is not complete. Why do countries not completely specialize?
a. Because not all goods are traded internationally
b. Because production of most goods involves increasing opportunity costs
c. Because tastes for products differ
d. All of the above

17. Which of the following is a source of comparative advantage?
a. Autarky
b. Absolute advantage
c. The relative abundance of capital and labor
d. All of the above

18. The term *external economies* refers to
a. the process of turning inputs into goods and services.
b. the reduction of production costs due to increased capacity utilization.
c. the reduction of costs resulting from increases in the size of an industry in a given area.
d. the benefits an industry derives from other industries located nearby.

19. Refer to the graph below. What does the light grey area represent?

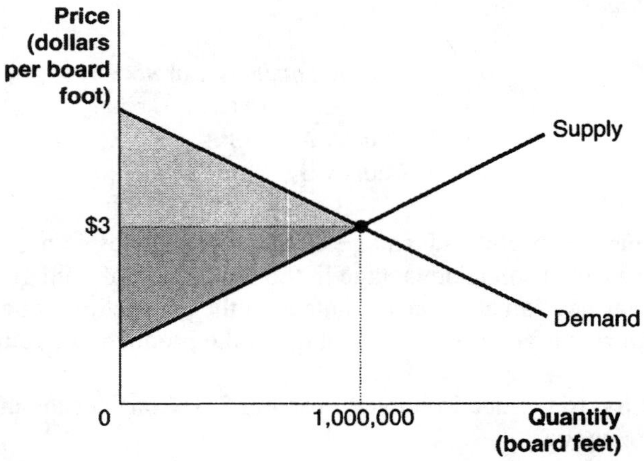

a. Autarky
b. Consumer surplus
c. Producer surplus
d. Economic surplus

20. Refer to the graph below. Under autarky, which area represents consumer surplus?

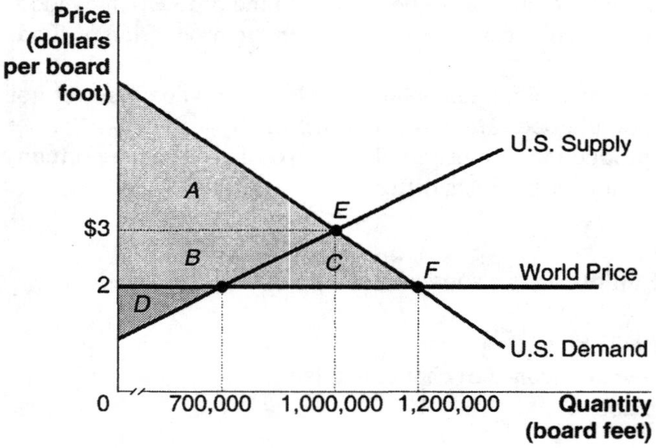

a. A
b. $A + B$
c. $A + B + C$
d. C only

21. Refer to the graph below. Under autarky, which area represents the total economic surplus?

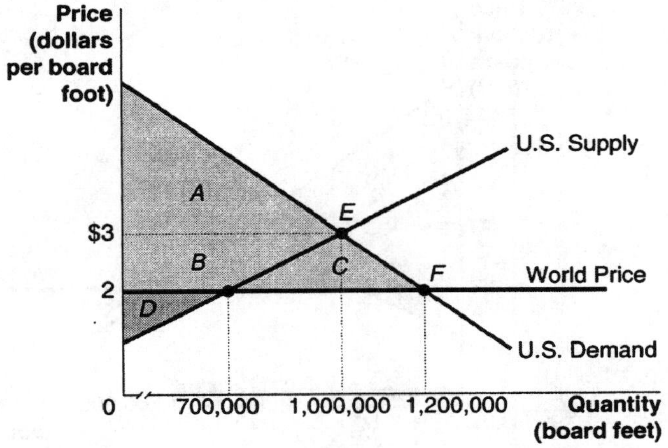

a. *A*
b. *A* + *B*
c. *A* + *B* + *C*
d. *A* + *B* + *D*

22. Refer to the graph below. How many board feet of lumber are imported when imports are allowed into the United States?

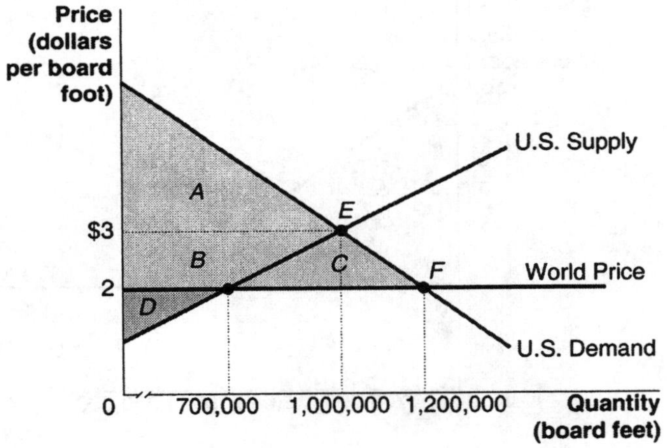

a. 1,000,000
b. 500,000
c. 700,000
d. 1,200,000

23. Refer to the graph below. Which situation results in higher domestic producer surplus?

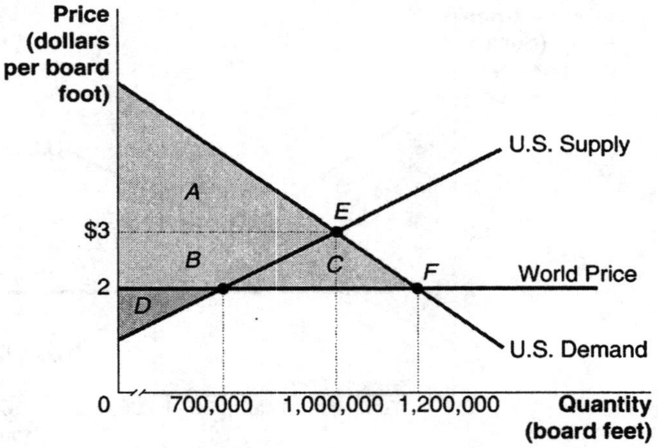

a. Autarky
b. The economy with imports
c. Both autarky and the economy with imports result in the same amount of producer surplus.
d. Any situation other than autarky or imports

24. Refer to the graph below. Which area represents the net benefit from opening the economy to imports?

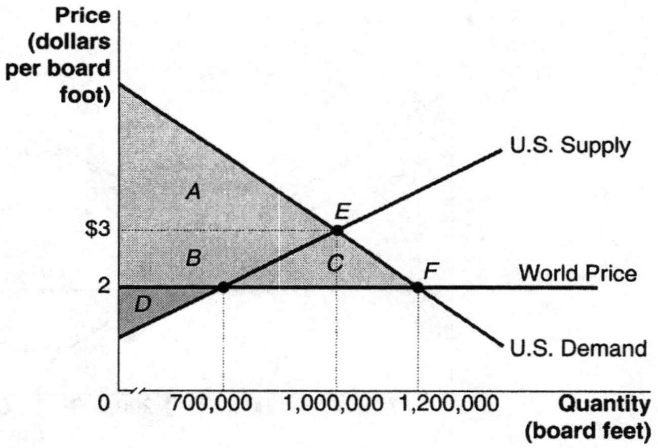

a. Area *A*
b. Area *B* + *C*
c. Area *C*
d. Area *D*

25. Refer to the graph below. The figure shows the effect of a $0.50 per board foot tariff on lumber. Which area represents the deadweight loss from this tariff?

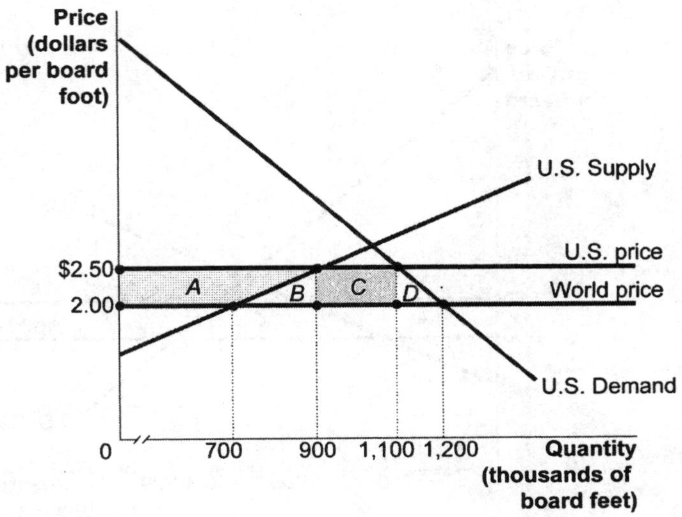

a. *A*
b. *C*
c. *B* + *D*
d. *B* + *C* + *D*

26. Refer to the graph below. The graph shows the effect of a $0.50 per board foot tariff on lumber. What is the quantity of lumber supplied (in thousands of board feet) by domestic producers after the tariff?

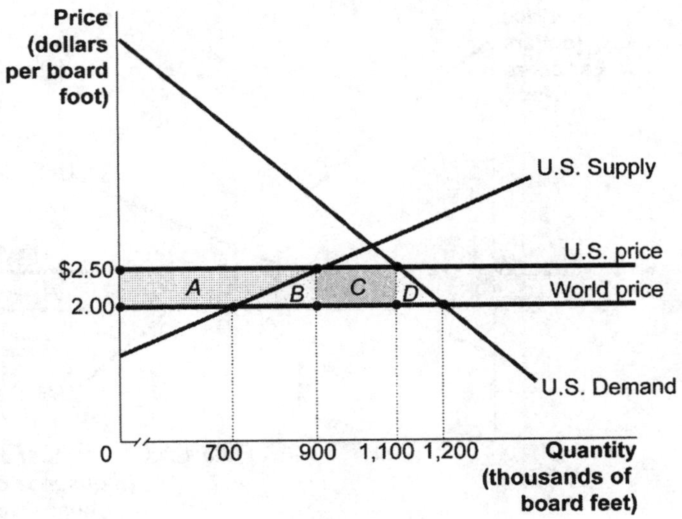

a. 700
b. 900
c. 1,100
d. 1,200

27. Refer to the graph below. The graph shows the effect of a $0.50 per board foot tariff on lumber. What is the reduction in U.S. lumber consumption (in thousands of board feet) as a result of the tariff?

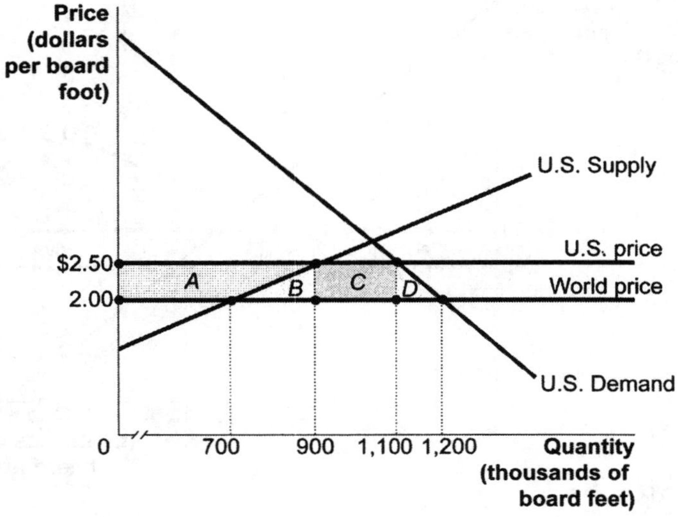

a. 100
b. 200
c. 300
d. 500

28. Refer to the graph below. The graph shows the effect of a $0.50 per board foot tariff on lumber. Which area represents the revenue collected by government from the tariff?

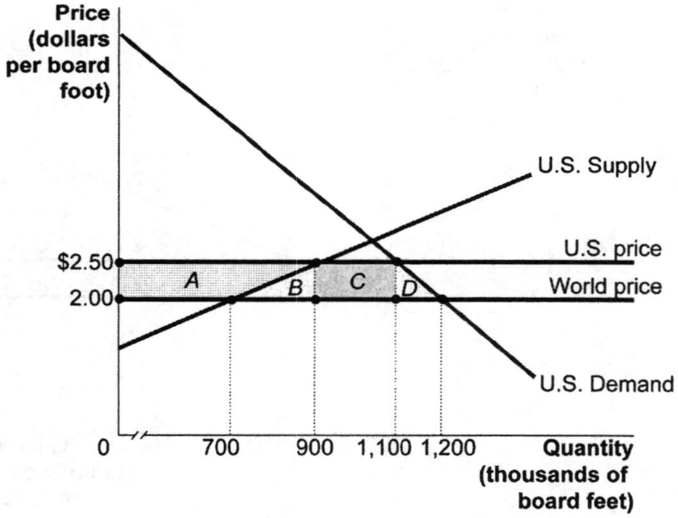

a. $A + B + C + D$
b. $B + D$
c. C
d. A

29. What is a *quota*?
    a. A quota is a numerical limit on the quantity of a good that can be imported.
    b. A quota is an agreement negotiated between two countries that places a numerical limit on the quantity of a good that can be imported by one country from the other country.
    c. A quota is the same thing as a voluntary export restraint.
    d. All of the above

30. What is a *voluntary export restraint*?
    a. A numerical limit on the quantity of a good that can be imported
    b. An agreement negotiated between two countries that places a numerical limit on the quantity of a good that can be imported by one country from the other country
    c. A quota imposed by the WTO
    d. The same as a tariff

31. In countries like the United States and Japan, the cost of saving jobs through trade barriers such as tariffs and quotas is
    a. very low in both countries.
    b. very high in both countries.
    c. high for the United States but small for Japan.
    d. low for the United States but high for Japan.

32. Which of the following acronyms applies to the international trade agreement that covers services and intellectual property as well as goods?
    a. GATT
    b. WTO
    c. NTB
    d. NAFTA

33. Which of the following are characteristics of the process of globalization that began in the 1980s?
    a. An increase in tariffs and restrictions on foreign trade and investment
    b. An increase in tariffs and elimination of restrictions on foreign trade and investment
    c. A decrease in tariffs and opening to foreign trade and investment
    d. A decrease in tariffs and restrictions on foreign trade and investment

34. Which of the following groups of people are significant sources of opposition to the WTO?
    a. People who want to protect domestic firms
    b. People who believe that low-income countries gain at the expense of high-income countries
    c. People who favor globalization
    d. All of the above

35. The opponents of globalization contend that
    a. globalization destroys cultures.
    b. globalization causes factories to relocate from low-income to high-income countries.
    c. globalization means that workers in poor countries lose jobs.
    d. All of the above

36. The use of trade barriers to shield domestic companies from foreign competition is called
    a. protectionism.
    b. dumping.
    c. dlobalization.
    d. patriotism.

37. Which of the following arguments is used to justify protectionism?
    a. Tariffs and quotas save jobs.
    b. Tariffs and quotas protect national security.
    c. Tariffs and quotas protect infant industries.
    d. All of the above

38. Which of the following statements about NAFTA is correct?
    a. NAFTA resulted in reduced consumption for the countries involved.
    b. NAFTA led to an overall loss of jobs.
    c. NAFTA reduced wages for both U.S. and Mexican workers.
    d. None of the above

39. What is the name given to the sale of a product for a price below its cost of production?
    a. Bargain pricing
    b. Cut-throat pricing
    c. Grim-trigger pricing
    d. Dumping

40. Which of the following is an example of positive economic analysis?
    a. Measuring the impact of the sugar quota on the U.S. economy.
    b. Asserting that the sugar quota is bad public policy and should be eliminated.
    c. Justifying the profits of U.S. sugar companies based on the number of workers they employ.
    d. All of the above

Short Answer Questions

1. The textbook notes that: "The effect of a quota is very similar to the effect of a tariff." If the effects are similar, why would a nation impose a quota rather than a tariff on an imported good?

____

____

____

2. Tables 8-5 and 8-6 list the high cost of trade restrictions to consumers in the United States and Japan for each job saved in several product markets. Because the number of jobs saved is much smaller than the number of consumers who must pay high prices to save these jobs, why do the governments of the United States and Japan maintain these trade restrictions?

____

____

____

3. Comparative advantage is used to explain why nations export products that they can produce at a lower opportunity cost than other nations. How, then, can one explain why the United States both exports and imports automobiles?

4. David Ricardo's explanation of comparative advantage is considered to be one of the most important contributions to the history of economic thought. Why is comparative advantage so important?

5. The World Trade Organization (WTO) allows member nations to impose tariffs on imported products if dumping can be demonstrated. Why is it difficult to prove accusations of dumping?

True/False Questions

T F 1. As a percentage of GDP, U.S. imports and exports have both decreased during the past 20 years.

T F 2. Demand for the Boeing 747 has increased due to international trade.

T F 3. Although imports and exports are a small fraction of GDP in the United States, they are a much larger fraction of the GDP for smaller nations such as Japan.

T F 4. One reason why countries do not specialize completely in production is that not all goods and services are traded internationally.

T F 5. Although United States firms were able to produce consumer electronics goods more cheaply and with higher quality than Japanese firms in the 1970s and 1980s, Japanese firms used superior process technology to move ahead of U.S. firms by 2005.

T F 6. Firms in Dalton, Georgia developed a comparative advantage in carpet-making because of external economies.

T F 7. Between 1994, when the North American Free Trade Agreement (NAFTA) went into effect, and 2007, the number of jobs in the U.S. declined by 21 million. Some of this decrease was due to NAFTA.

T F 8. Barriers to international trade include health and safety requirements that are more strictly imposed on imported goods than goods produced by domestic firms.

T F 9. The Smoot-Hawley Tariff of 1930 lowered average tariff rates in the U.S. by about 50 percent.

T F 10. One reason why countries do not specialize completely in production is that complete specialization requires countries to have an absolute advantage in the products they produce.

T F 11. Although countries gain from international trade, some individuals are harmed, including some workers who lose their jobs.

T F 12. The terms of trade refers to the length of trade agreements (for example, NAFTA) signed by officials from countries that are parties to these agreements.

T F 13. Each year the United States exports about 50 percent of its wheat crop.

T F 14. Germany is the leading exporting country, accounting for about 10 percent of total world exports.

T F 15. A tariff imposed on imports of textiles will raise the price of textiles in the importing country and create a deadweight loss in the domestic textile market.

Answers to the Self-Test

Multiple-Choice Questions

Question	Answer	Explanation
1	a	The sugar quota creates winners—U.S. sugar companies and their employees—and losers—U.S. companies that use sugar, their employees, and U.S. consumers who must pay higher prices for goods that contain sugar.
2	d	Improvements in transportation and communications have created a global marketplace.
3	b	Tariff rates have fallen. In the 1930s, the United States charged an average tariff rate above 50 percent. Today, the rate is less than 2 percent.
4	b	Imports are goods and services bought domestically but produced in other countries. Exports are goods and services produced domestically, but sold to other countries.
5	b	Not all sectors of the U.S. economy have been affected equally by international trade.
6	b	Exports have been less than imports since 1982.
7	a	The United States is the leading exporting country, accounting for about 10 percent of total world exports.
8	c	International trade is less important to the United States than to most other countries, with the significant exception of Japan.
9	b	Boeing received a significant increase in demand for the 747 to transport air freight.
10	c	The country with a lower opportunity cost of production has a comparative advantage in the production of that good.
11	d	If you can pick apples at a lower opportunity cost than your neighbor can, you have a comparative advantage in picking apples. Your neighbor is better off specializing

		in picking cherries, and you are better off specializing in picking apples. You can then trade some of your apples for some of your neighbor's cherries and both of you will end up with more of both fruit.
12	a	Absolute advantage is the ability of an individual, firm, or country to produce more of a good or service than competitors using the same amount of resources.
13	d	Countries gain from specializing in producing goods in which they have a comparative advantage and trading for goods in which other countries have a comparative advantage.
14	a	Country A can produce more food and more clothing in one day than Country B.
15	c	A worker in Country A can produce 6 times as many units of food as a worker in Country B, but only 1.5 as many units of clothing. Country A is more efficient in producing food than clothing relative to Country B.
16	d	The three reasons above are the explanations given in the textbook.
17	c	The main sources are: climate and natural resources, the relative abundance of labor and capital, technology, and external economies.
18	c	The advantages include the availability of skilled workers, the opportunity to interact with other companies in the same industry, and being close to suppliers. These advantages result in lower costs to firms located in the area. Because these lower costs result from increases in the size of the industry in an area, economists refer to them as external economies.
19	b	The light grey area represents consumer surplus and the dark grey area represents producer surplus.
20	a	Autarky refers to equilibrium without trade. Area A is consumer surplus when price equals domestic price, or $3 per board foot.
21	d	The total economic surplus is the area between the demand and supply curves out to the domestic equilibrium.
22	b	Imports will equal 500,000 board feet, which is the difference between U.S. consumption and U.S. production at the world price.
23	a	The area of surplus under autarky is B + D.
24	c	Area C is additional consumer surplus that did not exist under autarky.
25	c	The areas B and D represent deadweight loss.
26	b	After the tariff is imposed, the quantity supplied domestically is 900 board feet, at a price of $2.50.
27	a	At a price (before tariff) of $2.00, U.S. consumption is 1,200. After the tariff is imposed, U.S. consumption falls to 1,100, so the decrease is 100.
28	c	Government revenue equals the tariff multiplied by the number of board feet imported, or $0.50 x (1,100,000 – 900,000) = $0.50 x 200,000 = $100,000.
29	a	A quota is a numerical limit on the quantity of a good that can be imported, and it has an effect similar to a tariff. Government revenue equals the tariff multiplied by the number of board feet imported, or $0.50 x (1,100,000 – 900,000 = $0.50 x 200,000 = $100,000).
30	b	That is a voluntary export restraint.
31	b	Tables 8-5 and 8-6 show how expensive it is to save jobs in each country.
32	b	In the 1940s, most international trade was in goods, and the GATT agreement covered only goods. In the following decades, trade in services and in products incorporating intellectual property, such as software programs and movies grew in importance. Many GATT members pressed for a new agreement that would cover services and intellectual property, as well as goods. A new agreement was negotiated, and in January 1995, the World Trade Organization (WTO), headquartered in Geneva, Switzerland, replaced the GATT.

33	c	During the years immediately after World War II, many developing countries erected high tariffs and restricted investment by foreign companies. When these policies failed to produce much economic growth, many of these countries decided during the 1980s to become more open to foreign trade and investment. This process became known as globalization.
34	a	The WTO favors the opening of trade and opposes most trade restrictions.
35	a	Some believe that free trade and foreign investment destroy the distinctive cultures of many countries.
36	a	Protectionism is the use of trade barriers to shield domestic companies from foreign competition.
37	d	According to the textbook, all of the reasons above, in addition to protecting high wages, are in support of protectionism.
38	d	The results of NAFTA were the precise opposite of those listed.
39	d	Dumping is selling a product for a price below its cost of production. The results of NAFTA were the precise opposite of those listed.
40	a	Positive economics concerns "what is." Measuring the impact of the sugar quota on the U.S. economy is an example of positive analysis.

Short Answer Responses

1. Quotas may be used to restrict trade when there are legal and political obstacles to raising tariffs. Quotas may also be used when there is a desire to limit imports by a specified amount. It is difficult to know the impact of a tariff rate on the amount of imports before the tariff is imposed.

2. Because the benefits are concentrated among relatively few workers, these workers and their employers have strong incentives to lobby for trade restrictions. Although many consumers are negatively affected, the impact is widely spread so that no individual has a strong incentive to lobby for the removal of the trade restrictions.

3. Real markets are more complex than the simple models used to explain comparative advantage. Automobiles are not standardized products that all look and perform in exactly the same way. One reason why the United States imports automobiles from some nations (for example, Japan) is that these nations specialize in producing the types of automobiles that appeal to certain consumers (consumers who desired relatively small fuel-efficient cars). The United States exports different types of automobiles that may appeal to consumers with different tastes in automobiles (for example, SUVs).

4. Comparative advantage explains why domestic and international trade is mutually beneficial under very general conditions, even when one of the parties to a trade has an absolute advantage in both traded goods. Nobel Laureate Paul Samuelson commented on a conversation he had with a mathematician who asked him to "name me one proposition in all of the social sciences which is both true and non-trivial." After much thought, Samuelson provided this response: comparative advantage. "That it is logically true need not be argued before a mathematician; that it is not trivial is attested by the thousands of important intelligent men who have never been able to grasp the doctrine for themselves or to believe it after it was explained to them."

Source: P.A. Samuelson, "The Way of an Economist," in *International Economic Relations: Proceedings of the Third Congress of the International Economic Association.* Macmillan: London, pp. 1-11.

5. Dumping (selling a good below its cost of production) is difficult to prove for two main reasons. First, it can be difficult to measure the true cost of production for firms from countries different from the country where the dumping allegedly occurred. Second, what is dumping to a firm harmed by the practice may be normal business practice to the firm that does the selling.

True/False Answers

1. F U.S. imports and exports have both increases as a fraction of GDP.
2. T See Making the Connection "How Expanding International Trade Has Helped Boeing."
3. F Although the ratio of exports and imports to GDP is greater in some nations that are smaller than the U.S., the ratio for Japan is smaller.
4. T Since not all goods are traded internationally, countries will have to produce some goods domestically to satisfy the demands of the domestic consumers.
5. F Japanese firms were producing consumer electronics goods more cheaply and with higher quality than U.S. firms in the 1970s and 1980s. U.S. firms used superior process technology to move ahead of Japanese firms by 2005.
6. T See Making the Connection "Why is Dalton, Georgia, the Carpet-Making Capital of the World?"
7. F The number of jobs *increased* by about 21 million during this time period.
8. T
9. F The Smoot-Hawley Tariff raised average tariffs rates to more than 50 percent.
10. F You need not have an absolute advantage in any good in order to specialize and gain from trade.
11. T There are winners and losers in international trade and the workers who work in the industry that competes with the imported goods often lose their jobs.
12. F Terms of trade refers to the ratio at which goods trade between two countries.
13. T See page 244.
14. F The United States is the leading export country.
15. T

Chapter 9

Consumer Choice and Behavioral Economics

Chapter Summary

As you learned in Chapter 1, economists assume that people are rational and try to make themselves as well off as possible. Economists therefore assume that when consumers spend their income they are trying to maximize their utility. **Utility** means enjoyment or satisfaction. The **marginal utility** a person receives from consuming an additional unit of a good or service will diminish as more is consumed in a given period of time. If you like Pepsi, your satisfaction will increase less from drinking a second glass than it did from drinking the first glass, and less from drinking a third glass than it did from drinking the second glass. Consumers maximize their utility when the marginal utility per dollar for each good consumed is equal.

In Chapter 3, you learned about demand curves. Demand curves slope downward because of the **income** and **substitution effects** from a change in price. A fall in price makes a good cheaper relative to substitutes—the substitution effect—but also allows a consumer to purchase more with a given among of money—the income effect. For normal goods, the income and substitution effects both lead consumers to buy more of a good after its price falls. For inferior goods, the income effect associated with a decrease in price causes a decrease in quantity demanded, whereas the substitution effect causes quantity demanded to increase.

Social factors affect consumer choices. Firms such as Coca-Cola and Nike have long used celebrity endorsements to induce consumers to buy their products because some consumers want to buy products associated with celebrities. There are **network externalities** in the consumption of a product if the usefulness of the product increases with the number of people who use it. Your cell phone is useful because many other people also own one. Though consumer choice theory assumes consumers are rational, many people like to be treated fairly and try to treat others fairly even if this makes them worse off financially. Examples of this behavior are voluntary tipping in restaurants and donating to charities. A new area of economics, **behavioral economics**, studies consumer decisions such as these that appear not to be rational.

One of the goals of economics is to suggest ways for people to make better decisions. Consumers can improve their decision making by avoiding common pitfalls. Among the most common of these pitfalls are (1) ignoring the nonmonetary **opportunity costs** of choices (2) failure to ignore **sunk costs** and (3) being overly optimistic about future behavior.

Learning Objectives

When you finish this chapter, you should be able to:

1. **Define utility and explain how consumers choose goods and services to maximize their utility.** Utility is the satisfaction people receive from consuming goods and services. A consumer's goal is to spend available income so as to maximize utility. Utility maximization occurs when the additional (marginal) utility received per dollar spent on each good or service is equal.

2. **Use the concept of utility to explain the law of demand.** When the price of a good decreases, a consumer's purchasing power increases, causing an income effect due to the price change. The income effect increases the quantity demanded of a normal good but decreases the quantity demanded of an inferior good. The substitution effect of a decrease in price increases the marginal utility per dollar of the good. This will increase the quantity demanded of this good and decrease the quantity demanded of substitutes for this good.

3. **Explain how social influences can affect consumption choices.** Some people receive utility from consuming goods they believe are popular. Some consumers buy products associated with celebrities because using these products makes them feel closer to the celebrity endorsers or more fashionable. Technology can help explain why consumers buy products other consumers are buying since the usefulness of some products increases with the number of other consumers who use them.

4. **Describe the behavioral economics approach to understanding decision making.** Recognizing nonmonetary opportunity costs and ignoring sunk costs, which have been paid and cannot be recovered, will increase consumers' utility and make better use of their scarce resources. Being unrealistic about future behavior inhibits consumers' ability to achieve their long run goals.

Appendix: Use indifference curves and budget lines to understand consumer behavior. Your instructor may cover the appendix to this chapter. While the chapter assumes that we can measure a consumer's satisfaction, or utility, the appendix uses the more realistic assumption that consumers can *rank* different combinations of goods and services.

Chapter Review

Chapter Opener: Can Jay-Z Get You to Drink Cherry Coke? (pages 284-285)

Firms often hire celebrities to endorse their products with the expectation that the endorsements will increase their sales. For example, for nearly 100 years Coca-Cola has used movie stars and other celebrities in their advertising. One theme in this chapter, and several following chapters, is that firms try to distinguish their products from the products of rival firms (as Coke, for example, tries to distinguish itself from Pepsi) in the minds of consumers.

Helpful Study Hint

An ***Inside Look*** at the end of this chapter describes some additional examples of using celebrities to pitch firms' products. You may believe that advertising only increases the costs of marketing products, which are then passed on to consumers in higher prices. But advertising also provides the consumer with information. Ads that firms place in newspapers and magazines, in particular, provide consumers with valuable information including dates and locations of special sales. Information is a valuable, though intangible, product for consumers. Often, consumers incur costs to obtain useful information. In practice, it is very difficult to distinguish between advertising spending that provides information and advertising that is intended to keep firms that cannot afford a large advertising budget from entering an industry.

Economics in YOUR Life! asks if you make consistent decisions. If you purchased a $75 concert ticket, would you sell it to someone for $90? Keep this question in mind as you read the chapter. The authors will answer this question at the end of the chapter.

9.1 LEARNING OBJECTIVE

9.1 Utility and Consumer Decision Making (pages 286-295)

Learning Objective 1 Define utility and explain how consumers choose goods and services to maximize their utility.

Utility is the enjoyment or satisfaction people receive from consuming goods and services. Economists assume consumers spend their limited budgets on the bundle of goods and services that provides them with the most utility, although utility cannot be measured exactly. If we assume that utility can be measured, then a certain number of "utils" (units of utility or satisfaction) are associated with each unit of a product.

Marginal utility (*MU*) is the change in total utility a person receives from consuming one additional unit of a good or service. The **law of diminishing marginal utility** states that consumers experience less additional satisfaction as they consume more of a good or service during a given period of time.

Because consumers have limited income, they try to receive the most utility they can as they spend their income. A **budget constraint** refers to the limited amount of income available to consumers to spend on goods and services. The model of consumer behavior can be used to determine the optimal amounts of goods a consumer will purchase given (a) knowledge of the marginal utilities (*MU*) of the goods, (b) the prices of the goods, and (c) the consumer's budget constraint. This model applies a key economic principle you learned about in Chapter 1: optimal decisions are made at the margin.

The following information is taken from Table 9-2 on page 290 of the text. It is assumed that the price of pizza is $2 per slice, the price of a cup of Coke is $1, and the consumer has $10 to spend on pizza and Coke.

Slices of pizza	*MU* per dollar (pizza)	Cups of Coke	*MU* per dollar (Coke)
1	10	1	20
2	8	2	15
3	5	3	10
4	3	4	5
5	1	5	3

The consumer maximizes utility by first buying the good for which the *MU* per dollar is higher. Because the first cup of Coke has a higher *MU* per dollar (20) than the *MU* per dollar from the first slice of pizza (10), the consumer will first spend $1 on a cup of Coke. Because of the law of diminishing marginal utility, the *MU* of Coke and pizza declines as more of each is consumed. The consumer will compare the *MU* per dollar of the next unit of each good in deciding how to spend his income. The consumer will maximize his utility when:

1. *MU*/Price is equal for each good consumed and
2. total spending on all goods equals the income available.

The consumer's optimal consumption is 3 slices of pizza (at $2 each, spending $6 on pizza) and 4 Cokes (at $1 each, spending $4 on Coke). Total spending is equal to the consumer's budget, $10. Marginal utility per dollar is 5 for both pizza and Coke at this equilibrium.

The rule of equal marginal utility per dollar can be used to analyze a consumer's response to a price change. Using the previous example, if the price of pizza were to fall to $1.50, there would be a substitution and income effect on the quantity of pizza demanded.

Slices of pizza	*MU* per dollar (pizza)	Cups of Coke	*MU* per dollar (Coke)
1	13.3	1	20
2	10.7	2	15
3	6.7	3	10
4	4	4	5
5	1.3	5	3

The decrease in the price of pizza has raised the *MU* per dollar of pizza. Previously, the consumer's $10 budget was used to buy 3 slices of pizza and 4 cups of Coke. At the lower price of pizza, the same combination of goods costs only $8.50. This increase in purchasing power is the income effect of the price change. And the consumer will now purchase 4 slices of pizza, but will still buy 4 Cokes as this is the consumption bundle where the entire budget is spent and the marginal utility per dollar of the last unit consumed is the same for both goods.

The **income effect** is the change in the quantity demanded of a good that results from a change in price caused by the altered consumer purchasing power, holding all other factors constant. If pizza is a normal good, the income effect of a decrease in price will lead to an increase in the quantity demanded of pizza. If pizza is an inferior good, the income effect of a decrease in price will lead to a decrease in the quantity demanded. The **substitution effect** is the change in quantity demanded of a good that results from a change in price that makes the good more or less expensive relative to other goods, holding constant the effect of the price change on consumer purchasing power.

Helpful Study Hint

The assumption that we can measure utility exactly is unrealistic. We can't strap a consumer into a chair and measure how many "utils" she receives from eating a slice of pizza. But it is realistic to assume a consumer can determine whether he or she prefers a certain amount of one product to an amount of another, or that he or she is indifferent between consuming two different products. Economists do not believe in "cardinal utility" – utility measured in utils. Economists do believe in "ordinal utility" – that consumers can rank products, or combinations of products, based on their preferences. Cardinal and ordinal measurements can be found on newspapers' sports pages. A list of baseball teams' won-loss records from first to last is an ordinal ranking. For example, reproduced below are the standings for baseball's National League West division for the 2007 season. The Arizona Diamondbacks team finished first, the Colorado Rockies team finished second, and so on. Baseball standings also include the number of games teams are behind the first place club. This is a cardinal ranking since it provides information regarding how far from first place each team is. For example, in 2007 the Rockies finished 1/2 game behind the Diamondbacks, the San Diego Padres finished 1 1/2 games behind the Diamondbacks (and 1 game behind the Rockies), and so on.

National League West	W	L	Games Behind
Arizona	90	72	--
Colorado	90	73	1/2
San Diego	89	74	1 1/2
Los Angeles	82	80	8
San Francisco	71	91	19

Helpful Study Hint

You may have difficulty understanding why consumers will equate the *MU* per dollar for all goods and services they consume. Imagine a consumer in a store with a shopping cart with all of the items she wishes to purchase. Because this consumer has not yet bought the items, it is possible to have a "utility inspector" with a magical ability to know the *MU* of each item in the cart and who will suggest ways to make the consumer better off. Assume that the *MU* per dollar for two items is unequal and the price of each item is the same (for example, $1). Also assume there is more than one can of peas (*MU* per dollar = 20) and more than one can of corn (*MU* per dollar = 10) in the cart. The inspector can make the consumer better off by taking away one can of corn and replacing it with one more can of peas. The total dollar value of the goods in the cart has not changed, but there is a net gain of 10 utils (20 minus 10). As similar exchanges are made, the *MU* of corn will become more than 10 – this represents the last can placed in the cart – and the *MU* of peas will decrease from 20 because there are now additional cans of peas in the cart.

Extra Solved Problem 9-2

Chapter 9 in the textbook includes two Solved Problems. Here is an extra Solved Problem to help you build your skills solving economic problems.

Supports Learning Objective 2: Use the concept of utility to explain the law of demand.

Deriving Lee's Demand Curve for Ice Cream

The following table represents Lee's marginal utility per dollar for ice cream cones and cans of lime fizz as derived in Step 4 of Solved Problem 9-1 in the textbook. The optimal level of consumption, given Lee's $7 budget constraint and the price of $2 per cone and $1 per can of lime fizz, is 1 ice cream cone and 5 cans of lime fizz.

	Ice Cream Cones $2 each		Cans of Lime Fizz $1 each	
Quantity	*MU*	*MU/P*	*MU*	*MU/P*
1	30	15	40	40
2	25	12.5	35	35
3	20	10	26	26
4	15	7.5	18	18
5	10	5	15	15
6	5	2.5	7	7

a. Assume that the price per can of lime fizz remains $1.00. What is the optimal level of consumption if the price per ice cream cone falls to $1.50? What is the optimal level of consumption if the price per cone falls to $1.00? (Hint: Select the *MU* per *P* ratios to be as close as possible.)

b. Use the optimal consumption bundles for each of the three prices of ice cream cone to derive Lee's demand curve for ice cream cones.

SOLVING THE PROBLEM

Step 1: Review the chapter material.
This problem is about optimal consumption bundles and how to derive a demand curve, so you may want to review the section "Where Demand Curves Come From," which begins on page 295 of the textbook.

Step 2: Calculate the marginal utility per dollar of spending for each of the two prices proposed in part (a).
Since only the price of ice cream cones is changing we can focus on the marginal utility of ice cream cones. See the table below for the results of the calculations:

	Ice Cream Cones $1.50 each		Ice Cream Cones $1.00 each	
Quantity	*MU*	*MU/P*	*MU*	*MU/P*
1	30	20	30	30
2	25	17	25	25
3	20	13	20	20
4	15	10	15	15
5	10	7	10	10
6	5	3	5	5

Step 3: Determine the optimal consumption bundle for Lee given his $7 budget for each of the new possible price of ice cream cones.

At a price of $1.50 per ice cream cone, Lee will consume 2 ice cream cones and 4 cans of lime fizz as this is the point where the marginal utilities per dollar are closest and still within the $7.00 budget. Similarly, when the price is $1.00 per cone, Lee will consume 3 ice cream cones and 4 cans of lime fizz.

Step 4: Use the optimal bundles to generate Lee's demand curve for ice cream cones.

At a price of $2.00, Lee will consume 1 ice cream cone. At $1.50 per cone, Lee will consume 2 cones and at $1 per cone, he will consume 3 cones.

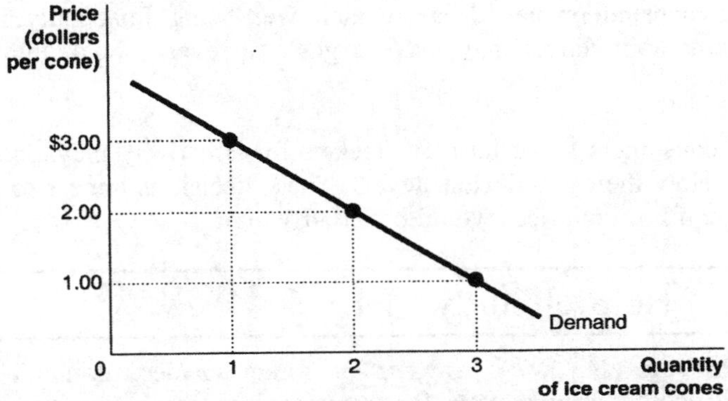

9.2 LEARNING OBJECTIVE

9.2 Where Demand Curves Come From (pages 295-297)

Learning Objective 2 Use the concept of utility to explain the law of demand.

The substitution and income effects of price changes explain why demand curves for normal goods are downward sloping. As price decreases, the good becomes attractive relative to available substitutes, so the quantity demanded of the good will rise. This same price decrease causes an increase in the consumer's purchasing power, which causes an increase in the quantity demanded of normal goods. Although the substitution and income effects of price changes for inferior goods have opposite effects on quantity demanded, the income effect is typically quite small. So, as the price decreases, the quantity demanded will increase for nearly all goods. Economists have statistically estimated millions of demand curves using real-world data. In nearly every case, the demand curve slopes downward. The law of demand is based on real-world evidence, not economic theory alone.

9.3 LEARNING OBJECTIVE

9.3 Social Influences on Decision Making (pages 298-303)

Learning Objective 3 Explain how social influences can affect consumption choices.

Consumer decisions appear to be influenced by the actions and perceptions of other consumers. Some people obtain utility from consuming goods that others consume. Firms use celebrity endorsements to sell products because consumers often wish to be identified with products used by celebrities. Celebrity endorsements can be particularly effective when consumers believe celebrities are knowledgeable about the products they endorse. For example, consumers know that Tiger Woods is knowledgeable about golf clubs and therefore trust his endorsement.

Consumer decisions can be affected by **network externalities**. The utility of some products increase as more consumers use them. For example, you will not find a fax machine useful if no one else owns one. Consumers' willingness to buy new technologies, such as Blu-Ray DVD players, is enhanced when they know many others have bought them, because this will ensure these technologies will be available in the future and that complementary products—such as DVDs in the Blu-Ray format—will be widely available.

Recent studies of consumer behavior indicate consumers think about fairness when they make decisions, which means that consumers may decrease their well-being financially for the sake of fairness. For example, some restaurant diners may leave a good tip even though they do not expect to visit that restaurant again.

Firm realize that consumers value fairness. Tickets for Broadway plays, concerts, and sporting contests are often priced below their equilibrium levels. These decisions appear to be a response to consumers' concerns that the equilibrium prices would be unfairly high.

Helpful Study Hint

Prior to the 1970s, owners of foreign-made automobiles often had difficulty locating parts for their cars and mechanics who could repair them. One would usually need hard-to-find metric wrenches to do even simple repair work. The rapid increase in oil and gasoline prices beginning in 1973 caused a surge in demand for the smaller, more fuel-efficient automobiles offered by Japanese and German automakers. By the late twentieth century, foreign manufacturers had gained significant market share in the United States. The availability of parts, mechanics, and tools was no longer an issue for buyers of domestic or foreign automobiles. This is an example of the importance of network externalities.

Helpful Study Hint

Consumers' concern for fairness explains the social stigma attached to the practice of ticket scalping. In some cities, the practice is illegal despite the voluntary nature of the transactions. Scalpers buy tickets for events well before the events take place. They sell tickets at a premium if the demand for the event increases, but they suffer losses if the demand falls due to bad weather or when a sports game has no playoff implications for the teams involved. Most economists see the actions of scalpers as benign or beneficial for consumers. However, many other people disagree and perceive scalping as an unfair practice. For an example of the affect of fairness on decision making see ***Making the Connection*** "Professor Krueger Goes to the Super Bowl."

Extra Solved Problem 9-3

Chapter 9 in the textbook includes two Solved Problems. Here is an extra Solved Problem to help you build your skills solving economic problems.

Supports Learning Objective 3: Explain how social influences can affect consumption choices.

"Ladies and gentlemen: In this corner, the undisputed heavyweight champion of the marketing world: George Foreman!"

After stunning losses to Muhammad Ali and Jimmy Young, former heavyweight boxing champion George Foreman retired from the ring and spent over a decade in near obscurity. At age 40, he began an improbable comeback that resulted in his regaining the heavyweight title in 1994 at age 45. But even more improbable has been Foreman's emergence as one of the most successful celebrity endorsers of any era. Salton Inc., the manufacturer of The George Foreman Grill, sold more than 55 million grills since the product was first launched in 1995. Foreman has endorsed other products as well, including Meineke Mufflers and the George Foreman Signature Collection, a clothing line sold by the Casual Male Big and Tall retail chain. By the end of 2004, Foreman had earned about $240 million from celebrity endorsements, nearly three times what he earned from boxing. An important part of Foreman's success is his amiable persona, a contrast with the sullen image he had in his early boxing years. Foreman recognizes the importance of his positive image.

> He tries all potential new products – gathering approvals from his wife and children – before putting his name on anything. John Bellamy, CEO of Knockout Group Inc., says Foreman went so far as to put an ethics clause in Knockout's contract prohibiting it from selling the company to anyone involved in alcohol, tobacco, pornography, or gambling…"The most important thing to him is image," Bellamy says.

Source: "George Foreman: Marketing Champ of the World," *BusinessWeek Online*. December 20, 2004.

a. Why do consumers buy products endorsed by George Foreman?

b. Celebrity endorsers are some dropped from product endorsements, as happened in recent years to Whoopi Goldberg and Mary-Kate Olsen. Contrast Foreman's success with these marketing failures.

SOLVING THE PROBLEM

Step 1: Review the chapter material.
This problem is about how celebrity endorsements influence consumer choice, so you may want to review the section "Social Influences on Decision Making," which begins on page 298 of the textbook.

Step 2: Answer question (a).
Part of Foreman's appeal stems from his personality. Many consumers know and like Foreman and want to own products he endorses because they know other people who own these products. Consumers may also believe Foreman is knowledgeable about the products he endorses, such as George Foreman's Grills and his line of "Big and Tall" men's clothing.

Step 3: Answer question (b).

Goldberg and Olsen received adverse publicity for behavior that made companies unwilling to continue using them in their advertising campaigns. In contrast, Foreman carefully selects the products he endorses to maintain his credibility with consumers and the firms whose products he endorses.

9.4 LEARNING OBJECTIVE

9.4 Behavioral Economics: Do People Make Their Choices Rationally? (pages 303-308)

Learning Objective 4 Describe the behavioral economics approach to understand decision making.

Some economists have questioned whether consumers make decisions rationally. Consumers sometimes make poor choices. Among the most important reasons for poor choices are: failure to account for nonmonetary opportunity costs, failure to ignore sunk costs, and overly optimistic assessments of future behavior.

Helpful Study Hint

Sunk costs are often ignored not only by consumers but by government officials and even baseball executives. Before the 2002 baseball season, Allard Baird, the general manager of the Kansas City Royals, decided to release pitcher José Rosado. Writing about this decision Rany Jazayerdi wrote: "[I]t's the first piece of evidence…that Baird understands…sunk costs. Rosado was paid $3.5 million to make five starts in 2000…$3.25 million again in 2001 to do absolutely nothing. He's already guaranteed $533,000 this year…it must be awfully tempting to keep him on the roster…in hope that, after so much time and so much money, their investment might finally pay some dividends…Baird cut Rosado because he compared Rosado to the other [pitching] options…and came to the…conclusion that the only thing Rosado had on [other pitchers] is service time and income."

Source: Rany Jazayerdi, "Rany on the Royals: Cutting Bait," posted on the website baseballprospectus.com, March 12, 2002.

Helpful Study Hint

Economics in YOUR Life! asked if you make consistent decisions. If you purchased a $75 concert ticket, would you sell it to someone for $90? The cost of going to see the concert is what you have to give up for the ticket. Initially, the cost was just $75—the dollar price of the ticket. This amount was also the most you were willing to pay. However, once someone offers you $90 for the ticket, the cost of seeing the concert rises to $90. The reason the cost of the concert is now $90 is that once you turn down an offer of $90 for the ticket you have incurred a nonmonetary opportunity cost of $90 if you use the ticket yourself. The endowment effect explains why some people would not sell the ticket for $90 even though they would not have bought it at the same price. People seem to value things that they have more than things that they do not have. Therefore, a concert ticket you already own may be worth more to you than a concert ticket you have yet to purchase. Behavioral economists study situations like this where people make choices that do not appear to be economically rational.

Key Terms

Behavioral economics. The study of situations in which people make choices that do not appear to be economically rational.

Budget constraint. The limited amount of income available to consumers to spend on goods and services.

Endowment effect. The tendency of people to be unwilling to sell a good they already own even if they are offered a price that is greater than the price they would be willing to pay to buy the good if they didn't already own it.

Income effect. The change in the quantity demanded of a good that results from the effect of a change in price on consumer purchasing power, holding all other factors constant.

Indifference curve. A curve that shows the combinations of consumption bundles that give the consumer the same utility.

Law of diminishing marginal utility. The principle that consumers experience diminishing additional satisfaction as they consume more of a good or service during a given period of time.

Marginal rate of substitution. The slope of an indifference curve, which represents the rate at which a consumer would be willing to trade off one good for another.

Marginal utility (MU). The change in total utility a person receives from consuming one additional unit of a good or service.

Network externalities. The situation where the usefulness of a product increases with the number of consumers who use it.

Opportunity cost. The highest-valued alternative that must be given up to engage in an activity.

Substitution effect. The change in the quantity demanded of a good that results from a change in price, making the good more or less expensive relative to other goods, holding constant the effect of the price change on purchasing power.

Sunk cost. A cost that has already been paid and cannot be recovered.

Utility. The enjoyment or satisfaction people receive from consuming goods and services.

Appendix

Using Indifference Curves and Budget Lines to Understand Consumer Behavior (pages 317-331)

LEARNING OBJECTIVE: Use indifferent curves and budget lines to understand consumer behavior.

Consumer Preferences

Rather than assume utility is measured in utils, it is more realistic to assume that consumers rank different combinations of goods and services by how much utility they provide. If a consumer is presented with two alternative consumption bundles (*A* and *B*) one can assume she will be able to decide on one of the following:

1. the consumer prefers *A* to *B*, or
2. the consumer prefers *B* to *A*, or
3. the consumer is indifferent between *A* and *B* because she receives equal utility from *A* and *B*.

Economists assume the consumer's preferences are transitive. This means that if a consumer prefers *A* to *B* and *B* to *C*, then she must prefer *A* to *C*. Given the assumptions made, we can draw a map of a consumer's preferences using indifference curves. An **indifference curve** is a curve that shows the combinations of consumption bundles that give the consumer the same utility. Indifference curves assume that consumption bundles consist of various amounts of only two goods. Each possible combination of two goods – for example, cans of Coca-Cola and slices of pizza – has an indifference curve passing through it. A consumer is indifferent among all the consumption bundles that are on the same indifference curve.

In a graph of indifference curves, the further to the right a curve is the greater the utility it represents. Along an indifference curve the slope (which is called the **marginal rate of substitution (*MRS*)**) indicates the rate at which a consumer is willing to trade off one product for another, keeping total utility constant. The *MRS* decreases as we move down the indifference curve. This decrease in the *MRS* means the indifference curves are bowed in or convex.

Indifference curves do not cross. If two indifference curves (I_1 and I_2) crossed, they would share a common point (point *X*). Assume that *Y* is a point on I_2 so that the consumer would be indifferent between points *X* and *Y*. Assume that point *Y* lies on the portion of I_2 that is above I_1. *Z* is another point on I_1 so that the consumer is indifferent between *X* and *Z*. Because of the transitivity assumption, the consumer should be indifferent between points *Z* and *Y*, but *Y* represents more of both Coke and pizza. The violation of the transitivity assumption proves that indifference curves cannot cross.

Helpful Study Hint

Be sure you understand Figure 9A-1 on page 318 and Figure 9A-2 on page 319 and the description of these graphs in the text. Notice that the indifference curves do not bend backward, or become positively sloped. This means that receiving more Coke and pizza always increases utility.

If indifference curves were positively sloped, this would mean that receiving more of one good (for example, pizza) would lower consumer utility and require more of the other good to maintain utility at the same level. (Positively sloped indifference curves are sometimes used to model economic "bads" such as pollution and risk.)

The Budget Constraint

A consumer's budget constraint is the amount of income the consumer has to spend on goods and services. Knowing a consumer's income and the prices of two goods he or she can buy allows us to draw a budget line in a graph with the amount of either good measured on the vertical and horizontal axes of the graph. The vertical intercept of the budget line is the maximum amount of a good (for example, cans of Coke) that can be bought with the consumer's income (for example, $10) and the price of the good (for example, $1). The horizontal intercept of the budget line is the maximum of the other good (for example, slices of pizza) that can be bought with the consumer's income.

The slope of the budget constraint is constant and is equal to the ratio of the price of pizza (the good measured on the horizontal axis) to the price of Coke (the good measured along the vertical axis) multiplied by negative 1.

Helpful Study Hint

Budget lines are similar to the production possibilities frontiers introduced in chapter 2. Figure 9A-3 on page 320 illustrates a budget line for Dave, a representative consumer. Points on the budget line represent maximum alternative combinations of two goods, points inside the budget line represent affordable but inefficient consumption bundles, and points above the budget line represent unaffordable consumption bundles.

Choosing the Optimal Consumption of Pizza and Coke

To maximize utility, a consumer needs to be on the highest indifference curve, given the consumer's budget constraint. The combination of goods that will maximize utility subject to a consumer's budget constraint is at the tangency of the budget line with an indifference curve. If the price of one of the goods changes, the budget line will change. For example, when the price of pizza decreases to $1, more consumption bundles can be purchased than were previously possible. The change in the budget line from a price decrease results in a new combination of goods that will maximize utility.

By changing the price of one of the goods and determining amount of the good that will be purchased after the price change, one can derive the demand curve for the good. Indifference curves and budget constraints can be used to analyze the income and substitution effects from a price change. Assume that a consumer is maximizing utility at the tangency of a budget line and indifference curve I_1. Assume a change in the price of pizza from $2 to $1. The budget line changes to reflect the price change and the lines' new slope. The consumer maximizes utility at the tangency of the new budget line and indifference curve I_2 as in Figure 9A-6.

Drawing a line parallel to the new budget line (that is, with the new line's slope) tangent to the I_1 illustrates the substitution effect of the price change. The change in consumption from the tangency of a line parallel to the new budget line and I_1 to the tangency of the new budget line and I_2 illustrates the income effect of the change in price. Increases in income shift the budget line outward and enable consumers to reach higher indifference curves.

Helpful Study Hint

It is much easier to understand how the optimal combination of goods is determined and how price changes change the optimal combination with graphs rather than with words alone. Be sure you understand the graphs in Figures 9A-4 through 9A-8, ***Making the Connection, Dell Determines the Optimal Mix of Products,*** and ***Solved Problem 9A-1***.

The Slope of the Indifference Curve, the Slope of the Budget Line, and the Rule of Equal Marginal Utility per Dollar Spent

At the point of optimal consumption, the *MRS* is equal to the ratio of the price of the product on the horizontal axis to the price of the product on the vertical axis. The slope of the indifference curve is the rate at which a consumer is *willing* to trade off one good for the other. The slope of the budget line is the rate at which a consumer is *able* to trade off one good for the other. Only at the point of optimal consumption is the rate at which a consumer is willing to trade off one good for the other equal to the rate which she can trade off one good for the other.

Indifference curves and budget lines can be used to explain the rule of equal marginal utility per dollar. When a consumer moves downward along an indifference curve, more of one good (for example, pizza) and less of another good (for example, Coke) is consumed but utility is constant. Moving along an indifference curve results in a loss in utility equal to the change in the quantity of Coke multiplied by the marginal utility of Coke:

$$= -\Delta\text{Coke} \times MU_{\text{Coke}}$$

and a gain in utility equal to the change in the quantity of pizza multiplied by the marginal utility of pizza.

$$= +\Delta\text{pizza} \times MU_{\text{pizza}}$$

The loss in utility from consuming less Coke equals the gain in utility from consuming more pizza because the consumer remains on the same indifference curve. The change in utility can be written:

$$-\Delta\text{Coke} \times MU_{\text{Coke}} = +\Delta\text{pizza} \times MU_{\text{pizza}}$$

This can be rewritten:

$$\frac{-\Delta\ \text{Coke}}{+\Delta\ \text{pizza}} = -\frac{\text{MUpizza}}{\text{MUCoke}}$$

$$\text{MRS} = -\frac{\text{MUpizza}}{\text{MUCoke}}$$

Since the slope of the indifference curve (MRS) equals the slope of the budget line at the point of optimal consumption then:

$$-\frac{MU_{pizza}}{MU_{Coke}} = -\frac{P_{pizza}}{P_{Coke}}$$

$$\frac{MU_{pizza}}{MU_{Coke}} = \frac{P_{pizza}}{P_{Coke}}$$

Rewriting this equation yields marginal utility per dollar:

$$\frac{MU_{pizza}}{P_{pizza}} = \frac{MU_{Coke}}{P_{Coke}}$$

Key Terms – Appendix

Indifference curve. A curve that shows the combinations of consumption bundles that give the consumer the same utility.

Marginal rate of substitution (*MRS*). The slope of an indifference curve, which represents the rate at which a consumer would be willing to trade off one good for another.

Self-Test

(Answers are provided at the end of the Self-Test.)

Multiple-Choice Questions

1. When total utility is maximized, which of the following is true concerning marginal utility?
   a. Marginal utility is equal to total utility.
   b. Marginal utility equals zero.
   c. Marginal utility is also maximized.
   d. Marginal utility is minimized.

2. If marginal utility is negative, what must be true about total utility?
   a. Total utility increases with additional consumption.
   b. Total utility decreases with additional consumption.
   c. Total utility remains constant regardless of the number of units consumed.
   d. Total utility equals zero.

3. Which of the following statements concerning total utility and marginal utility is correct?
   a. Marginal utility is usually larger than total utility.
   b. Total utility is the sum of marginal utilities.
   c. Marginal utility is the sum of total utility.
   d. Marginal utility is maximized when total utility is zero.

4. According to the law of diminishing marginal utility, as the consumption of a particular good increases,
   a. total utility increases by more and more.
   b. marginal utility increases.
   c. total utility decreases.
   d. marginal utility decreases.

5. Refer to the table below. Total utility derived from consuming three ice cream cones equals

Ice Cream Cones	Total Utility	Marginal Utility
1	10	?
2	18	?
3	?	6
4	28	?
5	?	2

   a. 34.
   b. 6.
   c. 22.
   d. 24.

6. Refer to the table below. The marginal utility of consuming the second ice cream cone equals

Ice Cream Cones	Total Utility	Marginal Utility
1	10	?
2	18	?
3	?	6
4	28	?
5	?	2

   a. 10.
   b. 9.
   c. 8.
   d. 18.

7. Refer to the graph below. Marginal utility is

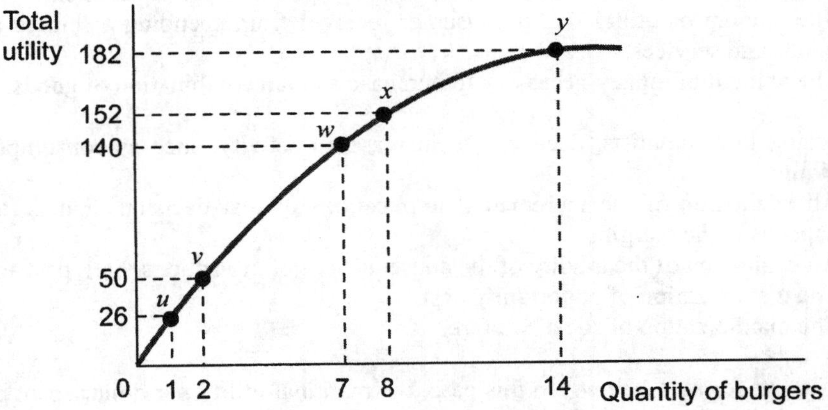

a. greater at points *u* and *v* than at points *w* and *x*.
b. greater at points *w* and *x* than at points *u* and *v*.
c. the same at points *u* and *v* than at points *w* and *x*.
d. greatest at point *y*.

8. Refer to the graph below. From the information in the graph, we can deduce that the marginal utility curve would be

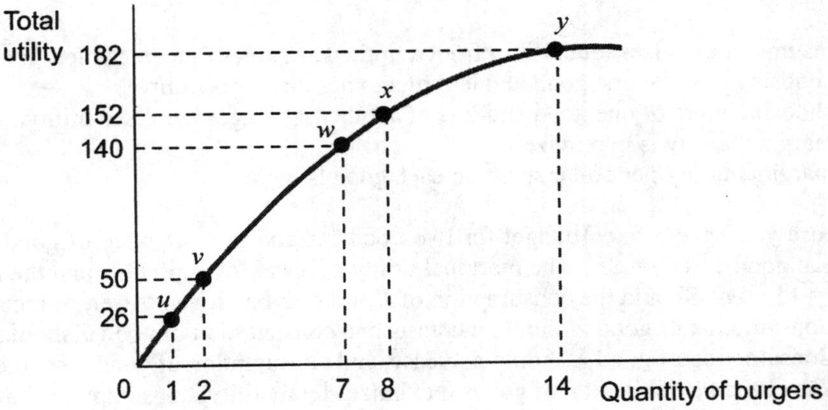

a. downward sloping.
b. upward sloping.
c. horizontal.
d. vertical.

9. What is a budget constraint?
   a. The limited amount of income available to consumers to spend on goods and services.
   b. The amount of income that yields equal marginal utility per dollar spent.
   c. The amount of utility that a consumer receives from spending a limited amount of income on goods and services.
   d. The amount of money necessary to purchase a given combination of goods.

10. According to economists, decisions to increase an activity, such as consumption, are based on the following:
   a. An evaluation of the incremental implications of that decision, that is, an evaluation of what happens at the margin.
   b. An evaluation of the totality of the consequences of our actions, both past and present.
   c. The maximization of opportunity cost.
   d. The maximization of social welfare.

11. Refer to the formula below. In this case, the marginal utility per dollar spent on good *X* is less than the marginal utility per dollar spent on good *Y*. According to the rule of equal marginal utility per dollar spent, what can a consumer do to increase total utility from consumption of goods *X* and *Y*?

$$\frac{\text{Marginal utility of good X}}{\text{Price of good X}} < \frac{\text{Marginal utility of good Y}}{\text{Price of good Y}}$$

   a. Increase the consumption of good *X*
   b. Increase the consumption of good *Y*
   c. Increase the consumption of both goods
   d. Decrease the consumption of both goods

12. A consumer maximizes total utility from a limited amount of income when
   a. choosing more of one good and less of another increases utility.
   b. choosing more of one good and less of another no longer increases utility.
   c. marginal utility is maximized.
   d. marginal utility per dollar spent on each good is highest.

13. Suppose you have a fixed budget for two goods, *X* and *Y*. The price of good *X* is $P_x = \$10$ and the price of good *Y* is $P_y = \$5$. The marginal utility of *X* is $MU_x = 60$ utils and the marginal utility of *Y* is $MU_y = 15$ utils. Should the consumption of *X* and/or *Y* be higher, lower, or remain the same?
   a. Consumption of good *X* should increase, and consumption of good *Y* should decrease.
   b. Consumption of good *X* should decrease, and consumption of good *Y* should increase.
   c. The current combination of goods maximizes total utility; consumption should remain the same.
   d. The consumption of goods *X* and *Y* should both increase.

14. Refer to the table below. As stated in the first row, the income of the consumer (I) equals \$20. The price of good X (P_x) equals \$4.00 and the price of good Y (P_y) equals \$2.00. Total utility derived from consuming X and Y is listed. What combination of goods X and Y will maximize utility subject to her budget constraint?

I =	\$20.00	PX= 4.00		PY=	\$2.00		
X	Total Utility	MUX	MUX/PX	Y	Total Utility	MUY	MUY/PY
0	0	-		0	0	-	
1	40			1	35		
2	65			2	55		
3	85			3	70		
4	100			4	80		
5	108			5	84		
6	114			6	85		

a. 6 units of X and 6 units of Y
b. 5 units of X
c. 3 units of X and 4 units of Y
d. 4 units of X and 3 units of Y

15. Refer to the table below. As stated in the first row, the income of the consumer (I) equals \$20. The price of good X (P_x) equals \$3.00 and the price of good Y (P_y) equals \$2.00. Total utility derived from consuming X and Y is listed. What combination of goods X and Y will maximize utility subject to her budget constraint?

I = \$20.00		PX= \$3.00		PY= \$2.00			
X	Total Utility	MUX	MUX/PX	Y	Total Utility	MUY	MUY/PY
0	0	-		0	0	-	
1	40			1	35		
2	65			2	55		
3	85			3	70		
4	100			4	80		
5	108			5	84		
6	114			6	85		

a. 6 units of X and 6 units of Y
b. 6 units of X and 1 unit of Y
c. 4 units of X and 3 units of Y
d. 4 units of X and 4 units of Y

16. Fill in the blanks. The change in the quantity demanded of a good that results from ____________, holding all other factors constant, is known as the *substitution effect*.
a. the effect of a change in price on consumer purchasing power
b. a change in price making the good more or less expensive relative to other goods
c. an increase in the usefulness of a product as the number of consumers who use it increases
d. the tendency of people to be unwilling to sell something they own

17. Fill in the blanks. The change in the quantity demanded of a good that results from ____________, holding all other factors constant, is known as the *income effect*.
   a. the effect of a change in price on consumer purchasing power
   b. a change in price, making the good more or less expensive relative to other goods
   c. an increase in the usefulness of a product as the number of consumers who use it increases
   d. the tendency of people to be unwilling to sell something they own

18. How do the income and substitution effects work when the price of a normal good decreases?
   a. Both the income effect and the substitution effect cause an increase in the quantity demanded of the good.
   b. Both the income effect and the substitution effect cause a decrease in the quantity demanded of the good.
   c. The income effect causes an increase in the quantity demanded and the substitution effect causes a decrease in the quantity demanded.
   d. The income effect causes a decrease in the quantity demanded and the substitution effect causes an increase in the quantity demanded.

19. How do the income and substitution effects work when the price of an inferior good decreases?
   a. Both the income effect and the substitution effect cause an increase in the quantity demanded of the good.
   b. Both the income effect and the substitution effect cause a decrease in the quantity demanded of the good.
   c. The income effect causes an increase in the quantity demanded and the substitution effect causes a decrease in the quantity demanded.
   d. The income effect causes a decrease in the quantity demanded and the substitution effect causes an increase in the quantity demanded.

20. What is the inclination of the demand curve for an inferior good if the income effect prevails over the substitution effect?
   a. Downward sloping
   b. Upward sloping
   c. Horizontal
   d. Vertical

21. Refer to the graph below. The graph shows your weekly demand for pizza. How was this demand curve constructed?

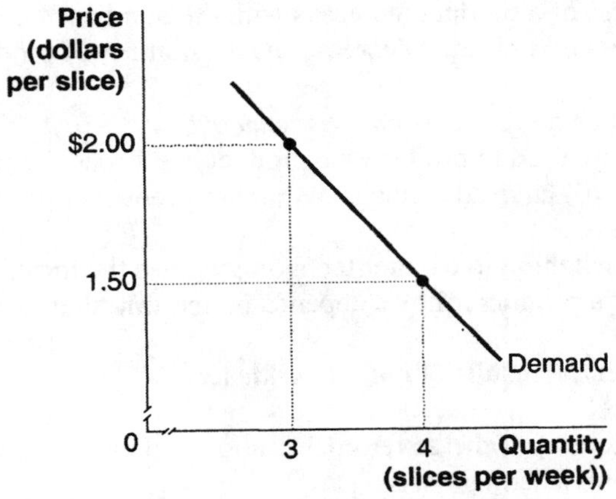

a. By computing your optimal consumption of pizza at the various prices shown, all else the same.
b. By computing your consumption of pizza when the price of pizza remains constant.
c. By computing your consumption of pizza when both the price of pizza and the number of slices you consume per week remain constant.
d. By computing your consumption of pizza at various prices, regardless of utility gained.

22. What are the characteristics of *Giffen* goods?
a. Giffen goods have downward-sloping demand curves.
b. Giffen goods are normal, not inferior goods.
c. Giffen goods are inferior goods for which the income effect prevails over the substitution effect when price changes.
d. All of the above

23. Which of the following factors best explains why consumers would prefer to go to a restaurant that was popular than another restaurant that had similar décor and serves similar food but had fewer customers?
a. Network externalities
b. Some people receive utility from goods they believe are popular.
c. Income and substitution effects
d. Celebrity endorsements

24. Whenever consumption takes place publicly, what does your decision to buy a product depend on?
a. The decision depends strictly on the characteristics of the product.
b. The decision depends strictly on how many other people are buying the product.
c. The decision depends both on the characteristics of the product and on how many other people are buying the product.
d. The decision depends on factors other than the characteristics of the product or how many people are buying it.

25. What happens when *network externalities* are present?
   a. The usefulness of telecommunications equipment rises.
   b. The usefulness of networks diminishes with the number of consumers who enter them.
   c. The usefulness of a product increases with the number of consumers who use it.
   d. The usefulness of a product decreases as the number of products rises.

26. What happens when a product is *path dependent*?
   a. The technology used to produce the product has a specific growth path.
   b. The product will have advantages over other products if it was the first one to be introduced in the market.
   c. The cost of switching to a better technology gives the initial technology an advantage.
   d. The path that a product follows depends on the firm that uses the best technology to produce it.

27. What are the potential results of *path dependence*?
   a. Market failure
   b. A loss of efficiency if the government chooses to intervene in these markets
   c. A reduction in switching costs
   d. All of the above

28. In considering consumers' attitudes toward fairness, which of the following is supported by a great deal of evidence?
   a. People are interested mainly in making themselves as well off as possible.
   b. People attempt to treat others fairly, even if doing so makes them worse off financially.
   c. People attempt to treat others fairly, but only if doing so makes them better off financially.
   d. People usually ignore fairness when making spending decisions.

29. Which of the following is consistent with the general view of fairness by consumers?
   a. In order to part with their money, consumers need to receive something material in return.
   b. Making donations gives people more utility than if they had kept the money and spent it on themselves.
   c. People leave tips but only if they anticipate returning to the same restaurant again.
   d. All of the above

30. In the *ultimatum game*, if neither the allocator nor the recipient cared about fairness, what would be the optimal distribution of $20.00?
   a. $19.99 for the allocator and $0.01 for the recipient
   b. $10.00 for the allocator and $10.00 for the recipient
   c. $19.99 for the recipient and $0.01 for the allocator
   d. $20.00 for the allocator and nothing for the recipient

31. In the *ultimatum game*, when the allocator and the recipient care about fairness, how is the distribution of $20.00 affected?
   a. Allocators receive everything and recipients nothing.
   b. Recipients usually reject offers of less than a 10 percent share.
   c. Allocators usually offer recipients a very small share.
   d. Allocators and recipients always end up sharing the $20.00 equally.

32. Refer to the graph below. At what price level is there a shortage of tickets?

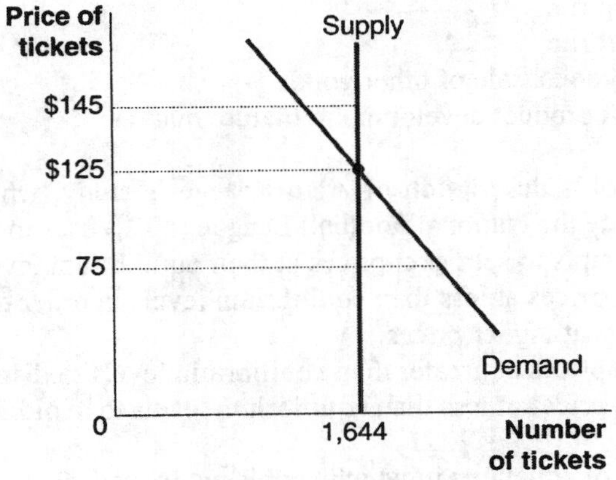

a. At $75
b. At $125
c. At $145
d. At all three prices

33. Refer to the graph below. When producers take fairness into account, which of the following would most likely be true?

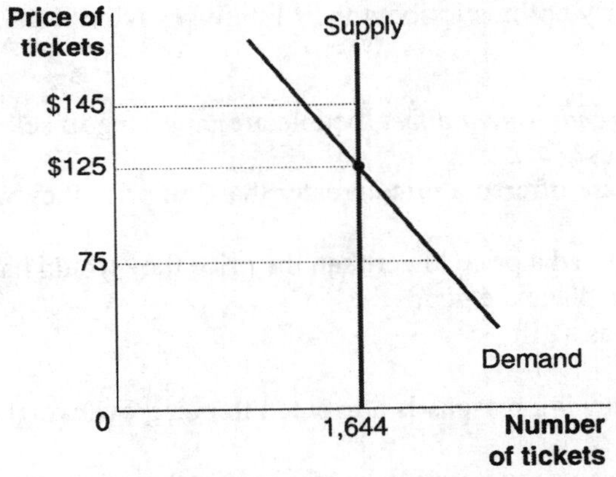

a. The market will almost always settle in equilibrium at $125.
b. Producers could charge $75 even though the result would be a shortage.
c. Producers could charge $145 in anticipation of stronger demand.
d. Producers could raise prices gradually as demand strengthens.

34. Fill in the blanks. Which of the following has been found by researchers in surveys of consumers? Most people considered it _________ for firms to raise their prices following an increase in costs ___________ to raise prices following an increase in demand.

a. fair; and fair
b. fair; but unfair
c. unfair; but fair
d. unfair; and unfair

35. Fill in the blanks. Researchers have found that sometimes firms will give up some profits in the ________ to keep their customers happy and increase their profits in the ________.
    a. short run; long run
    b. long run; short run
    c. sale of some goods; sale of other goods
    d. early stages of product development; mature market

36. Based the textbook's description of Alan Krueger's study, which of the following statements best describes the policy the National Football League (NFL) uses to set the prices of Super Bowl tickets?
    a. The NFL attempts to set ticket prices at their equilibrium levels.
    b. The NFL sets prices at less than equilibrium levels in order to allow corporate sponsors and teams to resell tickets at higher prices.
    c. The NFL sets prices at greater than equilibrium levels to discourage ticket scalping.
    d. The NFL sets prices at less than equilibrium levels to avoid alienating football fans.

37. What is the study of situations in which people act in ways that are not economically rational called?
    a. Normative economics
    b. Rational economics
    c. Behavioral economics
    d. The economics of fairness

38. Which of the following mistakes do consumers commonly commit when making decisions?
    a. They take into account monetary costs but ignore nonmonetary opportunity costs.
    b. They fail to ignore sunk costs.
    c. They are overly optimistic about their future behavior.
    d. All of the above

39. According to the *endowment effect*, people are unwilling to sell a good they already own in which of the following cases?
    a. Even if they are offered a price greater than the price they would pay if they did not already own the good
    b. If they are offered a price lower than the price they would have to pay to replace the good
    c. If they can't replace the good
    d. If the good was a gift

40. Which of the following reasons is attributed to being overweight according to economists who study this problem?
    a. People undervalue the utility to be received in the future.
    b. People overvalue the utility from current choices.
    c. People's preferences are not consistent over time.
    d. All of the above

Short Answer Questions

1. Is it possible for a normal good to have an upward-sloping demand curve? Explain briefly.

2. A Congressional representative explained his support for a spending project in his district by arguing "The bridge that is being built has cost the taxpayers of the United States $15 million. If we don't spend an additional $20 million to finish the bridge, the initial $15 million will be wasted. We owe it to the taxpayers to finish this project." Explain the decision-making mistake the representative made in this statement.

3. In Table 9-2 (page 290) from the textbook, you have a budget of $10 to spend on pizza and coke and the pizza costs $2 per slice while Coke is $1.00 per cup. You would maximize your utility by consuming 3 slices of pizza and 4 Cokes. What quantities of Coke and pizza would you consume if your budget increased to $13?

4. Some consumers argued that VHS video recorders used technology that was inferior to the technology used by Sony Betamax recorders. Nevertheless, VHS technology dominated the market for video recorders, and by the end of the twentieth century, Betamax recorders were so rare that their owners found it to be nearly impossible to purchase movies taped in Betamax format. Is this an example of market failure?

5. Approximately 20 percent of U. S. adults smoke cigarettes despite the documented health risks associated with smoking. Explain how the prevalence of smoking can be cited as an example of irrational decision-making.

True/False Questions

T F 1. Coca-Cola has used celebrity endorsements to sell their products since the 1700s.

T F 2. Marginal utility is the total utility a person receives from consuming one additional unit of a good or service.

T F 3. One of the conditions for maximizing utility is that total spending on goods must be equal to the amount available to be spent.

T F 4. For an inferior good, a price decrease increases a consumer's purchasing power and causes the quantity demanded to increase.

T F 5. Gary Becker and Kevin Murphy are among the economists who believe that social factors such as culture, customs, and religion do not explain the choices consumers make.

T F 6. Economists use the phrase "network externalities" to describe the role technology plays in explaining why consumers buy products that other consumers are already buying.

T F 7. Switching costs can explain why consumers buy products that have inferior technologies.

T F 8. A Giffen good has an upward-sloping demand curve.

T F 9. When the price of a normal good decreases, the substitution effect causes the quantity demanded to increase. When the price of an inferior good decreases, the substitution effect causes the quantity demanded to decrease.

T F 10. Economists believe that it is possible to measure utility in units called "utils."

T F 11. When economists state "optimal decisions are made at the margin" they mean that most decisions people make involve doing a little more of one thing or a little more of an alternative.

T F 12. Firms pay celebrities to endorse their products because they believe this will increase the demand for these products.

T F 13. Firms will sometimes not raise their prices, even when there is a large increase in demand for their products, because they fear consumers will consider the price increases unfair.

T F 14. Consumers often commit the mistake of ignoring sunk costs when they make decisions.

T F 15. The endowment effect is used to describe the mistake a consumer makes when he accounts for the monetary costs of his decisions but ignores the nonmonetary opportunity costs.

Answers to the Self-Test

Multiple-Choice Questions

Question	Answer	Explanation
1	b	Maximum total utility is consistent with zero marginal utility. Remember, marginal utility is the slope of the total utility curve. At its maximum, the slope of the total utility curve is zero.
2	b	Figure 9-1 on page 288 in the textbook shows this clearly.
3	b	The table in Figure 9-1 on page 288 in the textbook confirms this fact.
4	d	According to the law of diminishing marginal utility, consumers experience diminishing additional satisfaction as they consume more of a good or service during a given period of time.
5	d	Total utility is the sum of marginal utilities. Therefore, total utility = 18 + 6 = 24.
6	c	Marginal utility is the additional utility caused by the consumption of one additional ice cream cone, so 18 – 10 = 8.
7	a	As total utility increases, marginal utility decreases.
8	a	For successive units of *X* consumed, the values of marginal utility would be: 40, 25, 20, 15, 8, and 6, so the marginal utility is negatively sloped.
9	a	This is the textbook's definition of a budget constraint.
10	a	Optimal decisions are made at the margin.
11	b	Increasing the consumption of good Y causes the marginal utility of good Y to decrease, thus lowering the numerator of that fraction and bringing both fractions into equality.
12	b	When a consumer maximizes utility subject to the budget constraint, the marginal utility of the last dollar spent on each good is the same.
13	a	Apply the utility maximizing rule: (60/10) > (15/5). Since the marginal utility per dollar spent on *X* is greater than the marginal utility per dollar spent on *Y*, the quantity of *X* consumed should increase. As the quantity consumed of good X increases, the *MU*x decreases, lowering the numerator and bringing both fractions into equality. At the same time, the quantity consumed of *Y* should decrease. This will increase the marginal utility of *Y*, raising the numerator of the right side of the equation and also bringing both fractions into equality.
14	c	The marginal utility per dollar spent on the third unit of *X* (20/$4 = 5) equals the marginal utility per dollar spent on the fourth unit of *Y* (10/$2 = 5).
15	d	The marginal utility per dollar spent on the fourth unit of *X* (15/$3 = 5) equals the marginal utility per dollar spent on the fourth unit of *Y* (10/$2).

16	b	If we hold constant the effect of the price change on your purchasing power, and just focus on the effect of the price being lower relative to the price of the other good, we have isolated the substitution effect of the price change.
17	a	An increase in purchasing power is essentially the same thing as an increase in income. The change in the quantity of pizza you will demand because of this increase in purchasing power—holding all other factors constant—is the income effect of the price change.
18	a	The lower price increases purchasing power and lowers the opportunity cost of consuming the good.
19	d	Refer to the effects of a price change in Table 9-4 on page 294 in the textbook.
20	b	When the price of an inferior good falls, the income and substitution effects work in opposite directions: The income effect causes consumers to decrease the quantity of the good they demand, whereas the substitution effect causes consumers to increase the quantity of the good they demand. It is possible, then, that consumers might actually buy less of a good when the price falls. If this happened, then the demand curve would be upward-sloping.
21	a	A consumer responds optimally to the fall in the price of a product by consuming more of that product. When the price of pizza falls from $2 per slice to $1.50, the optimal quantity of slices consumed rises from 3 to 4. We assume that tastes and preferences, income and the price of related goods remain constant. When we graph this result, we have the consumer's demand curve.
22	c	For a demand curve to be upward sloping, the good would have to be an inferior good, and the income effect would have to be larger than the substitution effect. Goods that have both of these characteristics are called Giffen goods.
23	b	Although economists have traditionally believed social influences on consumer choice are unimportant, some consumers appear to receive utility from consuming goods that are popular with other consumers.
24	c	Whenever consumption takes place publicly, many consumers will base their purchasing decisions on what other consumers buy. Examples include eating in restaurants, attending sporting events, wearing clothes or jewelry, or driving cars. In all these cases, the decision to buy a product will depend partly on the characteristics of the product and partly on how many other people are buying the product.
25	c	There are network externalities in the consumption of a product if the usefulness of the product increases with the number of consumers who use it. For example, if you owned the only telephone in the world, it would not be very useful.
26	c	Once a product becomes established, consumers may find it too costly to switch to a new product that contains a better technology. The selection of products may be *path dependent*. That means that because of switching costs, the technology that was first available may have advantages over better technologies that were developed later.
27	a	Some economists have argued that because of path dependence and switching costs, network externalities can result in market failures.
28	b	There is a great deal of evidence that people like to be treated fairly and that they usually attempt to treat others fairly, even if doing so makes them worse off financially. Tipping servers in restaurants is an example.
29	b	There are many other examples where people willingly part with money when they are not required to do so and when they receive nothing material in return. The most obvious example is making donations to charity.
30	a	If neither the allocator nor the recipient cared about fairness, optimal play in the ultimatum game is straightforward: The allocator should propose a division of the money in which the allocator receives $19.99 and the recipient receives $0.01. The

		allocator has maximized his or her gain. The recipient should accept the division, because the alternative is to reject the division and receive nothing at all.
31	b	When the ultimatum game experiment is carried out, both allocators and recipients act as if fairness is important. Allocators usually offer recipients at least a 40 percent share of the money, and recipients almost always reject offers of less than a 10 percent share.
32	a	At this price level, the quantity demanded is greater than the quantity supplied.
33	b	The theater could have raised prices for the musical. Instead, the theater kept the price of tickets at $75, even though the result was a shortage of seats.
34	b	Most people considered it fair for firms to raise their prices following an increase in costs but unfair to raise prices following an increase in demand.
35	a	Knetsch and Thaler have concluded that firms may sometimes not raise their prices even when the demand for their product is greater than the supply out of fear that in the long run they will end up losing customers who believe the price increases were unfair.
36	d	When asked whether it would "be fair for the NFL to raise the [price of tickets] to $1,500 if that is still less than the amount most people are willing to pay for tickets," 92 percent of the fans surveyed answered "no." Even 83 percent of the fans who had paid more than $1,500 for their tickets answered "no." Krueger concluded that whatever the NFL might gain in the short run from raising ticket prices, it would more than lose in the long run from alienating football fans.
37	c	Behavioral economics is the study of situations in which people act in ways that are not economically rational.
38	d	Consumers commonly commit the following three mistakes when making decisions: They take into account monetary costs but ignore nonmonetary opportunity costs. They fail to ignore sunk costs. They are overly optimistic about their future behavior.
39	a	The *endowment effect* is the tendency of people to be unwilling to sell something they already own even if they are offered a price that is greater than the price they would be willing to pay to buy the good if they didn't already own it.
40	d	Because you are unrealistic about your future behavior, you underestimate the costs of choices—like overeating or smoking—that you make today. A key way of avoiding this problem is to be realistic about your future behavior.

Short Answer Responses

1. No. Assume that the price of a normal good (apples) increased. The substitution effect from this price change would cause the quantity of apples demanded to decrease. Because apples are a normal good, the income effect would cause the quantity demanded to decrease also. If was apples were an inferior good, the income effect would cause quantity demanded to increase. Apples would have an upward-sloping demand curve only if (a) it was an inferior good and (b) the income effect of the price increase was greater than the substitution effect.

2. The representative fails to recognize that the $15 million spent on bridge construction is a sunk cost that should be ignored when deciding whether the project merits additional spending so that the bridge can be finished. The representative should ignore the money that has already been spent and explain why the additional expenditure of $20 million is justified.

3. You should consume the quantity of pizza and Coke that makes the marginal utility per dollar equal and spends your entire budget. If the budget increases to $13, you would want to consume 4 slices of pizza and 5 cups of Coke to maximize your utility.

4. Some economists argue that because of switching costs and path dependence, network externalities can result in market failure. In their view, the triumph of VHS technology can be seen as market failure. But other economists, such as Stephen Margolis and Stan Leibowitz, argue that network externalities do not lock consumers into using inferior technology and that the evidence that Betamax technology was truly superior is unconvincing. This is an area where there is no consensus opinion among mainstream economists.

5. This is an example of people being unrealistic about their future behavior. Those who are addicted to nicotine have difficulty quitting because of the withdrawal effects, including nervousness, irritability, and weight gain. As a result, the decision to quit smoking is put off into the future even though the withdrawal effects will not be avoided. No doubt most adults who smoke would like to quit in the long run but their short run decisions are inconsistent with their long run goals.

True/False Answers

1. F Coca-Cola has used celebrity endorsements since the 1910s. Wedgwood china was probably the first product that received celebrity endorsements and this began in the 1700s. Josiah Wedgwood offered china dishware to celebrities of the day at a reduced price hoping to receive publicity from these sales.
2. F Marginal utility is the *increase* in total utility a person receives from consuming one additional unit of a good or service.
3. T To maximize utility we must spend our total budget.
4. F This describes the income effect for a normal good, not an inferior good.
5. F These economists believe that the mentioned factors *do* influence decision making.
6. T The product becomes more useful as more consumers purchase and use the product.
7. F Switching costs can explain why consumers continue to use a previously purchased product that presently contains inferior technology.
8. T For Giffen goods, as the price increases so does the quantity demanded.
9. F If the price of either a normal good or an inferior good decreases, the substitution effect will cause quantity demanded to increase.
10. F At one time, some economists believed that this might be possible.
11. T Marginal decision making involves small, incremental changes.
12. T Consumers may buy product endorsed by celebrities in order to be cool or to feel closer to the celebrity.
13. T See the section entitled "Does Fairness Matter?" that begins on page 300.
14. F In fact, consumers should ignore sunk costs when they make decisions, but they often don't.
15. F The endowment effect is the tendency of people to be unwilling to sell a good they already own even if they are offered a price that is greater than the price they would be willing to pay to buy the good if they didn't already own it.

Chapter 10

Technology, Production, and Costs

Chapter Summary

In Chapter 9, we considered consumer decision making and the demand curve. In this chapter, we look at decisions of firms and the supply curve. The basic activity of a firm is to use inputs to produce goods and services using existing technology, where **technology** is defined as the process a firm uses to turn inputs into outputs. Firms separate the relationship between production and costs into the short run and long run. In the **short run**, the firm's technology and physical plant are fixed, but other inputs (such as labor and raw materials) are variable. In the **long run**, the firm can vary the quantities of all inputs, adopt new technology, and change the size of its physical plant.

Total cost is the cost of all the inputs used in production. In the short run, the costs of fixed inputs are **fixed costs.** Examples of fixed costs include lease payments on a store or warehouse or interest payments on a loan used to buy machinery and equipment. In the short run, the costs of variable inputs are **variable costs.** Examples of variable costs include the worker salaries and raw material.

$$\text{Total Cost } (TC) = \text{Fixed Cost } (FC) + \text{Variable Cost } (VC)$$

When a firm spends money on salaries or utility bills, it incurs an **explicit cost** or accounting cost. When a firm uses resources its owns—such as the time and talent of the owner—to produce goods, it incurs an implicit cost. **Implicit costs** are the nonmonetary **opportunity costs** of production. Economic costs include both accounting and implicit costs.

The firm's **production function** is the relationship between the inputs employed by the firm and the maximum output it can produce with those inputs. A short-run production function shows the relationship between the inputs and outputs where at least one of the inputs is fixed. The firm's **average total cost** (*ATC*) equals the total cost divided by the quantity of output produced (TC/Q). Typically, *ATC* has a U-shape: Falling for low levels of output before rising at higher levels of output.

In the short run, adding more and more of a variable input, such as labor, to the same amount of a fixed input, such as capital (such as machinery, equipment, or structures), will eventually cause the **marginal product of labor** to decline. This principle is called the **law of diminishing returns**. When only a small amount of the variable is being used, the marginal product of the variable input increases. This is caused by specialization and the division of labor. The marginal product of labor is the change in output that results from changing the number of workers hired. The **average product of labor** equals total output divided by the total number of workers hired. When the marginal product of labor is greater than the average product of labor, the average product increases, and when the marginal product of labor is less than the average product of labor, the average product of labor decreases.

Here is a summary of the costs you will learn about in this chapter:

Term	What it means	Equation
Marginal cost (*MC*)	The change in total cost from producing one more unit of output	$\frac{\Delta TC}{\Delta Q}$
Average total cost (*ATC*)	Total cost divided by total output	$\frac{TC}{Q}$
Average variable cost (*AVC*)	Total variable cost divided by total output	$\frac{VC}{Q}$
Average fixed cost (*AFC*)	Total fixed cost divided by total output	$\frac{FC}{Q}$

In the long run, all costs are variable. Many firms experience **economies of scale,** which means long run average cost falls as output increases. **Constant returns to scale** occur when long run average cost is unchanged as output increases. **Diseconomies of scale** exist when long run average cost rises as output increases.

Learning Objectives

When you finish this chapter, you should be able to:

1. **Define technology and give examples of technological change**. Technology is the processes a firm uses to turn inputs into outputs of goods and services. Positive technological change results in the production of more output using the same quantity of inputs or production of the same amount of output with a smaller quantity of inputs. An example of positive technological change is a firm installing machinery or equipment that increases output produced per worker. Negative technological change can result from damage to machinery or equipment from an accident or a natural disaster such as a hurricane. Negative technological change decreases the quantity of output produced from the same quantity of inputs.

2. **Distinguish between the economic short run and the economic long run.** The short run is a time period during which at least one of the firm's inputs is fixed so that changes in the rate of output result from varying the use of other variable inputs. In the long run, the firm changes the rate of output by varying all inputs. In other words, there are no fixed inputs in the long run.

3. **Understand the relationship between the marginal product of labor and the average product of labor.** The marginal product of labor is the additional output a firm produces by hiring one more worker. The average product of labor equals total output produced by a firm divided by the number of its workers. When the marginal product of labor is greater than the average product of labor, the average product increases. When the marginal product of labor is less than the average product of labor, the average product decreases.

4. **Explain and illustrate the relationship between marginal cost and average total cost.** Marginal cost is the change in total cost caused by producing one more unit of output. Average total cost equals total cost divided by total output. When marginal cost is greater than average total cost, average total cost increases. When marginal cost is less than average total cost, average total cost decreases.

5. **Graph average total cost, average variable cost, average fixed cost, and marginal cost.** The average fixed cost curve declines continuously as output increases. The average total cost curve and the average variable cost curve are U-shaped. The marginal cost curve crosses both of these curves from below at their lowest points. The distance between the average total cost curve and the average variable cost curve equals average fixed cost.

6. **Understand how firms use the long-run average cost curve in their planning.** The long-run average total cost curve shows the lowest cost at which a firm can produce a given amount of output in the long run. This curve shows the impact on cost of expanding output by, for example, building a larger factory or store.

Appendix: Use isoquants and isocost lines to understand production and cost. Your instructor may cover the appendix of this chapter. While the chapter covers the relationship between a firm's level of production and its costs, the appendix looks more closely at how firms choose the *combination of inputs* to produce a given level of output.

Chapter Review

Chapter Opener: Sony Uses a Cost Curve to Determine the Price of Radios (pages 332-333)

The introduction to the chapter uses a story related by Sony Corporation chairman Akio Morita regarding the behavior of his firm's average costs of production. Sony's cost per unit, or average cost, changes as it increases its rate of output. At first, average cost falls as output increases, but eventually increases as output increases further. The U-shape of Sony's average total cost curve is typical of most firms' average total cost curves.

Helpful Study Hint

At the end of the chapter, ***An Inside Look*** describes how an increase in the supply of the components for the production of flat panel TVs affects the costs of the firms that produce flat panel TVs. This reading complements the treatment of long run average total costs and economies of scale in the latter part of the chapter.

Economics in YOUR Life! asks you to imagine owning a furniture store and planning to buy recliners from a manufacturer for $300 and selling them for a price of $500 each. Your competitor, Bob's Big Chairs, buys recliners from the same manufacturer and prices them at $450 each. How can Bob sell recliners at a profit when he is charging only $450 rather than $500? Keep this question in mind as you read the chapter. The authors will answer this question at the end of the chapter.

10.1 LEARNING OBJECTIVE

10.1 Technology: An Economic Definition (pages 334-335)

Learning Objective 1 Define technology and give examples of technological change.

Technology is the processes a firm uses to turn inputs into outputs of goods and services. **Technological change** is a change in the ability of a firm to produce a given level of output with a given quantity of inputs. Positive technological change results from changes such as rearranging the layout of a store and purchasing faster or more reliable machinery. Positive technological change causes more output to be produced from the same inputs or the same output from fewer inputs. Negative technological change may result from changes such as hiring less-skilled workers or damage to buildings due to inclement weather. The result is a decline in the quantity of output that can be produced from a given quantity of inputs.

Helpful Study Hint

Do not confuse technological change with invention. An invention is the development of a new product or process for making a product. An invention or discovery of new information, such as a chemical formula, is not technological change. Technological change results from the application of new or old knowledge to a production process. ***Making the Connection*** "Improving Inventory Control at Wal-Mart" provides an example of technological change in which Wal-Mart uses electronic point-of-sale information and just-in-time (JIT) delivery to manage its inventories and supply chain in order to fulfill the needs of the customer and grow the business. A number of other firms have followed in Wal-Mart's footsteps by incorporating JIT and electronic inventory controls into their production process to increase their efficiency.

Extra Solved Problem 10-1

Chapter 10 in the textbook includes two Solved Problems. Here is an extra Solved Problem to help you build your skills solving economic problems.

Supports Learning Objective 1: Define technology and give examples of technological change.

Technological Change: Wright and Wrong

Decades can pass before a new idea is developed to the point where it can be widely used. For instance, the Wright Brothers first achieved self-propelled flight at Kitty Hawk, North Carolina, in 1903. But the Wright Brothers' plane was very crude and it wasn't until the introduction of the DC-3 by Douglas Aircraft in 1936 that regularly scheduled intercity flights became common in the United States. Similarly, the development of the first digital electronic computer – the ENIAC – occurred in 1945. But the first IBM personal computer was not introduced until 1981. It wasn't until the 1990s that widespread use of computers began to have a significant effect on the productivity of American business.

In 1999, Hershey Foods, manufacturer of Hershey's bars and Reese's Peanut Butter Cups, installed a new software program designed by the German company SAP to coordinate almost all of the company's operations. Unfortunately, it took Hershey many months to get the software to work properly. During the period when the software was not working well, Hershey failed to send out some shipments and other shipments contained less candy than they were supposed to. Software problems made it difficult for Hershey to keep track of what was shipped out and to whom it had been shipped. The company lost $150 million worth of sales before the problem was corrected and the software began to work as it was intended.

Sources: For DC-3 and ENIAC, David Mowery and Nathan Rosenberg, "Twentieth Century Technological Change," in Stanley L. Engerman and Robert Gallman, eds., *The Cambridge Economic History of the United States, Vol. III: The Twentieth Century*, Cambridge: Cambridge University Press, 2000. For Hershey: Emily Nelson and Evan Ramstad, "Trick or Treat: Hershey's Biggest Dud Has Turned Out to Be Its New Technology," *Wall Street Journal*, October 29, 1999 and "Hershey Foods Warns 1999 Earnings Will Be Worse Than Initially Feared," *Dow Jones Business News*, December 28, 1999.

a. Define technology and technological change.

b. Was the Wright Brothers' 1903 flight at Kitty Hawk an example of technological change? Was the development of the ENIAC computer an example of technological change?

c. Explain why the widespread use of computers in the 1990s resulted in positive technological change.

d. Did Hershey's use of a new software program in 1999 result in positive or negative technological change?

SOLVING THE PROBLEM

Step 1: **Review the chapter material.**
This problem is about technology and technological change, so you may want to review the section "Technology: An Economic Definition," which begins on page 334 in the textbook.

Step 2: **Answer question (a) by defining technology and technological change.**
A firm's technology is the processes it uses to turn inputs into outputs of goods and services. Technological change is the change in the ability to produce a given level of output with given quantities of inputs.

Step 3: **Answer both of the questions in (b).**
Neither the Wright Brothers' 1903 flight at Kitty Hawk nor the development of ENIAC represents technological change because there was no effect on the ability of firms to produce output with a different quantity of inputs.

Step 4: **Answer question (c) by discussing the effect of computers on technological change.**
The widespread use of computers has led to a widespread improvement in productivity. Many firms were able to produce the same output of goods and services with fewer inputs or more output with the same quantity of inputs.

Step 5: **Answer question (d) by discussing the results of the installation of the new software program at Hershey in 1999.**
The initial use of the software produced negative technological change since Hershey's output was less with the same quantity of inputs. After the major "bugs" were eliminated, the use of this software produced a positive technological change.

10.2 LEARNING OBJECTIVE

10.2 The Short Run and the Long Run (pages 335-339)

Learning Objective 2 Distinguish between the economic short run and the economic long run.

The **short run** is a period of time during which at least one of the firm's inputs is fixed. The **long run** is a period of time long enough to allow a firm to vary all of its inputs, to adopt new technology, and to increase or decrease the size of its physical plant. **Total cost** is the cost of all the inputs a firm uses in production. **Variable costs** are costs that change as output changes. **Fixed costs** are costs that remain constant as output changes.

$$\text{Total Cost } (TC) = \text{Fixed Cost } (FC) + \text{Variable Cost } (VC)$$

In the long run, all costs are variable because the quantities of all inputs are variable.

Total costs can also be divided into explicit and implicit costs. An **explicit cost** is a cost that involves spending money. An **implicit cost** is a nonmonetary opportunity cost. Recall from Chapters 1 and 2 that the **opportunity cost** of an activity is the highest-valued alternative that must be given up to engage in the activity. **Average total cost** (*ATC*) is total cost divided by the quantity of output produced, or the cost of producing the average unit. The **production function** is the relationship between the inputs employed by the firm and the maximum output it can produce with those inputs. In the short run, at least one input is fixed, so the short-run production function shows the level of output the firm can produce with different levels of the variable inputs and a constant quantity of the fixed input. The long-run production function shows the maximum quantity of output the firm can produce using various levels of all inputs.

Helpful Study Hint

An example may help you to understand the difference between a short-run and a long-run production function. Your hometown probably has a theater, stadium, or auditorium. Various events are held at these venues during the year, some of which may sell out while others do not. In the short run, the size of the facility is a fixed input and variations in crowd size can be accommodated by changes in the use of variable inputs (such as ticket takers, ushers, parking attendants, and food at refreshment stands). It is unlikely that the owners will decide to increase or decrease the capacity of the facility unless they expect a permanent change in average expected attendance. Such a permanent change could be the result of an increase or decrease in the population served by the facility or the acquisition or loss of a permanent tenant; for example, a professional sports franchise or a philharmonic orchestra. Expanding or contracting the size of the facility (usually by tearing down the existing structure and building a new one) is an example of a long-run production decision. See ***Making the Connection*** "Fixed Costs in the Publishing Industry" for a discussion of fixed costs in the editing and marketing of books. Because the number of editors, designers, and marketing people does not vary with the number of copies of books that are sold in a given year, publishers treat the salaries and benefits of people in these job categories as fixed costs.

Extra Solved Problem **10-2**

Chapter 10 in the textbook includes two Solved Problems. Here is an extra Solved Problem to help you build your skills solving economic problems.

Supports Learning Objective 2: Distinguish between the economic short run and the economic long run.

Apple Picking

Suppose that you own an apple orchard and the following chart represents the number of apples that can be picked from your orchard on a per-hour basis with a given quantity of capital equipment, such as baskets and ladders.

Quantity of Workers	Apples	Fixed Cost	Variable Cost	Total Cost	Cost per Apple (*ATC*)
0	0	$10	$0		
1	100	10	5		
2	210	10	10		
3	300	10	15		
4	380	10	20		
5	450	10	25		

a. Complete the table above by calculating the total cost and the average total cost.

b. Does the total cost in the table represent your short-run or long-run total cost?

SOLVING THE PROBLEM

Step 1: **Review the chapter material.**
This problem is about distinguishing short-run and long-run costs, so you may want to review the section, "The Short Run and the Long Run in Economics," which begins on page 335 in the textbook.

Step 2: Answer question (a) by computing the total cost and the average total cost.
Total cost is calculated by adding the fixed costs to the variable costs. The average total cost is the total cost divided by the quantity. The table below provides the results of the calculations.

Quantity of Workers	Apples	Fixed Cost	Variable Cost	Total Cost	Cost per Apple (ATC)
0	0	$10	$0	$10	–
1	100	10	5	15	$ 0.15
2	210	10	10	20	0.10
3	300	10	15	25	0.08
4	380	10	20	30	0.08
5	450	10	25	35	0.08

Step 3: Answer question (b) by determining whether the costs and production function shown in the table are representative of the short run or the long run.
To determine whether this is the short run or the long run, we need to determine if all inputs are variable or if at least one input is fixed. In the description of the problem, we see that the number of ladders and baskets is fixed, so we are looking at the short-run condition. This is reinforced by the fact that your orchard is experiencing a positive and constant fixed cost.

10.3 LEARNING OBJECTIVE

10.3 The Marginal Product of Labor and the Average Product of Labor (pages 339-342)

Learning Objective 3 Understand the relationship between the marginal product of labor and the average product of labor.

The **marginal product of labor** is the additional output a firm produces as a result of hiring one more worker. The increases in marginal product of labor that occur at low rates of output result from specialization and the division of labor. Consider for instance, a firm that initially employs only one worker. Adding a second or third worker, for example, would typically reduce the time the workers spend moving from one activity to the next and allow them to become more specialized at their tasks. At some point, adding more of a variable input, such as labor, to the same amount of a fixed input, such as capital, will cause the marginal product of the variable input to decline. This principle is called the **law of diminishing returns**.

The **average product of labor** is the total output produced by a firm divided by the quantity of workers. When the marginal product of labor is greater than the average product of labor, the average product of labor must be increasing. When the marginal product of labor is less than the average product of labor, the average product of labor must be decreasing. The marginal product of labor equals the average product of labor for the quantity of workers where the average product of labor is at a maximum.

Helpful Study Hint

The relationship between the marginal and average product of labor is similar to many other marginal-average relationships. You will better understand the relationship between the marginal product and average product of labor after reviewing the example of GPAs illustrated in Figure 10-3. Also read ***Making the Connection*** "Adam Smith's Famous Account of the Division of Labor in a Pin Factory" for a discussion of how the division of labor can increase the average output per worker. Smith describes how workers become very specialized in a particular part of the production process with the division of labor and, thus, become more productive.

Extra Solved Problem 10-3

Chapter 10 in the textbook includes two Solved Problems. Here is an extra Solved Problem to help you build your skills solving economic problems.

Supports Learning Objective 3: Understand the relationship between the marginal product of labor and the average product of labor.

Apple Picking - Continued

Suppose that you own an apple orchard and the following chart represents the number of apples that can be picked from your orchard on a per-hour basis with the given capital equipment, including five baskets.

Quantity of Workers	Quantity of Baskets	Apples	Marginal Product of Labor	Average Product of Labor
0	5	0		
1	5	100	100	100
2	5	210	110	105
3	5	300	90	100
4	5	380	80	95
5	5	450	70	90

a. Complete the table above by calculating the marginal product of labor and the average product of labor.

b. Describe the relationship between marginal product of labor and the orchard's total production. Does the law of diminishing returns apply to the orchard's production?

c. Describe the relationship between the marginal product of labor and the average product of labor.

SOLVING THE PROBLEM

Step 1: Review the chapter material.

This problem is about marginal and average product of labor, so you may want to review the section "The Marginal Product of Labor and the Average Product of Labor," which begins on page 339 of the textbook.

Step 2: Answer question (a) by computing the marginal product of labor and the average product of labor.

The marginal product of labor is the additional output a firm produces as a result of hiring one more worker. This is calculated by dividing the change in the quantity of apples produced by the changing in the quantity of labor used to produce the apples. The average product of labor is the total output produced by a firm divided by the quantity of workers used to produce that output. The results of these calculations are displayed in the table below.

Quantity of Workers	Quantity of Baskets	Apples	Marginal Product of Labor	Average Product of Labor
0	5	0		
1	5	100	100	100
2	5	210	110	105
3	5	300	90	100
4	5	380	80	95
5	5	450	70	90

Step 3: Answer question (b) by explaining the relationship between the marginal product and the total output.

When the marginal product is increasing rapidly the firms total output increases rapidly. As the gains from specialization and the division of labor are exhausted, an additional increase in labor causes the marginal product to fall. Total output continues to increase but at a decreasing rate as the marginal product falls. See Figure 10-2 on page 341 of the textbook to see an example of this.

Step 4: Answer question (c) by describing the relationship between the marginal product of labor and the average product of labor.

When the marginal product of labor is greater than the average product of labor, the average product of labor will increase. When the marginal product of labor is lower than the average product of labor, the average product of labor will decrease. (See the GPA example on page 342 of the textbook for an example of how the marginal drives the average.)

10.4 LEARNING OBJECTIVE

10.4 The Relationship between Short-Run Production and Short-Run Cost (pages 342-345)

Learning Objective 4 Explain and illustrate the relationship between marginal cost and average total cost.

In the short run, the behavior of the marginal product of the variable factor is represented in the behavior of marginal cost. **Marginal cost** is the change in a firm's total cost from producing one more unit of a good or service. The U-shape of the average total cost curve is determined by the shape of the marginal cost curve. Marginal cost (*MC*) can be expressed mathematically as

$$MC = \frac{\Delta TC}{\Delta Q}$$

where Δ represents "change in," *TC* is total cost, and *Q* is output.

The law of diminishing returns explains the behavior of the marginal product of the variable factor in the short run. This is illustrated in Figure 10-4 on page 344 of the textbook. The table in this figure shows how the marginal product of labor rises for the first and second workers and the marginal cost falls as these first two workers are hired. As diminishing returns set in, the marginal product of labor falls and the marginal cost rises as the last four workers are hired. The marginal cost of production falls and then rises—a U-shape—because the marginal product of labor rises and then falls.

Helpful Study Hint

Solved Problem 10-4 shows how, as diminishing returns set in, the average and marginal costs of production rise. Work-related end-of-chapter problems 4.5 and 4.6 for further help in understanding the law of diminishing returns and its relationship to costs.

10.5 LEARNING OBJECTIVE

10.5 Graphing Cost Curves (Page 346)

Learning Objective 5 Graph average total cost, average variable cost, average fixed cost, and marginal cost.

Several related average cost measures can be described mathematically.

Average total cost (*ATC*) equals total cost (*TC*) divided by the quantity of output produced.

$$ATC = \frac{TC}{Q}$$

Average fixed cost (*AFC*) equals fixed cost divided by the quantity of output produced.

$$AFC = \frac{FC}{Q}$$

Average variable cost (*AVC*) equals variable cost divided by the quantity of output produced.

$$AVC = \frac{VC}{Q}$$

The *MC*, *ATC*, and *AVC* curves are all U-shaped. Here are key points about these curves:

- When *MC* is below *AVC* or *ATC*, it causes them to decrease.
- The *MC* curve intersects the *AVC* and *ATC* curves at their minimum points.
- When *MC* is above *AVC* or *ATC*, it causes them to increase.
- As output increases, the difference between *ATC* and *AVC* (this is equal to *AFC*) gets smaller because *AFC* gets smaller and smaller as output increases.

Helpful Study Hint

Practice drawing these cost curves by working through the ***Extra Solved Problem*** that appears next. To draw the curves accurately, it is best to draw the *MC* curve first. Then draw *ATC* but start by putting your pencil or pen on the *MC* curve and drawing the left half of *ATC*. Go back to the *MC* curve and then draw the right half of *ATC*. Follow the same procedure to draw *AVC*. When you draw the left half of AVC make sure that the difference between *ATC* and *AVC* becomes greater as output decreases. When you draw the right half of *AVC*, make the difference between *ATC* and *AVC* smaller as output increases. Remember that the difference between *ATC* and *AVC* is *AFC* (average fixed cost).

Extra Solved Problem 10-5

Chapter 10 in the textbook includes two Solved Problems. Here is an extra Solved Problem to help you build your skills solving economic problems.

Supports Learning Objective 5: Graph average total cost, average variable cost, average fixed cost, and marginal cost.

Apple Picking - Continued

Suppose that you own an apple orchard and the following chart represents the quantity of apples that can be picked from your orchard per hour with a given quantity of capital equipment, such as baskets and ladders.

Quantity of Workers	Apples	Fixed Cost	Variable Cost	Total Cost	Cost per Apple (*ATC*)	*MC*	*AVC*	*AFC*
0	0	$10	$0	$10				
1	100	10	5	15	$ 0.15			
2	210	10	10	20	0.10			
3	300	10	15	25	0.08			
4	380	10	20	30	0.08			
5	450	10	25	35	0.08			

a. Complete the table above by calculating the marginal cost, average variable cost, and the average fixed cost.

b. Graph the marginal cost, average total cost, average variable cost, and average fixed cost curves.

SOLVING THE PROBLEM

Step 1: Review the chapter material.
To complete this problem you may want to review the section Graphing Cost Curves that begins on page 346 of the textbook.

Step 2: Answer question (a) by computing the marginal cost, the average variable cost, and the average fixed cost.
The average fixed cost is the fixed cost divided by the quantity of output produced. Average variable cost is calculated by dividing variable cost by the quantity of units produced. The marginal cost is the change in a firm's total cost from producing one more unit of a good or service. The results of these calculations are presented below. (Hint: Students often make the mistake of using the quantity of workers in these calculations, but you should use the quantity of apples produced.)

Quantity of Workers	Apples	Fixed Cost	Variable Cost	Total Cost	Cost per Apple (*ATC*)	*MC*	*AVC*	*AFC*
0	0	10	0	10				
1	100	10	5	15	$0.150	$0.050	$0.050	$0.100
2	210	10	10	20	0.095	0.045	0.048	0.048
3	300	10	15	25	0.083	0.056	0.050	0.033
4	380	10	20	30	0.079	0.063	0.053	0.026
5	450	10	25	35	0.078	0.071	0.056	0.022

Step 3: **Answer question (b) by graphing the cost curves.**
To graph each of the average cost curves and the marginal cost curve, you should consider what the cost is for each given quantity. The graph of the curves is as follows:

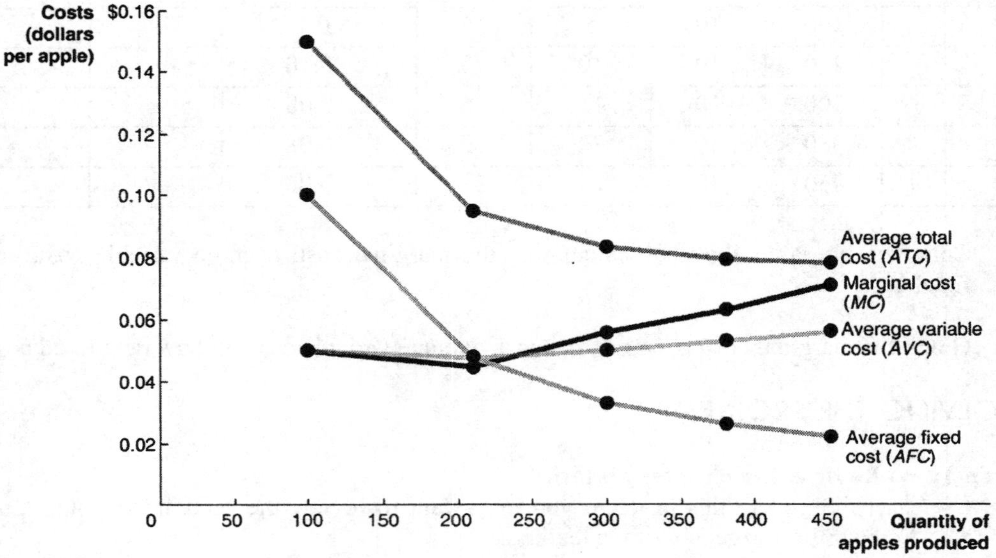

10.6 LEARNING OBJECTIVE

10.6 Costs in the Long Run (pages 346-351)

Learning Objective 6 Understand how firms use the long-run average cost curve in their planning.

There are no fixed costs in the long run, so total cost equals variable cost. In the short run, managers of firms decide how they will operate their current store, office, or factory. In the long run, managers decide whether the firm would be more profitable if the store, office, or factory were made larger or smaller.

A **long-run average cost curve** shows the lowest cost at which the firm is able to produce a given quantity of output in the long run, when no inputs are fixed. **Economies of scale** is the situation when a firm's long-run average total costs fall as it increases output. **Constant returns to scale** is the situation when a firm's long-run average costs remain unchanged as it increases output. **Minimum efficient scale** is the level of output at which all economies of scale have been exhausted. **Diseconomies of scale** is the situation when a firm's long-run average costs rise as it increases output.

Economies of scale may result from several factors. The firm's technology may make it possible to increase production with a smaller than proportional increase in at least one input. As output expands, both workers and managers may become more specialized, enabling them to be more productive. Large firms may be able to purchase inputs at lower costs than smaller competitors. Diseconomies of scale result when managers have difficulty coordinating a firm as it grows in scale.

Helpful Study Hint

Long-run average cost curves, such as those shown in Solved Problem 10-6, are drawn as smooth U-shaped curves. Do not confuse these curves with short-run average total cost curves. Read ***Don't Let This Happen to YOU!*** "Don't Confuse Diminishing Returns with Diseconomies of Scale," which explains why there are different explanations for the U-shape of the short-run and long-run curves. The smooth long-run average cost curve is similar to the optical illusion of a motion picture. A motion picture is essentially a series of still photographs that when projected sequentially (and rapidly) give the viewer the illusion of live, continuous motion. Similarly, the long-run average cost curve is made up of a series of short-run *ATC* curves, each of which contributes a small portion (one point) of the long-run average cost curve. As the plant size increases or decrease, the effect of the plant size on the production cost (that is, economies and diseconomies of scale) determines the shape of the long-run average cost curve. The shape of the short-run average cost curve, on the other hand, is determined by diminishing returns.

Solved Problem 10-6 describes how Motorola and Siemens both produced mobile phone handsets and wireless infrastructure. The companies decided that they would exchange businesses, so that each company specialized in only one of the two goods. In doing this, each firm was able to increase the size of its operations and take advantage of scale economies, which means that each firm is able to produce the same quantities of the goods at lower costs.

Henry Ford and the Ford Motor Company learned a hard lesson that bigger is not always better. Read ***Making the Connection***, "The Colossal River Rouge: Diseconomies of Scale at Ford Motor Company," which explains that Ford experienced economies of scale by building larger factories in the early years of the company. Ford expected that by building the colossal River Rouge plant he would continue to reduce his average costs of producing automobiles. However, the River Rouge plant turned out to be too large and Ford encountered diseconomies of scale, which raised his average cost of production.

Helpful Study Hint

Economics in YOUR Life! asked you to consider why Bob (a competing retailer) can sell his recliners at a lower price than you can. Bob is selling more recliners than you are at a lower price per recliner and is still able to make a profit. Bob can do this because as he increases his sales, the average fixed cost per recliner decreases, and so does his average total cost. If his average total cost is lower than yours, he can sell his recliners at a lower price and still make a profit.

Key Terms

Average fixed cost. Fixed cost divided by the quantity of output produced.

Average product of labor. The total output produced by a firm divided by the quantity of workers.

Average total cost. Total cost divided by the quantity of output produced.

Average variable cost. Variable cost divided by the quantity of output produced.

Constant returns to scale. The situation when a firm's long-run average costs remain unchanged as the firm increases output.

Diseconomies of scale. The situation when a firm's long-run average costs rise as the firm increases output.

Economies of scale. The situation when a firm's long-run average costs fall as the firm increases output.

Expansion path. A curve that shows a firm's cost-minimizing combination of inputs for every level of output.

Explicit cost. A cost that involves spending money.

Fixed costs. Costs that remain constant as output changes.

Implicit cost. A nonmonetary opportunity cost.

Isocost line. All the combinations of two inputs, such as capital and labor, that have the same total cost.

Isoquant. A curve that shows all the combinations of two inputs, such as capital and labor, that will produce the same level of output.

Law of diminishing returns. The principle that, at some point, adding more of a variable input, such as labor, to the same amount of a fixed input, such as capital, will cause the marginal product of the variable input to decline.

Long run. A period in which a firm can allow a firm to vary all of its inputs, adopt new technology, and increase or decrease the size of its physical plant.

Long-run average cost curve. A curve showing the lowest cost at which the firm is able to produce a given quantity of output in the long run, when no inputs are fixed.

Marginal cost. The change in a firm's total cost from producing one more unit of a good or service.

Marginal product of labor. The additional output a firm produces as a result of hiring one more worker.

Marginal rate of technical substitution (*MRTS*). The slope of an isoquant, or the rate at which a firm is able to substitute one input for another while keeping the level of output constant.

Minimum efficient scale. The level of output at which all economies of scale have been exhausted.

Opportunity cost. The highest-valued alternative that must be given up to engage in an activity.

Production function. The relationship between the inputs employed by the firm and the maximum output it can produce with those inputs.

Short run. The period of time during which at least one of the firm's inputs is fixed.

Technological change. A change in the ability of a firm to produce a given level of output with a given quantity of inputs.

Technology. The processes a firm uses to turn inputs into outputs of goods and services.

Total cost. The cost of all the inputs a firm uses in production.

Variable costs. Costs that change as output changes.

Appendix

Using Isoquants and Isocosts to Understand Production and Costs

LEARNING OBJECTIVE: Use isoquants and isocost lines to understand production and cost.

The chapter covers the relationship between a firm's level of production and its costs. This appendix looks more closely at how firms choose the *combination of inputs* to produce a given level of output.

Isoquants

Firms search for the cost-minimizing combination of inputs that will allow them to produce a given level of output. The cost-minimizing combination of inputs depends on technology and input prices. An **isoquant** is a curve showing all the combinations of two inputs, such as capital and labor, that will produce the same level of output. The farther an isoquant is from the origin – the farther to the right on the graph – the more output the firm is producing. There are many isoquants, one for every possible level of output.

The **marginal rate of technical substitution (*MRTS*)** is the slope of an isoquant. The *MRTS* represents the rate at which a firm is able to substitute one input for another while keeping the level of output constant. The slope of an isoquant becomes less steep as one moves downward along the isoquant. This is a consequence of diminishing returns.

Helpful Study Hint

Figure 10A-1 illustrates three isoquants, each of which represents various combinations of capital (measured on the vertical axis) and labor (measured on the horizontal axis) that enable Jill to produce a given number of pizzas per week. Isoquants are similar to indifference curves in several respects. If you understand the analysis of indifference curves in the appendix to Chapter 9, you should understand isoquants.

Isocost Lines

The relationship between the quantity of inputs used and the firm's total cost can be shown with an **isocost line**. An isocost line shows all the combinations of two inputs, such as capital and labor, that have the same total cost. An isocost line intersects the vertical axis at the maximum amount of an input (for example, capital) that can be purchased with a given budget, or total cost. The same isocost line intersects the horizontal axis at the maximum amount of another input (for example, labor) that can be purchased with the same budget. One input is substituted for another as one moves along an isocost line, but the total expenditure on inputs is the same. The slope of an isocost line is constant and equals the change in the quantity of one input (capital) divided by the change in the quantity of the other input (labor). The slope of an isocost line is equal to the ratio of the price of the input on the horizontal axis divided by the price of the input on the vertical axis, multiplied by negative 1. A change in the price of an input causes the slope to change, which is a rotation of the isocost line. Higher levels of total cost shift the isocost line outward, and lower levels of cost shift the isocost line inward.

Helpful Study Hint

Figure 10A-2 on page 366 of the textbook illustrates an example of an isocost line. The analysis of isocost lines is similar to the analysis of budget lines in the appendix to Chapter 9.

Choosing the Cost-Minimizing Combination of Capital and Labor

If diminishing returns exist, there will be only one combination of inputs that will produce a given amount of output at the lowest total cost. The lowest cost combination of inputs that will produce a given level of output is found at the tangency of an isocost line with the isoquant that represents the given output level. The cost-minimizing choice of inputs is determined jointly by available production technology and input prices. A change in technology affects the position of isoquants and may affect the choice of inputs. If input prices change the position of isocost lines will change and the choice of inputs may also change.

At the point of cost minimization, the *MRTS* is equal to the price of the input measured on the horizontal axis (for example, the wage rate or price of labor) divided by the price of the input measured on the vertical axis (for example, the rental price of capital). The slope of an isoquant, or the *MRTS*, is the rate at which a firm can substitute labor for capital given the existing technology. The slope of an isocost line, or the price ratio, is the rate at which a firm is able to substitute labor for capital at given current input prices.

Helpful Study Hint

Making the Connection "The Changing Input Mix in Walt Disney Film Animation" describes how Disney has substituted away from the now relatively expensive input, animators, toward the less expensive input of computers in order to minimize the costs of production for their highly-popular animated films.

Moving along an isoquant, the output is constant while changes the amounts of two inputs change. The marginal product of capital (MP_K) equals the change in output from using an additional unit of capital. The marginal product of labor (MP_L) equals the change in output from using an additional unit of labor. The change in output from moving down an isoquant is equal to:

$$-\Delta \text{ quantity of capital x } MP_K = \Delta \text{ quantity of labor x } MP_L$$

Rewriting this equation:

$$-\frac{\Delta \text{ quantity of capital}}{\Delta \text{ quantity of labor}} = MRTS = \frac{MP_L}{MP_K}$$

The slope of the isocost line equals the wage rate (w) divided by the rental price of capital (r). At the point of cost minimization, the slope of the isoquant equals the slope of the isocost line. Therefore:

$$\frac{MP_L}{MP_K} = \frac{w}{r}$$

or, after rearranging, $\frac{MP_L}{w} = \frac{MP_K}{r}$

The last equation implies that to minimize cost, a firm should hire inputs up to the point where the last dollar spent on each input results in the same increase in output.

Helpful Study Hint

Solved Problem 10A-1 explains how Jill can find the cost minimizing combination of inputs to produce pizza. A firm should purchase or hire inputs up to the point where the ratio of the marginal product to the price of the input is the same for every input used. If one input has a higher marginal product for the last dollar spent, then the firm should hire more of that input and less of the other input in order to minimize the costs of production. See ***Making the Connection*** "Do National Football League Teams Behave Efficiently?" for a discussion of how NFL team managers often overestimate the marginal productivity of top draft picks relative to the marginal productivity of lower draft picks. Therefore, they tend to pay salaries to the top draft picks that are too high relative to their marginal productivity. By more efficiently allocating their salaries, NFL teams would be able to win more games at the same cost.

The Expansion Path

An **expansion path** is a curve showing a firm's cost-minimizing combination of inputs for every level of output. The expansion path represents the least-cost combination of inputs to produce a given level of output in the long run when the firm is able to vary the levels of all of its inputs. In the short run, at least one of the firm's inputs is fixed. The expansion of output is possible only by varying the firm's variable input(s), so the firm's minimum total costs of production are lower in the long run than in the short run.

Key Terms – Appendix

Expansion path. A curve that shows a firm's cost-minimizing combination of inputs for every level of output.

Isocost line. All the combinations of two inputs, such as capital and labor, that have the same total cost.

Isoquant. A curve that shows all the combinations of two inputs, such as capital and labor, that will produce the same level of output.

Marginal rate of technical substitution (*MRTS*). The slope of an isoquant, or the rate at which a firm is able to substitute one input for another while keeping the level of output constant.

Self-Test

(Answers are provided at the end of the Self-Test.)

Multiple-Choice Questions

1. The process a firm uses to turn inputs into outputs of goods and services is ___________.
   a. technology
   b. technological change
   c. the short run
   d. the production function

2. The term used to describe the ability of a firm to produce more output using the same inputs, or the same output using fewer inputs is ____________.
   a. technology
   b. technological change
   c. the long run
   d. the production function

3. What is the *short run*?
   a. A period of time during which a firm can vary all of its inputs.
   b. A period of time during which a firm can adopt a new technology.
   c. A period of time during which a firm can increase or decrease the size of its physical plant.
   d. A period of time during which at least one of the firm's inputs is fixed.

4. Which costs are affected by the level of output produced?
   a. Fixed costs
   b. Variable costs
   c. All costs
   d. Sunk costs

5. If the number of people in a publishing company does not go up or down with the quantity of books it publishes, then how should we categorize the salaries and benefits paid to these employees?
   a. They are part of fixed cost.
   b. They are part of variable cost.
   c. They are an implicit cost.
   d. They are not considered a part of the cost of production.

6. Which of the following is known as the highest-valued alternative that must be given up in order to engage in that activity?
   a. Opportunity cost
   b. Explicit cost
   c. Total cost
   d. Variable cost

7. Refer to the table below. Which of the following costs are *implicit costs*?

Paper	$20,000
Wages	$48,000
Lease payment for copy machines	$10,000
Electricity	$6,000
Lease payment for store	$24,000
Foregone salary	$30,000
Foregone interest	$3,000
Total	$141,000

   a. The foregone salary and interest
   b. The lease payments
   c. The payments for paper, wages, and electricity
   d. All of the above

8. Which of the following are sometimes called *accounting costs*?
   a. Economic costs
   b. Implicit costs
   c. Explicit costs
   d. Total variable costs

9. What is the *production function*?
   a. A representation of the firm's costs
   b. A relationship between the inputs employed by a firm and the maximum output it can produce with those inputs
   c. The total cost divided by the quantity of output produced
   d. All of the above

10. Fill in the blanks. When graphing a conventional *short-run production function*, we place ________________ in the horizontal axis and ________________ in the vertical axis.
   a. output; the variable input
   b. the variable input; the fixed input
   c. the fixed input; the variable input
   d. the variable input; output

11. Refer to the graphs below. Which graph is representative of a typical *average total cost* curve?

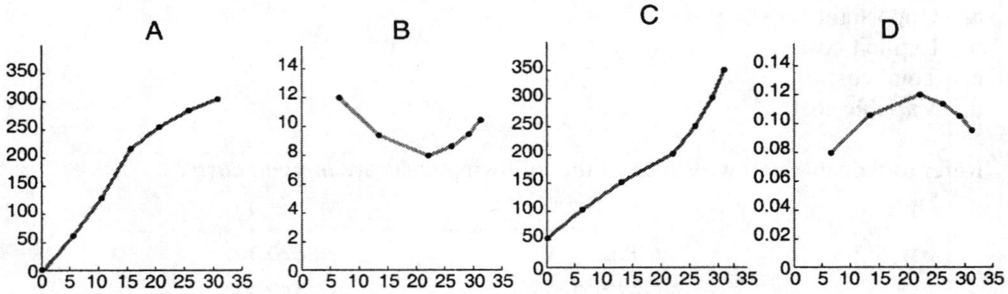

a. A
b. B
c. C
d. D

12. Which of the following is true?

i. Total cost = fixed cost + variable cost
ii. Total cost = explicit costs + implicit costs
iii. Economic cost = accounting cost + implicit costs

a. i only
b. ii only
c. i and ii only
d. i, ii, and iii

13. What is the additional output that a firm produces as a result of hiring one more worker called?

a. The production function
b. Average total cost
c. Marginal product of labor
d. Average product of labor

14. Refer to the table below. When do diminishing returns in the production of copies start?

QUANTITY OF WORKERS	QUANTITY OF PIZZA OVENS	QUANTITY OF PIZZAS	MARGINAL PRODUCT OF LABOR
0	2	0	—
1	2	200	200
2	2	450	250
3	2	550	100
4	2	600	50
5	2	625	25
6	2	640	15

a. When the second worker is hired
b. When the third worker is hired
c. When the fourth worker is hired
d. When the fifth worker is hired

15. Refer to the graph below. In moving along the curve from point A to point *B*, which of the following is more likely to occur?

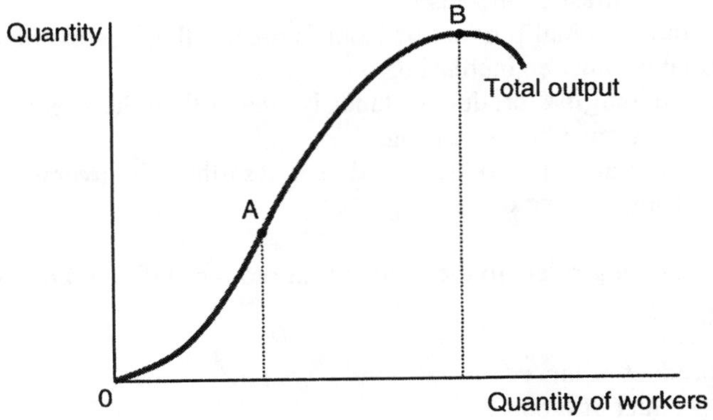

a. Specialization
b. Diminishing returns
c. Division of labor
d. None of the above

16. Refer to the graph below. From the origin up until point *A*,

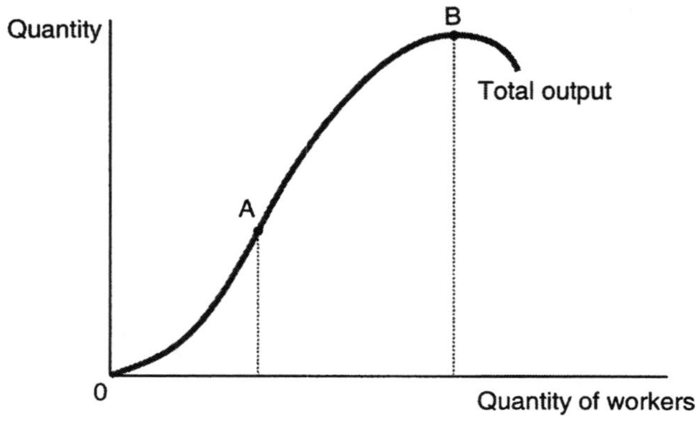

a. output increases at an increasing rate.
b. output increases at a decreasing rate.
c. output increases at a constant rate.
d. the effect of diminishing returns is greater than the effect of specialization.

17. Which of the following statements about the relationship between marginal and average product is correct?
a. Whenever the marginal product of labor is less than the average product of labor, the average product of labor must be increasing.
b. Whenever the marginal product of labor is greater than the average product of labor, the average product of labor must be increasing.
c. Whenever the marginal product of labor is greater than the average product of labor, the marginal product of labor must be decreasing.
d. Whenever the marginal product of labor is less than the average product of labor, the marginal product of labor must be decreasing.

18. Which of the following refers to the total output produced divided by the quantity of workers?
a. Average total cost
b. Marginal cost
c. Average product of labor
d. Marginal product of labor

19. Refer to the graph below. Based on the relationship between *marginal product* and *average product*, which curve appears to be *average product*?

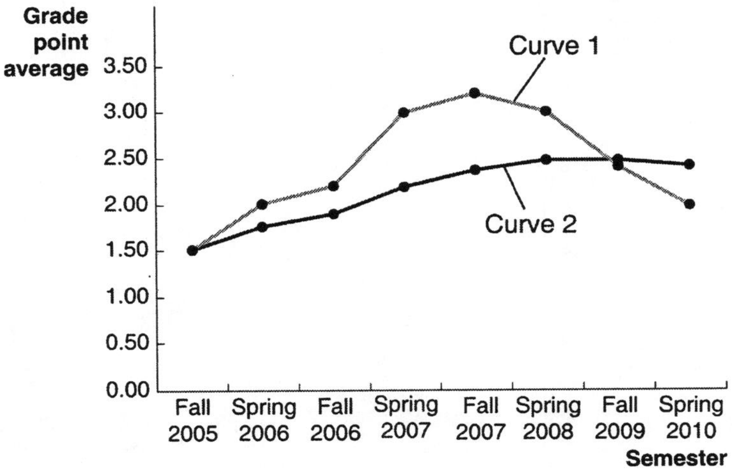

a. Curve 1
b. Curve 2
c. Both curves appear to be average product curves.
d. Neither curve

20. Refer to the table below. What is the *marginal cost* of producing the 200th pizza?

Quantity of Workers	Quantity of Pizzas	Marginal Product of Labor	Total Cost of Pizzas
0	0	–	$800
1	200	200	1450
2	450	250	2100
3	550	100	2750
4	600	50	3400
5	625	25	4050
6	640	15	4700

a. Zero
b. $2.60
c. $3.25
d. $650

21. Refer to the graph below. Based on the relationship between average cost and marginal cost, which of the curves below appears to be *average cost*?

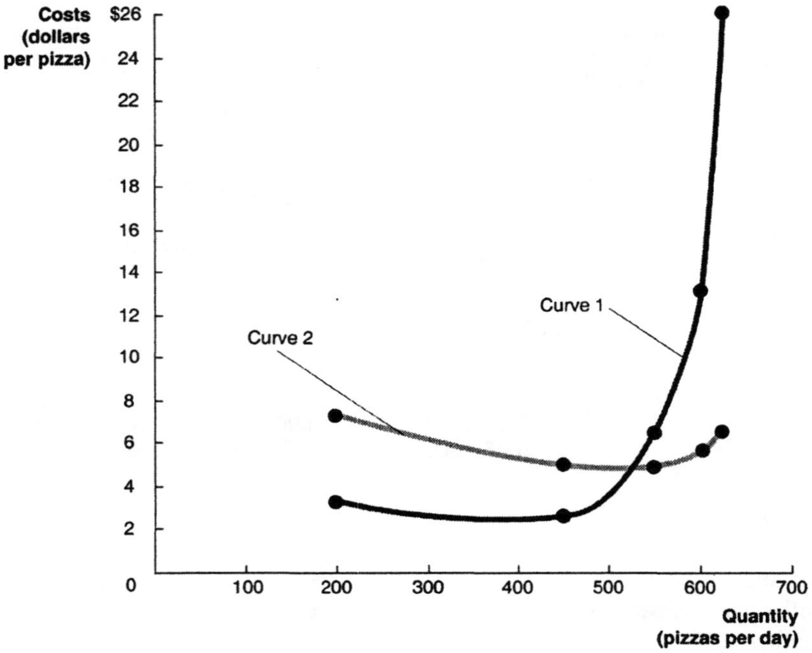

a. Curve 1
b. Curve 2
c. Both curves appear to be average cost curves.
d. Neither curve

22. Refer to the graph below. For a certain output range (or quantity produced per day), marginal cost is greater than average cost. Which output range is that?

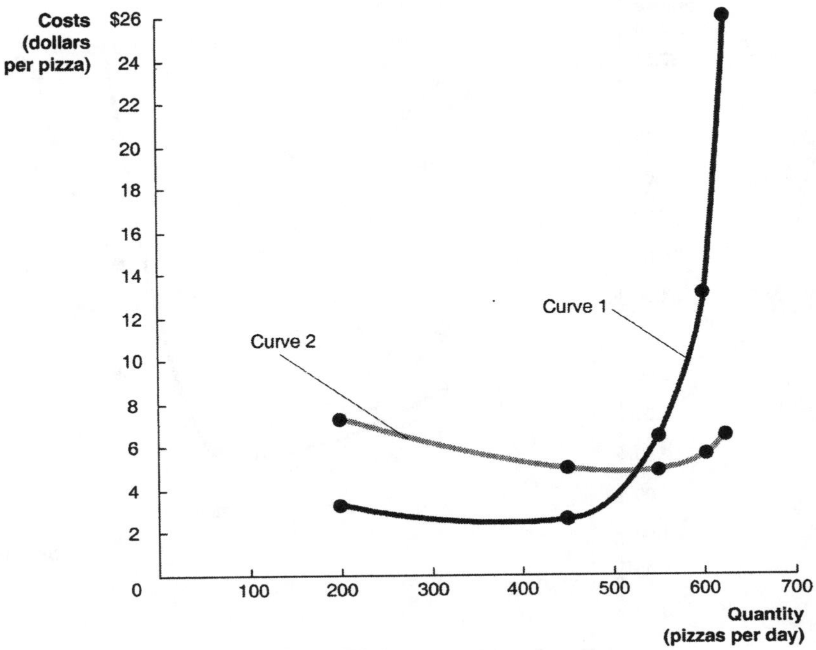

a. From zero to about 525 units.
b. The output range after about 525 units.
c. The entire output range, from zero to about 640 units.
d. Exactly 640 units.

23. What measure do we obtain by dividing the fixed cost by the quantity of output produced?
a. Total variable cost
b. Average fixed cost
c. Total cost
d. Average variable cost

24. What cost measure do we obtain from $AFC + AVC$?
a. Total cost
b. Average total cost
c. Marginal cost
d. Total variable cost

25. Refer to the graph below. What does curve 4 represent?

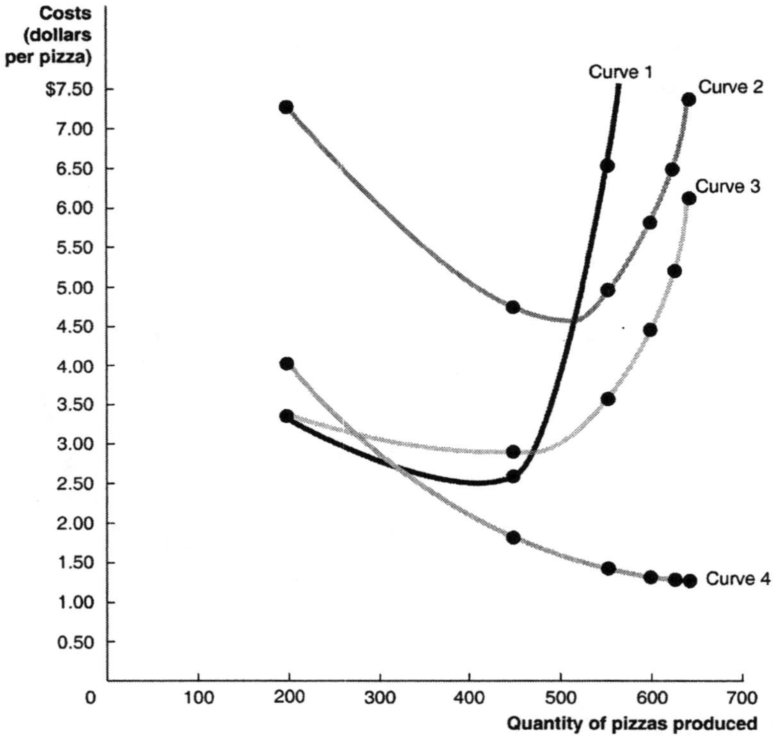

a. Average variable cost
b. Average total cost
c. Average fixed cost
d. Marginal cost

26. Refer to the graph below. What is the distance between curves 2 and 3 equal to?

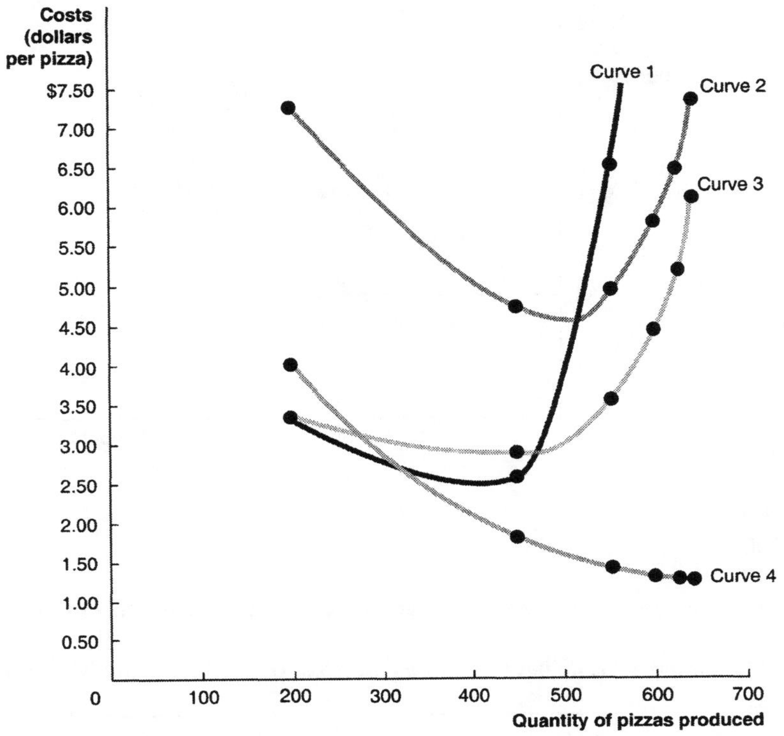

a. Curve 1
b. Curve 4
c. Total cost
d. Marginal cost

27. The following cost measures reach their minimum points when they are equal to the value of marginal cost, except one. Which one?
   a. Average variable cost
   b. Average total cost
   c. Average fixed cost
   d. There is no exception; all three measures above reach their minimum values when they are equal to the value of marginal cost.

28. What does the term "spreading the overhead" refer to?
   a. Lowering average fixed cost by selling more output.
   b. Lowering average total cost by selling more output.
   c. Lowering average variable cost by selling more output.
   d. Lowering total cost by selling more output.

29. Refer to the graph below. How much is the value of *total fixed cost*?

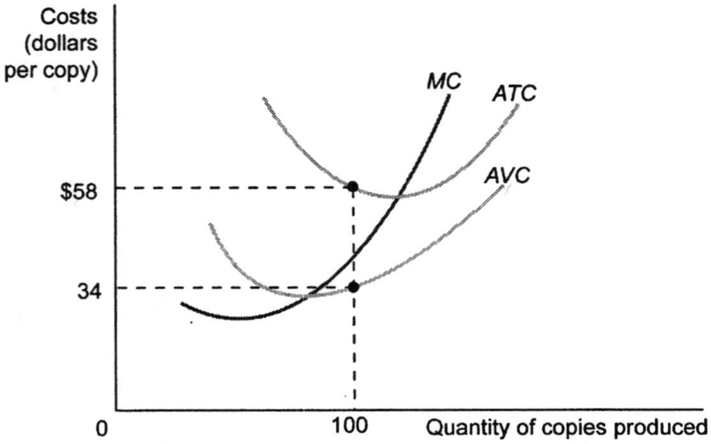

a. $2,400
b. $3,400
c. $5,800
d. None of the above; total fixed cost cannot be computed using this graph.

30. Refer to the table below. What is the *marginal cost* of producing the 640th pizza?

Quantity of Workers	Quantity of Ovens	Quantity of Pizzas	Cost of Ovens (Fixed cost)	Cost of Workers (Variable cost)	Total Cost of Pizzas
0	2	0	$800	$0	$800
1	2	200	800	650	1,450
2	2	450	800	1,300	2,100
3	2	550	800	1,950	2,750
4	2	600	800	2,600	3,400
5	2	625	800	3,250	4,050
6	2	640	800	3,900	4,700

a. $43.33
b. $650.00
c. $4050.00
d. $4700.00

31. Refer to the table below. What is the *average total cost* of producing 5,300 copies?

Quantity of Workers	Quantity of Ovens	Quantity of Pizzas	Cost of Ovens (Fixed cost)	Cost of Workers (Variable cost)	Total Cost of Pizzas
0	2	0	$800	$0	$800
1	2	200	800	650	1,450
2	2	450	800	1,300	2,100
3	2	550	800	1,950	2,750
4	2	600	800	2,600	3,400
5	2	625	800	3,250	4,050
6	2	640	800	3,900	4,700

a. $5.67
b. $6.48
c. $13.00
d. $26.00

32. What happens to the difference (or distance) between average variable cost and average total cost as the level of output increases?
a. The difference increases.
b. The difference decreases.
c. The difference remains the same.
d. The difference first increases then decreases.

33. Which of the following statements is correct?
a. In the long run, all costs are variable.
b. In the long run, all costs are fixed.
c. In the long run, there are no fixed or variable costs.
d. In the long run, at least one input remains fixed.

34. Which of the following terms refers to the lowest cost at which a firm is able to produce a given level of output in the long run, when no inputs are fixed?
a. The long-run marginal cost curve
b. The long-run average cost curve
c. The variable inputs curve
d. Economies of scale

35. What happens when firms experience *economies of scale*?
a. Firms can produce more output in smaller plants.
b. The firm's long run average costs fall as output increases.
c. The possibility of lowering long run average costs is exhausted.
d. Only a single plant size minimizes the long run average cost of production.

36. Refer to the graph below. Which change in output represents *economies of scale* in bookselling?

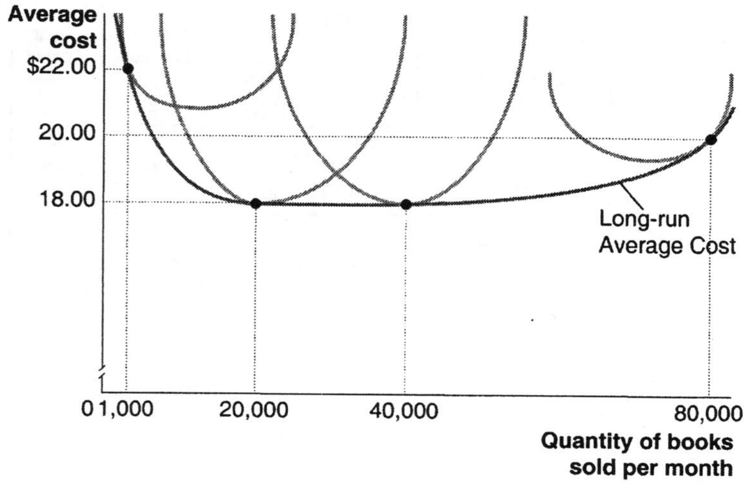

a. The move from 1,000 to 20,000 books sold per month.
b. The move from 20,000 to 40,000 books sold per month.
c. The move from 40,000 to 80,000 books sold per month.
d. None of the above. Economies of scale cannot be achieved anywhere on the graph.

37. Refer to the graph below. Which level of output represents the *minimum efficient scale*?

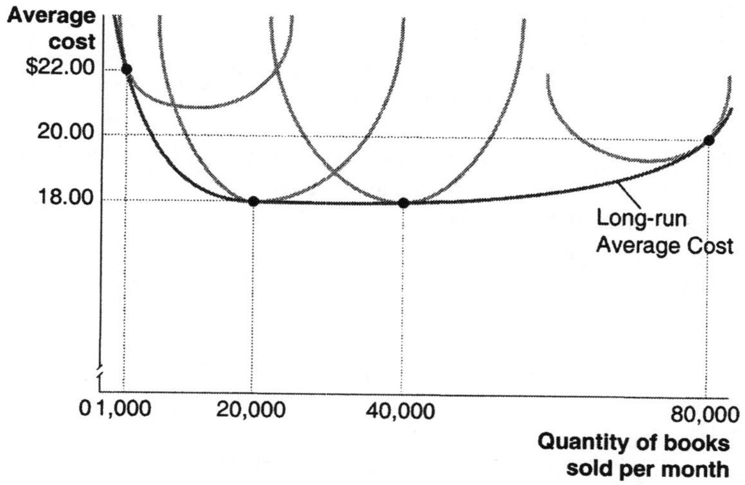

a. 1,000 books
b. 20,000 books
c. 40,000 books
d. 80,000 books

38. Refer to the graph below. In what output range do we find *constant returns to scale*?

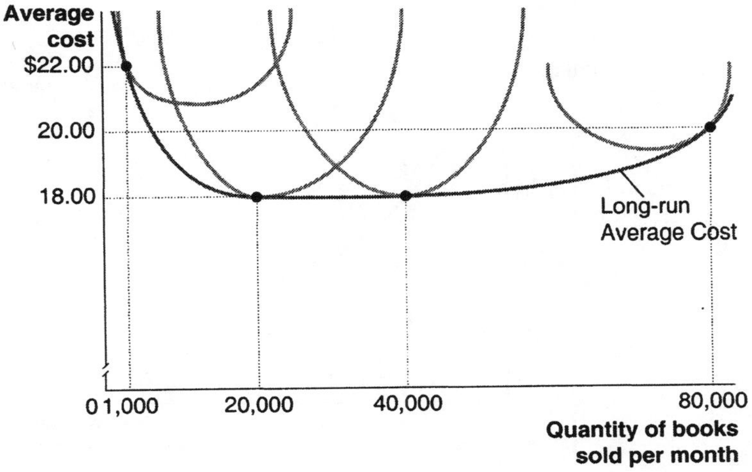

a. Between 0 and 1,000 books
b. Between 1,000 and 20,000 books
c. Between 20,000 and 40,000 books
d. Between 40,000 and 80,000 books

39. Refer to the graph below. Which bookstore is more likely to experience *diseconomies of scale*?

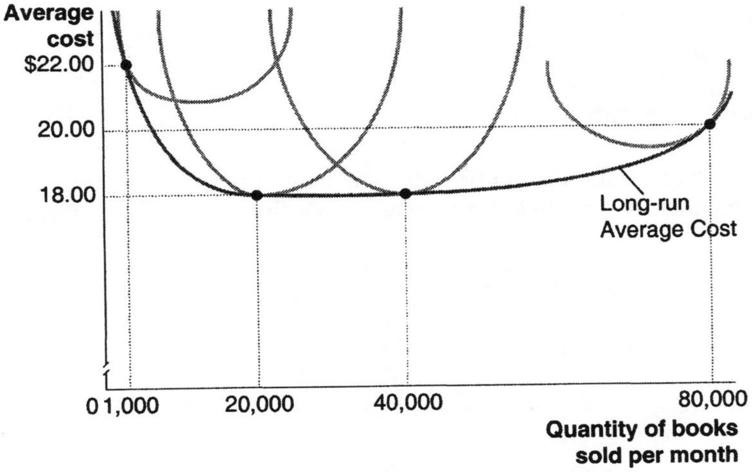

a. The bookstore selling 1,000 books per month
b. The bookstore selling 20,000 books per month
c. The bookstore selling 40,000 books per month
d. The bookstore selling 80,000 books per month

40. Refer to the graph below. Which point best illustrates several smaller companies producing a few phone handsets each rather than one large company producing many phone handsets?

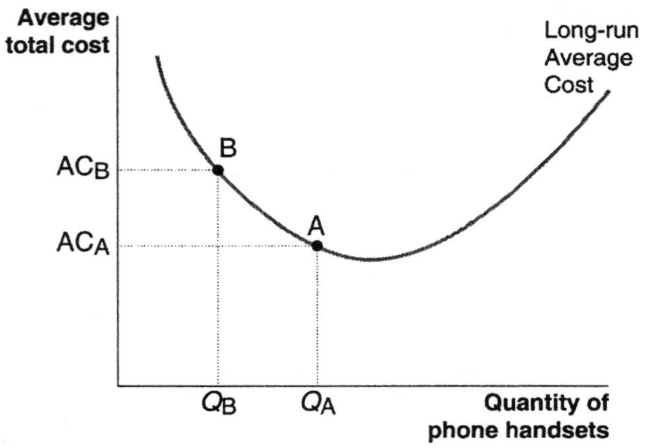

a. Point *A*
b. Point *B*
c. Either point *A* or point *B* depict two smaller companies.
d. Either point *A* or point *B* depict two larger companies.

41. When does the *law of diminishing returns* apply?
a. When there are *diseconomies of scale*
b. In the *short run* only
c. In the *long run* only
d. In both the *short run* and the *long run*

Short Answer Questions

1. Assume that the minimum efficient scale in an industry is equal to 25 percent of the total market for a product. Is it possible for more than four firms to survive in this market in the long run?

____

____

____

____

2. What is the difference between a sunk cost and an opportunity cost?

____

____

____

3. Figure 10-6 on page 348 of the textbook illustrates a bookstore's long run average total cost curve. The average total cost of selling 60,000 books per month ($20) is greater than the average total cost of selling 40,000 books per month ($18). If the bookstore sells 60,000 books at a cost of $20 each, is it producing inefficiently?

____

____

4. The last column of Table 10-3 on page 339 of the textbook shows the marginal product of labor at Jill Johnson's restaurant changes as additional workers are hired. The marginal product of the second worker (250 pizzas) is greater than the marginal product for any other worker. To make the most profit, should Jill hire two workers?

____

____

____

5. In his famous account of the division of labor in a pin factory, Adam Smith refers to "...the important business of making a pin..." Even in Smith's day the total value of pin production in the United Kingdom was not a large fraction of total output. Why would Smith use the word "important" in referring to the production of a seemingly insignificant product?

____

____

____

True/False Questions

T F 1. In the short run, as the marginal product of labor (the variable factor) rises, marginal cost falls (assuming the wage rate remains constant as the quantity of labor hired changes).

T F 2. The average product of labor equals the total output produced by the firm divided by the change in the quantity of workers.

T F 3. The increase in the supply of LCD panels allows flat-panel television producers to take advantage of increasing marginal returns that could not have been achieved without this increase in supply.

T F 4. Average fixed cost is constant in the short run.

T F 5. Explicit costs are opportunity costs; implicit costs are not.

T F 6. When the average product of labor increases, marginal cost decreases.

T F 7. In the short run, the change in total cost is equal to the change in variable cost.

T F 8. Isoquants are curves that represent all the combinations of two inputs that have the same total cost.

T F 9. In the short run, if an increase in output causes average total cost to increase, then marginal cost must be greater than average total cost.

T F 10. The relationship between the inputs employed by a firm and the maximum output it can produce with those inputs is a production function.

T F 11. A technological change results in the production of more output using the same inputs, or the same output using fewer inputs.

T F 12. In the long run, average fixed cost declines as output increases.

T F 13. According to the law of diminishing returns, as more workers are hired in the short run, the marginal product of labor always decreases.

T F 14. The average product of labor is the average of the marginal products of labor.

T F 15. In the long run, all costs are variable.

Answers to the Self-Test

Multiple-Choice Questions

Question	Answer	Explanation
1	a	The process a firm uses to turn inputs into outputs of goods and services is called technology.
2	b	Technological change is the term used to describe the ability of a firm to produce more output using the same inputs, or the same output using fewer inputs.
3	d	The short run is the period of time during which at least one of the firm's inputs is fixed.
4	b	Variable costs are the costs that vary with the amount of output produced. Read "The Difference between Fixed Costs and Variable Costs" on page 335 in the textbook.
5	a	Read Making the Connection "Fixed Costs in the Publishing Industry." The company's output is books published per year. The input in question is the quantity of labor. Since the quantity of labor does not change when the number of books published changes, labor must be a fixed input in this production process.
6	a	This is the definition of opportunity cost.
7	a	These are implicit costs.
8	c	Explicit costs are sometimes called *accounting costs.*
9	b	The relationship between the inputs employed by a firm and the maximum output it can produce with those inputs is called the firm's production function.
10	d	The short-run production function shows the quantity of output that can be produced by a variable input (i.e. labor), while another input (i.e. capital) remains fixed.
11	b	Average total cost is typically U-shaped.
12	d	Each of the equations is true.
13	c	The additional output produced by a firm as a result of hiring one more worker is called the marginal product of labor.
14	b	The marginal product of labor starts to decrease when the third worker is hired.
15	b	Because of specialization and the division of labor, output will at first increase at an increasing rate, with each additional worker hired causing production to increase by a greater amount than did the hiring of the previous worker. After point A, hiring more workers while keeping the amount of machinery constant results in diminishing returns. Once point *A*, or the point of diminishing returns, has been reached, production increases at a decreasing rate.
16	a	Because of specialization and the division of labor, output will at first increase at an increasing rate, with each additional worker hired causing production to increase by a greater amount than did the hiring of the previous worker.
17	b	When marginal is above average, average is rising. When marginal is below average, average is falling.
18	c	The average product of labor is the total output produced divided by the quantity of workers.

19	b	When the marginal is above the average, the average is rising.
20	c	Marginal cost is the change in total cost given (or divided by) a change in the level of output produced. The change in total cost from zero to 200 pizzas is $1450 – $800 = $650. The change in output is 200 – 0 = 200. Then $650/200 = $3.25.
21	b	When the marginal is above the average, the average rises, and when the marginal is less than the average, the average falls.
22	b	Marginal cost is above average cost when average cost is rising.
23	b	$AFC = FC/Q$.
24	b	$ATC = AFC + AVC$.
25	c	*AFC* gets smaller and smaller as output increases.
26	b	$ATC - AVC = AFC$.
27	c	When marginal cost equals average variable cost or average total cost, they must be at their minimums, but not average fixed cost, which decreases continuously as output increases.
28	a	Firms often refer to lowering average fixed cost by selling more output as "spreading the overhead."
29	a	$ATC - AVC = AFC$, or $58 – $34 = $24. Then *AFC* x *Q* = Total fixed cost, or $24 x 100 = $2,400.
30	a	Marginal cost is the change in total cost divided by the change in output. As output increases from 625 to 640 pizzas, the total cost increases from $4050 to $4700. Then, $650/15 = $43.33.
31	b	Average total cost equals total cost divided by output produced. Then, $4050/625 = $6.48.
32	b	As output increases, the difference between average total cost and average variable cost decreases because average fixed cost gets smaller as output increases.
33	a	In the long run, all costs are variable. There are no fixed costs in the long run.
34	b	The long-run average cost curve shows the lowest cost at which the firm is able to produce a given level of output in the long run, when no inputs are fixed.
35	b	Economies of scale means that a firm's long-run average cost falls as it increases the quantity of output it produces.
36	a	For the small bookstore, the average total cost of selling 1,000 books per month would be $22 per book. For a Barnes & Noble store, the average total cost of selling 20,000 books would be only $18 per book. This decline in average cost represents the economies of scale that exist in bookselling.
37	b	The first quantity where economies of scale have been exhausted is 20,000.
38	c	A bookstore selling 20,000 books per month and a bookstore selling 40,000 books per month will experience constant returns to scale and have the same average cost.
39	d	Very large bookstores will experience diseconomies of scale, and their average costs will rise as sales increase beyond 40,000 books per month.
40	b	By producing a larger target level of output, the single company can achieve economies of scale. Therefore, point *B* represents two smaller companies.
41	b	The law of diminishing returns applies in the short run, when at least one of the firm's inputs is fixed.

Short Answer Responses

1. A maximum of four firms can reach minimum efficient scale in this industry. But it may be possible for one or more firms to survive in the industry even if they do not achieve minimum efficient scale. These firms must be able to market their products to consumers on the basis of better quality, better service, etc. – qualities for which consumers are willing to pay prices higher than can be charged by firms that do reach minimum efficient scale.

2. A sunk cost is not an opportunity cost since it has been paid in the past and cannot be avoided.

3. No. $20 is the lowest long-run average total cost of selling 60,000 books. The store can reduce its average total cost only by selling fewer books with a smaller scale (for example, with a smaller size store). As long as the firm is producing output on its production possibilities frontier it is producing efficiently – regardless of costs!

4. One cannot determine Jill's profit or the optimal number of workers to hire without knowing the selling price of her services and her firm's costs. In Table 10-3 the marginal product of the sixth worker is only 15 pizzas, but if the revenue Jill earns from selling these pizzas is greater than the wage she pays to this worker, her profits would increase (assuming that labor is the only variable factor of production in the short run).

5. Smith used the example of how a pin was produced to show how using specialization and a division of labor in production could cause an enormous increase in the productivity of a nation's scarce resources. The lessons learned from Smith's example can be applied to many more products with similar effects on productivity. It was the process, not the product, that was important to Smith.

True/False Answers

1. T See the section "Why Are the Marginal and Average Cost Curves are U Shaped?" beginning on page 344 of the textbook.
2. F The average product of labor is the total quantity divided by the total amount of labor, not the change in the quantity of labor.
3. F The increase in the supply of LCDs causes the price of LCDs to fall, which causes the *ATC* of flat panel TVs to decrease.
4. F Fixed cost, not average fixed cost, is constant in the short run.
5. F Implicit costs are the nonmonetary opportunity costs.
6. F When the *marginal* product of labor increases, marginal cost decreases.
7. T The change in total cost is equal to the change in marginal cost due to fixed costs being constant in the short run.
8. F *Isocost* lines represent all the combinations of two inputs that have the same total cost.
9. T If quantity is such that the marginal cost is greater than the average total cost, then the average total cost increases.
10. T This is the definition of the production function.
11. F This describes only positive technological change. Technological change may also be negative.
12. F There are no fixed costs in the long run.
13. F In the short run, the marginal product of labor (the variable factor) increases initially but eventually decreases.
14. T See the section entitled "The Relationship between Marginal and Average Product" beginning on page 341 of the textbook.
15. T Since there are no fixed inputs in the long run, there are no fixed costs.

Chapter 11

Firms in Perfectly Competitive Markets

Chapter Summary

Economists group industries into one of four market structures: Perfect competition, monopolistic competition, oligopoly, and monopoly. In Chapter 11, you will learn about the first market structure – perfect competition. In a **perfectly competitive market,** there are many buyers and many firms, all of whom are small relative to the size of the total market. Products sold by these firms are identical and there are no barriers to new firms entering the market. Firms in a perfectly competitive market are **price takers**, meaning that they are unable to control the prices of goods they sell and are unable to earn economic profits in the long run. Consumers are also price takers in a perfectly competitive market.

Prices in perfectly competitive markets are determined by the interaction of market demand and market supply. The objective of the firm is to maximize profit. **Profit** is the difference between total revenue and total cost. The firm will produce the output for which the **marginal revenue** (*MR*) equals the marginal cost (*MC*). For perfectly competitive firms, price is equal to marginal revenue. In the short run, the firm's price:

a. will exceed its average total cost (*ATC*) which means it will make an **economic profit**, or
b. will equal *ATC* so its total cost will equal total revenue, which means the firm breaks even and earns no economic profit, or
c. will be less than *ATC*, which means the firm experiences an **economic loss**.

Remember that economic costs include all opportunity costs as well as explicit accounting costs.

A firm experiencing losses can continue to produce, stop production by shutting down temporarily, or go out of business. The first two are short-run options, while the third is a long-run option. In the short run, if by producing the firm would lose an amount greater than its fixed cost, the firm will shut down temporarily. If the firm's losses are less than the amount of its fixed cost, it will continue to produce. The firm will produce output *even though total profits remain negative* if total revenue is greater than total variable cost. This is identical to saying that the price of its output (*P*) must exceed average variable cost (*AVC*). The quantity where $P = AVC$ is called the **shutdown point**.

When firms earn short-run profits, other firms will enter the industry. Entry of new firms shifts the industry supply curve to the right and lowers the market price. Entry continues until economic profits are zero. When firms suffer short-run losses, some firms will exit the industry. The exit of firms shifts the industry supply curve to the left and the market price increases. Exit continues until economic profits are zero.

In a **long-run competitive equilibrium**, entry and exit of firms causes the typical firm to earn zero economic profits. The **long-run supply curve** in a perfectly competitive market shows the relationship between market price and quantity supplied. In the long run, firms will supply the quantity that consumers demand at a price equal to the minimum average total cost. A perfectly competitive market achieves **productive efficiency** and **allocative efficiency** in the long run.

Learning Objectives

When you finish this chapter, you should be able to:

1. **Define a perfectly competitive market and explain why a perfect competitor faces a horizontal demand curve.** A perfectly competitive market has many buyers and sellers, all firms sell identical products, and there are no barriers to new firms entering the market. A perfectly competitive firm faces a horizontal demand curve because if the firm tried to raise its price, consumers would buy from the firm's competitors. Because the firm can sell all the output it wants at the current market price, there would be no point trying to charge a lower price. If a firm increases the output it sells, the price will not decrease because each firm is too small to shift the market supply curve enough to lower equilibrium price.

2. **Explain how a firm maximizes profits in a perfectly competitive market.** To make profit as large as possible, a firm will produce that quantity of output for which marginal revenue equals marginal cost. Since marginal revenue equals price for a perfectly competitive firm, price will also equal marginal cost at the profit-maximizing quantity of output.

3. **Use graphs to show a firm's profit or loss**. The firm's profit-maximizing rate of output is determined by the intersection of the demand curve with the marginal cost curve. The position of the average total cost (*ATC*) curve in this graph will indicate whether the firm earns a profit (price exceeds *ATC*) or suffers a loss (price is less than *ATC*).

4. **Explain why firms may shut down temporarily.** A firm experiencing losses in the short run will shut down if the revenue from producing is insufficient to cover its total variable costs. By shutting down, the firm will avoid variable costs and minimize its losses. When the firm shuts down, it must still pay the fixed costs of production.

5. **Explain how entry and exit ensure that perfectly competitive firms earn zero economic profit in the long run**. If firms earn short run economic profits, other firms will enter the market. The entry of firms will shift the market supply curve to the right and lower price until the short run profits are eliminated. If firms suffer short run losses, some firms will leave the market. The exit of firms will shift the market supply curve to the left and raise price until the short run losses are eliminated.

6. **Explain how perfect competition leads to economic efficiency.** In the long run, competitive forces will drive the market price to the minimum average total cost of the typical firm. This means that perfect competition results in productive efficiency. Firms also produce at the point where the marginal cost of producing another unit equals the marginal benefit consumers receive from consuming that unit. This means that perfect competition achieves allocative efficiency.

Chapter Review

Chapter Opener: Perfect Competition in the Market for Organic Apples (pages 376-377)

The market for organic apples grew rapidly in the late 1990s. In response to rising demand and high profits, many apple growers switched to organic methods. The entry of new firms rapidly increased supply, which decreased the price and profit associated with the production of organic apples. Today, the industry has the characteristics of a perfectly competitive market. Each apple producer has only a small share of the overall market; therefore each firm is a price taker.

Helpful Study Hint

An ***Inside Look*** at the end of this chapter features a newspaper article about organic foods and includes graphs that describe the effect of the entry of firms on profits in a competitive market. The increase in the popularity of organic foods will increase the price of organic foods and the profits associated with producing these foods. This will provide an incentive for firms to enter, supply will shift to the right, and prices will fall until economic profit becomes zero. The market for organic apples is used to describe the impact of the entry and exit of firms in Figures 11-8 and 11-9 on pages 394 and 396 of the textbook. ***Making the Connection*** "The Decline of Apple Production in New York State" addresses the decline of apple production in the state of New York. In New York, the demand for land has risen, increasing the profitability of using land for nonagricultural purposes. This means that the opportunity cost of using the land for growing apples increases, so land is being converted from apple production to a more profitable use, such as housing.

Economics in YOUR Life! asks you to consider your entrepreneurial ventures. Maybe you babysat, mowed lawns, or shoveled snow. How did you select a price to charge? Keep this question in mind as you read the chapter. The authors will answer this question at the end of the chapter.

11.1 LEARNING OBJECTIVE

11.1 Perfectly Competitive Markets (pages 379-381)

Learning Objective 1 Define a perfectly competitive market and explain why a perfect competitor faces a horizontal demand curve.

A **perfectly competitive market** is a market that meets the conditions of (1) many buyers and sellers, (2) all firms selling identical products, and (3) no barriers to new firms entering the market. Prices in perfectly competitive markets are determined by the intersection of market demand and supply. Consumers and firms must accept the market price if they want to buy and sell in a competitive market.

A **price taker** is a buyer or seller that is unable to affect the market price. A firm in a perfectly competitive market is a price taker because it is very small relative to the market and sells exactly the same product as every other firm. Consumers are also price takers. Although the market demand curve has the normal downward shape, the demand curve for a perfectly competitive firm is horizontal at the market price because the firm is unable to affect the market price.

Helpful Study Hint

Spend some time reviewing Table 11-1 on page 378 because it provides an overview of the four market structures. This chapter focuses on perfect competition. You will see the other three market structures in the upcoming chapters.

Don't Let This Happen to YOU! "Don't Confuse the Demand Curve for Farmer Parker's Wheat with the Market Demand Curve for Wheat" reinforces the idea that the individual firm is a price taker, so he faces a flat (perfectly elastic) demand curve not the market demand curve.

The perfectly competitive firm's demand curve represents what happens to quantity demanded for the smallest increase in price—quantity demanded drops to zero even if the price is increased by only a penny! Since the firm can sell all it is able to at the market price, the question "what happens to quantity if price is decreased?" is irrelevant. The firm would not choose to lower price. Consider a farmer offering to sell wheat at $2.95 per bushel if he can sell all he produced for a price of $3.00.

Extra Solved Problem 11-1

Chapter 11 in the textbook includes two Solved Problems. Here is an extra Solved Problem to help you build your skills solving economic problems.

Supports Learning Objective 1: Define a perfectly competitive market and explain why a perfect competitor faces a horizontal demand curve.

Analyze the following statement: "When an individual firm in a perfectly competitive industry increases its production, the price of the good will likely fall."

Step 1: Review the chapter material.
This problem is about the definition of a perfectly competitive market and the effect of market structure on the firm's ability to control price, so you may want to review the section "Perfectly Competitive Markets," which begins on page 379 of the textbook.

Step 2: Determine whether the statement is true or false and explain your answer.
The statement is false. Firms in a perfectly competitive industry do not have the ability to affect the price. If a single firm or several firms increase the number of units they produce, this increased production has no effect on the market price because the production of these firms is only a tiny fraction of total production in the market. Firms in a perfectly competitive industry are price takers who are unable to affect the market price no matter how much or how little they produce.

11.2 LEARNING OBJECTIVE

11.2 How a Firm Maximizes Profit in a Perfectly Competitive Market (pages 381-384)

Learning Objective 2 Explain how a firm maximizes profits in a perfectly competitive market.

Economists assume that the objective of a firm is to maximize profits. **Profit** is the difference between total revenue (*TR*) and total cost (*TC*):

$$\text{Profit} = TR - TC$$

Therefore, a firm will produce that quantity of output where the difference between *TR* and *TC* is as large as possible. A firm's **average revenue (*AR*)** equals total revenue divided by the number of units sold. Average revenue is the same as market price. For a firm in a perfectly competitive market, price is also equal to marginal revenue. **Marginal revenue (*MR*)** is the change in total revenue caused by producing and selling one more unit:

$$\text{Marginal revenue} = MR = \frac{\Delta TR}{\Delta Q}$$

The marginal revenue curve for a perfectly competitive firm is the same as its demand curve.

The marginal cost (*MC*) of production for a perfectly competitive firm first falls, then rises. So long as *MR* exceeds *MC* the firm's profits are increasing and production will increase. The firm's profits will decrease if production is increased beyond the output for which *MC* exceeds *MR*. The profit maximizing level of output is where $MR = MC$. Since $P = MR$ for these firms, profit will be maximized when $P = MC$.

Helpful Study Hint

Students often ask "Why would the firm produce a unit of output for which $MR = MC$, since it would not earn any profit from this last unit?" Included in the cost of production is a normal return so that the revenue earned from the profit maximizing unit of output is just enough to compensate the firm's owner(s) for the effort made to produce it.

Extra Solved Problem 11-2

Chapter 11 in the textbook includes two Solved Problems. Here is an extra Solved Problem to help you build your skills solving economic problems.

Supports Learning Objective 2: Explain how a perfect competitor decides how much to produce.

Cost and Revenue for "Apples R' Us"

Sally Borts owns "Apples R' Us," an orchard located in Washington State. Sally is one of about 7,500 apple producers in the United States who produced over 9 billions pounds of apples in 2004. Although the price of apples reached nearly $0.30 per pound in 2003, it fell to less than $0.20 in 2005. Sally believes she would be able to sell her apples for $0.20 in 2006, or $200 per thousand lbs. She estimated her revenue and costs of production for various quantities of apples based on the number of pounds her orchard would yield per acre.

Output (000 lbs.)	Total cost (000)	Marginal cost (000)	Total revenue (000)	Marginal revenue (price per 1,000 lbs)
0	$50	-----	$0	-----
1	150	$100	200	$200
2	225	75	400	200
3	275	50	600	200
4	375	100	800	200
5	525	150	1,000	200
6	725	200	1,200	200
7	1,000	275	1,400	200
8	1,500	500	1,600	200

Sources: http://www.usapple.org/media/industry/index.shtml. Agricultural Prices, U.S. Department of Agriculture, National Agricultural Statistics Service.

a. Determine whether "Apples R' Us" is a perfectly competitive firm.

b. Explain how Sally will decide how much to produce.

SOLVING THE PROBLEM

Step 1: **Review the chapter material.**
This problem is about how a firm maximizes profits, so you may want to review the section "How a Firm Maximizes Profit in a Perfectly Competitive Market," which begins on page 381 of the textbook.

Step 2: **Determine if "Apples R' Us" is a perfectly competitive firm.**
Sally is one of thousands of apple producers and her output is a small fraction of the total number of apples produced. Within each variety of apples (Red Delicious, McIntosh, Granny Smith, etc.) apple growers sell an identical product and new firms are free to enter the market. Therefore, "Apples R' Us" is a perfectly competitive firm. Also, marginal revenue is constant, which means that price must also be constant, and the demand curve must be horizontal. Price and marginal revenue are constant and the demand curve is horizontal only in a perfectly competitive market.

Step 3: **Explain how Sally will decide how much to produce.**
Sally should increase her production of apples so long as the marginal revenue exceeds her marginal cost of production. Sally's marginal revenue equals the $200 price of a thousand pounds of apples. Therefore, if the estimates for 2006 are accurate, Sally should produce 6 thousand pounds of apples because her marginal cost for this quantity of output also equals $200.

11.3 LEARNING OBJECTIVE

11.3 Illustrating Profit or Loss on the Cost Curve Graph (pages 385-390)

Learning Objective 3 Use graphs to show a firm's profit or loss.

Profit equals total revenue (*TR*) minus total cost (*TC*). Since *TR* equals price multiplied by quantity sold, this can be written as:

$$\text{Profit} = (P \times Q) - TC$$

Dividing both sides by *Q*:

$$\frac{\text{Profit}}{Q} = \frac{(P \times Q)}{Q} - \frac{TC}{Q}$$

This equation means that profit per unit (or average profit) equals price minus average total cost. Multiplying both sides of the equation by *Q* yields an equation that tells us a firm's total profit is equal to the quantity produced multiplied by the difference between price and average total cost. ($P - ATC$ is called the profit margin per unit.)

$$\text{Profit} = (P - ATC) \times Q$$

Figure 11-4 on page 385 of the textbook illustrates the situation where the firm is making a profit. Figure 11-5 on page 387 illustrates the situations where the firm is either breaking even or suffering a loss. The firm will make a profit if $P > ATC$. The firm will break even if $P = ATC$. The firm will experience losses if $P < ATC$.

Helpful Study Hint

Solved Problem 11-3 provides an example of an individual firm in a perfectly competitive market. Study this ***Solved Problem*** carefully and be sure you understand the graphs that show a firm's profit or loss. If properly drawn, graphs can help you to answer questions that would be more difficult to answer using only words or numbers. Here are tips to learning from these graphs:

(1) When a firm's demand curve intersects the *ATC* curve, price will exceed *ATC* for some level of output. That means the firm earns a profit.

(2) To show a firm suffering losses, the *ATC* curve is drawn everywhere above the demand curve, which would mean that the price is less than the average total cost.

(3) Always draw the demand curve and the *MC* curve first to determine the profit-maximizing output. This will make it easier to identify *ATC* and *AVC* at this same output.

Review the section ***Don't Let This Happen to YOU!*** "Remember That Firms Maximize Total Profit, Not Profit per Unit." Remember that $P - ATC$ is the profit per unit and at Q_1 the profit per unit would be maximized; that is, the distance between price and the average total cost curve would be greatest. But this is not the profit-maximizing level of output. At this quantity the marginal revenue is greater than the price, so if the firm adds additional units to output it will add more to revenue than it adds to cost. In other words, increasing production will increase profit. The firm should stop producing at the quantity where *MC* = *MR* in order to maximize profit.

Making the Connection "Losing Money in the Medical Screening Industry" provides an example of firms experiencing losses. The demand for preventative CT scans was so low that the price that consumers were willing to pay was lower than the firm's average total cost and firms experienced losses. This caused many firms to exit the market for preventative CT scans to avoid the losses.

11.4 LEARNING OBJECTIVE

11.4 Deciding Whether to Produce or to Shut Down in the Short Run (pages 390-393)

Learning Objective 4 Explain why firms may shut down temporarily.

In the short run, a firm suffering losses has two options: produce or shutdown. The firm will produce the profit-maximizing output if its total revenue is greater than its total variable cost. In this situation, even though the firm is suffering a loss, it is earning enough revenue to cover all of its variable costs and at least some of its fixed costs. The firm's second option is to stop production by shutting down temporarily (producing zero output). During a temporary shut down, a firm must still pay its fixed costs. If, by producing, the firm would lose an amount greater than its fixed costs (that is, the firm will not be able to cover all of its variable costs), it will shut down.

A **sunk cost** is a cost that has already been paid and cannot be recovered. The firm should treat its sunk costs as irrelevant to its decision making.

The firm's marginal cost curve is its supply curve only for prices at or above average variable cost. The **shutdown point** is the minimum point on a firm's average variable cost curve. If the price falls below this point, the firm shuts down production in the short run. The market supply curve can be derived by adding up the quantity that each firm in the market is willing to supply at each price.

Helpful Study Hint

The decision to shut down is not the same as deciding to leave the market or go out of business. Many firms sell goods or services only in certain seasons. Examples include ski resorts, retail stores near summer resorts, and Christmas tree vendors. These firms shut down temporarily during the off season. Going out of business permanently, however, is a long-run decision. See ***Making the Connection*** "When to Close a Laundry" for an example of a firm that is not making a profit. The laundry had \$3,300 per month in fixed costs and was losing \$4,000 per month while operating. If the laundry closed down it would only lose \$3,300 per month instead of \$4,000, so the firm should shut down. The owner of the laundry brought in a new manager who reorganized the business so that it was now only losing $2,000 per month. Under this reorganization, the firm should stay in business because it is only losing $2,000 per month while operating compared to the $3,300 per month that would be lost if it shut down.

Extra Solved Problem 11-4

Chapter 11 in the textbook includes two Solved Problems. Here is an extra Solved Problem to help you build your skills solving economic problems.

Supports Learning Objective 4: Explain why firms may shut down temporarily.

The table and graph below represent the cost curves for the perfectly competitive firm Apples R' Us. The cost curves were derived using the information for the firm from the table in Solved Problem 11-3 on page 386.

Quantity of apples (in thousands)	VC	ATC	MC	AVC
0	0			
1	100	$150.00	$100.00	$100.00
2	175	112.50	75.00	87.50
3	225	91.67	50.00	75.00
4	325	93.75	100.00	81.25
5	475	105.00	150.00	95.00
6	675	120.83	200.00	112.50

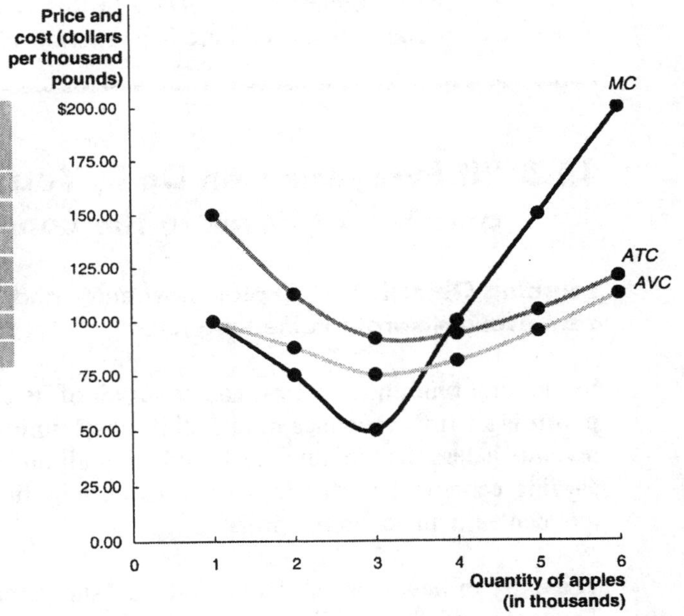

a. Determine the rule that Apples R' Us will use to determine whether it will produce at various market prices.

b. Should the firm produce and sell apples if the price is $100 per 1,000 pounds of apples or should the firm shut down? What about a price of $85 per 1,000 pounds of apples? What about at a price of $70 per 1,000 pounds?

Step 1: Review the chapter material.
This problem is about whether a firm should continue to produce or shut down at various possible market prices, so you may want to review the section "Deciding Whether to Produce or to Shut Down in the Short Run," which begins on page 390 of the textbook.

Step 2: Determine the rule that Apples R' Us will use to determine whether they should produce at each price mentioned in the problem.

Apples R' Us will compare the market price to the minimum value of average variable cost. If the price is greater than the minimum *AVC*, then the firm will produce. If the price is below the minimum *AVC*, then the firm will shut down in the short run. Apples R' Us should continue to produce in the short run as long as the price is greater than $75, which is the minimum value for *AVC*. If the price falls below $75, the firm will shut down temporarily because its loss will be greater than its fixed cost.

Step 3: Compare each price to the rule from step 2 to determine whether the firm will produce or shut down at each given price.

Apples R' Us will continue to produce in the short run when the price is $100 and $85 per thousand pounds of apples. The firm will receive a positive profit for the $100 price because the price is greater than the *ATC* for the 4,000 pounds of apples that will be produced. When the price is $85 per thousand pounds, the firm is suffering a loss, but the firm will continue to produce because its revenue is high enough that all the variable costs are covered and there is some money left over to put towards the fixed costs that the firm must pay. When the price falls to $70 per thousand pounds, the firm will shut down because the price has fallen below the minimum of the *AVC*. In this case the firm cannot collect enough revenue to cover its variable costs, so there is no money left over to pay down on the fixed costs.

11.5 LEARNING OBJECTIVE

11.5 "If Everyone Can Do It, You Can't Make Money at It": The Entry and Exit of Firms in the Long Run (pages 393-398)

Learning Objective 5 Explain how entry and exit ensure that perfectly competitive firms earn zero economic profit in the long run.

In the long run, unless a firm can cover all of its costs it will shut down and exit the industry. **Economic profit** is a firm's revenues minus all its costs, implicit and explicit. An **economic loss** means a firm's total revenue is less than its total cost, including all implicit costs. If firms in a perfectly competitive market are earning economic profits in the short run, new firms will have an incentive to enter the market so they, too, can earn an economic profit.

The entry of new firms shifts the industry supply curve to the right. As a result, the market price will fall. The entry of firms will continue until price is equal to average total cost. If firms in a perfectly competitive market are suffering losses in the short run, some of these firms will exit the industry because they will not be able to cover all of their costs. The exit of firms shifts the industry supply curve to the left. As a result, the market price will rise. The exit of firms will continue until price is equal to average total cost.

Long-run competitive equilibrium is the situation in which the entry and exit of firms have resulted in the typical firm just earning zero economic profits. The **long-run supply curve** shows the relationship in the long run between market price and the quantity supplied in the long run. A constant cost industry is an industry in which the typical firm's long-run average costs do not change as the industry expands. This means that the firm will have a horizontal long-run supply curve. An increasing cost industry is an industry in which the typical firm's long-run average costs increase as the industry expands. This means the firm will have an upward-sloping long-run supply curve. A decreasing cost industry is an industry in which the typical firm's long-run average costs decrease as the industry expands. This means that the firm will have a downward sloping long run supply curve.

Helpful Study Hint

Which firms are most likely to leave an industry that is experiencing economic losses? Even though we assume all firms are identical, that is not true in the real world. Some firms have more financial resources and are better able to withstand short periods of negative profits. Financially weaker firms are more likely to exit. For example, a corporate-owned Starbucks is more likely to sustain economic losses due to slow sales and remain in the industry than is a local coffee shop.

Extra Solved Problem 11-5

Chapter 11 in the textbook includes two Solved Problems. Here is an extra Solved Problem to help you build your skills solving economic problems.

Supports Learning Objective 5: Explain how entry and exit ensure that perfectly competitive firms earn zero economic profit in the long run.

Consider the perfectly competitive market in which Apples R' Us competes. There are many buyers and sellers in the market for apples, so many that all consumers and firms in the market are price takers. Suppose that the price is $85 per thousand pounds of apples and that all firms face the same cost curves as Apples R' Us.

a. What will happen to the supply in this industry in the long run? What is the effect of this change in supply on price?

b. What will happen to the long run profit of firms that remain in the market for apples?

Step 1: Review the chapter material.
This problem is about long-run losses, so you may want to review the section "'If Everyone Can Do It, You Can't Make Money at It': The Entry and Exit of Firms in the Long Run," which begins on page 393 of the textbook.

Step 2: Determine what the short run profit looks like for a typical firm in the industry and discuss the incentive effect that this profit has on the firm.
If each firm has the same costs as Apples R' Us, the price of $85 will be below minimum average total cost, and each firm in the industry will be suffering a loss. These losses give firms an incentive to exit the industry because the owners of the firms could receive a greater return on their investment somewhere else.

Step 3: Determine how this incentive will alter the market supply curve and the equilibrium price.
Because profits are negative, some firms will exit the apple market, which will cause the market supply curve to shift to the left. A decrease in supply means that the market price for apples will rise.

Step 4: **Consider the effect of exit on the profit of the remaining firms.**
As firms exit the industry, the price will continue to rise up to the point where it equals minimum average total cost and all firms in the industry will be achieving zero economic profit. The firms who remain are making the same return producing apples as could be achieved in their next best alternative, so there is no additional incentive for firms to exit the market.

11.6 LEARNING OBJECTIVE

11.6 Perfect Competition and Efficiency (pages 398-401)

Learning Objective 6 Explain how perfect competition leads to economic efficiency.

Productive efficiency is the situation in which a good or service is produced at the lowest possible cost. Perfect competition results in productive efficiency because the forces of competition drive the market price to the minimum average cost of the typical firm. Managers of firms strive to earn economic profits by reducing costs. But in a perfectly competitive market, other firms can quickly copy ways of reducing costs, so that in the long run consumers, not producers, benefit from cost reductions.

Allocative efficiency is a state of the economy in which production represents consumer preferences. In particular, every good or service is produced up to the point where the last unit produced provides a marginal benefit to consumers equal to the marginal cost of producing it. Entrepreneurs in a perfectly competitive market efficiently allocate resources to best satisfy consumer wants.

Helpful Study Hint

Critics of the perfectly competitive model complain that few industries feature sellers of identical products who are all price takers. These critics fail to understand either what an economic model is or how economists use these models. Although not many markets are perfectly competitive, many markets are very competitive and experience entry and exit in response to short-run profits and losses. The markets for televisions, calculators, personal computers, and even automobiles have changed over time as firms earned short-run profits or new technologies forced firms to adapt. The steel and coal industries experienced exit by firms in response to short-run losses, just as the model of perfect competition predicts. The model also provides policymakers and analysts with a valuable standard against which to judge the efficiency of real markets. When the price of a product is greater or less than marginal cost, one can argue that too little or too much of the product has been produced, a deviation from allocative efficiency.

Solved Problem 11-6 describes the benefits of competition in the market for such products as plasma televisions and DVD players. When new technology is developed, firms that enter a market early can earn positive economic profits. These profits will provide an incentive for other firms to enter, causing the market supply curve to shift to the right. This shift will decrease the price of the good and reduce the profit that the firms in the market can achieve. Firms will enter the market until the price equals the minimum average total cost for the typical firms. The result is productive efficiency. Competition ensures that the benefits from the production of any good are quickly passed onto the consumers.

Helpful Study Hint

The competition that teenagers face in markets such as babysitting and lawn mowing is the subject of the ***Economics in YOUR Life!*** in this chapter. Teenagers are unable to affect the low market price for services such as babysitting and lawn mowing because they supply these services in very competitive markets.

Key Terms

Allocative efficiency. A state of the economy in which production represents consumer preferences; in particular, every good or service is produced up to the point where the last unit provides a marginal benefit to consumers equal to the marginal cost of producing it.

Average revenue (AR). Total revenue divided by the quantity of the product sold.

Economic loss. The situation in which a firm's total revenue is less than its total cost, including all implicit costs.

Economic profit. A firm's revenues minus all its costs, implicit and explicit.

Long-run competitive equilibrium. The situation in which the entry and exit of firms has resulted in the typical firm breaking even.

Long-run supply curve. A curve that shows the relationship in the long run between market price and the quantity supplied.

Marginal revenue (MR). Change in total revenue from selling one more unit of a product.

Perfectly competitive market. A market that meets the conditions of (1) many buyers and sellers, (2) all firms selling identical products, and (3) no barriers to new firms entering the market.

Price taker. A buyer or seller that is unable to affect the market price.

Productive efficiency. The situation in which a good or service is produced at the lowest possible cost.

Profit. Total revenue minus total cost.

Shutdown point. The minimum point on a firm's average variable cost curve; if the price falls below this point, the firm shuts down production in the short run.

Sunk cost. A cost that has already been paid and that cannot be recovered.

Self-Test

(Answers are provided at the end of the Self-Test.)

Multiple-Choice Questions

1. Which of the following are characteristics of a perfectly competitive industry?
   a. Firms are unable to control the prices of the products they sell.
   b. Firms are unable to earn an economic profit in the long run.
   c. Firms sell identical products.
   d. All of the above

2. Which of the following conditions must exist in order to have a perfectly competitive market?
   a. There must be many buyers and many firms, all of whom are small relative to the market.
   b. The products sold by firms in the market must be different from each other.
   c. There must be some barriers to entry in order to protect perfect competition.
   d. All of the above

3. A buyer or seller that is unable to affect the market price is called?
   a. A price maker
   b. A price taker
   c. An independent producer
   d. A monopoly

4. Refer to the graph below. What is the graph trying to explain?

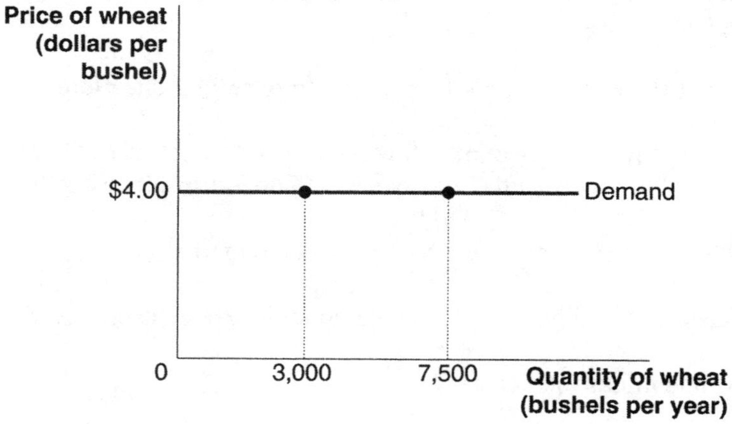

   a. The decision of a producer to charge $4.00 for 3,000 bushels or for 7,500 bushels
   b. Uncertainty about producing 3,000 or 7,500 bushels given the market price of $4.00
   c. How market demand and the firm's demand curve are one and the same in a perfectly competitive market
   d. The ability of the perfectly competitive firm to sell any amount of output as long as it accepts the market price of $4.00

5. If an individual firm in a perfectly competitive market increases its price, the firm will experience
   a. higher revenue.
   b. lower average total cost.
   c. increased sales.
   d. None of the above

6. To maximize profit, which of the following should a firm attempt to do?
   a. Maximize revenue
   b. Minimize cost
   c. Find the largest difference between total revenue and total cost
   d. All of the above simultaneously

7. Refer to the graphs below. What is this graph trying to explain?

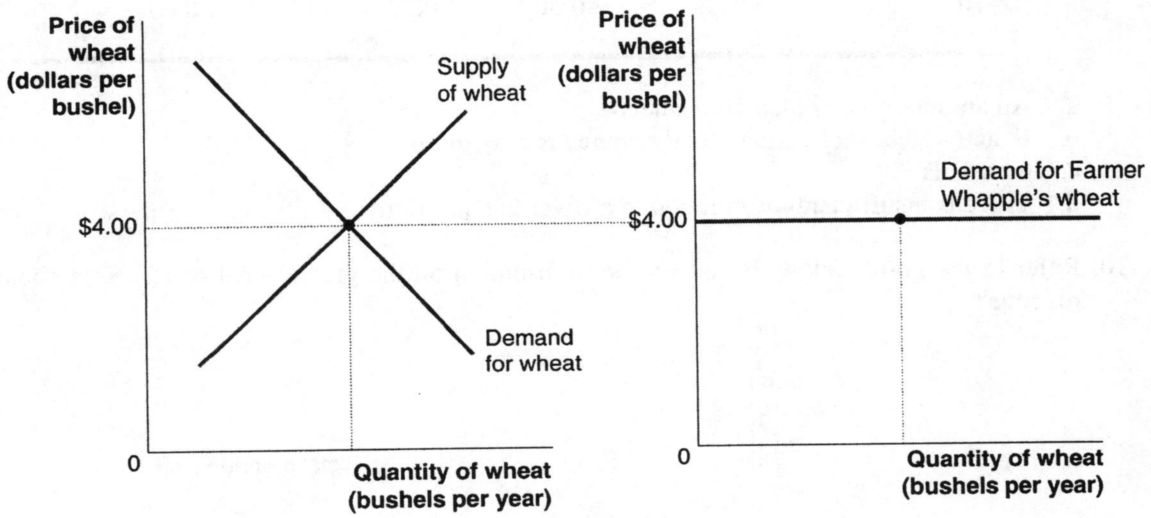

   a. The difference between a monopolistic market and a competitive market
   b. The way a competitive market sets the price taken by individual firms
   c. The ability of the firm to affect the market price of wheat
   d. Two possible demand curves that a perfectly competitive firm might have to confront

8. What is the relationship between price, average revenue, and marginal revenue for a firm in a perfectly competitive market?
   a. Price is equal to average revenue and greater than marginal revenue.
   b. Price is greater than average revenue and equal to marginal revenue.
   c. Price is equal to both average revenue and marginal revenue.
   d. Price, average revenue, and marginal revenue are usually all different values.

9. Refer to the table below. Based on the numbers on the table, how much should this farmer produce in order to maximize profit?

QUANTITY (BUSHELS) (*Q*)	TOTAL REVENUE (*TR*)	TOTAL COSTS (*TC*)	MARGINAL REVENUE (*MR*)	MARGINAL COST (*MC*)
4	16.00	9.50	4.00	2.00
5	20.00	12.00	4.00	2.50
6	24.00	15.00	4.00	3.00
7	28.00	19.50	4.00	4.50
8	32.00	25.50	4.00	6.00
9	36.00	32.50	4.00	7.00
10	40.00	40.50	4.00	8.00

a. An amount greater than 10 bushels
b. Exactly 10 bushels, where total revenue is maximum
c. 6 bushels
d. There is insufficient information to answer the question.

10. Refer to the graph below. Based on the information on the graph, what can be said about marginal revenue?

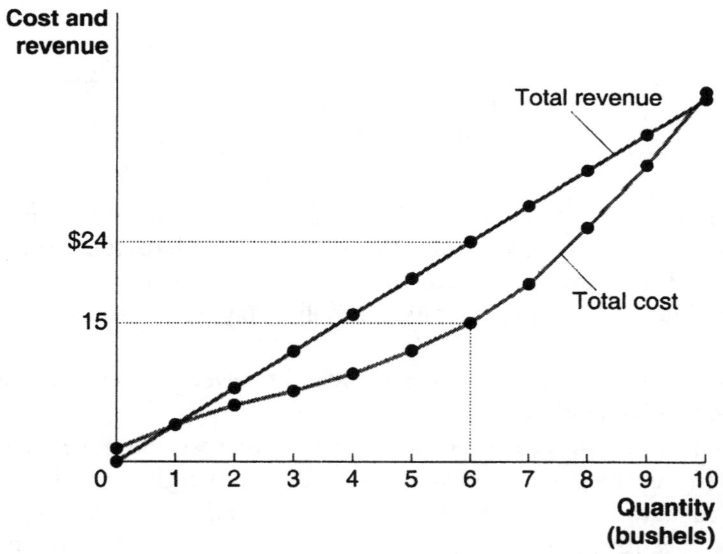

a. Marginal revenue increases as the quantity of bushels produced and sold increases.
b. Marginal revenue decreases with additional bushels produced and sold.
c. Marginal revenue remains constant as additional bushels are produced and sold.
d. There is insufficient information to deduct the behavior of marginal revenue from this graph.

11. Refer to the graph below. What is the profit-maximizing level of output (in whole units)?

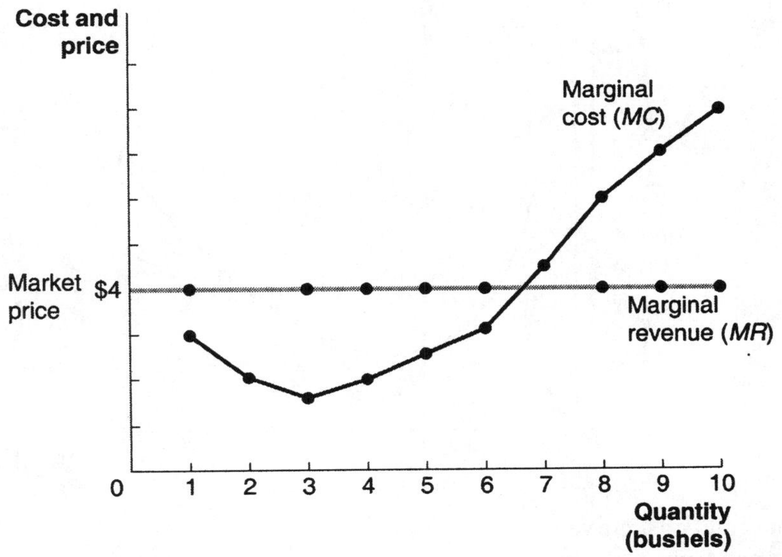

a. 3 bushels, where marginal cost is minimized
b. 10 bushels, where the distance between marginal cost and marginal revenue is the greatest
c. 6 bushels, where the proximity between marginal revenue and marginal cost is the closest and $MR > MC$
d. 7 bushels, where marginal cost rises slightly above marginal revenue

12. Refer to the graph below. Which of the following best represents profit per unit?

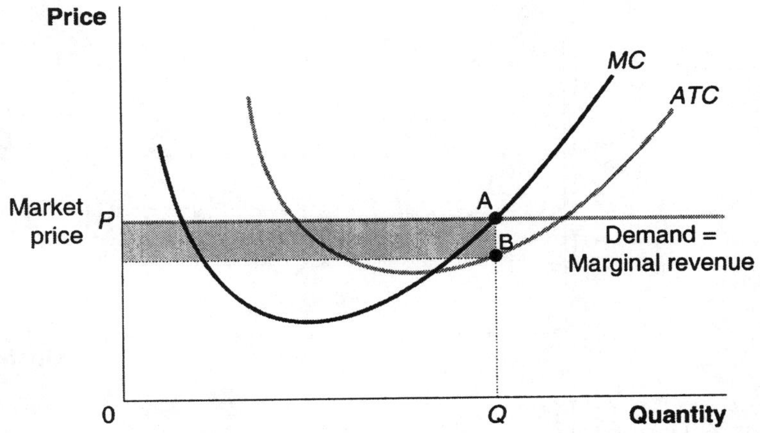

a. The shaded rectangle
b. The distance between points *A* and *B*
c. Market price, or the demand (marginal revenue) curve
d. None of the above

13. Refer to the graph below. One of the curves in this graph is not necessary in order to determine the profit-maximizing level of output. Which curve can be discarded?

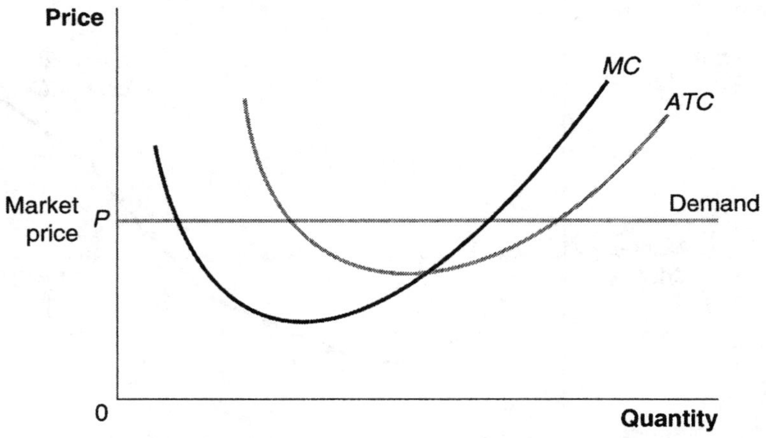

a. The marginal cost curve
b. The demand curve
c. The average total cost curve
d. None of the above; all three curves are needed to determine which level of output maximizes profit.

14. Refer to the graph below. One of the curves in this graph is not necessary in order to determine the amount of profit obtained from producing any level of output. Which curve can be discarded?

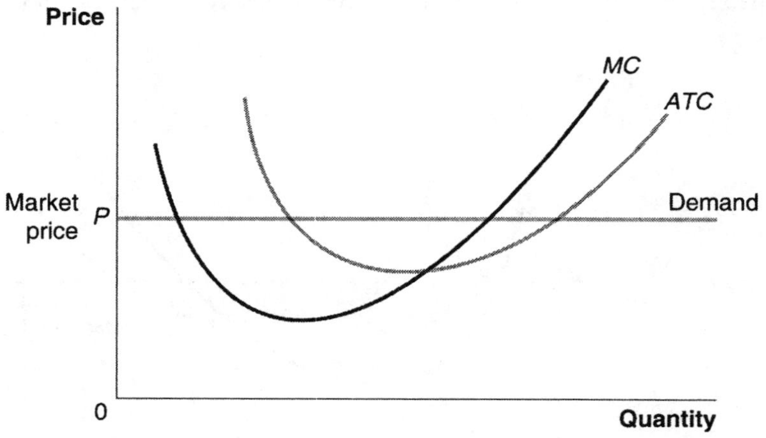

a. The marginal cost curve
b. The demand curve
c. The average total cost curve
d. None of the above; all three curves are needed to determine the amount of profit obtained from producing and selling any amount of output.

15. Refer to the graph below. At what level of output does the firm maximize profit?

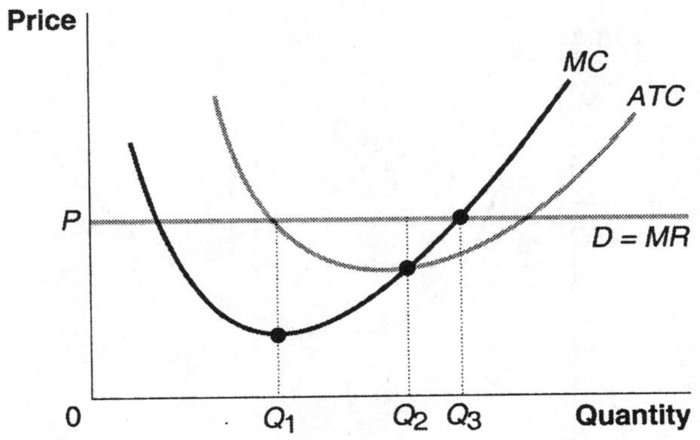

a. At Q_1, where output coincides with the minimum point on the *MC* curve
b. At Q_2, where output coincides with the minimum point on the *ATC* curve
c. At Q_3, where price is greater than *ATC*
d. None of the above

16. Refer to the graph below. What happens at point *A*?

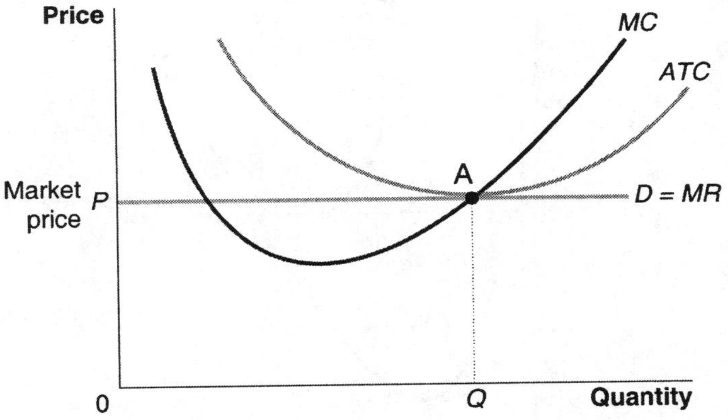

a. The firm earns zero accounting profit.
b. The firm suffers a loss.
c. The firm breaks even, which means that it earns some accounting profit.
d. The firm may or may not earn profit.

17. Refer to the graph below. What does the shaded area in the graph represent?

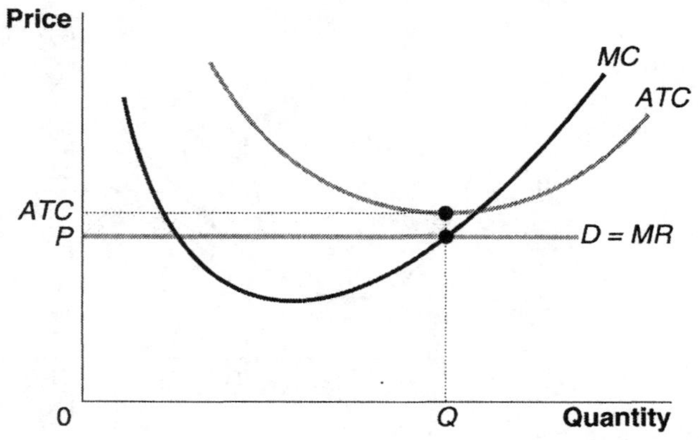

a. Positive economic profit
b. Accounting profit
c. Negative economic profit, or losses
d. Neither profits nor losses

18. Refer to the graph below. Which level of the demand curve results in economic losses?

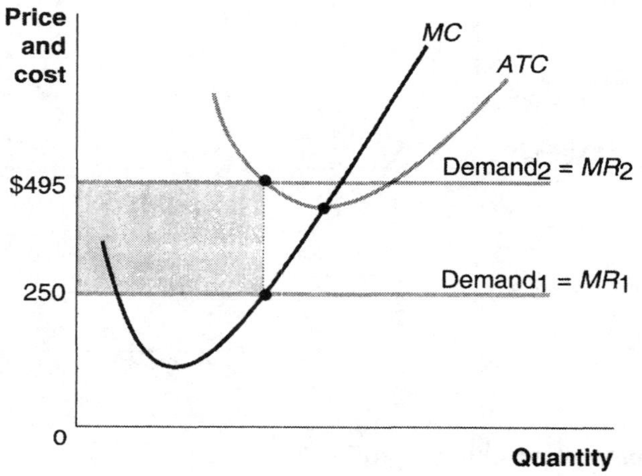

a. Demand when price is $495
b. Demand when price is $250
c. Any demand curve for prices above $495
d. Both levels of the demand curve shown on the graph result in losses for the firm.

19. What is the term given to a cost that has already been paid and cannot be recovered?
a. Unrecoverable cost
b. Variable cost
c. Sunk cost
d. Implicit cost

20. Refer to the graph below. Which demand curve is associated with the shutdown point?

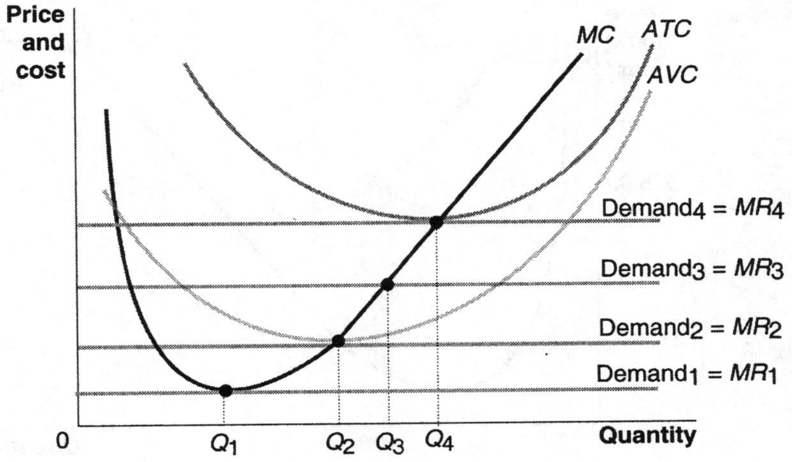

a. Demand$_1$
b. Demand$_2$
c. Demand$_3$
d. Demand$_4$

21. Refer to the graph below. When the demand curve is Demand$_3$, which of the following is true?

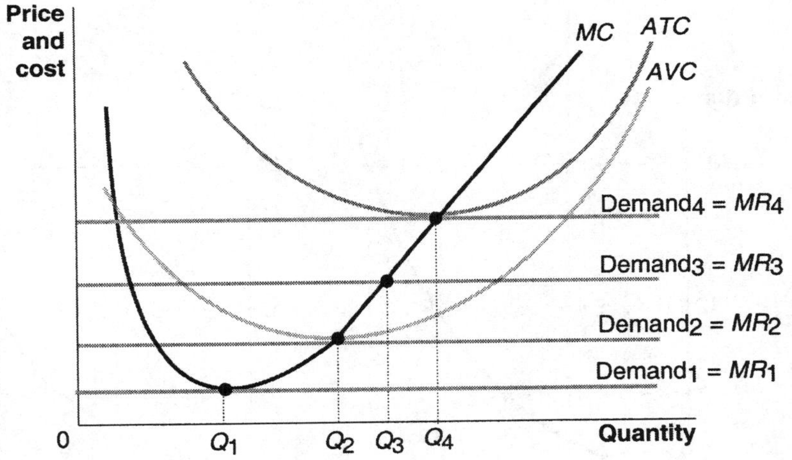

a. The firm can cover all of its fixed costs.
b. The firm should shut down.
c. The firm will suffer losses, but should continue to operate.
d. The firm does not suffer a loss, but earns only a small economic profit.

22. Refer to the graph below. What is the value of *total fixed cost*?

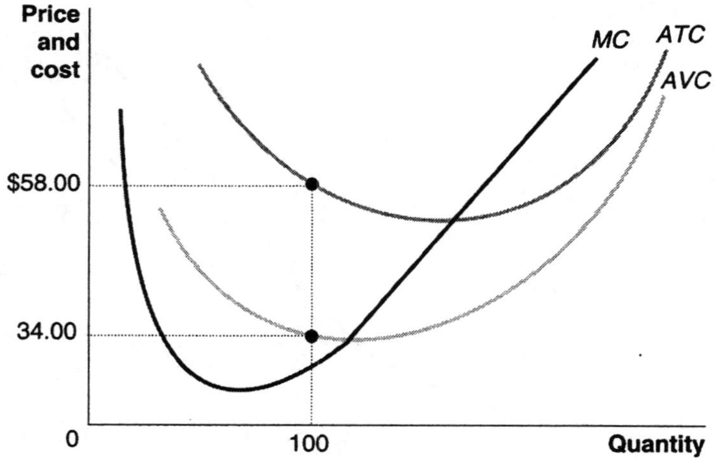

a. $3,400
b. $5,800
c. $2,400
d. None of the above; there is insufficient information to answer the question.

23. Refer to the graphs below. Suppose the graph on the left represents a typical firm's supply curve in a given industry. Suppose that there are 100 identical firms in the industry. Then the graph on the right represents:

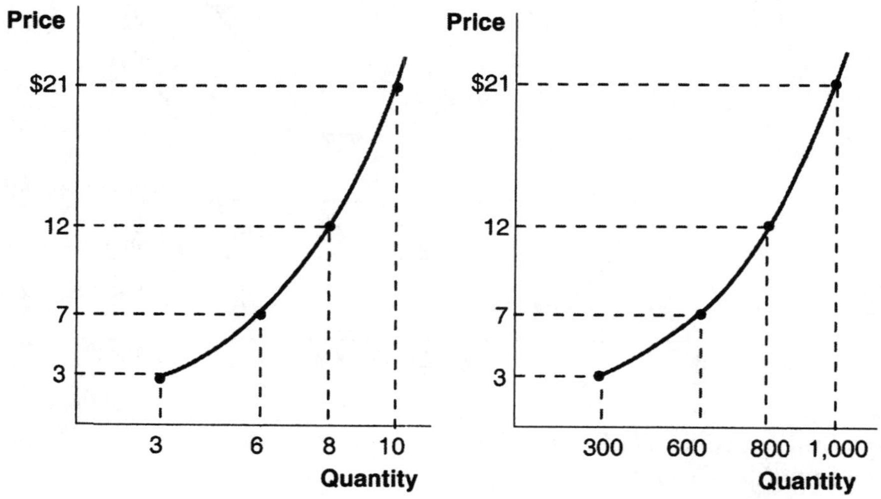

a. the market supply curve.
b. the average total cost curve for the industry.
c. the individual supply curve for each firm in the industry.
d. None of the above; there isn't sufficient information to establish what this curve represents.

24. Which term below best describes the minimum amount that a farmer needs to earn on her $100,000 investment in her farm to remain in a(perfectly competitive industry in the long run?
   a. Explicit cost
   b. Opportunity cost
   c. Economic profit
   d. Economic loss

25. Economic loss refers to a situation in which a firm's total revenue is less than its total cost. To calculate the amount of a loss, which of the following costs should be included?
   a. Explicit costs only
   b. Implicit cost only
   c. Both explicit costs and implicit cost
   d. Fixed costs only

26. Refer to the graphs below. The firms in this market are experiencing

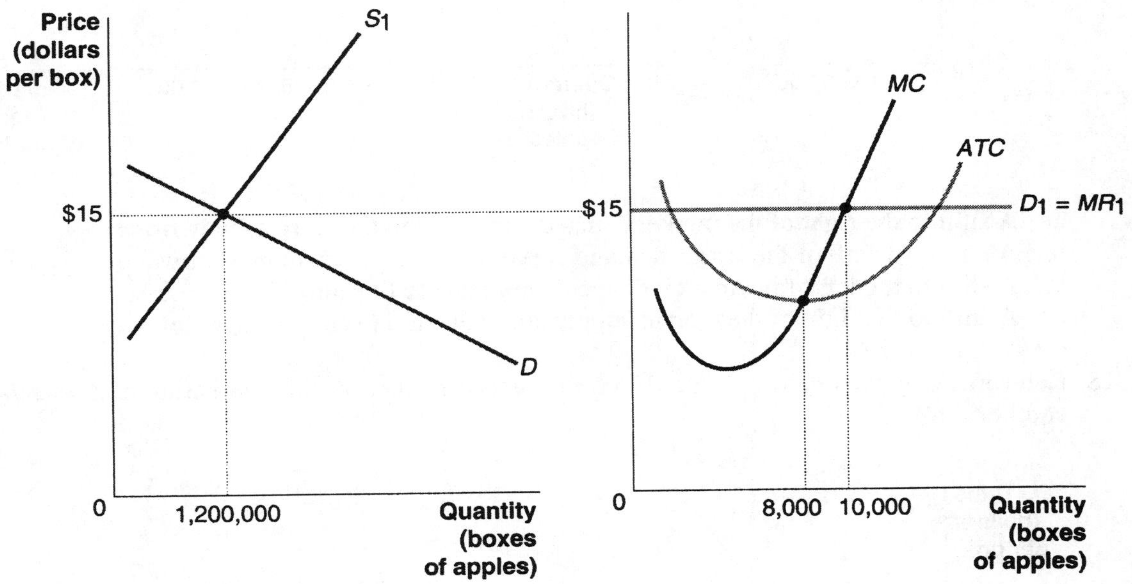

   a. a profit in the short run.
   b. a profit in the long run.
   c. a loss in the short run.
   d. a loss in the long run.

27. Refer to the graphs below. What do you expect to happen in this market as it approaches long-run equilibrium?

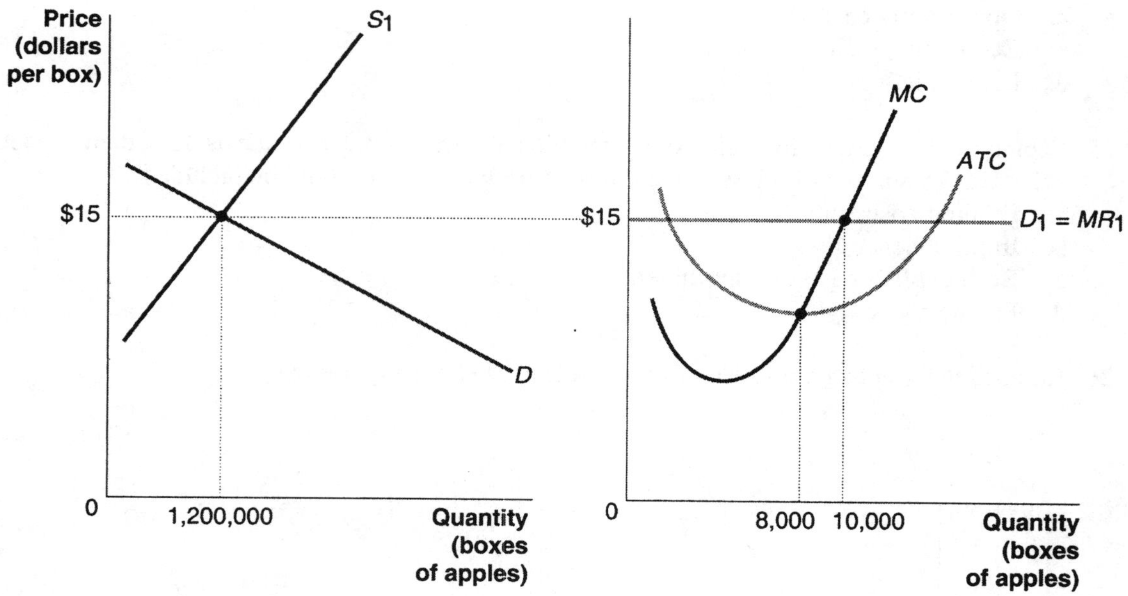

a. A shift to the right of the market demand curve due to the entry of new firms.
b. An upward shift of the firm's demand curve due to the entry of new firms.
c. A shift to the left of the market demand curve due to the entry of new firms.
d. A shift to the right of the market supply curve due to the entry of new firms.

28. Refer to the graphs below. What do you expect to happen in this market as it approaches long-run equilibrium?

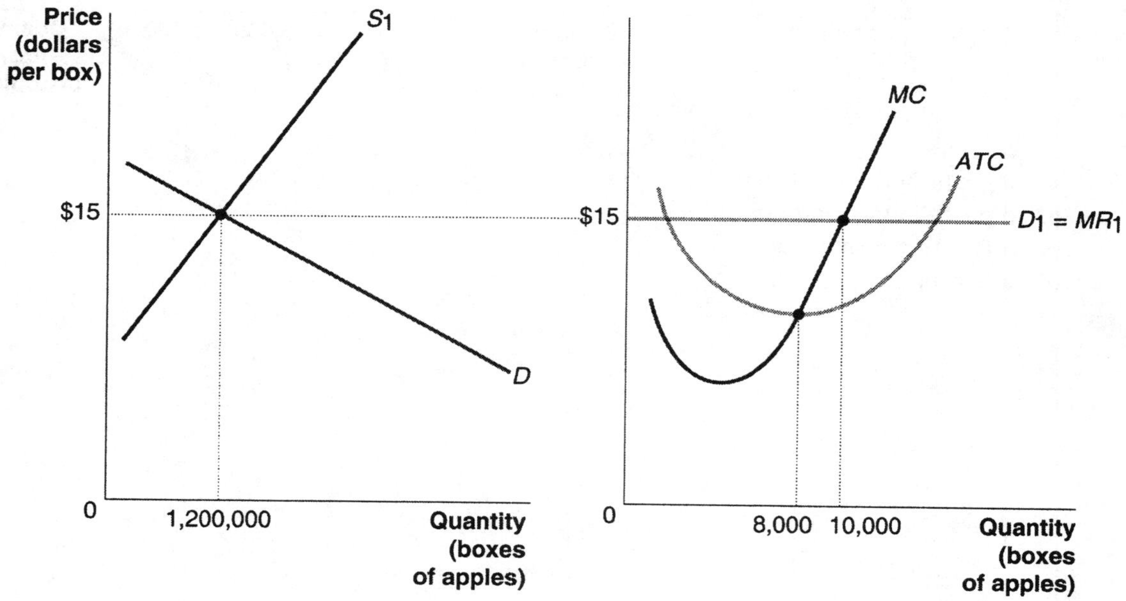

a. The price will increase and profits will become zero.
b. The price will decrease until it is equal to the minimum of average total cost, and profits will increase.
c. The price will decrease until it is equal to the minimum of average total cost, and profits will become zero.
d. Firms will exit because economic profit will become zero.

29. Refer to the graphs below. After the shift in the market demand curve, how will the firm react?

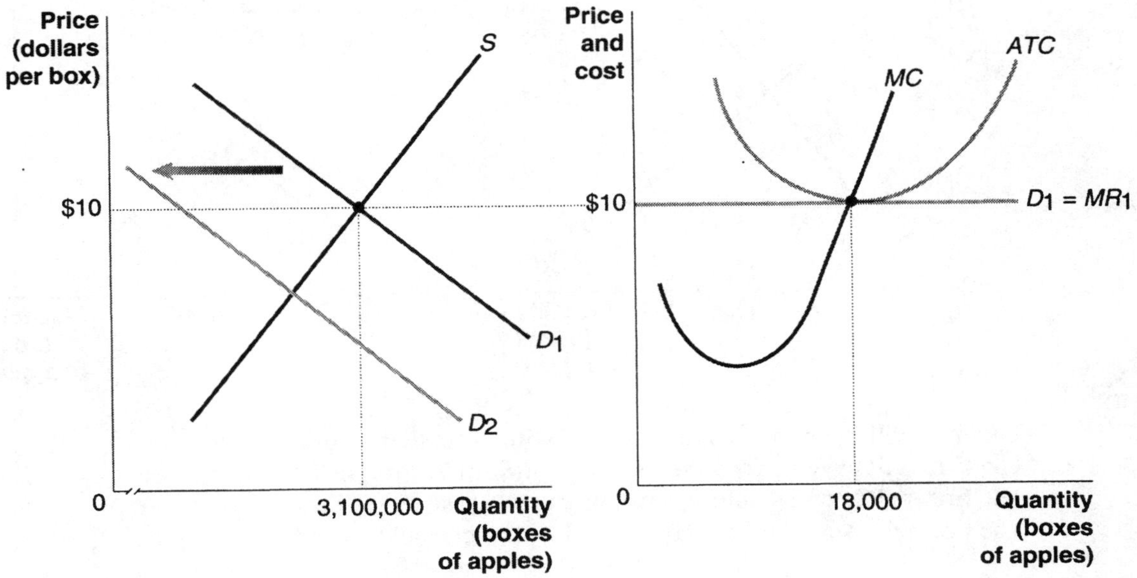

a. The firm will increase its output to increase its profits.
b. The firm will have to decrease its output and suffer losses.
c. The firm will maintain its output at the current level, but suffer losses.
d. The firm will decrease its output and earn higher profit.

30. Refer to the graphs below. When the market demand curve shifts to the right, how will the firm react?

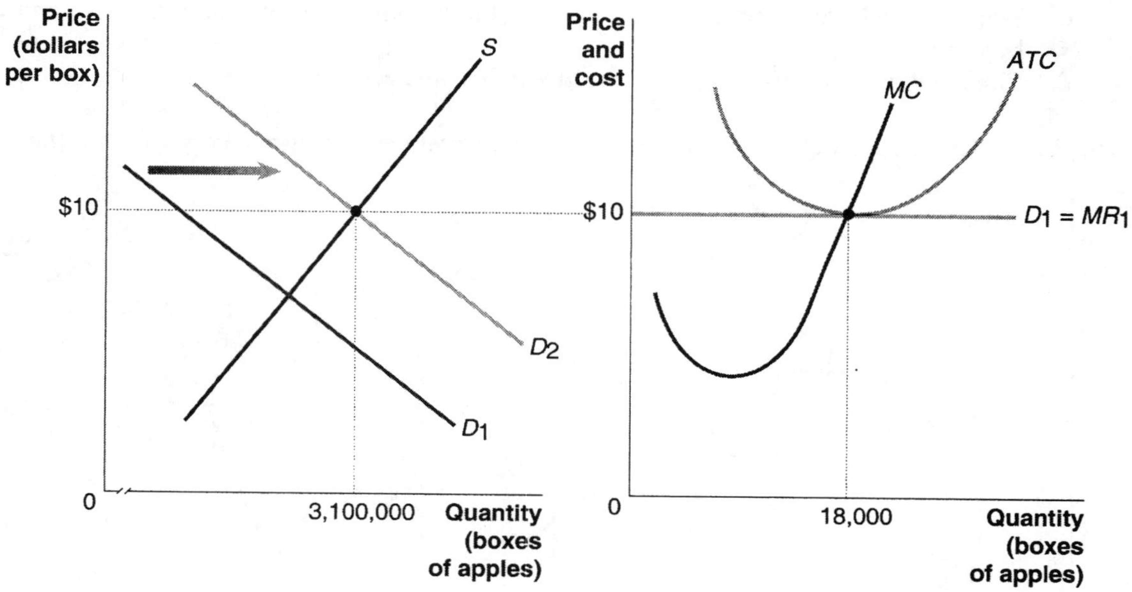

a. The firm will increase its output, which will increase its profits.
b. The firm will have to decrease its output and suffer losses.
c. The firm will keep its output constant, but increase its profits.
d. The firm will decrease its output, which will increase its profit.

31. What is *long-run competitive equilibrium*?
a. The situation in which the entry and exit of firms have resulted in the typical firm just breaking even.
b. A situation in which market price is at a level equal to the minimum point on the typical firm's marginal cost curve.
c. The end of a process during which firms are prevented from adjusting their production methods.
d. All of the above

32. Refer to the graphs below. After the market demand curve shifts to the left, which of the following would happen next in this perfectly competitive market as it adjusts to long-run equilibrium?

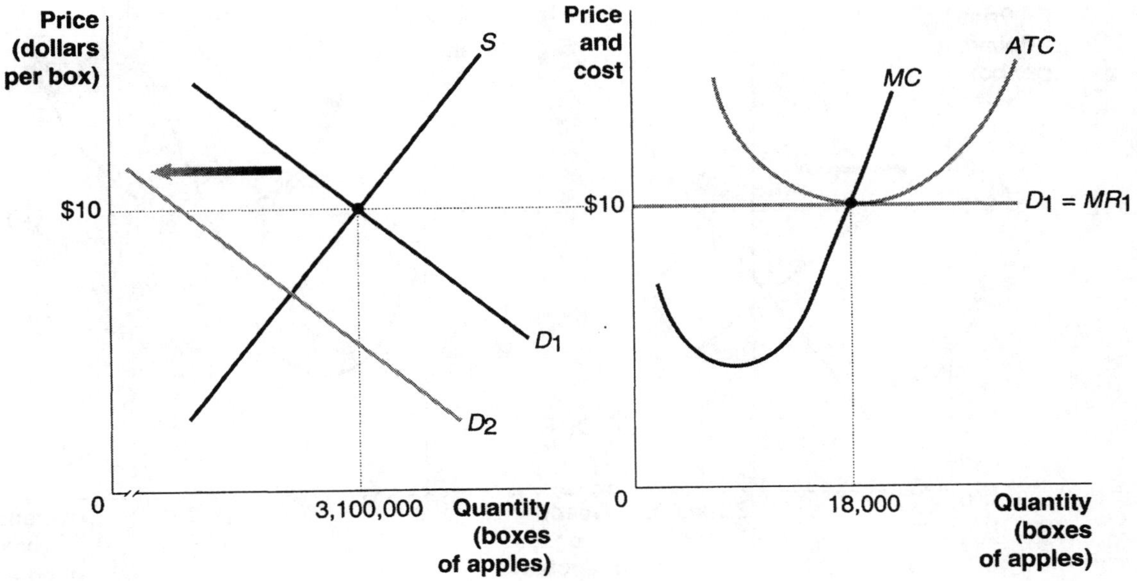

a. The market demand curve will shift back to the right.
b. The market supply curve will shift to the right.
c. The market supply curve will shift to the left.
d. The market demand curve will shift further to the left.

33. Refer to the graphs below. After the market demand curve shifts to the right, which of the following would happen next as this perfectly competitive market adjusts to long-run equilibrium?

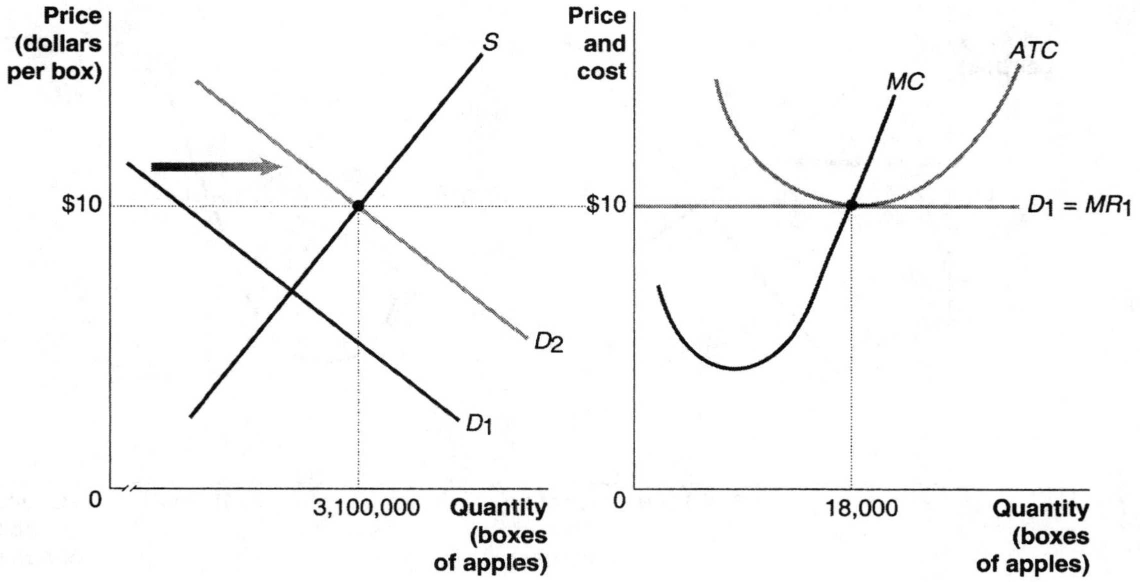

a. The market demand curve will shift back to the left.
b. The market supply curve will shift to the right.
c. The market supply curve will shift to the left.
d. The market demand curve will shift further to the right.

34. Refer to the graph below. Initially, the market is in long-run equilibrium at point *A*. If this is a constant-cost industry, after the increase in demand, through which point is the long-run supply curve most likely to cross?

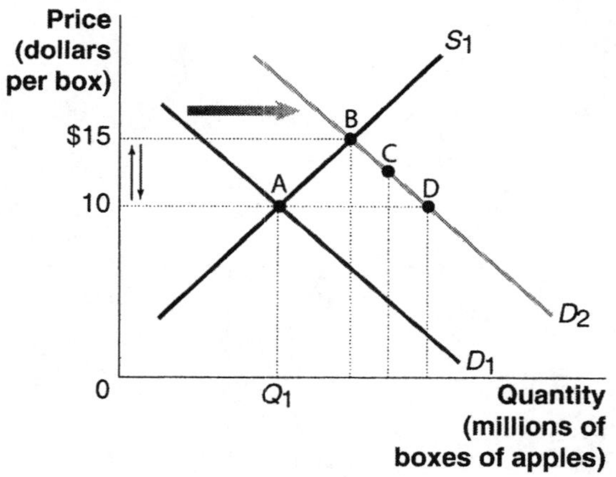

a. Through none of the points shown
b. Through point *B*
c. Through point *C*
d. Through point *D*

35. Refer to the graph below. Initially, the market is in long-run equilibrium at point *A*. Assume this is a constant-cost industry. Immediately after the decrease in demand, which point is likely to be a short-run equilibrium and which point is likely to be a final equilibrium?

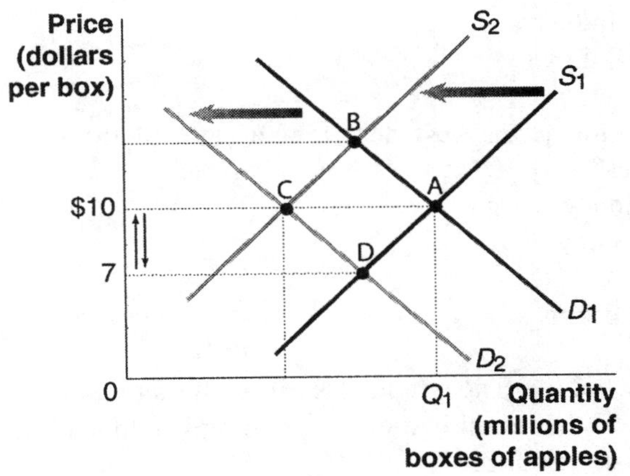

a. Point *B* is a short-run equilibrium and point *C* is a final equilibrium.
b. Point *D* is a short-run equilibrium and point C is a final equilibrium.
c. Point *C* is a short-run equilibrium and point *D* is a final equilibrium.
d. Point *C* is a short-run equilibrium and point *A* is a final equilibrium again.

36. What determines the position of the long-run supply curve?
a. Market price
b. The minimum point on the typical firm's marginal cost curve
c. The minimum point on the typical firm's average total cost curve
d. The minimum point on the typical firm's average variable cost curve

37. Refer to the graphs below. Which graph best depicts an industry in which the typical firm's average costs decrease as the industry expands production?

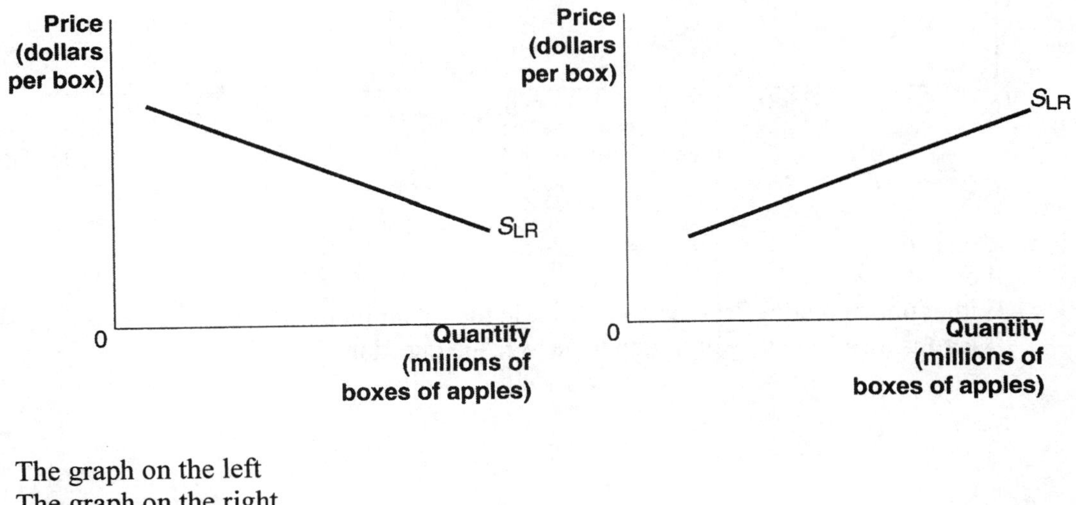

a. The graph on the left
b. The graph on the right
c. Either graph could be associated with that industry.
d. Neither graph

38. Which of the following terms best describes how the result of the forces of competition driving the market price to the minimum average cost of the typical firm?
    a. Allocative efficiency
    b. Productive efficiency
    c. Decreasing-cost industry
    d. Competitive markdown

39. Which of the following terms best describes a state of the economy in which production reflects consumer preferences?
    a. Allocative efficiency
    b. Productive efficiency
    c. Capitalism
    d. Consumer equilibrium

40. Refer to the graphs below. The graph describes the situation of a typical firm in the competitive plasma TV industry. What combination of price and output levels best describes the industry when plasma TVs were first introduced?

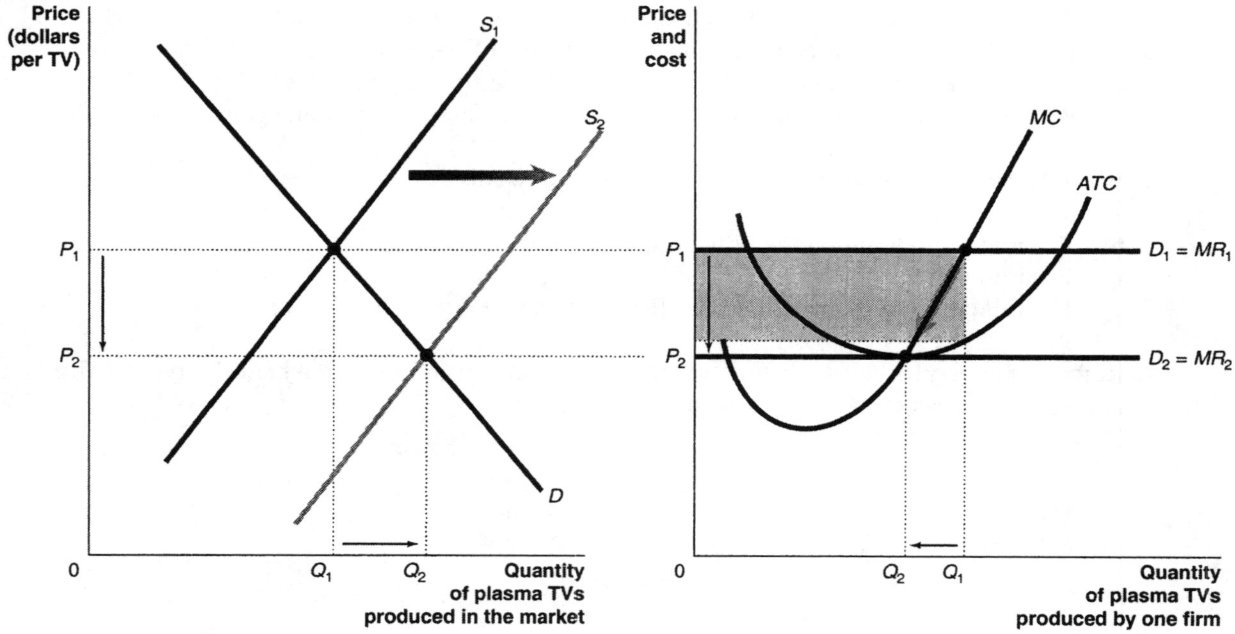

    a. Point *A*
    b. Point *B*
    c. Either point could reflect the conditions in the infant industry.
    d. There is insufficient information to answer the question.

41. Refer to the graphs below. The graph describes a typical firm in the competitive plasma TV industry. What combination of price and output levels best describes the existence of *productive efficiency* in the plasma TV industry?

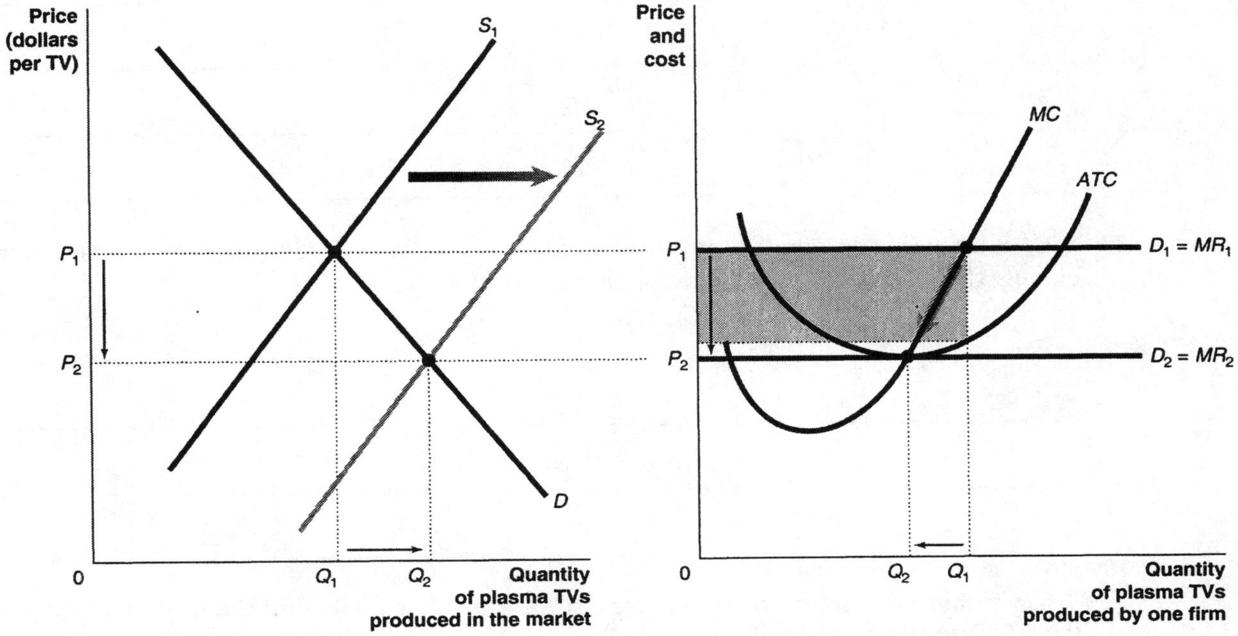

a. Point *A*
b. Point *B*
c. Both points reflect productive efficiency.
d. Neither point reflects productive efficiency.

42. When the market system allocates inputs efficiently to produce goods and services that best satisfy consumer wants, which of the following is true?
a. The price of a good represents the marginal benefit consumers receive from consuming the last unit of the good sold.
b. Perfectly competitive firms produce up to the point where the price of the good equals the marginal cost of producing the last unit.
c. Firms produce up to the point where the last unit provides a marginal benefit to consumers equal to the marginal cost of producing it.
d. All of the above

Short Answer Questions

1. Entry and exit ensure that perfectly competitive firms will not earn economic profits in the long run. Why would any firm remain in an industry if it cannot earn a profit?

____

____

____

2. Explain why the firm's short-run supply curve is that portion of its marginal cost curve that lies above its average variable cost curve.

____

____

____

____

3. Why must perfectly competitive firms produce at the lowest point on their average total cost curves when their markets are in long run equilibrium?

____

____

____

____

4. When firms suffer short-run losses, the exit of some firms will shift the market supply curve to the left. But some firms will remain in the industry. Which types of firms will leave the market?

____

____

____

____

5. Explain why a perfectly competitive firm would not advertise its product in order to attract consumers away from rival firms.

____

____

____

____

True/False Questions

T F 1. Perfectly competitive firms will lower their prices in response to price cuts of rival firms.
T F 2. The slope of the demand curve of a perfectly competitive firm equals zero.
T F 3. The firm's profit equals price minus average total cost.
T F 4. If a firm's price is less than average variable cost in the short run, it will temporarily shut down.
T F 5. The long run supply curve of a perfectly competitive industry is upward sloping.
T F 6. Allocative efficiency is achieved when a product is produced up to the point where the marginal benefit equals the marginal cost of the last unit sold.
T F 7. In the short run, a perfectly competitive firm will shut down if the total revenue from the quantity of output it sells is less than total cost.
T F 8. When perfectly competitive firms exit a market, the market supply curve shifts to the left.
T F 9. An increase in the firm's fixed costs will raise its price and reduce the quantity of output it sells.
T F 10. When a firm's price equals its average variable costs, it will break even.
T F 11. The market supply curve is derived by adding up the quantity that each firm in a perfectly competitive market is willing to supply at each possible price.
T F 12. The market demand curve for a perfectly competitive market is perfectly elastic.
T F 13. In a constant cost industry, the market demand curve is a horizontal line.
T F 14. Productive efficiency is achieved when firms produce the level of output that minimizes their variable costs.
T F 15. Allocative efficiency is achieved when a firm produces a good or service up to the point where average total cost of the last unit produced equals price.

Answers to the Self-Test

Multiple-Choice Questions

Question	Answer	Explanation
1	d	Firms in a perfectly competitive market are unable to control the prices of the goods they sell, and the owners are unable to earn economic profits in the long run.
2	a	The three conditions that make a market perfectly competitive are: 1) There must be many buyers and many firms, all of whom are small relative to the market; 2) The products sold by all firms in the market must be identical; and 3) There must be no barriers to new firms entering the market.
3	b	A buyer or seller that is unable to affect the market price; that is each is a price taker.
4	d	The firm can bring to the market any amount of output it chooses to produce, and sell it at the given market price of $4.00 per bushel.
5	d	If the firm increases its price, it will not sell any units of the good.
6	c	To maximize profits, a perfectly competitive firm should produce that quantity of the good where the difference between the total revenue he receives and his total cost is as large as possible.
7	b	This is the graph that describes the concept of a price-taker type of firm.
8	c	For a firm in a perfectly competitive market, price is equal to both average revenue and marginal revenue.

9	c	In order to maximize profit, the farmer should produce the level of output where marginal revenue equals marginal cost or the last unit of the good for which the $MR > MC$.
10	c	When total revenue is linear, marginal revenue is constant.
11	c	The closest the farmer can come to equalizing marginal revenue and marginal cost is by producing 6 bushels of wheat.
12	b	Profit per unit equals price minus average total cost, or the distance between points *A* and *B* on the graph.
13	c	Only marginal revenue and marginal cost are needed in order to determine the profit-maximizing level of output.
14	a	Marginal cost is not needed in the computation of profit.
15	c	Profit is maximized by setting marginal revenue equals marginal cost.
16	c	The firm earns normal profit, or an amount of profit equal to the opportunity cost to the firm's owners of remaining in this business.
17	c	Since average total cost is greater than price, the area represents losses or a negative economic profit.
18	b	Since average total cost is greater than price, the area represents losses.
19	c	Sunk cost is a cost that has already been paid and cannot be recovered.
20	b	At the price level indicated by this demand curve, the firm obtains exactly the amount of revenue necessary to cover the variable costs of production, leaving the firm with a loss equal to total fixed cost. At this point, the firm is indifferent between producing or shutting down. This is called the shutdown point.
21	c	When demand is $Demand_3$, the firm can cover all of the variable cost and part of the fixed cost, so the firm is better off producing than shutting down.
22	c	$TFC = TC - TVC$. $TC = \$58.00 \times 100 = \$5{,}800$. $TVC = \$34.00 \times 100 = \$3{,}400$. Then, $5,800 – $3,400 = $2,400.
23	a	The graph on the right represents the market's supply curve.
24	b	If a farmer could have earned a 10 percent return on her $100,000 in savings in the best alternative use, then her apple business incurs a $10,000 opportunity cost. We can also think of this $10,000 as being the minimum amount that the farmer needs to earn on her $100,000 investment in her farm to remain in the industry in the long run.
25	c	Economic loss is a situation in which a firm's total revenue is less than its total cost, including all implicit costs.
26	a	Since price is greater than average total cost, there is economic profit to be made in the short run.
27	d	Because price is greater than average total cost, there are economic profits to be made and firms will enter the market. As firms enter, the market supply curve shifts to the right.
28	c	As firms enter the market, the market price will decrease until it reaches the minimum of the *ATC* curve and the profit will become $0.
29	b	The lower equilibrium market price will force the firm to reduce its output to maintain the condition where price (marginal revenue) and marginal cost are equal (and avoid an even bigger loss if output remained the same).
30	a	The higher equilibrium market price would entice the profit-maximizing firm to increase its output so that price (marginal revenue) and marginal cost remain equal. The firm would increase its profits if it increases output rather than if it maintains the same level of output after the price increase.
31	a	In long-run competitive equilibrium, entry and exit have resulted in the typical firm just breaking even. The long-run equilibrium market price is at a level equal to the minimum point on the typical firm's average total cost curve.

32	c	Lower market demand results in losses that cause some firms to exit the industry, thereby shifting the market supply curve to the left.
33	b	Higher market demand results in economic profit that causes some firms to enter the industry, thereby shifting the market supply curve to the right.
34	d	An increase in demand for apples will lead to a temporary increase in price from \$10 to \$15 per box, as the market demand curve shifts to the right from D_1 to D_2. The entry of new firms shifts the market supply curve to the right, which in the case of the constant-cost industry will cause the price to fall to its long-run level of \$10.
35	b	A decrease in demand will lead to a temporary decrease in price from \$10 to \$7 per box, as the market demand curve shifts to the left from D_1 to D_2. The exit of firms shifts the market supply curve to the left from S_1 to S_2, which causes the price to rise to its long-run level of \$10.
36	c	The position of the long-run supply curve is determined by the minimum point on the typical firm's average total cost curve. Anything that raises or lowers the costs of the typical firm in the long run will cause the long-run supply curve to rotate up or down.
37	a	In the long run, competition will force the price of the product to fall to the level of the new lower average cost of the typical firm. In this case, the long-run supply curve will slope downward. Industries with downward-sloping long-run supply curves are called decreasing-cost industries.
38	b	*Productive efficiency* refers to the situation in which a good or service is produced at the lowest possible cost. As we have seen, perfect competition results in productive efficiency.
39	a	*Allocative efficiency* is a state of the economy in which production reflects consumer preferences; in particular, every good or service is produced up to the point where the last unit provides a marginal benefit to consumers equal to the marginal cost of producing it. When DVD players were first introduced, prices were high and only a few firms were in the market.
40	a	When plasma TVs were first introduced, prices were high and only a few firms were in the market.
41	b	Productive efficiency is achieved when plasma TVs are produced at the lowest possible cost.
42	d	When the market system allocates inputs efficiently to produce goods and services that best satisfy consumer wants: 1) the price of a good represents the marginal benefit consumers receive from consuming the last unit of the good sold; 2) perfectly competitive firms produce up to the point where the price of the good equals the marginal cost of producing the last unit; and 3) firms produce up to the point where the last unit provides a marginal benefit to consumers equal to the marginal cost of producing it.

Short Answer Responses

1. Remember that zero economic profit is not the same as zero accounting profit. The return that a perfectly competitive firm earns in the long run is equal to the value of the owner(s) opportunity cost. An economic profit is a return greater than this. In competitive markets, economic profits are possible only in the short run.

2. A supply curve shows the relationship between the price of a product and the quantity of the product supplied. The firm's marginal cost curve traces out the quantity the firm will supply at various prices. But for prices less than average variable cost, the firm will shut down temporarily and produce zero

units of output. This is why the firm's short-run supply curve coincides with only the portion of the marginal cost curve that lies above average variable cost. (Of course, the supply curve also includes the graph's origin.)

3. Since the demand curve for a perfectly competitive firm is horizontal, it has a zero slope. In long-run equilibrium the firm will earn zero economic profit. For this to be true, price must equal average total cost. This can only happen when the demand curve is tangent to the firm's long run average total cost curve and this tangency can only be where both the demand curve and the average total cost curve have slopes equal to zero. And the *ATC* curve will have a slope of zero only at its minimum point.

4. Owners of firms are in different locations and have different opportunity costs. Some will be more optimistic about the future of their markets than others. Owners who are less optimistic about the future prospects for profit are more likely to leave. Some firms are likely to have greater financial resources than others. The firms with lower financial resources are more likely to leave the market when they experience losses.

5. Successful advertising allows firms to gain sales at the expense of other firms and/or to raise the prices of the products they advertise. In perfectly competitive markets, firms can sell all the output they wish to sell at the market price and cannot raise their prices. Advertising would only add to cost and reduce profits.

True/False Answers

1. F The firm should charge the market price because it can sell as many or as few units of the good as desired at that price.
2. T The change in price over the change in quantity is zero.
3. F This defines profit per unit, not total profit.
4. T Because $P < AVC$, the firm cannot cover all the losses.
5. F The statement describes an increasing cost industry. A perfectly competitive market can have constant, increasing, or decreasing long run costs. (A decreasing cost industry will have a downward sloping long run supply curve. A constant cost industry will have a horizontal long run supply curve.)
6. T See the definition of allocative efficiency on page 401 of the textbook.
7. F The firm will continue to produce if total revenue exceeds total *variable* costs.
8. T A decrease in the number of firms in the market will cause the market supply curve to shift left.
9. F Changes in fixed costs will affect a firm's profit but not its output since this does not affect marginal cost. Changes in price result from changes in market supply and demand.
10. F Break even occurs when all costs are covered and there is no additional revenue left over, that is, when P = minimum of the *ATC* curve.
11. T See Figure 11-7 on page 392 of the textbook.
12. F The firm's, not the market's, demand curve is perfectly elastic.
13. F In a constant-cost industry, the long-run market supply curve is a horizontal line.
14. F Productive efficiency occurs when a firm produces the quantity associated with the minimum average total cost.
15. F Allocative efficiency is achieved when a firm produces up to the point where the marginal benefit of the last unit equals the marginal cost of producing it.

Chapter 12

Monopolistic Competition: The Competitive Model in a More Realistic Setting

Chapter Summary

In Chapter 11, you learned about the market structure of perfect competition. Growing wheat and growing apples are examples of perfectly competitive markets. Here in Chapter 12, you will learn about the more common market structure of monopolistic competition. If you shop at supermarkets and go to movie theaters, you are dealing with firms that are in monopolistically competitive markets. **Monopolistical competition** is the most common market structure in the United States. This structure has three characteristics:

1. There are many buyers and sellers
2. Barriers to entry are low
3. Firms compete by selling similar but differentiated goods and services

Each monopolistically competitive firm faces a downward-sloping demand curve, so marginal revenue is less than price. Firms maximize profit by producing the level of output that makes marginal revenue equal marginal cost. The firm may earn an economic profit or suffer an economic loss in the short run. Because there are low entry barriers, in the long run, economic profits will cause new firms to enter the market. A firm that earns short-run profits will earn zero economic profit in the long run as entry from new firms shifts the firm's demand curve to the left and causes it to become more elastic. If the typical firm in a monopolistically competitive market suffers economic losses in the short run, some firms will exit the market and the demand curves for each of the firms that remain in the industry will shift to the right and become less elastic. In the long run, the firm's demand curve will be tangent to its long-run average total cost curve, but average total cost will be not be at its minimum level.

Unlike perfectly competitive firms, monopolistically competitive firms charge a price greater than marginal cost, and they do not produce at minimum average total cost. A monopolistically competitive firm has excess capacity. If the firm increases its output, it could produce at a lower average cost. But consumers benefit from being able to purchase a product that is differentiated and more closely suited to their tastes.

Firms can use **marketing** to differentiate their products. Marketing tools include **brand management** and advertising. There are a number of factors that a firm can control that determine the firm's success, but market forces and luck also play an important role in the firm's profitability.

Learning Objectives

When you finish this chapter, you should be able to:

1. **Explain why a monopolistically competitive firm has downward-sloping demand and marginal revenue curves.** A monopolistically competitive firm is able to raise its price without losing all of its customers. Some customers are willing to pay the higher price because the firm has a favorable location, can offer better service, and has a higher quality product.

2. **Explain how a monopolistically competitive firm maximizes profit in the short run.** All firms maximize profits by producing where marginal revenue is equal to marginal cost. Since price is greater than marginal revenue, a monopolistically competitive firm produces where price is greater than marginal cost. The firm will earn economic profits if its price exceeds average total cost in the short run.

3. **Analyze the situation of a monopolistically competitive firm in the long run.** Since entry barriers are low in monopolistically competitive industries, short-run profits give entrepreneurs an incentive to enter the market and establish new firms. The entry of new firms will shift the demand curves of existing firms to the left and make them more elastic. If firms suffer short-run economic losses, some firms will exit the industry in the long run. This will shift the demand curves of remaining firms to the right and make them more inelastic. In the long run, the demand curve of a typical firm will be tangent to its average total cost curve. With price equal to average total cost in the long run, the firm's profit will be zero.

4. **Compare the efficiency of monopolistic competition and perfect competition.** In the long run, the profit-maximizing level of output for a monopolistically competitive firm occurs where price is greater than marginal cost and the firm is not at the minimum point of its average total cost curve. Unlike a perfectly competitive firm, a monopolistically competitive firm does not achieve allocative efficiency or productive efficiency.

5. **Define marketing and explain how firms use it to differentiate their products**. Marketing refers to all the activities necessary for a firm to sell a product to consumers. Firms use brand management and advertising to earn profits and defend profits from competitors.

6. **Identify the key factors that determine a firm's success.** The most important factors under a firm's control are its ability to differentiate its product and to produce at a lower average cost than competing firms. Other factors that affect profitability are not under a firm's control. These factors include the prices of the inputs it uses in production and random chance.

Chapter Review

Chapter Opener: Starbucks: Growth through Product Differentiation (pages 410-411)

Since the first Starbucks coffee shop opened in 1971, the firm has grown into a worldwide company. But the growth has been in the number of shops, over 13,000, rather than the size of the shops themselves. Starbucks faces competition from other firms. Neighborhoods often have three or more coffeehouses. Barriers to entry into the market for coffeehouses are low and firms differentiate their products by offering different menus and services.

Helpful Study Hint

An ***Inside Look*** at the end of this chapter features a newspaper story about how Dunkin' Donuts has tried to make their stores more upscale to attract more business. Dunkin' Donuts paid for a market research project designed to help them determine the differences between their stores and customers and those of Starbucks. Dunkin' Donuts concluded that the customers for the two stores were two completely kinds of people – upscale versus down-to-earth. In response to these findings, Dunkin' Donuts decided to redesign its stores to be more similar to those of Starbucks in the hope of attracting new customers without alienating current customer base. Redesigning stores represents another way for firms to differentiate their product.

Economics in YOUR Life! asks you to imagine opening your own restaurant. How do you decide the type of food to serve and the type of decor? How successful are you likely to be? Keep these questions in mind as you read the chapter. The authors will answer questions at the end of the chapter.

12.1 LEARNING OBJECTIVE

12.1 Demand and Marginal Revenue for a Firm in a Monopolistically Competitive Market (pages 412-415)

Learning Objective 1 Explain why a monopolistically competitive firm has downward-sloping demand and marginal revenue curves.

Monopolistic competition is a market structure in which barriers to entry are low and many firms compete by selling similar, but not identical, products. Because their products are differentiated, monopolistically competitive firms can raise their prices without losing *all* their customers. A price increase will, however, cause *some* customers to switch to another similar product. A monopolistically competitive firm faces down-sloping demand and marginal revenue curves. Monopolistically competitive firms have only limited control over their prices because they face competition from many firms selling similar products. McDonald's, for example, would sell very few Big Macs at a price of $10.

Helpful Study Hint

You should study Figure 12-3 on page 414 of the textbook to aid in your understanding of the downward-sloping demand and marginal revenue curves that a monopolistically competitive firm faces.

Restaurants, convenience stores, bookstores, and gas stations are all examples of monopolistically competitive firms. Gas stations display their prices so that consumers can easily compare differences between stations. Many motorists are willing to buy at a slightly higher per-gallon price if a station is in a more convenient location than a station that offers a lower price. Some consumers believe there are differences between various brands of gasoline. These customers are willing to pay a somewhat higher price for what they perceive as a superior product. The next time you drive or ride in a car, notice how much difference there is between the prices charged by the stations you pass.

Extra Solved Problem **12-1**

Chapter 12 in the textbook includes two Solved Problems. Here is an extra Solved Problem to help you build your skills solving economic problems.

Supports Learning Objective 1: Explain why a monopolistically competitive firm has downward-sloping demand and marginal revenue curves.

Suppose that the following table represents the demand for Luigi's Italian Restaurant pizza. Use this table to answer the questions below.

Price	Quantity
$26	30
24	60
22	90
20	120
18	150
16	180
14	210
12	240
11	255

a. Calculate Luigi's marginal revenue.

b. Is Luigi's a perfectly competitive firm or a monopolistically competitive firm? Explain.

SOLVING THE PROBLEM

Step 1: **Review the chapter material.**
This problem is about demand and marginal revenue, so you may want to review the section "Demand and Marginal Revenue for a Firm in a Monopolistically Competitive Market," which begins on page 412 of the textbook.

Step 2: **Answer question (a) by calculating Luigi's marginal revenue.**
To calculate marginal revenue, first total revenue by multiplying the price by the quantity demanded at that price. Then calculate the marginal revenue by dividing the change in total revenue by the change in quantity. For example, at a price of $22 total revenue is: $22 x 90 = $1,980. If Luigi cuts his price from $22 to $20 his marginal revenue equals: ($2,400 – $1,980)/(120 – 90) = $14.

Price	Quantity	Total Revenue	Marginal Revenue
$26	30	$ 780	-
24	60	1,440	$22
22	90	1,980	18
20	120	2,400	14
18	150	2,700	10
16	180	2,880	6
14	210	2,940	2
12	240	2,880	−2
11	255	2,805	−5

Step 3: **Answer question (b) by determining whether this is a monopolistically or perfectly competitive firm.**

To determine whether Luigi is a perfect competitor or a monopolistic competitor, consider his marginal revenue. A perfectly competitive firm faces a horizontal demand curve that is also its marginal revenue curve, while a monopolistically competitive firm faces downward-sloping demand and marginal revenue curves. The marginal revenue in the table above decreases as the quantity increases, so Luigi's is a monopolistically competitive firm.

12.2 LEARNING OBJECTIVE

12.2 How a Monopolistically Competitive Firm Maximizes Profits in the Short Run (pages 415-417)

Learning Objective 2 Explain how a monopolistically competitive firm maximizes profit in the short run.

As with firms in other markets, a monopolistically competitive firm will maximize profits by producing the level of output that makes marginal revenue (*MR*) equal to marginal cost (*MC*). Because the *MR* curve lies below the firm's demand curve, the firm will maximize profits where price (*P*) exceeds *MC*:

$$P > MC$$

Helpful Study Hint

Review the table and graph in Figure 12-4 on page 416 of the textbook for an example of a monopolistically competitive firm that makes a profit in the short run. Notice that
(a) the profit-maximizing quantity is where $MR = MC$,
(b) when firms earn profits the *ATC* curve crosses the demand curve at two points, and
(c) at the profit maximizing output $P > MR$ and $P > MC$.

Solved Problem 12-2 considers the situation many firms face when considering whether to produce an additional unit of the good. Managers often add up all of the costs associated with the production of the unit – the average total cost – and compare this to the revenue that unit will bring in. However, the manager should only consider the additional variable costs that go into the production of the unit of the good – the marginal cost of that unit – relative to the marginal revenue. If the marginal revenue is greater than the marginal cost, then the unit should be produced and sold.

12.3 LEARNING OBJECTIVE

12.3 What Happens to Profits in the Long Run? (pages 417-423)

Learning Objective 3 Analyze the situation of a monopolistically competitive firm in the long run.

When firms in a market are earning economic profits, entrepreneurs have an incentive to enter the market and establish new firms. As a result of this entry of new firms, the demand curve of an established firm shifts to the left and becomes more elastic. Entry will continue until the typical firm's demand curve is tangent to its *ATC* curve. In the long run, the typical firm's price will equal its average total cost and the firm will break even.

Economic losses will lead some firms to exit the market. As a result, the demand curve for a firm remaining in the market shifts to the right and becomes less elastic. The exit of firms continues until the typical firm can charge a price equal to its average total cost. In the long run, firms that remain in the industry will experience zero economic profit.

Helpful Study Hint

This section of the textbook contains several features to help you understand how a market moves from short-run to long-run equilibrium. ***Don't Let This Happen to You!*** warns you not to confuse economic and accounting profit. Economic profit is the revenue left over after all expenses have been paid, including the opportunity cost of any resources the owners supply to the firm, such as their time and financial investment. Accounting profit is the revenue left over after all monetary expenses have been paid. Economic profit is typically less than accounting profit because in calculating accounting profit certain opportunity costs are not included. If economic profit falls to zero, the firm is still earning positive accounting profits.

See Figure 12-5 on page 418 of the textbook for graphs that illustrate the short run for a firm earning profits and how the entry of competing firms eliminate these profits in the long run. Spend some time reviewing Table 12-2 on page 419, which is a comprehensive graphical summary of the short run and long run for a monopolistically competitive firm. Be sure that you understand (1) the difference between the short run and the long run and (2) the process of the transition between the short run and the long run.

Making the Connection "The Rise and Fall of Apple's Macintosh Computer" and ***Solved Problem 12-3*** use the experience of Apple's Macintosh computer to analyze the short run and long run under monopolistic competition. The Macintosh was a differentiated product, so Apple could charge a price well above marginal cost and continue to hold a large market share. Over time, competitors began to develop products that were able to compete directly with and were quite similar to Apple's products. Because Apple's Macintosh was no longer significantly different from the other products available in the market, Apple could no longer charge a higher price and maintain its high market share.

Making the Connection "Staying One Step Ahead of the Competition: Eugène Schueller and L'Oréal" describes the efforts of a cosmetics company to stay ahead of its competition. L'Oréal devotes significant resources to continually updating and improving its products. This allows the products to be continually differentiated from other firms in the cosmetic industry and, in turn, L'Oréal continues to receive a positive economic profit.

12.4 LEARNING OBJECTIVE

12.4 Comparing Perfect Competition and Monopolistic Competition (pages 423-425)

Learning Objective 4 Compare the efficiency of monopolistic competition and perfect competition.

There are two important differences between the long-run equilibrium in a perfectly competitive industry and in a monopolistically competitive industry. Unlike perfectly competitive firms, monopolistically competitive firms charge a price greater than marginal cost and they do not produce at minimum average total cost. Because price is greater than marginal cost, allocative efficiency is not achieved, and because price is greater than minimum average total cost, productive efficiency is not achieved. Monopolistically competitive firms also have excess capacity because they do not produce where average total cost is at a minimum. Despite these apparent inefficiencies, consumers benefit from purchasing products that are differentiated.

Helpful Study Hint

Although monopolistic competition appears to fall short of perfect competition in terms of economic efficiency, the textbook rightly notes that consumers are willing to pay for the variety offered by monopolistically competitive firms. Consider gas stations once again as an example. Let's say there are three gas stations on a single street corner. During most hours of the day, at least one or two of the stations are not busy. We can interpret this as excess capacity. But during rush hours, all three stations have customers. Enough drivers are willing to pay to keep all three stations operating for the convenience of not waiting in long lines during peak hours. Supermarkets offer another example of consumers' willingness to pay for greater convenience. Most supermarkets open additional check-out lines – some for consumers with just a few items to buy – when long lines start to form.

You should review Figure 12-6 on page 424 of the textbook to be sure that you understand the difference between a perfectly competitive firm's long run equilibrium and that of a monopolistically competitive firm. To reinforce this concept, you should work Problems and Applications 4.4 on page 436.

Making the Connection "Abercrombie and Fitch: Can the Product Be Too Differentiated?" provides another example of product differentiation and its effect on the firm. This article discusses the tradeoffs between being like everybody else and creating a niche market. Abercrombie and Fitch was willing to decrease the number of people who would be interested in shopping at its store to support its extremely narrow niche market program. Apparently Abercrombie and Fitch has created too narrow a niche because it has been experiencing decreased sales. If this decrease continues, Abercrombie and Fitch will likely have to change its niche market or eventually go out of business.

Extra Solved Problem 12-4

Chapter 12 in the textbook includes two Solved Problems. Here is an extra Solved Problem to help you build you skills solving economic problems.

Supports Learning Objective 4: Compare the efficiency of monopolistic competition and perfect competition.

Luigi's Italian Restaurant has the demand and revenue schedules below from Solved Problem 12-1. Assume that the marginal costs for Luigi's are as given in the last column in the table.

Price	Quantity	Total Revenue	Marginal Revenue	Marginal Cost
$26	30	$ 780	-	-
24	60	1,440	$22	$21
22	90	1,980	18	17
20	120	2,400	14	14
18	150	2,700	10	11
16	180	2,880	6	9
14	210	2,940	2	9
12	240	2,880	−2	12
11	255	2,805	−5	17

a. Compare Luigi's profit maximizing condition with that of the perfectly competitive firm's profit maximizing condition. Explain the inefficiency caused by Luigi's being a monopolistically competitive firm.

b. What do customers gain by participating in industries that are monopolistically competitive?

SOLVING THE PROBLEM

Step 1: Review the chapter material.
This problem is about perfect competition versus monopolistic competition, so you may want to review the section "Comparing Perfect Competition and Monopolistic Competition," which begins on page 423 of the textbook.

Step 2: Determine the profit-maximizing quantity for Luigi's and the profit-maximizing quantity if Luigi's was a perfectly competitive firm.
Luigi's will maximize profit where marginal revenue equals marginal cost. Marginal revenue and marginal cost both equal $14 per pizza when 120 pizzas are produced and sold. Note that at the quantity of 120 pizzas, a price of $20 will be charged, which is greater than the marginal revenue of $14. A perfectly competitive firm will produce where marginal cost equals price. Price and marginal cost both equal $12 per pizza when 240 pizzas will be produced.

Step 3: Compare the profit-maximization condition for Luigi's and the perfectly competitive firm, while being sure to note the inefficiency that arises due to monopolistic competition.
As a monopolistic competitor, Luigi's charges a price of $20 per pizza, which is significantly higher than the perfectly competitive price of $12. Luigi's also produces only 120 pizzas, while a perfectly competitive firm that was producing where price equals marginal cost would produce 240 pizzas. We can conclude that Luigi's, as a monopolistically competitive firm, has excess capacity and charges a price greater than its marginal cost.

Step 4: Discuss the gains to consumers that buy from monopolistically competitive firms.
Though consumers pay a higher price and cannot purchase as many units of the good when it is produced in a monopolistically competitive industry, they get to choose from a variety of products when making their consumption choices. The willingness of consumers to pay higher prices for differentiated goods indicates that consumers value these goods enough to be willing to pay the higher prices.

12.5 LEARNING OBJECTIVE

12.5 How Marketing Differentiates Products (pages 425-427)

Learning Objective 5 Define marketing and explain how firms use it to differentiate their products.

Firms can differentiate their products through marketing. **Marketing** refers to all the activities necessary for a firm to sell a product to a consumer. Firms use two marketing tools to differentiate their products:

1. **Brand management** refers to the actions of a firm intended to maintain the differentiation of a product over time. Economic profits are earned when a firm introduces a new product, but this leads to the entry of firms producing similar products and the profits are eliminated. Firms use brand management to delay the time when they will no longer be able to earn profits.

2. Advertising shifts the demand curve for a product to the right and makes the demand curve more inelastic. Successful advertising allows the firm to sell more at every price. Advertising also increases costs. If the increase in revenue from advertising exceeds the costs, profits will rise.

Once a firm, such as Coca-Cola or Apple, has established a brand name, it has an incentive to defend it. Firms can apply for a trademark. A trademark grants legal protection against other firms using a product's name. If firms do not prevent the unauthorized use of their trademarks, they may be no longer entitled to legal protection. Firms will spend substantial amounts to ensure that they do not lose legal protection for their trademarks.

Helpful Study Hint

See ***Solved Problem 12-5*** in this Study Guide for an example of the legal means 3Com Corporation uses to protect its trademarks.

Extra Solved Problem 12-5

Chapter 12 in the textbook includes two Solved Problems. Here is an extra Solved Problem to help you build your skills solving economic problems.

Supports Learning Objective 5: Define marketing and explain how firms use it to differentiate their products.

We Came. We Marketed. We Sold.

3Com Corporation is mentioned in the introduction to the first chapter of the textbook. The firm was incorporated in 1979 and specializes in providing computer network devices such as routers and network switches. Among 3Com's clients are businesses that want to improve the communication and security capabilities of their computer systems. 3Com is not a household name in the same way McDonald's or Microsoft are, but marketing is an important part of the company's success. It faces stiff competition from other computer service providers, such as Cisco Systems, and uses advertising and trademarks to influence its customers. 3Com's advertising efforts are aimed primarily at computer network managers; for example, an advertising agency developed a two-page ad for 3Com titled "We Came. We Saw. We Routed." Ads such as these are placed in publications most likely to be seen by the target audience. It would be less effective for 3Com to place ads in *People* or *Time* magazines, because few of their readers are computer network managers, than it would be to advertise in business publications. The importance of establishing and maintaining 3Com's trademarks is indicated by the guidelines the firm's legal experts issue to employees. The following is a small sample of these guidelines for over 40 company and product trademarks:

> Always Use a Trademark as an Adjective, Followed by the Appropriate Description(s). If not, the trademark could become generic...make sure that 3Com and the ® symbol (3Com®) precedes a trademark mention of the product or service.
>
> Correct: The 3Com® NBX® business telephone has powerful call processing features.
> Incorrect: NBX® has powerful call-processing features.

Sources: http://www.3com.com/corpinfo/en_US/legal/trademark/tmn_list.html
http://www.langstaffcommunications.com/Portfolio/Advertising/advertising.html

a. Define marketing and explain the importance of marketing to firms.

b. Explain how 3Com Corporation uses marketing to differentiate its products.

SOLVING THE PROBLEM

Step 1: Review the chapter material.
This problem is about marketing, so you may want to review the section "How Marketing Differentiates Products," which begins on page 425 of the textbook.

Step 2: Define marketing and explain the importance of marketing to firms.
Marketing refers to all the activities necessary for a firm to sell a product to a consumer. To earn profits, monopolistically competitive firms must differentiate their products. These firms use two marketing tools to do this: brand management and advertising.

Step 3: Explain how 3Com Corporation uses marketing to differentiate its products.
3Com Corporation uses brand management, including extensive use of trademarks, and advertising to differentiate its products. 3Com Corporation focuses its marketing strategies on its customers, who are primarily computer network managers.

12.6 LEARNING OBJECTIVE

12.6 What Makes a Firm Successful? (pages 427-428)

Learning Objective 6 Identify the key factors that determine a firm's success.

A firm can control some of the factors that allow it to make economic profits, while other factors are uncontrollable. Controllable factors include the ability of a firm to differentiate its product and produce it at a lower average total cost than competing firms. Factors that the firm cannot control include input prices, changes in consumer tastes, and random chance.

Helpful Study Hint

Making the Connection "Is Being the First Firm in the Market a Key to Success?" discusses whether "first-mover advantages" are the key to a firm's success. In some industries there are significant advantages to being the first firm in the industry. However, firms that enter an industry late can become more successful than the first-movers if their products are more reliable, less expensive, or more convenient.

Economics in YOUR Life! "Opening Your Own Restaurant" discusses what is likely to happen if you open a restaurant in your hometown. If your restaurant is successful, other entrepreneurs will have an incentive to copy the desirable characteristics of your restaurant. Because the restaurants will differ from one another in their food and ambience, each restaurant will be selling a differentiated product. As firms enter the restaurant industry, economic profit will eventually be driven to zero.

Key Terms

Brand management. The actions of a firm intended to maintain the differentiation of a product over time.

Marketing. All the activities necessary for a firm to sell a product to a consumer.

Monopolistic competition. A market structure in which barriers to entry are low and many firms compete by selling similar, but not identical, products.

Self-Test

(Answers are provided at the end of the Self-Test.)

Multiple-Choice Questions

1. Which of the following are characteristics of monopolistic competition?
   a. High barriers to entry
   b. Few firms compete
   c. Firms sell similar, but not identical, products
   d. All of the above

2. Why does a monopolistically competitive firm have a downward-sloping demand curve?
   a. Because its customers only buy goods that are being discounted from their original prices
   b. Because changing the price will affect the quantity sold
   c. Because the firm is a price taker, like a wheat farmer
   d. Because the firm's level of output produced depends on its cost structure

3. Refer to the graph below. According to this graph, what will happen if Starbucks increases the price of café lattes?

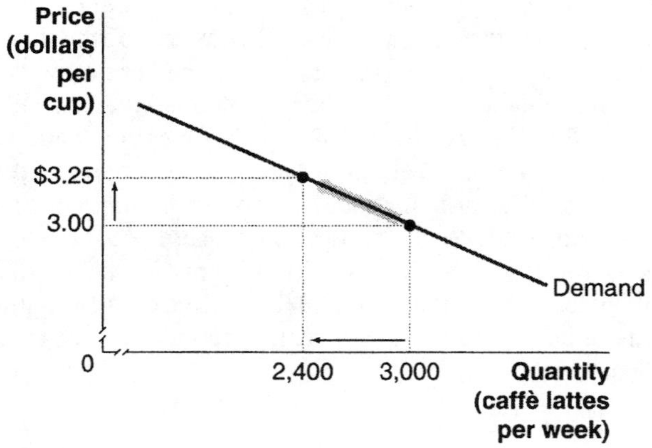

   a. It will not lose any customers.
   b. It will lose all of its customers.
   c. It will lose some, but not all, of its customers.
   d. It will gain customers.

4. In which case is the firm's demand curve the same as marginal revenue?
   a. In the monopolistically competitive case
   b. In the perfectly competitive case
   c. In both the monopolistically competitive case and the perfectly competitive case
   d. In neither the monopolistically competitive case nor the perfectly competitive case

5. If marginal revenue slopes downward, which of the following is true?
   a. The firm must cut the price to sell a larger quantity.
   b. The firm must increase the price to sell a larger quantity.
   c. The firm must cut its price if it wants to keep on selling the same quantity day after day.
   d. The firm is unable to adjust price in order to adjust quantity sold.

6. Which of the following measures is conceptually the same as price?
   a. Marginal revenue
   b. Total revenue
   c. Average revenue
   d. None of the above

7. Which of the following terms best describes the additional revenue associated with selling an additional unit of output?
   a. Price
   b. Average revenue
   c. Marginal revenue
   d. Total revenue

8. When a monopolistically competitive firm cuts price, good and bad things happen. Which of the following is considered a good thing for the firm?
   a. The price effect
   b. The output effect
   c. The revenue effect
   d. All of the above are good things.

9. When a monopolistically competitive firm cuts price, good and bad things happen. Which of the following is considered a bad thing for the firm?
   a. The price effect
   b. The output effect
   c. The revenue effect
   d. All of the above are good things.

10. Refer to the table below. What is the *average revenue* associated with the sixth unit of output produced and sold?

Caffé Lattes Sold per Week (Q)	Price (*P*)	Total Revenue (*TR*= *P* x *Q*)	Average Revenue	Marginal Revenue
4	$4.00	$16.00		
5	3.50	17.50		
6	3.00	18.00		

a. $3.00
b. $2.00
c. $0.50
d. None of the above; there is insufficient information to answer the question.

11. Refer to the table below. What is the *marginal revenue* associated with the sixth unit of output produced and sold?

Caffé Lattes Sold per Week (Q)	Price (*P*)	Total Revenue (*TR*= *P* x *Q*)	Average Revenue	Marginal Revenue
4	$4.00	$16.00		
5	3.50	17.50		
6	3.00	18.00		

a. $3.00
b. $2.00
c. $0.50
d. None of the above

12. Refer to the graph below. A downward move along the demand curve as price falls from $3.50 to $3.00 per cup results in a gain and a loss of revenue. Which area represents the loss of revenue?

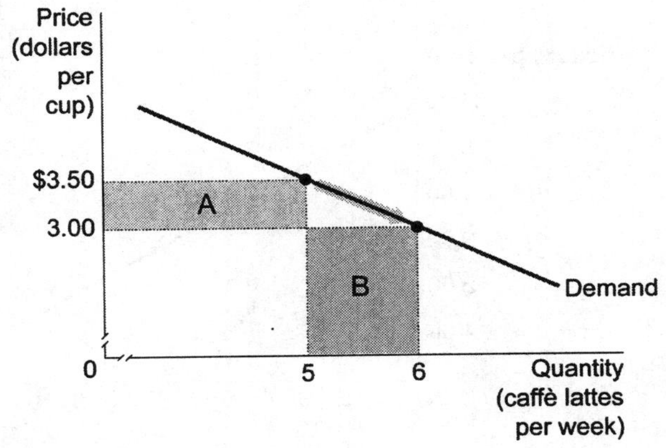

a. Area *A*
b. Area *B*
c. Both *A* and *B* represent revenue losses.
d. An area not shown.

13. Refer to the graph below. A downward move along the demand curve as price falls from $3.50 to $3.00 per cup results in a gain and a loss of revenue. Which area represents the revenue gain?

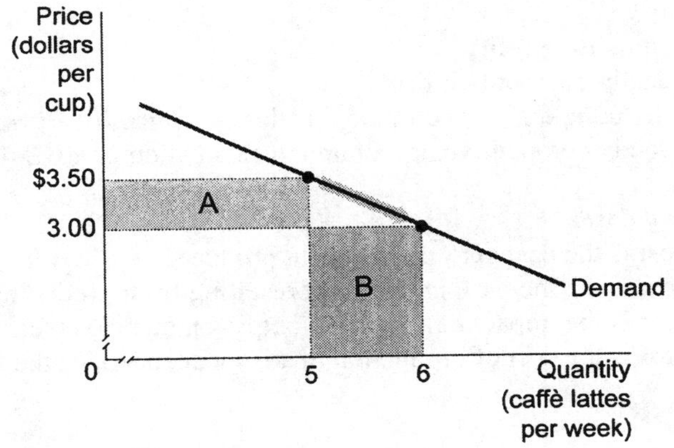

a. Area *A*
b. Area *B*
c. Both areas highlighted represent revenue gains.
d. An area not shown.

14. If a firm has the ability to affect the price of the good or service it sells, what is the relationship between its marginal revenue curve and its demand curve?
a. The firm will have a marginal revenue curve that is above its demand curve.
b. The firm will have a marginal revenue curve that is below its demand curve.
c. The firm will have a marginal revenue curve that is the same as its demand curve.
d. The firm will have an upward-sloping marginal revenue curve and a downward-sloping demand curve.

15. Refer to the graph below. In which portion of the marginal revenue curve is the additional revenue (from selling more) less than the revenue lost from receiving a lower price?

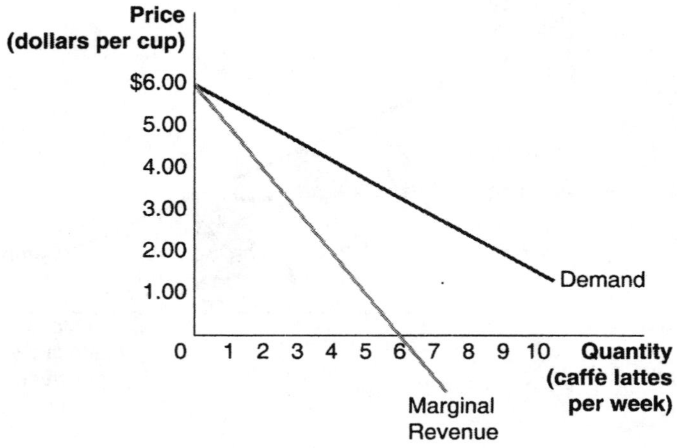

a. In the portion where marginal revenue is positive
b. In the portion where marginal revenue is negative
c. All the way throughout the marginal revenue curve
d. None of the above; the additional revenue gained is always greater than revenue lost.

16. Which of the following types of firms use the marginal revenue equals marginal cost approach to maximize profits?
a. Perfectly competitive firms
b. Monopolistically competitive firms
c. Both perfectly competitive and monopolistically competitive firms
d. Neither perfectly competitive nor monopolistically competitive firms

17. What is *marginal cost*?
a. Marginal cost is the cost per unit of output produced.
b. Marginal cost is the increase in total cost resulting from producing another unit of output.
c. Marginal cost is the impact of additional output on total fixed cost.
d. Marginal cost is the cost of production that is independent of the level of output produced.

18. Refer to the graph below. In order to maximize profit, what price should the firm charge?

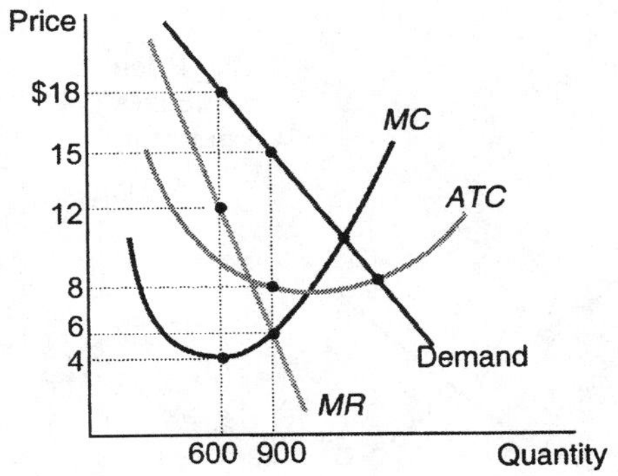

a. $18
b. $15
c. $8
d. $4

19. Refer to the graph below and select the best answer choice. Assume that the firm is producing 600 units. What should the firm do in order to maximize profit?

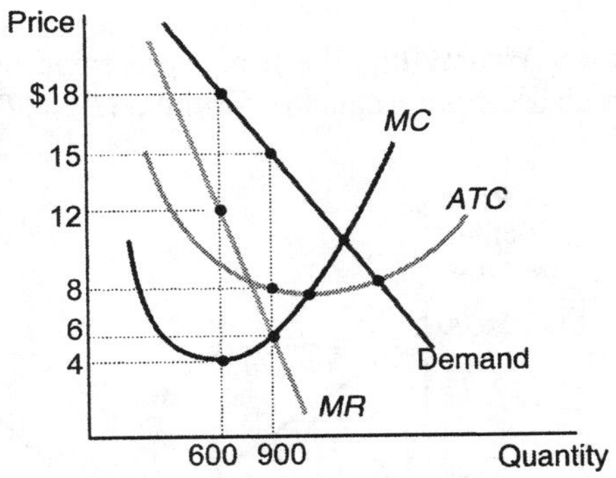

a. The firm should increase output because at 600 units price is above marginal cost.
b. The firm should maintain output at 600 units, because at this output level, marginal revenue is greater than marginal cost, marginal cost is minimized, and price is the highest.
c. The firm should increase the level of output because at 600 units, marginal revenue is greater than marginal cost.
d. The firm should increase the level of output until it reaches the minimum average cost.

20. Refer to the graphs below. Assume both firms are producing 5 cups per week, which firm is maximizing profits?

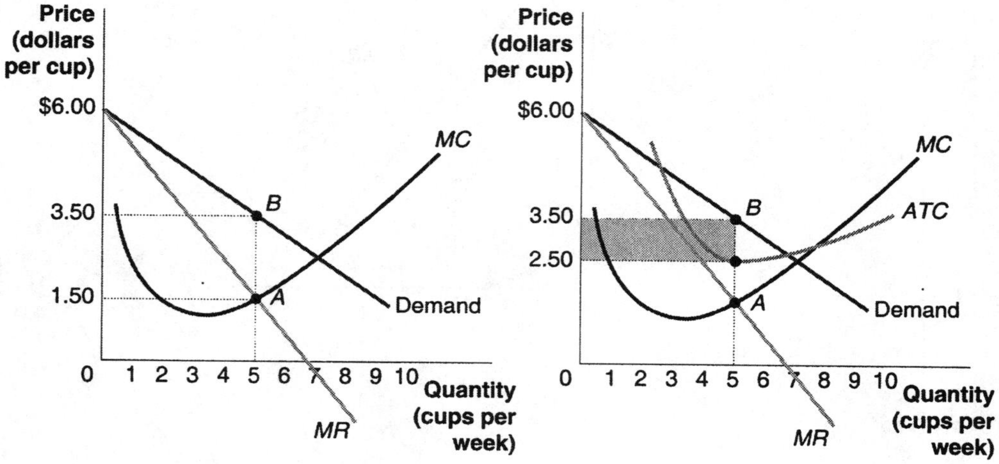

a. The firm on the left
b. The firm on the right
c. Both firms
d. Neither firm

21. Refer to the graph below. Assume that the firm represented by the cost and demand curves below is maximizing profit. Which area represents the formula: $(P - ATC)Q$?

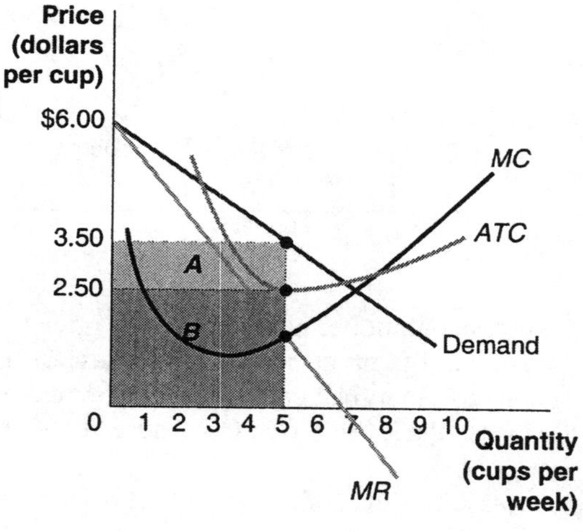

a. Area A
b. Area B
c. Area $A + B$
d. None of the above

22. Refer to the graph below. Assume that the firm represented by the cost and demand curves below is maximizing profit. The value of profits is

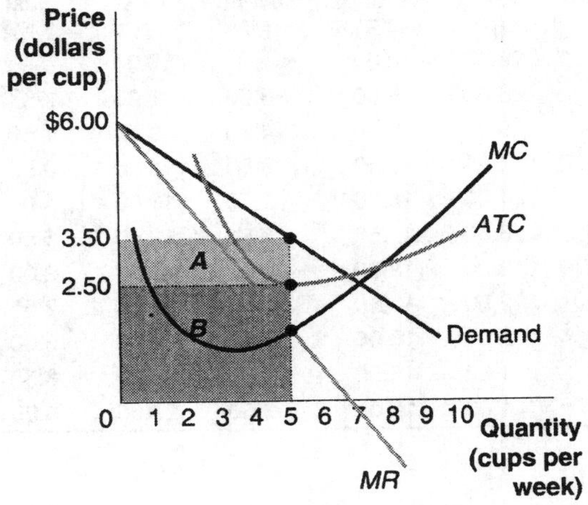

a. $17.50
b. $12.50
c. $5.00
d. None of the above; that information cannot be obtained from this graph.

23. Refer to the table below. When is average total cost minimized?

Cups Sold per Week (Q)	Price (P)	Total Revenue (TR)	Marginal Revenue (MR)	Total Cost (TC)	Marginal Cost (MC)	Average Total Cost (ATC)	Profit
0	$6.00	$0.00	-	$5.00	-		
1	5.50	5.50	$5.50	8.00	$3.00		
2	5.00	10.00	4.50	9.50	1.50		
3	4.50	13.50	3.50	10.00	0.50		
4	4.00	16.00	2.50	11.00	1.00		
5	3.50	17.50	1.50	12.50	1.50		
6	3.00	18.00	0.50	14.50	2.00		
7	2.50	17.50	-0.50	17.00	2.50		
8	2.00	16.00	-1.50	20.00	3.00		
9	1.50	13.50	-2.50	23.50	3.50		
10	1.00	10.00	-3.50	27.50	4.00		

a. At 1 unit of output
b. At 5 units of output
c. At 6 units of output
d. At 10 units of output

24. Refer to the table below. What level of output should be produced in order to maximize profit?

Cups Sold per Week (Q)	Price (P)	Total Revenue (TR)	Marginal Revenue (MR)	Total Cost (TC)	Marginal Cost (MC)	Average Total Cost (ATC)	Profit
0	$6.00	$0.00	-	$5.00	-		
1	5.50	5.50	$5.50	8.00	$3.00		
2	5.00	10.00	4.50	9.50	1.50		
3	4.50	13.50	3.50	10.00	0.50		
4	4.00	16.00	2.50	11.00	1.00		
5	3.50	17.50	1.50	12.50	1.50		
6	3.00	18.00	0.50	14.50	2.00		
7	2.50	17.50	-0.50	17.00	2.50		
8	2.00	16.00	-1.50	20.00	3.00		
9	1.50	13.50	-2.50	23.50	3.50		
10	1.00	10.00	-3.50	27.50	4.00		

a. 1 unit of output
b. 5 units of output
c. 6 units of output
d. 10 units of output

25. Refer to the graphs below. Which firm is a monopolistic competitor operating in the long run?

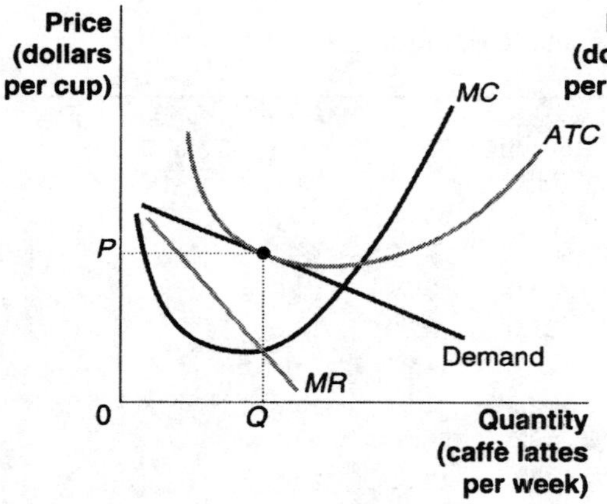

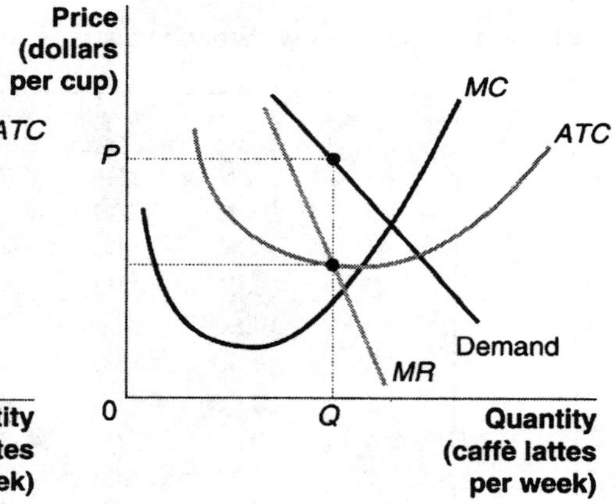

a. The firm on the left
b. The firm on the right
c. Both firms
d. Neither firm

26. How does the entry of new coffeehouses affect the profits of existing coffeehouses?
a. Entry will increase the profits of existing coffeehouses by shifting the market demand curve for coffee to the right.
b. Entry will increase the profits of existing coffeehouses by shifting each of their individual demand curve to the right.
c. Entry will decrease the profits of existing coffeehouses by shifting each of their individual demand curves to the left and making the demand curves more elastic.
d. Entry will not affect the profits of existing coffeehouses.

27. Suppose you invest $200,000 in a business. The return you could earn each year on a similar investment using that money is 10 percent, or $20,000. In an economic sense, the $20,000 is
   a. an economic cost.
   b. economic profit.
   c. an accounting cost.
   d. both economic profit and accounting profit.

28. Refer to the graphs below. Which graph depicts a situation in which some firms will exit the industry?

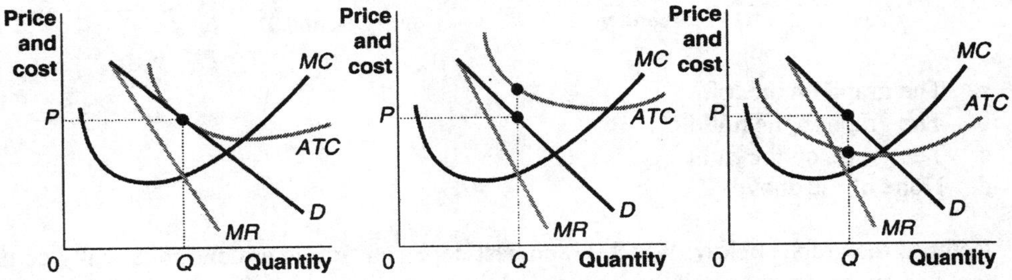

   a. The graph on the left
   b. The graph in the middle
   c. The graph on the right
   d. None of the above

29. Refer to the graphs below. Which graph best depicts the relationship between price and average total cost in the long run for a monopolistically competitive firm?

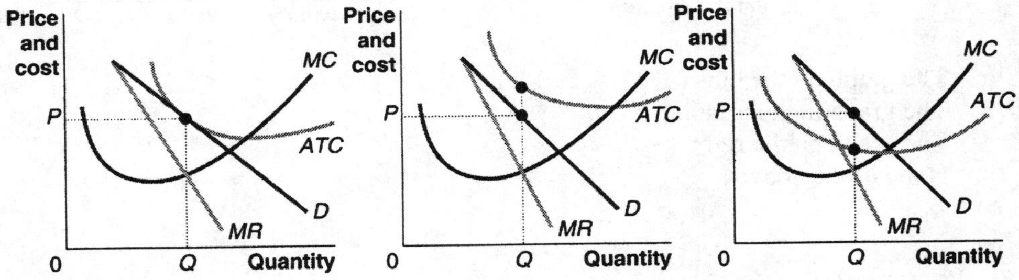

   a. The graph on the left
   b. The graph in the middle
   c. The graph on the right
   d. None of the above

30. Refer to the graphs below. Which graph best depicts the profit or loss situation for a monopolistically competitive firm in the long run?

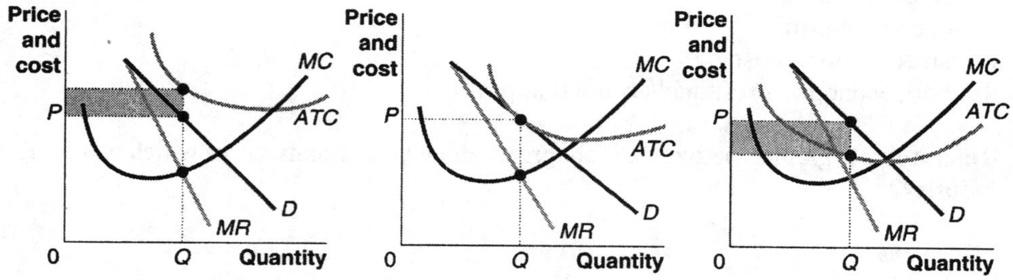

a. The graph on the left
b. The graph in the middle
c. The graph on the right
d. None of the above

31. Refer to the graphs below. Which graph best depicts a firm in a monopolistically competitive industry that has an incentive to exit the industry in the long run?

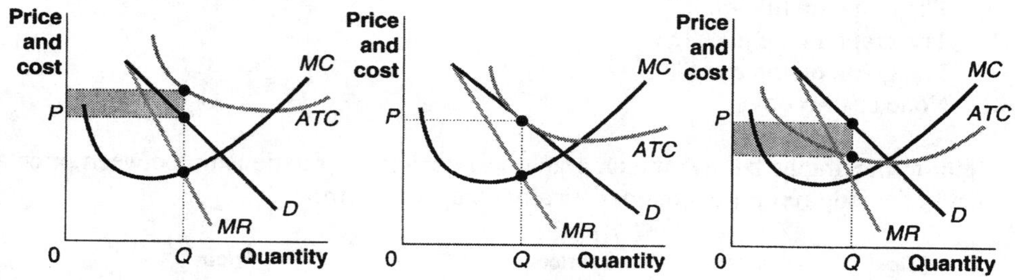

a. The graph on the left
b. The graph in the middle
c. The graph on the right
d. None of the above

32. Refer to the graphs below, which represent the situations facing typical firms in three different monopolistically competitive industries. Which graph best represents the situation where new firms are likely to enter the industry?

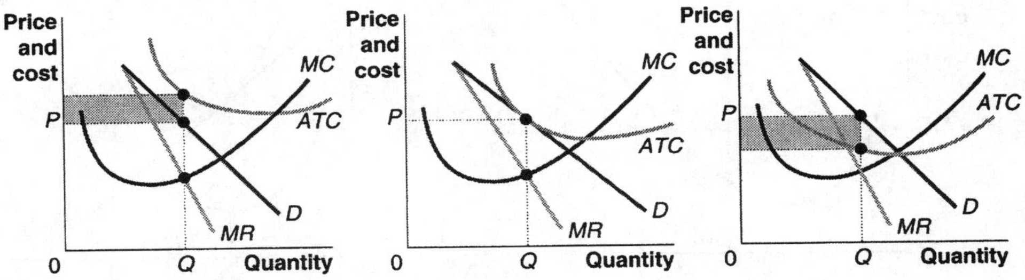

a. The graph on the left
b. The graph in the middle
c. The graph on the right
d. None of the above

33. Refer to the graph below. Which set of demand and marginal revenue curves for a typical firm is consistent with long-run equilibrium in the computer industry?

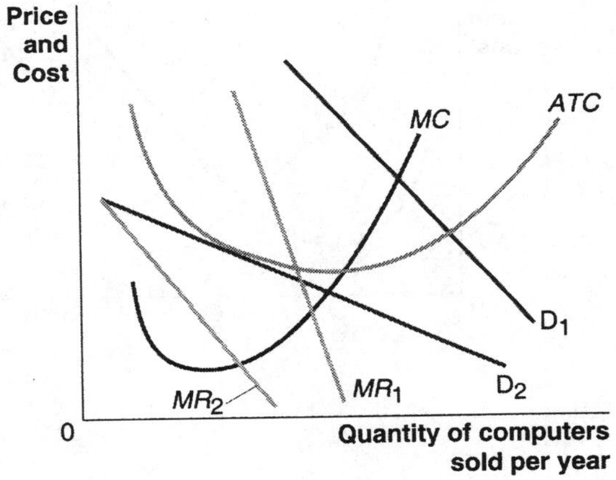

a. D_1 and MR_1
b. D_2 and MR_2
c. D_1 and MR_2
d. D_2 and MR_1

34. Is zero economic profit inevitable in the long run for a monopolistically competitive firm?
   a. Yes; there is nothing the firm can do to avoid zero economic profit in the long run.
   b. No; a firm could try to continue making a profit in the long run by producing a product identical to those of competing firms.
   c. No; a firm could try to continue making a profit in the long run by reducing production costs and improving its products.
   d. No; a firm could try to continue making a profit in the long run by simply offering goods that are cheaper to produce, even if they have less value than those offered by competing firms.

35. Refer to the graphs below. Which points on the graph coincide with *productive efficiency*?

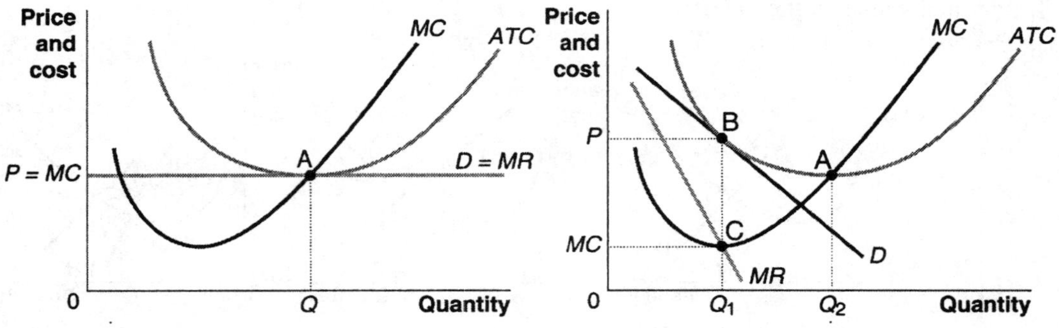

a. Point *A* on both graphs
b. Point *B* on the graph on the right
c. Point *C* on the graph on the right
d. Points *A*, *B*, and *C* on the graph on the right

36. Refer to the graph below. Which equilibrium level of output indicates excess capacity?

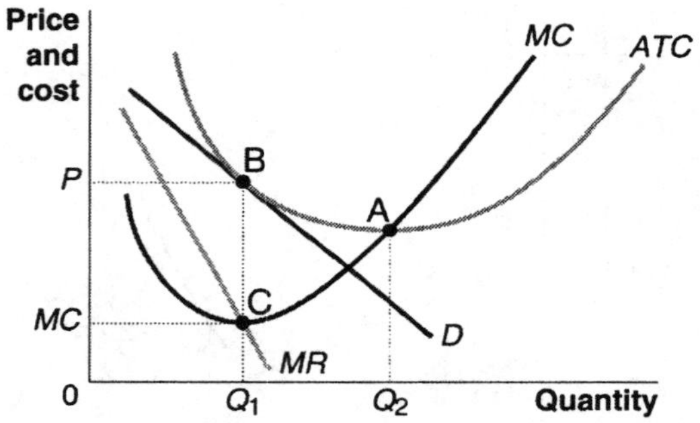

a. Q_1
b. Q_2
c. Both Q_1 and Q_2
d. Neither Q_1 nor Q_2

37. Which type of efficiency is achieved by a monopolistically competitive firm in the long run?
a. Allocative efficiency
b. Productive efficiency
c. Both allocative and productive efficiency
d. Neither allocative nor productive efficiency

38. What trade-offs do consumers face when buying a product from a monopolistically competitive firm?
    a. Consumers pay a lower price but also have fewer choices.
    b. Consumers pay a price greater than marginal cost but also have choices more suited to their tastes.
    c. Consumers pay a higher price but are happy knowing that the industry is highly efficient.
    d. Consumers pay a price as low as the competitive price but have difficulty finding and buying the product.

39. What is the term given to all the activities necessary for a firm to sell a product to a consumer?
    a. Brand management
    b. Advertising
    c. Marketing
    d. Product differentiation

40. What is the term given to the actions of a firm intended to maintain the differentiation of a product over time?
    a. Brand management
    b. Advertising
    c. Marketing
    d. Campaigning

41. Which of the following statements is correct?
    a. Brand names can be easily protected, especially as time goes by.
    b. Legally enforcing trademarks can be difficult.
    c. Establishing franchises is the best strategy to protect a firm's brand name.
    d. All of the above

42. Refer to the figure below. Which of the following terms is missing in the box on the right?

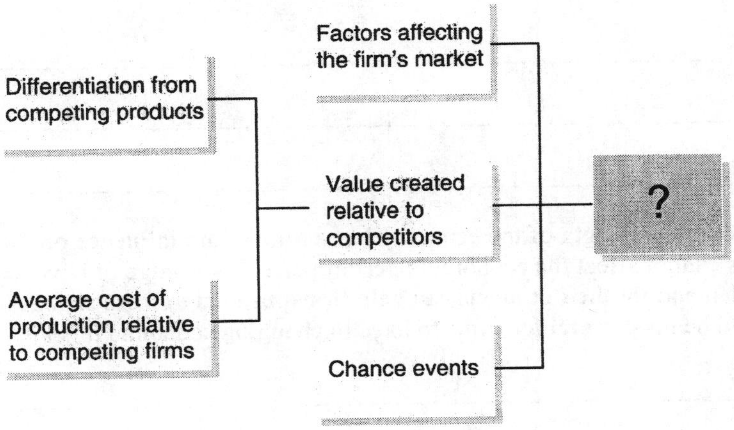

    a. Brand management
    b. Marketing
    c. Profitability
    d. Demand

Short Answer Questions

1. Describe how Starbucks has used brand management to differentiate its products.

2. What is the most important characteristic that perfectly competitive and monopolistically competitive firms have in common?

3. Why is it not possible for a monopolistically competitive firm to produce at minimum average total cost in long run equilibrium?

4. The overall strength of the economy has an important influence on the profits of firms. Although firms cannot affect the economy's performance, knowledge of how economy-wide changes affect the demand for their products can help firms respond to these changes. What product information would be most useful for firms to have in changing economic times?

5. The job of some of Coca-Cola's employees is to visit restaurants and bars and order mixed drinks. What motivation would Coca-Cola have to encourage their employees to "drink on the job?"

____

____

____

____

____

____

True/False Questions

T F 1. The marginal revenue curve lies below the demand curve for any firm that has the ability to affect the price of the product it sells.

T F 2. A firm's profit equals the total quantity sold times the difference between the price of the product minus total cost.

T F 3. Monopolistically competitive firms charge a price greater than marginal cost in both the short run and the long run.

T F 4. The market for coffeehouses, such as Starbucks, has many firms and the barriers to entering the market are low.

T F 5. Unlike perfectly competitive firms, monopolistically competitive firms earn long run profits.

T F 6. When some firms exit a monopolistically competitive market, the demand curves of firms that remain become less elastic.

T F 7. Among the factors that make a firm successful but are not under its control is the ability to differentiate its product.

T F 8. The word "thermos" was originally a brand name that become so widely used that it is no longer subject to legal protection.

T F 9. Brand management refers to all activities necessary for a firm to sell a product to a consumer.

T F 10. In 2006, the managers of the clothing store Abercrombie and Fitch experienced a decline in store sales because of a marketing campaign that narrowed its market too much.

T F 11. Unlike perfectly competitive firms, monopolistically competitive firms have excess capacity.

T F 12. Because a monopolistically competitive firm has a downward sloping demand curve, marginal revenue will always be lower than price.

T F 13. An important reason why Starbucks has been able to maintain control over the operations of its coffeehouses is that they are all company-owned, not franchises.

T F 14. Firms use brand management to postpone the time when they will no longer be able to earn economic profits.

T F 15. One motive for advertising is to make the demand for a product more elastic so that when price is lowered there will be a greater increase in quantity demanded.

Answers to the Self-Test

Multiple-Choice Questions

Question	Answer	Explanation
1	c	Monopolistic competition is a market structure in which barriers to entry are low, and many firms compete by selling similar, but not identical, products.
2	b	Because changing the price affects the quantity sold, a monopolistically competitive firm will face a downward-sloping demand curve, rather than the horizontal demand curve faced by a competitive firm, like a wheat farmer.
3	c	If Starbucks increases the price of café lattes, it will lose some, but not all, of its customers.
4	b	A perfectly competitive firm faces a horizontal demand curve and does not have to cut the price in order to sell a larger quantity. A monopolistically competitive firm, however, must cut the price to sell more, so its marginal revenue curve will slope downward and will be below its demand curve.
5	a	A monopolistically competitive firm must cut the price to sell more. Therefore, its marginal revenue curve and demand curve are both downward sloping.
6	c	Price is revenue per unit, or average revenue. Average revenue is equal to total revenue divided by quantity. Because total revenue equals price multiplied by quantity, dividing by quantity leaves just price. Therefore, average revenue is always equal to price. This will be true for firms in any of the four market structures.
7	c	The firm's marginal revenue shows how the amount of total revenue changes as the firm sells one more unit of output.
8	b	When the firm cuts the price, one good thing and one bad thing happen. The good thing: It sells one more unit of the good; we can call this the *output effect*. The bad thing: It receives less for each unit that it could have sold at the higher price; we can call this the *price effect*.
9	a	When the firm cuts the price one good thing and one bad thing happen. The good thing: It sells one more unit of the good; we can call this the *output effect*. The bad thing: It receives less for each unit that it could have sold at the higher price; we can call this the *price effect*.
10	a	Average revenue equals price, which is $3.00 when six units are sold. Or, average revenue equals total revenue divided by output, or $18.00/6 = $3.00.
11	c	Marginal revenue equals the change in total revenue divided by the change in output. As output increases from 5 to 6 units, the change in total revenue is 18.00 – 17.50 = $0.50, and the change in output is 6 – 5 = 1. Therefore, marginal revenue equals: $0.50/1 = $0.50.
12	a	Area *A* shows the loss of revenue from a price cut = $0.50 x 5 = $2.50.
13	b	This area shows the gain in revenue from the price cut = $3.00 x 1 = $3.00.
14	b	Every firm that has the ability to affect the price of the good or service it sells will have a marginal revenue curve that is below its demand curve. Only firms in perfectly competitive markets, which can sell as many units as they want at the market price, have marginal revenue curves that are the same as their demand curves.
15	b	Marginal revenue from the seventh through the tenth café latte is negative. This is because the additional revenue received from selling one more café latte is smaller than the revenue lost from receiving a lower price on the café lattes that could have been sold at the original price.

16	c	All firms use the same approach to maximize profits: Produce where marginal revenue is equal to marginal cost.
17	b	A firm's marginal cost is the increase in total cost resulting from producing another unit of output.
18	b	Marginal cost equals marginal revenue when 900 units of output are produced and sold. Consumers are willing to pay $15 for 900 units.
19	c	At 600 units of output, marginal revenue is $12 and marginal cost is $4. The firm is earning $12 – $4 = $8 additional profit for the next unit produced. The firm should produce that unit and continue to increase output as long as $MR > MC$.
20	c	In both cases, the output level is set where marginal revenue equals marginal cost.
21	a	Profit = $(P - ATC)\ Q$, so area A represents profit.
22	c	Correct. Profit = $(P - ATC)\ Q$ = ($3.50/cup – $2.50/cup) x 5 cups = $5.00.
23	c	When $Q = 6$, ATC = $14.50/6 = 2.42.
24	b	At this level of output, marginal revenue of $1.50 equals marginal cost.
25	a	In the long run, when the demand curve is tangent to the average cost curve, price is equal to average total cost, the firm is breaking even, and it no longer earns an economic profit.
26	c	As new coffeehouses open, the firm's demand curve will shift to the left. The demand curve will shift because the existing firms will sell fewer cups of coffee at each price now that there are additional coffeehouses in the area selling similar drinks. The demand curve will also become more elastic because consumers in the area now have additional coffeehouses from which to buy coffee, so existing firms will lose more customers if they raise their prices.
27	a	The annual opportunity cost of investing the funds in your own business is 10 percent of $200,000 or $20,000. This $20,000 is part of your profit in the accounting sense, and you would have to pay taxes on it. But in an economic sense, the $20,000 is a cost.
28	b	Since price is less than average total cost, the firm is suffering losses. Firm losses will lead to the exit of some firms in the industry.
29	a	In the long run, $P = ATC$ and the firm earns zero economic profit.
30	b	In the long run, a monopolistically competitive firm earns zero economic profit, or $P = ATC$.
31	a	The graph on the left shows a monopolistically competitive firm suffering losses, so there is an incentive for firms to exit.
32	c	The graph on the right shows a monopolistically competitive firm earning profits, so there is an incentive for firms to enter.
33	b	If the computer industry is monopolistically competitive, then in the long run the typical firm's demand curve will be tangent to its average cost curve and economic profit will equal zero.
34	c	Firms try to continue earning profits by reducing the cost of producing their products, by improving their products, or by convincing consumers their products are indeed different from what competitors offer. To stay one step ahead of its competitors, a firm has to offer consumers goods or services that they perceive to have greater value than those offered by competing firms.
35	a	At point A on both graphs, the firms produce where average total cost is at a minimum. When this happens, the firms are productively efficient.
36	a	The monopolistically competitive firm has excess capacity equal to the difference between its profit-maximizing level of output and the productively efficient level of output.

37	d	In a perfectly competitive market, both productive efficiency and allocative efficiency are achieved, but in a monopolistically competitive market, neither is achieved.
38	b	Consumers face a trade-off when buying the product of a monopolistically competitive firm: They are paying a price that is greater than marginal cost and the product is not being produced at minimum average cost, but they benefit from being able to purchase a product that is differentiated and more closely suited to their tastes.
39	c	Firms can differentiate their products through marketing. Marketing refers to all the activities necessary for a firm to sell a product to a consumer.
40	a	The actions of a firm intended to maintain the differentiation of a product over time are called brand management.
41	b	Legally enforcing trademarks can be difficult. Estimates are that each year U.S. companies lose hundreds of billions of dollars of sales worldwide as a result of unauthorized use of their trademarked brand names. U.S. companies have often found it difficult to enforce their trademarks in the courts of some foreign countries.
42	c	The factors under a firm's control—the ability to differentiate its product and the ability to produce it at lower cost—combine with the factors beyond its control to determine the firm's profitability.

Short Answer Responses

1. The textbook describes several brand management methods Starbucks uses to differentiate its products. "Competitors have found it difficult to duplicate Starbucks' European espresso bar atmosphere...Most importantly, Starbucks has continued to be very responsive to its customers' preferences..." In addition, company-owned coffeehouses (rather than franchise businesses) enable Starbucks to have greater control of the products sold and how they are marketed. Despite the success it has enjoyed, low entry barriers will eventually enable other firms to copy much of what Starbucks has done. Starbucks must continue to use brand management techniques to postpone the time when its economic profits are eliminated.

2. Low entry barriers are common to both market structures, so firms can easily enter and exit the industry. Ease of entry and exit ensures that firms earn zero economic profits in the long run.

3. The entry and exit of firms ensures that monopolistically competitive firms will earn zero economic profits in the long run. For this to be true, price must equal average total cost. This, in turn, requires a firm's demand curve to be tangent to its average total cost curve. Because the firm's demand curve is downward-sloping, this tangency must be to the left of the minimum point on the average total cost curve.

4. Changes in the overall economy's performance affect the growth of consumer income. When the economy expands, employment and income growth increase. When the economy slows, unemployment rises and income growth slows. Knowledge of the income elasticities of a firm's products allow it to respond to economy-wide changes. For example, automobiles and housing have high income elasticities. If the economy were to experience slow growth, firms know that the demand for these products will fall more than products with low or negative income elasticities.

5. Coca-Cola is very careful to protect its trademarked name. Some employees visit bars and restaurants to order "rum and Coke." If they are served another cola, they will inform their legal department. The offending bar or restaurant will be contacted and warned to either serve Coca-Cola or to inform customers that they do not serve "rum and Coke." Although such actions may seem petty to some people, they serve the important purpose of protecting a valuable trademark. Firms that have not taken positive steps to protect their trademarks have lost legal protection of their brand names.

True/False Answers

1. T See the section "Marginal Revenue for a Firm with a Downward-Sloping Demand Curve" on page 413.
2. F A firm's profit equals the total quantity sold times the difference between the price of the product minus *average total cost*.
3. T The firm has downward-sloping demand and marginal revenue curves and the marginal revenue curve lies below the demand curve. The firm will choose to produce where the marginal revenue intersects the marginal cost and then choose the price to charge by going up to the demand curve and charging the consumers' willingness to pay at that quantity.
4. T See the Chapter Opener on page 410 of the textbook.
5. F Low barriers to entry mean firms will enter and exit until economic profit equals zero.
6. T When firms exit, the demand curve for firms shifts right and becomes less elastic.
7. F This factor is under the firm's control.
8. T See "Defending a Brand Name" beginning on page 426 of the textbook.
9. F This is the definition of marketing.
10. T See Making the Connection "Abercrombie and Fitch: Can the Product Be Too Differentiated?" on page 425 of the textbook.
11. T Because $P > MC$ and the quantity is less than the quantity at the minimum average total cost, the firm has excess capacity.
12. T See the section "Marginal Revenue for a Firm with a Downward-Sloping Demand Curve" on page 413 of the textbook.
13. T See the Chapter Opener on page 410 of the textbook.
14. T Product differentiation and brand management help firms achieve economic profit longer.
15. F One motive for advertising is to make the demand for a product less elastic so that if price is raised, quantity demanded will not fall as much as it would without advertising.

Chapter 13

Oligopoly: Firms in Less Competitive Markets

Chapter Summary

In Chapters 11 and 12, you studied perfectly competitive and monopolistically competitive markets. You learned that firms maximize profits by producing where marginal revenue equals marginal cost. In this chapter, you will learn about another market structure – oligopoly. An **oligopoly** is a market structure in which a small number of interdependent firms compete. A measure of the extent of competition in an industry is the four-firm concentration ratio, which states the fraction of each industry's sales accounted for by the four largest firms.

Barriers to entry make it difficult for new firms to enter an oligopoly industry. Three barriers to entry are:

1. economies of scale.
2. ownership of a key input.
3. government-imposed barriers.

To analyze oligopolies, economists use **game theory**, which is the study of how people make decisions in situations where attaining their goals depends on their interactions with others. In oligopolies, interactions among firms are crucial in determining profitability because all firms are large relative to the market.

Michael Porter developed a model showing how five competitive forces determine the overall level of competition in an industry. These forces are: (1) competition from existing firms, (2) the threat from potential entrants, (3) competition from substitute goods or services, (4) the bargaining power of buyers, and (5) the bargaining power of suppliers.

Learning Objectives

When you finish this chapter, you should be able to:

1. **Show how barriers to entry explain the existence of oligopolies.** Barriers to entry make it difficult for new firms to enter an oligopoly market. The most important entry barrier is economies of scale. The greater the economies of scale, the fewer the number of firms in the industry. Another entry barrier is ownership of a key input. If production of a good requires a certain input, control over the supply of that input will be a barrier to entry. Government imposed barriers, such as patents, occupational licensing, or import restrictions (tariffs or quotas) may also limit entry of new firms.

2. **Use game theory to analyze the strategies of oligopolistic firms.** In oligopolies, the interaction of firms is crucial in determining profitability because firms are large relative to the market. Economists use game theory to predict the decisions of firms when their goals depend on interactions with other firms.

3. **Use sequential games to analyze business strategies.** Economists use sequential games to predict and explain the behavior of firms in business situations where the actions of one firm will lead to a response from another firm. Sequential games are used to analyze deterring entry and bargaining between firms.

4. **Use the five competitive forces model to analyze competition in an industry**. Michael Porter developed a model showing how five forces determine the overall level of competition in an industry. These forces are (1) competition from existing firms, (2) the threat from potential entrants, (3) competition from substitute goods or services, (4) the bargaining power of buyers, and (5) the bargaining power of suppliers.

Chapter Review

Chapter Opener: Competing with Wal-Mart

Wal-Mart started as a small business and grew to be one of the few large companies in the discount department store industry by following a specific business strategy. Wal-Mart would enter small towns, buy in bulk to get products at a reduce cost, and use advanced computer tracking for supply-chain management. Ford, Microsoft and Dell also started out small and developed into large firms industries that have only a few firms. These industries – discount department stores, automobile manufacturing, computer software, and personal computers – are all oligopolies.

Helpful Study Hint

Wal-Mart's growth has been due to innovative business practices as well as aggressive, and sometimes controversial, policies. At the end of this chapter, ***An Inside Look*** describes the business strategy of Target, one of Wal-Mart's competitors. Wal-Mart introduced a prescription drug plan where it offered about 150 generic prescriptions at $4 for a 30-day supply. Target responded to Wal-Mart's business strategy by implementing the same prescription plan in their Florida stores. Target's response was an attempt to maintain their market share in the prescription drug market.

Economics in YOUR Life! asks you to consider why you can't find a cheap PlayStation 3. Whether you go to Best Buy, Wal-Mart, or another store, you are likely to find PlayStation 3 with very similar prices. Keep this question in mind as you read the chapter. The authors will answer the question at the end of the chapter.

13.1 LEARNING OBJECTIVE

13.1 Oligopoly and Barriers to Entry

Learning Objective 1 Show how barriers to entry explain the existence of oligopolies.

Oligopolies are industries with only a few firms. Economists use concentration ratios to measure the fraction of sales accounted for by the largest firms in an industry. Most economists believe that a four-firm concentration ratio of 40 percent or more indicates an industry is an oligopoly. Concentration ratios have flaws. As usually calculated, the ratios do not include sales in the United States by foreign firms and concentration ratios are calculated for the national market even though competition in some markets is local.

An important reason why oligopolies exist is the presence of barriers to entry. A **barrier to entry** is anything that keeps new firms from entering an industry in which firms are earning economic profits. The most important barrier to entry is **economies of scale**, which exist when a firm's long-run average costs fall as it increases output. A second entry barrier is ownership of a key input. An example of this type of barrier is Ocean Spray's control of most of the supply of cranberries. A third type of barrier to entry is a government-imposed barrier. A patent is an entry barrier. A **patent** is the exclusive right to a product for a period of 20 years from the date the product was invented.

Helpful Study Hint

Table 13-1 on page 443 of the textbook lists some concentration ratios taken from the *2002 Economic Census*. Concentration ratios for many industries can be found in this source, which is available online from the U.S. Census Bureau. These ratios change over time in response to changes in industry demand and supply. Industries with high ratios in one year may have lower ratios in a subsequent year and vice versa.

Extra Solved Problem 13-1

Chapter 13 includes two Solved Problems. Here is an extra Solved Problem to help you build your skills solving economic problems.

Supports Learning Objective 1: Show how barriers to entry explain the existence of oligopolies.

Government Sanctioned Oligopoly

The European Union continues to experience growing pains as the economies of many countries are melded into a single economy. One adjustment that has needed is changes in the regulation of the electricity and natural gas industries. An article on this subject contains the following observations:

> Oligopoly is the best structure for a European Union gas and power market, a senior advisor to EU competition commissioner, Neelie Kroes, told an industry seminar in Brussels on May 11.

> "A market which requires such investment and is so technical is not effective if you have thousands of small operators," said Olivier Guersent, deputy head of Kroes' policy advisory team.

Source: "EU Commissioner: Oligopoly is Best Structure for Europe Union's Power and Gas Markets," *Global Power Report*, May 18, 2006.

Which barriers to entry discussed in the textbook are most relevant to this discussion?

SOLVING THE PROBLEM

Step 1: Review the chapter material.
This problem is about barriers to entry, so you may want to review the section "Oligopoly and Barriers to Entry," which begins on page 442 of the textbook.

Step 2: Discuss barriers to entry that apply to the European Union's gas and power market.
The barrier to entry that is most relevant to this discussion is economies of scale. The advisors to the EU competition commissioner suggest that there is a significant amount of fixed costs in the form of physical capital and intellectual capital. Due to these fixed costs, it is likely that if power and gas were supplied by many small firms, each firm's average cost would be quite high. As a result, consumers would have to pay high prices to cover these high average costs. To promote economic efficiency, the commissioner should recommend an oligopolistic market structure.

13.2 LEARNING OBJECTIVE

13.2 Using Game Theory to Analyze Oligopoly

Learning Objective 2 Use game theory to analyze the strategies of oligopolistic firms.

Game theory is the study of how people make decisions in situations where attaining their goals depends on their interactions with others. Economists use game theory to study the decisions of firms in industries where the profits of each firm depend on its interactions with other firms. Games share three characteristics:

1. rules that determine what actions are allowable,
2. strategies that players employ to attain their objectives in the game, and
3. payoffs that are the result of the interaction among the players' strategies.

A **business strategy** represents actions taken by a firm to achieve a goal, such as maximizing profits. A **payoff matrix** is a table that shows the payoffs that each firm earns from every combination of strategies by the firms. **Collusion** is an agreement among firms to charge the same price, or to otherwise not compete.

A **dominant strategy** is a strategy that is the best for a firm, no matter what strategies other firms use. An equilibrium where each firm chooses the best strategy, given the strategies chosen by other firms, is called a **Nash equilibrium**.

Some games result in a cooperative equilibrium. A **cooperative equilibrium** is an equilibrium in which players cooperate to increase their mutual payoff. An equilibrium in a game where players choose not to cooperate will be a **noncooperative equilibrium** in which players pursue their own self-interest. An example of a noncooperative equilibrium is a **prisoners' dilemma**, a game where pursuing dominant strategies results in noncooperation that leaves everyone worse off. Cooperation does not necessarily have to breakdown. If the business situation will recur, the business owners will be more likely cooperate to avoid retaliation in future situations. When a situation reoccurs, it is a repeated game.

A **cartel** is a group of firms that colludes by agreeing to restrict output to increase prices and profits. The Organization of Petroleum Exporting Countries (OPEC) is a cartel whose members meet periodically to agree on the quantities of oil each will produce. OPEC's production quotas are intended to reduce oil production below the competitive level and to increase the profits of member countries. Until recently, OPEC had difficulty sustaining member quotas and oil prices over time because when prices are high, each member has had an incentive to stop cooperating and increase output beyond its quota. In recent years, however, surging worldwide demand for oil has made it easier for OPEC to sustain high oil prices.

Helpful Study Hint

This section of the textbook includes numerous examples to help you understand game theory and how it can be applied to explain the behavior of oligopoly firms in different circumstances. Figure 13-2 on page 446 of the textbook is a payoff matrix that illustrates a simple duopoly game between Wal-Mart and Target. ***Don't Let This Happen to You!*** "Don't Misunderstand Why Each Manager Ends Up Charging a Price of $400" explains why firms may end up charging a low price when by cooperating and charging a high price they would earn greater profits.

Solved Problem 13-2 analyzes a prisoners' dilemma using advertising decisions by Pepsi and Coca-Cola. Both firms will maximize their profits by advertising, so advertising is each firm's dominant strategy.

Figure 13-3 is another payoff matrix showing a game between Wal-Mart and Target. Test your knowledge of the ***Making the Connections*** by doing related end-of-chapter problems 2.11, 2.16, 2.18, 2.19, and 2.20.

Making the Connection "A Beautiful Mind: Game Theory Goes to the Movies" explains how the movie makers incorrectly represented the concept of the Nash equilibrium in the bar scene from that movie.

Making the Connection "Is There a Dominant Strategy for Bidding on eBay?" explains how in second-price auctions like eBay the winner pays the bid of the runner up. Suppose Bob is bidding on a pair of tennis shoes on eBay. It is in Bob's best interest; that is, it is Bob's dominant strategy, to bid his willingness to pay for the good. If Bob is the highest bidder, he pays the second highest bidder's price and is better off. If Bob is outbid, then the person who outbid him had a higher willingness to pay for the good.

Making the Connection "American Airlines and Northwest Airlines Fail to Cooperate on a Price Increase" discusses a case where the two airlines were trying to agree to increase their fares due to the high fixed costs of providing this service. The airlines agreed to the price increase, but were not able to maintain the high price. The fares quickly came down from the agreed-upon level so that the firms could remain competitive with other airlines.

13.3 LEARNING OBJECTIVE

13.3 Sequential Games and Business Strategy

Learning Objective 3 Use sequential games to analyze business strategies.

In many business situations, one firm will make a decision and other firms will respond. These situations can be analyzed by using sequential games. For example, sequential games can be used to analyze strategies designed to deter entry by new firms or to analyze bargaining between firms. A decision tree as in Figure 13-6 on page 455 of the textbook can be used to illustrate a sequential game.

Helpful Study Hint

To understand how a sequential game works, you should read ***Solved Problem 13-3*** on page 455 of the textbook. This problem explains that deterring the entry of other firms is not always the best idea. A firm should attempt to deter entry of other firms into their industry only if the cost of deterrence is less than the benefits they would receive by deterring entry. Work related end-of-chapter Problems and Applications 3.3 to make sure you understand the concepts behind the ***Solved Problem***.

13.4 LEARNING OBJECTIVE

13.4 The Five Competitive Forces Model

Learning Objective 4 Use the five competitive forces model to analyze competition in an industry.

Michael Porter of the Harvard Business School developed a model to analyze the competitiveness of an industry using five competitive forces. The forces are (1) competition from existing firms, (2) the threat from new entrants, (3) competition from substitute goods or services, (4) the bargaining power of buyers, and (5) the bargaining power of suppliers.

Helpful Study Hint

Study Figure 13.8 on page 458 of the textbook, which illustrates Porter's model. Test your knowledge of the model by doing related end-of-chapter problem 4.3.

Making the Connection "Is Southwest's Business Strategy More Important Than the Structure of the Airline Industry?" discusses Southwest Airlines' advantage over its competitors. Southwest Airlines offers a distinct service to its customers. It provides flights that are short hops with stripped down service. This allows Southwest to provide fast turnarounds at airport gates. This niche service has proven itself to be very profitable for Southwest. Other airlines have attempted to copy Southwest's approach, but as of yet they have not be successful doing so.

Economics in YOUR Life! answers the question "Why Can't You Find a Cheap PlayStation 3?" All of the stores that sell the gaming device set the price at a nearly identical level. The firms did not engage in price competition for PlayStations. The firms set a high price and stick to it to achieve high profits and to avoid future price retaliation from the competition.

Extra Solved Problem **13-4**

Chapter 13 includes two Solved Problems. Here is an extra Solved Problem to help you build your skills solving economic problems.

Supports Learning Objective 4: Use the five competitive forces model to analyze competition in an industry.

Analyzing Competition in the Music Industry Using the Five Forces Model

Until 2004, the music industry was dominated by the Big Five major record companies, which accounted for about 75 percent of a $25 billion market in CDs and related products. A merger in 2004 between Sony Music Entertainment and BMG Entertainment reduced the Big Five to the Big Four: EMI, Sony-BMG, Warner Music Group and Universal Music Group. The following is a competitive analysis of the music industry prior to the late 1990s, before consumers began to download music on a wide scale over the Internet. The competitive analysis follows Michael Porter's five forces model, which is designed to assess the degree of competition in an industry.

1. **Competition from existing firms**. Significant competition among the largest firms, but little between the Big Five and smaller firms. Little change over time in the market share of the Big Five firms.

2. **The threat from new entrants.** Barriers to entry made the potential threat from new entrants negligible. The financial resources required to establish a recording artist or group were substantial. Sound and video recordings had to be made and distributed and contacts made with venues where the artists would perform. It was difficult for a new firm to become established.

3. **Substitute goods or services**. Music was essentially available and playable in one format, the CD, and from one source, the music company that owned the rights to an artist's recordings. Few substitutes were available.

4. **Bargaining power of buyers**. Buyers' options were limited. They could only obtain music in one format and the Big Five had considerable control over the prices of CDs.

5. **Bargaining power of suppliers**. Since recording artists were compelled to work with one of the Big Five, they had little negotiating power. Terms included in record contracts for new performers were very standardized.

Changes in the degree of competition in the industry have come about since the late 1990s primarily due to new technology. Widespread access to personal computers, MP3 encoding, and the Internet have made it possible for consumers to copy and distribute music at low cost.

Source: Google Answers: April 5, 2004. http://answers.google.com/answers/threadview?id=325373

Analyze the competitiveness of the music industry in the early twenty-first century using Porter's model.

SOLVING THE PROBLEM

Step 1: Review the chapter material.
This problem is about Michael Porter's model, so you may want to review the section "The Five Competitive Forces Model," which begins on page 457 of the textbook.

Step 2: Discuss the extent of competition from existing firms.
New music technology has reduced the start-up costs for new artists. High quality recordings can be made, copied, and marketed directly through the Internet. Some artists have even established their own companies, bypassing the Big Four. Competition is likely to erode the market share of the Big Four in the future.

Step 3: Discuss the threat from new entrants.
Entry barriers have been lowered by the new technologies. New artists are less dependent on the traditional marketing network. Music can be advertised and sold directly from the artists' web sites. The threat from entrants has increased.

Step 4: Discuss competition from substitute goods or services.
More substitutes are available for consumers. If the format used by record companies is not what consumers want, or if music is sold at high prices, consumers can easily download it through the Internet. Consumers who want only two or three songs from a CD with 10 or more songs can download only those they want.

Step 5: Discuss the bargaining power of buyers.
As the availability of substitutes has grown, so has the bargaining power of consumers. Because consumers can download songs at little cost beyond their time, the Big Four companies have had to offer consumers lower prices and different formats.

Step 6: Discuss the bargaining power of suppliers.
As noted in the previous steps, musicians and consumers can use the Internet to bypass the traditional distribution networks and are less dependent on established companies, in particular the Big Four. The bargaining power of suppliers has increased, because musicians can credibly threaten to sell their music directly to consumers if the Big Four are unwilling to offer the musicians favorable contracts.

Key Terms

Barrier to entry. Anything that keeps new firms from entering an industry in which firms are earning economic profits.

Business strategy. Actions taken by a firm to achieve a goal, such as maximizing profits.

Cartel. A group of firms that collude by agreeing to restrict output to increase prices and profits.

Collusion. An agreement among firms to charge the same price or otherwise not to compete.

Cooperative equilibrium. An equilibrium in a game in which players cooperate to increase their mutual payoff.

Dominant strategy. A strategy that is the best for a firm, no matter what strategies other firms use.

Economies of scale. The situation when a firm's long-run average costs fall as it increases output.

Game theory. The study of how people make decisions in situations in which attaining their goals depends on their interactions with others; in economics, the study of the decisions of firms in industries where the profits of each firm depend on its interactions with other firms.

Nash equilibrium. A situation in which each firm chooses the best strategy, given the strategies chosen by other firms.

Noncooperative equilibrium. An equilibrium in a game in which players do not cooperate but pursue their own self-interest.

Oligopoly. A market structure in which a small number of interdependent firms compete.

Patent. The exclusive right to a product for a period of 20 years from the date the product was invented.

Payoff matrix. A table that shows the payoffs that each firm earns from every combination of strategies by the firms.

Price leadership. A form of implicit collusion where one firm in an oligopoly announces a price change, which is matched by the other firms in the industry.

Prisoners' dilemma. A game in which pursuing dominant strategies results in noncooperation that leaves everyone worse off.

Self-Test

(Answers are provided at the end of the Self-Test.)

Multiple-Choice Questions

1. Which of the terms below is defined as follows: "A market structure in which a small number of interdependent firms compete?"
   a. Game theory
   b. Barriers to entry
   c. Oligopoly
   d. Economies of scale

2. Which of the terms below is defined as follows: "Anything that keeps new firms from entering an industry in which firms are earning economic profits?"
   a. Game theory
   b. Barriers to entry
   c. Oligopoly
   d. Economies of scale

3. According to the textbook, which of the following industries in the retail trade had the highest concentration ratios in the United States?
   a. Hobby, toy, and game stores, and radio, television, and other electronic stores
   b. College bookstores and athletic footwear stores
   c. Warehouse clubs and superstores, and discount department stores
   d. Pharmacies and drugstores

4. According to the textbook, which of the following industries in manufacturing had the highest concentration ratios in the United States?
   a. Aircraft and breakfast cereal
   b. Automobiles and dog and cat food
   c. Cigarettes and beer
   d. Computers

5. Economies of scale help determine the extent of
   a. market failure in an industry.
   b. competition in an industry.
   c. product differentiation in an industry.
   d. product innovation in an industry.

6. Economies of scale exist when a firm's ___________ average costs fall as it ___________ output.
   a. short-run; increases
   b. short-run; decreases
   c. long-run; increases
   d. long-run; decreases

7. Refer to the graph below. Which quantity is more likely to be the quantity produced by the typical firm in an oligopoly?

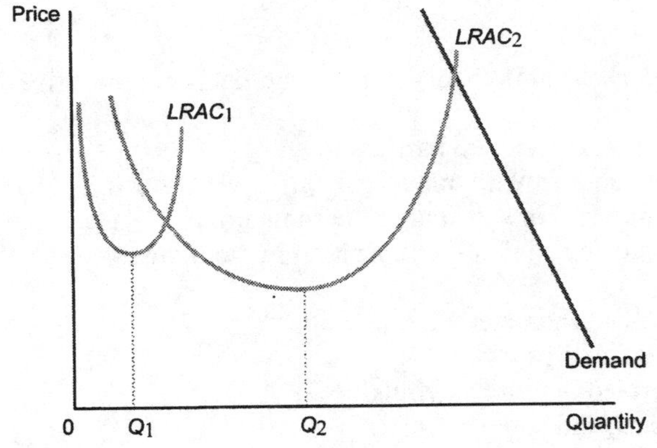

a. Q_1
b. Q_2
c. The sum of Q_1 and Q_2
d. There is insufficient information to determine the quantity requested.

8. Refer to the graph below. Fill in the blanks. When the level of output produced is Q_1, economies of scale in the industry are relatively ____________ and the industry will have a ___________ number of firms.

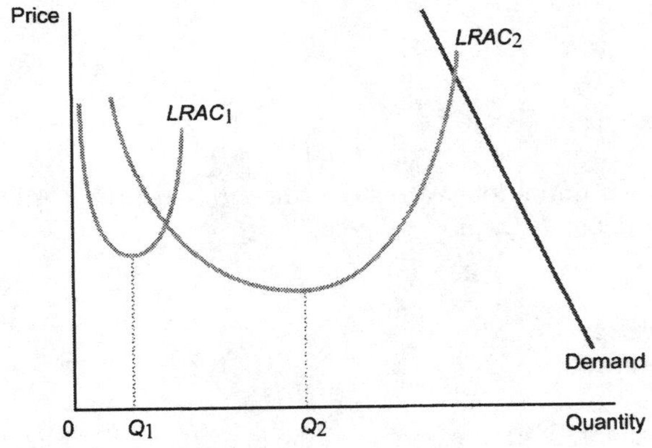

a. important; small
b. important; large
c. unimportant; small
d. unimportant; large

9. Which of the following is a barrier to entry?
a. Economies of scale
b. Ownership of a key input
c. Patents
d. All of the above are barriers to entry

10. A patent typically gives the holder exclusive rights to a product for a period of
    a. 10 years.
    b. 20 years.
    c. 30 years.
    d. 40 years.

11. In the broadest sense, game theory studies the decisions of firms in industries where the profits of each firm depend on
    a. the ability of a firm to set up barriers to entry.
    b. the firm's interactions with other firms.
    c. agreements among firms to charge the same price.
    d. the ability to achieve a dominant position in the industry.

12. Every game has these characteristics
    a. winners, losers, and payoffs.
    b. rules, an intermediary, and payouts.
    c. rules, strategies, and payoffs.
    d. strategies and defeats.

13. Which of the following is the definition of *business strategy*?
    a. A business strategy refers to the rules that determine what actions are allowable.
    b. A business strategy refers to actions taken by firms to attain their objectives.
    c. A business strategy is a study of how people make decisions.
    d. A business strategy is an agreement among firms to charge the same price.

14. Match the following definition with one of the terms below: "A situation where each firm chooses the best strategy, given the strategies chosen by other firms."
    a. Payoff matrix
    b. Collusion
    c. Dominant strategy
    d. Nash equilibrium

15. Match the following definition with one of the terms below: "An agreement among firms to charge the same price or to otherwise not compete."
    a. Payoff matrix
    b. Collusion
    c. Dominant strategy
    d. Nash equilibrium

16. Match the following definition with one of the terms below: "A strategy that is the best for a firm, no matter what strategies other firms use."
    a. Payoff matrix
    b. Collusion
    c. Dominant strategy
    d. Nash equilibrium

17. Refer to the payoff matrix below. Suppose that Wal-Mart and Target are selling Sony flat screen computer monitors for a price of either $150 or $200 each. Based on the information on the payoff matrix, what is the dominant strategy?

		Target	
		$200	$150
Wal-Mart	$200	Wal-Mart earns $10,000 profit; Target earns $10,000 profit	Wal-Mart earns $5,000 profit; Target earns $15,000 profit
	$150	Wal-Mart earns $15,000 profit; Target earns $5,000 profit	Wal-Mart earns $7,500 profit; Target earns $7,500 profit

a. Both firms will charge $150.
b. Both firms will charge $200.
c. Wal-Mart will charge $150, and Target will charge $200.
d. Wal-Mart will charge $200, and Target will charge $150.

18. Refer to the payoff matrix below. Suppose that Wal-Mart and Target are selling Sony flat screen computer monitors for a price of either $150 or $200 each. Based on the information on the payoff matrix, does a Nash equilibrium exist?

		Target	
		$200	$150
Wal-Mart	$200	Wal-Mart earns $10,000 profit; Target earns $10,000 profit	Wal-Mart earns $5,000 profit; Target earns $15,000 profit
	$150	Wal-Mart earns $15,000 profit; Target earns $5,000 profit	Wal-Mart earns $7,500 profit; Target earns $7,500 profit

a. Yes
b. No
c. Yes, but only for Wal-Mart.
d. Yes, but only for Target.

19. An equilibrium in a game in which players cooperate to increase their mutual payoff is called
a. a cooperative equilibrium.
b. a noncooperative equilibrium.
c. a prisoners' dilemma.
d. a dominant strategy.

20. A game where pursuing dominant strategies results in noncooperation that leaves everyone worse off is called
a. a cooperative equilibrium.
b. a noncooperative equilibrium.
c. a prisoners' dilemma.
d. a dominant strategy.

21. What type of auction is used in eBay?
    a. A first-price auction
    b. A second-price auction
    c. A zero sum game auction
    d. None; eBay does not conduct auctions.

22. What is the dominant strategy of eBay auction participants?
    a. To place a bid well below the subjective value you place on the item
    b. To place a bid equal to the maximum value you place on the item
    c. To place a bid well above the subjective value you place on the item
    d. There is no dominant strategy on eBay auctions.

23. Fill in the blanks. In a repeated game, the losses associated with not cooperating are _________ the losses of cooperating.
    a. greater than
    b. less than
    c. equal to
    d. either greater than or less than, depending on the circumstances

24. How does the prisoners' dilemma compare to the outcome of a repeated game?
    a. The equilibrium in both cases is identical.
    b. In a repeated game, two firms would end up charging the low price, even though they would be better off if they charged the high price.
    c. In a repeated game, two firms would end up charging the high price and receiving high profits.
    d. There are no comparisons to be made between the two.

25. A group of firms that colludes by agreeing to restrict output to increase prices and profits is called
    a. a duopoly.
    b. an oligopoly.
    c. a cartel.
    d. a conglomerate.

26. Fill in the blanks that best describe the history of OPEC. Sustaining high prices has been __________ because members often _________ their output quotas.
    a. easy; produce less than
    b. easy; exceed
    c. difficult; produce less than
    d. difficult; exceed

27. Refer to the graph below. The graph shows world oil prices. Which line shows the nominal (or stated) price of a barrel of oil in each year?

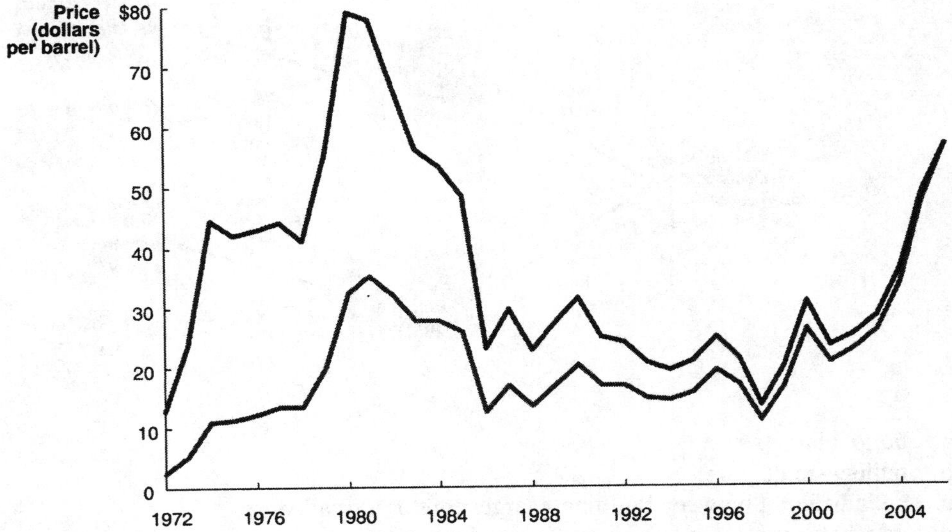

a. The top line
b. The bottom line
c. Both lines
d. Neither line

28. Refer to the payoff matrix below. The payoff matrix refers to the OPEC cartel with unequal members. Fill in the blanks. The equilibrium of this game will occur with Saudi Arabia producing a _______ output and Nigeria producing a _______ output.

		Nigeria	
		Low Output	High Output
Saudi Arabia	Low Output	Saudi Arabia earns $100 million profit; Nigeria earns $10 million profit	Saudi Arabia earns $75 million profit; Nigeria earns $15 million profit
	High Output	Saudi Arabia earns $80 million profit; Nigeria earns $7 million profit	Saudi Arabia earns $60 million profit; Nigeria earns $10 million profit

a. low; low
b. high; high
c. low; high
d. high; low

29. A game theory analysis of deterring entry concludes that
a. deterring entry is always a good idea.
b. deterring entry is always a bad idea.
c. deterring entry may be a good or a bad idea, depending on the circumstances.
d. it is difficult to predict whether deterring entry is a good or a bad idea.

30. Refer to the table below. The table is a decision tree for an entry game. In this case, Wal-Mart will

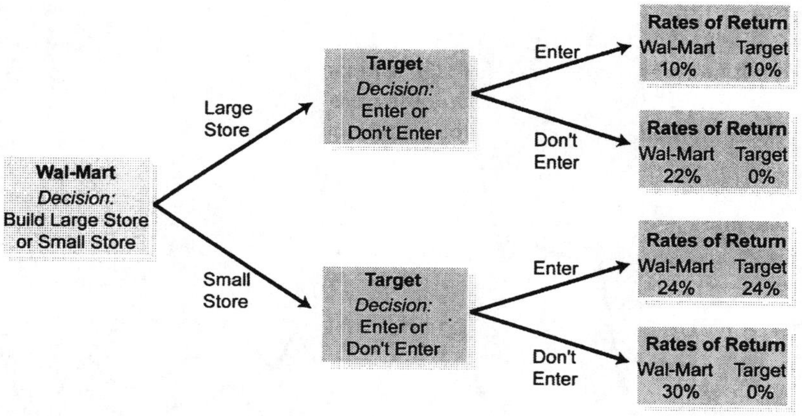

a. build a large store.
b. build a small store.
c. be indifferent between building a large store or a small store.
d. do whatever it takes to prevent Target from entering.

31. In Michael Porter's Competitive Forces Model, which term describes the threat of competition from firms that might enter the market?
a. Bargaining power of buyers
b. Bargaining power of suppliers
c. Competition from existing firms
d. Threat from new entrants

32. In terms of Michael Porter's Competitive Forces Model, which of the following is most likely to limit the profits earned by computer firms?
a. The bargaining power of buyers
b. The bargaining power of suppliers
c. Competition from existing firms
d. The threat from new entrants

33. During the 1940s, the Hollywood movie studios' interaction with the Technicolor Company can best be described as
a. competition from a substitute good.
b. a threat from a new entrant.
c. a reduction in profits caused by the bargaining power of a buyer.
d. a reduction in profits caused by the bargaining power of a supplier.

34. Fill in the blanks. If automobile companies have significant bargaining power when buying tires, you would expect that tire prices are _______ and the profitability of tire manufacturers is __________.
a. low; limited
b. low; unlimited
c. high; limited
d. high; unlimited

35. Fill in the blanks. Suppliers have more bargaining power when ______ firms can supply the input and the input _______ specialized.
   a. many; is
   b. many; is not
   c. few; is
   d. few; is not

36. Fill in the blanks. If an input is specialized and only a few firms can provide it, the profits of the firms that supply that input will be ______, and the firms will have ______ bargaining power with buyers.
   a. high; more
   b. low; less
   c. high; less
   d. low; more

37. Refer to the figure below. The figure shows the Competitive Forces Model. What is the name of the box in the center?

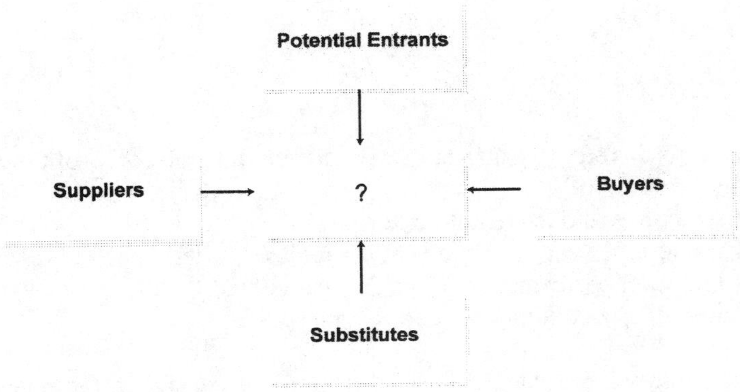

   a. Industry Competitors
   b. Bargaining Power
   c. Industry Threats
   d. Extent of Competition

38. Refer to the figure below. The figure shows the Competitive Forces Model. How many competitive forces are identified in this model?

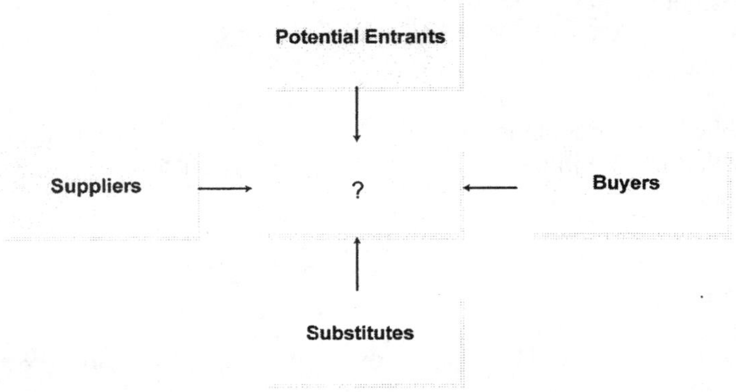

a. Three
b. Four
c. Five
d. Six

39. To explain how different firms can have different levels of profit, today economists put greater emphasis on the study of
a. market structures and barriers to entry.
b. firm characteristics and management strategies.
c. the stock market performance of the firms involved.
d. social rather than economic concerns.

40. Which of the following strategies has been more successful in the recent history of the U.S. airline industry?
a. Entering as many segments of the market as possible and confronting competitors through steep price cuts
b. Deterring entry by building a large fleet of airplanes and cutting labor costs
c. Identifying a segment of the market and shaping the company to fit that segment
d. Using game theory to analyze the actions of existing and potential firms in the market

Short Answer Questions

1. Assume that industry A and industry B each have a four firm concentration ratio of 80 percent. Both industries sell their products in national markets and firms in both industries face no competition from foreign firms. Can you conclude from this that the level of competition in both industries is similar?

____

____

____

____

____

2. The Organization of Petroleum Exporting Countries (OPEC) operates as a cartel. Representatives of OPEC countries meet periodically to agree on quotas, the quantities of oil each will produce. Why until recently did OPEC have difficulty maintaining high oil prices?

____

____

____

____

3. Occupational licensing laws in the United States require medical doctors and other practitioners to obtain licenses in order to operate legally. These laws are designed to protect the public – no one wants to be operated on by an unqualified surgeon – but critics point out that licensing restricts the number of people who enter the licensed professions. Is it necessary to have licensing laws to protect the public from using the services of unqualified medical doctors?

____

____

____

4. In a famous 1945 antitrust case, the Aluminum Company of America (Alcoa) was declared a monopoly because the company controlled nearly all of the world's known supplies of bauxite, an essential input in the production of aluminum. Could Alcoa have argued that it faced competition despite its control of the bauxite market?

____

____

____

5. The *Making the Connection* "American Airlines and Northwest Airlines Fail to Cooperate on a Price Increase" described the difficulty American Airlines had in raising ticket prices for business travelers in 2002. American subsequently lowered prices on some of its other routes in order to punish airlines for not matching its price increases. Why didn't American Airlines officials discuss its plans with other airline executives before prices were raised to find out if its strategy would be successful?

____

____

True/False Questions

T F 1. The Herfindahl-Hirschman Index is an alternative to concentration ratios as a measure of competition in an industry.

T F 2. In game theory, a Nash equilibrium is an equilibrium position where each firm chooses the best strategy, given the strategies chosen by other firms.

T F 3. The most important barrier to entry is ownership of a key resource.

T F 4. A prisoners' dilemma is a game that results in a cooperative equilibrium that leaves all parties better off.

T F 5. A duopoly is an oligopoly with two firms.

T F 6. John Nash won the Nobel Prize in economics for developing game theory in the 1940s.

T F 7. OPEC is a cartel that consists of 11 Arab countries that own about 75 percent of the world's proven oil reserves.

T F 8. Because the prisoners' dilemma assumes that a game will be played once, it does not describe most business situations.

T F 9. In a second-price auction, the winning bidder pays the price of the second-highest bidder.

T F 10. An oligopoly that results from ownership of a key input will result in a government-imposed barrier to entry.

T F 11. In repeated games, a retaliation strategy increases the chances of cooperative behavior.

T F 12. A patent grants exclusive rights to a product for a period of 15 years.

T F 13. Because the four-firm concentration ratio for college bookstores is greater than the concentration ratio for pharmacies and drugstores, competition is greater among pharmacies and drugstores.

T F 14. The large size of Wal-Mart stores was designed as a deterrent to entry of new firms.

T F 15. Most business situations are repeated games.

Answers to the Self-Test

Multiple-Choice Questions

Question	Answer	Explanation
1	c	An oligopoly is a market structure in which a small number of interdependent firms compete.
2	b	Barriers to entry refer to anything that keeps new firms from entering an industry in which firms are earning economic profits.
3	c	The concentration ratios for these retail industries were 92 percent and 95 percent respectively.
4	c	The concentration ratios for these retail industries were 95 percent and 91 percent respectively.
5	b	Economies of scale help determine the extent of competition in an industry.
6	c	Economies of scale exist when a firm's long-run average costs fall as it increases output.
7	b	In this case, the minimum point on the long-run average cost curve comes at a level of output that is a large fraction of industry sales (closer to market demand): thus the industry is an oligopoly.
8	d	Economies of scale are prevalent in industries where the minimum long-run average cost coincides with a large level of output relative to the market demand is being produced by a single firm.
9	d	All of the above are barriers to entry.
10	b	A patent typically gives the holder exclusive rights to a product for a period of 20 years.
11	b	Profits depend on strategy, or how a firm reacts to the moves made by other firms.
12	c	Rules determine what actions are allowable; strategies are used by players to attain their objectives in the game; and payoffs are the results of the interaction among the players' strategies.
13	b	Strategies are actions taken by a business firm to achieve a goal, such as maximizing profits.
14	d	Nash equilibrium is a situation where each firm chooses the best strategy, given the strategies chosen by other firms.
15	b	Collusion is an agreement among firms to charge the same price or to otherwise not compete.
16	c	A dominant strategy is a strategy that is the best for a firm, no matter what strategies other firms use.
17	a	This strategy leads to the highest possible profit no matter what the other firm will do.
18	a	Both firms would like to charge $200 but end up charging $150, so they are both forced to do what is best in light of what the other is doing, or forced to choose their dominant strategies.
19	a	Equilibrium in a game in which players cooperate to increase their mutual payoff is called a cooperative equilibrium.
20	c	The prisoners' dilemma is a game where pursuing dominant strategies results in noncooperation that leaves everyone worse off.
21	b	The winning bidder pays the price of the second-highest bidder. See the entitled "Is There a Dominant Strategy for Bidding on eBay?"
22	b	A strategy of placing the maximum value dominates.

23	a	In a repeated game, we are more likely to see cooperative behavior.
24	c	The firms end up charging the high price and receiving high profits.
25	c	A group of firms that colludes by agreeing to restrict output to increase prices and profits.
26	d	Sustaining high prices has been difficult because members often exceed their output quotas in order to increase their individual profit.
27	b	The lower line shows the nominal (or stated) price of a barrel of oil in each year, without regard to changes in the purchasing power of money over time.
28	c	The equilibrium of this game will occur with Saudi Arabia producing a low output and Nigeria producing a high output. Nigeria will choose a high volume of output because it will make them better off regardless of Saudi Arabia's production. Likewise, Saudi Arabia will choose a low volume of output because their profits will be higher regardless of Nigeria's output.
29	c	Deterrence is only worth pursuing if its costs are less than the benefits derived from deterrence.
30	b	In this case, Wal-Mart will build a small store because it can make greater profits and Target will enter.
31	d	Potential entrants refers to the threat of competition from new entrants.
32	c	Competition from existing firms imposes the most important limit on the profitability of firms in the computer industry.
33	d	In the 1940s, the movie studios could only produce color movies by using the cameras supplied by Technicolor. Technicolor took advantage of this situation to charge high prices, which reduced the profits of the movie studios.
34	a	This is an example of the bargaining power of buyers.
35	c	If few firms can supply an input and the input is specialized, the suppliers are likely to have the bargaining power to limit a firm's profits.
36	a	If many firms can supply an input and the input is not specialized, the suppliers are unlikely to have the bargaining power to limit a firm's profits.
37	a	This box is labeled "Industry Competitors." See Figure 13-8 on page 458.
38	c	This is Michael Porter's Five Competitive Forces Model.
39	b	Refer to the *Making the Connection* "Is Southwest's Business Strategy More Important Than the Structure of the Airline Industry?" in the textbook.
40	c	In the *Making the Connection* "Is Southwest's Business Strategy More Important Than the Structure of the Airline Industry?" the textbook states that many economists have argued that the best strategy for a company is to identify a segment of the market and shape the company to fit that segment.

Short Answer Responses

1. Not necessarily. A concentration ratio is the share of the market of the largest firms (usually the four largest) in an industry, not the distribution of market shares of among the largest firms. For example, the market shares of the four largest firms in industry A could be 20 percent each, while the market share of the largest firm in industry B could be 76 percent, with the other firms each having only a 1 percent share. In addition, concentration ratios do account for competitive forces included in Michael Porter's model. These include competition from existing firms, the threat from new entrants, competition from substitute goods, and the bargaining power of buyers and sellers.

2. OPEC quotas are designed to reduce oil production below the competitive level. This forces up the price of oil and increases the profits of OPEC members. But individual countries can gain market share and profits at the expense of other countries if they exceed their quotas and reduce

the price they charge for oil. Because all countries have the same incentive, when one member exceeds its quota, other countries are likely to do the same. As a result, oil prices and profits fall.

3. Even without licensing there would be a demand on the part of the public for information about the qualifications of medical doctors. Patients would likely make greater use of the Internet and other sources of information about how many operations a surgeon has performed, how many times a doctor or hospital has been sued for malpractice, etc.

4. One could argue that the company faced competition from substitute goods, one of the elements of Michael Porter's Five Competitive Forces Model. Steel and other materials are possible substitutes for aluminum in the construction of some products (for example, automobiles, machinery) and wax paper and plastic wrap are substitutes for aluminum foil. In fact, company officials made these arguments, albeit unsuccessfully.

5. Openly discussing pricing strategies is illegal in the United States. Airline officials would subject themselves and their companies to fines and possibly jail terms if they were found guilty of fixing prices.

True/False Answers

1. T See page 443 of the textbook.
2. T This is the definition of Nash Equilibrium.
3. F The most important barrier to entry is economies of scale.
4. F A prisoners' dilemma results in noncooperation that leaves everyone worse off.
5. T See the section "A Duopoly Game: Price Competition between Two Firms" beginning on page 445 of the textbook.
6. F Although Nash was a pioneer in the field, game theory was initially developed in the 1940s by John von Neumann and Oskar Morgenstern.
7. F Four members of OPEC are non-Arab countries.
8. T Most business situations involve repeated games, which is not the case in the prisoners' dilemma.
9. T See *Making the Connection*, entitled "Is There a Dominant Strategy for Bidding on eBay?" on page 449 of the textbook.
10. F Oligopolies may exist due to ownership of key inputs, but the government need not be involved in the market.
11. T If firms fear retaliation, they are less likely to cheat on a collusion agreement.
12. F Patent protection is granted for 20 years.
13. F The concentration ratio is a flawed measure of competition.
14. T See the section "Economies of Scale" beginning on page 443 of the textbook.
15. T See the section "Can Firms Escape the Prisoners' Dilemma?" beginning on page 450 of the textbook.

Chapter 14

Monopoly and Antitrust Policy

Chapter Summary

You saw in Chapter 11 that perfectly competitive markets are rare, but they show how firms act when there are many firms supplying the same product. Monopoly is the other extreme – where a firm is the only supplier of a particular product. A **monopoly** is a firm that is the only seller of a good or service that does not have a close substitute. For a monopoly to exist, barriers to entering the market must be so high that no other firms can enter. These entry barriers result from:

1. government blocking the entry of more than one firm into a market,
2. control over an input necessary to produce a product.
3. important network externalities.
4. economies of scale so large that one firm has a natural monopoly.

A monopoly firm maximizes profit by producing the quantity of output that makes marginal revenue equal to marginal cost. A monopoly firm's demand curve is the same as the market demand curve for the product it sells. If the monopolist's price exceeds its average total cost at the output where marginal revenue equals marginal cost, it will earn an economic profit. Because of high entry barriers, new firms will not be able to enter the market. If other things remain the same, the firm will be able to continue to earn economic profits, even in the long run. Generally, a monopoly will produce a smaller quantity and charge a higher price than would a perfectly competitive industry producing the same good. Because a monopolist's profit-maximizing price exceeds marginal cost, a monopoly generates a loss in economic efficiency relative to a perfectly competitive market.

The first important law regulating monopolies in the United States was the Sherman Act of 1890, which targeted firms that combined to form trusts. Other **antitrust laws** were passed in the twentieth century to regulate behavior not addressed in the Sherman Act. The Department of Justice and the Federal Trade Commission have developed guidelines to evaluate proposed mergers between firms. The guidelines have three main parts: market definition, measure of concentration, and merger standards. Firms that propose to merge must document the efficiencies that would result from their merger. It is typical for state or local regulatory commissions to set prices for natural monopolies. Most regulators allow owners of monopoly firms to earn a normal profit on their investment.

Learning Objectives

When you finish this chapter, you should be able to:

1. **Define monopoly.** The economic model of monopoly provides a benchmark for a firm that faces no competition from other firms supplying its product. The model is also useful for analyzing situations where firms agree to not compete and act as if they were a monopoly. A single seller in a small, local market may also find it has considerable monopoly power.

2. **Explain the four main reasons monopolies arise.** For a monopoly to exist, barriers to entering the market must be so high that no other firm can enter. The government may block the entry of firms by granting a patent or copyright to an individual or firm, or by granting a public franchise that makes one firm the exclusive provider of a good or service. Other barriers include control of a key input, network externalities, and economies of scale.

3. **Explain how a monopoly chooses price and output.** A monopoly maximizes profit by producing the quantity of output that makes marginal revenue equal marginal cost. Even if the monopolist earns economic profits, new firms will not be able to enter the market. Therefore, the monopolist can continue to earn economic profits, even in the long run.

4. **Use a graph to illustrate how a monopoly affects economic efficiency.** Compared to a perfectly competitive industry producing the same good, a monopolist (1) will charge a higher price and produce less, (2) will reduce the amount of consumer surplus, and (3) will increase the amount of producer surplus. By increasing the price and reducing the quantity produced, the monopolist reduces economic surplus and creates a deadweight loss, which represents the loss of economic efficiency due to monopoly.

5. **Discuss government policies toward monopoly.** Antitrust laws are used by governments to make illegal collusion and attempts by firms to form monopolies. Collusion is an agreement among firms to charge the same price for or otherwise not compete. Governments also regulate firms that are natural monopolies by controlling the prices they charge.

Chapter Review

Chapter Opener: Time Warner Rules Manhattan (pages 472-473)

Time Warner Cable, a division of the Time Warner Company, operates cable television systems in the United States. As the only provider of cable television in Manhattan, it has a monopoly in this market. There are few monopoly firms in the United States because when a firm earns an economic profit, other firms have an incentive to enter the market.

Helpful Study Hint

An ***Inside Look*** at the end of the chapter discusses monopoly in the cable television industry. Changing regulations have increased competition in the cable television market. This increase in competition has meant that consumers have a greater variety of cable companies to choose from and the price of cable television has fallen. The increased competition has meant huge benefits for consumers and an increase in economic efficiency.

If you enjoy watching football, you are probably aware that the National Football League began its own network – the NFL Network. ***Economics in YOUR Life!*** asks why some cable TV systems don't carry NFL Network and why you have to pay extra to access that network. Keep these questions in mind as you read the chapter. The authors will answer the questions at the end of the chapter.

14.1 LEARNING OBJECTIVE

14.1 Is Any Firm Ever Really a Monopoly? (pages 474-475)

Learning Objective 1 Define monopoly.

A **monopoly** is a firm that is the only seller of a good or service that does not have a close substitute. A narrow definition of monopoly is that a firm is a monopoly if it can ignore the actions of other firms. Broadly defined, a firm is a monopoly if it can retain economic profits in the long run.

Helpful Study Hint

Are all video games the same? ***Making the Connection*** "Is Xbox 360 a Close Substitute for PlayStation 3?" considers the meaning of the term "close substitute." Microsoft's Xbox included a hard disk and a version of the Windows operating system. These two features made the Xbox more expensive to produce than Sony's PlayStation 2. However, consumers considered the two products substitutes – which forced Microsoft to price the Xbox the same as Sony priced the PlayStation 2. In the next round of products, Sony repeated Microsoft's mistake. Sony produced PlayStation 3 to play Blu-ray DVDs, which increased its cost of production. Microsoft produced the Xbox 360 with the capability of playing older-format DVDs, while making available an add-on component to play HD-DVDs. Consumers were attracted to Microsoft's new product because it was $200 cheaper than Sony's new product.

Extra Solved Problem 14-1

Chapter 14 includes two Solved Problems. Here is an extra Solved Problem to help you build your skills solving economic problems.

Supports Learning Objective 1: Define monopoly.

Is the Cable Television Monopoly Over?

In June 2005, executives of Cablevision Systems Corp. offered to buy all public shares of the company for $7.9 billion. Cablevision, which has had a virtual monopoly on cable television service in Long Island and parts of New York City, was feeling the competitive heat from regulatory reform and new technology. The Satellite Home Viewer Improvement Act of 1999 allowed Digital Satellite Systems (DBS) to carry local broadcast signals back to their home markets. An aggressive campaign by DBS systems, such as DirecTV and DISH Network, to lure cable customers with low prices for equipment and service resulted in an increase in their national market share from 7 to 17 percent between 1998 and 2003.

But Cablevision had more to worry about. So-called Baby Bell phone companies were preparing to invade cable's turf by offering not only digital television programming, but high-speed Internet access and phone service. Ironically, the Baby Bell companies were formed after the breakup of AT&T, which for years had a monopoly on local and long-distance phone service. One of the Baby Bells is Verizon, which was awaiting local government approval to offer phone service in New York when Cablevision's announcement of its offer to go private was made. Verizon officials hinted they will offer more channels for less money than cable companies can charge. Industry analysts believe that Cablevision planned to invest more money in customer service and technology, moves that would lower its short-run profits and price of its stock if it were to remain a publicly-owned company.

Sources: "Cable System's New Weapon In Phone Battle: Going Private," by Peter Grant, *Wall Street Journal*, June 21, 2005.

"Cable TV Suffers From High Rate Increases, Lower Satisfaction," by Robyn Greenspan, *Hardware*. August 21, 2003.

a. What is the definition of monopoly?

b. Are cable television companies such as Cablevision monopolies?

SOLVING THE PROBLEM

Step 1: **Review the chapter material.**
This problem is about the definition of monopoly, so you may want to review the section "Is Any Firm Ever Really a Monopoly?" which begins on page 474 of the textbook.

Step 2: **Answer question (a) by defining monopoly.**
A monopoly is the only seller of a good or service that does not have a close substitute.

Step 3: **Answer question (b) by explaining whether Cablevision is a monopoly.**
The key to identifying a firm as a monopoly is determining whether the good or service it offers has close substitutes. Applying a narrow definition of monopoly, Cablevision is a monopoly if one can demonstrate Cablevision can ignore other firms' prices. Although this was true at one time, Cablevision cannot ignore the prices DBS companies and other competitors charge now that they can offer customers comparable services. A broader definition of monopoly would consider Cablevision to be a monopoly, even if there are substitutes for its service, if it can earn long-run economic profits. Using this definition, it is too early to state that Cablevision and other cable television companies have lost their monopoly status. But it will be increasingly difficult for cable companies to earn economic profits as more firms offer similar services in the future.

14.2 LEARNING OBJECTIVE

14.2 Where Do Monopolies Come From? (pages 475-481)

Learning Objective 2 Explain the four reasons monopolies arise.

A monopoly requires that barriers to entry into the market must be so high that no other firms can enter. There are four reasons entry barriers may be high enough to keep out competing firms:

1. Government can block the entry of more than one firm into a market by granting a patent or copyright or by granting a firm a public franchise. A **patent** is the exclusive right to a product for a period of 20 years from the date the product was invented. U.S. laws grant **copyright** protection to creators of books, films and music. State and local governments in the United States have granted **public franchises**—the legal right to be the sole provider of a good or service—to providers of electricity, natural gas, cable television, and water.

2. A firm can become a monopoly by controlling a key resource. Examples of this entry barrier include the Aluminum Company of America (until the 1940s), the International Nickel Company of Canada, and major professional sports teams.

3. **Network externalities** exist in the consumption of a product if the value of the product increases with the number of people who are using it. Some economists argue that network externalities are a barrier to entry, but other economists believe dominant positions by firms reflect their efficiency in satisfying consumer preferences.

4. Economies of scale are so large that one firm has a natural monopoly. A **natural monopoly** is a situation in which one firm can supply the entire market at a lower average total cost than can two or more firms.

Helpful Study Hint

Making the Connection "The End of the Christmas Plant Monopoly" and "Are Diamond Profits Forever? The De Beers Diamond Monopoly" describe the source of monopoly for firms in two different markets. The market for poinsettias was a monopoly for many years because the producers kept the production process a secret. Once the secret to the production process was revealed and became widely adopted by producers, the market was very competitive and the price of poinsettias plants fell. The market for diamonds was monopolized by De Beers for a significant number of years. The company maintained its monopoly by buying up new supplies as they were discovered, but the company was not able to buy all of the new supplies. De Beers no longer has a monopoly in the diamond market, but is trying to continue to earn economic profits by labeling their diamonds. Test your understanding by completing end-of-chapter problems 2.9 and 2.10.

Work through ***Solved Problem 14-2***, which provides an application of the long-run average total cost curve of a natural monopoly. Automatic Data Processing, Inc. is a company that provides reports to shareholders. This is an example of a natural monopoly because as the quantity of reports produced increases the average total cost of production for ADP decreases. Test your understanding by completing end-of-chapter problem 2.11.

14.3 LEARNING OBJECTIVE

14.3 How Does a Monopoly Choose Price and Output? (pages 481-485)

Learning Objective 3 Explain how a monopoly chooses price and output.

A monopoly maximizes profit by producing the level of output that makes marginal revenue equal to marginal cost. The monopoly's demand curve is the same as the market demand curve for the product. The monopolist is a price maker and has a downward-sloping demand curve. The monopoly's marginal revenue curve lies below its demand curve, so at any level of output its marginal revenue is less than its price. If the monopolist earns an economic profit, new firms will not be able to enter the market. Therefore, long-run economic profits can be earned.

Helpful Study Hint

Review Figure 14.2 on page 482 of the textbook, which shows how a monopoly such as Time Warner Cable calculates marginal revenue. Also review Figure 14.3 on page 483, which shows the profit-maximizing price and output for a monopoly.

Work through ***Solved Problem 14-3*** to learn the steps for finding the profit-maximizing price for Comcast, a cable provider. Comcast will maximize its profit by providing the quantity of cable service so that its marginal revenue equals its marginal cost. The profit is the revenue left over after all costs have been paid. Recall that profit is calculated by $(P - ATC) \times Q$. Practice your skills by completing related end-of-chapter problems 3.3 and 3.4.

Read ***Don't Let This Happen to You!*** to learn why charging a higher price won't guarantee more profits – even for a monopolist. It may seem logical for Comcast to increase its price for cable services to increase its profit, but the managers of firms must realize that as they increase price, the quantity demanded will fall. As the quantity demanded falls, the firm will no longer be producing the profit maximizing quantity and will no longer be receiving the highest possible profits.

Professional sports leagues such as Major League Baseball and the National Football League negotiate television contracts for all of their teams and they restrict the number of their franchises. In other words, they act as monopolists. But monopoly power does not guarantee a profit to each team. As is true in other industries, poor management or weak consumer demand can lead to economic losses. The Montreal Expos baseball franchise is one example of low consumer demand causing a firm to exit the industry. (The Expos moved to Washington D.C. a few years ago.) But successful franchises such as the Los Angeles Dodgers or the Kansas City Chiefs need not fear the entry of new teams into their markets.

14.4 LEARNING OBJECTIVE

14.4 Does Monopoly Reduce Economic Efficiency? (pages 485-488)

Learning Objective 4 Use a graph to illustrate how a monopoly affects economic efficiency.

Compared to equilibrium in a perfectly competitive market, which results in the maximum amount of economic surplus, a monopoly will produce less output and charge a higher price. This results in a reduction of economic surplus and a deadweight loss. Many firms that are not monopolies have some market power. **Market power** is the ability of a firm to charge a price greater than marginal cost. The loss of economic efficiency due to market power in the United States is small, probably less than 1 percent of total production. Some economists claim that the economy may benefit from firms having market power.

Firms with market power are more likely than competitive firms to earn profits that can be used to conduct research and develop new products. The argument that economic progress depends on technological change in the form of new products and that new technology pushes out old technology is closely associated with Joseph Schumpeter. For example, the computer you use replaced the typewriter your parents and grandparents used. However, many economists disagree with Schumpeter and argue that firms that started small, such as Apple and Google, have produced many new products.

Helpful Study Hint

Review Figure 14-4 and Figure 14.5, which compare economic efficiency under conditions of monopoly and perfect competition. Although small firms are one source of invention and innovation, firms with market power are better able to afford product development. Product development involves taking a new product or process, perhaps one developed by a small firm, and making it commercially successful. The failure rate for product development can be very high, over 50 percent in some industries, and it may take several years for new products to become profitable.

Extra Solved Problem **14-4**

Chapter 14 includes two Solved Problems. Here is an extra Solved Problem to help you build your skills solving economic problems.

Supports Learning Objective 4: Use a graph to illustrate how a monopoly affects economic efficiency.

Comcast Cable

The following table is reproduced from Solved Problem 14-3 in the textbook and represents the demand and costs that Comcast faces in the provision of cable television.

Price	Quantity	Total Revenue	Marginal Revenue	Total Cost	Marginal Cost
$17	3	$51	--	$56	--
16	4	64	$13	63	$7
15	5	75	11	71	8
14	6	84	9	80	9
13	7	91	7	90	10
12	8	96	5	101	11

a. Use a graph to show the profit-maximizing quantity and price that Comcast will produce and charge.

b. Use this graph to calculate the deadweight loss associated with this cable monopoly.

SOLVING THE PROBLEM

Step 1: Review the chapter material.
This problem is an extension of Solved Problem 14-3, so you may want to review this problem beginning on page 484 in the textbook. This problem also requires an understanding of the section "Does Monopoly Reduce Economic Efficiency?" which begins on page 485 of the textbook.

Step 2: Answer question (a) by drawing a graph representing the demand, marginal revenue, and marginal cost curves of the firm and indicate the profit maximizing quantity and price.
Comcast will choose to produce where the marginal revenue equals the marginal cost and charges the price that consumers are willing to pay for that quantity.

Price	Quantity	Total Revenue	Marginal Revenue	Total Cost	Marginal Cost
$17	3	$51		$56	
16	4	64	$13	63	$7
15	5	75	11	71	8
14	6	84	9	80	9
13	7	91	7	90	10
12	8	96	5	101	11

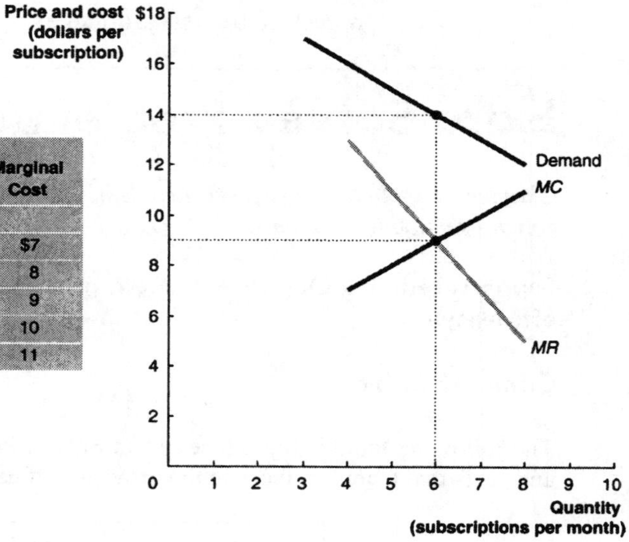

Step 3: Answer question (b) by showing the deadweight loss on your graph and use your graph to calculate the deadweight loss to society of the cable monopoly.
To calculate the deadweight loss associated with monopoly, we must first find what price and quantity would be in this market if the industry was perfectly competitive. The perfectly competitive quantity will be where price equals marginal cost, which occurs where the demand curve and the marginal cost curve intersect. Shade in the area between the monopoly's profit maximizing quantity and the perfectly competitive equilibrium and between the marginal cost and demand curves. See the graph below. To calculate this area, we calculate the area of a triangle:

½ x base x height =
½ x ($14/ subscription – $9/subscription) x (8.5 subscriptions – 6 subscriptions)
= $6.25 per month.

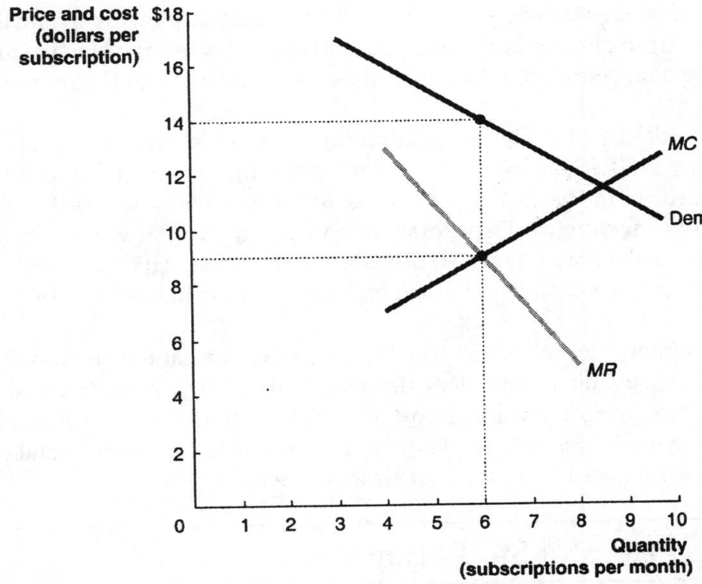

14.5 LEARNING OBJECTIVE

14.5 Government Policy toward Monopoly

Learning Objective 5 Discuss government policies toward monopoly.

Because monopolies reduce consumer welfare and efficiency, most governments regulate their behavior. **Collusion** refers to an agreement among firms to charge the same price or to otherwise not compete. **Antitrust laws** are laws aimed at eliminating collusion and promoting competition among firms. The passage of the first antitrust law was spurred by the formation of various "trusts" in the 1870s and 1880s. Trusts are combinations of firms in several industries that operate independently but are controlled by a common board of trustees.

The Sherman Act of 1890 was the first important law regulating monopolies in the United States. This Act prohibited price fixing, collusion, and monopolization. The Clayton Act of 1914 made a merger illegal if its effect was to lessen competition or if the merger tended to create a monopoly.

The federal government regulates business mergers because mergers can result in firms gaining market power. **Horizontal mergers** are mergers between firms in the same industry. **Vertical mergers** are mergers between firms at different stages of production of a good.

It is important to define the appropriate market when evaluating a proposed merger. The newly merged firm may be more efficient than the merging firms were individually. Merging firms must substantiate efficiency claims that would result from their proposed merger.

The Department of Justice and the Federal Trade Commission developed merger guidelines in 1982. The merger guidelines have three main parts:

1. Market definition. A market consists of all firms making products that consumers view as close substitutes.

2. Measure of concentration. A market is concentrated if a relatively small number of firms have a large share of total sales in the market. The guidelines use the Herfindahl-Hirschman Index (HHI) to measure concentration, which adds the squares of the market shares of each firm in an industry.

3. Merger standards. The HHI calculation for a market is used to evaluate proposed mergers. If the post-merger HHI is below 1,000, the merger will not be challenged because the market is not concentrated. If the post-merger HHI is between 1,000 and 1,800, this indicates the market is moderately concentrated. Depending on how much the HHI will be increased, the merger may be challenged. If the post-merger HHI is above 1,800, the market is highly concentrated. Mergers in this market may be challenged based on how much the merger will increase the HHI.

Local or state regulatory commissions usually set prices for natural monopolies. To achieve economic efficiency, regulators should require that the monopoly charge a price equal to marginal cost. Often, though, a natural monopoly's marginal cost will be less than its average total cost. In this case, most regulators will allow the monopoly to charge a price equal to its average total cost so that the owners of the monopoly can earn a normal return on their investment.

Helpful Study Hint

Making the Connection "Should the Government Prevent Banks from Becoming Too Big?" discusses whether the government should allow banks to merge or not. If there are large economies of scale that can be achieved by merging, then these mergers could increase economic efficiency. Regulations have been established by the federal government that will allow banks to merge only if merging means that no individual bank will control more than 10 percent of the deposits in the economy.

The actual regulation of natural monopolies is more complicated than the guidelines "set price equal to marginal cost" or "set price equal to average total cost" suggest. Regulatory commissions often recruit their members from the companies they regulate. Although these individuals have valuable knowledge regarding the regulated firm, they may be biased toward the firm's views, even at the expense of interests of the consumers, who they are supposed to represent. Other regulators may be biased against the firms they regulate. It is difficult to select commission members who are both knowledgeable and unbiased. Another problem is that allowing a firm to earn a normal profit may give it less incentive to reduce its costs than if it were unregulated. The firm would not earn higher profits from any cost-cutting actions and the commission might be willing to allow a price increase if higher average total costs could be documented.

Economics in YOUR Life! answers the question "Why Can't I Watch the NFL Network?" Because cable companies have market power, they may be able to increase their profits by not offering the NFL Network, just as monopolies typically can increase profits by producing a smaller quantity than would be produced in a competitive market.

Extra Solved Problem 14-5

Chapter 14 includes two Solved Problems. Here is an extra Solved Problem to help you build your skills solving economic problems.

Supports Learning Objective 5: Discuss government policies toward monopoly.

Does Microsoft Stifle Innovation?

In 2004, the European Commission found that Microsoft was using its market power to impede innovation and competition in the information technology market. Microsoft was fined Euros 497 million, or $675 million U.S. dollars. Microsoft appealed this ruling to the European Union's Court of First Instance and lost the appeal, so the original ruling that Microsoft was impeding competition was upheld.

Source: "Always Look On the Bright Side of Innovation" by Alan Burnside and Lars Liebeler, *Financial Times*, September 5, 2007.

Explain why the European Commission and the European Union's Court of First Instance would be concerned with Microsoft's actions that impeded competition.

SOLVING THE PROBLEM

Step 1: Review the chapter material.
European countries and the European Union have laws to increase and protect competition like those in the United States. To help understand why the European Union agents found Microsoft guilty of impeding competition, it would be useful for you to review the section "Government Policy toward Monopoly," which begins on page 488 of the textbook.

Step 2: Answer the question by discussing why the European Union's court system was with Microsoft's actions that impeded competition.
As in the United States, European governments have a strong desire to maintain a significant amount of competition in their markets to maximize the economic surplus in these markets. When a firm, in this case Microsoft, has market power, the firm has the ability to determine the price and quantity of a good that will be sold in the market. It may also mean that the firm has created artificial barriers to entry to keep other firms from competing against it in the market. The European Commission and the Court of First Instance is charged with maintaining competition in European markets. Therefore, if Microsoft has, in fact, been impeding competition, the European Commission will be obliged to take action.

Source: "Protect Innovators from Microsoft's Stifling Monopoly," by Maurits Dolmans and Thomas Graf, *Financial Times*, September 13, 2007.

Key Terms

Antitrust laws. Laws aimed at eliminating collusion and promoting competition among firms.

Collusion. An agreement among firms to charge the same price or otherwise not to compete.

Copyright. A government-granted exclusive right to product and sell a creation.

Horizontal merger. A merger between firms in the same industry.

Market power. The ability of a firm to charge a price greater than marginal cost.

Monopoly. A firm that is the only seller of a good or service that does not have a close substitute.

Natural monopoly. A situation in which economies of scale are so large that one firm can supply the entire market at a lower average total cost than can two or more firms.

Network externalities. The situation where the usefulness of a product increases with the number of consumers who use it.

Patent. The exclusive right to a product for a period of 20 years from the date the product was invented.

Public franchise. A designation by the government that a firm is the only legal provider of a good or service.

Vertical merger. A merger between firms at different stages of production of a good.

Self-Test

(Answers are provided at the end of the Self-Test.)

Multiple-Choice Questions

1. In which of the following situations can a firm be considered a monopoly?
   a. When a firm is surrounded by other firms that produce close substitutes
   b. When a firm can ignore the actions of all other firms
   c. When a firm uses other firms' prices in order to price its products
   d. When barriers to entry are eliminated

2. Using the broader definition of monopoly, in which of the following cases could we argue that Microsoft has a monopoly in computer operating systems?
   a. If Macintosh and Linux were not considered close substitutes for Windows
   b. If Microsoft charged prices similar to those that Macintosh and Linux charge for their operating systems in order to compete
   c. If Macintosh and Linux started to produce operating systems similar to Windows
   d. If Microsoft imposes barriers for Macintosh and Linux to enter the market

3. Which type of barrier to entry is the granting of a patent or copyright to an individual or firm considered?
   a. Entry blocked by government action
   b. Entry blocked by externalities
   c. Entry blocked by economies of scale
   d. Entry blocked by natural or technical constraints

4. Which of the following rights is given to the holder of a *patent*?
   a. The exclusive right to a new product
   b. Control over a key resource used in production of a good or service
   c. The exclusive right to a creation
   d. A public franchise

5. The more cell phones in use, the more valuable they become to consumers. Which of the following terms best ascribes to that assertion?
   a. Patent
   b. Network externalities
   c. Control of a key resource
   d. Natural monopoly

6. What is the name given to the situation where economies of scale are so large that one firm can supply the entire market at a lower average total cost than two or more firms?
   a. Network externalities
   b. Productive efficiency
   c. Natural monopoly
   d. Market power

7. Refer to the graph below. Which point corresponds to a natural monopoly serving this market and breaking even?

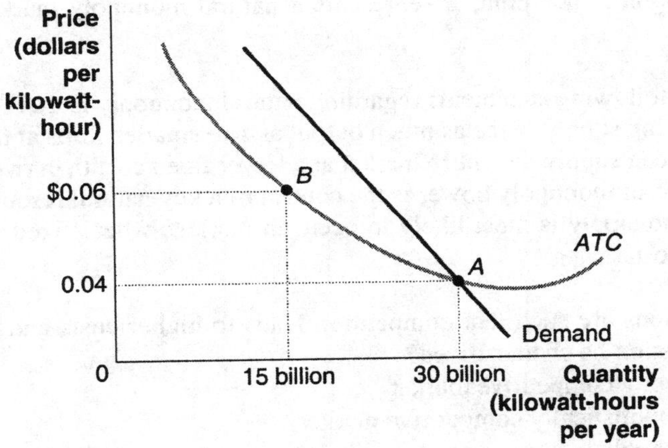

   a. Point *A*
   b. Point *B*
   c. Either point *A* or point *B* are associated with a natural monopoly breaking even.
   d. Neither point *A* nor point *B* is associated with a natural monopoly breaking even.

8. Refer to the graph below. Which point corresponds to a natural monopoly market being divided equally between two firms?

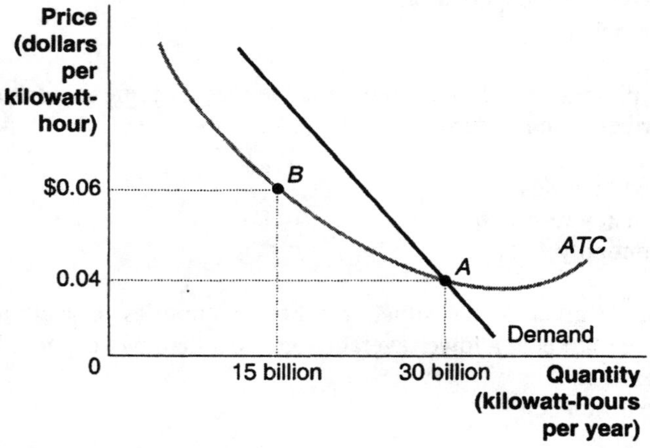

a. Point *A*
b. Point *B*
c. Both points *A* and B are associated with a natural monopoly market being divided between two firms.
d. Neither point *A* nor point *B* represents a natural monopoly market being divided between two firms.

9. Which of the following statements regarding natural monopoly is true?
a. One firm can supply twice as much output as two smaller firms at the same average total cost.
b. One firm can supply the entire market at a lower fixed cost than two or more firms.
c. The source of monopoly power is the control of a key natural resource.
d. Natural monopoly is most likely to occur in markets where fixed costs are very large relative to variable costs.

10. If cost conditions are such that competition leads to higher costs and higher prices, how should the market in question be characterized?
a. As a perfectly competitive market
b. As a monopolistically competitive market
c. As an oligopoly
d. As a natural monopoly

11. Which of the following types of firms use the marginal revenue equals marginal cost approach to maximize profits?
a. Perfectly competitive firms
b. Monopolistically competitive firms
c. Monopolies
d. All of the above

12. In which of the following cases is the firm's demand curve the same as the market demand for the product?
    a. In the perfectly competitive case
    b. In the monopolistically competitive case
    c. In the monopoly's case
    d. All of the above

13. Which firms face a downward-sloping demand curve and a downward-sloping marginal revenue curve?
    a. All price takers
    b. All price makers
    c. Monopolies only
    d. Monopolistic competitive firms only

14. When a firm's demand curve slopes down and the firm decides to cut price, which of the following happens?
    a. It sells more units and receives higher revenue per unit.
    b. It sells more units but receives lower revenue per unit.
    c. It sells fewer units and receives lower revenue per unit.
    d. It sells fewer units but receives higher revenue per unit.

15. Refer to the table below. How much is the *average revenue* associated with serving five subscribers per month?

Subscribers per Month (Q)	Price (P)	Total Revenue ($TR = P \times Q$)	Average Revenue ($AR = TR/Q$)	Marginal Revenue ($MR = \Delta TR/\Delta Q$)
0	$60	$0		
1	57	57		
2	54	108		
3	51	153		
4	48	192		
5	45	225		
6	42	252		
7	39	273		
8	36	288		
9	33	297		
10	30	300		

a. $33
b. $45
c. $5
d. None of the above

16. Refer to the table below. How much is the *marginal revenue* associated with serving seven subscribers per month?

Subscribers per Month (Q)	Price (P)	Total Revenue ($TR = P \times Q$)	Average Revenue ($AR = TR/Q$)	Marginal Revenue ($MR = \Delta TR/\Delta Q$)
0	$60	$0		
1	57	57		
2	54	108		
3	51	153		
4	48	192		
5	45	225		
6	42	252		
7	39	273		
8	36	288		
9	33	297		
10	30	300		

a. $39
b. $45
c. $21
d. None of the above

17. Refer to the graph below. In this graph, which curve is conceptually the same as *average revenue*?

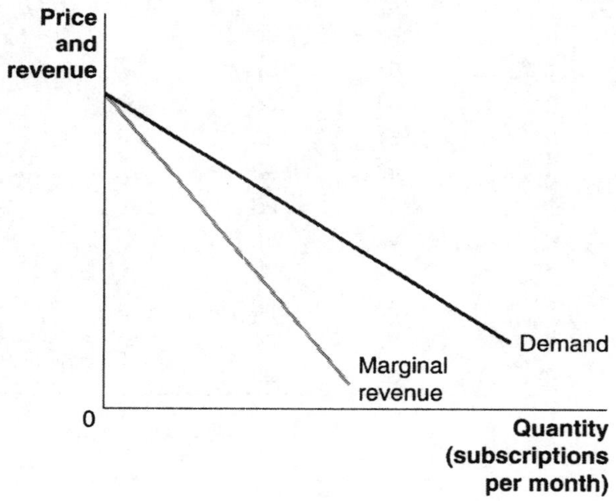

a. The demand curve
b. The marginal revenue curve
c. Both curves
d. Neither curve

18. Refer to the graph below. What is firm's profit when it sells six subscriptions per month?

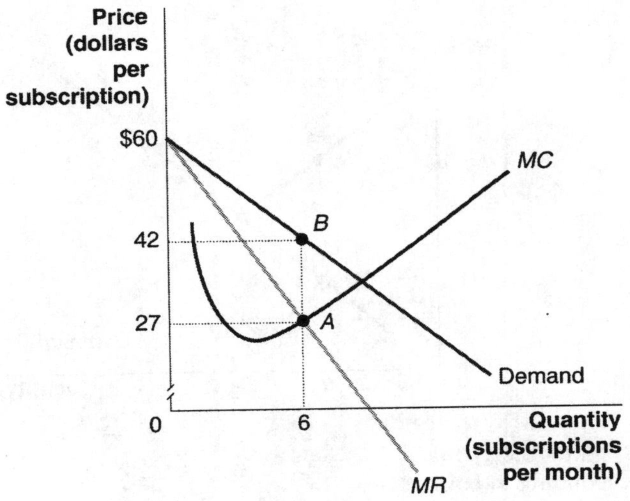

a. $90
b. $42
c. $27
d. None of the above; there is insufficient information to answer the question.

19. Refer to the graph below. What is firm's profit when it sells six subscriptions per month?

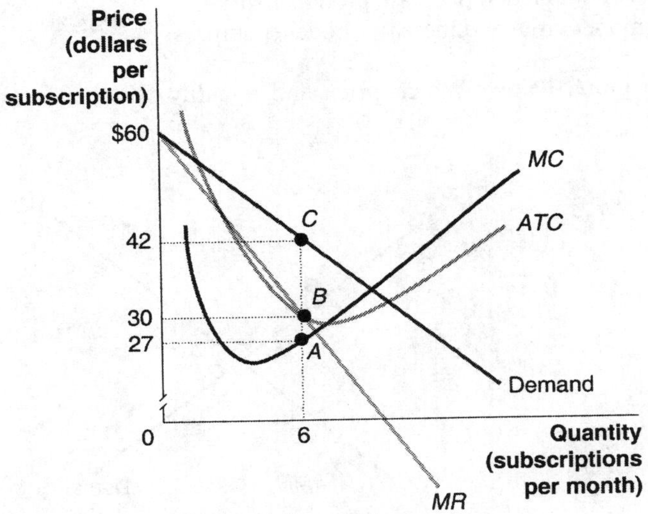

a. $90
b. $72
c. $42
d. $18

20. Refer to the graph below. Relative to the price and output produced by a perfectly competitive industry, what price and output levels correspond to a monopoly in this graph?

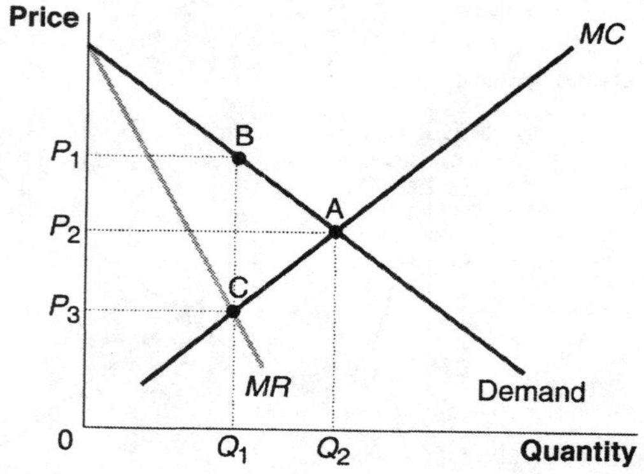

a. Those corresponding to point *A*
b. Those corresponding to point *B*
c. Those corresponding to point *C*
d. None of the above

21. Assume that an industry that began as a perfectly competitive industry becomes a monopoly. Which of the following describes a change in the market as a result of becoming a monopoly? Compared to when the industry was perfectly competitive, the monopolist will
a. charge a higher price and produce less output.
b. charge a higher price and increase consumer surplus.
c. produce less output and decrease producer surplus.
d. produce more output and increase producer surplus.

22. Refer to the graph below. Which price and quantity will prevail when the industry is perfectly competitive?

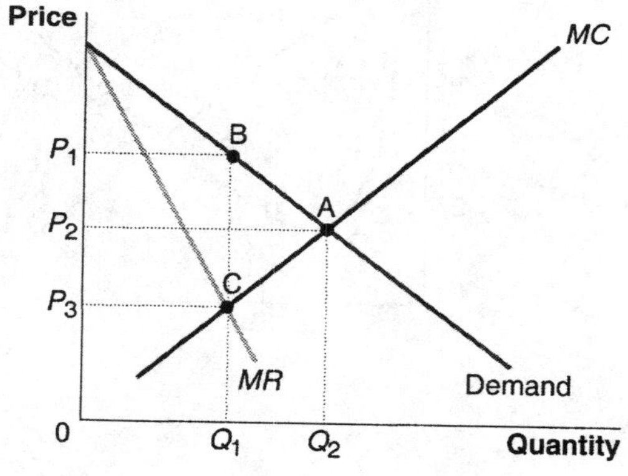

a. Those corresponding to point *A*
b. Those corresponding to point *B*
c. Those corresponding to point *C*
d. None of the above

23. Refer to the graph below. Which area shows the reduction in consumer surplus that results from this industry being a monopoly rather than perfectly competitive?

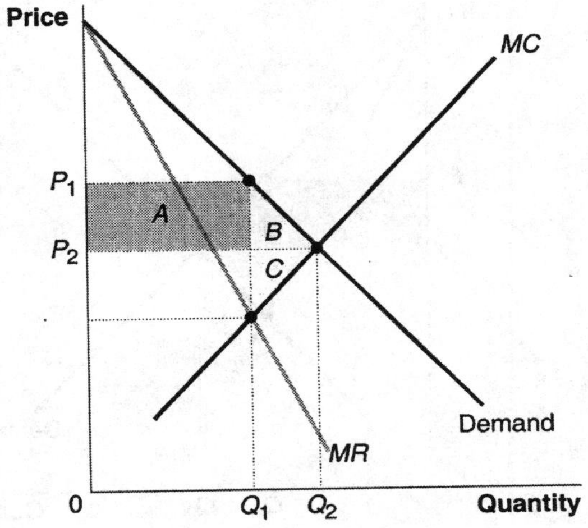

a. Area *A*
b. Area *B* + *C*
c. Area *A* + *B*
d. None of the areas indicated on the graph

24. Refer to the graph below. Which area shows a reduction in consumer surplus that becomes an increase in producer surplus as a result of this industry being a monopoly rather than being perfectly competitive?

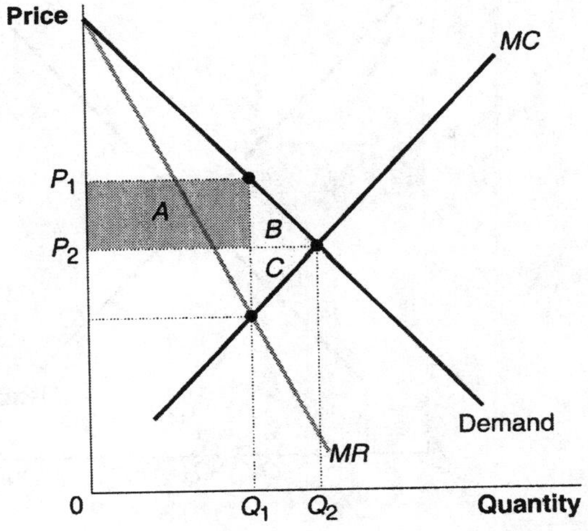

a. Area *A*
b. Area *B* + *C*
c. Area *A* + *B*
d. None of the areas indicated on the graph

25. Refer to the graph below. Which area is considered a reduction in *economic surplus* as a result of this industry being a monopoly rather than being perfectly competitive?

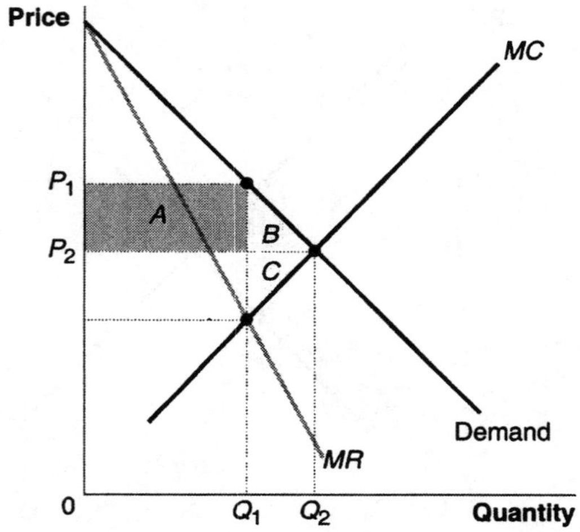

a. Area *A*
b. Area *B*
c. Area *C*
d. Area *B* + *C*

26. Refer to the graph below. If the industry changes from being perfectly competitive to being a monopoly, what happens to producer surplus?

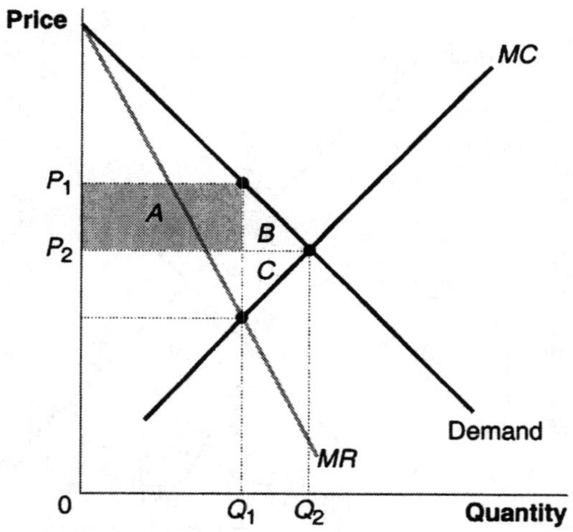

a. It increases by area *A* and decreases by area *B*.
b. It increases by area *A* and decreases by area *C*.
c. It increases by area *B* + *C*.
d. It increases by area *A* and decreases by area *B* + *C*.

27. Which of the following are effects of monopoly?
    a. Monopoly causes a reduction in consumer surplus.
    b. Monopoly causes an increase in producer surplus.
    c. Monopoly causes a reduction in economic efficiency.
    d. All of the above

28. What is the definition of *market power*?
    a. Market power is the same as inefficiency as measured by the amount of deadweight loss from a monopoly.
    b. Market power is the ability of a firm to eliminate competition.
    c. Market power is the ability of one firm to control other firms in the market.
    d. Market power is the ability of a firm to charge a price greater than marginal cost.

29. Refer to the graph below. How can the loss of economic efficiency resulting from this market being a monopoly rather than being perfectly competitive be estimated?

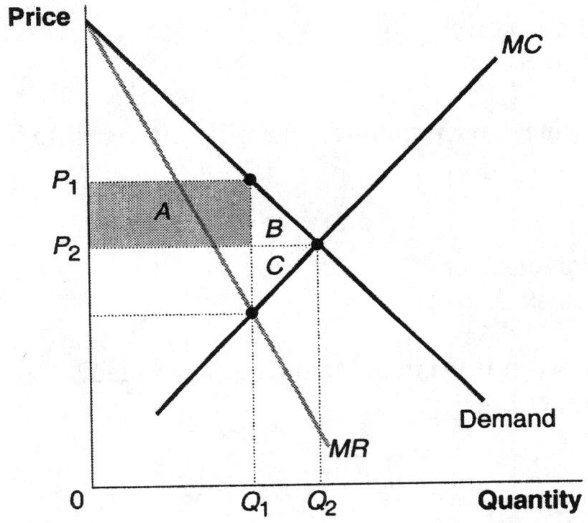

    a. By estimating the size of the triangle $B + C$
    b. By estimating the size of the rectangle A
    c. By estimating the size of the area $A + B + C$
    d. None of the above; the loss of economic efficiency cannot be estimated using this graph.

30. According to Joseph Schumpeter, what does economic progress depend on?
    a. Competition, especially price competition
    b. Technological change in the form of new products
    c. Government protection of competition
    d. The initial endowment of economic resources, such as the amount of labor and capital available

31. What does the term *collusion* refer to?
    a. Collusion refers to an agreement among firms to charge the same price or to otherwise not compete.
    b. Collusion refers to an agreement among existing firms to prevent potential competitors from entering an industry.
    c. Collusion refers to laws aimed at promoting competition among firms.
    d. Collusion refers to a price war among competing firms.

32. What are laws aimed at promoting competition among firms called?
    a. Collusion
    b. Antitrust laws
    c. Laws of comparative advantage
    d. Merger legislation

33. Which of the following laws outlawed monopolization?
    a. The Sherman Act
    b. The Clayton Act
    c. The Robinson-Patman Act
    d. The Cellar-Kefauver Act

34. Which of the following laws prohibited charging buyers different prices if the result would reduce competition?
    a. The Sherman Act
    b. The Clayton Act
    c. The Robinson-Patman Act
    d. The Cellar-Kefauver Act

35. What is a merger between firms in the same industry called?
    a. A horizontal merger
    b. A vertical merger
    c. A conglomerate
    d. A divestiture

36. Which of the following is more likely to increase market power?
    a. Horizontal mergers
    b. Vertical mergers
    c. Stricter enforcement of antitrust laws
    d. Divestitures

37. Refer to the graph below. Suppose that two firms each produce with a marginal cost of MC_1 and that when the two firms merge there are efficiency gains. As presented in Figure 14-6 of the textbook, which point on the graph shows how a merger results in efficiency gains?

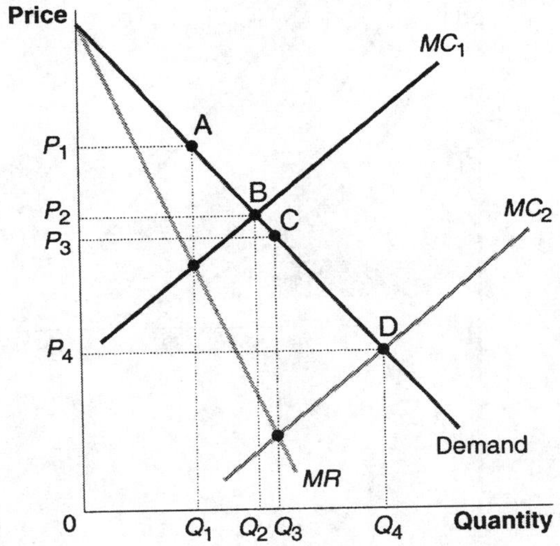

a. Point *A*
b. Point *B*
c. Point *C*
d. Point *D*

38. Which of the following is among the guidelines used by economists and attorneys to understand whether the government is likely to allow a merger or to oppose it?
a. Market definition
b. Measure of concentration
c. Merger standards
d. All of the above

39. What is the value of the Herfindahl-Hirschman Index (HHI) when there are four firms in an industry with each firm having an equal market share?
a. 4
b. 625
c. 2,500
d. 4,000

40. Refer to the graph below. If regulators want to achieve economic efficiency, how will they set the monopoly price?

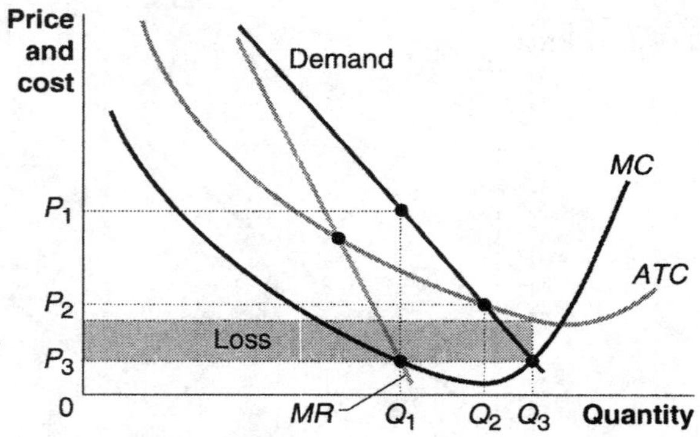

a. At P_1
b. At P_2
c. At P_3
d. None of the above

41. Refer to the graph below. If regulators want to ensure that the owners of the monopoly are able to earn a normal rate of return on their investment, how will they set the monopoly price?

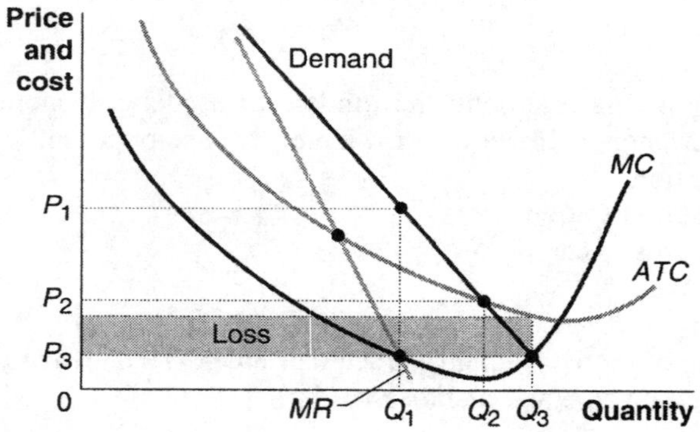

a. At P_1
b. At P_2
c. At P_3
d. None of the above

Short Answer Questions

1. The market shares of the four largest firms in Industry A are 75 percent, 2 percent, 2 percent and 1 percent. Each of the market shares of the four largest firms in Industry B equals 20 percent. Compare the four-firm concentration ratio and the Herfindahl-Hirschman Index (HHI) of concentration for both of these industries.

2. In the United States, regulatory commissions usually set prices for natural monopolies, such as firms selling natural gas. To achieve economic efficiency, commissions should require the firms they regulate to charge a price equal to marginal cost. If the price of natural gas was less than average total cost, could charging a price equal to marginal cost harm consumers?

3. Joseph Schumpeter argued that an economy may benefit from monopoly and oligopoly because firms with market power can afford costly research that leads to new technology. Perfectly competitive firms that earn zero economic profits in the long run can ill-afford to spend on research. Other economists argue that small, competitive firms have developed new products and technologies. Competition spurs firms to continually develop new products in order to stay ahead of competing firms. Are large firms with market power good or bad for an economy?

4. In the *Making the Connection* "The End of the Christmas Plant Monopoly," on page 476 of the textbook, the story of the Ecke family's development of a new variety of poinsettia plants was described. The Ecke family was able to maintain a monopoly on its poinsettias by keeping secret the technique they used to develop the plants. But the monopoly ended when a researcher discovered and published the technique. Did the Ecke family err in not obtaining a patent on the technique it used to develop its poinsettias?

5. In 2003 the Federal Trade Commission delayed Nestle's proposed acquisition of Dreyer's Ice Cream because the proposed merger had the potential to raise the price of "super-premium" ice cream. At the time there were only three producers of this type of ice cream in the U.S.: Nestle, Dreyer's and Ben and Jerry's. The FTC's objection to the merger (the merger was ultimately approved) received considerable criticism. Why should the FTC's concern for consumer welfare (reduced competition and, possibly, higher prices for some types of ice cream) have been criticized?

True/False Questions

T F 1. A broad definition considers a firm a monopoly if it can earn economic profits in the long run.
T F 2. A public franchise grants a firm an exclusive right to sell a good or service for 20 years.
T F 3. A merger between two firms in an industry with a Herfindahl-Hirschman Index value below 1,000 will not be challenged by the federal government.
T F 4. The Clayton Act (1890) prohibited price fixing and collusion.
T F 5. Joseph Schumpeter argued that small competitive firms are responsible for the development of most of the technological change that occurs over time.
T F 6. John D. Rockefeller organized the Standard Oil Trust.
T F 7. A monopolist will charge the highest price possible in order to make the most profit.
T F 8. A monopolist's demand curve is the same as the demand curve for the product it sells.
T F 9. A professional sports team's long-term stadium lease is an example of a barrier to entry.
T F 10. A broad definition of monopoly is that a monopolist can ignore the actions of all other firms.

T F 11. A public franchise is granted by the government to give one firm an exclusive right to provide a good or service.

T F 12. A "generic drug" refers to a drug that no longer is protected by a patent.

T F 13. A merger between two soft drink manufacturers is an example of a vertical merger.

T F 14. Department of Justice and Federal Trade Commission guidelines for evaluating proposed mergers use the Herfindahl-Hirschman Index to measure market concentration.

T F 15. In 2002, the Justice Department ruled that Microsoft had to charge the same price for its Xbox as Sony was charging for the PlayStation 2.

Answers to the Self-Test

Multiple-Choice Questions

Question	Answer	Explanation
1	b	A narrow definition of monopoly used by some economists is that a firm has a monopoly if it can ignore the actions of all other firms. In other words, other firms must not be producing close substitutes if the monopolist can ignore other firms' prices.
2	a	For most computer users, Linux and the Macintosh system are not close substitutes for Windows. So, using the broader definition, we can say that Microsoft has a monopoly in the market for computer operating systems.
3	a	Governments ordinarily try to promote competition in markets, but sometimes governments take action to block the entry of more than one firm into a market. In the United States, there are two main ways government blocks entry. One way is to grant a patent or copyright to an individual or firm, which gives it the exclusive right to produce a product. The second way is to grant a firm a public franchise, which makes it the exclusive legal provider of a good or service.
4	a	In the United States, there are two main ways government blocks entry. One way is to grant a patent or copyright to an individual or firm, which gives it the exclusive right to produce a product. The second way is to grant a firm a public franchise, which makes it the exclusive legal provider of a good or service.
5	b	There are network externalities in the consumption of a product if the usefulness of the product increases with the number of people who are using it. The more cell phones that are in use, the more useful they become to consumers.
6	c	A natural monopoly is a situation where economies of scale are so large that one firm can supply the entire market at a lower average total cost than two or more firms.
7	a	With a natural monopoly, the average total cost curve is still falling when it crosses the demand curve (point *A*). If there is only one firm producing electric power in the market and it produces where average cost intersects the demand curve, average total cost will equal $0.04 per kilowatt-hour of electricity produced.
8	b	If the market for electricity is divided between two firms, each producing 15 billion kilowatt-hours, then the average cost of producing electricity rises to $0.06 per kilowatt-hour (point *B*).
9	d	Natural monopoly occurs when firms must make a substantial investment in fixed costs (for example, machinery and equipment) in order to produce any output. As output increases, the increase in variable cost (marginal cost) is relatively small and average fixed cost falls. The net result is that average total cost falls continually until the entire market is supplied.

10	d	In certain markets, cost conditions are such that competition is likely to lead to higher costs and higher prices. These markets are natural monopolies that are well served by one firm.
11	d	Like every other firm, a monopoly maximizes profit by producing where marginal revenue equals marginal cost.
12	c	A monopoly differs from other firms in that a monopoly's demand curve is the same as the demand curve for the product. The textbook emphasizes in Chapter 11 that the market demand curve for wheat was very different from the demand curve for the wheat produced by any one farmer. But if that farmer had a monopoly on wheat production, then the two demand curves would be exactly the same.
13	b	Firms in perfectly competitive markets – such as a farmer in the wheat market – face horizontal demand curves. They are *price takers*. All other firms, including monopolies, are *price makers*. If they raise their price, they will lose some, but not all, of their customers. Therefore, they face a downward-sloping demand curve and a downward-sloping marginal revenue curve as well.
14	b	When a firm cuts the price of a product, one good thing and one bad thing happen. The good thing: It sells more units of the product. The bad thing: It receives less revenue from each unit than it would have received at the higher price.
15	b	Average revenue (*AR*) equals total revenue (*TR*) divided by output (*Q*). For five subscribers, $AR = 225/5 = P = \$45$.
16	c	The marginal revenue on the seventh subscription is \$273 – \$252 = \$21.
17	a	Demand is conceptually the same as average revenue. Total revenue is equal to the number of subscriptions sold per month times the price. Average revenue – or revenue per subscription sold – is equal to total revenue divided by the number of subscriptions sold.
18	d	Profit equals $(P - ATC)Q$. When six units are produced and sold, this amount equals $(\$42 - ATC) \times 6$. The average cost curve must be shown in order to estimate the amount of profit.
19	b	Profit equals $(P - ATC)Q$. When six units are produced and sold, this amount equals $(\$42 - \$30) \times 6 = \$72$.
20	b	A monopoly will produce the quantity that maximizes profit, i.e. the quantity that makes marginal revenue equal to marginal cost. The monopolist will charge the price that consumers are willing to pay as represented by the demand curve.
21	a	Price will be higher and there will be less output under monopoly. Because of this, there will be a decrease in consumer surplus and an increase in producer surplus.
22	a	If the industry is perfectly competitive, price and quantity are determined by the intersection of the supply (*MC*) and demand curves.
23	c	The higher price reduces consumer surplus by the area equal to the rectangle *A* and the triangle *B*.
24	a	Area *A* represents a transfer of consumer surplus to the monopoly.
25	d	Economic surplus is equal to the sum of consumer surplus plus producer surplus. By increasing price and reducing the quantity produced, the monopolist has reduced economic surplus by an amount equal to the areas of the triangles *B* and *C* (shaded in Figure 14-5). This reduction in economic surplus is called *deadweight loss* and represents the loss of economic efficiency due to monopoly.
26	b	We measure producer surplus as the area above the supply curve and below the market price. The increase in price due to monopoly increases producer surplus by an amount equal to rectangle *A*, and reduces it by an amount equal to triangle *C*. Because rectangle *A* is larger than triangle *C*, we know that a monopoly increases producer surplus.

27	d	We can summarize the effects of monopoly as follows: 1. Monopoly causes a reduction in consumer surplus. 2. Monopoly causes an increase in producer surplus. 3. Monopoly causes a reduction in economic efficiency, measured by the deadweight loss.
28	d	The only firms that do not have market power are firms in perfectly competitive markets, who must charge a price equal to marginal cost.
29	a	It is possible to put a dollar value on the loss of economic efficiency by estimating the size of the deadweight loss triangle – as in Figure 14-5.
30	b	Schumpeter argued that economic progress depended on technological change in the form of new products. Schumpeter was unconcerned that firms with market power would charge higher prices than perfectly competitive firms.
31	a	Collusion refers to an agreement among firms to charge the same price or to otherwise not compete.
32	b	Antitrust laws are laws aimed at eliminating collusion and promoting competition among firms.
33	a	The Sherman Act prohibited "restraint of trade," including price fixing and collusion. It also outlawed monopolization.
34	c	The Robinson-Patman Act prohibited charging buyers different prices if the result would reduce competition.
35	a	Horizontal mergers are mergers between firms in the same industry. Vertical mergers are mergers between firms at different stages of production of a good.
36	a	The government is most concerned with horizontal mergers, or mergers between firms in the same industry, because horizontal mergers are more likely to increase market power than vertical mergers.
37	c	When the merger realizes efficiency gains, marginal cost shifts to MC_2 and the profit maximizing level of output becomes Q_3 with a price of P_3.
38	d	One of the fruits of this economic expertise was the joint development by the Department of Justice and FTC of merger guidelines in 1982. The guidelines made it possible for economists and attorneys employed by firms considering a merger to understand whether the government was likely to allow the merger or to oppose it. The guidelines have three main parts: 1. Market definition 2. Measure of concentration 3. Merger standards
39	c	In this case, the Herfindahl-Hirschman Index (HHI) is calculated as follows: $25^2 + 25^2 + 25^2 + 25^2 = 2{,}500$.
40	c	To achieve economic efficiency, regulators should require that the monopoly charge a price equal to its marginal cost.
41	b	This price level corresponds to the level required to cover average total cost, which includes a normal rate of return.

Short Answer Responses

1. The four-firm concentration ratios for both Industry A and Industry B are 80 percent. The HHI for Industry A = $75^2 + 2^2 + 2^2 + 1^2 = 5{,}625$. The HHI for industry B = $20^2 + 20^2 + 20^2 + 20^2 = 1{,}600$. The HHI index indicates a higher level of concentration in Industry A than in Industry B because it accounts for the distribution of market shares among the largest firms in the industries. Concentration ratios do not account for the distribution of markets shares among firms. (In fact, the largest firm in industry A probably has considerable market power.)

2. If the regulated price was less than average total cost, the firm would suffer an economic loss. Investors would demand an interest premium for any funds lent to the firm and the firm's credit rating would suffer. If the firm was publicly owned, stockholders would sell their shares and buy shares of firms that offered a higher return. In the long run, the firm would go out of business. This may well leave consumers worse off than if they had to pay a price higher than marginal cost.

3. Both! Market power can be consistent with a lack of competition and high prices. But market power can be the result of offering consumers products that they want. Wal-Mart and Microsoft are large companies with market power, but they started out as small companies that grew because they offered consumers goods and services they wanted at acceptable prices. The ambivalence toward firms with market power is reflected in the government's policies toward mergers. Mergers that cause market power to increase may be approved if the merging firms can show that efficiencies will result.

4. A patent would have preserved the family's monopoly position but only for a limited time. The textbook explains that "…because the Ecke family kept the technique secret for decades, it was able to maintain a monopoly on the commercial development of the plants." Since the family was able to earn monopoly profits for decades, the absence of a patent probably had little impact on the firm's profits.

5. The first part of the FTC's merger guidelines, market definition, received the most criticism. The textbook notes that "A market consists of all firms making products that consumers view as close substitutes…If our definition of a market is too narrow, a price increase will cause firms to experience a…decline in sales – and profits – as consumers switch to substitutes." Rather than define the relevant market as the "market for ice cream" or the "market for frozen desserts," the FTC chose a more narrow market that seems less competitive. But if prices of "super-premium" ice cream rise, critics argued, consumers are free to buy other frozen deserts (including non-"super-premium" ice cream!) that are close substitutes.

True/False Answers

1. T See the section "Is Any Firm Ever Really a Monopoly?" beginning on page 474 of the textbook.
2. F A patent grants an inventor exclusive rights to a product for 20 years.
3. T See "Merger Standards" on page 492 of the textbook.
4. F The Sherman Act (1890) contained these provisions.
5. F Joseph Schumpeter argues that large firms are more readily able to have funds available to use for research and development.
6. T See the section "Antitrust Laws and Antitrust Enforcement" beginning on page 488.
7. F Charging the "highest price possible" means charging the price at the very top of the demand curve and (presumably) selling only one unit. That is rarely the profit-maximizing price.
8. T The monopolist faces the entire market demand curve as it is the only firm providing the good.
9. T The control of a key resource, in this case the stadium, is a barrier to entry.
10. F This is a narrow definition of monopoly.
11. T This is the definition of a public franchise.
12. T Generic drugs are drugs that are no longer protected by patents and are produced by a number of pharmaceutical companies.
13. F A merger between firms that produce the same product would be a horizontal merger.
14. T See the section "The Department of Justice and Federal Trade Commission Merger Guidelines" beginning on page 491.
15. F Microsoft discovered that it had to charge the same price as Sony due to competition. This price was not set by the government.

Chapter 15

Pricing Strategy

Chapter Summary

Pricing strategies are one way firms attempt to increase their economic profits. An example of a pricing strategy is **price discrimination**, which means charging different prices for the same good or service when the price differences are not due to cost differences. The possibility of **arbitrage**, buying a product in one market at a low price and reselling it in another market at a higher price, limits the ability of firms to use price discrimination. Successful price discrimination requires that (1) some consumers have a greater willingness to pay than other consumers and (2) firms must be able to segment the market for a product so arbitrage is not possible. If a firm is able to price discriminate in any way, it will charge a higher price to the consumer group with less elastic demand.

Perfect price discrimination occurs when a firm is able to charge the price each consumer is willing to pay, leaving consumers with zero consumer surplus. Perfect price discrimination is unlikely because it is difficult for firms to know each consumer's willingness to pay and to charge every consumer a different price. Some consumers are willing to pay more for a product when it is first introduced. Over time, firms will charge lower prices to attract consumers who have a lower willingness to pay.

Firms also use other pricing strategies to increase profits:

1. Odd pricing: The firm charges a price such as $4.98 rather than $5.00, to give consumers the illusion that the difference in price is greater than it actually is.
2. Cost-plus pricing: The firm sets a price by adding a mark-up to the average cost of production. Cost-plus pricing may be the best way to determine the optimal price when the firm's marginal cost and average cost are roughly equal and the firm has difficulty estimating its demand curve for each product it sells.
3. Two-part tariff: The firm requires consumers to pay an initial fee for the right to buy its product and an additional fee for each unit of the product purchased.

Learning Objectives

When you finish this chapter, you should be able to:

1. **Define the law of one price and explain the role of arbitrage**. The law of one price states that identical products should sell for the same price everywhere. This law holds only if there are no transactions costs. Arbitrage – buying a product at a low price and reselling it in another market at a high price – ensures that a product will sell for the same price everywhere.

2. **Explain how a firm can increase its profits through price discrimination**. Some consumers have a greater willingness to pay than other consumers. To profit from price discrimination, a firm must be

able to divide up the market for its product so that consumers who buy the product at a low price are not able to resell it at a high price. Price discrimination will not work if arbitrage is possible.

3. **Explain how some firms increase their profits through the use of odd pricing, cost-plus pricing, and two-part tariffs.** Many firms use odd pricing – for example, charging $4.95 instead of $5.00. There is some evidence that odd pricing results in a greater quantity demanded because the lower price seems more significant than it is. Firms use cost-plus pricing, which is setting price equal to average cost plus a percentage markup, when they have difficulty estimating the demand for a product or when marginal and average cost are nearly equal. A two-part tariff requires consumers to pay a fee for the right to buy a product and an additional fee for each unit purchased. Firms can use a two-part tariff to convert economic surplus into profit.

Chapter Review

Chapter Opener: Getting into Walt Disney World: One Price Does Not Fit All (pages 506-507)

Walt Disney World charges different consumers different prices for admission based on their willingness to pay. When Disneyland opened in 1955, the Disney company charged different prices for admission into the park *and* had a separate charge for rides. Today, there is a high price for admission to Disneyland and Walt Disney World but once a customer is in the park the rides are free. This change in strategy was designed to increase profits.

Helpful Study Hint

Test your understanding of Walt Disney's pricing strategy by working end-of-chapter problem 2.15. An ***Inside Look*** at the end of this chapter describes how colleges and universities offer different financial aid packages to different students. As a result, students pay a variety of actual tuition prices.

Economics in YOUR Life! asks you to think about why movie theaters often charge different groups of consumers different prices for admission, but not different prices for popcorn. Test your understanding of the material in this chapter by answering this question, then check your answer with the analysis the authors provide at the end of the chapter.

15.1 LEARNING OBJECTIVE

15.1 Pricing Strategy, the Law of One Price, and Arbitrage (pages 508-510)

Learning Objective 1 Define the law of one price and explain the role of arbitrage.

Firms sometimes increase their profits by practicing **price discrimination**, charging different prices to different consumers for the same product when the price differences are not due to differences in cost. The development of information technology has made it possible for firms to gather information on consumers' preferences and their responsiveness to price changes. This practice, called yield management, is particularly important to airlines and hotels. To practice price discrimination, firms must prevent arbitrage. Arbitrage is the process of buying a product in one market at a low price and reselling it in another market at a higher price. Arbitrage explains the law of one price: Identical products should sell for the same price everywhere.

The law of one price holds only if transactions costs are zero. **Transactions costs** are costs in time and other resources that parties incur in the process of agreeing to and carrying out an exchange of goods or services.

Helpful Study Hint

Arbitrage explains why differences in prices for shares of stock, commodities—such as gold or oil—and foreign currencies in different markets are short-lived. Buying and selling in these markets is done quickly and transactions costs are relatively small. Working through ***Solved Problem 15-1*** will help you understand how arbitrage serves a useful economic purpose. Auctions conducted through eBay, for example, provide benefits for both sellers and buyers.

15.2 LEARNING OBJECTIVE

15.2 Price Discrimination: Charging Different Prices for the Same Product (pages 510-519)

Learning Objective 2 Explain how a firm can increase its profits through price discrimination.

Charging different prices to different consumers for the same product when the price differences are not due to differences in cost is called **price discrimination**. Successful price discrimination has three requirements.

1. A firm must possess market power.
2. Some consumers must have a greater willingness to pay for the product than others, and the firm must know the prices consumers are willing to pay.
3. The firm must be able to segment the market so consumers who buy the product at a low price cannot resell it at a high price. Firms will charge a higher price to consumers whose demand is less elastic than other consumers.

Airlines have a strong incentive to use price discrimination to manage their prices because airline seats are a perishable product, and the marginal cost of flying one additional passenger is low. Airlines divide their customers into two main categories: business travelers who are not very sensitive to changes in price, and leisure passengers who are sensitive to changes in price. Airlines use yield management to make frequent price adjustments in response to fluctuations in demand.

Firms sometimes engage in price discrimination over time. These firms charge a higher price for a product when it is first introduced and a lower price later. This pattern was followed by firms that sold products such as HD-DVD players and digital cameras. Book publishers routinely use price discrimination over time to increase their profits. Hardcover editions of novels have much higher prices and are published months before paperback editions.

The Robinson-Patman Act of 1936 outlawed price discrimination *if* its effect is to reduce competition in an industry. In recent years, the courts have interpreted Robinson-Patman to allow firms to use common types of price discrimination.

Helpful Study Hint

Read ***Solved Problem 15-2*** to understand how price discrimination can increase profits from selling Dell computers. Figure 15-2 shows how airlines can sell seats on the same flight for many different prices. The first ***Making the Connection*** feature in this section describes an example of price discrimination you should find interesting: offering different financial aid packages to college students based on differences in the price elasticity of demand. A second ***Making the Connection*** describes a different type of price discrimination: charging the same price for goods or services of different quality. ***Don't Let This Happen to YOU!*** explains the difference between price discrimination and other types of discrimination. You can test your understanding of the topics described in this section by completing end-of-chapter problems 2.12, 2.14, 2.17, and 2.18.

15.3 LEARNING OBJECTIVE

15.3 Other Pricing Strategies (pages 519-524)

Learning Objective 3 Explain how some firms increase their profits through the use of odd pricing, cost-plus pricing, and two-part tariffs.

In addition to price discrimination, firms can use the strategy of odd pricing. Odd pricing refers to charging prices just less than even dollar amounts—for example, \$3.98 instead of \$4.00—to give the appearance that the price is less than it really is. Some evidence supports the effectiveness of odd pricing in increasing profits, but this evidence is not conclusive.

Another pricing strategy is cost-plus pricing. Cost-plus pricing involves adding a percentage markup to average cost to determine prices. This technique may be a good way to approximate the profit-maximizing price when marginal cost or marginal revenue are difficult to estimate. A **two-part tariff** is another pricing strategy. This is a situation in which consumers pay one price (or tariff) for the right to buy as much of a related good as they want at a second price. An amusement park that charges an admission fee and also separate fees for rides is using a two-part tariff.

Helpful Study Hint

Making the Connection in this section describes how the publishing industry uses cost-plus pricing.

Recall that ***Economics in YOUR Life!*** at the beginning of this chapter asked you to explain why movie theaters charge different prices for admission based on differences in consumers' willingness to pay, but do not charge different prices for popcorn. After reading this chapter, you probably have solved this mystery. Theaters can prevent consumers who pay low prices for admission tickets from reselling these tickets to consumers who are willing to pay higher prices. For example, the theater can require identification to gain admission with a discounted student or senior citizen ticket. It is much more difficult to prevent resale of popcorn and other movie concessions, which are sold to all customers for the same prices.

Extra Solved Problem 15-3

Chapter 15 includes two Solved Problems. Here is an extra Solved Problem to help you build your skills solving economic problems.

Supports Learning Objective 3: Explain how some firms increase their profits through the use of odd pricing, cost-plus pricing, and two-part tariffs.

Tennis Anyone?

The Topeka (Kansas) Racquet Club charges club members a monthly membership fee as well as an hourly fee to use its indoor tennis courts. The following graph illustrates the Racquet Club's demand, marginal revenue and marginal cost curves. Because marginal cost is constant, it is also equal to average cost ($2). The graph shows that if the Club charges a fee of $11 per hour, Club members will use the tennis courts a total of 9,000 hours in a month. This is the quantity where marginal revenue equals marginal cost. The Club's profit from its court fees for one month is equal to area *A* in the diagram ($11 – $2) x 9,000 = $81,000.

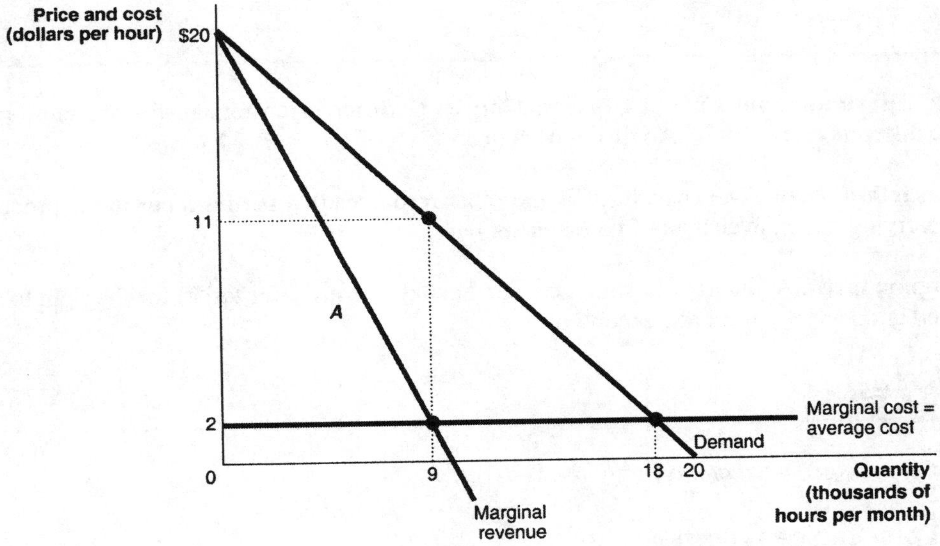

a. What is the maximum amount the Club can charge as a monthly fee if it charges an $11 per hour court fee?

b. Is it possible for the Club to charge a different hourly court fee and increase its profit?

SOLVING THE PROBLEM

Step 1: Review the chapter material.
This problem is about pricing strategies, so you may want to review the section "Other Pricing Strategies" which begins on page 519 of the textbook.

Step 2: Answer question (a) by calculating the maximum monthly fee the Club can charge.
When Club charges an $11 hourly fee, members receive a total consumer surplus of [1/2 x ($20 – $11) x 9,000 = $40,500]. Assuming that Club members are only interested in joining the Club to play tennis and the club is able to perfectly price discriminate in setting the monthly fee, total revenue from monthly fees can be as much as $40,500. If the Club has no other costs, then the maximum total profit it would receive would be $81,000 + $40,500 = $121,500.

Step 3: Answer question (b) by explaining whether the Club can increase its profits by changing its court fee from $11 per hour.
Club members would receive the maximum amount of consumer surplus if there were no hourly court fee. Consumer surplus would equal the areas under the demand curve: ½ x $20 x 20,000 = $200,000. This is the maximum total revenue the Club could receive from monthly membership fees. If members used the courts 20,000 hours, the Club's total cost would be $2 x 20,000 = $40,000. Assuming the Club received the maximum amount of revenue in the form of monthly fees, the Club's profit would be: $200,000 – $40,000 = $160,000. More profit would result if the club charged a $2 per hour court fee (this would cover all of its costs) and received the value of the consumer surplus (1/2 x 18 x 18,000 = $162,000).

Key Terms

Price discrimination. Charging different prices to different customers for the same product when the price differences are not due to differences in cost.

Transactions costs. The costs in time and other resources that parties incur in the process of agreeing to and carrying out an exchange of goods or services.

Two-part tariff. A situation in which consumers pay one price (or tariff) for the right to buy as much of a related good as they want at a second price.

Self-Test

(Answers are provided at the end of the Self-Test.)

Multiple-Choice Questions

1. Which of the following is the main purpose of pricing strategies?
   a. To increase economic profit
   b. To gain market share
   c. To find information about consumers
   d. To stay ahead of the competition

2. What name is given to the practice of gathering information on consumers' preferences and using it to rapidly adjust prices?
   a. Price discrimination
   b. Arbitrage
   c. Yield management
   d. Odd pricing

3. According to the *law of one price*, which of the following must be true?
   a. Identical products should sell for the same price everywhere.
   b. Perfectly competitive firms must end up charging the same price for their products.
   c. In a homogeneous economy, all goods should be sold for the same price.
   d. Market forces ensure that the price in a market is always a single price.

4. What name is given to the practice of buying a product in one market at a low price and almost simultaneously reselling it in another market at a high price?
   a. Price discrimination
   b. Speculation
   c. Arbitrage
   d. Cost-plus pricing

5. What name is given to the costs in time and other resources that parties incur in the process of agreeing to and carrying out an exchange of goods and services?
   a. Shoe-leather costs
   b. Arbitrage profits
   c. Shipping costs
   d. Transactions costs

6. When does the *law of one price* hold exactly?
   a. When transactions costs are zero
   b. When transaction costs are minimized
   c. When transaction costs are maximized
   d. When it is impossible to resell a product

7. When will firms be able to price discriminate?
   a. When the law of one price does not hold and it is impossible to resell a product
   b. When the law of one price holds and it is possible to resell a product
   c. When the law of one price does not hold but it is possible to resell a product
   d. When the law of one price holds but it is not possible to resell a product

8. According to economists, does the practice of selling and reselling goods on eBay have a useful economic purpose?
   a. No; selling and reselling does not add any value to the goods exchanged.
   b. Yes; if people are willing to participate, they must be made better off.
   c. Yes, but the value added is difficult to measure.
   d. No; participants usually end up paying more on eBay than they would have paid elsewhere.

9. Table 15-1 of the textbook is reproduced below. How is the difference in prices explained in the textbook?

PRODUCT: *HARRY POTTER AND THE DEATHLY HALLOWS*	
COMPANY	PRICE
Amazon.com	$18.89
BarnesandNoble.com	18.89
WaitForeverForYourOrder.com	17.50
JustStartedinBusinessLastWednesday.com	16.75

   a. The law of one price appears to be violated in this case.
   b. Booksellers must not be offering identical products.
   c. Competitors must be competing strictly on the basis of price.
   d. All of the above

10. When is charging different prices to different buyers *not* considered price discrimination?
   a. If the difference in price is due to differences in cost
   b. If the difference in price is due to differences in demand
   c. If the difference in price is due to differences in consumer preferences
   d. If the difference in price is due to differences in elasticity

11. Which of the following is a requirement for successful price discrimination?
   a. A firm must possess market power.
   b. Some consumers must have a greater willingness to pay for the product than other consumers, and the firm must be able to know what prices customers are willing to pay.
   c. The firm must be able to divide up – or segment – the market.
   d. All of the above

12. Which of the following is true if *arbitrage* is possible?
   a. Price discrimination will work.
   b. Price discrimination will not work.
   c. Price discrimination will work but only under specific conditions.
   d. The market cannot be segmented.

13. If products cannot be resold, which of the following is true?
   a. Firms can practice price discrimination.
   b. The law of one price is contradicted.
   c. Firms can only charge the market price.
   d. Firms must be perfectly competitive.

14. Refer to the graphs below. Which strategy will maximize profit?

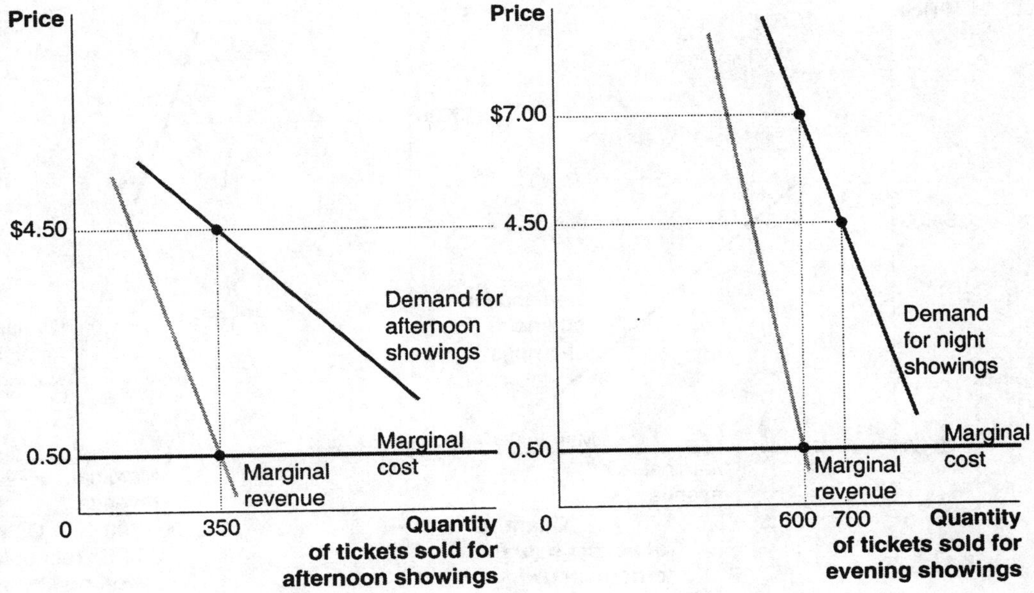

a. Charging $4.50 to all customers.
b. Setting marginal revenue equal to marginal cost in the market shown on the left.
c. Charging $7.00 to all customers.
d. None of the above

15. Refer to the graphs below. Which demand curve is relatively more elastic?

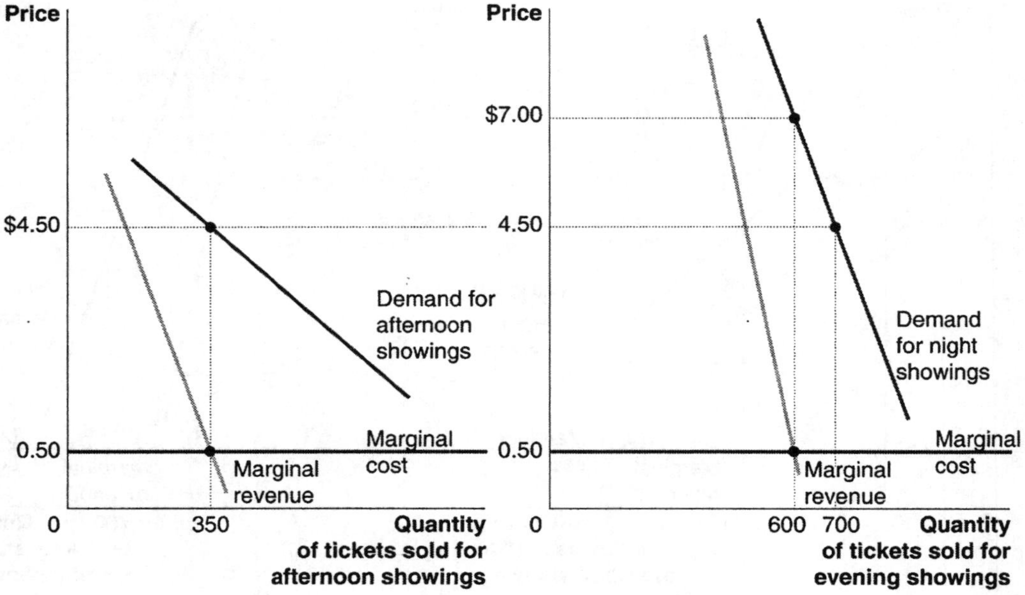

a. The demand curve for afternoon showings
b. The demand curve for night showings
c. Both demand curves have the same elasticity value.
d. Neither demand curve is elastic; they are both relatively inelastic.

16. Refer to the graphs below. Which customers have a lower price elasticity of demand?

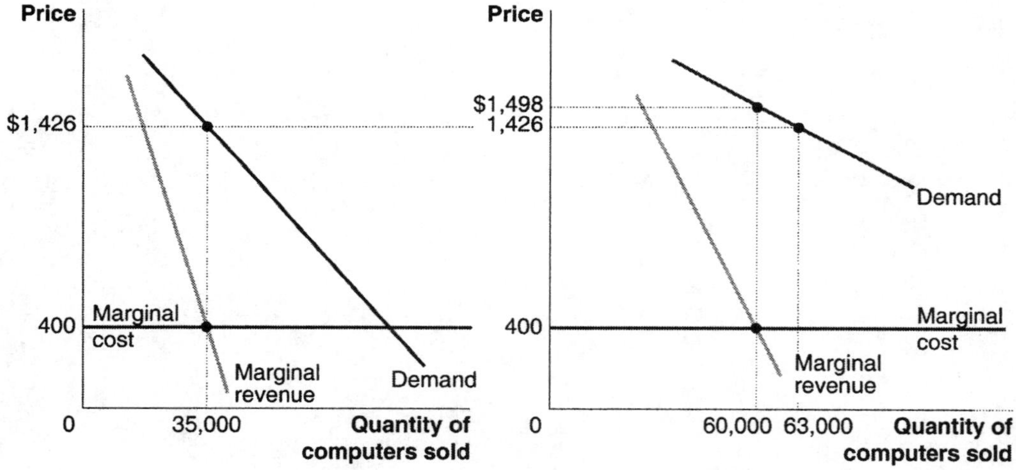

(a) Health-care customers **(b) Education customers**

a. The health-care customers
b. The education customers
c. Both have the same elasticity of demand.
d. Education workers have a higher elasticity but only when charged the higher price.

17. Refer to the graphs below. How can a price-discriminating firm maximize profit?

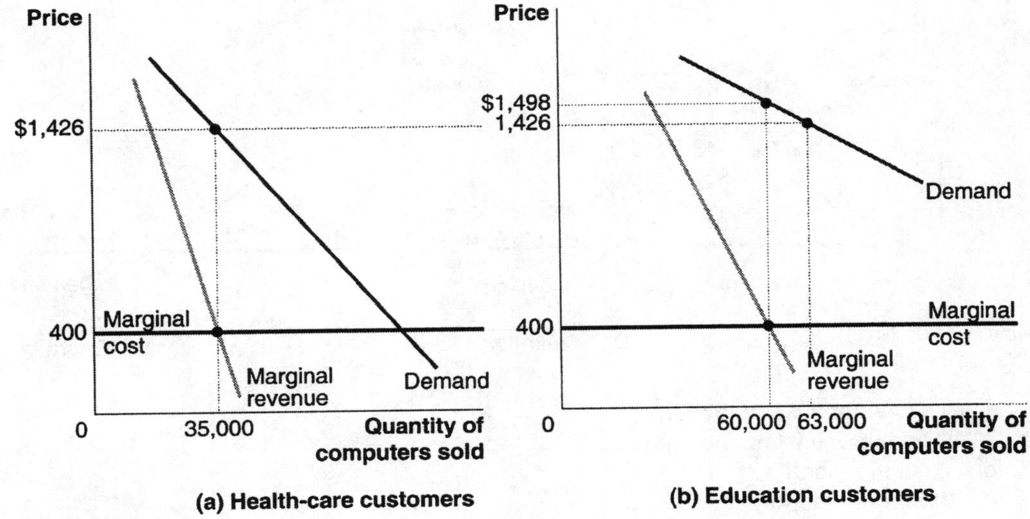

a. By setting marginal revenue equal to marginal cost in the health-care segment and charging all customers the corresponding price.
b. By setting price in each segment according to the price elasticity of demand and charging each segment the corresponding price.
c. By charging a higher price to education customers since they have a higher price elasticity of demand.
d. By charging the highest prices to consumers with the greatest incomes.

18. Which of the following industries uses sophisticated methods to calculate the price of each unit sold each day?
a. College education
b. Airlines
c. Wheat producers
d. All of the above

19. Which of the following is known as *first-degree price discrimination*?
a. Perfect price discrimination
b. Imperfect price discrimination
c. Zero price discrimination
d. Exponential price discrimination

20. Which of the following is a result of *perfect price discrimination*?
a. Maximum consumer surplus
b. Price is greater than marginal cost
c. Zero consumer surplus
d. Infinite consumer surplus

21. Refer to the graphs below. Which monopolist is practicing perfect price discrimination?

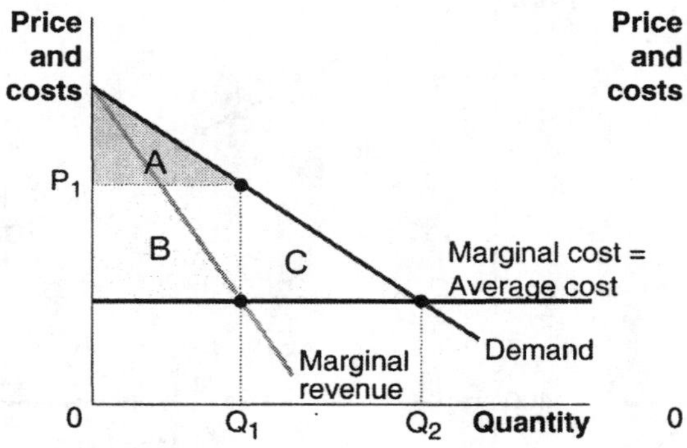

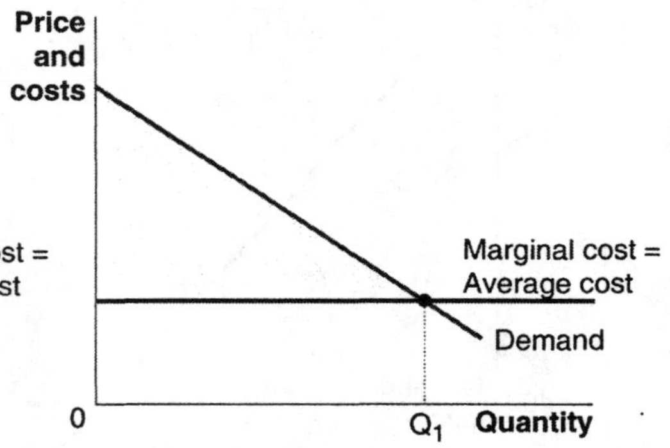

a. The monopolist on the left
b. The monopolist on the right
c. Both monopolies
d. Neither monopoly

22. Refer to the graphs below. In which case does the existence of a monopoly result in a larger amount of consumer surplus?

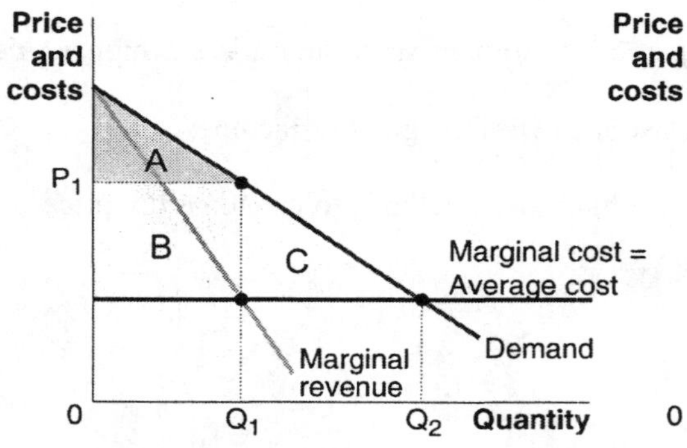

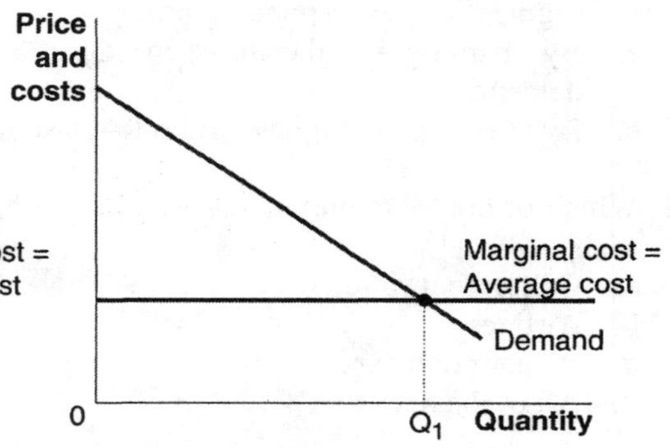

a. In the case of the monopolist on the left
b. In the case of the monopolist on the right
c. In both cases
d. In neither case

23. Refer to the graphs below. In which case does the existence of a monopoly result in a larger deadweight loss?

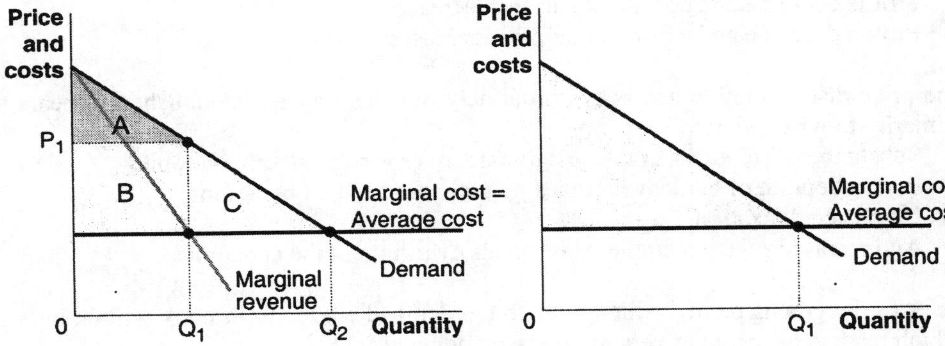

a. In the case of the monopolist on the left
b. In the case of the monopolist on the right
c. In both cases
d. In neither case

24. Refer to the graphs below. With which monopolist is economic efficiency the highest?

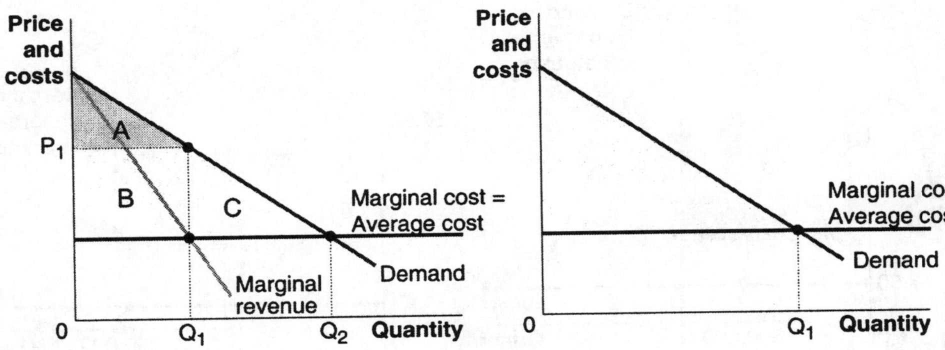

a. The monopolist on the left
b. The monopolist on the right
c. Both monopolists
d. Neither monopolist

25. Which of the following statements is true about price discrimination?
a. Under certain circumstances, price discrimination could improve economic efficiency.
b. In some cases, except for perfect price discrimination, other types of price discrimination could reduce economic efficiency.
c. No general conclusion can be drawn about the effects of price discrimination on economic efficiency.
d. All of the above.

26. Which of the following are key results of price discrimination?
    a. Profits increase and consumer surplus increases
    b. Profits increase and consumer surplus decreases
    c. Profits decrease and consumer surplus decreases
    d. Profits decrease and consumer surplus increases

27. The price discrimination across time routinely practiced by book publishers appears to be attributed primarily to what event?
    a. Substantial differences in the cost of hardcover versus paperback copies
    b. Early adoption of hardcover copies by the most devoted book fans
    c. Unexpected taxation
    d. An increase in the general level of prices over time in the economy

28. Refer to the graphs below, which refer to the demand curves for a book written by a popular author. Which readers have a relatively more elastic demand?

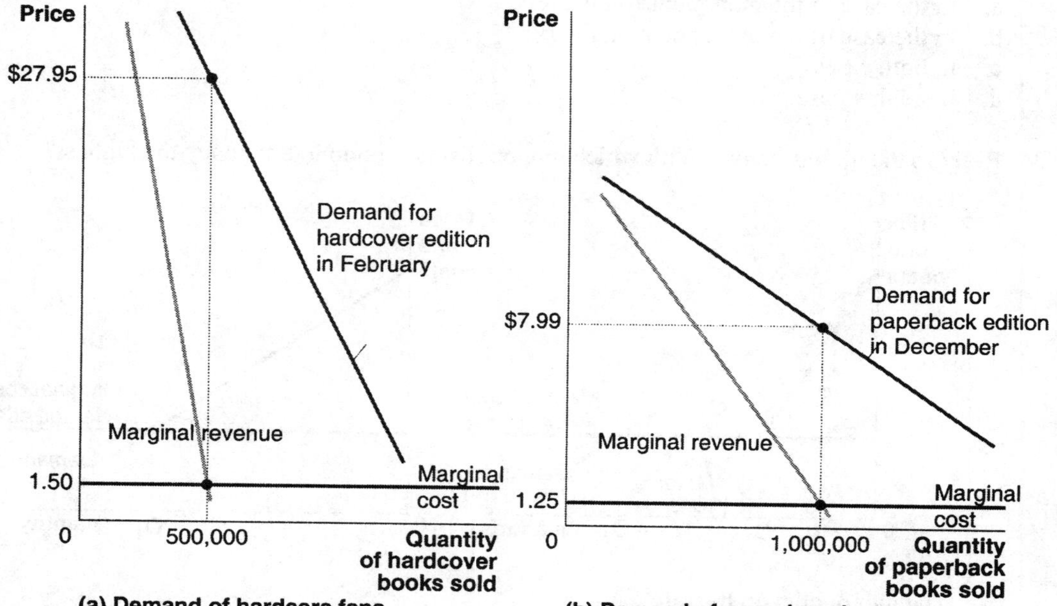

(a) Demand of hardcore fans (b) Demand of casual readers

    a. Casual readers
    b. Hardcore fans
    c. Both have very elastic demands
    d. Neither casual readers nor hardcore fans have elastic demands; they both have inelastic demands.

29. Which of the following price-discriminating strategies used by insurance companies has been accepted by the courts?
    a. Charging women lower prices than men for automobile insurance
    b. Charging blacks higher life insurance prices than whites (who have longer life spans)
    c. Discriminating on the basis of arbitrary characteristics
    d. All of the above

30. Which of the following facts related to odd pricing was found in surveys of consumers about their willingness to purchase a product?
    a. People connect odd prices with high-quality goods.
    b. The quantity demanded of goods with odd prices was greater than predicted using an estimated demand curve.
    c. Odd prices prevent employee theft.
    d. All of the above

31. In *cost-plus pricing*, a percentage markup is added to which of the following measures?
    a. Average cost
    b. Marginal cost
    c. Total cost
    d. Implicit cost

32. In a firm selling multiple products, what is the intent of *cost-plus pricing*?
    a. To segment the market
    b. To cover all costs, including those that are difficult to assign
    c. To increase economic profit
    d. To obtain a better idea of the demand curve

33. What are the views of economists about *cost-plus pricing*?
    a. Cost-plus pricing is simply a mistake that firms should avoid.
    b. Cost-plus pricing ignores demand.
    c. Cost-plus does not appear to maximize profits since it ignores marginal cost.
    d. All of the above

34. According to economists, which of the following is a condition under which cost-plus pricing could be the best way to determine the optimal price?
    a. When marginal cost differs substantially from average cost
    b. When the firm has difficulty estimating its demand curve
    c. Both of the above
    d. None of the above

35. Fill in the blanks: In general, companies that take demand into account will charge __________ markups on products that are ________ price elastic.
    a. higher; more
    b. lower; more
    c. zero; less
    d. zero; relatively

36. Which of the following are pricing schemes associated with a *two-part tariff*?
    a. Annual memberships and hourly court rental fees at tennis clubs
    b. Monthly fees for cellular phone subscriptions
    c. Fees for shopping privileges at a certain store
    d. All of the above

37. Refer to the graphs below. Which graph shows a higher profit obtained from the sale of ride tickets?

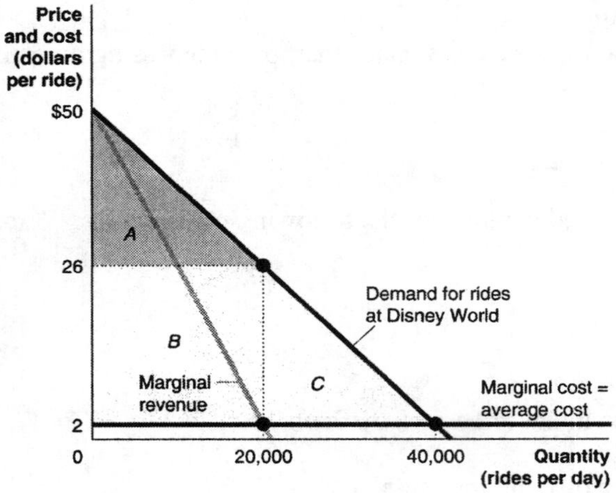

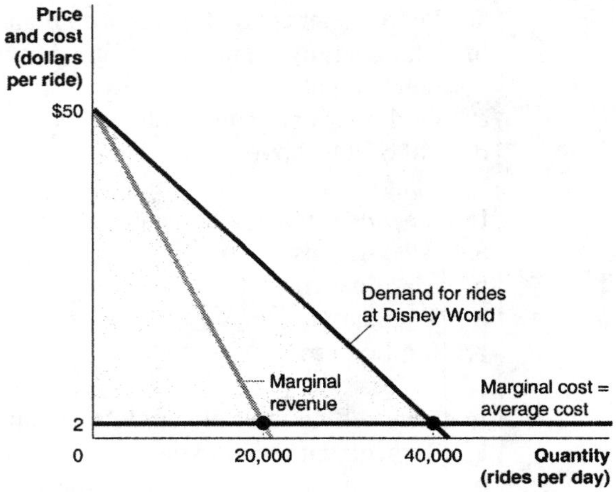

a. The graph on the left
b. The graph on the right
c. The amount of profit is the same in both graphs.
d. None of the above; neither graph shows any profit associated with the sale of ride tickets.

38. Refer to the graphs below. Which graph shows a larger deadweight loss?

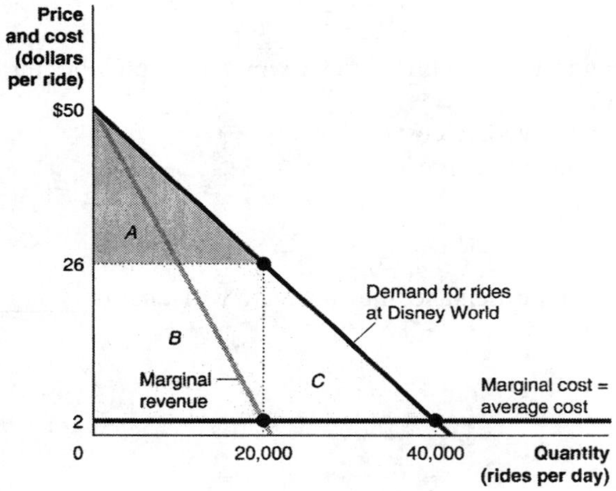

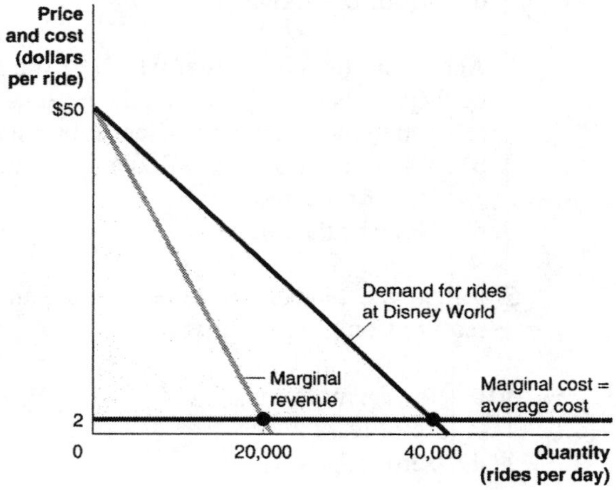

a. The graph on the left
b. The graph on the right
c. The amount of profit is the same in both graphs.
d. None of the above; neither graph shows any profit associated with the sale of ride tickets.

39. Refer to the graphs below. Which case results in a higher profit for the monopolist?

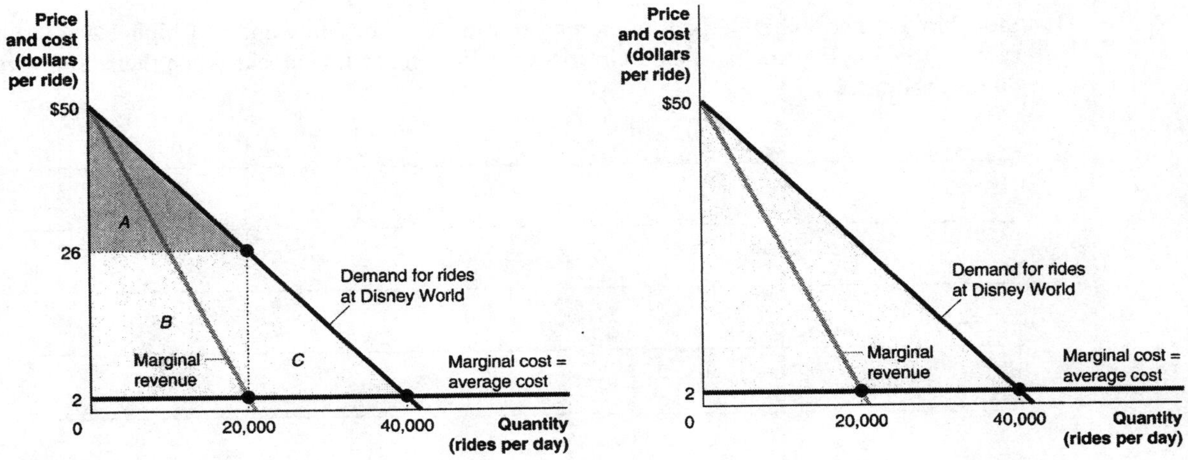

a. The graph on the left
b. The graph on the right
c. The amount of profit is the same in both graphs.
d. None of the above; neither graph shows any profit associated with the sale of ride tickets.

40. Refer to the graphs below. Which outcome is economically efficient?

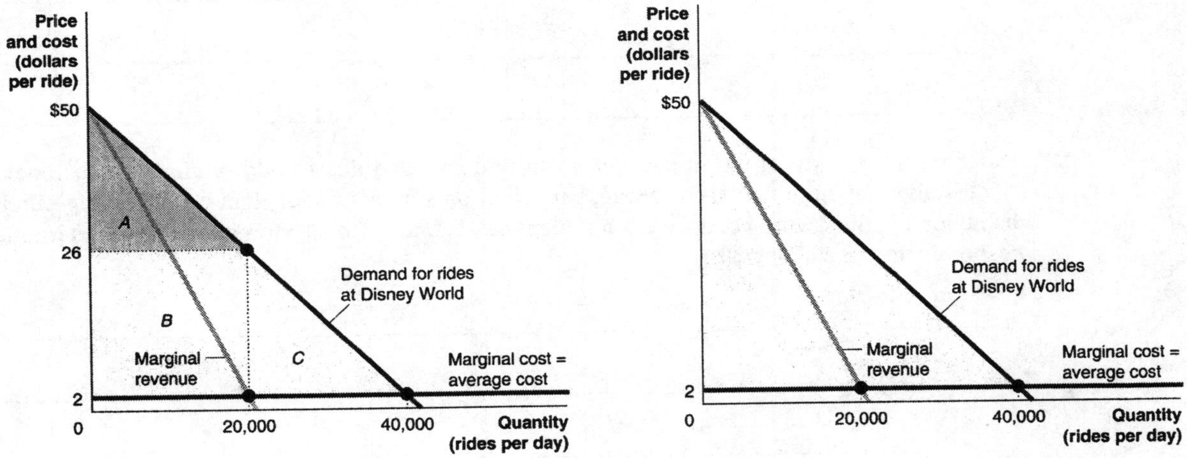

a. The outcome shown in the graph on the left.
b. The outcome shown in the graph on the right.
c. Both outcomes are economically efficient.
d. Neither outcome is economically efficient.

Short Answer Questions

1. Stockbrokers know that the key to earning profits is to "buy low and sell high." Are the profits earned from buying stocks when their prices are low and selling stocks when their prices are high due to arbitrage?

2. The web site of Priceline.com featured the following advertisement: "Last-Minute Cruises – Sail within 30 days and Save!" Why do cruise lines offer discount fares on Priceline.com?

3. Referring to a study of the impact on quantity demanded due to odd pricing, the textbook says: "The study was not conclusive because it relied on surveys rather than on observing purchasing behavior…" Why would consumers not respond accurately to surveys designed to determine their responses to price changes?

4. An economist from a university in California noted that the parking lots on his campus offer a good example of price discrimination. There are "faculty only" parking spaces in lots located close to university classrooms and offices while student spaces are located in more remote locations. Price discrimination requires a firm (in this case, the university) to segment its market so that consumers with a greater willingness to pay than other consumers can be identified. How can the university identify those students who have the greatest willingness to pay for parking spaces located close to classroom buildings?

____

____

____

____

____

____

5. The ***Making the Connection*** features on page 515 in this chapter describe the yield management techniques colleges and universities use to maximize tuition revenue and improve the quality of students they enroll. Since students are charged different prices (tuition minus financial aid) for the same service, yield management results in price discrimination. Is this form of price discrimination legal?

____

____

____

____

____

____

True/False Questions

T F 1. The profits received from engaging in arbitrage are referred to as *transactions profits*.

T F 2. Yield management refers to the gathering of information on consumer preferences and consumers' responsiveness to price changes in order to adjust prices rapidly.

T F 3. There is no evidence that odd-pricing is an effective pricing strategy.

T F 4. The Sherman Act (1890) made price discrimination illegal if its effect is to reduce competition in an industry.

T F 5. *Early adopters* are consumers who are willing to pay a high price to be among the first to own a product.

T F 6. Price discrimination causes consumer surplus to decrease.

T F 7. Perfect price discrimination results in no consumer surplus.

T F 8. Two-part tariffs result in a reduction in economic efficiency because consumers pay higher prices than they would if they paid only one price.

T F 9. Cost-price pricing is the best way to determine the optimal price when the marginal cost of production is much lower than the average cost of production.

T F 10. Book publishers often engage in price discrimination over time.

T F 11. Perfect price discrimination is often used by natural monopolies because of their high barriers to entry.

T F 12. Colleges that use yield management techniques typically offer less generous financial aid packages (other things being equal) to students who apply for early admission.

T F 13. Perfect price discrimination can convert a deadweight loss and consumer surplus into profit.

T F 14. Price discrimination occurs only in monopoly and oligopoly markets.

T F 15. Transactions costs are incurred in the process of carrying out an exchange of goods or services.

Answers to the Self-Test

Multiple-Choice Questions

Question	Answer	Explanation
1	a	Pricing strategies are one way firms attempt to increase their economic profits.
2	c	The practice of gathering information on consumers' preferences and the responsiveness of consumers to changes in prices, and using it to rapidly adjust prices is called *yield management*.
3	a	According to the law of one price, identical products should sell for the same price everywhere.
4	c	Buying a product in one market at a low price and reselling it in another market at a high price is referred to as *arbitrage*.
5	d	The costs of carrying out a transaction – by, for example, listing items on eBay and shipping them across the country – are called transactions costs.
6	a	The law of one price holds exactly only if transactions costs are zero.
7	a	In cases where it is impossible to resell a product, the law of one price will not hold and firms will be able to price discriminate.
8	b	Both the person who sold and the person who bought an item from eBay must have been made better off by the deals, or they would not have made them.
9	b	The difference in the prices of products offered on web sites does not violate the law of one price. A book offered for sale by Amazon.com is not the same product as a book offered for sale by JustStartedinBusinessLastWednesday.com.
10	a	Charging different prices to different customers for the same product, when the price differences are not due to differences in cost, is called *price discrimination*.
11	d	There are three requirements for a successful strategy of price discrimination: 1. A firm must possess market power. 2. Some consumers must have a greater willingness to pay for the product than other consumers, and the firm must be able to know what prices customers are willing to pay. 3. The firm must be able to divide up – or segment – the market.
12	b	The firm must be able to divide up – or segment – the market for the product so that consumers who buy the product at a low price are not able to resell it a high price. In other words, price discrimination will not work if arbitrage is possible.

13	a	Only firms that can keep consumers from reselling a product are able to practice price discrimination. Because the product cannot be resold, the law of one price is not contradicted.
14	d	To maximize profits, the theater should charge $4.50 for afternoon showings and $7.00 for night showings.
15	a	Since demand for afternoon showings is more elastic, these customers will pay a lower price than customers at night who have less elastic demands.
16	b	Because education customers are being charged the higher price, they must have a lower price elasticity of demand than health care customers.
17	b	The firm maximizes its profits by charging education customers a higher price than health-care customers.
18	b	Airlines have a strong incentive to manage prices so that as many seats as possible are filled on each flight.
19	a	If a firm knew every consumer's willingness to pay – and could keep consumers who bought at a low price from reselling the product – it could charge every consumer a different price. This is the case of *perfect price discrimination* – also known as *first-degree price discrimination*.
20	c	In this case of perfect price discrimination – also known as first-degree price discrimination – each consumer would have to pay a price equal to his willingness to pay and, therefore, would receive no consumer surplus.
21	b	The monopolist on the right is able to perfectly price discriminate by charging a different price to each consumer.
22	a	This monopoly leaves some consumer surplus in existence, while the monopolist on the right turns all consumer surplus into profit.
23	a	In this case, there is a deadweight loss equal to area *C*, while in the case of the monopolist on the right, there is no deadweight loss.
24	b	This monopolist on the right produces the same amount of output as a perfectly competitive industry, at Q_1.
25	d	Less than perfect price discrimination often will improve economic efficiency. But under certain circumstances, it may actually reduce economic efficiency, so we can't draw a general conclusion.
26	b	The two key results of price discrimination are that profits increase and consumer surplus decreases.
27	b	The difference in price between the hardcover and paperback is driven primarily by differences in demand. The author's most devoted fans want to read his next book at the earliest possible moment and are not too sensitive to price. Many casual readers are also interested in this author's books, but will read something else if the price is too high.
28	a	In panel (b), the more elastic demand of casual readers and the slightly lower marginal cost results in a profit-maximizing output of 1,000,000 for the paperback edition, sold at a price of $7.99.
29	a	The courts have ruled that this is not illegal discrimination under the civil rights laws because women, on average, have better driving records than men. Because the costs of insuring men are higher than insuring women, insurance companies are allowed to charge men higher prices.
30	b	Researchers surveyed consumers about their willingness to purchase different products at a series of prices. Ten of the prices were either odd cent prices – 99 cents or 95 cents – or odd dollar prices – $95 or $99. For 9 of these 10 odd prices there was an odd price effect, with the quantity demanded being greater than predicted using the estimated demand curve.

31	a	Many firms use cost-plus pricing, which involves adding a percentage markup to average cost. With this pricing strategy, the firm first calculates average cost at a particular level of production, usually equal to the firm's expected sales.
32	b	In a firm selling multiple products, the markup is intended to cover all costs, including those that the firm cannot assign to any particular product. Many firms have costs that are difficult to assign to one particular product.
33	d	Economists have two views of cost-plus pricing. One is that cost-plus pricing is simply a mistake that firms should avoid. The other view is that cost-plus pricing is a good way to at least come close to the profit-maximizing price when marginal revenue or marginal cost is difficult to calculate. The most obvious problems with cost-plus pricing are that it ignores demand and focuses on average cost, rather than marginal cost.
34	b	Economists conclude that cost-plus pricing may be the best way to determine the optimal price when: 1. Marginal cost and average cost are roughly equal. 2. The firm has difficulty estimating its demand curve.
35	b	In general, companies that take demand into account will charge lower markups on products that are more price elastic and higher markups on products that are less price elastic.
36	d	A *two-part tariff* is a situation where consumers pay one price (or tariff) for the right to buy as much of a related good as they want at a second price.
37	a	In the graph on the left, Disney charges the monopoly price of $26 per ride ticket, and sells 20,000 ride tickets. Its profit from ride tickets is shown by the area of triangle *B*, $480,000. In the graph on the right, the profit from ride tickets equals zero.
38	a	In this case, Disney charges the monopoly price of $26 per ride ticket, and sells 20,000 ride tickets. The deadweight loss equals area *C*. In the graph on the right, there is no deadweight loss.
39	b	In this case, Disney sets the price of admission to capture the entire consumer surplus from the rides.
40	b	In this case, because price equals marginal cost at the level of output supplied, the outcome is economically efficient.

Short Answer Responses

1. No. Arbitrage refers to buying a product in a market where the price is low and selling it in a market where the price is high *at the same time*. Although arbitrage transactions do take place in stock markets, most buying occurs with the expectation that stocks can be sold at a higher price at some time in the future. Traders profit from selling stocks when the prices they sell at are higher than the prices at which they bought the stocks at some earlier period of time.

2. Both airlines and cruise ships have high fixed costs but very low marginal costs from adding passengers to what would otherwise be a partially full cruise. Even at prices drastically lower than prices paid by other passengers who booked their travel well ahead of the cruise, almost all of the discount fares will add to profits.

3. Survey responses may be inaccurate even when responses are truthful. This is especially true when consumers are asked for their responses to price changes for items they do not buy on a regular basis. It is difficult for respondents to determine what a "high" or "low" price is for an item they have not recently purchased. What someone says she will do can differ from what she actually will do. This does not mean she has lied. Inevitably, survey responses are less accurate than actual purchasing behavior.

4. In order to restrict access to the faculty parking lots, the university fines students who park in faculty-designated spaces. University officials can identify these students by their license numbers or the numbers on their parking stickers. Those students with the most fines over a given period of time have the greatest willingness to pay. (The economist who made this observation also noted that the university's decision to locate faculty parking spaces in the most desirable locations differs from the practice used by retail stores. These stores usually require employees to park in remote locations in order to accommodate their customers.)

5. The Robinson-Patman Act (1936) outlawed price discrimination that reduced competition. One can argue that yield management increases competition among schools so that this type of price discrimination is legal. However, the Department of Justice investigated Ivy League schools and MIT for possible violations of the Sherman Antitrust Act because of their practice of collectively adopting a financial aid policy. Collusion, rather than price discrimination, was the focus of the investigation. School officials would meet each spring to jointly determine a student's contribution to tuition if the student was admitted to more than one of the schools. A settlement was reached in 1993 that allowed school officials to meet, but placed restrictions on the policies they used to award financial aid.

True/False Answers

1. F They are referred to as *arbitrage profits*.
2. T See the section "Arbitrage" on page 508 of the textbook.
3. F Some evidence based on consumer surveys supports the effectiveness of this strategy but the evidence is not conclusive. See the section "Odd Pricing: Why Is the Price $2.99 Instead of $3.00?" that begins on page 519.
4. F The Robinson-Patman Act (1936) made price discrimination illegal if its effect is to reduce competition in an industry.
5. T See the section "Price Discrimination across Time" on page 517.
6. T See the section "Perfect Price Discrimination" beginning on page 515.
7. T See the section "Perfect Price Discrimination" beginning on page 515.
8. F When the price (tariff) is set equal to marginal cost, the outcome is economically efficient.
9. F Cost-plus pricing may be the best way to determine the optimal price if marginal and average costs are about equal or when the firm has difficulty estimating its demand curve.
10. T See "Price Discrimination across Time" on page 517.
11. F It is unlikely that any firm would know each consumer's willingness to pay and could prevent consumers who buy a product at a low price from reselling it to consumers willing to pay a higher price. Perfect price discrimination requires both of these conditions.
12. T See ***Making the Connection*** "How Colleges Use Yield Management" on page 515.
13. T See the section "Perfect Price Discrimination" that begins on page 515.
14. F Price discrimination may be practiced by any firm that possesses market power. Perfectly competitive firms cannot practice price discrimination but firms in other types of market structures may be able to do so.
15. T See the section "Arbitrage" on page 508.

Chapter 16

The Markets for Labor and Other Factors of Production

Chapter Summary

Beginning with chapter 3, your study of markets has focused on demand and supply of final goods and services. The demand for labor, unlike the demand for goods and services, is a *derived* demand. A **derived demand** is the demand for a factor of production that is derived from the good the factor produces. If consumers increase their demand for iPods, Apple will demand more labor. The demand curve for labor is also the marginal revenue product of labor curve. The **marginal revenue product of labor** is the change in a firm's revenue as a result of hiring one more worker.

In constructing the demand curve for labor, we hold constant all variables that affect the willingness of firms to demand labor – except for the wage. The four most important factors that cause the demand for labor to change are:

1. Increases in human capital
2. Changes in technology
3. Changes in the price of the product
4. Changes in the quantity of other inputs

The labor supply curve is the relationship between the wage rate and the quantity of labor supplied. The three most important factors that cause supply to change are:

1. Increases in population
2. Changing demographics
3. Changing alternative employment opportunities

Equilibrium in the labor market occurs where the quantity of labor demanded equals the quantity supplied. Changes in demand and supply change the equilibrium wage rate and quantity of labor.

Differences in marginal revenue products are the most important reason for wage differences, although wages can differ for other reasons as well. **Compensating differentials** refer to higher wages for workers who have dangerous or otherwise unpleasant jobs. **Economic discrimination** on the basis of race, gender, or other irrelevant characteristics can also explain some wage differences. Workers who are members of labor unions earn higher wages than non-union members.

Personnel economics examines human resources issues, such as how firms hire, train, and promote workers and set wages and benefits. The markets for capital and natural resources can be analyzed using the approach used to analyze the market for labor. The **marginal productivity theory of income distribution** states that individuals receive income equal to the marginal contribution to production of the factors of production they own, including labor. The more factors of production an individual owns, and the more productive those factors are, the higher the individual's income will be.

Learning Objectives

When you finish this chapter, you should be able to:

1. **Explain how firms choose the profit-maximizing quantity of labor to employ.** Firms compare the additional revenue earned from hiring a worker (the marginal revenue product of labor) to the cost of paying a worker. As long as the marginal revenue product is greater than the worker's wage rate, the firm will continue to hire more workers.

2. **Explain how people choose the quantity of labor to supply.** The higher the wage someone earns from working, the higher the opportunity cost of leisure. As the wage increases, people choose less leisure and work more. Although most individuals have upward-sloping labor supply curves, it is possible that these curves are backward-bending (positively sloped) at high wages.

3. **Explain how equilibrium wages are determined in labor markets.** The equilibrium wage is determined at the intersection of the demand and supply curves for labor. Changes in the demand and supply for labor will change the equilibrium wage rate.

4. **Use demand and supply analysis to explain how compensating differentials, discrimination, and labor unions cause wages to differ.** Higher wages are needed to compensate workers for jobs that are dangerous or have unpleasant aspects. Wage differentials can be explained by economic discrimination, but most gaps between wages of white males and other groups is explained by differences in education, experience and differing preferences for jobs. Holding other factors constant, being in a union increases a worker's wages but most economists believe that unions have not raised the total amount of wages received by workers.

5. **Discuss the role personnel economics can play in helping firms deal with human resources issues.** A new focus of labor economics applies economic analysis to issues such as how firms hire, train, and promote workers and set their wages and benefits.

6. **Show how equilibrium prices are determined in the markets for capital and natural resources.** The demand for capital and the demand for natural resources are based on their marginal revenue products. Firms that produce capital goods face increasing marginal costs so the supply curve for capital goods is upward sloping. The supply of land is usually upward sloping but the quantity of some land is perfectly inelastic. In equilibrium, suppliers of capital and land receive prices equal to their marginal revenue products.

Chapter Review

Chapter Opener: Why Are the Chicago Cubs Paying Alfonso Soriano $18 per Year? (pages 534-535)

If you are a baseball fan, you are aware of the high salaries many players earn and you may wonder why players such as Alfonso Soriano can earn millions of dollars annually for playing a game. Wages and salaries for professional athletes are determined in the labor market by the demand and supply of labor, just as the price of any good is determined by its demand and supply. But unlike the markets for goods and services, concepts of fairness arise more frequently in labor markets.

Helpful Study Hint

An ***Inside Look*** at the end of this chapter explains why an increase in the popularity of auto racing in the 1990s has increased the salaries of Nascar pit crews.

Although the salaries earned by such star players as Alfonso Soriano make headlines, many fans are less upset about salaries earned by star players than they are with salaries of lesser talents. During the 2006-07 NBA season, the payroll of the champion San Antonio Spurs was about $65 million. The payroll of the Cleveland Cavaliers, their opponents in the NBA finals, was about $50 million. Salaries for players on these teams seemed to many fans as money well spent, but fans of the New York Knicks, a team with a 33-49 record that did not make the playoffs, weren't pleased that their team paid its players over $80 million. Test your understanding of the topics of the chapter opening by working through end-of-chapter problems 4.5 and 4.12.

If you have a job, you probably hope that your boss will reward your good work habits with a raise. ***Economics in YOUR Life!*** asks you to think of a convincing argument to use with your boss. After you read this chapter, you can compare your argument with one suggested by your authors.

16.1 LEARNING OBJECTIVE

16.1 The Demand for Labor (pages 536-540)

Learning Objective 1 Explain how firms choose the profit-maximizing quantity of labor to employ.

A **derived demand** is the demand for a factor of production that is derived from the demand for the good the factor produces. The demand for labor is dependent on the amount of output produced and the additional revenue received from selling that output. The **marginal product of labor (*MRP*)** is the additional output a firm produces as a result of hiring one more worker. Because of the law of diminishing returns, the marginal product of labor declines as a firm hires more workers. To decide how many workers to hire, a firm must compare the additional revenue it earns from hiring another worker to the increase in costs from paying the worker.

The marginal revenue product of labor (*MRP*) curve is the demand curve for labor. In constructing the demand curve for labor, all variables, except the wage rate, that affect the willingness of firms to demand labor are held constant. A change in the wage rate causes a change in the quantity of labor demanded. If any of the non-wage variables change, the demand curve will shift.

There are four important non-wage factors that affect the demand for labor:

1. Increases in human capital. Human capital represents the accumulated training and skills that workers possess.

2. Changes in technology. As new and better machinery is developed, workers become more productive and the labor demand curve shifts to the right.
3. Changes in the price of the product. Higher prices increase the marginal revenue product of labor and the labor demand curve shifts to the right.
4. Changes in the quantity of other inputs. Workers are able to produce more if they have more machinery and other inputs to work with.

Helpful Study Hint

Working through ***Solved Problem 16-1*** to understand how a firm decides how many workers to hire in order to maximize its profits. This problem uses Apple's production of iPods as an example. After reading the ***Solved Problem***, work through related end-of-chapter problem 1.5.

16.2 LEARNING OBJECTIVE

16.2 The Supply of Labor (pages 540-543)

Learning Objective 2 Explain how people choose the quantity of labor to supply.

The opportunity cost of leisure is the wage. The higher the wage you can earn from working, the higher the opportunity cost of leisure. Normally the labor supply curve is upward sloping, but it is possible for the curve to be backward bending at high wages. An increase in the wage raises the opportunity cost of leisure and causes a worker to devote more time to working. This is the substitution effect from a wage change. Because leisure is a normal good, as the wage rises, the income effect of a wage change causes a worker to devote less time to working and more time to leisure. Whether a worker supplies more or less labor following a wage increase depends on whether the substitution effect is greater than the income effect.

The supply curve of labor is constructed holding constant all variables other than the wage. If any of the nonwage variables change, the supply curve will shift. The most important nonwage variables are:

1. Increases in population
2. Changing demographics
3. Changing alternatives in other labor markets

Helpful Study Hint

Make sure you do not confuse the supply of *labor* with the supply of *jobs*. You are used to viewing yourself as consumer rather than as a producer. When you search for a job, you represent the supply side of the labor market, while employers represent the demand side.

Extra Solved Problem 16-2

Chapter 16 in the textbook includes two Solved Problems. Here is an extra Solved Problem to help you build your skills solving economic problems.

Supports Learning Objective 2: Explain how people choose the quantity of labor to supply.

Dear Adam: I'm confused. Help!

The following letter was written to an advice column titled "Dear Adam." The column provides online advice to college economics students who have difficulty understanding economics concepts.

> Dear Adam:
>
> I am a college microeconomics student from Santa Fe. My hometown passed a law in 2003 that raised the minimum wage for all businesses in the city with 25 or more workers. In 2006, the minimum wage was $9.50 and was raised to $10.50 in 2008. My friends have expressed different opinions about this law, but what I am confused about is the effect it has on the market for jobs. A local business owner wrote a letter to the magazine *City Journal* complaining that the law "is driving existing businesses out of town." If this is true, it means that the higher wage will reduce the quantity supplied of jobs. But we learned in my microeconomics class that the labor supply curve was upward sloping!
>
> After the New Mexico state court upheld the minimum wage ordinance, a lawyer who supported the law claimed that it will "benefit the low-wage workers of Sante Fe." This statement implies that the quantity demanded of jobs will rise as the minimum wage rises; I thought the demand curve for labor was downward sloping.
>
> I have an exam in two weeks on the labor market. Help!
>
> Yours truly,
>
> Hopeless in Sante Fe

Sources: "Court Upholds Sante Fe Wage Ordinance," Brennan Center for Justice, June 25, 2004. Christopher Chantrill, "Minimum Wage Hits $9.50 in Santa Fe," *American Thinker*, January 26, 2006.

Write a reply to Hopeless in Sante Fe explaining:

a. The supply curve for labor.

b. The impact of an increase in the minimum wage on workers in Sante Fe.

SOLVING THE PROBLEM

Step 1: **Review the chapter material.**
This problem is about the supply of labor, so you may want to review the section "The Supply of Labor," which begins on page 540 of the textbook.

Step 2: **Answer question (a) by explaining the supply curve for labor to Hopeless.**
Dear Hopeless: You made a common mistake in believing the market for labor was a market for jobs. The labor supply curve is the relationship between the quantity supplied of labor – not jobs – and the price of labor, or the wage rate. Understand, too, that the demand for labor refers to business firms' demand for workers, not jobs. It should make sense to you that the business owner you referred to believed that the increase in the wage firms have to pay for workers would reduce the quantity demanded (of *workers*, not jobs!).

Step 3: **Answer question (b) by explaining the impact of the minimum wage.**
P.S. – Increases in the minimum wage increase the quantity supplied of workers because the opportunity cost of one hour of work is an hour spent doing something else. Let's call this "something else" leisure, because the opportunity cost of working will be different for different people. At $5.15, fewer people would choose to work, or would work fewer hours, than at a wage rate of $8.50 or $10.50. But this does not mean all who are willing to work will be able to find jobs. I am sure you learned in your course that a worker will be hired only if the marginal revenue product he or she produces per hour is greater than the wage rate. Good luck on your exam!

Yours truly,
Adam

16.3 LEARNING OBJECTIVE

16.3 Equilibrium in the Labor Market (pages 543-547)

Learning Objective 3 Explain how equilibrium wages are determined in labor markets.

Demand and supply determine equilibrium in the labor market. Changes in demand and supply cause changes in the equilibrium wage and the level of employment. Increases in labor productivity cause increases in the demand for labor, which lead to increases in the equilibrium wage and in the number of workers employed. An increase in the labor supply, if the labor demand is unchanged, will decrease the equilibrium wage and increase the number of workers employed.

Helpful Study Hint

The ***Making the Connection*** on page 544 of the textbook describes the signaling hypothesis and discusses whether the courses you take while in college are likely to affect your future salary. The ***Making the Connection*** on page 546 explains that wages did not fall in the United States as a result of the large increase in the population in the early 1900s due to immigration because the demand for labor increased rapidly as technological progress increased. Some economists today argue that immigration may contribute to increasing income inequality by reducing the wages of low-income workers. Economists differ on the degree of the effect.

Extra Solved Problem 16-3

Chapter 16 in the textbook includes two Solved Problems. Here is an extra Solved Problem to help you build your skills solving economic problems.

Supports Learning Objective 3: Explain how equilibrium wages are determined in labor markets.

Help Wanted: K-12 Teachers (Knowledge of Spanish a Plus)

A survey conducted by the American Federation of Teachers found that the average salary of K-12 teachers (kindergarten through 12th grade) in 2004-05 in the United States was $47,602. The same survey estimated the average beginning salary for K-12 teachers in 2004-05 was $31,753. Average salaries differ by region as well as grade level and subject area. For example, Spanish-speaking mathematics and science teachers can command higher than average salaries in the Southwest and Western states. Several factors have affected the market for K-12 teachers in the United States in the first decade of the 21st century. Among these factors are:

1. Increased numbers of retirements of teachers who began their careers in the 1950s and 1960s when the "baby boom" generation (those born between the mid 1940s and early 1960s) increased the demand for teachers.
2. Increased enrollments of K-12 students as children of baby boomers began to attend school.
3. Government efforts to reduce student-teacher ratios resulted in more funding for local school districts.

Source: "2005 Survey and Analysis of Teacher Salary Trends," American Federation of Teachers. http://www.aft.org/salary/

a. Draw a demand and supply curve for beginning K-12 teachers for 2004-05. Assume that the equilibrium beginning salary is $30,000 and the equilibrium quantity was 200,000. This is about the number of new teachers hired annually.

b. How is the market for new teachers different from the market for other factors of production?

c. Explain how the three factors listed above will affect the market for beginning teachers.

SOLVING THE PROBLEM

Step 1: Review the chapter material.
This problem is about equilibrium, so you may want to review the section "Equilibrium in the Labor Market," which begins on page 543 of the textbook.

Step 2: Answer question (a) by drawing a demand and supply graph.
Note that the demand curve represents school or school district officials (for example, school board members) who determine how many teachers will be hired. The supply curve represents applicants for K-12 teacher positions. Most of these applicants will be undergraduate education majors, but some may be people who switch careers from private business or government to education. The salary measured on the vertical or price axis should

be considered a combination of salary and benefits. Benefits, such as medical insurance, are an important part of teachers' compensation.

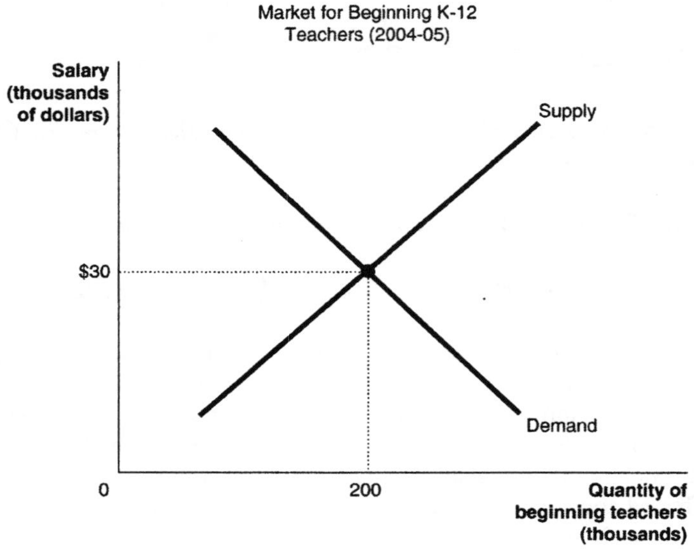

Step 3: Answer question (b) by explaining how the market for teachers is different from the market for other factors of production.

Markets for teachers, especially public school teachers, are different in several ways from the markets for other factors of production. First, unlike private firms, schools do not seek to maximize profits. Second, tax revenue is the source of funding for teaching positions in public school systems. Voters may not approve requests for additional teaching positions and other budget items. This means that while a school district may want to hire more teachers (willingness), taxpayers may not provide the funds necessary to hire the additional teachers (ability). Thus, the actual demand curve for beginning teachers will not increase (shift to right).

Step 4: Answer question (c) by discussing the effect of the three factors listed in the problem.

Each of these factors should result in an increase in demand for beginning teachers. For example, assume that greater numbers of retired teachers result in an increase in the quantity demanded of beginning teachers to 220,000 at a salary of $30,000. There would be a new equilibrium salary and quantity of beginning teachers and a shortage at the former equilibrium salary of $30,000. There will be a tendency for salaries to rise but, as noted in Step 3, funding for teaching positions could be subject to budget approval on the part of voters.

16.4 LEARNING OBJECTIVE

16.4 Explaining Differences in Wages (pages 548-557)

Learning Objective 4 Use demand and supply analysis to explain how compensating differentials, discrimination, and labor unions cause wages to differ.

Differences in marginal revenue product are the most important factor in explaining differences in wages. The more productive a worker is and the higher the price the worker's output can be sold for, the higher the wage the worker will receive. Compensating differentials can also explain wage differences. **Compensating differentials** are higher wages that compensate workers for unpleasant aspects of a job.

In the United States white males, on average, earn more than other groups. One possible explanation for this difference is economic discrimination. **Economic discrimination** refers to paying a person a lower wage or excluding a person from an occupation on the basis of an irrelevant characteristic such as race or gender. Excluding groups from certain jobs or paying one group more than another is illegal in the United States, but some employers may ignore the law.

Most economists believe that only a small amount of the gap between the wages of white males and other groups is due to discrimination. Most of the gap in wages is due to differences in education, differences in experience, and differing preferences for jobs. Many economists argue that economic discrimination is no longer a major factor in labor markets in the United States because employers pay an economic penalty if they engage in economic discrimination.

Workers' wages can differ depending on whether they are members of labor unions. A **labor union** is an organization of employees that has the legal right to bargain with employers about wages and working conditions. A smaller fraction of the U.S. labor force is unionized than in most other industrial countries. In the United States, union workers receive higher wages than workers who are not in unions.

Helpful Study Hint

Don't Let This Happen To YOU! uses Adam Smith's famous diamond-water example to explain that prices and wages are determined at the margin. ***Making the Connection*** explains how technological advances – such as DVDs, cable television, and Internet streaming video – have increased the number of viewers of sporting events and films and therefore have raised the salaries of superstar performers in sports and entertainment relative to average performers in these fields. ***Solved Problem 16-4*** describes the arguments for and against comparable worth legislation. Work through related end-of-chapter problems 4.6, 4.9, 4.10, 4.15 and 4.16 to better understand the concepts discussed in this section's features.

16.5 LEARNING OBJECTIVE

16.5 Personnel Economics (pages 557-559)

Learning Objective 5 Discuss the role personnel economics can play in helping firms deal with human resources issues.

Personnel economics is the application of economic analysis to human resources issues. Personnel economics analyzes the link between differences in jobs and differences in the way workers are paid. Firms need to design compensation policies that take into account differences in the skill requirements of jobs, working environments, and the extent of interaction among workers.

One compensation policy firms consider is whether workers will receive a certain wage or salary per week or month or be paid a commission or piece-rate pay. Although a commission or piece-rate system of compensation can be more profitable than a salary system for some firms, other firms have good reasons to choose a salary system. Firms choose a salary system when there is difficulty in measuring output and attributing output to a particular worker, or when firms have concerns about output quality. Many workers dislike the risk inherent in a piece-rate or commission compensation system.

Helpful Study Hint

Read the ***Making the Connection*** on page 558 for an interesting example of the successful introduction of a piece-rate system of compensation at the Safelite AutoGlass company. Work through related end-of-chapter problem 5.7.

Extra Solved Problem 16-5

Chapter 16 in the textbook includes two Solved Problems. Here is an extra Solved Problem to help you build your skills solving economic problems.

Supports Learning Objective 5: Discuss the role personnel economics can play in helping firms deal with human resources issues.

"Hey You, Sewing Jeans. Get Outta My Face!"

The ***Making the Connection*** in this section describes Edward Lazear's study of Safelite AutoGlass. Worker productivity and profits both increased when the firm abandoned a straight-time pay system in favor of a piece-rate system. Lazear found different results for Levi Strauss when the clothing company changed its compensation scheme in the opposite direction.

> Levi's is a worker-oriented company. It had good intentions when the piecework system was abandoned in 1992. Under that system, individual workers performed single, specialized tasks and were paid according to the work they completed. Under the new system, groups of 10-35 workers shared tasks and were paid according to the work they completed...instead of motivating workers...it damaged morale and triggered corrosive infighting. Skilled workers were pitted against slower colleagues. Threats and insults became common...the quantity of pants produced per hour plunged in 1993 to 77 percent of pre-team levels...labor and overhead costs raced up 25 percent. It was a disaster.

Source: Edward P. Lazear. "Personnel Economics and Economic Approaches to Incentives." *The Hong Kong Centre for Economic Research Letters*, vol. 61. September/October 2000.

But Lazear found that a team incentive approach worked very well for British Petrol and Exploration (BPE). A team incentive approach rewards workers based on the output produced by a group of workers. The firm has an oil field in Prudhoe Bay, Alaska with about 300 workers. Six months after introducing its team bonus approach, productivity increased more than 12 percent.

a. Why did the team incentive approach fail at Levi Strauss but was successful at BPE?

b. Under what circumstances are piecework systems and team incentive approaches likely to be successful?

SOLVING THE PROBLEM

Step 1: Review the chapter material.
This problem is about personnel economics, so you may want to review the section "Personnel Economics," which begins on page 557 of the textbook.

Step 2: Answer question (a) by explaining why the team incentive approach failed at Levi Strauss but was successful at BPE.
The team incentive approach failed at Levi Strauss because producing jeans does not require teamwork. As was true with production at Safelite AutoGlass, each task is easily performed by individual workers and can be monitored. When the team incentive approach was used at Levi Strauss there was a tendency for some workers to be "free riders" – to not work very hard, let others do most of the work but still get paid the same. At BPE's Prudhoe Bay field, output could not be produced by one worker. Teamwork at BPE was necessary to produce oil. Team-based pay was effective because production was truly a team effort.

Step 3: Answer question (b) by discussing under what circumstances piecework systems and team incentive systems are likely to be successful.
In summarizing the lessons learned from the experience of Levi Strauss and BPE, Lazear wrote: "For production workers, pay [based] on output is very effective. However, many firms are reluctant to tie compensation to tangible measures of output...It is easier to simply pay everybody the same...Team-based pay is only effective when production is truly a team effort. Often times, team incentives are weak and may cause resentment."

16.6 LEARNING OBJECTIVE

16.6 The Markets for Capital and Natural Resources (pages 560-563)

Learning Objective 6 Show how equilibrium prices are determined in the markets for capital and natural resources.

The markets for other factors of production are analyzed in much the same way as the market for labor. The demand for capital is a derived demand. Physical capital includes machinery, equipment, and buildings. The marginal revenue product of capital curve is the demand curve for capital. The supply curve for capital goods is upward sloping because the firms that produce capital goods face increasing marginal costs.

The marginal revenue product curve for natural resources is the demand curve for natural resources. The supply curve for natural resources is usually upward sloping. In some cases, the quantity of a natural resource is fixed and will not change as price changes. **Economic rent** (or **pure rent**) is the price of a factor of production that is in fixed supply.

Monopsony refers to a firm that is the sole buyer of a factor of production. A lumber mill in a small town is an example. A monopsony firm restricts the quantity of a factor demanded to force down the price of the factor and increase the firm's profits. A firm with a monopsony in a labor market will hire fewer workers and pay lower wages than a perfectly competitive firm would.

The **marginal productivity theory of income distribution** is the theory that the distribution of income is determined by the marginal productivity of the factors of production that individuals own. The more factors of production an individual owns, and the more productive those factors are, the higher the individual's income will be.

Helpful Study Hint

Be careful when deciding whether the quantity of a natural resource is fixed. For example, many people believe the supply curve for oil is vertical because "there's a limited amount of oil in the earth's crust." These people have confused the stock of oil with the flow of newly produced oil. Quantity supplied is the flow of newly pumped oil. As the price of oil rises, it becomes economical to reopen closed oil wells and pump oil from fields where extraction is costly, increasing the flow supply. So the supply curve for oil is not vertical after all. Review Figures 16-11 and 16-12, which illustrate equilibrium in the market for capital and natural resources.

Recall that ***Economics in YOUR Life!*** concerns making a case to your boss for a higher wage. After studying this chapter, you should understand why the authors suggest that you demonstrate to your boss that your marginal revenue product – the amount of revenue your are responsible for producing – justifies giving you a raise.

Extra Solved Problem **16-6**

Chapter 16 in the textbook includes two Solved Problems. Here is an extra Solved Problem to help you build your skills solving economic problems.

Supports Learning Objective 6: Show how equilibrium prices are determined in the markets for capital and natural resources.

Old King Coal

Energy consumers in the United States expressed concern in 2004 about price increases of nearly 20 percent and even higher increases through 2007. These consumers were managers of electric utilities who complained of the higher cost of coal. Although much of the oil consumed in the United States is imported, all 1,015 million short tons (a short ton, or metric ton, is equal to 2,000 lbs.) of coal consumed in 2004 were mined at home. Most of the coal was used by firms as a factor of production and most of these firms were electric utilities. Over 90 percent of the coal mined in the United States is used to generate electricity. Because transportation is a large part of the cost of using coal, the price is typically stated as a delivered price. In 2004, electric utilities paid an average delivered price of $27.28 per short ton of coal. Coal is usually not thought of as a clean energy source, but over 1/3 of the coal mined in the United States is from Wyoming's Powder River Basin (PRB). Coal from this source is very low in sulfur. Since the 1990 amendments to the Clean Air Act, electric utilities have faced restrictions on the amount of sulfur dioxide they can emit. Higher coal prices are due, in part, to an increase in demand as consumers sought substitutes for higher priced oil. But demand increased more for PRB coal because of the increase in the price of sulfur dioxide emissions allowances. Utilities are allowed to emit one ton of sulfur dioxide for each allowance they hold but may buy additional allowances from other utilities (this market-based tradeable emissions allowances program is described in Chapter 5). PRB coal is relatively inexpensive to mine, so despite the cost of moving PRB coal to the Midwest and East where most of the electric utilities are located, the delivered price of low sulfur coal is very competitive with delivered prices of coal mined in Kentucky and West Virginia.

Sources: Matthew Dalton, "Price for Wyoming Coal Surges," *Casper Star Tribune*. April 14, 2005. Table 25. "U.S. Coal Consumption by End-Use Sector." Department of Energy, September 21, 2007. Table 34. "Average Price of Coal Delivered to End Use Sector by Census Division and State." Department of Energy.

a. Show how the equilibrium price is determined in the market for coal.

b. Describe the how the marginal revenue product of coal affects the equilibrium price.

SOLVING THE PROBLEM

Step 1: Review the chapter material.
This problem is about capital and natural resources, so you may want to review the section "The Markets for Capital and Natural Resources," which begins on page 560 of the textbook.

Step 2: Answer question (a) by drawing a demand and supply curve for coal.
The graph shown below illustrates the market for coal in 2004. It assumes the average delivered price of coal is the equilibrium price and the quantity of coal consumed in 2004 is the equilibrium quantity. Demand and supply determine prices in resource markets just as they do in the markets for goods and services, but the demand for coal is a derived demand. Much of the demand for coal is because it is a source of energy used to power electric utilities. The graph includes a higher dashed demand curve. Due, in part, to higher prices for oil, a substitute energy source, the price of coal rose through the years from 2005 to 2007.

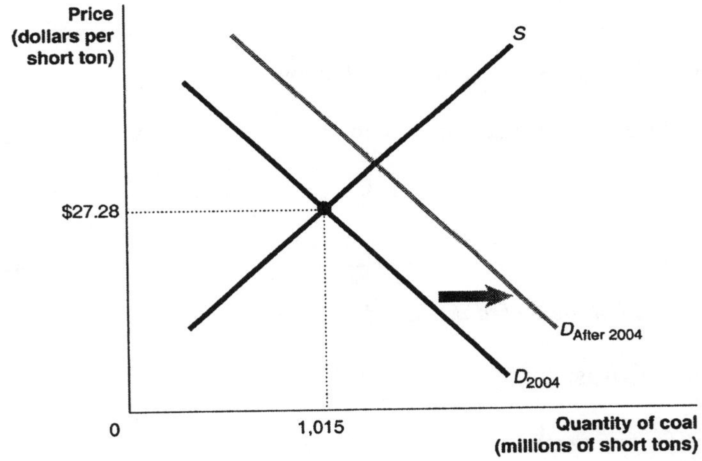

Step 3: Answer question (b) by describing how the marginal revenue product of coal affects the equilibrium price.
The marginal revenue product for coal is similar to the marginal revenue product for any natural resource. It is the change in a firm's revenue as a result of employing one more unit of the resource. It is also the demand for the resource. Therefore, the demand curves in the graph represent the marginal revenue product for coal.

Key Terms

Compensating differentials. Higher wages that compensate workers for unpleasant aspects of a job.

Derived demand. The demand for a factor of production that is derived from the demand for the good the factor produces.

Economic discrimination. Paying a person a lower wage or excluding a person from an occupation on the basis of an irrelevant characteristic such as race or gender.

Economic rent (or **pure rent**). The price of a factor of production that is fixed in supply.

Factors of production. Labor, capital, natural resources, and other inputs used to produce goods and services.

Human capital. The accumulated training and skills that workers possess.

Labor union. An organization of employees that has the legal right to bargain with employers about wages and working conditions.

Marginal product of labor. The additional output a firm produces as a result of hiring one more worker.

Marginal productivity theory of income distribution. The theory that the distribution of income is determined by the marginal productivity of the factors of production that individuals own.

Marginal revenue product of labor (*MRP*). The change in the firm's revenue as a result of hiring one more worker.

Monopsony. The sole buyer of a factor of production.

Personnel economics. The application of economic analysis to human resources issues.

Self-Test

(Answers are provided at the end of the Self-Test.)

Multiple-Choice Questions

1. Which of the following is a factor of production?
   a. Labor
   b. Natural resources
   c. Capital
   d. All of the above

2. Why do economists say that labor demand is a derived demand?
   a. Because in order to derive labor demand, we must derive labor supply first
   b. Because the demand for labor is derived from the demand for the products produced by workers
   c. Because the demand for labor depends on the amount of capital available; without capital there is no need for labor
   d. Because the demand for labor depends entirely on the willingness of the firm to hire workers

3. Link one of the terms below to the following definition: "__________ is the additional output a firm produces as a result of hiring one more worker."
   a. Marginal cost
   b. Marginal revenue
   c. Marginal product of labor
   d. Marginal revenue product of labor

4. Link one of the terms below to the following definition: "__________ is the change in the firm's revenue as a result of hiring one additional worker."
   a. Marginal cost
   b. Marginal revenue
   c. Marginal product of labor
   d. Marginal revenue product of labor

5. Which of the following formulas is correct?
   a. Product price = marginal product of labor x marginal revenue product
   b. Marginal product of labor = product price x marginal revenue product
   c. Marginal revenue product = product price x marginal product of labor
   d. None of the above

6. What happens as the number of workers increases?
   a. Marginal product of labor decreases and marginal revenue product of labor increases
   b. Marginal product of labor increases and marginal revenue product of labor decreases
   c. Both the marginal product and the marginal revenue product of labor increase
   d. Both the marginal product and the marginal revenue product of labor decrease

7. Let *MRP* equal the marginal revenue product of labor and *W* the wage. When should a firm hire more workers in order to increase profit?
   a. When $MRP > W$
   b. When $MRP < W$
   c. When $MRP = W$
   d. When $MRP = 0$

8. Which of the following is the equivalent of the demand curve for labor?
   a. The marginal revenue product curve
   b. The marginal product of labor curve
   c. The firm's demand curve for its product
   d. The firm's total revenue curve

9. Refer to the table below. Which two columns must a firm compare in order to determine the profit-maximizing quantity of workers to hire?

Number of Workers	Output of Televisions per Week	Marginal Product of Labor (television sets per week)	Product Price	Total Revenue	Marginal Revenue Product of Labor (dollars per week)	Wage (dollars per week)	Additional Profit from Hiring One More Worker (dollars per week)
(1)	(2)	(3)	(4)	(5)	(6)	(7)	(8)
0	0	–	$200		–	$500	–
1	6	6	180			500	
2	11	5	160			500	
3	15	4	140			500	
4	18	3	120			500	
5	20	2	100			500	
6	21	1	80			500	

a. Columns 4 and 6
b. Columns 6 and 7
c. Columns 5 and 6
d. Columns 3 and 4

10. Refer to the table below. How many workers should the firm hire in order to maximize profit?

Number of Workers	Output of Televisions per Week	Marginal Product of Labor (television sets per week)	Product Price	Total Revenue	Marginal Revenue Product of Labor (dollars per week)	Wage (dollars per week)	Additional Profit from Hiring One More Worker (dollars per week)
(1)	(2)	(3)	(4)	(5)	(6)	(7)	(8)
0	0	–	$200		–	$500	–
1	6	6	180			500	
2	11	5	160			500	
3	15	4	140			500	
4	18	3	120			500	
5	20	2	100			500	
6	21	1	80			500	

a. 2
b. 3
c. 4
d. 5

11. What name is given to the accumulated training and skills that workers possess?
a. The marginal product of labor
b. Human capital
c. Physical capital
d. Productivity

12. Which of the factors listed below does *not* cause the demand curve for labor to shift?
   a. A change in the wage
   b. A change in human capital
   c. A change in technology
   d. A change in the price of the product

13. Which of the following shifts the demand curve for labor to the right?
   a. A decrease in the wage
   b. An increase in the wage
   c. An increase in the price of the product
   d. A decrease in the quantity of inputs other than labor

14. According to the substitution effect, what is the impact of an increase in the wage?
   a. An increase in the opportunity cost of leisure
   b. An increase in the opportunity cost of work
   c. A decrease in the opportunity cost of leisure
   d. An increase in purchasing power

15. Which of the following best describes the change in consumer purchasing power as a result of a price change?
   a. The substitution effect
   b. The income effect
   c. The opportunity cost of leisure
   d. A shift of the labor supply curve

16. Along a backward-bending supply curve, which effect is larger at low wage levels?
   a. The substitution effect is larger than the income effect.
   b. The income effect is larger than the substitution effect.
   c. The tax effect is larger than the income effect.
   d. The work effect is larger than the leisure effect.

17. Which of the following factors shifts the labor supply curve?
   a. A change in demographics
   b. A change in alternatives available in other labor markets
   c. A change in population
   d. All of the above

18. A change in which of the following factors would cause a movement along the labor supply curve rather than a shift of the curve?
   a. A change in demographics
   b. A change in alternatives available in other labor markets
   c. A change in population
   d. A change in the wage

19. Refer to the graph below. Which of the following could have caused the shift in the labor demand curve?

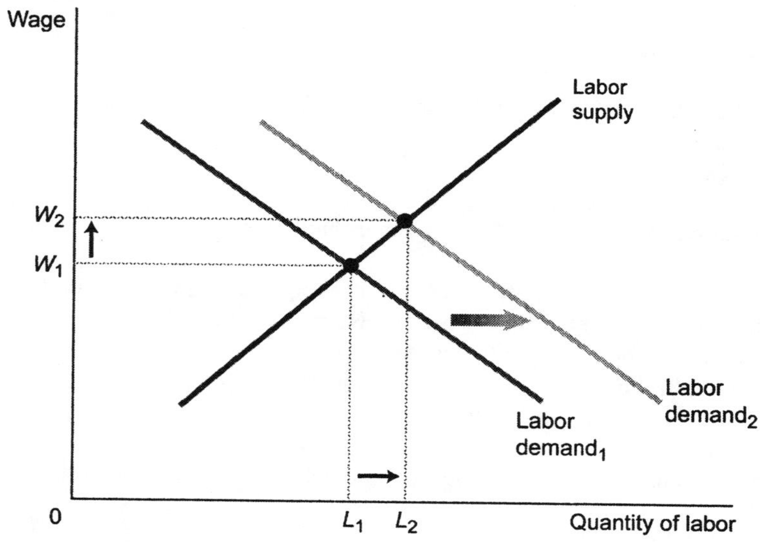

a. A change in labor productivity
b. A change in the substitution effect
c. A change in the income effect
d. All of the above

20. According to the *signaling hypothesis*, what signal does a college education send to prospective employers about a college graduate?
   a. College graduates require higher wages without necessarily being more productive than non-college graduates.
   b. College graduates possess certain desirable characteristics such as self-discipline and the ability to meet deadlines.
   c. A college graduate has knowledge that is worth paying for.
   d. A college graduate deserves a job because she has made an investment in education.

21. Refer to the graphs below. Which of the graphs below best depicts the impact of an increase in population on the labor market?

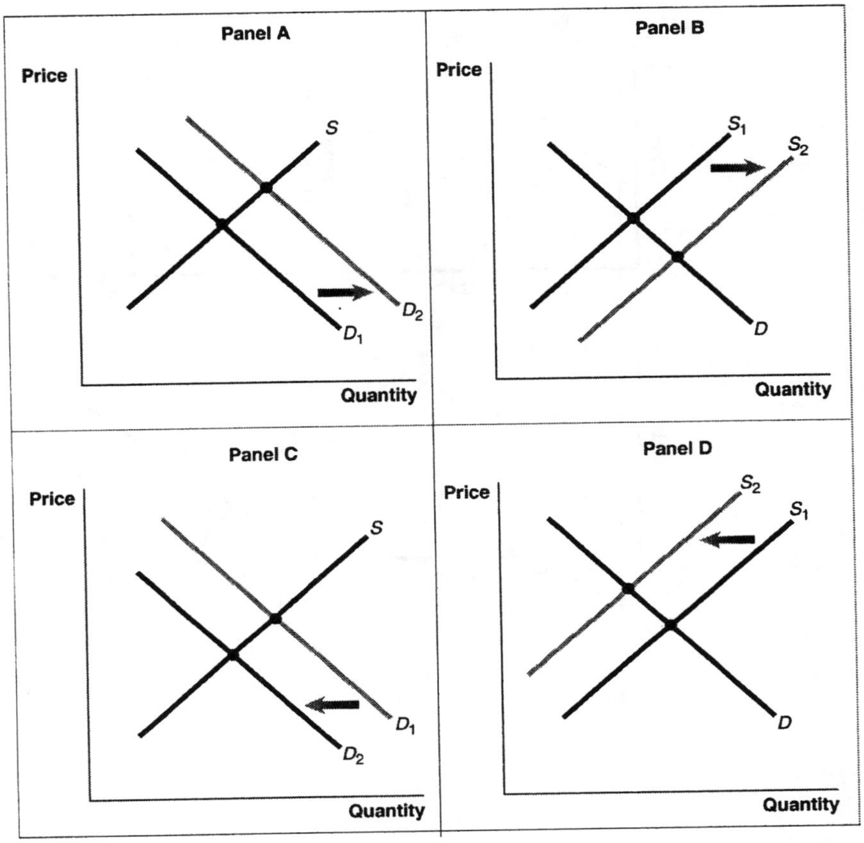

a. A
b. B
c. C
d. D

22. Refer to the graphs below. Judging by the relative position of supply and demand in each of these labor markets, which occupation appears to offer more desirable working conditions, all else the same?

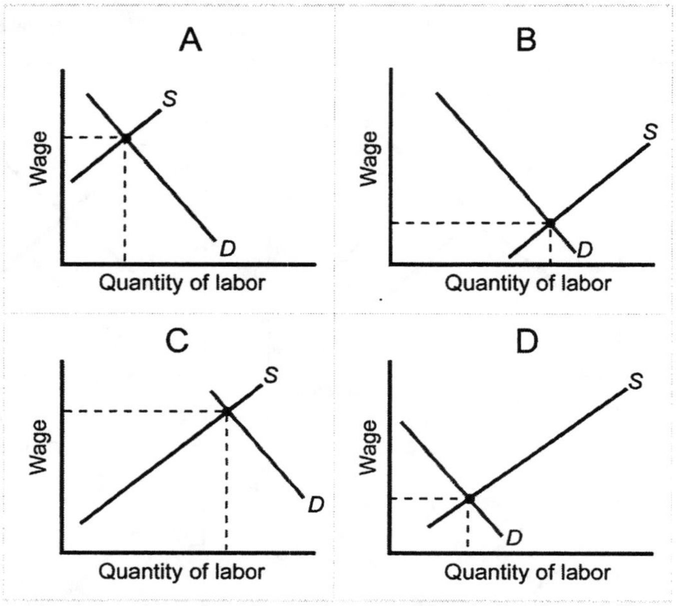

a. A
b. B
c. C
d. D

23. Refer to the graph below. According to the graph, who has a higher marginal revenue product of labor?

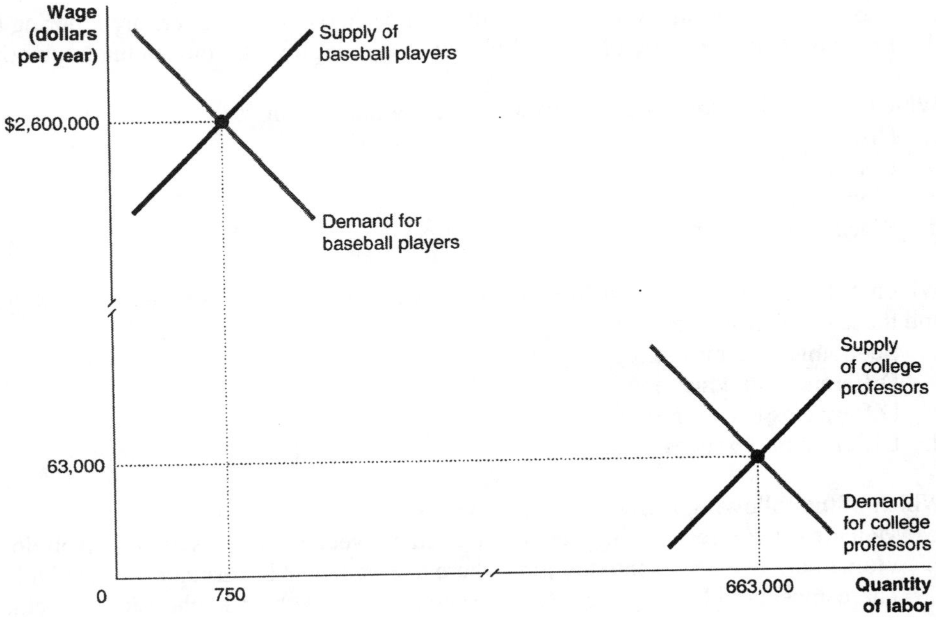

a. A college professor
b. A baseball player
c. There is insufficient information to answer the question.
d. No one; college professors and baseball players appear to have the same marginal revenue product of labor.

24. Which of the following is more relevant in determining the wages of baseball players?
a. The total value of the baseball games
b. The marginal value of baseball games
c. Both the total value and the marginal value are equally important.
d. The educational level of baseball players

25. When an employer pays higher wages to compensate workers for unpleasant aspects of their jobs, which of the following is the employer offering?
a. A discriminating wage
b. A labor union wage
c. A compensating differential
d. A risk premium

26. What does the term *cognitive dissonance* refer to?
a. The tendency for workers to ignore the going wage rate in a labor market
b. A distortion to the free labor market created by compensating differentials
c. The tendency for workers to underestimate the true risks of their jobs
d. The willingness of some workers to accept low wages for jobs involving high risk

27. Which of the following is true about *economic discrimination*?
    a. Economic discrimination is illegal, therefore impossible.
    b. Economic discrimination is both legal and possible.
    c. Economic discrimination is illegal, but it is possible that employers are ignoring the law.
    d. Economic discrimination is legal, but few if any employers would actually practice it.

28. Which of the following groups earns the lowest annual earnings?
    a. Hispanic males
    b. Hispanic females
    c. Black females
    d. Black males

29. Which of the following is least likely to be the cause of differences between the wages of white males and those of other groups?
    a. Economic discrimination
    b. Differences in education
    c. Differences in experience
    d. Different preferences for jobs

30. Which of the following is true about men's jobs versus women's jobs?
    a. Men are overrepresented in jobs where average weekly earnings are relatively low.
    b. Women are overrepresented in jobs where average weekly earnings are relatively low.
    c. There appears to be no preference between men and women in choosing particular jobs.
    d. Women tend to take jobs where work experience is very important.

31. Which of the following is a textbook argument about employer discrimination of workers?
    a. Employers who discriminate pay an economic penalty because very few workers are willing to work for a discriminating employer.
    b. Employers who discriminate pay an economic penalty imposed by the market system and by competition.
    c. Employers who discriminate receive an economic reward by keeping only the most productive workers.
    d. Employers who discriminate are rewarded by authorities who usually ignore their criminal behavior.

32. If discrimination makes it difficult for a member of a group to find employment in a particular occupation, his or her incentive to be trained to enter that occupation is reduced. Which of the terms below is more closely associated with this condition?
    a. Worker discrimination
    b. Customer discrimination
    c. Negative feedback loop
    d. Irrational expectations

33. In which of the following countries is the percentage of the labor force that belongs to unions the lowest?
    a. Sweden
    b. Canada
    c. Germany
    d. The United States

34. In the United States, how do the average weekly earnings of union workers compare with the earnings of nonunion workers?
   a. The earnings of union workers are higher than the earnings of nonunion workers.
   b. The earnings of union workers are lower than the earnings of nonunion workers.
   c. The earnings of union workers are almost identical to the earnings of nonunion workers.
   d. There is no way to compare the two.

35. What is the term given to the application of economic analysis to human resources issues?
   a. Labor economics
   b. Personnel economics
   c. Human resource management
   d. Occupational economics

36. Refer to the graph below. According to the textbook analysis of compensation, which line represents the compensation of a sales person based on commission?

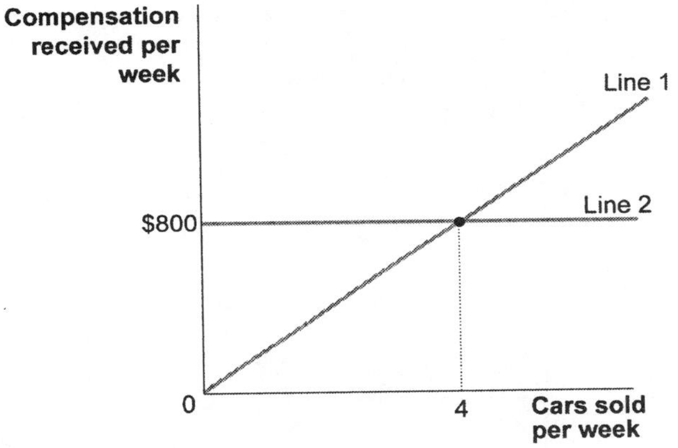

   a. Line 1
   b. Line 2
   c. Both lines
   d. Neither line

37. Which of the following is a reason for choosing a salary system rather than the more profitable commission, or piece-rate system of compensation?
   a. Difficulty in measuring output
   b. Concerns about quality
   c. Worker dislike of risk
   d. All of the above

38. What is the definition of *economic rent*?
   a. The price of a resource when that price is strictly determined by supply
   b. The marginal revenue product of natural resources
   c. The price received by a factor of production that is in fixed supply
   d. The earnings of a landlord

39. Which of the following is caused by the existence of a firm with a *monopsony* in the labor market?
    a. More workers will be hired at higher wages.
    b. More workers will be hired at lower wages.
    c. Fewer workers will be hired at higher wages.
    d. Fewer workers will be hired at lower wages.

40. Which of the statements below best describes the premise of the *marginal productivity theory of income distribution*?
    a. Workers become productive and receive income only at the margin.
    b. Income is distributed in such a way as to encourage workers to increase their productivity.
    c. The distribution of income is determined by the marginal productivity of the factors of production that individuals own.
    d. Income and productivity necessarily increase with additional hours spent at work.

Short Answer Questions

1. A professor in the Department of Foreign Languages at a Midwestern college complained that his salary is much less than an accounting professor at the same college. Both professors have Ph.D. degrees, 20 years of teaching experience, and similar research records. Is this difference in salary due to a compensating differential, economic discrimination, or some other factor?

____

____

____

____

____

____

____

2. Between 2005 and 2010, members of the "baby boom" generation will begin to reach retirement age (over 62 years). How will this affect the labor market in the United States?

____

____

____

3. Clergymen and clergywomen (ministers, rabbis, priests, etc.) work long hours and provide services to people at times of personal stress such as illness, death, and marriage problems. Economic reasoning would suggest that to attract people to these professions, a compensating differential would be needed. But economist Daniel Hamermesh estimated that male clergy in the United States earn less than 60 percent of the income earned by otherwise identical workers. How can this be explained?

____

____

____

____

____

____

4. Left-handed pitchers in Major League Baseball earn higher average salaries than right-handed pitchers of similar ability. Lefty pitchers Jesse Orosco, Terry Mulholland, and John Franco found employment with Major League teams despite being over 40 years old. Aaron Jerslid, a scout for the Toronto Blue Jays, commented on the difference in teams' desire for right-handed and left-handed pitchers: "Veteran scouts tell me 'A lefty should give you a reason not to like him. A right-hander has to show you something.'" (It's important to note that the demand for left-handed pitchers is strongly influenced by the fact that left-handed pitchers are more successful against left-handed batters.)

Source: "When it comes to pitching, left-handers get extra benefits," by Mel Antonen. June 6, 2006. USATODAY.com

Why do teams pay a premium for left-handed pitchers?

____

____

____

____

____

____

____

5. Table 16-2 on page 551 of the textbook lists annual earnings for different racial and gender groups. The annual earnings of black males ($33,248) exceed the annual earnings of Hispanic males ($26,769). Is this difference due to discrimination?

____

____

____

True/False Questions

T F 1. The price received by a factor of production that has a perfectly *inelastic* supply curve is called an economic rent.

T F 2. Economists refer to the wage premium paid to those who work in dangerous or unpleasant jobs hazard pay.

T F 3. If the price of iPods increases, the demand for iPod workers will shift to the right.

T F 4. Leisure is a normal good. Therefore, as wages increase, the substitution effect will cause a worker to devote less time to work and more time to leisure.

T F 5. Research has shown that increases in the number of science and mathematics courses students take in college (*ceteris paribus*) increase their future earnings.

T F 6. Salaries paid to movie stars today are greater than salaries paid to movie stars of the 1930s and 1940s mainly because of advances in technology.

T F 7. The differences between the salaries of white males and black males are due mostly to racial discrimination.

T F 8. An increase in the wage rate causes an increase in the demand for labor.

T F 9. Pure rent is another name for economic rent.

T F 10. Between 1900 and 1914, wages rose in the United States because the demand for labor increased more than the supply of labor.

T F 11. Compensating differentials explain why college graduates receive incomes higher than incomes of other workers who are 25 years of age and older.

T F 12. If the demand for labor is unchanged, an increase in the supply of labor will decrease the equilibrium wage rate and increase the number of employed workers.

T F 13. Although the labor force participation of women increased from 1950 to over 60 percent in 1970, the rate has fallen to less than 50 percent today as more women have left the labor market and become full-time undergraduate and graduate students.

T F 14. Between 1995 and 2004, the average unemployment rates in the United Kingdom, France, Germany, Italy and Spain were about twice as high as the average unemployment rate in the United States.

T F 15. Increases in human capital will cause workers to have more skills and be more productive. This will cause a shift the supply curve of labor.

Answers to the Self-Test

Multiple-Choice Questions

Questions	Answers	Explanation
1	d	Firms use factors of production – the most important of which are labor, capital, and natural resources – to produce goods and services.
2	b	Economists say that labor demand is a derived demand—that is, derived from the demand for the products produced by workers.
3	c	The *marginal product of labor* is the change in a firm's output from having one additional worker.
4	d	What matters is how much the firm's revenue will rise when it sells the additional output it can produce by hiring one more worker. We can calculate this amount by multiplying the additional output produced by the product price. This amount is called the marginal revenue product of labor (*MRP*).
5	c	The marginal revenue product of labor (*MRP*) is defined as the extra revenue generated by one additional worker.
6	d	Because of diminishing returns, the marginal product of labor (the change in output from one additional worker) decreases as the number of workers increases. Because the marginal product drops as the number of workers increases, the *MRP* curve is negatively sloped.
7	a	When $MRP > W$, the value of an additional worker to the firm exceeds the cost of hiring that worker. The difference is additional profit. Therefore the firm will hire the additional worker.
8	a	The *MRP* curve is also the firm's short-run demand curve for labor.
9	b	To determine the profit-maximizing quantity of workers to hire, we need to compare the marginal revenue product of labor with the wage. Column 8 does this by subtracting the wage (column 7) from the marginal revenue product (column 6). As long as the values in column 8 are positive, the firm should continue to hire workers.
10	a	The marginal revenue product of the second worker is $680 and her wage is $500, so column 7 shows that hiring her will add $180 to the firm's profits. The marginal revenue product of the third worker is $340 and his wage is $500, so hiring him would reduce the firm's profits by $160. Therefore, the firm will maximize profits by hiring 2 workers.
11	b	*Human capital* refers to the accumulated training and skills that workers possess.
12	a	An increase or decrease in the wage causes an increase or decrease in the *quantity of labor demanded*, which we show by a movement along the demand curve. If any variable other than the wage changes, the result is an increase or decrease in the *demand for labor*.
13	c	The marginal revenue product of labor depends on the price the firm receives for its output. A higher price increases the marginal revenue product and shifts the labor demand curve to the right. (Decreasing the quantities of other inputs may shift the labor demand curve in either direction depending on whether those other inputs are substitutes for labor or complements to labor in production.)
14	a	As the wage increases, the opportunity cost of leisure increases, causing individuals to supply a greater quantity of labor. Therefore, the labor supply curve is upward sloping. But this occurs only if the substitution effect prevails over the income effect.

15	b	The income effect of a price change refers to the change in the quantity demanded of a good that results from the effect of a change in the good's price on consumer purchasing power.
16	a	The substitution effect of a wage increase causes a worker to supply a larger quantity of labor. The backward-bending labor supply curve shows the typical case of the substitution effect being larger than the income effect at low levels of wages – so the worker supplies a larger quantity of labor as the wage rises.
17	d	These are the main determinants of labor supply other than the wage.
18	d	A change in quantity supplied or quantity demanded is always caused by a change in price. The wage rate is the price of labor.
19	a	Higher productivity will result in an increase in the demand for labor.
20	b	According to the signaling hypothesis, employers see a college education as a signal that workers possess certain desirable characteristics: self-discipline, the ability to meet deadlines, and the ability to make a sustained effort, even if these characteristics are not related to the specifics of a particular job.
21	b	Increases in labor supply will cause the equilibrium wage to fall, but the equilibrium level of employment to rise. As population increases, the labor supply curve shifts to the right; the equilibrium wage falls, and the equilibrium level of employment increases.
22	b	Labor supply is relatively high in this market, meaning that more workers are attracted to it; therefore, labor supply is abundant.
23	b	The marginal revenue product for baseball players is very high and the supply of people with the ability to play major league baseball is low. The result is that the 750 major league baseball players receive an average wage of $2 million. The marginal revenue product for college professors is much lower and the supply of people with the ability to be college professors is much higher. The result is that the 663,000 college professors in the United States receive an average wage of $73,000, far below that of baseball players. (Since $MRP = W$ in equilibrium, it's clear from comparing the wage rates of the two groups that baseball players have a higher *MRP*.)
24	b	Wages – like prices – do not depend on total value, but on marginal value, or the value of the additional baseball games the Mets expect to win.
25	c	Higher wages that compensate workers for unpleasant aspects of a job are called compensating differentials.
26	c	A psychological principle known as *cognitive dissonance* might cause workers to underestimate the true risk of their jobs. According to this principle, people prefer to think of themselves as intelligent and rational and tend to reject evidence that seems to contradict this image.
27	c	Economic discrimination is illegal in the United States since the passage of the Equal Pay Act of 1963 and the Civil Rights Act of 1964. Nevertheless, it is possible that employers are ignoring the law and practicing economic discrimination.
28	b	Among the groups listed in Table 16-2, Hispanic females have the lowest annual earnings.
29	a	Most economists believe that only a small amount of the gap between the wages of white males and the wages of other groups is due to discrimination. Instead, most of the gap is explained by three main factors: 1) differences in education; 2) differences in experience; and 3) differing preferences for jobs.
30	b	As Table 16-3 shows, women are overrepresented in some jobs where average weekly earnings are less than $500 per week and men are overrepresented in some jobs where weekly earnings are greater than $700 per week.

31	b	Many economists argue that economic discrimination is no longer a major factor in labor markets in the United States. One reason is that employers who discriminate pay an economic penalty in the form of higher wages, as Figure 16-8 illustrates.
32	c	In the textbook example, an unfortunate feedback loop occurred when few women prepared to become lawyers because many law firms discriminated against women and non-discriminating law firms were unable to drive discriminating law firms out of business because there were too few women lawyers available.
33	d	As Figure 16-9 shows, a smaller fraction of the U.S. labor force is unionized than in most other industrial countries.
34	a	As Table 16-4 shows, in the United States, workers in unions receive higher wages than workers who are not in unions.
35	b	Personnel economics is the application of economic analysis to human resources issues.
36	a	With a straight salary, she receives $800 per week, no matter how many cars she sells. This outcome is shown by the horizontal line in the figure. If she receives a commission of $200 per car, her compensation will increase with every car she sells. This outcome is shown by the upward-sloping line in the figure.
37	d	All of the above are reasons why companies choose a salary system rather than the more profitable commission, or piece-rate system of compensation.
38	c	The price received by a factor of production that is in fixed supply is called an *economic rent*, or a *pure rent*.
39	d	A firm with a monopsony in a labor market will hire fewer workers and pay lower wages than would be the case in a competitive market.
40	c	Individuals will receive income equal to the marginal contributions to production from the factors of production they own, including their labor. The more factors of production an individual owns, and the more productive those factors are, the higher the individual's income will be. This approach to explaining the distribution of income is called the *marginal productivity theory of income distribution*.

Short Answer Responses

1. It is highly doubtful that the accounting professor's higher salary was due to a compensating differential. Although the professional responsibilities of professors vary by department, the accounting professor's job is not more dangerous or unpleasant enough to warrant a compensating differential. Economic discrimination would explain this difference, only if it could be demonstrated that the accounting professor was paid more on the basis of race, gender or some other irrelevant characteristic. A more plausible explanation is that there are more people who want to be foreign language professors, relative to the demand for these positions, and relatively fewer people who want to be accounting professors, relative to the demand for these positions. There is a greater demand for accountants than foreign language specialists by private firms. The Midwestern college competes with private firms as well as other colleges and universities for the services of their accounting professors.

2. As baby boomers retire, there will be an increase in the demand for labor to replace those who retire. Holding everything else constant, this will increase the wages and salaries of the replacement workers because of the greater number of retired baby boomers compared to the number of new entrants into the labor force.

3. It seems clear that many clergy members choose their professions for reasons other than the salary and benefits offered. A large number of these people must enjoy helping other people (they may be said to receive "psychic income" from their work) and believe they are responding to a spiritual, rather than a monetary, calling. However, the number of people choosing this profession has declined

over time in several religious denominations. This has led some to suggest other ways to attract clergy, including advertising, loosening restrictions on personal behavior (for example, allowing Catholic priests to marry), and permitting non-clergy to perform some religious tasks. Not all of these suggestions have been adopted, but if recent trends continue, religious leaders will be forced to consider alternative means of recruiting clergy and providing services.

4. Because of the angles from which pitches are thrown, many right-handed batters hit more effectively against left-handed pitchers and many left-handed batters have greater success against right-handed pitchers. Many batters, even those who throw right-handed, learn to bat left-handed to take advantage of the greater number of right-handed pitchers. Using data for 2005, about 31 percent of Major League hitters batted left-handed, 56 percent batted right-handed and 12 percent were switch-hitters. (Switch-hitters usually bat right-handed against left-handed pitchers and left-handed against right-handed pitchers.) Only about 10 percent of the general population is left-handed. Although the supply of left-handed pitchers is not vertical, it is relatively inelastic. This means that salaries can increase substantially without a large increase in quantity supplied. It is common for Major League teams to hire left-handed pitchers to pitch to only one or two left-handed hitters per game. The premium paid to left-handed pitchers compared to right-handed pitchers of similar ability reflects their relative scarcity.

5. It is impossible to rule out discrimination as one factor responsible for the earnings gaps among groups divided by gender or race. But it is likely that this earnings gap can be explained by other factors as well, including differences in education, experience and preferences for jobs.

True/False Answers

1. T Economic rent or pure rent refers to the price of a factor of production that is in fixed supply. The supply curve of this factor is vertical, or perfectly inelastic.
2. F "Compensating differential" is the term economists use to describe this wage premium.
3. T The demand curve for labor is the same at the marginal revenue product of labor curve. The marginal revenue product of iPods equals the product price multiplied by the additional output produced by iPod workers. Therefore, if the price of iPods rises the demand for iPod workers will shift to the right.
4. F The income effect of a wage change has this effect. See the section "The Supply of Labor" beginning on page 540.
5. T Research by Daniel Hamermesh and Stephen Donald found this to be true. See *Making the Connection* on pages 544-545.
6. T DVDs, Internet streaming video, and other technologies developed since the 1930s and 1940s have resulted in large increases in revenue earned by popular movies and, in turn, large increases in salaries paid to those who star in these movies. See *Making the Connection* on pages 549-550.
7. F Most, but not all, of this difference is explained by differences in education, experience and preferences for jobs.
8. F An increase in the real wage caused by a shift of the supply curve causes the quantity demanded of labor to decrease. If the increase in the real wage was caused by a shift in the demand for labor, the causality would run in the opposite direction.
9. T See the explanation for answer number 1 above.
10. T The increase in demand is especially significant because of the large increase in immigration that occurred between 1900 and 1914. See the *Making the Connection* on pages 546-547.
11. F Compensating differentials explain the higher wages workers receive for dangerous or unpleasant jobs.
12. T See the section "The Effect on Equilibrium Wages of a Shift in Labor Supply" beginning on page 545.

13. F The current labor force participation rate for women is still about 60 percent.
14. T The average unemployment rate in the United States was about 5 percent versus about 10 percent in these European countries.
15. F Increases in human capital will cause changes in the *demand* for labor.

Chapter 17

The Economics of Information

Chapter Summary

You learned in Chapters 11 through 15 how firms determine the prices of the goods and services they sell in different types of markets. Some firms face special challenges when they set their prices due to a lack of information. Insurance companies, for example, have difficulty in pricing insurance policies because of **asymmetric information**, which happens when one party to a transaction has less information than the other party. Asymmetric information is present in the market for used cars because if someone is selling you a used car, that person has more information about the car than do you. Asymmetric information leads to **adverse selection**, which occurs when one party to a transaction takes advantage of knowing more than the other party. The insurance industry is also subject to **moral hazard**, which is the tendency of people to change their actions because they have insurance. For example, if you have insurance for your laptop or iPod, you may reduce your care of those objects. Insurance companies use deductibles and co-payments to reduce moral hazard.

Adverse selection and moral hazard also affect firms and investors in financial markets. When a firm has sold stocks and bonds, it may spend the funds in ways not in the owners' best interests. Moral hazard can also be present in labor markets. Once hired, workers may shirk their obligations and not work hard. Firms deal with this form of moral hazard by closely monitoring workers and making their jobs seem more valuable than other jobs.

Information problems can occur in auctions. In some auctions, neither the bidder nor the seller has complete information about what is being auctioned. One possible outcome of auctions, the **winner's curse**, occurs when the winning bidder overestimates the value of the item and ends up worse off than the losers.

Learning Objectives

When you finish this chapter, you should be able to:

1. **Define asymmetric information and distinguish between adverse selection and moral hazard.** Asymmetric information occurs when one party to an economic transaction has less information than the other party. Adverse selection refers to a situation in which one party to a transaction takes advantage of having more information than the other party. Moral hazard occurs when people change their actions as a result of having insurance.

2. **Apply the concepts of adverse selection and moral hazard to financial markets.** Asymmetric information exists in financial markets because firms know more about their financial situation than potential buyers of the firms' stocks and bonds. Moral hazard exists in financial markets because firms may use funds raised through the sale of stocks and bonds to reduce profits. The larger the firm and the more carefully analysts follow the firm's activities, the less likely moral hazard will be a problem.

3. **Apply the concepts of adverse selection and moral hazard to labor markets.** Workers have more information about their work ethic than their employers. After workers are hired they may shirk their obligations and not work hard.

4. **Explain the winner's curse and why it occurs.** The winner's curse refers to the tendency in certain auctions for winning bidders to overstate the value of the good they bid on. In competitive bidding, winning bidders are those that are most optimistic about the value of the item on which they bid. The average bid is often closer to the actual value of the item.

Chapter Review

Chapter Opener: Why Does State Farm Charge Young Men So Much More Than Young Women for Auto Insurance? (pages 574-575)

State Farm Insurance charges different prices for automobile insurance based on a driver's gender, age, and other factors. State Farm and other insurance companies attempt to match the prices they charge with the costs they are likely to incur on each policy. Many insurance companies use sophisticated computer models to predict the chance that a driver will have an accident. As a result, in recent years there has been an increase in the variety of prices insurance companies charge drivers.

Helpful Study Hint

An ***Inside Look*** explains how insurance companies use the credit reports of their customers as one factor in determining premiums, a procedure that has been criticized by some consumer groups. Complete related end-of-chapter problem 1.13 to test your understanding of the chapter opener.

Economics in YOUR Life! asks you to assume you are in the market for a used car and can choose between buying from a local dealer or an individual seller. Would you be willing to pay the same price for an apparently identical car from either seller? Think about your answer before you read what the textbook authors suggest you might do at the end of this chapter.

17.1 LEARNING OBJECTIVE

17.1 Asymmetric Information (pages 576-580)

Learning Objective 1 Define asymmetric information and distinguish between adverse selection and moral hazard.

The difficulty in correctly pricing insurance policies arises from asymmetric information. **Asymmetric information** is a situation in which one party to an economic transaction has less information than the other party. For example, if someone drinks, smokes, doesn't sleep well, and has heart disease in his or her family, a health insurance company does not necessarily have that information when pricing a policy. Guarding against the effects of asymmetric information is a major objective of sellers in the insurance market and of buyers in financial markets.

The study of asymmetric information began with the study of used car markets or the market for "lemons." Sellers of used cars have more information about the cars they sell than do buyers. Most used cars offered for sale will be lemons. This is due to adverse selection. **Adverse selection** is a situation in which one party to a transaction (for example, a used car dealer) takes advantage of knowing more than the other party to the transaction (for example, the car buyer). Used car dealers can take steps to assure buyers they are not selling lemons by offering warranties that guarantee repair or replacement over a certain time period. Sellers can also build a reputation for selling reliable cars.

Buyers of insurance will always know more than insurance companies about the likelihood of the event being insured against happening. For example, people with bad health habits and histories of health problems will have a better idea of the probability that they will suffer a heart attack or other health problem than will insurance companies. Insurance companies cover their costs only if they set the prices (premiums) of their policies at levels that represent how many payment claims the people they have insured are likely to submit. The adverse selection problem can be reduced if people are automatically covered by insurance. For example, state governments require drivers to have automobile insurance. Adverse selection problems can also be reduced by offering group coverage to large companies and other organizations.

The insurance market is also subject to moral hazard. **Moral hazard** is the tendency of people who have insurance to change their actions because of the insurance or, more broadly, actions taken by one party to a transaction that are different from what the other party expected at the time of the transaction. An example of moral hazard is a firm that has taken out fire insurance may be less careful about avoiding fire hazards. Insurance companies use deductibles and co-payments to reduce moral hazard.

Helpful Study Hint

Making the Connection on pages 578-580 explains why some people do not have health insurance:

1. Some healthy young adults between the ages of 18 and 24 don't expect to need medical care and so do not want to pay the monthly premiums to buy insurance they don't expect to need. Because of adverse selection, some insurance companies charge higher prices to young, healthy people than they are willing to pay.
2. Many low-income people qualify for government health insurance through the Medicaid program. But some of these do not take advantage of the program or are not eligible.

Don't Let This Happen to YOU! on page 580 explains how you can understand the difference between adverse selection and moral hazard:

- Adverse selection happens at the time you enter into the transaction. Example: You sell your roommate a computer that crashes on you every three or four weeks.
- Moral hazard refers to what happens after you enter into the transaction. Example: You get insurance for your apartment and are less careful about locking the door when you leave in the morning.

Work through related end-of-chapter problems 1.11, 1.12, and 1.14 to understand the concepts referred to in these features.

Extra Solved Problem **17-1**

Chapter 17 includes two Solved Problems. Here is an extra Solved Problem to help you build your skills solving economic problems.

Supports Learning Objective 1: Define asymmetric information and distinguish between moral hazard and adverse selection.

The Nub of the Matter (Warning - Content may be unsuitable for sensitive readers!)

Although most people with health and life insurance are honest, insurance companies are always subject to the problem of adverse selection. Some people change their behavior as a result of having insurance. Among the most conspicuous examples of behavioral change are those involving people who lie about their circumstances or take deliberate actions that endanger their health. There are reported cases of self-mutilation in order to collect on disability insurance. Perhaps the most bizarre story concerns a town in Florida that acquired the macabre nickname of "Nub City" in the 1970s.

> Over 50 people in the town have suffered "accidents" involving the loss of various organs and appendages, and claims of up to $300,000 have been paid out by insurers. Their investigators are positive the maimings are self-inflicted; many witnesses to the "accidents" are prior claimants or relatives of the victims, and one investigator notes that "somehow they always shoot off parts they seem to need least."

Another type of moral hazard involves staging automobile accidents. The following is a brief description of how this is done.

> *How do I get started?* For a "paper accident" try inflicting "controlled damage" on a couple of cars with a sledgehammer in a dark parking lot. Insert passengers. Summon a witness. Gather broken glass in bags for re-use.
>
> *That was easy, what next?* "Staged" accidents: Buy rustbuckets, insure one and run it into another one full of recruited claimants-to-be ("cows"). If you're nice, give them pillows...
>
> *How do I keep from getting caught?* Vary your fact patterns. Don't stamp a doctor's name on medical reports months after he's died. Don't lose your ledger – needed to keep hundreds of accidents straight – or your scripts and tip sheets.

Sources: "Moral Hazard and Adverse Selection." http://ingrimayne.saintjoe.edu/econ/RiskExclusion/Risk.html
Walter Olsen, "New Trends in Highway Robbery," *Wall Street Journal*, December 20, 1996.

a. Use the two passages above to describe asymmetric information.

b. Use the two passages to distinguish adverse selection and moral hazard.

SOLVING THE PROBLEM

Step 1: Review the chapter material.
This problem is about asymmetric information, so you may want to review the section "Asymmetric Information," which begins on page 576 of the textbook.

Step 2: Answer question (a) by defining asymmetric information.
Asymmetric information is a situation in which one party to an economic transaction has less information than the other party. Those who are insured obviously have more knowledge of their circumstances than the companies that insure them.

Step 3: Answer question (b) by explaining the difference between adverse selection and moral hazard.
Adverse selection occurs when people take advantage of knowing more about their circumstances than the insurance companies do. This is the case with those who are alleged to commit insurance fraud. The guilty parties demonstrate moral hazard, which is the tendency for insurance to alter behavior. The possibility of collecting on an insurance policy is the motivation for self-mutilation and staging phony automobile accidents.

17.2 LEARNING OBJECTIVE

17.2 Adverse Selection and Moral Hazard in Financial Markets (pages 581-583)

Learning Objective 2 Apply the concepts of adverse selection and moral hazard to financial markets.

Adverse selection and moral hazard pose problems for the managers of firms and for their owners. Because firms know more about their financial situations than stockholders, the firm can use the funds in ways that reduce profits. For example, a firm that has no debt on its balance sheet may suddenly issue a large quantity of bonds. This increases the risk to current owners of their stock.

Congress created the Securities and Exchange Commission (SEC) in 1934 to regulate the stock and bond markets. The SEC requires firms to register stocks and bonds they wish to sell, increasing the amount of information available to investors.

Helpful Study Hint

This section's ***Making the Connection*** on page 582 uses moral hazard to explain the accounting scandals of 2002. These scandals led to Congress and the President passing the Sarbanes-Oxley Act, which aimed at making future scandals less likely and restoring investor confidence in financial markets. Two key parts of this Act are that

1. A government board now oversees the auditing of financial statements and has authority to take legal action against auditors who fail to ensure the accuracy of corporate financial statements.
2. Chief executive officers are responsible for certifying financial statements and are subject to prison sentences for violating the Sarbanes-Oxley Act.

Work through related end-of-chapter problem 2.7 to check your understanding of moral hazard in financial markets.

Extra Solved Problem 17-2

Chapter 17 includes two Solved Problems. Here is an extra Solved Problem to help you build your skills solving economic problems.

Supports Learning Objective 2: Apply the concepts of adverse selection and moral hazard to financial markets.

The Fall of the House of Rigas

In early 2002, a large firm unveiled plans for a new corporate headquarters in downtown Buffalo, New York. The $125 million project would house 1,000 workers and serve as a catalyst for other development efforts in the city's Inner Harbor area. James Allen, executive director of the Amherst and Erie County Industrial Development Agencies commented, "We need a signature project on the waterfront and this gives us that project." Unfortunately, the building project was proposed by Adelphia Communications. On June 24th of that same year Adelphia filed for bankruptcy. On June 20, 2005, a court sentenced John Rigas, Adelphia's founder and longtime CEO, to 15 years in jail for looting the company's finances and concealing over $2 billion in debt from investors. Rigas' son Timothy received a 20-year sentence after being convicted on the same charges as his father: conspiracy, bank fraud and securities fraud. During the Rigas trial, U.S. attorneys accused the Rigases of using Adelphia as a "private piggy bank" to pay for such personal expenses as millions of dollars in cash advances, $13 million to build a golf course, and even 100 pairs of bedroom slippers. The elder Rigas had even used a company jet to send a Christmas tree to his daughter in New York City. When he found out the tree was the wrong size, he had another tree sent – at company expense.

Despite being a publicly held firm, Adelphia was run like a family business. John Rigas and three of his sons and one son-in-law held five of the nine seats on the company's board of directors. The family's mismanagement was hidden from investors through fraudulent financial statements. After the collapse of Internet stock prices following a rapid climb in the 1990s and the slowdown of the overall U.S. economy in 2001, investors began looking more closely at questionable managerial and accounting practices that made debt-ridden firms such as Adelphia and Enron appear in better financial condition than they actually were.

Sources: James Fink, "Adelphia Picks HOK for Downtown Office Design," *Buffalo Business First*, January 16, 2002. James Fink, "John Rigas Sentenced to 15 Years in Prison," *Buffalo Business First*, June 21, 2005.
"Rigases Looted Adelphia, Jurors Told" http://www.smh.com.au/articles/2004/03/02/1078191325849.html

a. What characteristic of Adelphia Communications' management structure demonstrates adverse selection?

b. Use the actions of the Rigas family to illustrate the consequences of moral hazard in financial markets.

SOLVING THE PROBLEM

Step 1: Review the chapter material.
This problem is about adverse selection and moral hazard, so you may want to review the section "Adverse Selection and Moral Hazard in Financial Markets," which begins on page 581 of the textbook.

Step 2: Answer question (a) by discussing Adelphia Communications' management structure.
The strong overall performance of the U.S. economy and U.S. financial markets masked the fraudulent behavior of the Rigases during the 1990s. Perhaps the most important characteristic of the company's management structure was that Rigas family members held a majority of the seats on Adelphia's board of directors. This meant that the family had effective control over the company and could prevent other board members from overruling questionable practices.

Step 3: Answer question (b) by discussing the consequences of moral hazard in financial markets.
It is critically important for investors and analysts to have access to timely and accurate information regarding a publicly-owned company. Had the true financial condition of the company been known earlier, the financial markets would have penalized Adelphia with lower stock prices. The company could have been forced to change the composition of the board of directors or to be sold to another company.

17.3 LEARNING OBJECTIVE

17.3 Adverse Selection and Moral Hazard in Labor Markets (pages 583-584)

Learning Objective 3 Apply the concepts of adverse selection and moral hazard to labor markets.

Economists refer to the conflict between the interests of shareholders and the interests of top management as a principal-agent problem. The **principal-agent problem** is caused by an agent pursuing his own interests rather than the interests of the principal who hired him. In labor markets, this problem arises because workers may shirk their obligations and not work hard.

Firms may reduce shirking through close monitoring of workers or by making a worker's job seem more valuable. Firms may pay efficiency wages, which are higher-than-equilibrium wages used to give workers an incentive to work harder.

A seniority system that rewards workers who have been with the firm longer with higher pay and other benefits may also reduce shirking. Profit sharing provides workers with a share of the firm's profits; the harder the employee works, the more profit the firm earns and the higher the employee's income. But this may not work well in large firms where there is only a slight connection between an individual worker's effort and the firm's profitability.

Helpful Study Hint

Read ***Solved Problem 17-3*** to understand how changes in a firm's compensation system can reduce moral hazard. Working through end-of-chapter problem 3.4 will further increase your understanding of this topic.

17.4 LEARNING OBJECTIVE

17.4 The Winner's Curse: When Is It Bad to Win an Auction? (pages 585-589)

Learning Objective 4 Explain the winner's curse and why it occurs.

In some auctions, neither the bidder nor the seller has complete information about what is being auctioned. The **winner's curse** is the idea that the winner in certain auctions may overestimate the value of the good, thus ending up worse off than the losers. When there is uncertainty regarding the value of the item auctioned, the average competitive bid is likely to be close to the true value. The winning bid in an auction will be one that is most optimistic and, therefore, greater than the true value. The winner's curse applies to auctions of common-value assets that would be given the same value by bidders if they had perfect information. The winner's curse does not apply to auctions of private-value assets when the value to each bidder depends on the bidder's own preferences.

Helpful Study Hint

You've probably heard statistics that about 40 percent of marriages end in divorce. The ***Making the Connection*** on page 586 of the textbook suggests that the winner's curse can explain why marriages often end in divorce: Some people overestimate another person's value as a spouse. The ***Making the Connection*** on page 588 describes another example of the winner's curse through a classroom experiment. ***Solved Problem 17-4*** further explores the winner's curse using an auction of Alaskan oil fields. Working through end-of-chapter problems 4.5, 4.7 and 4.10 will increase your understanding of this material.

Key Terms

Adverse selection. The situation in which one party to a transaction takes advantage of knowing more than the other party to the transaction.

Asymmetric information. A situation in which one party to an economic transaction has less information than the other party.

Moral hazard. The actions people take after they have entered a transaction that make the other party to transaction worse off.

Principal-agent problem. A problem caused by agents pursuing their own interests rather than the interests of the principal who hired them.

Winner's curse. The idea that the winner in certain auctions may have overestimated the value of the good, thus ending up worse off than the losers.

Self-Test

(Answers are provided at the end of the Self-Test.)

Multiple-Choice Questions

1. What is the reason for the existence of *asymmetric information*?
   a. Asymmetric information exists when people who have insurance change their actions because of the insurance.
   b. Asymmetric information exists when one party to an economic transaction has less information than the other party.
   c. Asymmetric information exists when parties to an economic transaction must pay different prices to obtain the same information.
   d. Asymmetric information exists when adverse selection leads to moral hazard.

2. Fill in the blanks: Guarding against the effects of asymmetric information is a major objective of __________ in the insurance market and __________ in financial markets.
   a. buyers; sellers
   b. sellers; buyers
   c. buyers; buyers
   d. sellers; sellers

3. If potential buyers have difficulty separating lemons from good used cars, what will they do?
   a. They will take this into account in the prices they are willing to pay.
   b. They will not take this into account in the prices they are willing to pay.
   c. They will be absolutely indifferent between cars, and will pay the same price for either type of car.
   d. They will pay a price for a car that is always too high.

4. When adverse selection exists in the used car market, which of the following will prevail?
   a. Buyers will generally offer a very high price, closer to the price of a good car.
   b. Buyers will generally offer a very low price, closer to the price of a lemon.
   c. Buyers will generally offer a price somewhere between the price they would be willing to pay for a good car and the price they would be willing to pay for a lemon.
   d. All buyers will end up buying a car.

5. Suppose that half of used cars offered for sale are reliable and half are unreliable. If potential buyers are willing to pay $5,000 for a reliable car, but only $2,500 for an unreliable one, how much will buyers offer for a car?
   a. $2,500
   b. $3,750
   c. $5,000
   d. $4,999

6. When uninformed buyers are willing to pay a price for used cars that is the average of the value of a lemon and the value of a good used car, which of the following will occur?
   a. Most used cars offered for sale will be lemons.
   b. Most used cars offered for sale will not be lemons.
   c. The quantity supplied of lemons will be identical to the quantity supplied of good used cars.
   d. Only good used cars will be offered for sale.

7. What is the impact of *adverse selection* on economic efficiency in a market?
   a. Adverse selection will increase economic efficiency.
   b. Adverse selection will reduce economic efficiency.
   c. Adverse selection does not have any impact on economic efficiency in a market.
   d. Consumer wants will shift toward the goods left in the market.

8. Which of the following is a way of reducing adverse selection in the car market?
   a. Providing manufacturer warranties
   b. Providing dealer warranties
   c. Building a good reputation
   d. All of the above

9. Which of the following is true about *lemon laws*?
   a. Lemon laws require a full refund if a new car needs several major repairs within the first two years.
   b. Car manufacturers have actually supported lemon laws.
   c. Most states today have enacted lemon laws and strictly enforce them.
   d. All of the above

10. Asymmetric information problems are particularly severe in the market for insurance. This is true because
    a. insurance companies will always know more about the likelihood of an event happening than will buyers of insurance.
    b. buyers of insurance will always know more about the likelihood of an event happening than will insurance companies.
    c. insurance companies and buyers of insurance cannot distinguish between good and bad information.
    d. insurance companies are non-depository financial institutions.

11. Which of the following groups tends to worsen the problem of adverse selection?
    a. Good drivers
    b. Sick people
    c. People living in houses made entirely of rock
    d. All of the above

12. Which of the following makes the adverse selection problem in the health insurance market worse?
    a. Charging high premiums for insurance coverage
    b. Refusing to offer insurance policies to certain people
    c. Requesting a medical examination for new applicants
    d. All of the above

13. How can insurance companies reduce adverse selection?
    a. By offering policies mostly to individuals rather than groups of people
    b. By offering group coverage rather than individual coverage
    c. By *not* requiring that every patient buy health insurance
    d. By increasing the price of participation in the health insurance program

14. When is it easier for insurance companies to estimate the average number of claims likely to be filed?
    a. When they offer policies to individuals, not groups
    b. When they offer group coverage rather than individual coverage
    c. When they insure small groups rather than large groups
    d. When they reduce the number of participants so as to deal with a small rather than large number of customers

15. Insurance companies can reduce the problems that arise from adverse selection by offering group coverage to large firms. Group coverage is an example of
    a. risk abatement.
    b. risk aversion.
    c. risk pooling.
    d. hazard reduction.

16. Which of the following is a consequence of the adverse selection problems insurance companies face?
    a. Insurance companies charge young women higher prices for automobile insurance than they charge young men.
    b. Insurance companies sometimes refuse to offer health insurance to people with chronic illnesses.
    c. Insurance companies sometimes refuse to offer group insurance to large companies because there are too many insured people to accurately price this insurance.
    d. The equilibrium quantity of health insurance is greater that it would be in the absence of adverse selection.

17. Which of the following is true about adverse selection and moral hazard?
    a. Adverse selection is a consequence of asymmetric information; asymmetric information is a consequence of moral hazard.
    b. Insurance companies can eliminate adverse selection by charging deductibles and co-insurance, but charging deductibles and co-insurance increases the risk of moral hazard.
    c. Adverse selection only affects the market for automobile insurance; moral hazard only affects the markets for health and life insurance.
    d. Adverse selection refers to what happens at the time of entering into a transaction; moral hazard refers to what happens after entering into a transaction.

18. Match one of the terms below to the following definition: Actions taken by one party to a transaction that are different from what the other party expected at the time of the transaction.
    a. Adverse selection
    b. Moral hazard
    c. The Coase Theorem
    d. Winner's curse

19. Which of the following actions is an attempt by a fire insurance company to reduce *moral hazard*?
    a. Requiring a warehouse to install a sprinkler system
    b. Reserving the right to inspect the warehouse for fire hazards
    c. Establish a system of deductibles and co-payments
    d. All of the above

20. Which of the following refers to a system in which the insurance company pays only a percentage of any claim, not a certain dollar amount?
    a. A deductible
    b. A co-payment
    c. Both deductibles and co-payments
    d. Neither deductibles nor co-payments

21. Fill in the blanks: There are two consequences of asymmetric information. ________________ refers to what happens *at the time* of entering a transaction, while ________________ refers to what happens *after* entering into the transaction.
    a. Adverse selection; moral hazard
    b. Moral hazard; adverse selection
    c. Imperfect information; economic inefficiency
    d. Voluntary exchange; involuntary participation

22. If your medical insurance policy has a $100 deductible and a 10 percent co-payment, how much will you pay on a medical bill of $1,000?
    a. $100
    b. $900
    c. $110
    d. $190

23. What is the effect of adopting deductibles and co-payments for all holders of insurance policies?
    a. Holders will have an incentive to file more claims.
    b. Holders will have an incentive to avoid filing claims.
    c. The moral hazard problem in the insurance market will be greater.
    d. The adverse selection problem in the insurance market will be greater.

24. When will potential investors be reluctant to buy the stocks and bonds of particular companies?
    a. When the firm knows more about its financial situation than does the potential investor
    b. When a great deal of public information is available about the firm
    c. When asymmetric information is absent
    d. All of the above

25. Which firms have an easier time selling stocks and bonds to potential investors?
    a. Firms that are studied closely by investment analysts
    b. Small corporations rather than large corporations
    c. Firms for which little public information is made available
    d. All of the above

26. If the managers of a corporation use funds in ways that actually reduce profits, which of the following problems is present?
    a. Diminishing returns to labor
    b. Moral hazard
    c. Adverse selection
    d. The winner's curse

27. Fill in the blanks: The _________ the firm is and the more carefully investment analysts follow its activities, the _________ likely moral hazard is to be a problem.
    a. larger; more
    b. smaller; less
    c. larger; less
    d. smaller; more

28. Which agency was established by Congress in 1934 to regulate the stock and bond markets?
    a. The Federal Reserve System
    b. The Federal Trade Commission
    c. The Commerce Department
    d. The Securities and Exchange Commission

29. What did the creation of the Securities and Exchange Commission do for financial markets?
    a. It made the problems of adverse selection and moral hazard worse, and reduced the number of firms that could raise funds by selling stocks and bonds.
    b. It helped reduce adverse selection and moral hazard and increased the number of firms that could raise funds by selling stocks and bonds.
    c. It helped reduce adverse selection and moral hazard, but decreased the number of firms that could raise funds by selling stocks and bonds.
    d. It increased adverse selection and moral hazard but also increased the number of firms that could raise funds by selling stocks and bonds.

30. Which of the following financial statements reports the profits of a firm over a period of time?
    a. The balance sheet
    b. The income statement
    c. The prospectus
    d. The audit

31. The news that Enron and other firms had "cooked the books" is an example of which of the following?
    a. Adverse selection
    b. Moral hazard
    c. The winner's curse
    d. Profit sharing

32. What was the objective of the Sarbanes-Oxley Act of 2002?
    a. To reduce the number of factors that can affect a firm's profits
    b. To eliminate the auditing of corporations by independent accounting firms
    c. To prevent chief executive officers from serving prison terms for financial crimes
    d. To restore confidence in the financial system and strengthen the country's security laws

33. Which of the following are provisions of the Sarbanes-Oxley Act of 2002?
    a. To establish a government board to oversee the auditing of financial statements
    b. To increase prison terms for violating securities laws
    c. To require chief executives and chief financial officers to personally certify the accuracy of financial statements
    d. All of the above

34. What is the term given to the problem caused by an agent pursuing his own interests rather than the interests of the principal who hired him?
    a. The principal-agent problem
    b. Adverse selection
    c. The capture theory of regulation
    d. Organizational misbehavior

35. Which of the following is most closely associated with the term "shirking"?
    a. Making an effort to report accurate information on financial statements.
    b. The possibility that a worker may be hired at a wage that is higher than the equilibrium wage in a given labor market.
    c. The possibility that workers, once hired, may not work as hard as anticipated.
    d. Actions by managers and workers designed to reduce the risk of being fired.

36. What is an *efficiency wage*?
    a. A wage designed to give workers an incentive to work harder
    b. Any minimum wage is an efficiency wage
    c. A wage usually below the equilibrium wage
    d. All of the above

37. Which of the following compensation schemes would reduce moral hazard among salespeople?
    a. Compensation based on a straight salary without commission
    b. Compensation that depends on how much workers sell, such as straight commission
    c. Compensation based on a set fee for services rendered rather than an hourly salary or commission
    d. None of the above

38. What is the idea behind the *winner's curse*?
    a. The act of winning a good in a certain auction may cause the bidder to build too much confidence and end up overbidding in subsequent auctions.
    b. In certain auctions, the winner may have overestimated the value of the good, and so ended up worse off than the losers.
    c. In certain auctions, the winner may have underestimated the value of the good, and so ended up far better off than the losers.
    d. Bad luck usually strikes those who win an auction.

39. In an auction for a common-value asset, if there are seven bids (in millions) of $32, $18, $11, $8, $6, $4, and $3, respectively, what is the most likely value of the asset?
    a. Close to $32
    b. Close to $3
    c. Close to $12
    d. None of the above; there is insufficient information to answer the question.

40. In which of the following auctions is the *winner's curse* most applicable?
   a. In auctions of private-value assets
   b. In auctions where the value to each bidder depends on the bidder's own preferences
   c. In auctions of common-value assets, such as oil fields
   d. In auctions where bidders place different bids even when they have perfect information

Short Answer Questions

1. Most colleges and universities have a tenure system for their faculty. After faculty members have been granted tenure, they receive a degree of employment security rare among other professions. One reason for the tenure system is that it promotes academic freedom. With tenure, a faculty member need not worry about being dismissed for stating controversial beliefs in his or her classroom. Does the tenure system also result in moral hazard? Explain your answer.

2. The ***Making the Connection*** on page 586 of the textbook noted that over 40 percent of marriages in the United States end in divorce. The high rate of divorce may be evidence of a winner's curse in the so-called *marriage market*. If divorce were banned in the United States, would this result in a lower percentage of people who are dissatisfied with their marriages?

3. In 2007, the baseball Barry Bonds hit for his record-breaking 756th home run was auctioned. The winning bid was over $750,000. Does the "winner's curse" explain why the auction resulted in such a high winning bid for this baseball?

____

____

____

____

4. Many fast-food restaurants pay their workers no more than the national minimum wage ($5.85 in 2007, with increases scheduled for 2008 and 2009), but some pay *more* than the minimum wage. Are these above-minimum wages also efficiency wages? Explain your answer.

____

____

____

____

____

____

____

5. Each academic term, a large number of students decide to take principles of economics courses. Most universities offer several sections of these courses. Explain how asymmetric information influences a student's decision about which principles of economics section to enroll in.

____

____

____

____

____

True/False Questions

T F 1. Adverse selection causes many used cars offered for sale to be "lemons" and reduces the total quantity of used cars sold.

T F 2. The "lemon laws" passed by most states include a provision that car manufacturers must indicate whether a used car they offer for sale was repurchased from the original owner as a lemon.

T F 3. Michael Spence began the study of asymmetric information with an analysis of the market for used cars.

T F 4. The Securities and Exchange Commission requires firms to take actions that reduce the problems associated with adverse selection and moral hazard in financial markets.

T F 5. Equilibrium wages paid to workers that reflect their marginal revenue products are called efficiency wages.

T F 6. The accounting scandals of 2002, involving Enron, WorldCom, and Adelphia Communications, are examples of moral hazard.

T F 7. Insurance companies can reduce problems caused by adverse selection by offering group coverage to large firms.

T F 8. A warehouse owner who purchases a fire insurance policy may become less careful about reducing potential fire hazards in his warehouse. This is an example of adverse selection.

T F 9. Pacific Telesis used economic reasoning and a knowledge of the winner's curse to successfully bid on licenses that allowed it to operate a wireless communication network.

T F 10. A firm can use a seniority system for its workers to reduce the incidence of moral hazard.

T F 11. A *co-payment* requires the holder of an insurance policy to pay a certain dollar amount of a claim.

T F 12. One reason for the Enron and WorldCom accounting scandals of 2002 was that their financial statements were audited by accountants employed by these firms.

T F 13. Profit-sharing typically does not overcome the risk of moral hazard on the part of employees because profits are affected by many factors that are unrelated to how hard a particular employee works.

T F 14. The winner's curse applies only to auctions of private-value assets.

T F 15. Lemon laws apply to both new and used car markets.

Answers to the Self-Test

Multiple-Choice Questions

Question	Response	Explanation
1	b	Asymmetric information is a situation where one party to an economic transaction has less information than the other party.
2	b	Guarding against the effects of asymmetric information is a major objective of sellers in the insurance market, and of buyers in financial markets. But it was in the market for used automobiles that economists first began to carefully study the problem of asymmetric information.
3	a	If potential buyers of used cars know that they will have difficulty separating the good used cars from the bad used cars, or "lemons," they will take this into account in the prices they are willing to pay.
4	c	When adverse selection in the used car market exists, buyers will generally offer a price somewhere between the price they would be willing to pay for a good car and the price they would be willing to pay for a lemon.

5	b	This price is halfway between the price they would pay if they knew for certain the car was a good one and the price they would pay if they knew it was a lemon.
6	a	To sellers of lemons, an offer of the average price is above the true value of the car and they will be quite happy to sell. As sellers of lemons take advantage of knowing more about the cars they are selling than buyers do, the used car market will fall victim to adverse selection: most used cars offered for sale will be lemons.
7	b	Adverse selection reduces the total quantity of used cars bought and sold in the market because few good cars are offered for sale. As a result, we can conclude that information problems reduce economic efficiency in a market.
8	d	All of the above are suggested ways of reducing adverse selection in the car market.
9	a	Most lemon laws have two main provisions. One is that new cars that need several major repairs during the first year or two after the date of original purchase may be returned to the manufacturer for a full refund. The other is that car manufacturers must indicate whether a used car they are offering for sale was repurchased from the original owner as a lemon. Although popular with consumers, opposition from manufacturers has resulted in lemon laws being enacted in fewer than 20 states. Enforcement has also been spotty.
10	b	Asymmetric information problems are particularly severe in the market for insurance. Buyers of insurance policies will always know more about the likelihood of the event being insured against happening than will insurance companies.
11	b	The adverse selection problem arises because sick people are more likely to want medical insurance than healthy people, reckless drivers are more likely to want automobile insurance than careful drivers, and people living in homes that are fire hazards are more likely to want fire insurance than people living in safe homes.
12	a	Insurance companies are reluctant to charge higher premiums because it increases the likelihood that only people who are almost certain to make a claim will purchase a policy.
13	b	Insurance companies can reduce adverse selection problems by offering group coverage. Everyone employed by a firm with group coverage is insured. If the group is large enough, coverage is likely to represent the proportions of healthy and unhealthy people in the general population.
14	b	As long as the group is large enough, it is likely to represent the proportions of healthy and unhealthy people found in the general population. That makes it easier for insurance companies to estimate the average number of claims likely to be filed under a group medical insurance or life insurance policy, than it would be to predict the number of claims likely to be filed under an individual policy.
15	c	See the section "Reducing Adverse Selection in the Insurance Market" beginning on page 577.
16	b	See the ***Making the Connection*** on pages 578-580.
17	d	See the ***Don't Let This Happen to YOU!*** on page 580.
18	b	Moral hazard is the tendency of people who have insurance to change their actions because of the insurance, or, more broadly, actions people take after they have entered into a transaction that make the other party to the transaction worse off.
19	d	Insurance companies can take steps to reduce moral hazard problems. For example, a fire insurance company may insist that a firm install a sprinkler system in a warehouse in order to offset any increased carelessness once the policy is in place. Or it may reserve the right to inspect the warehouse periodically to check for fire hazards. Insurance companies also use deductibles and co-payments to reduce moral hazard.

20	b	A deductible requires the holder of the insurance policy to pay a certain dollar amount of a claim. With a co-payment, the insurance company pays only a percentage of any claim.
21	a	Adverse selection refers to what happens at the time the transaction is entered into. Moral hazard refers to what happens after the transaction has been entered into.
22	d	If you have a medical insurance policy with a $100 deductible and a 10 percent co-payment and you have a medical bill of $1,000. You must pay the first $100 of the bill and 10 percent of the other $900, or $100 + $90 = $190.00.
23	b	Deductibles and co-payments give the holders of the insurance policy an incentive to avoid filing claims.
24	a	Asymmetric information is a key reason why only large corporations are able to raise funds by selling stocks and bonds. Every firm knows more about its financial situation than does any potential investor. Because investors have trouble distinguishing between well-run firms and poorly-run firms, they are reluctant to buy the stocks and bonds of companies unless there is a great deal of public information available about these companies.
25	a	Because investors have trouble distinguishing between well-run firms and poorly-run firms, they are reluctant to buy the stocks and bonds of companies unless there is a great deal of public information available about these companies. In practice, this means that unless firms are studied closely by investment analysts working for brokerage firms and investment companies, firms will have difficulty selling stocks and bonds to investors.
26	b	Investors are worried about moral hazard. Once a firm has sold stocks and bonds, the possibility exists that the company will use the funds in ways that reduce profits.
27	c	The larger the firm is and the more carefully investment analysts follow its activities, the less likely moral hazard is to be a problem. This is a reason why investors will be willing to buy the stocks and bonds of large firms, but not of small firms.
28	d	When firms failed to provide investors with clear information about their true financial positions, Congress responded by establishing the Securities and Exchange Commission (SEC) in 1934 to regulate the stock and bond markets.
29	b	The SEC succeeded in increasing the amount of information available to potential investors. This helped reduce the adverse selection and moral hazard problems in financial markets and increased the number of firms that have been able to raise funds by selling stocks and bonds.
30	b	The basic information on the financial condition of a company is contained in its financial statements, particularly its income statement and balance sheet. A firm's income statement reports its profits over a period of time, and its balance sheet shows the net value of the firm, based on the value of everything it owns minus the value of everything it owes.
31	b	The news that Enron and other firms had "cooked the books" illustrates the difficulty that moral hazard poses for investors. The management of a firm knows far more about the firm's finances than any outside investor can.
32	d	To help restore confidence in financial statements, Congress passed and President George W. Bush signed into law the Sarbanes-Oxley Act to strengthen the country's securities laws. The bill authorized the SEC to set up a government board to oversee the auditing of financial statements.

33	d	The bill authorized the SEC to set up a government board to oversee the auditing of financial statements. The bill also requires chief executive officers and chief financial officers to personally certify the accuracy of financial statements. The maximum prison term for violating the securities laws was raised to 25 years.
34	a	The principal-agent problem is caused by an agent pursuing his own interests rather than the interests of the principal who hired him.
35	c	The moral hazard behind the principal-agent problem between the managers of a firm and its workers is that once hired, workers may shirk their obligations and not work hard.
36	a	An efficiency wage is a higher than equilibrium wage used by firms to give workers an incentive to work harder.
37	b	Compensation that depends on how much workers sell reduces the risk associated with moral hazard since workers will not get paid for shirking.
38	b	In an auction for a common-value asset, the winning bidder may overestimate the value of the good, and so end up worse off than the losing bidders.
39	c	Mistakes of sometimes being too high would tend to offset the mistakes of sometimes being too low, so the average estimate would be close to the asset's value. In this case, it is likely that the true value of the asset in the auction is about $11.7 million, or the average of the seven bids.
40	c	The winner's curse applies only to auctions of *common-value assets* – such as oil fields – that would be given the same value by all bidders if they had perfect information. The winner's curse does not apply to auctions of *private-value assets* where the value to each bidder depends on the bidder's own preferences.

Short Answer Responses

1. Some critics of the tenure system argue that moral hazard may be a by-product of granting tenure to members of a college's faculty. Prior to receiving tenure, faculty have strong incentives to demonstrate excellence in teaching and research, two criteria used to evaluate faculty performance. After tenure is granted, some faculty will not work as hard on their teaching and research unless they have other incentives to do so. (Most universities have an additional promotion step to full professor that gives tenured associate professors some additional incentive to demonstrate continued excellence in teaching and research.)

2. It is possible that some people would take longer to select a marriage partner – and may choose not to marry at all – if divorce were made illegal in the United States. But keep in mind that people often make mistakes when they make decisions (recall from Chapter 9 that one common mistake is that consumers are overly optimistic about their future behavior) so it is highly unlikely that banning divorce would lead to a large increase in the number of successful marriages. The law would make it more likely that people would remain in unhappy marriages (not necessarily a better outcome) and would certainly lead some people to seek divorces in other countries where the practice was legal. Such a law might also encourage extra-legal solutions to the problem of unhappy marriages.

3. Many people believe that paying such a high price for a baseball must leave the buyer worse off, but the winner's curse applies only to common-value assets that would be given the same value by all bidders if they had perfect information. This is not the case with the Barry Bonds baseball, assuming that the winning bid reflected the buyer's true preferences. The buyer had full and complete information about the product being sold. The exchange was voluntary. Therefore, no "winner's curse" resulted from this auction.

4. It is possible that an above-minimum wage is an equilibrium wage. An equilibrium wage is one that equates the quantity demanded with the quantity supplied in a given market. Some fast-food restaurants pay wages that exceed the minimum wage because they face competition from other employers who also pay more than the minimum wage. Other firms pay more than the minimum wage because local economic conditions make it impossible to hire enough workers for the minimum wage. This does not mean that some fast-food restaurants do not pay efficiency wages. The motive for doing so is not only to provide an incentive for workers to work harder and not shirk (as the textbook explains), but to reduce worker turnover. Many service firms have difficulty retaining workers. Retaining experienced workers reduces training costs and may result in better customer service.

5. Most colleges and universities offer a number of sections of principles of microeconomics and macroeconomics each academic term. Freshmen and transfer students as well as non-majors often have little information about the teaching styles and course requirements of the course instructors. Students who have taken other courses from these instructors and the instructors themselves provide some of this information through conversation, course syllabi and (increasingly) through web sites that summarize course content and students' opinions of the instructors whose courses they have taken.

True/False Answers

1. T See the section "Asymmetric Information" beginning on page 576 of the textbook.
2. F Another provision included in the laws is that new cars that need several major repairs during the first year or two after the original purchase date may be returned for a full refund.
3. F George Akerlof was the author of the study of asymmetric information in the market for used cars.
4. T See the section "Adverse Selection and Moral Hazard in Financial Markets" on pages 581-582. By requiring firms to register the stocks and bonds they wish to sell with the SEC and requiring each firm to provide potential investors with a prospectus, the problems associated with adverse selection and moral hazard are reduced.
5. F An efficiency wage is a greater-than-equilibrium wage paid to encourage workers to work harder.
6. T See the *Making the Connection* beginning on page 582.
7. T See the section "Asymmetric Information" beginning on page 576.
8. F This is an example of moral hazard, since the warehouse owner changed his actions as a result of obtaining fire insurance.
9. T Pacific Telesis paid less for licenses in Los Angeles than other companies paid for licenses in other cities. See the section "The Winner's Curse: When Is It Bad to Win an Auction?" beginning on page 585.
10. T A seniority system grants higher pay and other benefits to workers who have served with a firm for a long time.
11. F A *deductible* requires the holder of an insurance policy to pay a certain dollar amount of a claim.
12. F All firms that issue stock to the public have their statements audited by employees of accounting firms, not the firms whose statements they audit.
13. T See the section "Adverse Selection and Moral Hazard in Labor Markets" beginning on page 583.
14. F The winner's curse applies only to auctions of common value assets, not private-value assets.
15. T See the section "Asymmetric Information" beginning on page 576.

Chapter 18

Public Choice, Taxes, and the Distribution of Income

Chapter Summary

You learned in Chapter 2 that government plays an important role in a market system by providing secure property rights and a legal system that enforces private contracts. In Chapter 5, you learned that the government sometimes supplies public goods that private firms cannot supply. In this chapter, you learn how the government decides which policies to adopt and the principles governments use to create tax policy.

Economists use the public choice model to analyze how government policymakers arrive at their decisions. The model assumes that policymakers will likely pursue their own self-interest, even if their self-interest conflicts with the public interest.

Governments must raise the revenue needed to pay for the services they provide, including public schools, highways, and homeland security. The purpose of most taxes is to raise revenue, but some taxes are used to discourage undesirable behavior such as smoking. The federal government in the United States raises most of its revenue through income and social insurance taxes. The largest source of revenue for state and local governments is grants from the federal government. Most states also raise substantial amounts of revenue from sales taxes. Many local governments depend heavily on property taxes to fund public schools.

While income in the United States is unequally distributed, there have been no dramatic changes in the distribution of income over time. The federal government defines the **poverty line** as an income level three times the amount needed to purchase the minimum amount of food required for adequate nutrition. Given this definition, the percentage of the U.S. population that was poor fell between 1960 and 1973 from 22 percent to 11 percent. The federal government defines the **poverty rate** as the percentage of the population that is poor according to the federal government's definition. Since 1973, the poverty rate has shown little change.

Two factors that have increased inequality are technological change and expanding international trade. Development of new technology has led to the relative decline in wages of unskilled workers. Expanding trade has put more U.S. workers in competition with foreign workers and the relative wages of unskilled workers have declined as a result.

Income data do not account for the effects of government programs designed to reduce poverty. Transfer payments received by individuals, such as Social Security payments, are not included in income data used to measure poverty. Individuals with low incomes also receive noncash benefits such as food stamps, free school lunches, and rent subsidies. In other countries, progress in reducing poverty is mixed. In China and other parts of Asia and in Latin America, the poverty rate fell significantly from 1970 to 2000. But in Sub-Saharan Africa, the poverty rate increased.

Learning Objectives

When you finish this chapter, you should be able to:

1. **Define the public choice model and explain how it is used to analyze government decision making.** The public choice model applies economic analysis to government decision making. A key insight of the model is that policymakers are no different from consumers or managers of firms in that they pursue their own self-interest; in particular, we expect that public officials will take actions that are likely to result in their being re-elected.

2. **Understand the tax system in the United States, including the principles that governments use to create tax policy.** The federal government raises more than 80 percent of its revenue from the individual income tax and social security taxes. The largest source of revenue for state and local governments is federal government grants. Most states raise substantial revenue from sales taxes. Local governments rely heavily on property taxes. In selecting which taxes to impose, governments take into account the following principles: the goal of economic efficiency, the ability-to-pay principle, the horizontal equity principle, the benefits received principle, and the goal of attaining social objectives.

3. **Understand the effect of price elasticity on tax incidence.** When a tax is imposed on the sale of a good or service, the incidence of the tax is the division of the burden of the tax between buyers and sellers. When the demand for a product is less elastic than the supply, consumers pay the majority of the tax. When the demand for a product is more elastic than the supply, firms pay the majority of the tax on the product.

4. **Discuss the distribution of income in the United States and understand the extent of income mobility.** In 2005, the 20 percent of Americans with the lowest incomes received only about 3.4 percent of all income, while the 20 percent with the highest incomes received 50.4 percent of all income. There was a decline in income inequality from 1936 to 1980, but an increase in inequality during the 1990s and early 2000s. One study has shown that of the people who were in poverty in 1996, 50.5 percent remained in poverty in 1999.

Chapter Review

Chapter Opener: Should the Government Use the Tax System to Reduce Inequality? (pages 598-599)

Tax laws affect economic incentives and can also affect perceptions of fairness. The debate over the tax system was an important part of the 2008 presidential campaign. The design of the tax system and the criteria to use in evaluating it are important questions.

Helpful Study Hint

An ***Inside Look*** at this chapter's end features an analysis of income inequality in the United States by Ben Bernanke, the Chairman of the Federal Reserve Board. He cites several causes of rising inequality, including:

1. Technological change that has reduced demand for unskilled labor and increased the demand for skilled labor
2. Increased trade
3. Increased immigration
4. New technologies, like computers, have increased the demand—and thus the relative pay—for educated workers.

You receive benefits from the government, but someone has to pay for these benefits. ***Economics in YOUR Life!*** asks you to think about what your fair share of the burden of government taxes should be. Compare your opinions on this issue with the analysis the authors provide at the end of the chapter.

18.1 LEARNING OBJECTIVE

18.1 Public Choice (pages 600-604)

Learning Objective 1 Define the public choice model and explain how it is used to analyze government decision making.

The **public choice model** applies economic analysis to government decision making. The model assumes that policymakers are likely to pursue their own self-interest, even if this conflicts with the public interest. We expect public officials to take actions that are likely to result in their re-election.

The **voting paradox**, which is the failure of majority voting to always result in consistent choices, demonstrates that politicians do not simply represent the views of voters. The **median voter theorem** is the proposition that the outcome of a majority vote is likely to represent the preferences of the voter who is in the political middle.

The public choice model assumes policymakers behave in their own self-interest. There are three reasons for this behavior:

1. Renting seeking, which refers to attempts by individuals and firms to use government action to make themselves better off at the expense of others. Because firms can benefit from government intervention in the economy, they are willing to make campaign contributions to politicians who vote for special interest legislation the firms will benefit from.
2. Logrolling, which refers to the situation where a member of Congress votes to approve a bill in exchange for favorable votes from other members on other bills.
3. Rational ignorance, which means that voters often lack an economic incentive to become informed about legislation because the cost of the time and effort required to do so exceeds the benefit.

The government sometimes intervenes in the economy by establishing a regulatory agency or commission with authority over a particular industry or product. When this happens, the affected firms have an incentive to try to influence the agency's actions. In extreme cases, this may lead to the agency making decisions that benefit the regulated firms, even if these actions are not in the public interest. In these cases, the agency is said to be subject to regulatory capture.

Public choice analysis indicates that government failure can occur where government intervention reduces economic efficiency rather than increases it.

Extra Solved Problem 18-1

Chapter 18 includes two Solved Problems. Here is an extra Solved Problem to help you build your skills solving economic problems.

Supports Learning Objective 1: Define the public choice model and explain how it is used to analyze government decision making.

The Public Choice Model

Traditional political theory holds that government agents (elected politicians, appointed bureaucrats, and other government employees) put aside their private interests and attempt to achieve goals that are in the general public's interest. Alternatively, public choice theory uses the same assumption that economists make about people's actions in private markets and applies them to collective, or government, decision making; namely, people are motivated mainly by self-interest. Self-interest is also assumed to motivate voters, who are largely ignorant about political issues, including those involving taxes. This ignorance is rational because the impact of a well-informed vote on an election is essentially nil. Even if the voter's preferred candidate is elected, the candidate cannot bring about policy changes without the support of other elected officials. Elected officials are also assumed to act in their own interest. These officials make decisions to use other people's resources to promote the "public interest." But interest groups that benefit from government programs have strong incentives to provide campaign funds to those politicians who agree with, and vote for, these programs. As a result, public officials often support special interest programs that are costly for taxpayers. Public choice economists point to "logrolling" or vote trading as an important example of political self-interest that can result in inefficient legislation. Logrolling refers to politicians voting for special interest legislation that favors interests in other legislative districts in order to win the votes of politicians in those districts for their own special interest legislation. Public choice economists recognize that government regulation or provision of services is necessary in some cases. If government action is required, they prefer that it take place at the local level whenever possible. This provides an opportunity for competition and experimentation among local governments. Citizens can move to areas that provide superior public services and governments have incentives to provide services efficiently.

Source: Jane S. Shaw, "Public Choice Theory," *The Concise Encyclopedia of Economics*, http://www.econlib.org/Library/Enc/PublicChoiceTheory.html

Citizens Against Government Waste (CAGW) is a private non-profit organization founded in 1984 to "eliminate waste, fraud, abuse and mismanagement in the federal government." Each year CAGW publishes the *Congressional Pig Book*, which lists federal government spending projects the organization believes are of questionable value to taxpayers. The 2007 *Pig Book* found 2,658 questionable projects in just one piece of legislation, the Defense and Homeland Security Appropriations Act. The projects have a total cost of over $13 billion. Since 2000, Alaska and Hawaii received the greatest amount of pork spending per capita from these sources. CAGW claims that Senators Ted Stevens (R-Alaska) and Daniel Inouye (D-Hawaii), among the longest serving members of the Senate, served their states "more than their fair share of bacon."

a. How would the public choice model explain the large amount of pork spending in federal government's budget?

b. Why would Alaska and Hawaii top other states in per capita pork spending?

Source: Citizens Against Government Waste. http://www.cagw.org/site/PageServer

SOLVING THE PROBLEM

Step 1: Review the chapter material.

This problem is about public choice, so you may want to review the section "Public Choice," which begins on page 600 of the textbook.

Step 2: Answer question (a) by using the public choice model to explain the large amount of pork spending in the federal government's budget.

The public choice model would claim that pork spending is a result of (1) The self-interest of voters; because each taxpayer pays a small fraction of any program, he or she has little incentive to become well-informed or to vote for or against a candidate who supports these programs. (2) A bias in favor of special interest projects; the money spent for government projects is concentrated so that the recipients have a strong incentive to lobby and provide financial support for politicians who vote in favor of their projects.

Step 3: Answer question (b) by explaining why Alaska and Hawaii top other states in per capita pork spending.

Even though these states have small populations, they have Congressional Representatives and Senators who have a great deal of seniority. More senior politicians often have a greater ability to push special interest legislation through Congress. Politicians commonly use logrolling to garner support from colleagues for programs that benefit their states, even if these programs produce benefits that do not exceed their costs.

18.2 LEARNING OBJECTIVE

18.2 The Tax System (pages 604-612)

Learning Objective 2 Understand the tax system in the United States, including the principles that governments use to create tax policy.

Taxes are necessary to raise the funds required to provide public goods and various government activities at the federal, state, and local levels. Taxes are also used to discourage what society views as undesirable behavior. In the United States, the federal government, most state governments, and some local governments tax the incomes of households and the profits of firms. This individual income tax is the largest source of revenue for the federal government. The federal government taxes wages and salaries to raise revenue for the Social Security and Medicare programs. The federal and state governments also tax wages and salaries to fund unemployment insurance programs.

Most state and local governments tax retail sales of most products. Most local governments use property taxes – taxes on homes, offices, and factories and the land they are built on – to fund public schools. Excise taxes are levied by the federal government and some state governments on the sale of specific goods. The federal government raises more than 80 percent of its revenue through individual income and social insurance taxes. Over the past 40 years, federal revenues as a share of gross domestic product have ranged between 17 and 23 percent.

Economists categorize taxes based on how much people with different levels of income pay relative to their incomes. A **regressive tax** is a tax for which people with lower incomes pay a higher percentage of their income in tax than do people with higher incomes. A **progressive tax** is a tax for which people with lower incomes pay a lower percentage of their income in tax than do people with higher incomes. The federal income tax is a progressive tax. Every taxpayer is allowed to exclude from taxation a certain amount of income, called the personal exemption. Deductions are used to reduce the amount of income subject to tax.

The fraction of each additional dollar of income that must be paid in taxes is the **marginal tax rate**. The **average tax rate** is the total tax paid divided by total income. When a tax is progressive, the marginal and average tax rates will differ. Economists focus on the marginal tax rate when considering a change in tax policy. The marginal tax rate tells economists how a tax change will affect people's willingness to work, save, and invest.

The federal government taxes the profits earned by corporations with the corporate income tax. Some economists argue that if the purpose of the tax is to tax the owners of corporations, it would be better to do this directly by taxing owners' incomes rather than indirectly through the corporate income tax.

In selecting which taxes to use, governments take into account several goals and principles:

- The goal of economic efficiency
- The ability-to-pay principle
- The horizontal-equity principle
- The benefits-received principle
- The goal of attaining social objectives

The **excess burden** of a tax is the efficiency loss to the economy that results from a tax causing a reduction in the quantity of a good produced. This is also known as the deadweight loss from a tax. A tax is efficient if it imposes a small excess burden relative to the revenue it raises. Taxation can have substantial effects on economic efficiency by altering the incentives to work, save, and invest.

Although tax simplification would reduce the administrative burden and deadweight loss from taxation, complicated tax loopholes benefit certain taxpayers who would oppose simplification. Taxes are sometimes used to attain social objectives, such as to discourage smoking or drinking alcohol.

Helpful Study Hint

The ***Making the Connection*** on page 607 of the textbook provides statistics on which income groups pay the most in federal taxes. Review the table on that page and notice that the 20 percent of taxpayers with the highest incomes pay more than 86 percent of federal income taxes. The ***Making the Connection*** on page 611 discusses a proposed shift from an income tax to a consumption tax. Some economists oppose this shift because they believe a consumption tax will be more regressive than an income tax and would impose a burden on people with very low incomes.

Work through related end-of-chapter problems 2.9 and 2.11 to test your understanding of the concepts in these features.

Extra Solved Problem 18-2

Supports Learning Objective 2: Understand the tax system in the United States, including the principles that governments use to create tax policy.

The Evolution of the Income Tax System

The United States did not have an income tax prior to the Civil War. Before then, the federal government's revenue came from such sources as excise taxes, customs duties, and the sale of public lands. The demands placed on government because of the war forced Congress to pass a law in 1862 that raised excise taxes and imposed a 3 percent tax on incomes up to $10,000. Higher incomes were taxed at 5 percent. As the war ended, the government's revenue needs waned. The income tax was abolished in 1872, and until 1913 the federal government derived most of its revenue from excise taxes and tariffs. By the early 1900s, the nation was becoming increasingly aware that tariffs and excise taxes were neither efficient nor fair as they fell disproportionately on lower income citizens. Proposals for a new income tax were championed by Congressional representatives from agricultural states who feared the possibility of a tax on land. By 1913, 36 states had ratified the 16th Amendment to the Constitution, which allowed Congress to impose a new income tax. In October, Congress passed a law that levied a tax beginning at 1 percent on incomes between $3,000 and $20,000 (which was a very large income in 1913), with a top rate of 7 percent on incomes above $500,000. Because most people had incomes of less than $3,000 in 1913, less than 1 percent of the population paid any income tax.

The entry of the United States into World War I increased the revenue needed by the federal government. The Revenue Act of 1916 raised the lowest tax rate to 2 percent and the top rate to 15 percent for incomes in excess of $1.5 million. Other revenue acts followed. Still, in 1918 only 5 percent of the population paid income taxes. As the economy boomed in the 1920s, Congress cut tax rates five times. But after the economy plunged into the Great Depression, tax receipts fell. Congress raised tax rates by passing the Tax Act of 1932. Another tax hike followed in 1936. The lowest tax rate was 4 percent and the top rate reached 79 percent. Individual and corporate taxes were raised in 1940 and 1941. Once again, wartime spending led to greater demands for tax revenues. By the end of the war, taxpayers with taxable incomes of only $500 were subject to a tax rate of 23 percent, while taxpayers with incomes over $1 million faced a top rate of 94 percent. Federal taxes as a share of national income rose from 7.6 percent in 1941 to 20.4 percent in 1945.

Source: Fact Sheets: *Taxes. History of the U.S. Tax System.* United States Treasury. http://www.treas.gov/education/fact-sheets/taxes/ustax.shtml

a. Why did the United States first institute an income tax system?

b. Use one goal or principle of taxation to evaluate the decision to pass the 16th Amendment to the U.S. Constitution.

SOLVING THE PROBLEM

Step 1: Review the chapter material.
This problem is about the tax system, so you may want to review the section "The Tax System," which begins on page 604 of the textbook.

Step 2: Answer question (a) by explaining why the federal government instituted an income tax.

Prior to the Civil War, federal government spending was a relatively small percentage of national income. The government's revenue needs could be met through excise taxes, tariffs and sales of public land. Many people paid little or no taxes. But wartime spending required much more revenue. The government needed a broader tax base; that is, a tax or taxes that would affect many more people.

Step 3: (b).

Even before the 16th Amendment was passed, income taxes were progressive, because people with lower incomes paid a lower percentage of their income in taxes than people with higher incomes. Since the Amendment was passed, progressive tax rates have always been a characteristic of the income tax system. This is a response to the ability-to-pay principle. One could also argue that an income tax scores higher on the benefits-received principle than the alternatives of a land tax, excise tax, or tariff. As government spending grew, especially during times of war, the benefits of government programs and services were broadly spread across the population. Hence, a broader tax was justified.

18.3 LEARNING OBJECTIVE

18.3 Tax Incidence Revisited: The Effect of Price Elasticity (pages 612-615)

Learning Objective 3 Understand the effect of price elasticity on tax incidence.

Tax incidence is the actual division of the burden of a tax between buyers and sellers in a market. When a tax is imposed on the sale of a product, consumers pay the majority of the tax when the price elasticity of demand is smaller than the price elasticity of supply. When the elasticity of demand for a product is larger than the elasticity of supply, firms pay the majority of the tax.

Helpful Study Hint

Don't Let This Happen to YOU! cautions you not to confuse the burden of tax with who pays it. Although your receipt for a product tells you the amount of sales tax you paid, the seller also shares the burden of that tax. Review Figure 18-4 on page 613 of the textbook and the figure caption in the margin to understand this point.

Making the Connection describes the consequences of the imposition of a corporate income tax and explains why some economists have called for the reform of this tax. Most economists agree that some of the burden of the corporate income tax is passed on to consumers in the form of higher prices. Review Table 18-4 on page 609 for a comparison of corporate income taxes in nine countries. Notice that Ireland has a corporate tax rate of 13 percent, while the United States has a corporate tax rate of 40 percent.

Solved Problem 18-3 examines how the burden of a tax is dependent on the elasticities of demand and supply of the good that is taxed.

Complete related end-of-chapter problems 3.5, 3.6, 3.7, and 3.9 to increase your understanding of these topics.

18.4 LEARNING OBJECTIVE

18.4 Income Distribution and Poverty (pages 615-623)

Learning Objective 4 Discuss the distribution of income in the United States and understand the extent of income mobility.

The distribution of income in the United States is unequal, and there have been no dramatic changes in the distribution of income over time. According to the federal government's definition, a family is poor if it is below the poverty line. The **poverty line** is a level of annual income equal to three times the amount of income necessary to purchase the minimal quantity of food required for adequate nutrition. The **poverty rate** is the percentage of the population that is poor according to the federal government's definition. Between 1960 and 1973, the poverty rate declined from 22 percent to 11 percent, but since 1973, the poverty rate has shown little change. Figure 18-5 on page 617 in the textbook shows the poverty rate over time.

For most people, the most important factor of production they own is their labor. The income they earn depends on how productive they are and on the prices of the goods and services their labor helps to produce. Therefore, the distribution of income is related to the productivity of labor and ownership of other productive resources.

Income inequality has increased in the United States over the past 25 years. Rapid technological change contributed to this trend as computers and other machines were substituted for labor. Another contributing factor has been the expansion of international trade, which has put more U.S. workers in competition with foreign workers. As a result, the wages of unskilled workers have been reduced relative to the wages of other workers.

A **Lorenz curve** is a curve that shows the distribution of income by arraying incomes from lowest to highest on the horizontal axis and indicating the cumulative fraction of income earned by each fraction of households on the vertical axis. The Gini coefficient is a way to summarize the information provided by the Lorenz curve. If the income distribution were completely equal, the Gini coefficient would equal 0. If the income distribution were completely unequal, the Gini coefficient would equal 1.

Measures of poverty and the distribution of income are misleading. These measures do not account for income mobility. For example, a family below the poverty line one year may be above the line the next year. One study showed that only 50.5 percent of people who were in poverty in 1996 remained in poverty in 1999. Also, measures of poverty and income distribution ignore the effect of government programs meant to reduce poverty. Conventional statistics do not include transfer payments such as Social Security payments and noncash benefits, such as food stamps. Because the income tax system is progressive, income after taxes is more equally distributed than is income before taxes.

Although poverty remains a problem in high-income countries such as Australia, Canada, and Japan, it is a much larger problem in poor countries. The percentage of the population in poverty in countries in Sub-Saharan Africa was over 35 percent in 1970 and has risen since. Poverty reduction occurred in Asia and Latin America between 1970 and 2000 due to relatively rapid rates of economic growth.

Helpful Study Hint

Although the poverty rate in the United States has not fallen below 10 percent in any year, ***Solved Problem 18-4*** explains that the percentage of the population who remain in poverty for many years is smaller than 10 percent.

After reading this chapter you should have a better understanding of how governments raise revenue to provide the public with goods and service. At the beginning of this chapter, ***Economics in YOUR Life***! asked you to think about what your fair share of the tax burden is. For many teenagers, their first experience with this question occurs when they receive their first paycheck and realize that deductions have been made for income and payroll taxes. But you also pay taxes whenever you buy an item subject to sales tax. Because income taxes in the United States are progressive, the percentage of your income that will be taxed will rise as your income rises.

Key Terms

Arrow impossibility theorem. A mathematical theorem that holds that no system of voting can be devised that will consistently represent the underlying preferences of voters.

Average tax rate. Total tax paid divided by total income.

Excess burden. The efficiency loss to the economy that results from a tax causing a reduction in the quantity of a good produced; also known as the deadweight loss.

Lorenz curve. A curve that shows the distribution of income by arraying incomes from lowest to highest on the horizontal axis and indicating the cumulative fraction of income earned by each fraction of households on the vertical axis.

Marginal tax rate. The fraction of each additional dollar of income that must be paid in taxes.

Median voter theorem. The proposition that the outcome of a majority vote is likely to represent the preferences of the voter who is in the political middle.

Poverty line. A level of annual income equal to three times the amount necessary to purchase the minimal quantity of food required for adequate nutrition.

Poverty rate. The percentage of the population that is poor according to the federal government's definition.

Progressive tax. A tax for which people with lower incomes pay a lower percentage of their income in tax than do people with higher incomes.

Public choice model. A model that applies economic analysis to government decision making.

Regressive tax. A tax for which people with lower incomes pay a higher percentage of their income in tax than do people with higher incomes.

Rent seeking. The attempts by individuals and firms to use government action to make themselves better off at the expense of others.

Tax incidence. The actual division of the burden of a tax between buyers and sellers in a market.

Voting paradox. The failure of majority voting to always result in consistent choices.

Self-Test

(Answers are provided at the end of the Self-Test.)

Multiple-Choice Questions

1. A key insight of the public choice model is that
   a. most politicians are dishonest.
   b. majority voting will fail to result in policies that represent the median voter.
   c. majority voting may result in inconsistent policy choices.
   d. votes in the U.S. Senate will result in more consistent policy choices than votes taken in the House of Representatives because the Senate has fewer voting members.

2. The voting paradox refers to the proposition that the outcome of a majority vote
   a. will not represent the preferences of the voter who is in the political middle.
   b. will result in consistent choices, but the choices will result turn out not to be transitive.
   c. will result in rent seeking behavior.
   d. will fail to always result in consistent choices.

3. Kenneth Arrow developed a theorem stating that no system of voting can be devised that will consistently represent the underlying preferences of voters. This is called the Arrow
   a. voting paradox.
   b. median voter theorem.
   c. inconsistency theorem.
   d. impossibility theorem.

4. One way in which the government intervenes in the economy is by establishing a regulatory agency or commission that has authority over a particular industry or product. Because the firms that are regulated have an incentive to influence those actions, regulation may lead to
   a. logrolling, where regulators will support legislation that increases the power of the agency or commission.
   b. rational ignorance, where voters do not have an incentive to become informed about how the agency or commission reaches its regulatory decisions.
   c. the voting paradox.
   d. regulatory capture.

5. Which of the following is an example of logrolling?
   a. Congressman Hacker votes for an increase in the defense budget even though he knows that a majority of other representatives will vote against the increase. Hacker's vote demonstrates to his constituents that he supports national defense.
   b. Congressman Hacker votes in favor of funding for a national park in Congresswoman Sleet's district because Sleet has promised to vote in favor of funding for a new highway in Hacker's district.
   c. Congressman Hacker supports funding in his district for a bridge despite several analyses that show the cost of the bridge is far in excess of the benefits the bridge will provide.
   d. Congressman Hacker votes in favor of a government subsidy program that will benefit farmers because of a strong lobbying effort by farmers in his district.

6. Which of the following statements is correct about the U.S. tax system?
   a. Most taxes are intended to discourage behavior rather than to raise revenue.
   b. The largest source of revenue for the federal government is the corporate income tax.
   c. "Payroll taxes" include Social Security and Medicare taxes.
   d. The sales tax is the largest source of funds for public schools.

7. Refer to the figure below. The figure shows the sources of government revenue. Which segments correspond to corporate income taxes on these pies?

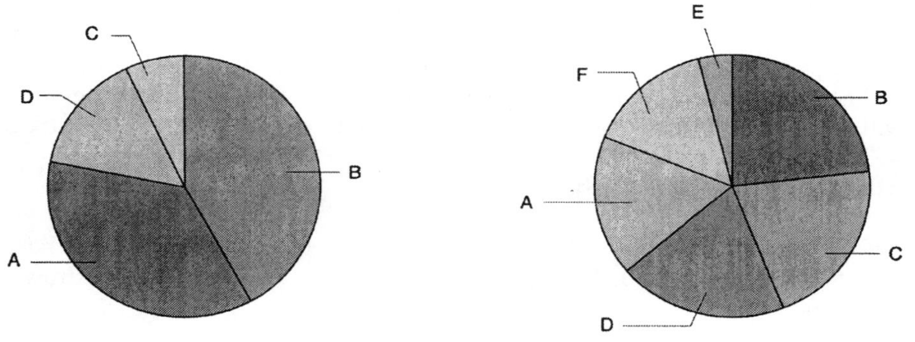

(a) Sources of federal govenment revenue, 2007

(b) Sources of state and local government revenue, 2007

   a. A on the left and B on the right
   b. C on the left and C on the right
   c. D on the left and E on the right
   d. B on the left and D on the right

8. Refer to the figure below. Which letter corresponds to the segment of a pie chart that shows sales taxes?

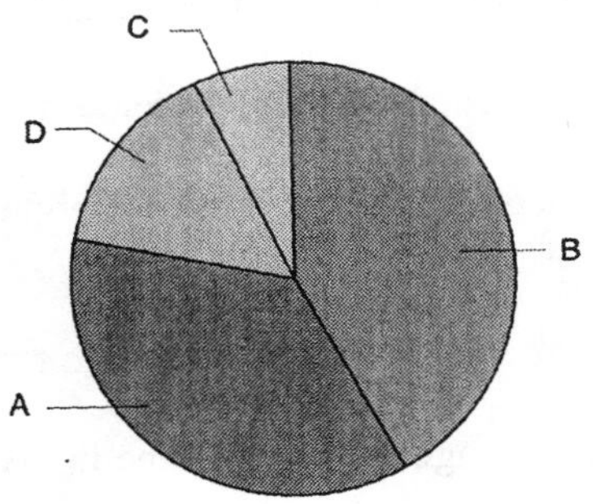

(a) Sources of federal govenment revenue, 2007

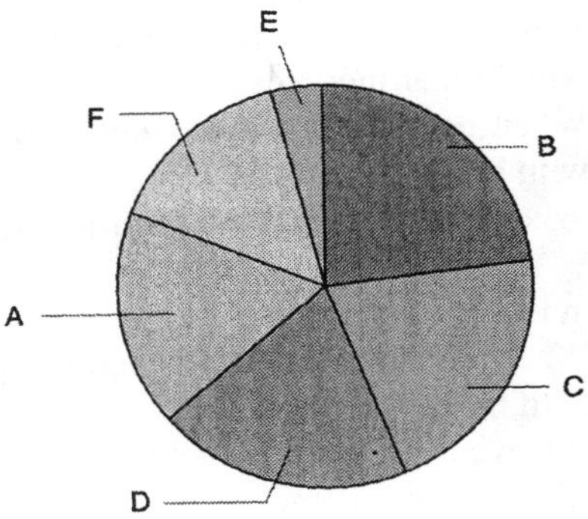

(b) Sources of state and local government revenue, 2007

a. A on the right
b. B on the right
c. E on the right
d. D on the left and E on the right

9. Refer to the figure below. Which letter corresponds to the segment of a pie chart that shows social insurance taxes?

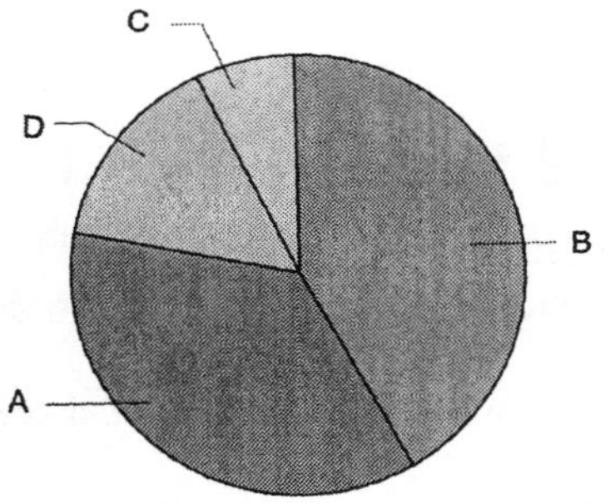

(a) Sources of federal govenment revenue, 2007

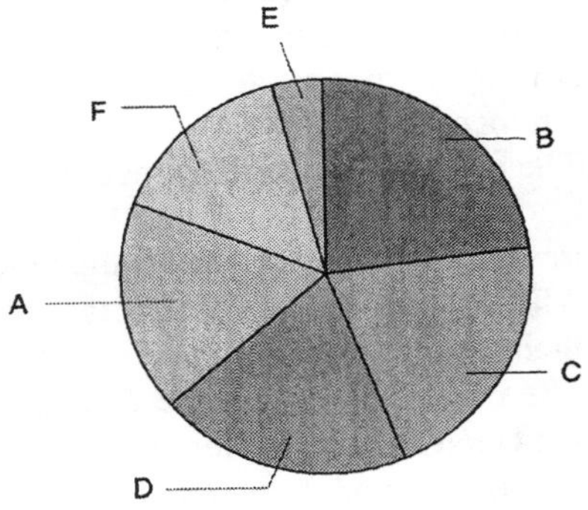

(b) Sources of state and local government revenue, 2007

a. A on the left
b. C on the right
c. D on the left
d. E on the right

10. Which of the following statements about U.S. government revenues is correct?
a. In 2006, federal revenues amounted to about $2.5 trillion, or $8,400 per person.
b. Federal revenues as a share of Gross Domestic Product have ranged between 17 and 23 percent for a long time.
c. The largest source of revenue for state and local government is grants from the federal government intended to pay for *federal mandates*.
d. All of the above.

11. When is a tax *regressive*?
    a. When people with lower incomes pay a higher percentage of their income in tax than do people with higher incomes.
    b. When people with lower incomes pay a lower percentage of their income in tax than do people with higher incomes.
    c. When people with lower incomes pay the same percentage of their income in tax as do people with higher incomes.
    d. When people who are poorer pay lower taxes and people who are richer pay higher taxes.

12. When is a tax *progressive*?
    a. When people with lower incomes pay a higher percentage of their income in tax than do people with higher incomes.
    b. When people with lower incomes pay a lower percentage of their income in tax than do people with higher incomes.
    c. When people with lower incomes pay the same percentage of their income in tax as do people with higher incomes.
    d. When people who are poorer pay lower taxes and people who are richer pay higher taxes.

13. Which of the following types of tax is the federal income tax?
    a. A progressive tax
    b. A regressive tax
    c. A proportional tax
    d. None of the above

14. Which of the following does a *tax rate* refer to?
    a. A percentage of income
    b. A range of income
    c. An income group
    d. The portion of income earned that is exempt from taxes

15. As presented in the text, how is the federal income tax structured?
    a. All taxpayers pay the same tax rate. The dollar amount of the tax is equal to this tax rate times their taxable income.
    b. The rate at which income is taxed increases as income increases. Additional amounts of income are taxed at ever greater rates.
    c. The rate at which income is taxed decreases as income increases. Additional amounts of income are taxed at ever lower rates.
    d. Most taxpayers pay taxes only on a portion of their incomes, not on their entire incomes.

16. Refer to the table below. Based on the information on the table, how much in federal income taxes will someone owe who earns $150,000?

INCOME	TAX RATE
$0–$7,82	10%
$7,826–$31,850	15
$31,851–$77,100	25
$77,101–$160,850	28
$160,851–$349,700	33
Over $349,70	35

a. $36,507
b. $42,000
c. $49,500
d. $14,653

17. Which of the following groups pays the most in federal taxes?
a. The lowest 20 percent of income earners
b. The third highest 20 percent of income earners
c. The fourth highest 20 percent of income earners
d. The top 20 percent of income earners

18. Which of the following groups bears a greater share of all the federal taxes paid?
a. The 40 percent of taxpayers with the lowest incomes
b. The 20 percent of taxpayers with the lowest incomes
c. The 20 percent of taxpayers with the highest incomes
d. None of the above; in the United States, everyone pays the same portion of the total taxes paid.

19. Which of the following is the *average tax rate*?
a. The fraction of each additional dollar of income that must be paid in taxes
b. The total tax paid divided by total income
c. The income range within which a tax rate applies
d. The tax rate paid by the average taxpayer

20. If the last dollar of income earned by individuals with the highest incomes is taxed at a rate that is less than the average tax rate which of the following is correct?
a. The marginal tax rate is equal to the average tax rate.
b. The income tax is a progressive income tax.
c. The income tax is a regressive income tax.
d. The individuals with the highest incomes will pay less in taxes than those with the lowest incomes.

21. Which of the following tax rates is a better indicator of people's willingness to work, save, and invest?
a. The average tax rate
b. The marginal tax rate
c. The average and the marginal tax rates are equally good indicators
d. Neither the average tax rate nor the marginal tax rate affects those decisions.

22. Which of the following statements is correct?
    a. The individual income tax is progressive but the corporate income tax is regressive.
    b. Most corporations are taxed at the highest tax rate of 35 percent.
    c. The corporate income tax eliminates the double taxation of dividends.
    d. All of the above

23. Refer to the graph below. Which of the following represents the government's revenue from a tax?

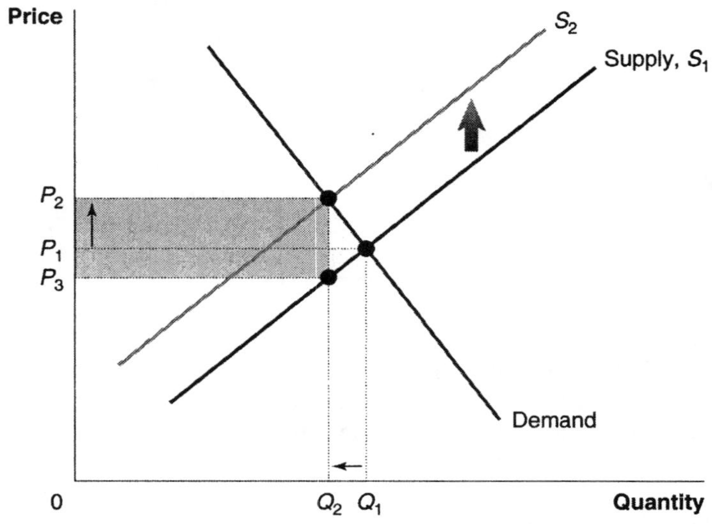

a. The triangular area to the right of the shaded rectangle
b. The shaded rectangle
c. The arrow showing an increase in price, from P_1 to P_2
d. The arrow showing a decrease in quantity, from Q_1 to Q_2

24. Refer to the graph below. Which of the following represents the excess burden of the tax?

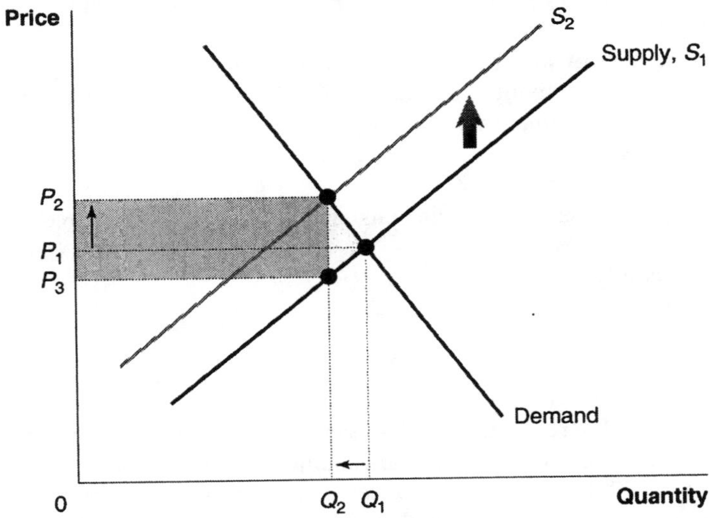

a. The triangular area to the right of the shaded rectangle
b. The shaded rectangle
c. The arrow showing an increase in price, from P_1 to P_2
d. The arrow showing a decrease in quantity, from Q_1 to Q_2

25. Which term is given to a tax that imposes a small excess burden relative to the revenue it raises?
a. Fair
b. Efficient
c. Vertically equitable
d. Horizontally equitable

26. Which of the following is a tax associated with a high deadweight loss?
a. A tax on leisure
b. A tax on cigarettes
c. A tax on interest earned from saving
d. All of the above

27. If a CD offers a 3 percent interest rate and the interest is subject to a tax rate of 33 percent, what is the after-tax return on the investment in the CD?
a. 1 percent
b. 2 percent
c. 4 percent
d. −30 percent

28. Which of the following is an accurate statement associated with the debate over whether the United States should switch from an income tax to a consumption tax?
    a. Under a consumption tax, present consumption would be taxed more favorably than future consumption.
    b. A better measure of well-being is income rather than consumption.
    c. Individuals whose savings are mainly in IRAs or 401(k) plans are already in effect paying consumption taxes rather than income taxes.
    d. All of the above

29. Which term below is associated with raising more taxes from people with high incomes than from people with low incomes?
    a. Horizontal equity
    b. Vertical equity
    c. Benefits received principle
    d. Tax incidence

30. Which of the following represents the *horizontal equity* principle of taxation?
    a. People in the same economic situation should be treated equally.
    b. Two people with the same income receive equal utility from consumption.
    c. A greater share of the tax burden should be borne by people who have a greater ability to pay.
    d. People who receive the benefits from a government program should pay the taxes that support that program.

31. Why is a sales tax inconsistent with the *ability to pay* principle?
    a. Because a sales tax does not treat two people who are in the same economic situation equally
    b. Because the revenue from a sales tax is used to benefit people who don't pay the tax
    c. Because poorer people tend to spend a larger fraction of their income than do richer people
    d. Because sales taxes are progressive

32. Refer to the graph below. When do consumers bear more of the burden of a tax?

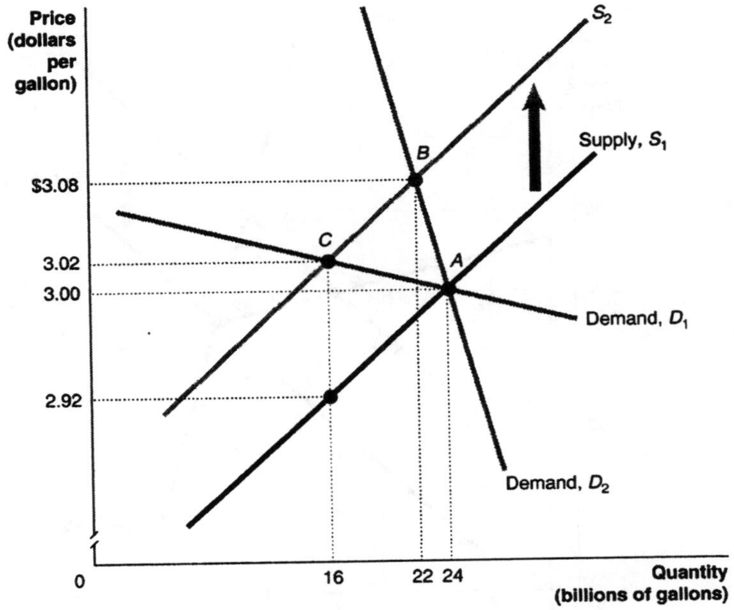

a. When demand is D_1
b. When demand is D_2
c. The tax burden to consumers is identical for both demand curves.
d. When the elasticity of supply is very small

33. What name is given to the actual division of the burden of a tax between buyers and sellers in a market?
a. Horizontal equity
b. Vertical equity
c. Tax incidence
d. The benefits-received principle

34. Refer to the graph below. In which case do firms end up paying the majority of the tax?

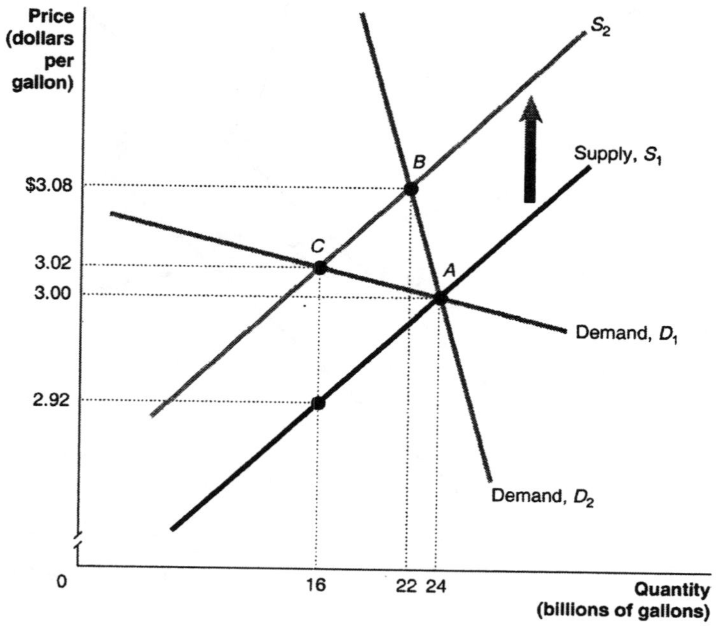

a. When demand is D_1
b. When demand is D_2
c. When supply is S_1
d. When the excess burden is small

35. Which of the following is true about the distribution of income in the United States over time?
a. Over time, there has been a dramatic decline in income inequality.
b. Over time, there has been a dramatic increase in income inequality.
c. Over time, there have been no dramatic changes in the distribution of income.
d. Over time, the distribution of income has been very volatile, with both large increases and large declines in income equality.

36. What do you call the level of annual income equal to three times the amount necessary to purchase the minimal quantity of food required for adequate nutrition?
a. The poverty rate
b. The poverty line
c. The Lorenz curve
d. The Gini coefficient

37. Which of the following is a true statement about the poverty rate in the United States?
a. Over the last 30 years, the poverty rate has fluctuated between 11 and 15 percent of the population.
b. Over the last 30 years, the poverty rate declined substantially, from 35 percent to 9 percent.
c. The poverty rate increased, from 16 percent in 1970 to over 23 percent in 2003.
d. Over the last 30 years, the poverty rate has remained constant at about 4 percent of the population.

38. Which of the following statements about poverty in the United States is correct?
    a. Individuals who are less productive or who help to produce goods and services that can be sold for only a low price will earn lower incomes.
    b. Ownership of capital is more equally distributed than income earned from labor.
    c. Poverty in the United States has increased dramatically in the last 20 years.
    d. All of the above

39. One of the following factors *does not* appear to contribute to income inequality. Which one?
    a. Expanding international trade
    b. Technological change
    c. Changes in tax rates
    d. None of the above; all of the above factors contribute to income inequality.

40. Refer to the graph below. Which of these curves shows a more unequal distribution of income?

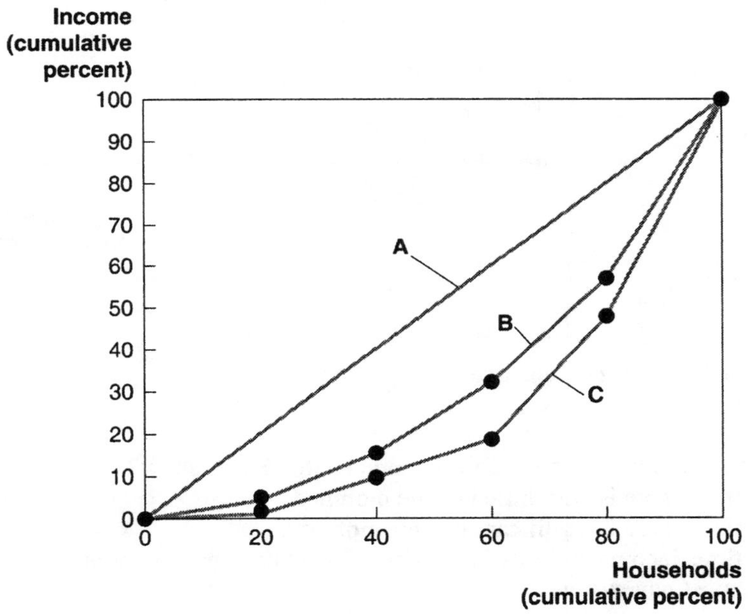

    a. A
    b. B
    c. C
    d. None of the above; the distribution of income is the same along all three curves.

41. Refer to the graph below. When the income distribution is described by the line labeled A, what is the value of the Gini coefficient?

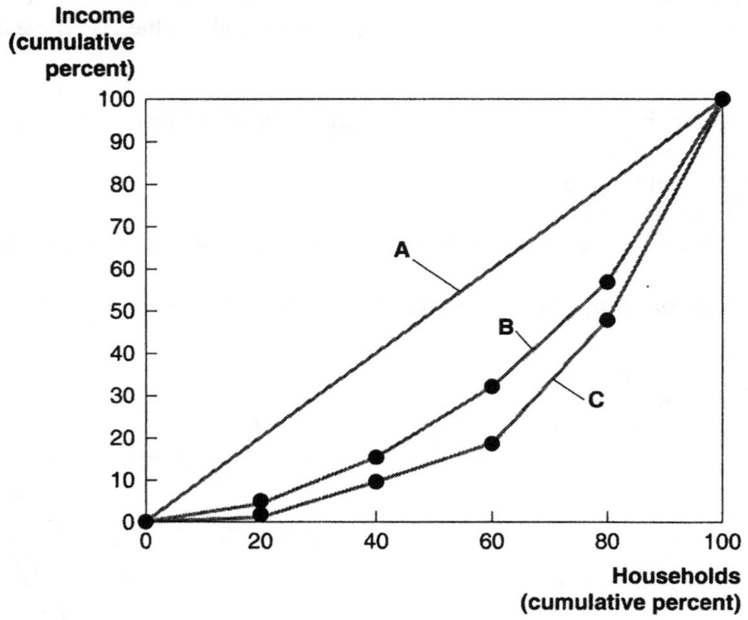

a. Zero
b. One
c. A value between zero and one
d. 45

42. What do statistics on income mobility in the United States show?
a. Over time, there is very little income mobility.
b. Over time, there is significant income mobility.
c. Over time, income mobility has varied. Sometimes income mobility is significant and other times it is almost nonexistent.
d. There are no studies on income mobility because income mobility is impossible to measure.

43. Which of the following statements about poverty in the United States is correct?
a. The people who fall into poverty in any one year are likely to remain in poverty for many years.
b. If 10 percent of the population is in poverty in a given year, the same 10 percent is likely to be in poverty in the next ten years.
c. The number of people who remain in poverty for many years is much smaller than the number who are in poverty during any one year.
d. None of the above

44. Which of the following statements about the effect of taxes and transfers on income distribution is correct?
    a. The Social Security system has failed to reduce poverty among people older than 65.
    b. The distribution of income worsens when we take transfer payments into account.
    c. Income after taxes is more equally distributed than income before taxes.
    d. All of the above

45. Which of the following statements about the distribution of income around the world is correct?
    a. The distribution of income in the United States is more equal than in some moderate-income countries, such as Brazil and Chile.
    b. The United States has the most unequal distribution of income of any high-income country in the world.
    c. The U.S. distribution of income is significantly less equal than some high-income countries, such as Norway and Japan.
    d. All of the above

Short Answer Questions

1. In the song "Taxman," George Harrison of The Beatles wrote this line:

   Let me tell you how it will be;
   There's one for you, nineteen for me

   What marginal tax rate does this imply? What percentage of George Harrison's total income would be paid in taxes at this tax rate?

   ____

   ____

   ____

   ____

   ____

   ____

2. U.S. taxpayers may reduce their federal income tax liability by deducting the amount they pay for mortgage interest and real estate taxes on their homes. If these deductions were eliminated, how would this affect the housing market?

3. Investment in research and capital are important means for less developed countries to increase their rates of economic growth. In order to encourage saving and investment, should a less developed country use a consumption tax rather than an income tax to raise revenue needed for government expenditures?

4. If the current federal income tax system was replaced by a consumption tax, what impact would this have on the demand for accountants and lawyers and firms who assist taxpayers to complete their tax forms?

5. A 2001 study of the impact of cigarette prices on smoking found that the price elasticity of demand for high school smokers was about −1.0. This compares to an estimated price elasticity of demand for adults of about −0.4. Assume that the overall elasticity is −0.8. Who would bear the greater burden—consumers or producers—of a 10 percent increase in the price of cigarettes as a result of a federal excise tax increase?

Source: H. Ross and F. Chaloupka, "The Effect of Cigarette Prices on Youth Smoking," http://repositories.cdlib.org/tc/reports/YO4.

____

____

____

____

____

True/False Questions

T F 1. In the United States, income after taxes is more equally distributed than income before taxes.

T F 2. From 1970 to 2000, the poverty rate in Sub-Saharan Africa and south Asia declined but rose in Latin America.

T F 3. The closer the value of the Gini coefficient is to 1, the more unequal the distribution of income.

T F 4. Reductions in marginal tax rates in the United States from the 1950s to the 1990s have led to an increase in the degree of income inequality.

T F 5. Most economists favor increasing the corporate income tax because it is the most efficient tax imposed by the federal government.

T F 6. A consumption tax imposes the same tax rate on income spent and saved.

T F 7. The ability-to-pay principle states that people who receive benefits from a particular government program should pay for that program.

T F 8. Differences in tax rates on work explain much of the difference in the average annual number of hours worked in Europe and the United States.

T F 9. A progressive income tax system is consistent with the ability-to-pay principle of taxation.

T F 10. An excise tax is a tax imposed on the sale of a specific good.

T F 11. In the United States, sales taxes and excise taxes are the main source of funds for public schools.

T F 12. Medicaid is a federally funded program that provides medical assistance to the elderly.

T F 13. The public choice model can be used to conclude that Congress should abolish the Food and Drug Administration and the Federal Trade Commission.

T F 14. The Arrow impossibility theorem is used to explain why logrolling and rational ignorance help explain why rent-seeking makes efficient government regulation impossible.

T F 15. In a regressive income tax system, the marginal tax rate rises as income rises.

Answers to the Self-Test

Multiple-Choice Questions

Question	Response	Explanation
1	c	This result is known as the voting paradox. See pages 600-601 of the textbook.
2	c	The voting paradox refers to the failure of majority voting to always result in consistent choices.
3	d	See the discussion of the Arrow impossibility theorem on page 601 of the textbook.
4	d	Regulatory capture occurs in extreme cases where the influence of regulated firms leads the agency to make decisions that are not in the public interest. Some economists use the now-abolished Interstate Commerce Commission as an example of regulatory capture.
5	b	Logrolling occurs when a member of Congress votes to approve a bill in exchange for favorable votes from other members of Congress on other bills.
6	c	See the section "The Tax System," which begins on page 604.
7	c	Corporate income taxes amount to 15 percent of federal tax receipts and 4 percent of state tax receipts in 2006. Refer to Figure 18-2 in the textbook.
8	b	Sales taxes are collected only by state and local governments. They are the largest source of revenue for state and local governments.
9	a	Social insurance taxes comprised 36 percent of federal government revenue in 2006.
10	d	Over the past 40 years, federal revenues as a share of Gross Domestic Product have remained in a fairly narrow range between 17 and 23 percent. The largest source of revenue for state and local government is grants from the federal government. These grants are intended in part to pay for programs that the federal government requires states and local governments to carry out. These programs are often called *federal mandates*.
11	a	A tax is regressive if people with lower incomes pay a higher percentage of their income in tax than do people with higher incomes.
12	b	A tax is progressive if people with lower incomes pay a lower percentage of their income in tax than do people with higher incomes.
13	a	As income rises, tax rates on additional income also rise.
14	a	A *tax rate* is the percentage of income paid in taxes. A *tax bracket* refers to the income range within which a tax rate applies.
15	b	Federal income taxes are paid according to predetermined tax brackets, or income ranges. The rate at which income is taxed increases as additional income moves taxpayers into higher brackets.
16	a	Her first $7,825 of income is in the 10 percent bracket, so she pays $782.50 on this income. Her next $24,025 of income is in the 15 percent bracket, so she pays $3,603.75 on this income. Her next $45,250 of income is in the 25 percent bracket, so she pays $11,312.50 on this income. Her last $72,900 of income is in the 28 percent bracket, so she pays $20,412, which brings her total federal income tax bill to $36,110.75.
17	d	The highest 20 percent of income earners pay over 85 percent of the total federal individual income taxes and more than 70 percent of the total federal taxes. Refer to *Making the Connection* "Which Groups Pay the Most In Federal Taxes?" on pages 607-608.